FREE AT LAST

FREE AT LAST

A DOCUMENTARY HISTORY OF SLAVERY, FREEDOM, AND THE CIVIL WAR

IRA BERLIN

BARBARA J. FIELDS

STEVEN F. MILLER

JOSEPH P. REIDY

LESLIE S. ROWLAND

THE NEW PRESS · NEW YORK

OTHER PUBLICATIONS OF
THE FREEDMEN AND SOUTHERN SOCIETY PROJECT

Freedom: A Documentary History of Emancipation, 1861–1867

Series 1, volume 1, *The Destruction of Slavery*, ed. Ira Berlin, Barbara J. Fields, Thavolia Glymph, Joseph P. Reidy, and Leslie S. Rowland (1985)

Series 1, volume 2, *The Wartime Genesis of Free Labor: The Upper South*, ed. Ira Berlin, Steven F. Miller, Joseph P. Reidy, and Leslie S. Rowland (forthcoming, 1993)

Series 1, volume 3, *The Wartime Genesis of Free Labor: The Lower South*, ed. Ira Berlin, Thavolia Glymph, Steven F. Miller, Joseph P. Reidy, Leslie S. Rowland, and Julie Saville (1990)

Series 2, *The Black Military Experience*, ed. Ira Berlin, Joseph P. Reidy, and Leslie S. Rowland (1982)

Slaves No More: Three Essays on Emancipation and the Civil War, by Ira Berlin, Barbara J. Fields, Steven F. Miller, Joseph P. Reidy, and Leslie S. Rowland (1992)

PUBLISHED IN THE UNITED STATES BY THE NEW PRESS, NEW YORK.
DISTRIBUTED BY W.W. NORTON & COMPANY, INC.
500 FIFTH AVENUE, NEW YORK, NY 10110

Library of Congress Cataloging-in-Publication Data

Free at last : a documentary history of slavery, freedom, and the Civil War /
[edited by Ira Berlin] . . . [et al.].
p.   cm.
Includes bibliographical references and index.
ISBN 1-56584-120-4
1. Slaves—United States—Emancipation—History—Sources.
2. United States—History—Civil War, 1861–1865—Afro-Americans—Sources.
3. Afro-Americans—History—To 1863—Sources.
4. Afro-Americans—History—1863–1877—Sources.
I. Berlin, Ira, 1941–

E185.2.F8 1992
973.04'96073—dc20
92-53726 CIP

PRINTED IN THE UNITED STATES OF AMERICA

CONTENTS

ACKNOWLEDGMENTS   *vii*

INTRODUCTION   *ix*

EDITORIAL METHOD   *xix*

    Editorial Symbols   *xxii*

    Symbols Used to Describe Manuscripts   *xxiii*

SHORT TITLES AND ABBREVIATIONS   *xxv*

CHRONOLOGY   *xxvii*

CHAPTER I.   *A War for the Union*   3

CHAPTER II.   *A War for Freedom*   95

CHAPTER III.   *Life and Labor within Union Lines*   167

CHAPTER IV.   *Free Labor in the Midst of War*   241

CHAPTER V.   *Slavery within the Union*   333

CHAPTER VI.   *Soldiers and Citizens*   435

NOTES   541

SUGGESTIONS FOR FURTHER READING   549

INDEX   555

ACKNOWLEDGMENTS

So many years have elapsed since this volume was conceived that its origins can never be fully recovered. The debts incurred along the way cannot easily be forgotten, and it is with pleasure that we acknowledge them.

André Schiffrin of The New Press believed in the endeavor from the first and waited more or less patiently for its completion. Teachers in colleges, universities, and secondary schools in the United States and abroad—especially participants in the 1989 Institute on High School History, administered by the Woodrow Wilson National Fellowship Foundation—sustained us with assurances of the utility of a single volume based on documents from *Freedom: A Documentary History of Emancipation*. They also assisted in the construction of such a volume by lobbying for documents that "had to be included." Students at the various universities with which we have been associated—the University of Maryland, Howard University, the University of Michigan, and Columbia University—and elsewhere provided similar insights into what "worked." We hope they find enough old friends in *Free at Last* to reward their investment in it.

In bringing this volume into print, Terrie Hruzd, administrative assistant of the Freedmen and Southern Society Project, played a variety of roles, including computer technician, proofreader, and production coordinator. With her deep knowledge of both the project and the workings of the University of Maryland, she solved many problems before we realized they were problems. Cynthia Kennedy-Haflett applied her quiet competence to the drudgery of proofreading and fact-checking and her lively historical imagination to a close reading of the volume in draft. Ed Cohen copyedited the manuscript with a welcome combination of technical rigor and intellectual engagement. Charles Nix designed a book worthy of its subject.

The National Historical Publications and Records Commission and the University of Maryland have provided generous material support for the Freedmen and Southern Society Project since its inception. The National Endowment for the Humanities has also been a long-time and much-appreciated source of both funding and encouragement. Grants from the H. W. Wilson Foundation and the Philip Morris Companies, Inc., helped push this volume to completion. We thank them all.

INTRODUCTION

"$\mathfrak{M}$R PRESIDENT IT IS MY DESIRE TO BE FREE. TO GO TO see my people on the eastern shore. my mistress wont let me you will please let me know if we are free. and what i can do. I write to you for advice. please send me word this week. or as soon as possible and oblidge." With that concluding hint of urgency, Annie Davis, a slave in a small town about twenty miles northeast of Baltimore, posted a carefully written note to President Abraham Lincoln in August 1864.[1] Lincoln never answered Davis's letter. He probably never saw it. Occupied as he was during the nation's fourth year of civil war, his secretaries routinely shielded him from the glut of unofficial correspondence.* For, as the Civil War touched the lives of more and more Americans, thousands of ordi-

---

*Had Lincoln responded, he probably would have noted that, because of Maryland's standing in the Union, state laws pertaining to slavery remained in effect; unless her owner supported the Confederacy, Davis was still legally a slave.

nary men and women felt impelled to address the president and others who wore the badge of high office. Many of them wrote in a rough hand, suggesting greater familiarity with a plow than with a pen. Untutored in the niceties of the written language, they invented their own conventions of spelling and punctuation. Like Annie Davis, however, they had questions so pressing that they demanded the attention of those in positions of power, even the president of the United States.

Davis wrote as a petitioner, but she and the others who addressed high-ranking officials were not mere suppliants. Their letters were informed by a powerful sense of entitlement. "Now Your Excellency," wrote James Henry Gooding, a black corporal who spoke with the voice of a general, "We have done a Soldiers Duty. Why cant we have a Soldiers pay?"[2] "I have defended the country in the field," declared a veteran several months after the war had ended, "and most respectfully request that I be protected at home."[3]

As befitted their experience, soldiers spoke with special force. But others did as well. Hearing rumors that the Emancipation Proclamation might be retracted, Hannah Johnson, daughter of a slave and mother of a soldier, implored Lincoln "don't do it" and then gently summoned the president to his place in history. "When you are dead and in Heaven, in a thousand years that action of yours will make the Angels sing your praises I know it." Johnson did not stop there. Having, she supposed, gained the president's ear, she advanced her own understanding of the wrong of slavery and the right of freedom. "Ought one man to own another, law for or not,   who made the law, surely the poor slave did not.   so it is wicked, and a horrible Outrage, there is no sense in it,   because a man has lived by robbing all his life and his father before him, should he complain because the stolen things found on him are taken.   Robbing the colored people of their labor is but a small part of the robbery   their souls are almost taken, they are made bruits of often." Perhaps fearing that she had overstepped her station in lecturing the Great Emancipator on the meaning of emancipation, Johnson added a barely audible, "You know all about this."[4]

Hannah Johnson thought the president needed a reminder and believed it her right—even her duty—to provide it, for she saw herself as a full partner in the remaking of the American republic. Johnson's direct mode of address and her sense of fellowship in a larger struggle characterized much of the correspondence received by Lincoln and other federal officials. "I hope When these few Badly Written lines Reach you they Will find you in the Best of Health," began a soldier soliciting help from the secretary of war.[5]

The combination of familiar tone and prescriptive address reflected the former slaves' newfound conviction that the federal government stood with them and would act in their interest. Sergeant Joseph Harris, whose regiment was serving in Florida, did not hesitate to ask "the granterfurction of a Small favor" from the general who had supervised recruitment in his home state of Louisiana. Indeed, even as he formulated his request, the appeal became a directive. "[W]ill you ples to Cross the Mississippia River at Bayou Sar La. with your Command," he wrote, "& jest on the hill one mile from the little town you will finde A plantation Called Mrs Marther. H. Turnbuill & take a way my Farther & mother & my brothers wife with all their Childern & U take them up at your He[d] Quarters. & write to me." The mission, Harris assured the general, would not take long; "it isent mor then three or four Hours trubel."[6]

Rather than appeal for federal assistance, some former slaves themselves assumed the mantle of the government. After assuring his daughters that they would be free "if it cost me my life," Spotswood Rice, a soldier in Missouri, wrote to the woman who held one of them as her slave.

"[M]ary is my Child and she is a God given rite of my own," he announced, articulating one of the former slaves' most sacred beliefs. "[M]y Children is my own," he repeated after predicting the place in eternity that awaited his daughter's mistress: "you may hold on to hear as long as you can but…the longor you keep my Child from me the longor you will have to burn in hell and the qwicer youll get their." As Private Rice reflected on the prospects of uniting his family and establishing a domestic life worthy of a free people, he also deemed it appropriate to instruct his daughter's owner in the etiquette of the new order. "[W]hen I get ready to come after mary I will have bout a powrer and autherity to bring hear away and to exacute vengencens on them that holds my Child   you will then know how to talke to me   I will assure that and you will know how to talk rite too." Rice knew what he was talking about when he contemplated such earthly reversals of deference and power. He himself had been transformed from a slave to a free man and a soldier in the army of the Republic. "I have no fears about geting mary out of your hands," he concluded. "[T]his whole Government gives chear to me and you cannot help your self."[7]

The momentous changes that gave "chear" to Spotswood Rice affected other Americans, high and low. The Northern soldiers—few of them abolitionists—who hooted slaveholders out of their camps when they tried to retrieve runaways felt those changes. So did some of their officers, who violated military etiquette and challenged their superiors by denouncing slavery as a relic of the past, arming runaway slaves, and promulgating their own proclamations of emancipation. So too did the nonslaveholders who advocated the enlistment of slaves into the Union army, who hired freedpeople despite the threats of slaveholders, and who resisted the introduction of new forms of coercion in slavery's stead. Horrified by the "Bands Prowling apon Horse Back around the Country armed with Revolvers and Horse Whips threatning to Shoot every Negroe that gives Back the first word after they Lacerate his flesh with the Whip," Thomas B. Davis, an impoverished lighthouse keeper, demanded of a judge in Baltimore, "In the Name of Humanity is there no Redress for those poor ignorant down troden Wreches."[8]

In ordinary times, lighthouse keepers do not query judges, enlisted men do not direct generals, slaves do not threaten slaveholders, and former slaves do not lecture presidents. Although those who enjoy political power and social authority speak their minds and indulge their inclinations freely and often, their subordinates generally do not. Only in the upheaval of accustomed routine can the lower orders freely give voice to the assumptions that guide their world as it is and as they wish it to be.

The Civil War was such an upheaval. In four years of internecine war—"century like years," as one Union officer described them[9]—American society underwent a social revolution of mammoth proportions. The government was transformed, social classes rearranged, citizenship redefined, billions of dollars of property expropriated without compensation, and the relations of free labor forcibly substituted for those of slavery. Few men and women were unchanged. White Southerners surrendered the right to own other human beings. White Northerners became the enemies of slavery and the allies of slaves, often despite their intentions. Free-black people lost the special position they had occupied when most people of African descent were slaves. And slaves became free men and women; before long, some of them marched in the ranks of the Union army, voted in elections, and held high public office.

Hannah Johnson's letter to Lincoln, like those of Annie Davis and Spotswood Rice, were products of the revolution that accompanied emancipation. Drawing strength from the momentous changes that were transforming them and their society, Johnson, Davis, Rice, and other such men and women abandoned their usual caution in favor of direct speech and even more direct action. Their letters demonstrate that under the pressure of unprecedented events, ordinary men and women can become extraordinarily perceptive and articulate. They also suggest the ways in which revolutionary change emboldens common people to challenge the assumptions of the old regime and proclaim a new social order.

Some of their wisdom had the ring of age-old maxims. "[W]hen the rich grumble God help the poor," wrote one mother to her soldier son, "for it is a true saying that 'poverty is no disgrace but very unhandy.'"[10] But just as often, the heat of the moment fired new revelations. "Wee are said to be U S Soldiers and behold wee are U S Slaves," exclaimed a long-suffering private.[11] Nor were pithy aphorisms confined to former slaves. "The great civilizer here is the 'dime,'" testified a resident of Massachusetts who had inherited a South Carolina plantation, summarizing the laws of political economy that were now to govern the South.[12]

Whatever their rank, Americans caught up in the drama of war and emancipation often spoke with uncommon eloquence, in some measure because their culture prized that quality. When arguments turned on a deft formulation, an apt image, or the appropriate word, men and women learned how to turn a phrase. Had black men done their duty as soldiers? asked James Henry Gooding rhetorically. His response was worthy of his subject. "Let their dusky forms, rise up, out the mires of James Island, and give the answer. Let the rich mould around Wagners parapets be upturned, and there will be found an Eloquent answer. Obedient and patient, and Solid as a wall are they. all we lack, is a paler hue, and a better acquaintance with the Alphabet."[13]

The revolution that accompanied emancipation helped to capture this wisdom and uncommon eloquence by placing the American people in close contact with numerous governmental agencies: the offices of the president and his cabinet, the U.S. Army at every level of command, the Bureau of Colored Troops, the American Freedmen's Inquiry Commission, the Freedmen's Bureau, and many others. The bureaucratic structure of these agencies provided a mechanism for the preservation of many documents by and about people who are generally dismissed as historically mute. The documents are now housed in the National Archives of the United States, as are the records of the Confederate government— among the spoils that went to the victors in the Civil War.

Scattered among the official reports that crowd the shelves of the National Archives, letters by former slaves—numbering into the thousands—reveal aspirations, beliefs, and behavior that have previously gone unnoted. Not only did extraordinary numbers of former slaves, many of them newly literate, put pen to paper in the early years of freedom, but hundreds of others, entirely illiterate, gave depositions to government officials, placed their marks on resolutions passed at mass meetings, testified before courts-martial and Freedmen's Bureau courts, and dictated letters to more literate black men and women and to Northern officers and teachers. This written record constitutes an unparalleled outpouring from people caught up in the process of emancipation. Although many of the documents—like Annie Davis's letter to Abraham Lincoln—requested some official action, others originated in relationships entirely outside the purview of federal authorities. They include correspondence between black soldiers and their families and between kinfolk who had been separated during slavery and even—as with Spotswood Rice—letters to a daughter's owner. That such letters fell, for various reasons, into the bureaucratic net of government agencies, and thus were preserved along with official records, should not obscure their deeply personal origins.

These documents convey, as perhaps no historian can, the experiences of the liberated: the quiet personal satisfaction of meeting an old master on equal terms, as well as the outrage of exclusion from the ballot box; the elation of a fugitive slave enlisting in the Union army, and the indignation of a laborer cheated out of hard-earned wages; the joy of a family reunion after years of forced separation, and the distress of having a child seized for apprenticeship to a former owner; the hope that freedom would bring a new world, and the fear that, in too many ways, life would be much as before. The documents also offer insight into the diverse reactions of planters, Union soldiers, and Southern yeomen—men and women who faced emancipation with interests and expectations frequently at odds with those of former slaves. They, too, were transformed by the revolution that accompanied emancipation. Their words—though sometimes harsh and mean-spirited—reveal just as much about that revolution as do those of the former slaves. There is no hierarchy that assigns greater value to some documents than others because they represent more "authentic" voices, nor do sources come in color, class, or sex. The notion of "black" sources and "white" sources, "male" sources and "female" sources, "slave" sources and "slaveholder" sources proves on examination to be a fiction.

The recovery of "voices" from the past is, in any case, an impossible task. The voices of the past have long since been stilled by the deaths of their owners. What remains are not voices but words: words that, appropriately considered and critically evaluated, may help those reading them today to decipher the thoughts and actions of people in the past. The words that serve that purpose may be those of slaves, of slaveholders, of army officers, of politicians, of ordinary citizens. The documents that appear in this volume have been selected, not on the basis of their supposed authenticity as voices, but on the basis of the effectiveness with which they help to explain an important aspect of the past.

The Freedmen and Southern Society Project was established in 1976 to write a history of emancipation in the words of the men and women caught up in its drama: Unionists and Confederates, soldiers and civilians, slaveholders and slaves. For three years, the project's editors combed the National Archives in search of material from which to construct a documentary history of emancipation; they selected some 40,000 documents—perhaps 2 percent of the records examined. From that collection, the editors are selecting a still smaller number for publication in their multivolume study, *Freedom: A Documentary History of Emancipation, 1861–1867.* *

During the past decade, four volumes of *Freedom* have reached print. *The Destruction of Slavery* analyzes the process by which slavery collapsed under the pressure of federal arms and of the slaves' determination to place their own liberty on the wartime agenda; it documents the transformation of a war for the Union into a war against slavery. *The Wartime Genesis of Free Labor: The Upper South* and *The Wartime Genesis of Free Labor: The Lower South* concern the evolution of freedom in Union-occupied areas of the South. Detailing the experiences of former slaves as military laborers, residents of government-sponsored "contraband camps," and wage-workers in both countryside and city, they explore the freedpeople's struggle to attain economic independence in difficult wartime circumstances. *The Black Military Experience* demonstrates how the enlistment and military service of almost 200,000 black soldiers and sailors—most of them former slaves—hastened the transformation of the Civil War into a war for universal liberty.

Free at Last: A Documentary History of Slavery, Freedom, and the Civil

---

*For further information about the Freedmen and Southern Society Project, see the prefatory material that appears in each volume of *Freedom*.

War brings together many of the most telling documents from the first four volumes of *Freedom*. They have been selected because they help unravel the history of emancipation and explain how a people with little power and few weapons secured its freedom against the will of those with great power and many weapons. The tale is not one of unalloyed success. Those in power ignored more often than they heeded the words of the Spotswood Rices, Hannah Johnsons, and Annie Davises. Legal freedom did not guarantee the social order for which the freed men and women hoped and struggled. But if victories were few, costly, and incomplete, they were victories nonetheless. At war's end, a new truth prevailed where slavery once had reigned: men and women could never again be owned and citizenship belonged by right to all. American life had been set on a new course.

EDITORIAL METHOD

The editors have approached the question of transcription with the conviction that readability need not require extensive editorial intervention and, indeed, that modernization (beyond what is already imposed by typesetting) can compromise the historical value of a document.

Therefore, the textual body of each document in this volume is reproduced *exactly* as it appears in the original manuscript—to the extent permitted by modern typography. (Exceptions to this general principle will be noted hereafter.) All peculiarities of syntax, spelling, capitalization, and punctuation appear in the original manuscript. Illegible or obscured words that can be inferred with confidence from textual evidence are printed in ordinary roman type, enclosed in brackets. If the editors' reading is conjectural or doubtful, a question mark is added. When the editors cannot decipher a word by either inference or conjecture, it is represented by a three-dot ellipsis enclosed in brackets. An undecipherable passage of more than one word is represented in the same way, but a foot-note reports the extent of the illegible material. (A summary of editorial symbols follows this essay.)

Some adaptations are employed to designate characteristics of hand-written letters that cannot be exactly or economically reproduced on the printed page. Words underlined once in the manuscript appear in *italics*. Words underlined more than once are printed in SMALL CAPITALS. Inter-nally quoted documents that are set off in the manuscript by such devices as extra space or quotation marks on every line are printed in smaller type. Interlineations are simply incorporated into the text at the point marked by the author, without special notation by the editors unless the interlineation represents a substantial alteration. Finally, the beginning of a new paragraph is indicated by indentation, regardless of how the au-thor set apart paragraphs.

The editors deviate from the standard of faithful reproduction of the textual body of the document in only two significant ways. First, the end-ings of unpunctuated or unconventionally punctuated sentences are marked with extra space. Second, some of the documents are not printed in their entirety. Each editorial omission is indicated by a four-dot ellip-sis.

The editors intervene without notation in the text of manuscripts in three minor ways. When the author of a manuscript inadvertently re-peated a word, the duplicate is silently omitted. Similarly, most material crossed out by the author is omitted without note, since it usually repre-sents false starts or ordinary slips of the pen. When, however, the editors judge that the crossed-out material reflects an important alteration of meaning, it is printed as ~~canceled type~~. In printed documents (of which there are few), silent correction is made for jumbled letters, errant punc-tuation, and transpositions that appear to be typesetting errors. All other editorial interventions in the textual body of a document are clearly identified by being placed in italics and in brackets. These include descriptive interpolations such as [*In another handwriting*] or [*Endorsement*], expansion of unusual abbreviations, the addition of words or letters omitted by the author, and the correction of misspelled words and erroneous dates. The editors exercise restraint in making such additions, however, intervening only when the document cannot be understood or is seriously misleading as it stands. In particular, no effort is made to correct misspelled personal and place names. When material added by the editors is conjectural, a question mark is placed within the brackets.

In the interest of saving space, the editors have adopted the following procedures for treating the peripheral parts of manuscripts. The inside address and return address of a letter are omitted. (Instead, the text preceding each document conveys information about the sender and recipient, and the source citation supplies their names and titles exactly as they appear in the document.) The place and date are printed on a single line at the beginning of the document regardless of where they appear in the manuscript. The salutation and complimentary closing of a letter are run into the text regardless of their positions in the original. Multiple signatures are printed only when there are twelve or fewer names. For documents with more than twelve signatures, the editors indicate only the number of signatures on the signature line, for example, [*86 signatures*]. The formal legal apparatus accompanying documents such as sworn affidavits—including the names of witnesses and the name and position of the official who administered the oath—is omitted without notation. Postscripts that concern matters unrelated to the body of a letter are also silently omitted.

A technical description symbol follows each document, usually on the same line as the signature. The symbol describes the physical form of the manuscript, the handwriting, and the signature. (For a list of the symbols employed, see p. xxiii.)

The source citations for the documents published in *Free at Last* are to the volumes of *Freedom: A Documentary History of Emancipation* where they appear and where full information may be found regarding their location in the National Archives.

EDITORIAL SYMBOLS

[roman]

Words or letters in roman type within brackets represent editorial inference or conjecture of parts of manuscripts that are illegible, obscured, or mutilated. A question mark indicates doubt about the conjecture.

[. . .]

A three-dot ellipsis within brackets represents illegible or obscured words that the editors cannot decipher. If there is more than one undecipherable word, a footnote reports the extent of the passage.

. . .*

A three-dot ellipsis and a footnote represent words or passages entirely lost because the manuscript is torn or a portion is missing. The footnote reports the approximate amount of material missing.

~~canceled~~

Canceled type represents material written and then crossed out by the author of a manuscript. This device is used only when the editors judge that the crossed-out material reflects an important alteration of meaning. Ordinarily, canceled words are omitted without notation.

[*italic*]

Words or letters in italic type within brackets represent material that has been inserted by the editors and is not part of the original manuscript. A question mark indicates that the insertion is a conjecture.

. . . .

A four-dot ellipsis centered on a separate line represents editorial omission of a substantial body of material. A shorter omission, of only one or two sentences, is indicated by a four-dot ellipsis between two sentences.

SYMBOLS USED
TO DESCRIBE MANUSCRIPTS

Symbols describing the handwriting, form, and signature of each document appear at the end of each document.

The first capital letter describes the handwriting of the document:

A   autograph (written in the author's hand)
H   handwritten by other than the author (for example, by a clerk)
P   printed
T   typed

The second capital letter, with lower-case modifier when appropriate, describes the form of the document:

L	letter	c	copy
D	document	d	draft
E	endorsement	f	fragment
W	wire (telegram)		

The third capital letter (or its absence) describes the signature:

S   signed by the author
Sr   signed with a representation of the author's name
     no signature or representation

The more common symbols include:

ALS (autograph letter, signed by author), HLS (handwritten letter, signed by author), HLSr (handwritten letter, signed with a representation), HLcSr (handwritten copy of a letter, signed with a representation), HD (handwritten document, no signature).

SHORT TITLES AND ABBREVIATIONS

SHORT TITLES

Black Military Experience
  Freedom: A Documentary History of Emancipation, 1861–1867.
  Series 2, *The Black Military Experience*, ed. Ira Berlin, Joseph P.
  Reidy, and Leslie S. Rowland (Cambridge, 1982).

Destruction of Slavery
  Freedom: A Documentary History of Emancipation, 1861–1867.
  Series 1, volume 1, *The Destruction of Slavery*, ed. Ira Berlin, Barbara
  J. Fields, Thavolia Glymph, Joseph P. Reidy, and Leslie S. Rowland
  (Cambridge, 1985).

Statutes at Large
  United States, *Statutes at Large, Treaties, and Proclamations of the
  United States of America*, 17 vols. (Boston, 1850–73).

Wartime Genesis: Lower South
  Freedom: A Documentary History of Emancipation, 1861–1867.
  Series 1, volume 3, *The Wartime Genesis of Free Labor: The Lower*

South, ed. Ira Berlin, Thavolia Glymph, Steven F. Miller, Joseph P. Reidy, Leslie S. Rowland, and Julie Saville (Cambridge, 1990).

Wartime Genesis: Upper South
  Freedom: A Documentary History of Emancipation, 1861–1867.
  Series 1, volume 2, *The Wartime Genesis of Free Labor: The Upper South*, ed. Ira Berlin, Steven F. Miller, Joseph P. Reidy, and Leslie S. Rowland (Cambridge, forthcoming, 1993).

ABBREVIATIONS

Asst.	*Assistant*	Lt., Lieut.	*Lieutenant*
Brig., Brigr.	*Brigadier*	Maj.	*Major*
Capt.	*Captain*	Obt. Servt.	*Obedient Servant*
Cav., Cav'y	*Cavalry*	Pro. Mar., Prov. Mar.	*Provost Marshal*
Co.	*Company*	Reg., Regt.	*Regiment*
Co.	*County*	Sergt., Sargt.	*Sergeant*
Col.	*Colonel*	Supt.	*Superintendent*
comdg.	*commanding*	USCI	*U.S. Colored Infantry*
Dept.	*Department*		
Dist.	*District*	USCT	*U.S. Colored Troops*
Gen., Gen'l	*General*	V., Vol., Vols.	*Volunteers (usually preceded by a state abbreviation)*
Hd. Qrs.	*Headquarters*		
Hon.	*Honorable*		
Inft., Infy.	*Infantry*	&c	*et cetera*
inst.	*instant; i.e., of the current month*		

CHRONOLOGY

*Unless otherwise specified, all entries pertain to the Union
rather than the Confederacy.*

1860

November

6 Abraham Lincoln elected president

December

20 South Carolina becomes the first Southern state to secede from the Union

1861

February

4 Convention of seceded states (South Carolina, Mississippi, Florida, Alabama, Georgia, Louisiana) meets in Montgomery, Alabama; adopts provisional constitution of the Confederate States of America (Feb. 8) and elects Jefferson Davis provisional president (Feb. 9)

March

2 U.S. Congress adopts and sends to the states a constitutional amendment (which ultimately failed of ratification) forbidding any subsequent amendment to "abolish or interfere . . . with the domestic institutions" of the states

4 President Lincoln inaugurated

April

12 Civil War begins with Confederate attack on federal garrison at Fort Sumter, South Carolina

15 President Lincoln issues proclamation calling for troops to put down the rebellion

May

20 Following Texas, Arkansas, Tennessee, and Virginia into the Confederacy, North Carolina becomes the last state to secede

24 Fugitive slaves at Fortress Monroe, Virginia, are received and put to work by Union general Benjamin F. Butler, who declares them "contraband of war"

July

21 Confederate victory at battle of Bull Run (Manassas) dashes Union hopes of quelling the rebellion quickly and without great loss of life

August

6 First Confiscation Act nullifies owners' claims to fugitive slaves who had been employed in the Confederate war effort

30 Invoking martial law, General John C. Frémont declares free the slaves of disloyal owners in Missouri; President Lincoln asks that he modify his order so as not to exceed congressional laws respecting emancipation

September

11 General Frémont having refused to modify his emancipation order, President Lincoln orders him to do so

December

1 Secretary of War Simon Cameron issues his annual report, from which President Lincoln had required the deletion of passages advocating emancipation and the employment of former slaves as military laborers and soldiers; Cameron is soon replaced by Edwin M. Stanton

1862

March

13   Congress adopts an additional article of war forbidding members of the army and navy to return fugitive slaves to their owners

April

3   General David Hunter, Union commander in the South Carolina Sea Islands, requests permission to arm black men for military service; receiving no response, he begins recruiting on his own authority in early May, but the War Department refuses to pay or equip the regiment and Hunter is therefore compelled to disband it

10   At Lincoln's request, Congress pledges financial aid to any state that undertakes gradual emancipation with compensation to owners

16   Congress abolishes slavery in the District of Columbia, with compensation to loyal owners, and appropriates money for the voluntary removal ("colonization") of former slaves to Haiti, Liberia, or other countries

May

9   General David Hunter declares free all slaves in South Carolina, Georgia, and Florida

19   President Lincoln issues a proclamation nullifying General Hunter's emancipation edict and urging the border states (Kentucky, Misssouri, Maryland, and Delaware) to embrace gradual, compensated emancipation

June

7   Congress adopts legislation enforcing the Direct Tax Act of 1861 in the seceded states; it provides for forfeiture to the government of land whose owners failed to pay the tax and for its subsequent lease or sale

19   Congress prohibits slavery in the territories

July

12   President Lincoln appeals to congressmen from the border states to support gradual, compensated emancipation, with colonization of freed slaves outside the United States, warning that if they do not act soon, slavery in their states "will be extinguished by mere friction and abrasion—by the mere incidents of the war"; two days later, a majority of the congressmen reject Lincoln's appeal

17   Second Confiscation Act frees the slaves of persons engaged in or assisting the rebellion and provides for the seizure and sale of other property owned

by disloyal citizens; it also forbids army and navy personnel to decide on the validity of any fugitive slave's claim to freedom or to surrender any fugitive to any claimant, and authorizes the president to employ "persons of African descent" in any capacity to suppress the rebellion

17 Militia Act provides for the employment of "persons of African descent" in "any military or naval service for which they may be found competent," granting freedom to slaves so employed (and to their families if they belong to disloyal owners)

22 President Lincoln announces to his cabinet his intention to issue a proclamation freeing slaves in the rebel states, but agrees to postpone it until after a suitable military victory

August

22 In New Orleans, General Benjamin F. Butler incorporates into Union forces several "Native Guard" units composed of free-black soldiers; soon thereafter he begins recruiting both free-black and ex-slave men for additional regiments

25 After having withheld its permission for months, the War Department authorizes recruitment of black soldiers in the South Carolina Sea Islands

September

17 Confederate invasion of Maryland repulsed at Antietam

22 Preliminary Emancipation Proclamation issued by President Lincoln; it announces that all slaves in those states or portions of states still in rebellion as of January 1, 1863, will be declared free, pledges monetary aid for slave states not in rebellion that adopt either immediate or gradual emancipation, and reiterates support for the colonization of freed slaves outside the United States

October

11 Confederate Congress exempts from conscription one white man on each plantation with twenty or more slaves

December

23 Confederate President Davis issues proclamation ordering that black Union soldiers and their officers captured by Confederate troops are not to be treated as prisoners of war; instead, they are to be remanded to Confederate state authorities

1863

January

1 Emancipation Proclamation issued by President Lincoln; it declares free all slaves in the Confederate states (except Tennessee, southern Louisiana, and parts of Virginia) and announces the Union's intention to enlist black soldiers and sailors. By late spring, recruitment is under way throughout the North and in all the Union-occupied Confederate states except Tennessee

March

16 American Freedmen's Inquiry Commission appointed by Secretary of War Stanton to investigate the condition of former slaves and recommend measures for their employment and welfare

May

22 Bureau of Colored Troops created within the War Department

27 Black soldiers play important role in failed assault on Port Hudson, Louisiana

June

7 Black soldiers repel Confederate attack at Milliken's Bend, Louisiana

July

1–3 Confederate offensive into Maryland and Pennsylvania repulsed at Gettysburg

4 Confederate surrender of Vicksburg, Mississippi

8 Confederate surrender of Port Hudson clinches Union control over the Mississippi River

18 Black soldiers spearhead failed assault on Fort Wagner, South Carolina

30 President Lincoln pledges that Union soldiers, black or white, are entitled to equal protection if captured by the enemy and threatens retaliation for Confederate enslavement of black prisoners of war

October

3 War Department orders full-scale recruitment of black soldiers in Maryland, Missouri, and Tennessee, with compensation to loyal owners

December

8 Proclamation of Amnesty and Reconstruction issued by President Lincoln; it offers pardon and restoration of property (except slaves) to Confederates who take an oath of allegiance to the Union and agree to accept emancipation; it also proposes a plan by which loyal voters of a seceded state can begin the process of readmission into the Union

1864

March

16 New Arkansas state constitution, which abolishes slavery, is ratified by pro-Union voters

April

8 Senate approves constitutional amendment abolishing slaver,

12 Confederate troops under General Nathan B. Forrest massacre black soldiers captured at Fort Pillow, Tennessee

June

7 Enlistment in Kentucky opened to slave men irrespective of their owners' consent, with compensation to loyal owners

15 House of Representatives fails to approve constitutional amendment abolishing slavery

15 Congress makes pay of black soldiers (which had been $10 per month for all ranks) equal to that of white soldiers ($13 per month for privates, larger amounts for higher ranks); the change is retroactive to January 1, 1864, or, for men who were free before the war, to the time of enlistment

20 Congress increases the pay of all privates, black and white, to $16 per month, with corresponding increases for higher ranks

September

5 New Louisiana state constitution, which abolishes slavery, is ratified by pro-Union voters

November

1 New Maryland state constitution, which abolishes slavery, takes effect, having been ratified in October

8 Abraham Lincoln is reelected president, defeating George B. McClellan

1865

January

11 Missouri state constitutional convention abolishes slavery

12 General William T. Sherman and Secretary of War Edwin M. Stanton meet with twenty black leaders in Savannah, Georgia, to discuss the future of the ex-slaves

16 General Sherman issues Special Field Order 15 setting aside part of coastal South Carolina, Georgia, and Florida for settlement exclusively by black people, settlers to receive "possessory title" to forty-acre plots

31 House of Representatives approves constitutional amendment abolishing slavery, sending it to the states for ratification

February

22 Amendment to Tennessee state constitution abolishes slavery

March

3 Congress approves a joint resolution liberating the wives and children of black soldiers

3 Congress establishes Bureau of Refugees, Freedmen, and Abandoned Lands (Freedmen's Bureau) to oversee the transition from slavery to freedom

13 Confederate Congress authorizes President Jefferson Davis to recruit slave men as soldiers, with the permission of their owners

April

9 Surrender of the army of Confederate General Robert E. Lee at Appomattox Court House, Virginia

14 President Lincoln assassinated; Vice-President Andrew Johnson succeeds to the presidency

December

18 Thirteenth Amendment to U.S. Constitution ratified; it abolishes slavery throughout the United States

FREE AT LAST

CHAPTER

I.

A WAR FOR
THE UNION

IT WOULD BE A WAR TO RESTORE NATIONAL UNITY, a war in which slaves would be, at best, interested spectators whose status and circumstances would remain unchanged. So said Abraham Lincoln, the new president, and nearly every other official in his administration. Generals in the field and politicians in Congress echoed those opinions.

Slaves had a different understanding of the war. Unmoved by public pronouncements and official policies, they recognized their centrality to the dispute and knew their future depended upon its outcome. Lacking political standing and public voice, and forbidden access to the weapons of war, slaves nonetheless acted resolutely to place their freedom and that of their posterity on the wartime agenda. By demonstrating their readiness to risk all for freedom and to put their loyalty, their labor, and their lives in the service of the Union, they gradually rendered untenable every policy short of universal emancipation.

The change did not come easily or at once. At first, Union political and military leaders freed slaves only hesitantly, under pressure

of wartime necessity. But slowly the Northern people and their representatives in Congress embraced emancipation, and a war for the
Union became a war against slavery. In September 1862, President
Lincoln informed the world that he would issue a proclamation of
emancipation on January 1, 1863. What had once been inconceiv-
able to all but the despised abolitionist and the lowly slave became
the official policy of the federal government. The president who had
sworn to uphold slavery became the Great Emancipator.

Even before the first battle, rumors of civil war threatened the balance of power between slave and master, putting at risk the stability of the Southern social order. Many white Southerners, slaveholders and nonslaveholders alike, feared that when white men
marched off to war, slaves would turn on their enslavers and seize
their liberty. To foil potential insurrectionists, one barely literate
Alabama farmer urged Confederate president Jefferson Davis to
imprison black men or enroll them in the army.

The State of Ala.   Monroe County   Bells Ldg   May th 4 /1861
Dear Sir   i havs to in form you that thire is a good meny pore men
with large famely to susport An if they have to go in to the Army there
famelys will sufer   thire is a Nother question to rise with us   the
Negroes is very Hiley Hope up that they will soon Be free so i think that
you Had Better order out All the Negroe felers from 17 years oald
up   Ether fort them up or put them in the army and Make them fite
like good fells for wee ar in danger of our lives hear among them   So i
Will close with my Best love to you

                                                        Wm H Lee[1]
ALS

The presumption that slaves understood the sectional conflict and
anticipated their imminent liberation was not confined to unlet-
tered white Southerners. An educated Georgian urged the Confed-

erate secretary of war to protect the home front, strengthen Confederate forces in the field, and teach the Yankees a well-deserved lesson by arming slave men against the Northern enemy.

Athens Ga 4th May 1861

Dear Sir

. . . .

Some of our people are fearful that when a large portion of our fighting men are taken from the country, that large numbers of our negroes aided by emissaries will ransack portions of the country, kill numbers of our inhabitants, and make their way to the black republicans;   There is no doubt but that numbers of them believe that Lincoln's intention is to set them all free.   Then, to counteract this idea, and make them assist in whipping the black republicans, which by the by would be the best thing that could be done, could they not be incorporated into our armies, say ten or twenty placed promiscuously in each company?   In this way there number would be too small to do our army any injury, whilst they might be made quite efficient in battle, as there are a great many I have no doubt that would make good soldiers and would willingly go if they had a chance.   They might be valued as you would a horse or other property, and let the government pay for them provided they was killed in battle, and it should be made known to them that if they distinguish^d themselves by good conduct in battle, they should be rewarded.   Could some plan of this sort be thought expedient and be carried out with propriety, it would certainly lessen the dangers at home, and increase our strength in the field, and would I have but little doubt, be responded to by large numbers of our people in all the States.   It is however only a suggestion, but one that I have thought might merit your consideration.   Very Respectfully your humble Servant

ALS

John J. Cheatham[2]

While some Confederate partisans foresaw a threat to slavery, President Abraham Lincoln and the U.S. Congress reiterated that the North sought only to preserve the Union. Desiring to reassure unionists in the slave states—particularly the border states of Maryland, Kentucky, and Missouri, which had not seceded—Lincoln promised that the army would respect the property rights of slaveholders. In the early months of the war, federal field commanders hewed closely to the president's policy. Writing to General William S. Harney, the commander at St. Louis, a Missouri unionist sought assurances that the government would protect slavery.

Saint Louis   Mo.   May 14, 1861.

Sir: In common with thousands who have perused your admirable proclamation of this morning,* I return you the thanks of a citizen of Missouri for its pratriotic tone and tranquilizing assurances.

There is nothing in this paper which is in my opinion needs explanation; yet I wish to be able to answer, with the authority of your name, a question which I have already replied to on my own judgment. Last evening, a gentleman, of the highest respectability, and intelligence, from Greene county, Mo. asked me whether I supposed it was the intention of the United States Government to interfere with the institution of negro slavery in Missouri or any Slave State, or impair the security of that description of property.   Of course, my answer was most unqualifiedly, and almost indignantly in the negative.   I told him that I had no means of forming an opinion which were not open to every other

---

*In a proclamation to the people of Missouri, General Harney warned that "the whole power of the Government of the United States, if necessary, will be exerted to maintain Missouri in her present position in the Union" and pledged himself to that end. Harney also vowed to use his authority to protect the "persons and property [of Missouri unionists] from violations of every kind." (*Destruction of Slavery*, p. 414n.)

private citizen; but that I felt certain that the force of the United States, would, if necessary, be exerted for the protection of this, as well as any other kind of property.   Will you be good enough to spare from your engrossing military duties so much time as may be required to say whether I answered correctly?

I have the honor to be, with the highest respect, your most obedient Servant.

HLcSr   (Sgd)   Thomas T. Gantt.[3]

General Harney was quick to reassure Gantt.

[*St. Louis, Mo.*]   May 14, 1861.
Sir: I have just received your note of this date, inquiring whether, in my opinion, you were correct in replying to a citizen of Southwestern Missouri as to the purpose of the United States Government respecting the protection of negro property.

I must premise my saying that I have no special instructions on this Head from the War Department.   But I should as soon expect to hear that the orders of the Government were directed towards the overthrow of any other kind of property as of this in negro slaves.

I entertain no doubt whatever that you answered the question you mention correctly.   I should certainly have answered it in the same manner, and I think with the very feelings you describe.   I am not a little astonished that such a question could be seriously put.   Already since the commencement of these unhappy disturbances, slaves have escaped from their owners, and have sought refuge in the camps of

United States troops from Northern states and commanded by a Northern General. They were carefully sent back to their owners. An insurrection of slaves was reported to have taken place in Maryland. A Northern General offered to the Executive of that State the aid of Northern troops under his own command, to suppress it. Incendiaries have asked of the President permission to invade the Southern States, and have been warned that any attempt to do this will be punished as a crime. I repeat it, I have no special means of knowledge on this subject, but what I have cited, and my general acquaintance with the statesmanlike views of the President, makes me confident in expressing the opinion above given. Very respectfully, Your obedt. Servant:

[*William S. Harney*]⁴

HLc

Slaves paid no heed to such pronouncements and instead fled slavery and sought refuge within Union lines. Their persistence eventually forced field commanders to reconsider the policies of their superiors. The first change came in late May 1861 at Fortress Monroe, Virginia, a federal bastion at the tip of the peninsula between the James and York rivers. Fugitive slaves, some of whom had been impressed to work on Confederate batteries, sought entry into the fortress. General Benjamin F. Butler, its commander, gave them food and shelter and put the able-bodied men to work. To his superiors in Washington, Butler justified these actions as a way to deprive the Confederacy of the benefits of slave labor and satisfy the Union army's labor requirements without necessarily disturbing its commitment to respect slave property. But men who had labored on Confederate fortifications were not the only slaves who fled to Fortress Monroe. The arrival of large numbers of women and children raised difficult questions, which Butler answered by accepting all applicants, employing the able-bodied at military labor, and issuing rations to both workers and nonworkers. He defended these measures to General-in-Chief Winfield Scott.

[*Fortress Monroe, Va.*]   May 27 /61

Sir

(Duplicate)

Since I wrote my last dispatch the question in regard to slave property is becoming one of very serious magnitude.   The inhabitants of Virginia are using their negroes in the batteries, and are preparing to send the women and children South.   The escapes from them are very numerous, and a squad has come in this morning to my pickets bringing their women and children.   Of course these cannot be dealt with upon the Theory on which I designed to treat the services of able bodied men and women who might come within my lines and of which I gave you a detailed account in my last dispatch.*   I am in the utmost doubt what to do with this species of property.   Up to this time I have had come within my lines men and women with their children—entire families—each family belonging to the same owner.   I have therefore determined to employ, as I can do very profitably, the able-bodied persons in the party, issuing proper food for the support of all, and charging against their services the expense of care and sustenance of the non-laborers, keeping a strict and accurate account as well of the services as of the expenditure having the worth of the services and the cost of the expenditure determined by a board of Survey hereafter to be detailed.   I know of no other manner in which to dispose of this subject and the questions

---

*In the earlier letter to Scott, Butler reported his receipt of three slave
men who had run away to avoid impressment for Confederate military
labor. Finding them "very serviceable" and being "in great need of
labor" for his own quartermaster's department, Butler had put the
men to work. "Shall [the Confederates] be allowed the use of this
property against the United States," he asked rhetorically, "and we
not be allowed its use in aid of the United States?" (*Destruction of
Slavery*, p. 72n.)

connected therewith.   As a matter of property to the insurgents it will
be of very great moment, the number that I now have amounting as I am
informed to what in good times would be of the value of sixty thousand
dollars.   Twelve of these negroes I am informed have escaped from the
erection of the batteries on Sewall's point which this morning fired upon
my expedition as it passed by out of range.   As a means of offence
therefore in the enemy's hands these negroes when able bodied are of
the last importance.   Without them the batteries could not have been
erected at least for many weeks   As a military question it would seem
to be a measure of necessity to deprive their masters of their
services   How can this be done?   As a political question and a question
of humanity can I receive the services of a Father and a Mother and not
take the children?   Of the humanitarian aspect I have no doubt.   Of the
political one I have no right to judge.   I therefore submit all this to your
better judgement, and as these questions have a political aspect, I have
ventured—and I trust I am not wrong in so doing—to duplicate the
parts of my dispatch relating to this subject and forward them to the
Secretary of War.

                                    .   .   .   .

HLcS   Benj. F. Butler[5]

General Scott approved Butler's course, as did Secretary of War
Simon Cameron. In a letter to Butler of May 30, 1861, Cameron
acknowledged the importance of enforcing federal laws (including
the fugitive-slave law), but argued that no "Federal obligations"
outweighed the suppression of armed rebellion. He therefore instructed Butler to "refrain from surrendering [fugitive slaves] to
alleged masters."[6] Needing no encouragement, Butler declared the
runaways "contraband of war"—property subject to seizure because of its military value to the enemy.[7] His bold stroke captured
the Northern imagination, and the designation "contrabands"

quickly gained general usage as a name for fugitive slaves within
Union lines. Butler continued to accept "contrabands," and before
long slaves from throughout eastern Virginia were seeking protection at Fortress Monroe.

Butler's policy also found support in Congress, especially after
the defeat at Bull Run in July 1861 dashed hope of a quick Union
victory. In August, Congress passed and Lincoln signed the First
Confiscation Act, which sought to weaken the Confederacy by making all property employed in support of the rebellion—including
slaves—"subject of prize and capture wherever found."[8] Although
it did not explicitly declare such slaves free, it nullified their owners' claim to them.

The shift in federal policy signaled by the confiscation act hardly
diminished the dangers of flight. If recaptured by their owners,
runaways faced certain punishment and sometimes death. After
the war, a Freedmen's Bureau official in Washington, D.C., gathered testimony describing the fate of a fugitive slave who had been
returned to his owner after reaching Union lines in 1861.

Washington D.C.   [*November 20,*] 1867

. . . .

On the 28th of May 1866, Henry Seward made affadavit that in
December 1861 while in Conversation with Mr. Samuel Cox living five
(5) miles South of Port Tobacco [*Maryland*], he (Cox) confessed that in
August 1861 he had murdered one of his Slaves, Jack Scroggins by
whipping him to death—

This statement is corroberrated by affadavits made by John Sims—
and William Jackson—(at a different time) who testify that Scroggins
was flogged to death for having escaped to the Federal lines, whence he

was recaptured— and on the 12th of May 1866—Wm Hill, col[*ore*]^d an employee at the Senate Post Office reports this case and states that in whipping Scroggins to death Cox was assisted by Frank Roly his overseer & 2 other men. all these parties are living now at the same place and have never been arrested

. . . .

HL_d   [*Charles H. Howard*][9]

The operation of Union armies in the border states put Northern soldiers in direct contact with slaves and slaveholders, often for the first time in their lives. Few soldiers began the war determined to destroy slavery; most had no commitment to abolition or racial equality. For many of these soldiers, however, encounters with desperate slaves and haughty slave owners illustrated the barbarity of slavery. The very presence of Northern troops, moreover, emboldened slaves to flee to their camps. Even soldiers with an active disdain for people of African descent found the fugitives useful in scouting the countryside, building fortifications, preparing meals, and cleaning camp. The ability of slaves to ingratiate themselves with individual soldiers disrupted slavery, angered slaveholding unionists, and obliged officers like General Charles P. Stone, commander of an observation corps on the Maryland side of the Potomac River, to remind his troops of their duty to uphold the laws of the United States.

Poolesville [*Md.*] Sept. 23^d 1861.

General Orders N° 16   The General Commanding has with great concern learned that in several instances soldiers of this Corps have so far forgotten their duty as to excite and encourage insubordination among the colored servants in the neighbourhood of their camps, in direct violation of the laws of the United States, and of the state of

Maryland in which they are serving.

The immediate object of raising and supporting this army was the suppression of rebellion, and the putting down by military power of those ambitious and misguided people, who (unwilling to subject themselves to the constitution and laws of the country) preferred the carrying out of their own ideas of right and wrong, to living in peace and good order under the established Government— While, therefore, it should be the pride of Every Army to yield instant and complete obedience to the laws of the land, it is peculiarly the duty of Every officer and Enlisted man in this Army to give an example of subordination and perfect obedience to the laws: and to shew to those in rebellion, that loyal national soldiers sink all private opinions in their devotion to law as it stands.   By order of Brig Gen[l] Stone[10]

HDc

When Union troops entered Kentucky in the fall of 1861, their commanders confronted the same problem Butler had faced in Virginia and Stone in Maryland. Federal soldiers employed fugitive slaves as scouts, personal servants, and laborers. Even commanders who cared nothing about the runaways' aspirations and worried that harboring them would alienate border-state slaveholders found fugitive slaves militarily useful. That was the dilemma facing General Alexander McDowell McCook, who appealed for guidance from his superior, General William T. Sherman.

Camp Nevin   Kentucky   November 5th 1861
General: The subject of Contraband negros is one that is looked to, by the Citizens of Kentucky of vital importance   Ten have come into my Camp within as many hours, and from what they say, there will be a

general Stampeed of slaves from the other side of Green River— They have already become a source of annoyance to me, and I have great reason to belive that this annoyance will increase the longer we stay— They state the reasons of their running away—there masters are rank Secessionists, in some cases are in the rebel army—and that Slaves of union men are pressed into service to drive teams &&c

I would respectfully suggest that if they be allowed to remain here, that our cause in Kentucky may be injured— I have no faith in Kentucky's loyalty, there-for have no great desire to protect her pet institution Slavery— As a matter of policy, how would it do, for me to send for their master's and diliver the negro's—to them on the out-side of our lines, or send them to the other side of Green River and deliver them up— What effect would it have on our cause south of the River— I am satisfied they bolster themselves up, by making the uninformed believe that this is a war upon African slavery— I merely make these suggestions, for I am very far from wishing these recreant masters in possession of any of their property—for I think slaves no better than horses in that respect—

I have put the negro's to work— They will be handy with teams, and generally useful. I consider the subject embarrassing and must defer to your better judgement

                    . . . .

The negros that came to me to day state that their master's had notified them to be ready to go south with them on Monday Morning, and they left Sunday night—

                    . . . .

ALS   A. M^cD. McCook[11]

In reply, Sherman formulated a policy many generals found attractive. He urged McCook to stay clear of the entire matter by excluding fugitive slaves from his lines.

Louisville Kenty   Nov 8, 1861

Sir   I have no instructions from Government on the subject of
Negroes,   my opinion is that the laws of the state of Kentucky are in full
force and that negroes must be surrendered on application of their
masters or agents or delivered over to the sheriff of the County.   We
have nothing to do with them at all and you should not let them take
refuge in Camp.   It forms a source of misrepresentation by which Union
men are estranged from our Cause

I know it is almost impossible for you to ascertain in any case the
owner of the negro, but so it is,   his word is not taken in evidence and
you will send them away   I am yours

HLcS   W. T. Sherman[12]

Although Union commanders ordered runaway slaves banished
from their camps, slaves continued to find allies within the army.
When a Maryland slave owner tried to recover his slave from a regiment of Massachusetts soldiers, he discovered that the fugitives'
friends could be a formidable lot. Driven from the camp in a hail of
epithets and brickbats, the beleaguered slaveholder appealed to
Thomas H. Hicks, the governor of Maryland, who in turn petitioned officials in Washington with plaintive tales of loyal men
abused while attempting to recover legally owned property. Declaring "the Devlish Nigger difficulty" irrelevant to the war, Hicks
urged Secretary of War Simon Cameron to enforce the law, protect
slave property, and thereby ensure the loyalty of Maryland.

Annapolis [*Md.*],   November 18 *1861*

My Dear Sir   A circumstance occurred at one of the Camps in the
vicinity of Annapolis, viz. the Massachusetts 25th Regiment, to day, that,
calls forth this communication.

The facts, I briefly, but, correctly narrate.   I was called on by a Mr
Tucker of this (Anne Arundel) County, who stated that he had a servant,
that had left him, and taken refuge in the Encampment of the 25th Regt.
from Mass, that he had repaired to the ground so occupied, and that Co[l]
Upton, Commanding, at first refused, afterward, said to him go through
and see if your man is here,   He proceeded, but a short distance, when
he *Tucker* was surrounded by quite a number, menaced him, and, applied
opprobious Epithets; such as Negro stealer, Negro catchers, and that the
negro was better than he, the master was &c &c until he was obliged to
leave the ground, without looking after his servant.   Now whilst in this
there is amusement, I must say there was much to provoke, and altho I
care little for what becomes of the negroes, yet these things produce bad
feeling and bad effect.   upon the representation of this case. I wrote to
Co[l] Upton, and at same time sent for Co[l] Morse Commanding the 21st
Mass. Regt. and here I discovered the necessity of obtrudeing a little
upon your closely occupied time, and patience; Gen[l] Burnside was not
here (gone to N.Y)   all here, were then equal in grade (Coln[s]) and none
to Issue orders, or command supremely.   the result is, the case stands
open.   Tucker has gone home much fretted, and his servant, at
large.   now a word as to how these things work;   we *all* delighted with
Gen[l] Dix, Proclamation, issued for the E. S. of Virginia;* rec[d], this
morning per mail; but taken quite aback this evening, by the occurrence
at Camp Hicks (I understand it is call[d]) in regard to this servant and his
master, with those offering insult—

.   .   .   .

---

*On November 13, 1861, General John A. Dix, who was about to
invade the Eastern Shore of Virginia, had assured residents of the
region that his army would threaten "no rights of person or property,"
and that their laws, institutions, and customs would be "scrupulously
respected." (*Destruction of Slavery*, pp. 79–80.)

you are fully aware sir of the difficulty we have had in M^d. things are
working right now. let us have no stumbling blocks placed in our
way— I care nothing for the Devlish Nigger difficulty, I desire to save
the union, and will cooperate with the Administration in everything
tending to that important result, that is proper. I know the difficulties
surrounding us, and do not wish to mingle and mix up too much with the
main design.

I labored to have M^d roll up a majority, that would smother
secessionism. We have given them a heavy dose. I hope to strike them
another blow by an early convocation of the Legislature of our state, and
if we can but keep away outside Issues, and all things foreign from the,
one, true, great design of all Patriots, we shall save the union— I will
attend early to your Telegram rec^d this evening. I have the Honor to be
with great respect y^r ob^t Servant

ALS   Tho. H. Hicks[13]

General Henry W. Halleck, commander of the Department of the
Missouri, was well aware of the political difficulties likely to follow
from accepting fugitive slaves, but he chose military, rather than
political, grounds to justify excluding them.

St. Louis, [Mo.] November 20th, 1861.

GENERAL ORDERS, No. 3.

I. It has been represented that important information respecting the
numbers and condition of our forces is conveyed to the enemy by means
of fugitive slaves who are admitted within our lines. In order to remedy
this evil, it is directed that no such persons be hereafter permitted to

enter the lines of any camp, or of any forces on the march, and that any now within such lines be immediately excluded therefrom.

II. The General Commanding wishes to impress upon all officers in command of posts and troops in the field the importance of preventing unauthorized persons of every description from entering and leaving our lines, and of observing the greatest precaution in the employment of agents and clerks in confidential positions. BY ORDER OF MAJOR GENERAL HALLECK.[14]

PD

> Even as General Halleck professed to fear that fugitive slaves might be serving as spies for the Confederacy, black freemen in the North were clamoring to fight for the Union. Although federal officials gave their petitions little heed, they continued to press for an opportunity to strike a blow against slavery and thereby strengthen their own claim to equality. In parts of the North, black men formed militia companies and began drilling on their own, hoping that their chance would soon come. Hearing rumors that the rebels were forcing black men, free and slave, to fight for the Confederacy,* a freeman in Ohio beseeched Secretary of War Simon Cameron.

Oberlin O.   Nov. 27th 1861

Sir:— Very many of the colored citizens of Ohio and other states have had a great desire to assist the government in putting down this injurious rebellion.

Since they have heard that the rebels are forming regiments of the free blacks and compelling them to fight against the Union as well as

---

*The rumors, which were false, perhaps derived from the fact that a few free-black militia units had offered their services to the Confederacy. (See below, p. 437.)

their Slaves. They have urged me to write and beg that you will receive one or more regiments (or companies) of the colored of the free States to counterbalance those employed against the Union by Rebels.

We are partly drilled and would wish to enter active service amediately.

We behold your sick list each day and Sympathize with the Soldiers and the government. We are confident of our ability to stand the hard Ships of the field and the climate So unhealthy to the Soldiers of the *North*

To prove our attachment and our will to defend the government we only ask a trial   I have the honor to remain your humble Servant

ALS   Wᵐ A. Jones[15]

Fugitive slaves hoped to find Union soldiers who would protect them from recapture, but unless they could demonstrate that they had been employed against the Union and were therefore entitled to freedom under the First Confiscation Act, federal policy required that they be returned to their owners. Many soldiers, mindful of the law and respectful of higher authority, followed orders to the letter. According to a report sent to Governor John A. Andrew of Massachusetts, soldiers from his state had returned several black people who entered their encampment in Maryland to sell baked goods. The complicity of Union soldiers in sustaining slavery angered abolitionists like Governor Andrew, who indignantly forwarded the report to Secretary of War Simon Cameron.

Boston [*Mass.*],   Dec 7, *186*1

Dear Sir   I wish to call your attention to the enclosed copy of a recent letter from a reliable source, in relation to the use to which Massachusetts soldiers are being put, (as is alleged) by Brigadier General Stone. I cannot for a moment beleive that the War Department will countenance such proceedings, and I invoke your interpostion not only now, but for the future, for the issue of such orders as will secure the soldiers of this Commonwealth from being participators in such dirty and despotic work. Massachusetts does not send her citizens forth to become the hunters of men or to engage in the seizure and return to captivity of persons claimed to be fugitive slaves, without any recognition of even the forms of law & I trust you will save our soldiers and our State from such dishonor, by the exercise of your official authority in such manner as will insure the protection of our men from such outrages in future and humanity itself from such infractions under color of military law and duty.   I remain with great respect Your Obedient Servant.

HLS   John A. Andrew[16]

[*Enclosure*]   Poolesville Md   Nov 28, 1861
                          (Copy)
                        . . . .*

   On Saturday last an order came down from General Stone giving a description of two Fugitive Slaves and directing their return (in case they should enter our camp,) to their owners "whoever they might be".   This order it appears was handed by Lieut Col Palfrey, to the Officer of the day, Mr Macy of Co I.   On Sunday morning several negroes came into Camp as usual for the purpose of selling cakes, pies &c to the Soldiers.

   Although having eatables for sale, some of these negroes were themselves almost famished and were treated to a breakfast by the men of one of our German Companies.†   About the time of guard mounting

---

*The ellipsis appears in the manuscript.

†I.e., companies from Massachusetts that were composed of German immigrants.

the vigilant eyes of Lieut Macy espied the negroes as they were
disposing of their wares through the Company streets, and, leaving the
new guard to be mounted as it might, he beckoned two of the negroes to
the Guard house when he ordered them into arrest and then
immediately *detailed a file of Soldiers under a sergeant with loaded
muskets to escort them to their supposed owners and deliver them up.*

The procedure was therefore unknown to all save the officers who
were parties to it and the parties who composed the escort had no
knowledge that their prisoners were suspected fugitives.[17]

HDc

> In response, Cameron instructed the general in whose command
> the episode had occurred that he should issue orders to "prevent
> similar complaints for the future, of injustice and oppression to ne-
> groes visiting the camps in the exercise of lawful occupations."[18]

———•—•———

> While opponents of slavery like Governor Andrew pressed the fed-
> eral government from the outside, abolitionists within Union ranks
> itched for an opportunity to put their principles into practice. Late
> in 1861, General John W. Phelps, a Vermont free-soiler, took com-
> mand of Ship Island, off the coast of Mississippi. While federal
> troops prepared for an invasion of Louisiana, Phelps issued a
> proclamation to the people of the region, denouncing slavery as a
> relic of the past that subverted republican principles and threat-
> ened American liberty. Expounding upon the ideals that had guid-
> ed one wing of the antislavery movement in the North for more
> than a generation, Phelps contrasted the virtues of free labor to the
> vice of slavery. Opponents of slavery applauded Phelps, but, as he
> later noted, "the government never seemed to recognize [the
> proclamation], either to approve or disapprove."[19]

Ship Island, Miss.   December 4th 1861

To the Loyal Citizens of the South-West: Without any desire of my own, but contrary to my private inclinations, I again find myself among you as an officer of the Government.*   A proper respect for my fellow countrymen renders it not out of place that I should make known to you the motives and principles by which my command will be governed.

We believe that every State that has been admitted as a Slave State into the Union, since the adoption of the Constitution, has been so admitted in direct violation of that Constitution.

We believe that the Slave States which existed, as such, at the adoption of our Constitution, are, by becoming parties to that compact, under the highest obligations of honor and morality to abolish Slavery.

It is our conviction that monopolies are as destructive as competition is conservative of the principles and vitalities of republican government; that slave-labor is a monopoly which excludes free-labor and competition; that slaves are kept in comparative ease and idleness in a fertile half of our arable national territory, while free white laborers, constantly augmenting in numbers from Europe, are confined to the other half, and are often distressed by want; that the free-labor of the North has more need of expansion into the Southern States, from which it is virtually excluded, than Slavery had into Texas in 1846; that free labor is essential to free institutions; that these institutions are better adapted and more congenial to the Anglo-Saxon race than are the despotic tendencies of Slavery; and, finally, that the dominant political principle of this North American Continent, so long as the Caucasian race continues to flow in upon us from Europe, must needs be that of free institutions and free government.   Any obstructions to the progress

---

*Presumably a reference to his service in the regular army before the Civil War.

of that form of Government in the United-States must inevitably be attended with discord and war.

Slavery, from the condition of a universally recognised social and moral evil, has become at length a political institution, demanding political recognition. It demands rights, to the exclusion and annihilation of those rights which are insured to us by the Constitution; and we must choose between them, which we will have, for we cannot have both. The Constitution was made for Freemen, not for Slaves. Slavery, as a social evil, might for a time be tolerated and endured; but as a political institution it becomes imperious and exacting, controlling, like a dread necessity, all whom circumstances have compelled to live under its sway, hampering their action, and thus impeding our national progress. As a political institution it could exist as a coordinate part only of two forms of government, viz, the despotic and the free; and it could exist under a free government only where public sentiment, in the most unrestricted exercise of a robust freedom, leading to extravagance and licentiousness, had swayed the thoughts and habits of the people beyond the bounds and limits of their own moderate constitutional provisions. It could exist under a free government only where the people in a period of unreasoning extravagance had permitted popular clamor to overcome public reason, and had attempted the impossibility of setting up, permanently, as a political institution, a social evil which is opposed to moral law.

By reverting to the history of the past, we find that one of the most destructive wars on record, that of the French Revolution, was originated by the attempt to give political character to an institution which was not susceptible of political character. The Church, by being endowed with political power, with its convents, its schools, its immense landed wealth, its associations, secret and open, became the ruling

power of the State, and thus occasioned a war of more strife and
bloodshed, probably, than any other war which has desolated the earth.

Slavery is still less susceptible of political character than was the
Church. It is as fit at this moment for the lumber-room of the past as
was in 1793 the monastery, the landed wealth, the exclusive privileges,
etc, of the Catholic Church in France. It behooves us to consider, as a
self-governing people, bred, and reared, and practiced in the habits of
self-government, whether we cannot, whether we *ought* not, to
revolutionize Slavery out of existence without the necessity of a conflict
of arms like that of the French Revolution.

Indeed, we feel assured that the moment Slavery is abolished, from
that moment our Southern brethren, every ten of whom have probably
seven relatives in the North, would begin to emerge from a hateful
delirium. From that moment, relieved from imaginary terrors, their
days become happy and their nights peaceable and free from alarm; the
aggregate amount of labor, under the new stimulus of fair competition,
becomes greater day by day; property rises in value; invigorating
influences succeed to stagnation, degeneracy and decay; and union,
harmony, and peace, to which we have so long been strangers, become
restored, and bind us again in the bonds of friendship and amity, as
when we first began our national career, under our glorious government
of 1789.

Why do the leaders of the rebellion seek to change the form of your
ancient government? Is it because the growth of the African element of
your population has come at length to render a change necessary? Will
you permit the free government under which you have thus far lived, and
which is so well suited for the developement of true manhood, to be
altered to a narrow and belittling despotism, in order to adapt it to the
necessities of ignorant slaves, and the requirements of their proud and

aristocratic owners?   Will the laboring men of the South bend their
necks to the same yoke that is suited to the slave?   We think not.   We
may safely answer that the time has not yet arrived when our Southern
brethren, for the mere sake of keeping Africans in slavery, will abandon
their long cherished free institutions, and enslave themselves.   It is the
conviction of my command, as a part of the national forces of the
United-States that labor—manual labor—is inherently noble; that it
cannot be systematically degraded by any nation without ruining its
peace, happiness, and power; that free labor is the granite basis on
which free institutions must rest; that it is the right, the capital, the
inheritance, the hope of the poor man every where; that it is especially
the right of five millions of our fellow countrymen in the Slave States as
well as of the four millions of Africans there; and all our efforts,
therefore, however small or great, whether directed against the
interference from governments abroad, or against rebellious
combinations at home, shall be for Free labor; our motto and our
standard shall be, here, and every where, and on all occasions—
FREE LABOR AND WORKING-MEN'S RIGHTS.   It is on this basis,
and this basis alone, that our munificent government—the asylum of
the nations—can be perpetuated and preserved.

ADeS   J. W. Phelps[20]

Other Northerners shared Phelps's hatred of slavery, and they condemned as morally bankrupt and militarily counterproductive the
policy of returning fugitive slaves to their owners. Writing to Secretary of War Simon Cameron, a Quaker in Michigan enumerated the
disastrous effects of that policy on military operations in Kentucky
and warned that driving away fugitive slaves would permanently
alienate them from the Union cause.

Battle Creek [*Mich.*]   Decr 5th 61

Freind Camron   a Fugitive from Tenesee a few nights Since on his way
to Canada Informed me that it is the Settled Intention of the Rebels to
Ere Long Arm the Slaves throughout the Entier South put them in the
front Ranks to Receive the fier & then Storm the Federal works in all
points.   he Sais its Talked of in all the Rebel Familys. Declaring that
Every Slave Shall first be Butchered before the Rebels will give up   he
Sais that Tens of Thousands of Slaves are in the greatest Alarm their
masters telling them that our officers & Army will Sell them to Cuba &
that 5 Slaves that was Sent over from Kentuckey by our Federal Troops
Say that the ware Badly Treated by our officers altho the offered to
work or Fight for the Government. but ware told to Clear out that the
officers wanted no D—D Niggers about them &c &c & ware actually
Driven over to their old Homes.   he Sais too that there is not a Slave
South but would Take up arms for our Troopes if the Could, but the
Treatment the Receive has almost Sett them Crasy.   the Expected
Friends of us in Stead of Enemys   the are Comeing through here
Constantly on their way to Canada.   now what a picture is this.   is our
Relatives to be Butcherd as the Are & we to add fuel to the Flames of
the Rebels to Continue the Destruction.   oh Can it be that this
Government is to Crush 4000000 of Human beings. to uphold the most
Blood Thirsty Sett of Tyrants on Earth.   your Document* is greatly
approved of, and if the Administration Dont put a Stop to the Ill
Treatment of the Slaves by our Army I greally fear that we will be the

---

*The reference is to Cameron's controversial annual report of
December 1, 1861, which advocated employing slaves on behalf of the
Union war effort—including arming them for military service—and
freeing all those so employed. President Lincoln forced Cameron to
delete the recommendation to arm and free slaves. (*Destruction of
Slavery*, p. 270n.)

Loosers thereby— I think that matter Cannot be Seen to, to Soon for I am Satisfyed that the Rebels will Resort to any Attrocious acts to Carry their points— Very Truly Yours

ALS   H. Willis[21]

Not all fugitive slaves received a hostile reception in Union camps. Some soldiers sheltered and protected fugitives, much to the discomfiture of federal commanders. Ordered by General Henry W. Halleck to exclude runaway slaves from his camps in Missouri, General Alexander S. Asboth dutifully informed his subordinates of the policy and demanded that they enforce it. Learning that fugitives nevertheless remained within his lines, Asboth directed regimental commanders in his division to report their compliance with Halleck's exclusion order.[22] Major George E. Waring, Jr., one of Asboth's subordinates, chafed under the assignment. His dilemma was compounded by the fact that fugitives, facing the loss of federal protection, frequently claimed to be legally free. For Waring, the potential injustice of enslaving free men and women and the inconvenience of losing valuable servants and laborers outweighed Halleck's desire to exclude the question of slavery by excluding the slaves.

Camp Halleck   near Rolla Mo.   Dec 19th 61

General: In obedience to the order contained in your circular (No. 2), received this day, I beg to report that on the receipt of your order No 23 communicating Gen. Order No. 3, from the Commanding General, ordering fugitive slaves to be excluded from the lines,* I caused all negroes in my camp to be examined, and it was reported to me that they all stoutly asserted that they were free.

Since that time a woman employed in my own mess as cook has been

---

*For the full text of General Order 3, see above, pp. 17–18.

claimed by one Captain Holland as the fugitive slave of his father-in-law. In compliance with your order, to that end, which he produced, she was given up to him.   Since the receipt of your circular of today, I have again caused an investigation to be thoroughly made which has resulted as in the first instance.

I beg now, General, to ask for your instructions in the matter.   These negroes all claim and insist that they are *free*.   Some of them, I have no question, are so; others I have as little doubt have been slaves,—but no one is here to prove it, and I hesitate to take so serious a responsibility as to decide, arbitrarily, in the absence of any direct evidence, that they are such.

If I turn them away, I inflict great hardship upon them, as they would be homeless and helpless.   Furthermore, such a course would occasion much personal inconvenience and sincere regret, to other officers no less than to myself.   These people are mainly our servants, and we can get no others.   They have been employed in this capacity for some time— long enough for us to like them as servants, to find them useful and trustworthy, and to feel an interest in their welfare.

The Commanding General, in his letter to Col. Blair, (as published in the Missouri Democrat of the 16th inst), says—in explanation of General order No 3.—"Unauthorized persons, black or white, free or slave, must be kept out of our camps."   The negroes in my camp are employed, in accordance with the Army Regulations, as officers servants, teamsters, and hospital attendants, and, with the exception of one little child are such as we are authorized to have in the camp.   It seems to me that they are without the pale of the order and the *intention* of the Commanding General, and I trust that I may be excused for awaiting more explicit instructions before doing what may be an extra-official act—at which my private feelings revolt.

I recognize the fact that obedience to Gen. Orders No. 3 is a part of my military duty, and I shall unflinchingly comply with it in the consciousness that I am in no way responsible therefore; but I *am* personally responsible for my decision, when it is to affect the happiness and security of others.

May I ask you, General, to relieve me of this responsibility by giving me your final decision at your earliest convenience. Very Respectfully Your Obedient Servant

ALS   Geo. E. Waring, Jr.[23]

Asboth referred Waring's letter to General Halleck, who responded that the return of the woman to her putative owner was "contrary to the intent" of General Order 3, which was to let civil authorities decide matters involving "[t]he relation between the slave and his master, or pretended master" and to "keep [the army] clear of all such questions." The order, Halleck further explained, did not apply to officers' servants or to other "negroes employed by proper authority in camps."[24]

For John Boston, a runaway slave from Maryland who took refuge with a New York regiment, the triumph of his own liberation was tainted by the resulting separation from his wife.

Upton Hill [*Va.*]   January [the] 12 1862

My Dear Wife   it is with grate joy I take this time to let you know Whare I am   i am now in Safety in the 14th Regiment of Brooklyn   this Day i can Adress you thank god as a free man   I had a little truble in giting away But as the lord led the Children of Isrel to

the land of Canon So he led me to a land Whare fredom Will rain in spite
Of earth and hell   Dear you must make your Self content i am free
from al the Slavers Lash   and as you have chose the Wise plan Of
Serving the lord i hope you Will pray Much and i Will try by the help of
god To Serv him With all my hart   I am With a very nice man and have
All that hart Can Wish But My Dear I Cant express my grate desire
that i Have to See you   i trust the time Will Come When We Shal meet
again   And if We dont met on earth We Will Meet in heven Whare
Jesas ranes   Dear Elizabeth tell Mrs Own[ees] That i trust that She
Will Continue Her kindness to you and that god Will Bless her on earth
and Save her In grate eternity   My Acomplements To Mrs Owens and
her Children   may They Prosper through life   I never Shall forgit
her kindness to me   Dear Wife i must Close   rest yourself Contented
i am free   i Want you to rite To me Soon as you Can Without
Delay   Direct your letter to the 14th Reigment New york State malitia
Uptons Hill Virginea In Care of M[r] Cranford Comary   Write my Dear
Soon As you C   Your Affectionate Husban   Kiss Daniel For me

John Boston

Give my love to Father and Mother[25]

ALS

It is not know whether Elizabeth Boston was a free woman or a
slave, nor is it clear whether she ever read her husband's letter. Intercepted either before or after she received it, the letter ended up
in the hands of a committee of the Maryland House of Delegates,
which presented it to General-in-Chief George B. McClellan and
demanded to know how John Boston's owner, "a loyal citizen of
Maryland," could recover his fugitive slave.[26]

The soldiers from Brooklyn who harbored John Boston were not
alone in defying orders to exclude fugitive slaves from their camps.

During the spring of 1862, attempts to enforce exclusion met increased hostility within the ranks. Mindful of the assistance fugitive slaves could render and weary of slaveholders who seemed to
value their slaves more highly than the Union, many Northern soldiers not only refused to assist in the rendition of runaways, but also turned on pursuing owners, sometimes violently. Learning of
numerous episodes in which soldiers had thwarted attempts to recover escaped slaves, a delegation of Maryland legislators protested
to Secretary of War Edwin M. Stanton.

[*Annapolis, Md.*]   March 10, 1862—
Sir   The Legislature of Maryland in the early part of its Session
appointed a committee to proceed to Washington & confer with Major
Genl McClellan in reference to the escapes of fugitive slaves within the
lines of the Army.   They presented for his consideration certain
resolutions & in response, the Committee have been informed, they were
transferred to the Secretary of War for his adjudication—   And not
receiving any communication from that Department they felt prompted
by the magnitude of the subject to depute Dr Bayne, one of the members
of the committee to solicit an interview with yourself.   He has reported
on his return, that the object of the resolutions meet with your
concurrence—And we have entertained the belief that Military Orders
would be enforced, which would not only prevent the further admission
of negroes within the lines of the Army but would have resulted in the
expulsion of those already there—   The Committee regret that the
Proclamation which has been issued in the Military Department near
the seat of Government has still continued to be inoperative—*   But

---

*In July 1861, the commander of the Department of Washington had
ordered that "[f]ugitive slaves will under no pretext whatever be
permitted to reside or be in any way harbored in the quarters and
camps of the troops serving in this department" or "to accompany
troops on the march." (*Destruction of Slavery*, p. 363n.)

they yet hope & believe that some plan will be adopted which will
accomplish the object & vindicate the rights of the loyal ctizens of
Maryland—

You advised the member of our Committee who had the honor of an
interview with you, to consult with the other members on his return &
ascertain, if some other suggestions could not be made additional to
those contemplated in the resolutions— In Military matters they defer
to your superior judgement, & still believe the plan indicated would be
the most successful & practicable one— In addition they will take the
liberty to suggest the organization of a Military Police consisting of a
few men, whose specific duty it should be to explore the Camps of every
regiment & expel therefrom every negro unless he could furnish
indubitable evidence of his freedom—

Genl Halleck has enforced orders prohibiting the admission of
fugitives within the lines of his Department— Genl Foster has done the
same most effectually at Annapolis— Genl Dix has pursued the same
course, & General Burnside has issued a similar proclamation in North
Carolina & we believe will have it executed faithfully— He has declared
in the most emphatic terms, that it is not the policy of the Government
in any way or manner to interfere with the laws of the State
constitutionally established, or their property or institutions in any
respect— And as we believe Maryland by her loyalty & geographical
position has contributed more to the preservation of the Capitol &
therby preventing a dismemberment of the Union than other State—We
therefore think we have a strong claim upon the Government for its
protection of every right guarrantied to us under the Constitution—

The Committee take the liberty to transmit a few affadavits to prove
that loyal citizens of Maryland have not only been treated with great
indignities, but have been violently contravened in the legitimate pursuit

of their property— Hundreds of similar cases could be obtained if
necessary— We have the honor to be most respectfully yr obt. servts

Jn°. H. Bayne   E. hammend

John S Sellman   Robert P. Dunlop

HLS   Washington Waters   G W Duvall[27]

[*Enclosure*]   State of Maryland Ch^s County 1st Mach 1862

On or about the 14th of november last I proceeded to Camp Fenton
near Port Tobacco to get three of my servants viz a man about Twenty
four years of age a boy about seventeen years of age and a boy some 13
or 14 years of age who had left their home and taken up their abode with
the soldiers at the above named camp   Col. Graham who was in
command at the time gave me an order to the officer of the day to search
the camp for my servants but at the same time intimated I might meet
with some difficulty as a portion of his troops were abolitionist   I
learned by some of the soldiers my servants were in Camp and soon as
my mission become general known a large crowd collected and followed
me crying shoot him, bayonet him, kill him, pitch him out, the nigger
Stealer the nigger driver   at first their threats were accompanied with
a few stones thrown at me which very soon became an allmost continued
shower of stones a number of which struck me, but did me no serious
damage.   Seeing the officer who accompanied me took no notice of what
was going on and fearing that some of the soldiers would put their
threats of shooting me into execution I informed him that I would not
proceed any farther,   about this time Lieutenant Edmund Harrison
came to my assistance and swore he would shoot the first man who
threw a stone at me,   the soldiers hooted at him and continued throwing.
I returned to Co^l Grahams quarters but was not permitted to see him

again.   I left the camp without getting my servants and have not been favored to get them yet

HDS   A. J. Smoot[28]

Perhaps more disturbing to border-state slaveholders than the opposition of soldiers in the field was the increasing indifference of officials in Washington. Whereas earlier appeals from prominent unionists had jolted the Lincoln administration into action, now a War Department aide offhandedly notified the Maryland delegation that the secretary of war would attend to their complaint "as soon as he is relieved from more important and pressing duties."[29]

The difficulty of excluding slaves increased as Northern soldiers advanced from the border states, where many slaveholders claimed fidelity to the Union, into the seceded states, where most slaveholders were sworn enemies. General Ambrose E. Burnside, commander of an expedition that invaded coastal North Carolina in early 1862, discovered the inefficacy of the old rules. Initially, he issued the customary assurances that the rights of loyal slaveholders would be respected. After capturing New Bern, however, he found few loyal slaveholders but many slaves who welcomed the Union invasion. Unsure how to proceed, he turned to Secretary of War Edwin M. Stanton for advice.

Newbern [*N.C.*]   Mch 21 /62

I have the honor to report the following movements in my department since my hurrid report of the 16" inst—

The detailed report of the Engagement on the 14" is not yet finished, but I hope will be ready to send by the next mail—

As I reported, our forces occupied this city & succeeded in restoring it
to comparative quietness by midnight on the 14", and it is now as quiet
as a New England village— I appointed Genl Foster Military Governor
of the city & its vicinity, and he has established a most perfect system of
guard & police— *nine tenth* of the depredations on the 14", after the
enemy & citizens fled from the town, were committed by the negroes,
before our troops reached the city— They seemed to be wild with
excitement and delight— they are now a source of very great anxiety to
us; the city is being overrun with fugitives from surrounding towns and
plantations— Two have reported themselves who have been in the
swamps for *five* years— it would be utterly impossible if we were so
disposed to keep them outside of our lines as they find their way to us
through woods & swamps from every side— By my next dispatch, I
hope to report to you a definite policy in reference to this matter, and in
the mean time shall be glad to receive any instructions upon the subject
which you may be disposed to give—

· · · ·

HLS   A. E. Burnside[30]

A week later, Burnside informed Stanton that "negroes continue to
come in, and I am employing them to the best possible advantage; a
principle part of them on some earth fortifications in the rear of the
city."[31]

Growing recognition of the fugitive slaves' military value eroded
the policy of exclusion not only in Union-occupied parts of the Confederate states but also in the border states. In March 1862, Congress adopted an article of war forbidding Union soldiers to return
fugitive slaves to their owners.[32] The new article strengthened the

hands of antislavery officers and marked a turning point in federal policy. General Abner Doubleday's instructions to the commander of a New York regiment, written by Doubleday's adjutant, cited the new article of war in requiring his troops to treat fugitive slaves "as persons and not as chattels" and to allow them into Union lines.

Washington [*D.C.*]   April 6th 1862

Sir   I am directed by Gen'l Doubleday to say in answer to your letter of the 2^d inst. that all negroes coming into the lines of any of the camps or Forts under his command, are to be treated as persons and not as chattels.

Under no circumstances has the commander of a Fort or camp the power of surrendering persons claimed as fugitive slaves as this cannot be done without determining their character   The additional article of war recently passed by Congress positively prohibits this.

The question has been asked whether it would not be better to exclude negroes altogether from the lines.   The General is of opinion that they bring much valuable information which cannot be obtained from any other source.   They are acquainted with all the roads, paths fords and other natural features of the country and they make excellent guides   They also Know and frequently, have exposed the haunts of secession spies and traitors and the existance of reble organization. They will not therefore be exclude.   The General also directs me to say that civil process [*to claim fugitive slaves*] cannot be served directly in the camps or Forts of his command without full authority obtained from the commanding officer for that purpose.   I am very respectfully your obt Servt.

HLcSr   (Signed)   E. P. Halsted³³

While Northern soldiers became practicing abolitionists, Radical Republicans in Congress pressed for legal emancipation. Their first target was the District of Columbia, where congressional authority over slavery was indisputable and most black people had already been free before the war. But as a proposal to emancipate slaves in the nation's capital made its way through the legislative process, Washington's City Council objected. It urged Congress to safeguard the District from an unwanted population, reminding the lawmakers that some of their own states prohibited the immigration of black people.

[*Washington, D.C. April, 1862*]

copy

Council No 59.

In Board of Alderman

Joint Resolution of Instruction

Be it Resolved by the Board of Aldermen and Board of Common Council of the City of Washington, That these councils, disclaiming any desire improperly to interfere with the business of the National Legislature, deem it not impertinent respectfully to express the opinion that the sentiment of a large majority of the people of this community is adverse to the *unqualified* abolition of slavery in this district at the present critical Juncture in our national affairs.

And be it further resolved, That the Joint Committee representing the interests of this Corporation before Congress be and are hereby instructed to urge respectfully upon the members of that honorable body as the constitutional guardians of the interests and rights of the people of this District, the expediency and the Justice of so shaping any legislation affecting the african race here as to provide Just and proper safe-guards against converting this city, located as it is between two

Slaveholding States, into an asylum for free negroes, a population undesirable in every american community, and which it has been deemed necessary to exclude altogether from some even of the non-Slaveholding States.

K Richards

W T. Dove[34]

HDcSr

In April 1862, despite protests from municipal officials and others, President Lincoln signed into law a bill emancipating all slaves in the District of Columbia. Although compromised by provisions that compensated slaveholders—and thus implicitly recognized the legitimacy of their claim to slave property—the law marked the first time the federal government had abolished slavery anywhere. Slaves and their allies celebrated jubilantly. The law also appropriated $100,000 "to aid in the colonization and settlement" of such black people in the District of Columbia "as may desire to emigrate to the Republics of Hayti or Liberia, or such other country beyond the limits of the United States."[35] Alienated by discrimination and abuse, some black people grasped at the opportunity to seek new homes. Hundreds had emigrated to Haiti during the first year of the war, and promoters were touting new destinations in Central America, notably the Chiriqui region (in present-day Panama). Forty men signed the following petition asking Congress to sponsor their resettlement in Central America.

[*Washington, D.C. April 1862*]

MEMORIAL.

To the Honorable the Senate and House of Representatives of the United States of America, in Congress assembled:

The undersigned, for themselves, their relatives, and friends, whom they represent; desire, by this memorial, most respectfully to show to the

Congress and people of this great country—of which, too, they are
natives, but humbly born—that they appreciate, to the fullest extent,
the humane actions which are now inaugurated to give freedom to their
so long oppressed colored race;* but they believe that this freedom will
result injuriously, unless there shall be opened to colored people a
region, to which they may immigrate—a country which is suited to their
organization, and in which they may seek and secure, by their own
industry, that mental and physical development which will allow them an
honorable position in the families of God's great world.

That there is ignorance in the mass of the colored race, is not to be
denied: this is caused by the peculiar condition in which they have been
raised—without the advantages of general education so wisely and
freely accorded to the white citizens.   But there are those amongst them
who have secured the blessings of knowledge, and who are capable of
informing their brethren of what is for their ultimate good, as the
leaders of the Pilgrim Fathers informed those who came with them to
plant civil and religious liberty upon this continent.

To these we are indebted for the knowledge that Liberia is too distant
from the land of our birth, and that however kindly and wisely the
original plans of colonization may have been laid for that country,
neither those plans, nor that region, are suited to our present condition,
and that it will be impossible for us ever to move there in sufficient
numbers to secure for us the full liberties of the human race, the
elements of which we have learned here.

From them, too, we have learned the deep degradation and
wretchedness in which our relatives were sunk, who were induced by

---

*In addition to the District of Columbia Emancipation Act, Congress
had recently approved a joint resolution offering monetary assistance
to any state that undertook gradual emancipation. (*Statutes at Large*,
vol. 12, p. 617.)

heartless speculators to immigrate to Hayti.*   Slavery, if it must be
borne, is more endurable under a race we have long been taught to look
up to and regard as superior, than under one originating in Africa,
degraded by abject slavery under Spanish and French greed, and still
further brutalized by unrestrained and licentious liberty, such as exists
with those who hold the power to control the poor immigrant in Hayti,
or either of the Africo-West India Islands.

Of our own will, we cannot go either to Liberia or these islands.   We
have, in the United States, been taught to venerate virtue, to strive to
attain it, and we can, with humble pride, point to as wide spread
examples of the benefit of these teachings, as can any similar number of
men, with no greater advantages than ourselves.   Therefore we wish to
shun those countries where the opposite of virtue rules, where vice
reigns supreme, where our very blood would be required if we opposed
its indulgence.

Though colored, and debarred from rights of citizenship, our hearts,
none the less, cling to the land of our birth.   We do not wish to be driven
beyond the Ocean, where old hands of kindness cannot reach us, where
we cannot hear from those with whom we have grown up, with all the
fond remembrances of childhood.

We now number as many souls as won the freedom of your sires from
British rule.   We may not *now* be as capable to govern ourselves as they
were, but we will, with your aid, be as zealous, and with God's blessing,
we will be as successful.

There is a land—part of this your own continent—to which we wish

---

*A reference to a scheme promoted by James Redpath, a white
abolitionist, whose Haitian Emigration Bureau sponsored the
relocation of 2,000 free-black people from the United States to Haiti
between 1860 and 1862. (John R. McKivigan, "James Redpath and
Black Reaction to the Haitian Emigration Bureau," *Mid-America* 69
[Oct. 1987]: 139–53.)

to go.   It is that portion generally called Central America.   There are lands there without inhabitants, yet bearing spontaneously all that is suited to our race.

Aid us to get there—protect us for a short while, and we will prove ourselves worthy and grateful.   The labor which, in servitude, has raised cotton, sugar, and tobacco, will do the same, not in the blood of bondage, but in the free spirit of liberty, and with the exultant knowledge, that it is to be part of your commerce, and to be given in exchange for the productions of our old native land.

If we are regarded as an evil here, (and we may become so by our competing with your white labor while here for the necessities of existence,) send us where, instead of being an evil, we may be made a blessing, by increasing the value of that white labor, while at the same time we offer to it greater comforts in reducing the costs in producing, by our own labor, those articles in abundance which all require for health and sustenance.

Do not, we beseech you, recognize and build up foreign nations of the black race, who have no sympathy in thought or language with that race which has grown up with you, and who only seek by such recognition, shaped, as it is, by European diplomacy, to sow discord and trouble with us here, that you and ourselves may be involved in a common ruin.

Send us—our prayer is, *send us*—to that country we have indicated, that we may not be wholly excluded from you, that we may aid in bringing to you that great commerce of the Pacific, which will still further increase the wealth and power of your country: and your petitioners will every pray.

PDS   [*40 signatures*][36]

Among the signers of another copy of the same petition was the
Reverend Henry M. Turner, a prominent clergyman in the African
Methodist Episcopal Church.

———•———

The dangers fugitive slaves continued to face even within sight of
the Capitol reinforced the suspicion that people of African descent
would never enjoy the full fruits of freedom in the United States.
Just before the enactment of emancipation in the District of Columbia, Grandison Briscoe escaped to Washington together with
his pregnant wife, an infant child, and his mother. Within days,
however, a slave catcher returned his loved ones to slavery in Maryland. Nearly two years after their recapture, Briscoe made the following affidavit describing their fate.

[*Washington, D.C.*]   6th day of February 1864
Grandison Briskoe being duly sworn says he is about 25 years of age
was born in Maryland & has been married to his wife since
1861   Came to reside with his wife in this City in April—4th day of
April 1862 & has resided in said City Since that period of time except a
part of the time   he has been in the Service of the United States all the
time & is now in Said Service in Virginia—   That his wife & his mother
were taken away from Washington in April (on the 7th day) 1862 & as
fugitive Slaves & taken to Piscatawa to Broad Creek to their master's
[farm?] whose name is John Hunter & My mothers masters name was &
is Robert Hunter—   They were both taken to the barn & severely
whipped   Their clothes were raised & tied over their heads to keep
their screams from disturbing the neighborhood & then were tied up &
whipped very severely whipped and then taken to Upper Marlborough to
jail   My wife had a Child about nine month's old which was taken from
her & died soon after.   Some six or eight months after my wife was

imprisoned she had a Child but the inhuman master & mistress though the knew she was soon to be Confined or give birth to a Child made no arrangements provided no Clothing nor anything for the Child or mother   I have sent them Clothing & other articles frequently until the first or near the first of January 1864 Since which the new jailor has refused to allow them to receive any thing from me

They have been in prison for the Crime of Coming to Washington to reside, ever since about the fourth of April 1862 now a year & ten months.   They are confined in Jail at Upper Marlborough Prince George's County Maryland

HDS   Grandison Briscoe[37]

The Civil War disrupted slavery not only in Union-held territory, but also within the Confederacy. Like Billy Yank, Johnny Reb found value in the services of fugitive slaves. Much to the slaveholders' disgust, runaways occasionally found refuge within the ranks of the Confederate army, whose soldiers cared less about the owners' property rights than about the comforts slave servants could provide. Lamenting the subversive effects of such practices, a Virginia slaveholder urged the Confederate secretary of war to prohibit soldiers from employing slaves without their owners' consent.

Etna P.O.   Hanover [*Va.*]   May 2 [*1862*]

Dear Sir   Many farmers in Virginia are injured by a practice which has become habitual and extensive among the soldiers of our own army. The soldiers employ runaway negroes to cook for the mess, clean their horses, and so forth.   The consequence is that negroes are encouraged to run away, finding a safe harbour in the army.   Two of my neighbours have each recovered runaway negroes within the last few weeks; who

were actually found in the employment of the soldiers on the Peninsula
and these negroes had been runaway many months.   I therefore write to
ask you to issue a general order forbidding this practice and anexing a
penalty sufficiently severe to break it up.

All that is necessary is to forbid the employment of any coloured
person unless he can show free papers or a pass from his master; and
hold the soldier responsible, for the genuineness of the free papers or
pass.

In this section of country a heavy draught has been made upon the
farmers (half of our available working force) to work on the
fortifications.   I, for one, rendered this tribute cheerfully to a cause
which is dear to my heart, though that, together with the excessive rains
will materially shorten my crop.   I think however, we ought to be
protected by the army authorities from the abuses above mentioned.
Yours &c

L. H. Minor

I can scarcely see to sign my name

One of my negro men has been runaway for many months and I have
reason to believe that he is in the service of the soldiers.[38]

ALS

No matter how many slaves escaped their owners' control by service with Confederate forces, it was the Union army that was becoming an army of liberation. The slaves' contributions to federal
military success became apparent as Northern troops advanced
more deeply into the Confederacy. After leading his division of the
Army of the Ohio into northern Alabama, General Ormsby M.
Mitchel informed Secretary of War Edwin M. Stanton that "[t]he
negroes are our only friends."[39]   Mitchel enlarged upon their importance in a subsequent telegram.

Huntsville [*Ala.*]   May 4 1862

I have this day written you fully embracing three topics of great importance.   The absolute necessity of protecting slaves who furnish us valuable information—the fact that I am left with out the command of my line of communications and the importance of holding Alabama north of the Tennessee.   I have promised protection to the slaves who have given me valuable assistance and information.   My River front is 120 miles long and if the Government disapprove what I have done I must receive heavy re enforcements or abandon my position.   With the assistance of the Negroes in watching the River I feel my self sufficiently strong to defy the enemy.

HWcSr   O. M. Mitchel[40]

Stanton's reply indicated that authorities in Washington had already reached a similar conclusion.

Washington [*D.C.*]   5 May 1862

General O M Mitchel,   Your Telegram of the 3[d] and 4th have been received   No General in the field has deserved better of his Government than yourself and the department rejoices to award credit to one who merits it so well.   The Department is advised of nothing that you have done but what it has approved   The assistance of slaves is an element of military strength which under proper regulations you are fully justified in employing for your security and the success of your operations.   It has been freely employed by the enemy: and to abstain from its use when it can be employed with military advantage would be a failure to employ means to suppress the Rebellion and retrieve the

authority of the Government.   Protection to those who furnish
information or other assistance is a high Duty

HWcSr   Edwin M Stanton[41]

Uneasiness about the loyalty of the border states weighed heavily
on federal policy regarding slavery. When abolitionist field officers
tried to advance emancipation on their own, Lincoln quickly over-
ruled their efforts. Such had been the fate of General John C. Frémont's order of August 1861 freeing the slaves of disloyal owners
in Missouri.[42] And such was the fate of General David Hunter's
proclamation in May 1862 freeing all the slaves in South Carolina,
Georgia, and Florida. In a proclamation abolishing Hunter's abolition, however, Lincoln also urged the border states to embrace a
proposal for gradual emancipation, with compensation to owners,
that Congress had recently approved.

Washington [*D.C.*] this nineteenth day of May,
in the year of our Lord one thousand eight hundred and sixty-two
By the President of the United States of America.
A Proclamation.
Whereas there appears in the public prints, what purports to be a
proclamation, of Major General Hunter, in the words and figures
following, to wit:

Head Quarters Department of the South,
Hilton Head, S.C.   May 9, 1862.
General Orders N° 11.—The three States of Georgia, Florida and
South Carolina, comprising the military department of the south,
having deliberately declared themselves no longer under the protection
of the United States of America, and having taken up arms against the
said United States, it becomes a military necessity to declare them

under martial law.   This was accordingly done on the 25ᵗʰ day of April, 1862.   Slavery and martial law in a free country are altogether incompatible; the persons in these three States—Georgia, Florida and South Carolina—heretofore held as slaves, are therefore declared forever free.

(Official)   David Hunter,
Major General Commanding.

Ed. W. Smith,
    Acting Assistant Adjutant General.

And whereas the same is producing some excitement, and misunderstanding; therefore

I, Abraham Lincoln, President of the United States, proclaim and declare, that the government of the United States, had no knowledge, information, or belief, of an intention on the part of General Hunter to issue such a proclamation; nor has it yet, any authentic information that the document is genuine—   And further, that neither General Hunter, nor any other commander, or person, has been authorized by the Government of the United States, to make proclamations declaring the slaves of any State free; and that the supposed proclamation, now in question, whether genuine or false, is altogether void, so far as respects such declaration.

I further make known that whether it be competent for me, as Commander-in-Chief of the Army and Navy, to declare the slaves of any State or States, free, and whether at any time, in any case, it shall have become a necessity indispensable to the maintenance of the government, to exercise such supposed power, are questions which, under my responsibility, I reserve to myself, and which I cannot feel justified in leaving to the decision of commanders in the field.   These are totally different questions from those of police regulations in armies and camps.

On the sixth day of March last, by a special message, I recommended to

Congress the adoption of a joint resolution to be substantially as follows:

Resolved, That the United States ought to co-operate with any State which may adopt a gradual abolishment of slavery, giving to such State pecuniary aid, to be used by such State in its discretion, to compensate for the inconveniences, public and private, produced by such change of system.

The resolution, in the language above quoted, was adopted by large majorities in both branches of Congress, and now stands an authentic, definite, and solemn proposal of the nation to the States and people most immediately interested in the subject matter.   To the people of those States I now earnestly appeal—   I do not argue, I beseech you to make the arguments for yourselves—   You can not if you would, be blind to the signs of the times—   I beg of you a calm and enlarged consideration of them, ranging, if it may be, far above personal and partizan politics.   This proposal makes common cause for a common object, casting no reproaches upon any—   It acts not the pharisee. The change it contemplates would come gently as the dews of heaven, not rending or wrecking anything.   Will you not embrace it?   So much good has not been done, by one effort, in all past time, as, in the providence of God, it is now your high privilege to do.   May the vast future not have to lament that you have neglected it.

In witness whereof, I have hereunto set my hand, and caused the seal of the United States to be affixed.

HDS   Abraham Lincoln[43]

Unwilling to bend to Lincoln's policies, some antislavery officers continued to press their cause. Stationed at Camp Parapet, Louisiana, near New Orleans, General John Phelps—who had an-

nounced slavery's doom in his proclamation from Ship Island*—
welcomed runaway slaves. They fled to Camp Parapet from the
swamps, from abandoned plantations, and from functioning estates. Their ragged condition and tales of barbarous treatment in-
censed Phelps, who ordered retributive raids upon the cruelest
slaveholders. The raids ignited the surrounding plantation district
with the spirit of freedom, intensifying the disruptive effect of military occupation and frightening unionist planters and their sympathizers within the federal army. Captain Edward Page, Jr., one
such officer, complained to the Union commander in southern
Louisiana, General Benjamin F. Butler.

Kenner   16 miles above New Orleans   May 27th 1862.
Sir,   From orders issued to me on May 23rd I understood that I was
ordered here to prevent the commission of excesses either on (the) part
of soldiers or laborers—   This Sir, I shall find impossible to do if
soldiers from Camp Parapet are allowed to range the country, insult the
Planters and entice negroes away from their plantations, and I regret I
must report this conduct on the part of soldiers from that camp. . . .†
   If on any of the Plantations here a negro is punished when he most
deserves it, the fact becoming known at Genl. Phelp's camp, a party of
soldiers are sent immediately to liberate them and with orders to bring
them to Camp.   A negro convicted of barn-burning and afterwards
riotous conduct on the plantation of Mrs. Butler Kannar (a lady who
has from you a safeguard and by which all officers and soldiers are
commanded to respect her property and to afford her every protection,)
was confined in the stocks that he might at the first opportunity be sent
to the city for trial, was [released] by a company of soldiers, sent by Gen.
Phelps, and afterwards taken to the Camp.   Yesterday an outbuilding

---

*See above, pp. 22–25.

†Ellipsis in the manuscript.

on Mrs. Fendeairs Plantation was broken open by these soldiers and
three negroes, confined there over night, taken out and carried to the
camp, notwithstanding the presence of the owners, who protested
against the act as one contrary to all orders.   The soldiers also broke
into the house and stole therefrom silver spoons, dresses and other
articles. . . .*

While Sir, such acts are permitted it is utterly impossible to call upon
the negroes for any labor, as they say they have only to go to the Fort to
be free and are therefore very insolent to their masters.   If these men
could be returned we should need no white men on the levee and much
expense might be saved the Government   I have now posted sentinels
to prevent any more negroes leaving and shall continue that duty until I
receive further orders from you—   There is much to be done here for
over three miles on the levee, and the planters are willing to take the
whole work upon themselves can they have their own necessary help.
From information received I should judge there was from One hundred
to One hundred and fifty *"Contrabands"* at Camp Parapet.   Awaiting
Orders I am Sir, Your most obdt. Servant

(signed)   Edward Page Jr.

Capt. 31st Regt.

Since writing the above Genl. Phelps has sent to me 80
"Contrabands," men, women and children, but I have no provisions and
shall therefore draw upon the Quarter Master for them. . . .†

Having no orders to dismiss the laborers they will continue their
duties.   Respectfully Yours

HLcSr   (Signed)   Edward Page Jr.[44]

---

*Ellipsis in the manuscript.

†Ellipsis in the manuscript.

The next day, General Butler warned Phelps that "the officers and men of your Command must be prevented from strolling without authority and without right, outside of your lines, and from interfering . . . without right in the domestic affairs of the people round about you."[45]

Among the fugitive slaves who took refuge at Camp Parapet in the fall of 1862 was Octave Johnson, who had fled from his owner more than a year earlier.

[New Orleans, La. February? 1864]

Deposition of Octave Johnson, Corporal Co. C, 15th Regt. Corps d'Afrique.

I was born in New Orleans;   I am 23 years of age;   I was raised by Arthur Thiboux of New Orleans;   I am by trade a cooper;   I was treated pretty well at home;   in 1855 master sold my mother, and in 1861 he sold me to S. Contrell of St. James Parish for $2,400;   here I worked by task at my trade;*   one morning the bell was rung for us to go to work so early that I could not see, and I lay still, because I was working by task;   for this the overseer was going to have me whipped, and I ran away to the woods, where I remained for a year and a half;   I had to steal my food; took turkeys, chickens and pigs;   before I left our number had increased to thirty, of whom ten were women;   we were four miles in the rear of the plantation house;   sometimes we would rope beef cattle and drag them out to our hiding place;   we obtained matches from our friends on the plantation;   we slept on logs and burned cypress leaves to

---

*I.e., he was assigned a quota of work to finish each day (a "task") and exercised some control over his working hours, provided he completed each day's task.

make a smoke and keep away mosquitoes; Eugene Jardeau, master of hounds, hunted for us for three months; often those at work would betray those in the swamp, for fear of being implicated in their escape; we furnished meat to our fellow-servants in the field, who would return corn meal; one day twenty hounds came after me; I called the party to my assistance and we killed eight of the bloodhounds; then we all jumped into Bayou Faupron; the dogs followed us and the alligators caught six of them; "the alligators preferred dog flesh to personal flesh;" we escaped and came to Camp Parapet, where I was first employed in the Commissary's office, then as a servant to Col. Hanks; then I joined his regiment.[46]

HD

Assurances of freedom by antislavery officers availed nothing where Confederate forces enjoyed the upper hand. Union troops had occupied the Sea Islands surrounding Port Royal Sound, off the coast of South Carolina, in November 1861, but their control was tenuous on outlying islands. In early June 1862, Confederate soldiers counterattacked on Hutchinson's Island, butchering scores of former slaves, carrying others back into slavery, and destroying the crops that they had hoped would guarantee their livelihood. A U.S. naval officer who surveyed the aftermath of the raid informed the commander of the South Atlantic Blockading Squadron of the woeful fate of ex-slaves unprotected in a war zone.

St Helena Sound   S.C.   June 13th 1862

Sir; This morning at 4 o'clock it was reported to me that there was a large fire on Hutchinson's Island, and shortly after that a preconcerted signal that the enemy were in the vicinity had been made from the house of our Pilot. I immediately started in the gig accompanied by the

tender "Wild Cat," Boats'n Downs, Launch, Act'g Mid'n Terry, 1st
Cutter, Act'g Master Billings, 2^{d} Cutter, Act'g Master Hawkins, and 3^{d}
Cutter Cox'n Shurtleff, up Horn, or Big River Creek, in the direction of
the fire.   Soon after leaving the ship a canoe containing three negroes
was met, who stated that the rebels, three hundred strong were at Mrs.
March's plantation killing all the negroes

As we advanced up the creek we were constantly met by canoes with
two or three negroes in them, panic stricken, and making their way to
the ship while white flags were to be seen flying from every inhabited
point around which were clustered groups of frightened fugitives.
When about two and half miles from Mrs March's, I was obliged to
anchor the "Wild Cat" from the want of sufficient water in the channel
with orders to be ready to cover our retreat if necessary.

On arriving at Mrs. March's the scene was most painful; her dwelling
and chapel were in ruins, the air heavy with smoke, while at the landing
were assembled over one hundred souls, mostly women and children in
the utmost distress.—

Throwing out a picket guard, and taking every proper measure
against surprise, I satisfied myself that the enemy were not in our
immediate neighborhood, the negroes assuring me that they had left the
island and returned to Fort Chapman.—

I then gathered the following particulars: The rebels during the night
landed on the island from Fort Chapman with a force of unknown
numbers and guided by a negro who for a long time had been on Otter
Island in the employ of the army, surrounded the house and chapel in
which a large proportion of the negroes were housed, posting a strong
guard to oppose our landing.

At early dawn they fired a volley though the house; as the alarmed
people sprang nearly naked from their beds and rushed forth frantic

with fear, they were shot, arrested or knocked down. The first inquiry of the rebels was for the "d—d Yankees," and at what time we were in the habit of visiting the Islands, mingled with exclamations of "be quick boys the people from the ship will be up,"—"Lets burn the houses,"— "Not yet, they will see the fire from the ship and come up."—

Having collected most of the chickens and despoiled many of the poor people of their very wretched clothing, and telling them that as they belonged to the estate or others nearly adjoining they would not molest them, they fired the buildings and fled.—

As the people were clamorous to be removed I filled the boats with them and pulled down to the Tender on board of which they were placed. On our return for the remainder they were observed as we approached the landing to be in the utmost confusion, dashing wildly into the marshes and screaming, "the Secesh* are coming back;" on investigation however it proved to be that the enemy in full sight about two miles off crossing an open space of ground were in hasty retreat instead of advancing. On our first visit they must have been concealed in a patch of woods not more than half a mile from our pickets.—

Having succeeded in removing or in providing with boats all who wished to remain to collect their little property, I returned to the ship bring with me about seventy, among them one man literally riddled with balls and buck shot; (since dead); another shot through the lungs and struck over the forehead with a clubbed musket laying the bone perfectly bare; one woman shot in the leg, shoulder, and thigh; one, far gone in pregnacy, with dislocation of the hip joint and injury to the womb caused by leaping from a second story window, and another, with displacement of the cap of the knee, and injury of the leg from the same cause.—

It appears that the negro who guided the party had returned to them

---

*I.e., secessionists.

after the evacuation of this place, told them all the troops had been withdrawn and that the Islands were entirely unprotected except by this ship; I am therefore at a loss to account for their extreme barbarity to negroes, most of whom were living on the plantation where they had been born, peacefully tilling the ground for their support, which their masters by deserting had denied them, and who were not even remotely connected with the hated Yankee.—

I would respectfully request that whenever one of the light draft steamers, such as the Planter, or the Ellen, can be spared for a day or two she may be allowed to visit this place. The Tender is, owing to the prevalence of sea breezes, almost useless in the narrow creeks except in advancing.— The occasional trip of a small steamer up the Ashepoo would make the wooding and watering of this ship less hazardous.

I trust you will approve my sending the contrabands to Hilton Head: had I not been unable to provide for such a large number, and so much embarrassed by the frequent demands made upon me for provisions by new arrivals, I should have waited for your orders in the matter.—

Last Tuesday we had an arrival of thirty from the main-land, and scarce a day passes without one or more arrivals always in a half-starved condition, whose appeals for food I have not yet been able to resist, though trespassing rather largely on the ships stores. All the new arrivals give the same account of the want and scarcity of provisions among the white population, and of their own dangers and sufferings in effecting their escape.—

Though exercising no control over the negroes on the neighboring islands I have, ever since the withdrawal of the troops, urged them to move to Edisto or St. Helena, and warned them that some night they would be visited by the rebels, but the majority insisted on remaining because it was their home while all seemed to have the most perfect faith in the protection of the ship though perhaps as was the case last night, ten or twelve miles distant from her.   Very Respectfully Your obdt. servant

HLcSr

(signed)   W. T. Truxtun[47]

> One of the Union officers most determined to make freedom universal was General David Hunter. Although President Lincoln had voided his proclamation of emancipation,* Hunter went on to enlist ex-slaves as soldiers without War Department authorization. When a congressional resolution sponsored by border-state representatives demanded an explanation, Hunter retorted that he had no fugitive slaves under arms, only men "whose late masters are 'Fugitive Rebels.'" Hunter's letter quickly became a featured story in the antislavery press, which employed his withering sarcasm to good effect.

Port Royal   S° C^a   June 23rd 1862

Sir: I have the honor to acknowledge the receipt of a communication from the Adjutant General of the Army, dated June 13th 1862, requesting me to furnish you with information necessary to answer certain resolutions introduced in the House of Representatives, June 9th 1862, on motion of the Hon. Mr. Wickliffe of Kentucky,—their substance being to inquire;

1st   Whether I had organized or was organizing a regiment of "Fugitive Slaves" in this Department.

2nd   Whether any authority had been given to me from the War Department for such organization;—and

3rd   Whether I had been furnished by order of the War Department

---

*See above, pp. 46–48.

with clothing, uniforms, arms, equipments and so forth for such a force?

Only having received the letter covering these inquiries at a late hour on Saturday night, I urge forward my answer in time for the Steamer sailing today (Monday),—this haste preventing me from entering as minutely as I could wish upon many points of detail such as the paramount importance of the subject calls for.   But in view of the near termination of the present session of Congress, and the wide-spread interest which must have been awakened by Mr Wickliffe's Resolutions, I prefer sending even this imperfect answer to waiting the period necessary for the collection of fuller and more comprehensive data.

To the First Question therefore I reply that no regiment of "Fugitive Slaves" has been, or is being organized in this Department.   There is, however, a fine regiment of persons whose late masters are "Fugitive Rebels,"—men who everywhere fly before the appearance of the National Flag, leaving their servants behind them to shift as best they can for themselves.—   So far, indeed, are the loyal persons composing this regiment from seeking to avoid the presence of their late owners, that they are now, one and all, working with remarkable industry to place themselves in a position to go in full and effective pursuit of their fugacious and traitorous proprietors.

To the Second Question, I have the honor to answer that the instructions given to Brig. Gen. T. W. Sherman by the Hon. Simon Cameron, late Secretary of War, and turned over to me by succession for my guidance,—do distinctly authorize me to employ all loyal persons offering their services in defence of the Union and for the suppression of this Rebellion in any manner I might see fit, or that the circumstances might call for.   There is no restriction as to the character or color of the persons to be employed, or the nature of the employment, whether civil or military, in which their services should be used.   I conclude, therefore that I have been authorized to enlist "Fugitive Slaves" as soldiers, could any such be found in this Department.— No such characters, however, have yet appeared within view of our most advanced pickets,—the loyal slaves everywhere remaining on their plantations to welcome us, aid us, and supply us with food, labor and information.— It is the masters who have in every instance been the "Fugitives", running away from loyal slaves as well as loyal soldiers, and whom we have only partially been able to see,—chiefly their heads over ramparts, or, rifle in hand, dodging behind trees,—in the extreme distance.— In the absence of any "Fugitive Master Law", the deserted Slaves would be wholly without remedy, had not the crime of Treason given them the right to pursue, capture and bring back those persons of whose protection they have been thus suddenly bereft.

To the Third Interrogatory, it is my painful duty to reply that I never have received any Specific authority for issues of clothing, uniforms, arms, equipments and so forth to the troops in question,—my general instructions from Mr Cameron to employ them in any manner I might find necessary, and the military exigencies of the Department and the country, being my only, but in my judgment, sufficient justification. Neither have I had any Specific authority for supplying these persons with shovels, spades and pick axes when employing them as laborers, nor with boats and oars when using them as lightermen,—but these are not points included in Mr. Wickliffe's Resolution.— To me it seemed that liberty to employ men in any particular capacity implied with it liberty, also, to supply them with the necessary tools; and acting upon this faith, I have clothed, equipped and armed the only loyal regiment yet raised in South Carolina.

I must say, in vindication of my own conduct, that had it not been for the many other diversified and imperative claims on my time and attention, a much more satisfactory result might have been hoped for; and that in place of only one, as at present, at least five or six well-drilled, brave and thoroughly acclimated regiments should by this time have been added to the loyal forces of the Union.

The experiment of arming the Blacks, so far as I have made it, has been a complete and even marvellous success.   They are sober, docile, attentive and enthusiastic, displaying great natural capacities for acquiring the duties of the soldier.   They are eager beyond all things to take the field and be led into action; and it is the unanimous opinion of the officers who have had charge of them, that in the peculiarities of this climate and Country they will prove invaluable auxiliaries,—fully equal to the similar regiments so long and successfully used by the British Authorities in the West India Islands.

In conclusion I would say it is my hope,—there appearing no possibility of other reinforcements owing to the exigencies of the Campaign in the Peninsula,—to have organized by the end of next Fall, and to be able to present to the Government, from forty eight to fifty thousand of these hardy and devoted soldiers.—   Trusting that this letter may form part of your answer to Mr Wickliffe's Resolutions, I have the honor to be, most respectfully, Your Very Obed^t Servt.

HLc   *[David Hunter]*[48]

Many members of Congress who remained unwilling to enlist black men as soldiers were nevertheless prepared to employ them as military laborers. In July 1862, Congress enacted and President Lincoln—despite reservations—approved a second confiscation act and a new militia act. The Second Confiscation Act expanded the legal basis by which slaves might gain their freedom, declaring the slaves of disloyal owners "forever free." It also moved beyond the article of war adopted in March by forbidding persons in federal service to decide upon the validity of a slave's claim to freedom "under any pretence whatever" or to "surrender up" any slave to a claimant.[49] In effect, the new law deemed free all fugitive slaves who came into Union lines professing that their owners were disloyal, as well as slaves who fell under federal control in enemy territory. The Militia Act, enacted the same day, provided for the employment of "persons of African descent" in "any military or naval service for which they may be found competent," and it granted freedom to slaves so employed, as well as to their mothers, wives, and children if they belonged to disloyal owners.[50]

———•———

Slaves who accompanied their owners into the Confederate army as personal servants often learned of federal emancipation policies before their families and friends. When they returned home, their knowledge spread quickly. A former slave from Georgia, who had been taken to the frontlines in Virginia, told a postwar federal commission of the result on his plantation.

[*McIntosh, Ga.   July 17, 1873*]

My name is Samuel Elliott   I was born in Liberty County a Slave and became free when the Army came into the County.   I belonged to Maybank Jones.   I am 54 years old.   I reside at Lauralview in Liberty County.   I am a farmer. . . .

I resided from the 1st of April 1861 to the 1st of June 1865 where I live now at Lauralview.   I worked for my master all the time.   I changed my business at one time when I was with my master as a waiter—in the rebel service   I was with him Eleven month.   I came home with him.   I told my son what was going on— he with 11 more ran off and joined the Army (the Yankee Army) on St Catherine Island. I dont remember the Year but it was soon after the battle at

Williamsburgh Va, and before the 7 days battle near Chickahomony.   I
mean that was the time I came home with my master.   I was with him at
Yorktown—   Soon after I came home My son with 11 others ran away &
joined the Union Army.   My Master had me taken up tied me and tried
to make me tell "What made them ran off"   I had to lie about it to
keep from getting killed.   the 11 slaves belonged to My Master
Jones   that stoped the slave owners from sending or taking slave into
the Army as waiters or anything else.   it stoped it in our neighborhood

· · · ·

his

HDSr   Samuel × Elliot[51]

mark

> By the summer of 1862, the flight of slaves to Union lines was
> causing great distress within the Confederacy. Planters in Liberty
> County, Georgia, estimated that the coastal counties of the state
> had lost 20,000 slaves, whose escape not only reduced the labor
> force but demoralized the remaining slave population. The clergy-
> man Robert Q. Mallard and his fellow planters asked General
> Hugh W. Mercer, the commander of Confederate forces in the re-
> gion, for stern action. Runaway slaves, they argued, should be re-
> garded as traitors and summarily executed. Whereas slaveholders
> had previously favored strict limits on the right of the courts to
> punish a slave without the owner's consent, Mallard and his neigh-
> bors now complained that civil courts lacked the power to mete out
> the swift and extreme punishment that the slaves' odious action de-
> manded.

[Liberty County, Ga.   August 1, 1862]

General: The undersigned Citizens of Liberty County of the Fifteenth
District, would respectfully present for your consideration a subject of

grave moment, not to themselves only but to their fellow Citizens of the
Confederate States, who occupy not only our territory immediately
bordering on that of the old United States, but the whole line of our sea
coast from Virginia to Texas.   We allude to the escape of our Slaves
across the border lines landward, and out to the vessels of the enemy
Seaward, & to their being also enticed off by those who having made
their escape, return for that purpose, and not unfrequently, attended by
the enemy.   The injury inflicted upon the interests of the citizens of the
Confederate States by this now constant drain is immense; independent
of the forcible seizure of Slaves by the enemy whenever it lies in his
power; and to which we now make no allusion, as the indemnity for this
loss, will in due time occupy the attention of our Government.—   From
ascertained losses on certain parts of our Coast, we may set down as a
low estimate, the number of Slaves absconded & enticed off from our
Seaboard as 20,000 & their value as from $12 to 15 millions of Dollars,
to which loss—may be added the insecurity of the property along our
borders & the demoralization of the negroes that remain, which
increases with the continuance of the evil & may finally result in perfect
disorganization and rebellion.—

    The absconding Negroes hold the position of Traitors, since they go
over to the enemy & afford him aid & comfort, by revealing the condition
of the districts and cities from which they come, & aiding him in erecting
fortifications & raising provisions for his support: and now that the
United States have allowed their introduction into their Army &, Navy,
aiding the enemy by enlisting under his branners & increasing his
resources in men, for our annoyance & destruction.   Negroes occupy the
position of Spies also, since they are employed in secret expeditions for
obtaining information, by transmission of newspapers & by other modes;
and act as guides to expeditions on the land & as pilots to their vessels

on the waters of our inlets and rivers.—

They have proved of great value, thus far, to the Coast operations of the enemy, & without their assistance, he could not have accomplished as much for our injury & annoyance as he has done; and unless some measures shall be adopted to prevent the escape of the negroes to the enemy, the threat of an Army of trained Africans for the coming fall & winter's campaigns may become a reality. Meanwhile the counties along the Seaboard will become exhausted of the Slave population, which should be retained as far as possible for the raising of provisions & supplies for our forces on the Coast.—

In the absence of penalties of such a nature as to ensure respect and dread, the temptations which are spread before the negroes are very strong, and when we consider their condition, their ignorance and credulity & love of change, must prove in too many cases decidedly successful. No effectual check being interposed to their escape, the desire increases among them in proportion to the extent of its successful gratification, & will spread inland until it will draw Negroes from Counties, far in the interior of the State; & Negroes will congregate from every quarter, in the counties immediately bordering on the Sea and become a lawless set of runaways, corrupting the Negroes that remain faithful, depredating on property of all kinds & resorting it may be to deeds of violence; which demonstrates that the whole State is interested in the effort to stop this evil: & already have Negroes from middle Georgia made their escape to the Seaboard Counties, and through Savannah itself to the enemy.—

After consulting the Laws of the State we can discover none that meet the case & allow of that prompt execution of a befitting penalty, which its urgency demands. The infliction of capital punishment is now confined to the Superior Court; & any indictment before that Court, would

involve incarceration of the Negroes for months with the prospect of
postponement of trial—long litigation—large expense & doubtful
conviction; and moreover, should the Negroes be caught escaping in any
numbers, there would not be room in all our Jails to receive them.   The
Civil Law therefore as it now stands cannot come to our protection.

Can we find protection under Military Law?   This is the question we
submit to the General in Command—   Under Military Law the severest
penalties are prescribed for furnishing the enemy with aid & comfort, &
for acting as Spies and Traitors; all which the Negroes can do as
effectually as white men, as facts prove and as we have already
suggested.   There can be but little doubt, that if Negroes are detected in
the act of exciting their fellow slaves to escape; or of taking them off; or
of returning after having gone to the enemy, to induce & aid others to
escape:—they may in each of these cases be summarily punished under
military authority.   But may not the case of Negroes *taken in the act of
absconding*, singly, (or in families) or in parties, without being directly
incited so to do by one or more others, be also summarily dealt with by
Military Authority?—   Were our white population to act in the same
way, would it not be necessary to make a summary example of them, in
order to cure the evil or put it under some salutary control?   If it be
argued, that in case of the Negroes, it would be hard to meet out a
similar punishment under similar circumstances, because of their
ignorance pliability, credulity, desire of change, the absence of the
political ties of allegiance & the peculiar status of the Race;—it may be
replied—that the Negroes, constitute a part of the Body politic, *in fact*;
and should be made to know their duty; that they are perfectly aware
that the Act which they commit is one of rebellion against the power &
authority of their owners & the Government under which they live; they
are perfectly aware that they go over to the protection & aid of the

enemy who are on the Coast for the purpose of killing their owners & of destroying their property; & they know further, that if they themselves are found with the enemy that they will be treated as the enemy— namely shot & destroyed:—   To apprehend such transgressors, to confine & punish them privately by owners or publicly by the Citizens of the County by confinement and whipping & then return them to the plantations will not abate the evil; for the disaffected will not thereby be reformed, but will remain a leaven of corruption in the mass & stand ready to make any other attempts that may promise success.   It is indeed a monstrous evil that we suffer.—   Our Negroes our property— the agracultural class of the Confederacy, upon whose order & continuance so much depends, may go off, (inflicting a great pecuniary loss both private & public) to the enemy—convey any amount of valuable information—and aid him by building his fortifications: by raising supplies for his armies—by enlisting as Soldiers—by acting as Spies & as guides & pilots on his expiditions on land & water & bringing in the foe upon us to kill & devastate; and yet if we catch them in the act of going to the enemy we are powerless for the infliction of any punishment adequate to their crime & adequate to fill them with salutary fear of its commission!   Surely some remedy should be applied & that speedily for the protection of the Country, aside from all other considerations.   A few executions of leading transgressors among them by hanging or shooting would dissipate the ignorance which may be supposed to possess their minds and which may be pleaded in arrest of judgement.—

We do not pray the General in Command to issue any order for the government of the Citizens in the matter, which of course is no part of his duty; but the promulgation of an order to the military for the execution of ring-leaders who are detected in stirring up the people to escape—for the execution of all who return having once escaped & for the execution of all who are caught in the act of escaping; will speedily be known & understood by the entire slave population, and will do away with all excuses of ignorance, & go very far towards an entire arrest of the evil. While it will enable the Citizens to act efficiently in there own sphere—whenever circumstances—require them to act at all— In an adjoining County which has lost some 200 since the shooting of two detected in the act of escaping not another attempt has been made & it has been several weeks since the two were shot.—

As Law abiding men we do not desire Committees of Vigalence, clothed with plenary powers; nor meetings of the body of our Citazens, to take the Law into their own hands, however justifiable it may be under the peculiar circumstances, & therefore in the failure of the Civil Courts to meet the emergency, we refer the Subject to the General in Command, believing that he has the power to issue the necessary order to the forces under him, covering the whole ground, and knowing that by so doing he will recieve the commendation and cordial support of the intelligent & Law abiding citizens inhabiting the military department over which he presides.   All which is Respectfully submited by Your friends & fellow citizens.—

R. Q. Mallard.

T. W. Fleming.

E. Stacy[52]

HDS

General Mercer sympathized with the planters but, in forwarding their petition to the Confederate secretary of war, urged caution about granting individual officers "the responsibility of life & death, so liable to be abused."[53]

With tens of thousands of black men and women working for the
Union army and navy, Northerners could not help but recognize the
importance of former slaves to the war effort. Their successful employment as laborers pushed to the fore the possibility of using
them as soldiers: if black men could wield a shovel they could also
shoulder a musket. By the summer of 1862, many Northerners
who cared little about emancipation and racial equality had come
to favor the enlistment of black soldiers on utterly pragmatic
grounds. In a letter to General-in-Chief Henry W. Halleck, Governor Samuel J. Kirkwood of Iowa suggested that a black man could
stop a bullet as well as a white man.

                              [*Des Moines*] Iowa   August 5 1862
General   You will bear me witness I have not trouble on the "*negro*"
subject but there is as it seems to me so much good sense in the
following extract from a letter to me from one of the best colonels this
state has in the service that I have yielded to the temptation to send it to
you—   It is as follows.   "I hope under the confiscation and
emancipation bill just passed by Congress* to supply my regiment with
a sufficient number of 'contrabands' to do all the 'extra duty' labor of
my camp.   I have now *sixty men on extra duty* as teamsters &c. whose
places could just as well be filled with *niggers*—   We do not need a single
negro in the army to fight but we could use to good advantage about one
hundred & fifty with a regiment as teamsters & for making roads,
chopping wood, policing camp &c.   *There are enough soldiers on extra
duty in the army to take Richmond or any other rebel city if they were in
the ranks instead of doing negro work.*"
    I have but one remark to add and that in regard to the negroes
fighting—   it is this—When this war is over & we have summed up the
entire loss of life it has imposed on the country I shall not have any

---

*The Second Confiscation Act and the Militia Act.

regrets if it is found that a part of the dead are *niggers* and that *all* are not white men—

. . . .

ALS　　　　　　　　　　　　　　　　Samuel J Kirkwood[54]

> Union general William T. Sherman was no friend of emancipation, but he too had concluded that winning the war required the use of every available resource—including slaves. Moreover, he believed that in seceding, the rebels had repudiated the U.S. Constitution and could no longer claim its protection for slave property. Thus when Thomas Hunton, a West Point classmate, requested assistance in reclaiming slaves who had fled to Union-occupied Memphis, Sherman offered a disquisition on why he could not cooperate.

Memphis Tenn.　Aug 24th 1862

My dear Sir,　I freely admit that when you recall the times when we were schoolfellows, when we were younger than now, you touch me on a tender point, and cause me to deeply regret that even you should style yourself a Rebel.　I cannot believe that Tom Hunton the Companion of Gaither, Rankin, and Irvin and many others long since dead, and of Halleck. Ord, Stevens and others still living can of his own free will admit the anarchical principle of secession or be vain enough to suppose the present Politicions Can frame a Government better than that of Washington Hamilton & Jefferson.　We cannot realize this but delude ourselves into the belief that by some strange but successful jugglery the manegers of our Political Machine have raised up the single issue, North or South, which shall prevail in America? or that you like others have been blown up, and cast into the Mississippi of Secession doubtful if by hard fighting you can reach the shore in safety, or drift out to the Ocean of Death, I know it is no use for us now to discuss this—war is on us. We are Enemies, still private friends. In the one Capacity I will do you all the harm I can, yet on the other if here. you may have as of old my last Cent, my last shirt and pants, You ask of me your negroes. and I will immediately ascertain if they be under my Military Control and I will moreover see that they are one and all told what is true of all— Boys if you want to go to your master, Go— You are free to choose, You must now think for yourselves. Your Master has seceded from his Parent Government and you have seceded from him—both wrong by law—but bothe exercising an undoubted natural Right to rebel, If your boys want to go, I will enable them to go, but I wont advise, persuade or force them— I confess I have not yet seen the "Confiscation Act," but I enclose you my own orders defining my position, I also cut out of a paper Grant's Orders, and I assert that the Action of all our Leading Military Leaders, Halleck, McClellan, Buell, Grant & myself have been more conservative of slavery than the Acts of your own men. The Constitution of the United States is your only legal title to slavery. You have another title, that of posession & Force, but in Law & Logic your title to your Boys lay in the Constitution of the United States. You may say you are for the Constitution of the United States, as it was— You know it is unchanged, not a word not a syllable and I can lay my hand on that Constitution and swear to it without one twang. But your party have made *another* and have another in force How can you say that you would have the old, when you have a new By the new if sucessful you inherit the Right of Slavery, but the new is not law till your Revolution is successful. Therefore we who contend for the old existing Law, Contend that you by your own act take away Your own title to all property save what is restricted by *our* constitution, your slaves included. You know I don't want your slaves; but to bring you to reason I think as a Military Man I have a Right and it is good policy to make *you all* feel that you are but men—that you have all the wants & dependencies of other men, and must eat, be clad &ᶜ to which end you must have property & labor, and that by Rebelling you risk both, Even without the Confiscation Act, by the simple laws of War we ought to take your effective slaves. I don't say to free them, but to use their labor & deprive you of it; as Belligerents we ought to seek the hostile Army and fight it and not the people.— We went to Corinth but Beaureguard declined Battle, since which time many are dispersed as Guerillas. We are not bound to follow them, but rightfully make war by any means that will tend to bring about an end and restore Peace. Your people may say it only exasperates, widens the breach and all that, But the longer the war lasts the more you must be convinced that we are no better & no worse than People who have gone before us, and that we are simply reenacting History, and that one of the modes of bringing People to reason is to touch their Interests pecuniary or property.

We never harbor women or children—we give employment to men, under the enclosed order. I find no negroes Registered as belonging to Hunton, some in the name of MᶜGhee of which the Engineer is now making a list— I see MᶜClellan says that the negroes once taken shall never again be restored.* I say nothing. My opinion is, we execute not make the Law, be it of Congress or War. But it is Manifest that if you

---

*On August 9, 1862, General George B. McClellan, commander of the Army of the Potomac, promulgated an executive order that instructed federal armies operating in rebellious states to seize property suitable for military purposes and to employ slaves. Slaves employed by the Union army, McClellan added, "have always understood that after being received into the military service of the United States in any capacity they could never be reclaimed by their former holders"; he promised such slaves "permanent military protection" against reenslavement. (*Destruction of Slavery*, p. 294n.)

wont go into a United States District Court and sue for the recovery of
your slave property You can never Get it, out of adverse hands.   No U.S.
Court would allow you to sue for the recovery of a slave under the
Fugitive Slave Law. unless you acknowledge allegiance.   Believing this
honesty, so I must act. though personally I feel strong frindship as ever,
for very many in the South   With Great Respect Your friend

HLcS   W. T. Sherman[55]

> By the fall of 1862, even conservatives like Sherman had concluded
> that striking against slavery in the Confederacy was politically jus-
> tified and militarily necessary. President Lincoln had reached this
> conclusion some time earlier. On July 22, he informed the cabinet
> of his intention to issue a proclamation of general emancipation. At
> the cabinet's recommendation, Lincoln agreed to withhold his pro-
> nouncement until after a Union victory. In late September, soon af-
> ter the battle of Antietam, he issued a preliminary proclamation,
> serving notice that on January 1, 1863, he would declare "then,
> thenceforward, and forever free" all slaves in those states still en-
> gaged in rebellion.[56]

> In those parts of the Confederacy that had already come under
> Union control, slavery eroded without any proclamation by the
> president. At times it disintegrated both quickly and violently. In
> southern Louisiana, where federal military might protected the
> property of unionist slaveholders, slaves took matters into their
> own hands. Often they had the assistance of abolitionist officers
> like General Phelps north of New Orleans and General Neal Dow
> south of the city. By issuing free papers to slaves who had been ex-
> pelled from their plantations after defying their owners, Dow en-
> raged sugar planters. One of them complained to General George
> F. Shepley, the military governor.

New Orleans [*La.*]   Sept 19. 1862.

Sir   In obedience to an order of Col J N French Provost Marshall, I respectfully submit the following statement—

On Monday last, while on a visit to my plantation, I was startled at the dawn of day by the announcement of my brother in law Mr Smith the manager of the place, that the negroes were in a state of insurection, some of them refusing to work— Proceeding immediately to the Cabin Yard, I found them gathered in different groups & on enquiry learned, that some of them would not work at all, & others wanted wages,   I informed them, I should not pay them wages, & being excited by their ingratitude & not wishing to feed and clothe those who would not work, & to avoid any difficulty, as my sister and her four small children were on the place, I said that it was better to part in peace & go off quietly & that I did not wish to lay eyes on them again, & they went away   I never drove any of them off the plantation, or told them according to the expression of Genl Dow to shift for themselves— So far from it, I sent a written notice to the rice planters below, forbidding them to employ them under the pains & risks of the law, in regard to employment of runaway slaves   about twenty five of them left the plantation, some few of them remained & went to work the next day—

On the 17th ins^t one of the revolted named Auguste, demanded from the overseer his gun, & not being able to find it endeavoured to get possession of the overseer's.   In reply to Mr Smith's question, "If he had a pass," he said Genl Dow had given him his free papers which he produced, & said moreover that Genl Dow had told him all the people were free, & that he, (Auguste) had come for what belonged to him— My brother in law, the overseer, and myself, knowing him to be a dangerous man, determined to bring him to the city & have the whole subject properly investigated— I started with him in my buggy,   M^r

Smith & the overseer on horseback—accompanyed me a short distance
and returned— His language was very offensive,   among other things
he said that he wished to go to Virginia, meaning thereby that he wished
to enlist— I succeeded with some assistance in securing him in the jail
of St Bernard—

Considering this boy as one of the ring-leaders & a dangerous
character on the plantation, I thought it best to remove him, & leave it to
the Provost Marshall to dispose of him as it may seem best—   There
are about twenty negroes with free papers from Genl Dow, a great
burthen to the place; a heavy tax on me & a bad example to the other
negroes—

Under this anamolous state of affairs, I pray that the Governor &
Provost Marshall, will take the necessary steps to examine into this
affair, & send an officer to verify this statement. & see into the condition
of things on the plantation, that a suitable protection be afforded my
sister and her children, that the negroes may be informed how far the
emancipation of Genl Dow may be valid, & the future conduct of the
place & themselves, may be put upon such a footing & will restore peace
& good order—   I am very respectfully your ob^t

HLS   John C. P. Wederstrandt[57]

Whatever advances emancipation made in federal policy, the actual
liberation of slaves depended upon the military fortunes of the federal government. In August 1862, as Lincoln prepared to issue his
preliminary proclamation, Confederate forces surged into Kentucky. The invasion galvanized midwesterners, who feared for the
safety of their homes. Thousands of volunteers from Illinois, Indiana, Ohio, Michigan, and Wisconsin rushed to repel the rebels. In
Kentucky, many of the new recruits got their first view of slavery
and, for the most part, they did not like what they saw. Obliged to

stand by while pursuing masters threatened fugitive slaves with deadly violence, many came to resent orders to exclude runaways from their camps. When masters followed runaways into federal encampments, they faced angry, armed soldiers with little respect for the self-proclaimed unionism of Kentucky slaveholders. Some of their officers had even less patience. Colonel Smith D. Atkins, commander of an Illinois regiment, informed a friend in Chicago of his determination not to allow himself or his regiment to do the bidding of the Kentucky slavocracy.

Mt. Sterling, Ky.   Nov. 2$^\text{d}$ 1862.

Dear Miller: I got your letter from Chicago, but until today I have not thought I had anything of interest to write you.   I arrived safely at Covington, & have had a pleasent march out, & am now, as you will see, by my order, in Command of this Post.   I am in the 3$^\text{d}$ Brigade of the 3$^\text{d}$ Division of Grangers. Army, under Genl Baird.   Col. Cochran of the 14$^\text{th}$ Ky. Vol. commands the Demibrigade in which I am. & his regiment is at Winchester.   Here I am, one regiment of Infantry, all alone, 20 miles from any support, just in the edge of the Cumberland Mountains, & they are full of Guerrilla Bands.   One of 300 strong has its headquarters at Hazel-Green.   [*Confederate General*] Humphrey Marshall with his Division 4000 strong is at Prestonburgh 60 miles distant by a good turnpike.   He has 400 cavalry & ten pieces of artilery. If he attacks us we are "gone up" but we are not apprehending an attack.   We are evidently doomed, to a winter of *ina[c]tion* in tents where snow falls 2 feet deep *guarding* a little sesesh hole that is too *cowardly* to guard itself, and our principle business is, expected to be returning niggers.   The old policy, is to prevail of cutting up the union forces to guard rebel property & let regiment after regiment fall by the enimies concentrationg, & then the loyal North must have a draft for a

new army. My superior Commanders order me to give up the niggers.
Ought I to do it? I love my country, Miller; I have risked my life in its
battles and am willing to do so again & again. I am deeply anxious to
do my whole duty. But under the Presidents proclamation of Sept 22^d
62.* I cannot conscientiously force my boys to become the slavehounds of
Kentuckians & I am determined I will not. You see my order.†
Doubtless before you get this I will under arrest, & undergoing Court
Martial, but I want my friends in Northern Illinois to know that it is not
for cowardice or disquallification but Simply because I will not make
myself & my regiment a machine to enforce the slave laws of Kentucky &
return slaves to rebel masters. If I go down in disgrace it will be with a
clean conscience; if I am *right* my friends must not let me go down. Let
me hear from you: Truly Thine

ALS

S. D. Atkins[58]

Colonel Atkins soon became embroiled with local slaveholders, who
mobilized civil officials and Atkins's own superiors—Generals Gordon Granger and Quincy A. Gillmore—against him. But Atkins
held his ground and refused to allow slaveholders to retrieve slaves
from his regiment. The ensuing controversy quickly found its way
into the Northern press.

---

*The preliminary emancipation proclamation, which in fact did not
pertain to Kentucky or the other slave states that had remained in the
Union.

†Enclosed was an order, issued November 2, 1862, in which Atkins
announced himself as commander of the post of Mt. Sterling,
Kentucky, and warned slave owners "to keep [their slaves] at home, as
no part of my command will in any way be used for the purpose of
returning fugitive slaves." (*Destruction of Slavery*, p. 530.)

[*Cleveland, Ohio   November? 1862*]

COL. SMITH D. ATKINS.

Since the publication of a letter in the Cincinnati *Commercial*, from Mt. Sterling, Kentucky, (which letter was copied, thoughtlessly as we believe, into several Illinois papers) containing charges of depredations on loyal citizens of Kentucky by the 92d Illinois regiment, Col. Smith D. Atkins, we have been at some pains to ascertain the facts in the case, and we believe they will be found to possess a considerable degree of public interest.   The charge against Col. Atkins and his regiment is the old one of "nigger stealing"—a phrase which signifies giving a black man his liberty.   We were told, in the letter referred to, that this practice was "having a most injurious effect upon the loyal sentiment here;" also that it was "heart-rending to a Union man;" likewise that this Illinois regiment "should be sent somewhere where they cannot ruin the loyal sentiment of the people."

Remarking first that the 92d Illinois regiment and its gallant colonel desire no earthly boon, so much as an order sending them out of Kentucky and into the presence of an enemy with bayonets and batteries, instead of bailiff's writs and bills in chancery, we proceed to the narration.   The regiment has been brigaded with certain Kentucky regiments, under Colonel Cochrane of the 14th Kentucky, acting brigadier general.   They were stationed for a short time at Mt. Sterling, Kentucky.   While there, fifteen negroes owned by notorious and avowed rebels came into Col. Atkins' camp.   They were employed as servants by commissioned officers of the regiment.   They were free by the terms of the confiscation act, and their employment by the officers of the 92d gave practical force and effect to the law—nothing more.   The claimants of the negroes applied to Gen. Gordon Granger for an order directing Col. Atkins to deliver them up.   General Granger, being mindful probably that the law forbade that method of determining the status of negroes, issued an order to Col. Atkins, directing him not to let any one, white or black, come within his lines.* This did not answer the case of the rebel owners, and accordingly they procured an order from Gen. G., most acceptable to the 92d, sending the regiment away from Mt. Sterling. At Winchester, on the road to Lexington, the citizens threatened, with the aid of the 14th Kentucky to "clean out," the Illinois boys. Col. Atkins accordingly marched through the town with fixed bayonets and loaded guns, and an excellent stomach for the fight. At Lexington the rabble came into the ranks of the 92d and tried to take one of the negroes, belonging to one of the worst secessionists in Kentucky. Col. Atkins went to the rear where the fracas was going on and told them that if they dared to interfere with his march he would fire a volley into them, so help him God! Whereupon they fell back in disorder. The regiment then continued its march toward Nicholasville.

But the negro hunters persevered. Two miles south of Lexington they came into the camp of the 92d with a hat full of documents, of which the following are samples:

ORDER FOR DELIVERY OF PROPERTY—SECTION 231.
Fayette Circuit Court—Order of Delivery,
Emily G. Hood, Plaintiff, *ag[ains]t.* Smith D. Atkins, Defendant.
The Commonwealth of Kentucky, to the Sheriff of Fayette county: You are commanded to take the slave Henry, of black complexion and 18 years old, in the petition of affidavit mentioned and of the value of $500, from the possession of the defendant, Smith D. Atkins, and deliver him to the plaintiff, Emily G. Hood, upon her giving the bond required by law: and you will make due return of this order on the 1st

---

*General Order 15, issued by General Granger on November 4, 1862, included the following provision: "No citizen nor non-combatant will be permitted within the camps or lines of this army, without special authority to that effect." (*Destruction of Slavery*, p. 534n.)

day of the next February term of the Fayette Circuit Court.

Witness: John B. Norton, Clerk of said Court, this 18th day of November, 1862.

JOHN B. NORTON, C.F.C.C.

SUMMONS—ORDINARY.

The Commonwealth of Kentucky—To the Sheriff of Fayette County, greeting: You are commanded to summon Smith D. Atkins to answer, on the first day of the next February term of the Fayette Circuit Court, a petition filed against him in said Court, by Emily G. Hood, and warn him that, upon his failure to answer, the petition will be taken for confessed, or he will be proceeded against for contempt, and you will make due return of this summons, on the first day of the next February term of said Court.

Witness: John B. Norton, Clerk of said Court, this 18th day of November, 1862.

JOHN B. NORTON, C.F.C.C.

LEXINGTON, Ky, Nov. 18, 1862.

COLONEL: It is reported to me that a civil process is to be served in your camp, and Judge Robertson requests me to drop you a line, intimating the course I pursue in such cases.

I invariably recognize the civil law in all its operations, as martial law does not exist here in Kentucky.

We have no right to resist the execution of any civil process, and an attempt to do so would render us amenable to the severe laws of this State. I can give you no order, but would, for the good of the cause recommend that the civil authorities be respected always. Your ob't servant.

Q. A. GILLMORE, Brig. Gen.

Col. ATKINS, Present.

To the latter document Col. Atkins made the following satisfactory and sensible reply:

IN CAMP TWO MILES SOUTH OF
LEXINGTON, Nov. 19th, 1862.

GENERAL: I have your note. I beg to state that I am under
orders to proceed southward with my command, and I do not know at
what moment I may find the enemy, and I cannot afford to piddle away
my time in hunting up niggers or in replying to bills in chancery filed
against me. When the war is over, and I am at leisure, I will answer
any civil process, but I beg to assure you, General, that I am now
altogether too busy with a terrible rebellion and bloody war, to be
fooling away my time in writing answers to bills in chancery filed by
secession sympathizers. I have not resisted and do not expect to, for I
have not a single nigger in my possession at all, but I cannot stop to
answer formally in court. Your ob't serv't.

SMITH D. ATKINS, Colonel.

Q. A. GILLMORE, Brigadier General.

Col. Atkins and the 92d need no defense at our hands.   Their services
can be had to fight rebels anywhere and at all times, but to return
negroes, to rebel masters, never!   All they ask is to be put into an
Illinois brigade and sent out of Kentucky, where they can see the white
of the enemy's eyes.   Is it an unreasonable demand?[59]

PD

> The behavior of Atkins and his regiment continued to infuriate
> slaveholders, some of whom were serving in the Union army. An of-
> ficer in a Kentucky regiment complained to the commander of the
> Army of Kentucky, in which both he and Atkins served.

[bluegrass area, Ky. November 24?, 1862]

("Paper")

I respectfully state to Major General Gordon Granger, that 3 negroes,
namely, Lyrus Moley & Henry, belonging to Chas Gilkey (an uncle to the

undersigned) were enticed from their owner at Mt Sterling Ky. by soldiers of the 92^d Illinois Regiment also Henry, slave of Mrs B. White, and Charles slave of James McGowan.   These negroes and about 30 more are now harbored in said regiment, and the Colonel says he will not give them up, unless, his Captains & Co. agree, as they are entitled to servants.   There was also 2 other negroes belonging to Thos Hill & James Hill^s estate, who came back to their Homes—   This Regiment is Commanded by Col Smith D. Atkins, and is now within 8 or 10 miles of Lexington, on Winchester Pike.   I can give to Genl Granger any reference he may desire as to veracity of statement, and respectfully ask of him if there is anything he can do for owners of said slaves, it will be appreciated, and we soldiers of Kentucky, can have some assurance, that our property is being protected at home, while we are away battling for our loved Country.   The above is respectfully submitted to General Granger.

HLeSr   Charles S. Rogers[60]

> Colonel Atkins admitted Rogers's charge without apology. In a let-
> ter to the headquarters of a superior officer (to whom Rogers's
> complaint had been referred), Atkins detailed the hostility he had
> faced in Kentucky and the measures he had been compelled to take
> to defend himself, his regiment, and the "servants" within his ranks.

Nicholasville Ky.   Nov. 25 /62.

Sir: In reply to your note of the 24th inst and paper enclosed, I have to report.

That I am not aware that any of the slaves mentioned in the paper, are within my lines at all, but presume they are.   There are now I am told fifteen colored persons employed by my Commissioned officers, as

servants; no more, I am certain.   The McGowan mentioned refused to
take a U.S. voucher for oats he had for sale, and I do not think myself
nor any of my officers, will spend much time in hunting up a slave for
him, without specific orders.   I tried at Mt Sterling to adopt a
conciliatory course, and on receiving, Maj Genl" Gordon Grangers Genl"
order No. 15,* turned out of Camp all that were not properly employed
as soldiers or servants—   no others are now within my regimental
lines—   Five to Eight hundred colored persons were sent to my
regiment on the 8th of November, evidently for the purpose of creating
trouble on this question.   At Winchester I was threatened by a mob, and
some of the 14th Ky. Infy. tried to take by force, servants from my lines,
while marching along.   We were compelled to march through the town
with bayonets fixed and guns loaded.   At Lexington a similar affair took
place, and a riot nearly occassioned.   I am sued in the civil courts of
Kentucky, for part of the slaves mentioned in the paper, although I have
not had a thing to do with any of them, since I came into the State.
Kentucky soldiers are no more willing to fight for our beloved Country,
than the sons, of Illinois, as the History of this war has already
demonstrated.   Illinois is loyal without conditions,   She imposes no
"ifs" in her devotion to the Union.   Illinois loves the Union, and her
volunteer soldiers are in the field to fight for it as Commanded by the
Commander In Chief of the Armies of the United States.   I have the
honor to be Captain Your Very Obt Sevt.

HLcS   Smith D. Atkins[61]

> Union commanders might officially enjoin their subordinates from
> interfering with either slaves or slaveholders, but in practice they
> had wide latitude to indulge personal inclinations. To Colonel Mar-

---

*For a summary of the order, see above, p. 77n.

cellus Mundy, a slaveholder who commanded a Kentucky regiment, the Union army had degenerated into "a mere negro freeing machine."[62] Defying military protocol, he wrote directly to the president to complain that this transformation violated his understanding of the cause for which he was prepared to sacrifice his life.

Louisville [Ky.],   Nov 27th *1862*

M[r] President. I deem it my privilege as a Citizen to make the following Complaint directly to you. While I have been absent from my home serving our Country in the field to the utmost of my humble ability, I have not only suffered large pecuniary loss from rebel depredations but worse still, federal officers, particularly those of the 18th Michigan Infantry Volunteers have taken within their lines and hold the negroes of my loyal neighbours and myself. That regiment has now not less than twenty five negroes in Camp at Lexington Ky, who belong to loyal union men who have been masters for loyalty's sake, and among the rest one of mine. I called upon the officer Commanding the regiment and mildly remonstrated against this injustice, particularly to myself, and requested him to have my negro turned out of his lines, which he flatly refused to do, justifying his detention by virtue of Your proclimation* and the new article of war. My father-in-law, Col E. N. Offutt had in the mean time, during my absence, as the best means of recovering my slave which they refused him permission to take, issued a writ of replevin for the negro which was duly served by the Sheriff of Fayette County—but was disobeyed by the officer and the Civil authorities defied. Another fact I should mention in this Connection, which is, that our negroes are being taught by the abolition officers from Michigan and other northern states now serving in Kentucky, that on the first day of January next, they are

---

*The preliminary emancipation proclamation.

all to be free, and will have a right even to kill their masters who may
attempt to restrain them, which has aroused a lively apprehension in the
minds of Citizens in Central Kentucky of a servile insurrection at that
time unless prevented by such orders as will check the evil— This is
neither slander upon those officers or idle rumor; but a fact for which I
and hundreds of citizens can vouch. Mr President I deem it unnecessary
to resort to argument to show to you the magnitude of the injustice in
this case to me— When I became a soldier I sacrificed a large and
lucrative practice as an attorney in Philadelphia and placed my property
in this state at the mercy of our enemies—who have revenged themselves
largely upon me—and now my utter ruin is to be Completed by our own
officers to promote a fanatical partizan theory—which not only ignores
gratitude as a principle; but does me and many loyal men of my state
bold wrong for a supposed benefit to another race. Mr President is this
right and will you sanction it? While in opinion I must dissent from
your policy of *freeing* the slaves of rebels, which would result in great
wrong to loyal slave owners, as well as to all loyal men burthened with
this immense war debt—I approve of the *Confiscation* of the slaves and
all property of rebels to weaken the resources of our enemy and relieve
the tax burthen of our friends. Being a soldier whether palatable or
impalatable, I am always ready to execute the orders of the President as
my Commander in Chief; but Mr President were I Commander in Chief I
would never trample upon the Constitutional rights of a loyal people in a
loyal state whereby our friends would be estranged and our enemies
advantaged   I need not reassure you sir of my abiding faith in your
goodness, integrity of purpose and sense of justice of which this appeal is
the evidence   I have the Honor to be Your Ob^t Servt

ALS

M Mundy[63]

The approach of January 1 and the promised promulgation of emancipation worried slaveholders throughout the South. Many believed that there would be a general insurrection sometime between Christmas and the new year, a week when slaves customarily enjoyed a respite from work and an opportunity to socialize with other slaves. Although similar forebodings had been common in the antebellum period, the forthcoming proclamation intensified unease. In southern Louisiana, a few regiments of black soldiers had recently been incorporated into federal ranks, and their presence gave slaveholders additional cause for anxiety. One planter, Pierre Soniat, addressed his worries to the Union military commander, General Nathaniel P. Banks.

Parish of St Charles [*La.*]   December 20 1862

General   my advanced age, my position as a planter, and my perfect knowledge of the country, make it my duty to present a few remarks which I hope you will receive favorably.   We have suffered greatly during this unfortunate war, and we undoubtedly will have much more to suffer before order is restored and peace smiles again on this country. So far we have, to regret in most instances, only the ruin and desolation which have extended to crops & farms; but the evil that threatens us is far more terrible than the loss of fortunes; our very lives are at stake!   As far as the memory of man can go, there has existed among the negro population a tradition which has caused us many a sleepless night.   They imagine that they are to be freed by Christmas.   Vague reports are spread about that they intend, taking whatever weapons they can find, to come in vast numbers and force the federal government to give them their freedom.   Having been deceived in their expectation, great crimes might be committed by them.   The negro regiments, in particular, being organized and armed are especially to be feared. General I have no conduct to dictate to you, but if I were allowed to make a suggestion, I would tell you to disarm the negroes at least for the present and place white men, to see to their behavior   Respectfully Submitted

ALS   P^{re} Soniat[64]

> While planters trembled at the prospect of the Emancipation Procla-
> mation, slaves and free people of color prepared to celebrate the
> Day of Jubilee. In New Orleans, the officers of a "union association"
> asked General Banks to allow its members to observe the day in a
> manner befitting an event their people had awaited more than two
> hundred years.

New orleans [*La.*]   Dec 22th 1862

In obedience To Th High chift an Command of Th Head quarters Department of Th Gulf Maggor Gen N P Bank We Th members of Th union association Desir Th & Respectfully ask of you Th privirliges of Salabrating Th first Day of January th 1863 by a Large procesion on that Day & We Wish to pass th Head quarters of th union officers High in a authority that is if it Suit your approbation & We also Wish to Give a Grand union Dinner on th Second Day of Januay that is if it so pleas you & th profit of th Dinner Will Go To th poor people in th Camp th Colour Woman & childeren   Your Most Homble obedien servant

J M Marshall   th president of th union association

HLSr   Henry clay   th Superintender of th Dinner[65]

"Contrabands" crossing the Rappahannock River in Virginia,
August 1862. (Library of Congress)

Former slaves in Richmond, Virginia, April 1865. (Library of Congress)

"Contrabands" taken aboard the U.S.S. *Vermont*.
(New-York Historical Society)

Slaves seeking admittance to Fortress Monroe,
Virginia, only weeks after the beginning of the Civil War.
(*Frank Leslie's Illustrated Newspaper*, June 8, 1861)

Fugitive slaves coming into Union lines at New Bern, North Carolina.
(*Harper's Weekly*, February 21, 1863)

Former slaves follow General William T. Sherman's troops across Georgia.
(*Frank Leslie's Illustrated Newspaper*, March 18, 1865)

Slaves from the plantation of Confederate president
Jefferson Davis arrive at Chickasaw Bayou, Mississippi.
(*Frank Leslie's Illustrated Newspaper*, August 8, 1863)

Fugitive slaves coming into Union lines near
Culpeper Court House, Virginia, November 8, 1863.
(Pencil drawing by Edwin Forbes, Library of Congress)

A fugitive reports his successful escape. (See pp. 29–30)

A slave writes the president. (See p. 349)

Slaves escaping by boat. (*Harper's Weekly*, April 9, 1864)

Former slaves greet black soldiers marching into Charleston, South Carolina, February 21, 1865. (*Harper's Weekly*, March 18, 1865)

Black soldiers lead Emancipation Day celebration on Port Royal Island,
South Carolina, January 1, 1863.
(*Frank Leslie's Illustrated Newspaper*, January 24, 1863)

CHAPTER

II.

A WAR FOR
FREEDOM

ON NEW YEAR'S DAY 1863, PRESIDENT ABRAHAM Lincoln fulfilled his promise of the previous September. The Emancipation Proclamation, issued under the president's powers as commander-in-chief, declared, in simple, straightforward language, "that all persons held as slaves" within the states still in rebellion "are, and henceforward shall be, free."[1] Applying as it did only to the seceded states, the proclamation left slavery untouched in the loyal border states. In addition, it exempted Tennessee, several counties of Virginia, and most of the sugar-growing region of southern Louisiana—areas in which local unionists (including unionist slaveholders) had already taken steps to resume their allegiance to the United States. In and of itself, the Emancipation Proclamation did not immediately free a single slave. Nevertheless, it fundamentally transformed the character of the war. The war for the Union became a war against slavery. After January 1, 1863, every advance of federal arms expanded the domain of freedom. Moreover, the liberated themselves became liberators, for the proclamation also announced the acceptance of black men into the Union army and navy.

In the years following the Emancipation Proclamation, slavery disintegrated unevenly on both sides of the line of battle. Federal military campaigns brought freedom within reach of more and more slaves, and newly freed slaves struck out to rescue families and friends. Confederate offensives and federal retreats, by contrast, reversed the process of liberation, throwing men and women who had tasted freedom back into bondage. As Northern armies came to depend upon black soldiers and military laborers, Confederates found that their slaves, once the foundation of Southern agricultural and military productivity, had been turned against them. Confederate authorities, endeavoring to counter the North's emancipation policy and to mobilize slaves to sustain rebel armies, unintentionally undermined the authority of slaveholders, subverted slave discipline, and strained relations between slaveholders and nonslaveholders. The slaves took full advantage, chipping away at their bondage from within while Union armies pounded it from without.

Slaves who had fled to the federal post of Corinth, in northeastern Mississippi, welcomed news of the Emancipation Proclamation. Emboldened by the pronouncement of freedom and armed by Union officers, they set out for their old homes to liberate others. When one of them was captured some sixty miles from Corinth, a Confederate cavalry officer sought instructions from department headquarters about how to deal with such *"missionaries"* of freedom.

Okolona Miss   Jany 8th 1863

You will oblige me by sending instructions in reference to the manner of disposing of negroes—runaways—caught by my scouts and not giving correct statement of the names of their owners and residence.   It is difficult by any manner to ascertain where they belong, and the number is increasing beyond convenience.

On yesterday a negro was caught armed and killed two dogs in the attempt to catch him and finally shot himself inflicting a severe wound, after which he stated that he was from Corinth; and that on the night of the 1st inst the negroes (or most of them) were assembled at that place and officers attended making lectures and stating they were free. The negroes after receiving each a pistol (six shooter) were instructed to go to the vicinity of their respective homes and act as *missionaries* (or "in the recruiting service.") I wish to know how to deal with them when caught. Very Respectfully By order of C R Barteau Lt Col Comdg

ALS
                                                   Pleas. Smith[2]

In reply, an adjutant at the headquarters of the Confederate Department of Mississippi and East Louisiana instructed Colonel Barteau to remand to the civil authorities all recaptured slaves who withheld the names of their owners or furnished incorrect information. "When you take Negroes with arms evidently coming out from the enemie's camp," he continued, "proceed at once to hold a drum head court martial and if found guilty hang them upon the spot."[3]

Former slaves who carried the gospel of freedom to those still in bondage often did so in order to liberate their own kin. A few days after the Emancipation Proclamation, a group of black men in eastern North Carolina—an area occupied by Union forces since 1862—seized the family and household goods of one of their number. According to a participant in the expedition, the liberating force included stewards from a federal naval vessel and the servants of Northern army officers.[4] Outraged by the audacity of the military laborers, slaveholders sought the assistance of Edward Stanly, a North Carolina unionist whom President Lincoln had appointed military governor; Stanly took their protest to the federal military commander.

New Berne [*N.C.*] Jany 20th 1863

General, I have just received a letter from Edenton, of date the 6th Inst. informing that a band of negroes & Soldiers, "*armed*," visited the premises of a Mrs Page of that town, and carried away Several negroes, and a parcel of bedding & other furniture: that they were very insolent in their conduct and threatened to have the town shelled if they were interfered with.

My correspondent says that they came, as he heard, from on board the Ocean Wave:

A negro man, formerly living on the plantation of the venerable James C. Johnston, named "Matthew" was the person commanding the party

This negro, is one of desperate character.

The Citizens of Edenton beg your protection from outrages of this Kind: they desire to know whether it can be afforded them, or must they take redress into their own hands?

I have written and informed my correspondent—a gentleman of the highest character—that I would call your attention to this case, & have no doubt you will, as heretofore, take effectual steps to protect peacable citizens and punish such outrages. I have the honor to be &c

ALS   Edw Stanly[5]

Early in the war, most of the slaves who escaped to federal military camps had been men who set out alone or in small bands. By 1863, however, with freedom the announced policy of the federal government, slaves increasingly fled in family groups. Sometimes entire plantation populations ran away en masse. In Tennessee, which had been exempted from the Emancipation Proclamation, the volume and changing character of slave flight confounded the efforts of federal authorities to retain the allegiance of slaveholding unionists. Aware that federal law and military orders prohibited him from returning slaves to their owners, a general in the southwestern part of the state sought guidance from the headquarters of the 16th Army Corps.

Lagrange, Tenn.,   March 27th *1863.*

Sir   I wrote a few days ago asking instructions with regard to the large number of contrabands now finding their way into our Camps—   The evil is a most perplexing one.   Whole families of them are stampeding and leaving their masters, and I am applied to daily for the return of those belonging to loyal Masters.   I know that our General Orders do not permit me to yield to such applications: but something should be done to shield our service from the charge of furnishing an Asylum to the Servants of loyal men living in districts not affected by the emancipation proclamation.   Very Respectfully Your obedt Servt.

HLS   W[m] Sooy Smith[6]

By virtue of their early occupation by federal troops and the unionism of many resident slaveholders, thirteen sugar-plantation parishes* of southern Louisiana were also exempted from the Emancipation Proclamation. As in Tennessee, however, the erosion of slavery proceeded apace. An army circular denying rumors of emancipation nevertheless enumerated a farrago of military regulations and federal laws that both demonstrated and contributed to the unraveling of bondage.

---

*In Louisiana, a parish is a unit of civil administration equivalent to a county.

CIRCULAR.

New Iberia, La., April 24, 1863.

The generally received impression, that the slaves of this Parish, are free, by force of the presence of the Union army, *is erroneous.*

This Parish, (St. Martin) is excepted by name, in the Emancipation Proclamation, of President Lincoln, issued at Washington, D. C., January 1, 1863.

No farther interference, with the institution of slavery will be allowed by the Army Authorities, than may necessarily result from the police regulations.

United States Army Officers, are forbidden, by law of Congress, to use force in the restoration of slaves to masters.

If slaves flee from their masters, they must work on Government works, receiving therefor, full rations, for full day's work.

If slaves voluntarily return to their masters, they will not be molested.

If masters use force, in abducting run-away slaves, the masters will be arrested.

If masters inhumanly punish or whip their slaves, they must be arrested.

No punishment of slaves, will be permitted, except such as are practiced in the Army.

                        A. B. LONG,
                  Capt., & Provost Marshal,
                        Commanding Post,

7

The Northern armies that left winter quarters for the spring campaigns of 1863 marched under a new banner, for emancipation had become central to federal military policy. Recognizing the importance of slavery to the Confederacy and the value of ex-slaves to the Union, most Northerners had come to regard the mobilization of black laborers and soldiers as militarily necessary. From the War Department in Washington, Henry W. Halleck, who had become general-in-chief of the army the previous July, privately advised General Ulysses S. Grant about the changing purposes of the war and the military benefits of emancipation. As a general in the field, Halleck had steadfastly disavowed interference with slavery,* and he felt little enthusiasm for the new policy. Nevertheless, he too acknowledged that measures once thought radical had become common sense.

Washington [*D.C.*],   March 31st/63

(Unofficial)

Genl,   It is the policy of the government to withdraw from the enemy as much productive labor as possible.   So long as the rebels retain and employ their slaves in producing grains, &c, they can employ all the whites in the field.   Every slave withdrawn from the enemy, is equivalent to a white man put *hors de combat*.†

Again, it is the policy of the government to use the negroes of the South so far as practicable as a military force for the defence of forts, depôts, &c.   If the experience of Genl Banks near New Orleans should be satisfactory, a much larger force will be organized during the coming summer; & if they can be used to hold points on the Mississippi during the sickly season, it will afford much relief to our armies.   They certainly can be used with advantage as laborers, teamsters, cooks, &c.

---

*See above, pp. 17–18, 27–29.

†Out of combat; disabled.

And it is the opinion of many who have examined the question without passion or prejudice, that they can also be used as a military force. It certainly is good policy to use them to the very best advantage we can. Like almost anything else, they may be made instruments of good or evil. In the hands of the enemy they are used with much effect against us. In our hands we must try to use them with the best possible effect against the rebels.

It has been reported to the Secretary of War that many of the officers of your command not only discourage the negroes from coming under our protection, but, by ill treatment, force them to return to their masters. This is not only bad policy in itself, but it is directly opposed to the policy adopted by the government. Whatever may be the individual opinion of an officer in regard to the wisdom of measures adopted and announced by the government, it is the duty of every one to cheerfully and honestly endeavour to carry out the measures so adopted. Their good or bad policy is a matter of opinion before they are tried; their real character can only be determined by a fair trial. When adopted by the government it is the duty of every officer to give them such a trial, and to do everything in his power to carry the orders of his government into execution.

It is expected that you will use your official and personal influence to remove prejudices on this subject, and to fully and thoroughly carry out the policy now adopted and ordered by the government. That policy is, to withdraw from the use of the enemy all the slaves you can, and to employ those so withdrawn, to the best possible advantage against the enemy.

The character of the war has very much changed within the last year. There is now no possible hope of a reconciliation with the rebels. The union party in the South is virtually destroyed. There can be no peace but that which is enforced by the sword. We must conquer the rebels, or

be conquered by them.   The north must either destroy the slave-
oligarchy, or become slaves themselves;—the manufacturers—mere
hewers of wood and drawers of water to southern aristocrats.

This is the phase which the rebellion has now assumed.   We must
take things as they are.   The government, looking at the subject in all
its aspects, has adopted a policy, and we must cheerfully and faithfully
carry out that policy.

I write you this unofficial letter, simply as a personal friend, and as a
matter of friendly advice.   From my position here, where I can survey
the entire field, perhaps I may be better able to understand the tone of
public opinion, and the intentions of the Government, than you can from
merely consulting the officers of your own army.   Very respectfully Your
obt servt

HLdS   H. W. Halleck[8]

> The freedom promised by the Emancipation Proclamation was not
> always enforced by federal authorities, even within Union lines.
> Twelve-year-old Amy Moore, along with three younger sisters and
> her mother, all of whom had been liberated by federal troops in
> northern Alabama, were reenslaved in early 1863 under a Ken-
> tucky law forbidding freed slaves from entering the state on pain of
> arrest as runaways. Seized by civil authorities and jailed, members
> of the Moore family were sold at auction to four different pur-
> chasers. Still held as a slave months after the end of the Civil War,
> Amy Moore swore the following affidavit before a federal military
> officer.

[*Louisville, Ky.   August 14?, 1865*]

Amy Moore Colored, being duly Sworn deposeth and Says, that in the
Summer of 1863 [*1862*] the United States Soldiers under command of

Major McMillen came to her masters house in Huntsville Alabama, (her master and his family having left them) and carried away deponent together with her mother and three Sisters,   that they brought us all to Nashville Tenn where we were put on board of a transport and Started for Cincinnati Ohio   that when we arrived at Louisville Ky we were arrested by a man who Said he was a watchman and taken to the Slave pen on Second Street Louisville Ky and kept there two or three days when we were taken to the Depot of the Louisville and Nashville Rail Road and there another watchman took charge of us and took us to Shepherdsville Ky and kept us confined several weeks when we were sold at auction by the Sherriff of Bullett County Ky.   Dr. McKay bought deponent and paid for her the sum of Five Hundred (500) dollars   *James Funk* bought deponents mother and youngest Sister paying Six Hundred (600) dollars for the two, and Soon after Sold her mother to *Judge Hoegner* who now holds her as a Slave   *James Shepherd* bought my Sister Nora and *Richard Deets* bought my sister Ann, and further deponent saith that she and her mother and Sisters have been held as Slaves Since the above Sale and Still continue to be so held.

her
Amy ✕ Moore[9]
mark

HDSr

Hundreds of former slaves from the seceded states forfeited their newly won freedom when they tried to travel northward through Kentucky, where slavery remained intact. Even freedpeople with protection papers from high-ranking military officers were halted at the Ohio River under state laws forbidding public conveyances to transport slaves without their owners' consent. State and local officials arrested the freedpeople as fugitive slaves, advertised for their masters, and sold them to new owners when no one registered a claim. They had escaped slavery in the Confederacy only to be reenslaved in the Union. A congressman from Michigan described the circumstances to General Ambrose E. Burnside, commander of the Department of the Ohio.

St Louis [*Mo.*] May 4th/63

General   I was in Louisville K'y lately on my return from Nashville and wish to call your attention to the manner in which Contrabands are treated in that City—   Colored men from Arkansas Tennessee Miss and other Rebel States who have Certificates of their freedom signed by Generals in the field are siezed—imprisoned, and sold for costs &c—   The temptation to kidnap them is very great as the man who takes them up gets $75" each & the Jailor is well paid also and these poor fellows have no friends to help them   The Ferry Boat which crosses the Ohio will not let a Contraband cross no matter tho' Gen'l Rosecrans should certify in writing that he is a free man   Many—yes a great many colored men who have rendered great service to the army & secured the good will of officers, who wished to send them to Ohio or Michigan have been siezed in spite of all these papers or Certificates & sold into slavery—sent no one knows where—   This infernal treatment of such men ought to call down the vengeance of Heaven on all who permit it

Let me state a case   I was in Franklin Tennessee in Maj Gen'l Grangers Camp—the last Sunday in April—when a very intelligent Contraband came in & told us his master was a Mississi Officer & he had run away   He told Gen Granger how to surprise two Camps & Gen G— did capture all in one of them the same night without the loss of a man—& would have taken the other but for an accident—   This fugitive

did all he could for us—& would do more & yet if I wished to take him to
Michigan & Gen'l Rosecrans certified to all these facts & that he was
legally free I could not get him over the Ohio River   A Louisville
kidnapper can sieze & imprison him & unless I will stay & see to it he
must be sold—

Kentucky is called a loyal State & is exempted by the Pres't from the
operation of the Proclamation   Protect them then & enforce the return
of *their* fugitive slaves but devise some way by which Officers of a certain
rank can certify to the freedom—of any colored man *not* a resident of
K'y who wishes to go North & compel these Ferry men to respect them

Orders should be issued regulating the passage of these men over the
River & Officers app'ted who should see these orders enforced   I
believe Col Moore does all he dare do without your orders* & I hope you
will adopt some course to remedy this grivious wrong— You must
pardon me for writing at such length for I cannot see *humble* & poor
men—who have done us often great service treated so inhumanely—   I
met you several times in Washington & you may remember
me   Perhaps too you have this subject under consideration now & I
cannot help feeling you will do what is necssary & right   I have the
honor to be Your Obt Serv't

F W Kellogg[10]

ALS

---

*Colonel Orlando H. Moore, who was from Michigan, was a provost
marshal in Louisville; on May 1, 1863, he had issued an order
prohibiting "all unlawful interference with the authorized negro
servants of officers of the United States Army and negroes legally
entitled to their freedom, passing from Kentucky to Indiana," but it
was immediately countermanded by Colonel Marcellus Mundy, a
Kentucky slaveholder and the commander of the Post of Louisville.
(*Destruction of Slavery*, p. 579n.)

By the time he received Kellogg's letter, General Burnside had already issued an order declaring "void" any sale in Kentucky of "slaves made free by the war measures of the President of the United States, by Congress, or by capture during the war."[11] Enforcing the order was, however, a difficult matter. At the end of the year, federal officers charged with releasing enslaved freedpeople acknowledged that many of them—perhaps hundreds—were still held in bondage by Kentucky purchasers.[12]

The promise of freedom announced by the Emancipation Proclamation was a beacon that reached deep into the Confederacy. Outposts controlled by Union forces, like Fortress Monroe in southeastern Virginia, drew fugitive slaves from hundreds of miles away. Runaways who set out to test the intentions of the Yankees subsequently ventured back to their old homes to claim their families, spreading word of freedom in the process. Captain Charles B. Wilder, the superintendent of contrabands at Fortress Monroe, explained in testimony before a War Department commission that such communication between Union- and Confederate-controlled territory informed slaves about the opportunities that beckoned behind federal lines.

[*Fortress Monroe, Va.,*]   May 9, 1863.
. . . .

Question   How many of the people called contrabands, have come under your observation?

Answer   Some 10,000 have come under our control, to be fed in part, and clothed in part, but I cannot speak accurately in regard to the number.   This is the rendezvous.   They come here from all about, from Richmond and 200 miles off in North Carolina   There was one gang that started from Richmond 23 strong and only 3 got through.

. . . .

Q In your opinion, is there any communication between the refugees and the black men still in slavery?

A. Yes Sir, we have had men here who have gone back 200 miles.

Q In your opinion would a change in our policy which would cause them to be treated with fairness, their wages punctually paid and employment furnished them in the army, become known and would it have any effect upon others in slavery?

A Yes—Thousands upon Thousands. I went to Suffolk a short time ago to enquire into the state of things there—for I found I could not get any foot hold to make things work there, through the Commanding General, and I went to the Provost Marshall and all hands—and the colored people actually sent a deputation to me one morning before I was up to know if we put black men in irons and sent them off to Cuba to be sold or set them at work and put balls on their legs and whipped them, just as in slavery; because that was the story up there, and they were frightened and didn't know what to do. When I got at the feelings of these people I found they were not afraid of the slaveholders. They said there was nobody on the plantations but women and they were not afraid of them   One woman came through 200 miles in Men's clothes. The most valuable information we recieved in regard to the Merrimack and the operations of the rebels came from the colored people and they got no credit for it. I found hundreds who had left their wives and families behind. I asked them "Why did you come away and leave them there?" and I found they had heard these stories, and wanted to come and see how it was. "I am going back again after my wife" some of them have said "When I have earned a little money"   What as far as that?" "Yes"   and I have had them come to me to borrow money, or to get their pay, if they had earned a months wages, and to get passes. "I am going for my family" they say. "Are you not afraid to risk it?" "No

I know the Way"   Colored men will help colored men and they will
work along the by paths and get through.   In that way I have known
quite a number who have gone up from time to time in the neighborhood
of Richmond and several have brought back their families; some I have
never heard from.   As I was saying they do not feel afraid now.   The
white people have nearly all gone, the blood hounds are not there now to
hunt them and they are not afraid,   before they were afraid to stir.
There are hundreds of negroes at Williamsburgh with their families
working for nothing.   They would not get pay here and they had rather
stay where they are.   "We are not afraid of being carried back" a great
many have told us and "if we are, we can get away again"   Now that
they are getting their eyes open they are coming in.   Fifty came this
morning from Yorktown who followed Stoneman's Cavalry when they
returned from their raid.   The officers reported to their Quartermaster
that they had so many horses and fifty or sixty negroes.   "What did you
bring them for"   "Why they followed us and we could not stop them."
I asked one of the men about it and he said they would leave their work
in the field as soon as they found the Soldiers were Union men and
follow them sometimes without hat or coat.   They would take best horse
they could get and every where they rode they would take fresh horses,
leave the old ones and follow on and so they came in.   I have questioned
a great many of them and they do not feel much afraid; and there are a
great many courageous fellows who have come from long distances in
rebeldom.   Some men who came here from North Carolina, knew all
about the [*Emancipation*] Proclammation and they started on the belief
in it; but they had heard these stories and they wanted to know how it
was.   Well, I gave them the evidence and I have no doubt their friends
will hear of it.   Within the last two or three months the rebel guards
have been doubled on the line and the officers and privates of the 99th

New York between Norfolk and Suffolk have caught hundreds of
fugitives and got pay for them.

Q Do I understand you to say that a great many who have escaped
have been sent back?

A Yes Sir, The masters will come in to Suffolk in the day time and
with the help of some of the 99th carry off their fugitives and by and by
smuggle them across the lines and the soldier will get his $20. or $50.

. . . .13

HD

> Some slaves became free when their owners abandoned them. But
> theirs was often a pinched and hard-pressed freedom, for masters
> and mistresses generally removed their most valuable slaves out of
> range of Union forces, leaving behind only the old, sick, and crip-
> pled. A Treasury Department inspector of plantations in southern
> Louisiana described an estate where, despite grave disadvantages,
> a group of abandoned slaves had managed to secure an indepen-
> dent livelihood.

New Orleans [*La.*]   August 18" 1863

On the 14th of August, I visited the plantation Evacuated by the rebel,
Dick Robinson;   Some of the hovels are occupied by five or six negroes
in a destitute condition— The dwelling house is abandoned and
stripped of the little furniture it contained,   one fine Piano is in the
possession of Mrs Baker in the town of Houmas— The old negroes
appear to share the old house of their Master,   it is open to the weather
and is in a very filthy condition; the miserable hovels occupied by the
Negroes are fast going to decay; the Sugarhouse also is in a very
miserable Condition

The Negroes remaining on the plantation have cultivated Small
parcels of ground, and made Sufficient Corn and vegetables to Supply

them; they have Some Cane, I have given them written permission to grind it for their own use— These Negroes have succeeded beyond rebel Expectations in living without the assistance of white men—

Robinson took all his good or able Negroes to Texas, and left these old and crippled ones to starve— No White men in Louisiana could have done more or better than these Negroes & they well deserve the reward of their labor (the Crop) and the Encouragement of the Government— One old waggon, two Condemned Mules— two old ploughs and Six old hoes Comprise the inventory of this *joint Stock Company*— The condition of the Negro Cabins, no floors, no chimneys, built of pickets without regard to Comfort or Convenience, and their venerable appearance Confirms the Stories of cruelty related by the old Negroes of Dick Robinson the planter who made annualy 600 H[*ogs*]h[*ea*]ds Sugar—

This plantation is situated 82 miles above this City on the Grand Cailloux, Parish Terrebonne, I could not obtain any Correct information of the size of the plantation

HDcSr   H. Styles[14]

> Other slaves gained freedom at the hands of black soldiers. An out-
> raged provost marshal in southern Louisiana described to the
> provost marshal general at departmental headquarters how re-
> cruiting expeditions undermined slavery and opened the doors to
> freedom.

                    St. Bernard [*Parish, La.*], August, 21, *1863.*
General   I have the honor to report that four negro soldiers representing themselves as belonging to the 1st La. Native Guards with

passes signed by the A[*ssistant*]. A[*djutant*]. G[*eneral*]. of Brig. Gen.
Ullman, came into this parish yesterday for the alleged purpose of
recruiting.   That under this guise they visited plantations of loyal &
peaceable men, putting guards over their houses, threatening to shoot
any white person attempting to leave the houses, and then siezing horses
carts & mules for the purpose of transporting men women & children
from the plantations to the city of New Orleans.   That a band of
negroes thus assembled to the number of seventy five went singing,
shouting & marauding through the Parish disturbing the peace.

The property thus siezed has mostly been returned to the proper
owners & the women & children have been advised to return [*to*] thir
several plantations.

These Recruiting negroes have promised to return in a day or two to
convey all the negroes who desire it to the City.   Thus great
insubordination and confusion has been caused.   Today five more negro
soldiers with passes similar to the others visited the Plantation of Mr. E.
Villerie loaded their muskets in front of his door and demanded some
colored women whom they called their wives—

I most respectfully submit that such a method of Recruiting for the
Service of the U.S. Army is improper & await further instructions in
regard to it.   Your Most Obt Servt

ALS   Geo G. Davis[15]

> The increase of federal military activity in a shrinking Confederacy
> provoked slaveholders to tighten discipline, making escape more
> difficult and punishment more severe. After the war, a former slave
> from Tennessee described the horrific consequences of his failed at-
> tempt to reach Union lines.

Memphis, Tenn.,   Sept 13th *1865.*

Statement of Archy Vaughn.   Last spring [*1864*] I was living with *Bartlet Ciles* about 8 miles from Somerville—near M[c]Culloughs and one eving some Confederate soldiers or Guerillas came along and he told me to feed their horses. and I was at the barn gitting corn. and staied longer than he thought I should and when I went back to the house—he told me he was going to whip me in the morning—   that night I took an old mare and went to the ferry across Wolf River.   I was going to Laffayette Depot to get into the federal lines and Andrew Johnson who lives close to the ferry. took me and kept me until Billy Simons came along and he gave me to him to carry me back to Bartlet Ciles. When he Ciles took me down to the woods. and tied my hands, and pulled them over my knees and put a stick through under my knees. and then took his knife and *castrated* me and then cut off the lop of my left ear,   he made a colord man named Dallas help hold me—   he drove me off from his plantation some time in June—I think.

HDSr

his
Archy ✕ Vaughn[16]
mark

Grim punishment also awaited many former slaves who attempted to liberate their families. The Union military commander in Kansas informed his counterpart in Missouri of an instance in which the assailants were not Confederate partisans, but Missouri militiamen serving under federal auspices.

Fort Leavenworth [*Kans.*],   Mar 13 *1864*

General   A negro "Sam Marshall" who resides in Leavenworth, reports to me that yesterday he went over to Platte City Missouri, to get his children, who he was told would be allowed to come away free. The children were at a Mr Greens. Sam went in day light, with a team, driven by a white man, and made no demonstration of insolance or disrespect to any body. He was arrested by the Military, Commanded by one Captain David Johnson of the Mo Militia, who talked to him about the impropriety of his conduct. The Sheriff one Jesse Morris also lectured him, and told him the Captain would send a guard to take him away, as it was a wonder he was not killed. About a dozen of the soldiers did escort him about half a mile out of Platte City, where they tied him to a tree, and stripping him to the waste lacerated his back with a cow skin the marks of which Sam will carry to his grave. They told him they were "introducing him to the Pawpaw Militia" and that if Col Jennison would come to Platte City, they would treat him in the same way.

The Militia were dressed in Federal uniform, and armed with revolvers

Two of them Sam knew. They are young—"Chinn", and a young "Cockeril".

Sam is a quiet well behaved negro, whose tears and sorely lacerated back, seem to attest the truth of his statement.

The white man that drove the wagon, was arrested, but had sufficient influence (as formerly a citizen of the County) to get off without being harmed.

I call your attention to the use made of Federal troops, or troops clothed, fed, and foraged if not paid by the Federal Government.

I most respectfully suggest General, that on both sides, it is far better that troops unconnected with old border difficulties, and negro katching and negro whipping, should be substituted for such miserable wretches as those who disgrace their uniforms, and humanity, by acts of cruelty and baseness.

I hope General you will not suppose I hold you accountable for such

transactions in a Command to which you have so recently been assigned;
but I know a Sense of duty and disgust must be awakened by any loyal
Citizen acquainted with such brutality, and I report Such matters to
you, for early correction.—

   They called "Sam" a Jayhawker,* and pretended that he had run off
horses; but all this was no doubt a mere subterfuge; as probably the only
real offense "Sam" has been guilty of, was to run himself off, with a son
who has entered the Federal Army.—

   Platte City, is only about 6 miles from my lines and Such treatment of
men from here going into that place, is well Calculated to induce fierce
resentments from this Side, which of course I shall restrain; Conscious
of your own desire to correct such outrages.   I remain General Very
Respectfully Yours

ALS   S. R. Curtis[17]

   Only on rare occasions could former slaves turn the tables on their
   masters by administering the punishments they had long received.
   General Edward A. Wild, the commander of a brigade of black soldiers, reported one such occasion to General Edward W. Hinks,
   commander of the federal Department of Virginia and North Carolina; Hinks had demanded an explanation for the whipping of a
   prisoner in Wild's camp.

                  Wilson's Wharf, James River [*Va.*]   May 12th 64
Sir—
                       . . . .

   On Tuesday May 10th William H. Clopton, was brought in by the
Pickets.   He had been actively disloyal so that I held him as Prisoner of

---

   *An antislavery guerrilla operating along the Kansas–Missouri border.

War, and have sent him as such to Fortress Monroe. He has acquired a
notoriety as the most cruel Slave Master in this region, but in my
presence he put on the character of a Snivelling Saint. I found half a
dozen *women* among our refugees, whom he had often whipped
unmercifully, even baring their whole persons for the purpose in
presence of *Whites and Blacks.* I laid him bare and putting the whip
into the hands of the Women, three of Whom took turns in settling some
old scores on their masters back. A black Man, whom he had abused
finished the administration of Poetical justice, and even in this scene the
superior humanity of the Blacks over their white master was manifest in
their moderation and backwardness. I wish that his back had been as
deeply scarred as those of the women, but I abstained and left it to
them— I wish it to be distinctly understood by Brig. Genl. Hinks that
I shall do the same thing again under similar circumstances. I forgot to
state that this Clopton is a high minded Virginia Gentleman, living for
many years next door to the late John Tyler ExPresident of the U.S. and
then and still intimate with his family.

. . . .

HLcSr

(Signed)   Edwd. A. Wild[18]

Questioning Wild's "soundness of mind," General Hinks recommended that he be either court-martialed or relieved from command.*

———•—•———

---

*The following month, a court-martial found Wild guilty of
disobedience of orders, but his conviction was reversed on the grounds
that, owing to prejudice against officers commanding black troops, his
trial had not been impartial. (*Destruction of Slavery*, pp. 97–98n.)

Freedpeople sometimes had assistance in rescuing their families from slavery. Three freedmen employed as military laborers in the District of Columbia hired two white teamsters with whom they had worked to take them to southern Maryland to liberate their wives and children. Although the men carried papers from a military official authorizing the mission, civil authorities in Maryland arrested and imprisoned them while they were returning to Washington with their families. The wife of one of the teamsters appealed to the War Department for her husband's release, and an endorsement by a Union general in Maryland described the circumstances of the case.

Washington City [*D.C.*]   May 25th 1864

Mrs Laura A. Moody, of Washington, D.C., applies for the release of her husband Geo. A. Moody, who while attempting to bring from Piscataway, Md some negro women to their husbands, living in this city under Government employ, was arrested and imprisoned in Lower Marlboro Jail.   Mr Moody had a pass and had been informed he would not be interfered with, or if he was so interfered with that he would be protected by Government[19]

HD

[*Endorsement*]   Hd. Qrs. First Separate Brigade Relay House [*Md.*] June 1" 64.   Respectfully returned to Depm't. Hd. Qrs. with the information that Detective Wm W. Wood was intrusted with the investigation of this case and reports that Geo A. Moody and a Mr. Jones, were employed by three (3) Negro's (contrabands then in the employ of the U.S. Govm't) to go to Piscataway after the wives and children of these contrabands, who accompanied Moody and Jones on papers purporting to be issued by Cap't Shutz Provost Marshal.   In the execution of what they supposed to be authorized by these papers, they, collected the women & children and were on their way to Washington with them, when they were arrested by a Constable, by the name of Kirby (Jones and one colored man eluding the officer) who took Moody, two of the negro men with the women and children before Dr. G. [F]. Harris a justice of the Peace, who ordered them committed to jail. Subsequently Jones who had returned to Washington, at the solicitation of Moody's wife accompanied her to Upper Marlboro Jail to see her husband; On their arrival, Jones was arrested and confined in Jail with Moody.

It appears that Moody and Jones were employed by these colored men because of their having a wagon and horses with which to transport their women and children, and having made their acquaintance while engaged upon the same work for the Govm't near Washington.   It appears further that these men (Moody & Jones) are very poor and ignorant, and their families dependent entirely upon their efforts for daily subsistence   being brothers in law, they had obtained a team and wagon with which they performed such jobs as they could get from the Govm't and private parties who might require their service.

Being employed occasionally at the [Correll] where these Negroes were at work, and being offered a paying price for this job, they undertook it and fell into the hands of the *Phillistines.*

Their ignorance and utter destitution [. . .]* idea of any intention to commit a crime [. . .] [with] them a Provost Marshals pass would be regarded a passport to the realms of eternal bliss if it was so written. In as much as they supposed they were acting under the authority of proper Military Power, I would recommend if it can be done, that their cases be investigated by a Military commission   E. B. Tyler—Brig Genl:

---

*Approximately two words obscured by an ink blot.

Several weeks later, General Tyler informed his department commander that the four men were still in custody.

Relay House [*Md.*]   June 15th *1864.*

Colonel,   On visiting Port Tobacco on Monday last, I learned that Moody, Jones and two negro men whose cases had been referred to me from the Secretary of War and Secretary of State, were as I had reported, confined in Charles County Jail having been transferred from Prince Georges.   Being informed that they were not properly treated I called on the Sheriff and requested an interview with the prisoners; he very politely complied by showing me to a building to all appearances well secured with bars and bolts, at both doors, and windows.   After unbolting two doors, I was shown into a medium sized room, where I found the four men heavily chained to the floor with fetters upon their feet, and was told the four were handcuffed together at night.   I inquired of the Sheriff by what authority he held the prisoners, and he produced an order from a Prince George' County Magistrate, directed to the Sheriff of Prince George Co. for the commitment of Jones in the Jail of his (Prince George) County, and said the others were charged with running off slaves; but exhibited no authority for holding them and I think he had none.   At my suggestion the Irons were taken off.

These men complained very bitterly of the treatment they had received in Prince George and Charles County Jails—and strongly disavowed any intention of committing an offence in what they did, believeing as they did, the pass of Provost Marshal Shutz of Washington all the authority they required.   There is evidently a strong prejudice in the minds of a majority of the citizens of Prince George and Charles Counties against these parties and all who sympathize with the slave, and in the death struggle of their cherished institution they appear anxious to vend their spite upon any one that may fall in their power.

Moody Jones and the colored men, claim to have been in the employ of the Government by the Military Authorities, and left that employment temporarily under the sanction and authority of the Military Provost Marshal and now urgently request its protection.   I am Colonel, Very Respectfully Your Ob't Serv't

HLS   E. B. Tyler[20]

> When the secretary of war learned of the continued incarceration, he ordered General Lew Wallace, the federal commander in Maryland, "to take measures to secure the release of the parties imprisoned." General Wallace asked the governor of Maryland to direct their release from the Charles County jail, but the governor refused to intervene. Wallace therefore had "no choice" but to liberate the prisoners by military authority.[21]

> Perhaps recognizing the risk of acting on his own and the futility of applying to civil authorities, another former slave from Maryland asked Secretary of War Edwin M. Stanton to aid him in reuniting his family.

Boston [*Mass.*]   July 26th 1864

Dear Sir   I am Glad that I have the Honour to Write you afew line   I have been in troble for about four yars   my Dear wife was taken from me Nov 19th 1859 and left me with three Children and I being a Slave At the time Could Not do Anny thing for the poor little Children for my master it was took me Carry me some forty mile from them So I Could Not do for them and the man that they live with half feed them and half Cloth them & beat them like dogs & when I was admited to go to see

them it use to brake my heart & Now I say agian I am Glad to have the
honour to write to you to see if you Can Do Anny thing for me or for my
poor little Children   I was keap in Slavy untell last Novr 1863.   then
the Good lord sent the Cornel borne [*William Birney?*] Down their in
Marland in worsester Co   So as I have been recently freed I have but
letle to live on but I am Striveing Dear Sir   but what I went too know
of you Sir is is it possible for me to go & take my Children from those
men that keep them in Savery   if it is possible will you pleas give me a
permit from your hand then I think they would let them go   I Do Not
know what better to Do but I am sure that you know what is best for me
to Do

my two son I left with Mr Josep Ennese & my litle daughter I left with
Mr Iven Spence in worsister Co [. . .] of Snow hill

Hon sir will you please excuse my Miserable writeing & answer me as
soon as you can   I want get the little Children out of Slavery, I being
Criple would like to know of you also if I Cant be permited to rase a
Shool Down there & on what turm I Could be admited to Do so   No
more At present Dear Hon Sir

John Q A Dennis

Hon Sir will you please direct your letter to No 4 1/2 Milton St Boston
mass[22]

ALS

There is no indication that the War Department acknowledged
Dennis's letter.

If high-ranking officials only occasionally responded to the petitions of former slaves, some freedpeople received assistance from
less exalted Northern officers. Like former slaves in many parts of

the Union-occupied South, a group of military laborers in eastern Virginia returned home to liberate families and friends. They were accompanied by a detachment of black soldiers, whose brigade commander reported the outcome of the dangerous expedition.

Newport-News, Va. Sept. 1st, 1864.

Sir, I have the honor to report that some Government employees (colored) came up here from Fort Monroe and Hampton Hospitals, having been allowed a short leave of absence for the purpose of getting their families if possible. I told them I had no boats, but would help them with men. They reappeared the next day with sailboats. I sent with them a Captain and 15 men (dismounted Cavalry). The families were in and about Smithfield. I gave them strict instructions to abstain from plundering—to injure no one if possible—to get the women and children merely, and come away as promptly as possible. They were to land in the night. They followed these directions closely: but became delayed by the numbers of women and children anxious to follow, whom they packed in extra boats, picked up there, and towed along. They also had to contend against a head tide, and wind calm. So that their progress down Smithfield Creek in the early morn was exceedingly slow. The inhabitants evidently gathered in from some concerted plan of alarm or signals. For, 3 miles below, the party were intercepted by a force of irregular appearance, numbering about 100—having horses and dogs with them;—armed variously with shot guns, rifles, &c, and posted behind old breastworks with some hurried additions. They attacked the leading boats, killed a man and woman, and wounded another woman therein. The contrabands then rowed over to the opposite bank and scattered over the marshes. How many more have been slaughtered we know not. Two (2) men have since escaped to us singly.— When the rear boats, containing the soldiers, came up, the Captain landed, with

the design of attacking the rebels.   But then the firing revealed their
full numbers.   He found they outnumbered him, more than 6 to 1, and
that the REVOLVERS of our Cavalry, in open boats or on the open beach,
would stand no chance against their rifles behind breastworks.   He
embarked again, and they made their way past the danger, by wading
his men behind the boats, having the baggage and bedding piled up like
a barricade.   They then had a race with 3 boats, which put out from
side creeks to cut them off.   But for the coolness and ingenuity of Capt.
Whiteman, none would have escaped.   None of the soldiers are known
to have been severely wounded; but 3 are missing in the marshes and
woods.   We have since learned that there are signal Stations in that
neighborhood— which ought to be brooken up.   I would also earnestly
recommend the burning of a dozen or 20 houses in accordance with *your*
General Order No. 23.*   Very respectfully Your obt. Servant

HLS   Edwd A. Wild[23]

> For some slaves, the price of freedom included the loss of property
> they had painstakingly accumulated in bondage. Nancy Johnson
> remained in slavery until Union troops under General William T.
> Sherman reached the coast of Georgia at the end of 1864. Several
> years after the war she told a federal commission that the hungry
> soldiers who freed her and her husband also stripped them of the
> means of providing for themselves. Seeking to establish that the
> seized property had been their own and that they had been adher-
> ents of the Union cause (and thus were entitled to federal compen-
> sation), Johnson recounted the rigors of life in the Confederacy
> and the tribulations of an impoverished freedom.

---

*Issued on August 20, 1864, by the commander of the District of
Eastern Virginia, the order announced that Confederate guerrillas
thereafter captured in an adjoining section of North Carolina were to
be treated as spies rather than prisoners of war, and that citizens who
aided the guerrillas would be imprisoned and their houses burned.
(*Destruction of Slavery*, p. 99n.)

[*Savannah, Ga. March 22, 1873*]

General Interrogatories by Special Com'r— My name is Nancy
Johnson. I was born in Ga. I was a slave and became free when the
army came here. My master was David Baggs. I live in Canoochie
Creek   The claimant is my husband. He was a good Union man
during the war. He liked to have lost his life* by standing up for the
Union party. He was threatened heavy. There was a Yankee prisoner
that got away & came to our house at night; we kept him hid in my house
a whole day. He sat in my room. White people didn't visit our house
then. My husband slipped him over to a man named Joel Hodges & he
conveyed him off so that he got home. I saw the man at the time of the
raid & I knew him. He said that he tried to keep them from burning my
house but he couldn't keep them from taking everything we had. I was
sorry for them though a heap. The white people came hunting this man
that we kept over night; my old master sent one of his own grandsons &
he said if he found it that they must put my husband to death, & I had to
tell a story to save life. My old master would have had him killed   He
was bitter. This was my master David Baggs. I told him that I had
seen nothing of him. I did this to save my husbands life. Some of the
rebel soldiers deserted & came to our house & we fed them. They were
opposed to the war & didn't own slaves & said they would die rather than
fight. Those who were poor white people, who didn't own slaves were
some of them Union people. I befriended them because they were on
our side. I don't know that he [*her husband*] ever did any thing more
for the Union; we were way back in the country, but his heart was right
& so was mine. I was served mighty mean before the Yankees came
here. I was nearly frostbitten: my old Missus made me weave to make
clothes for the [*Confederate*] soldiers till 12 o'clock at night & I was so

---

*I.e., nearly lost his life.

tired & my own clothes I had to spin over night. She never gave me so much as a bonnet. I had to work hard for the rebels until the very last day when they took us. The old man [*her former master*] came to me then & said if you won't go away & will work for us we will work for you; I told him if the other colored people were going to be free that I wanted to be. I went away & then came back & my old Missus asked me if I came back to behave myself & do her work & I told her no that I came to do my own work. I went to my own house & in the morning my old master came to me & asked me if I wouldn't go and milk the cows: I told him that my Missus had driven me off—well said he you go and do it— then my Mistress came out again & asked me if I came back to work for her like a "*nigger*"— I told her no that I was free & she said be off then & called me a stinking bitch. I afterwards wove 40 yds. of dress goods for her that she promised to pay me for; but she never paid me a cent for it. I have asked her for it several times. I have been hard up to live but thank God, I am spared yet. I quit then only did a few jobs for her but she never did anything for me except give me a meal of victuals, you see I was hard up then, I was well to do before the war.

Second Set of Interrogatories by Spec'l Com'r.

1 I was present when this property was taken.

2 I saw it taken.

3 They [*the Union soldiers*] said that they didn't believe what I had belonged to me & I told them that I would swear that it belonged to me. I had tried to hide things. They found our meat, it was hid under the house & they took a crop of rice. They took it out & I had some cloth under the house too & the dishes & two fine bed-quilts. They took them out. These were all my own labor & night labor. They took the bole of cloth under the house and the next morning they came back with it made into pantaloons. They were starved & naked almost. It was Jan &

cold, They were on their way from Savannah. They took all my
husbands clothes, except what he had on his back.

4 These things were taken from David Bagg's place in Liberty
County. The Yankees took them. I should think there were thousands
of them. I could not count them. They were about a day & a night

5 There were present my family, myself & husband & this man Jack
Walker. He is way out in Tatnal Co. & we can't get him here

6 There were what we called officers there. I don't know whether
they ordered the property taken. I put a pot on and made a pie & they
took it to carry out to the head men. I went back where the officers
camped & got my oven that I cooked it in back again. They must have
ordered them or else they could not have gone so far & they right there.
They said that they stood in need of them. They said that we ought not
to care what they took for we would get it all back again; that they were
obliged to have something to eat. They were mighty fine looking men.

7 They took the mare out of the stable; they took the bacon under
the house, the corn was taken out of the crib, & the rice & the lard.
Some of the chickens they shot & some they run down; they shot the hogs.

8 They took it by hand   the camp was close by my house.

9 They carried it to their camps; they had lots of wagons there.

10 They took it to eat, bless you! I saw them eating it right there in
my house. They were nearly starved.

11 I told one of the officers that we would starve & they said no that
we would get it all back again, come & go along with us; but I wouldn't
go because the old man had my youngest child hid away in Tatnal
Co: he took her away because she knew where the gold was hid & he
didn't want her to tell. My boy was sent out to the swamp to watch the
wagons of provisions & the [*Union*] soldiers took the wagons & the boy,
& I never saw him anymore. He was 14 yrs. old. I could have got the

child back but I was afraid my master would kill him; he said that he would & I knew that he would or else make his children do it: he made his sons kill 2 men big tall men like you. The Lord forgive them for the way they have treated me. The child could not help them from taking the horses. He [*her master*] said that Henry (my boy) hallooed for the sake of having the Yankees find him; but the Yankees asked him where he was going & he didn't know they were soldiers & he told them that he was going to Master's mules.

12 I didn't ask for any receipt.

13 It was taken in the day time, not secretly.

14 When they took this property, the army was encamped. Some got there before the camps were up. Some [*of the property*] was hung up in the house. Some people told us that if we let some hang up they wouldn't touch the rest, but they did, they were close by. They commenced taking when they first came. They staid there two nights. I heard a heap of shooting, but I don't think that they killed anybody. I didn't know any of the officers or quartermasters.

15 This horse was as fine a creature as ever was & the pork &c were in good order.

16 *Item No. 1.* I don't know how old the mare was. I know she was young. She was medium sized. She was in nice order, we kept a good creature. My husband bought it when it was a colt, about 2 years old. I think he had been using it a year & a little better. Colored people when they would work always had something for themselves, after working for their masters. I most forgot whether he paid cash or swapped cows. He worked & earned money, after he had done his masters work. They [*the Union soldiers*] bridled & carried her off; I think they jumped right on her back

Item No. 2. We had 7 hogs & we killed them right there. It was pickled away in the barrel: Some was done hung up to smoke, but we took it down & put it into the barrels to keep them from getting it. He [*her husband*] raised the hogs. He bought a sow and raised his own pork & that is the way he got this. He did his tasks & after that he worked for himself & he got some money & bought the hogs and then they increased. He worked Sundays too; and that was for ourselves. He always was a hardworking man. I could not tell how much these would weigh; they were monstrous hogs, they were a big breed of hogs. We had them up feeding. The others were some two years old, & some more. It took two men to help hang them up. This was the meat from 7 hogs.

Item No. 3. I had half a barrel of lard. It was in gourds, that would hold half a bushel a piece. We had this hid in the crib. This was lard from the hogs.

Item No. 4 I could not tell exactly how much corn there was but there was a right smart. We had 4 or 5 bushels ground up into meal & they took all the corn besides. They carried it off in bags and my children's undershirts, tied them like bags & filled them up. My husband made baskets and they toted some off in that way. They toted some off in fanners & big blue tubs.

Item No. 5. I don't know exactly how much rice there was; but we made a good deal. They toted it off in bundles, threshed out— It was taken in the sheaf   They fed their horses on it. I saw the horses eating it as I passed there. They took my tubs, kettles &c. I didn't get anything back but an oven.

Item No. 7. We had 11 hogs. They were 2 or 3 years old. They were in pretty good order. We were intending to fatten them right next year— they killed them right there.

Item No. 8. I had 30 or 40 head of chickens. They took the last one.

They shot them. This property all belonged to me and my husband. None of it belonged to Mr. Baggs   I swore to the men so, but they wouldn't believe I could have such things.   My girl had a changable silk dress & all had [talanas?] & they took them all—   It didn't look like a Yankee person would be so mean.   But they said if they didn't take them the whites here would & they did take some of my things from their camps after they left.

her
Nancy X Johnson[24]
mark

HDSr

Johnson's husband had submitted a claim of $514.50 for the property seized by Union soldiers; he was awarded $155.[25]

WHEREAS THE UNION ONLY GRADUALLY ACKNOWL-edged slavery's centrality to the Civil War, the Confederacy understood from the beginning. Confederate authorities acted quickly to mobilize slaves on behalf of Southern independence. By producing the food crops necessary to sustain both soldiers and civilians, slaves would enable the Confederacy to put a larger proportion of its white men into the army. Slave laborers would construct fortifications, manufacture ordnance, and move the supplies required by armies in the field. Finally, in serving as the mudsill of Southern society, slaves would assure the unity of white Southerners in a time of crisis.

As the war proceeded, however, Confederates found their great asset transmuted into an enormous liability. Not only did the Union threaten slavery from without, but the Confederacy's own war effort undermined the stability of the institution from within,

setting slaveholders at odds with Confederate officials and exacer-
bating conflicts among white Southerners. The slaves' resistance to
working for the rebel cause magnified the growing divisions in
Southern society. Their refusal to sustain the old obedience and
their hidden actions on behalf of the Union compromised slavery
even in regions that remained under Confederate control to the end
of the war.

————•———

Governor John Milton of Florida appreciated the importance of
slave labor to the South's agricultural production and hence to the
achievement of Confederate independence. But keeping the slaves
at work and preventing insubordination required strict discipline.
Milton therefore proposed to the Confederate secretary of war that
the government exempt overseers from military conscription. Failure to do so, he argued, would play directly into the hands of the
Yankees.

Tallahassee. Fla: February 17th. 1863.
Sir   The maintenance of our armies in the field—of the families of
those in Military Service—of the civil Government of the Confederate
States and the States seperately—in a word, not only the liberty, but the
lives of the people of the State, depend upon Agricultural labor.   The
advocates of Slavery, in our National Councils and throughout the
various forms of arguments to sustain it, have contended forcibly and
truthfully, that negroes had not the inclination or ability to labor
successfully, without the superior skill of the White man to direct and
enforce their labor.

Upon slave labor, the Agriculture of the Southern States is mainly
dependent, and consequently overseers for the management and
direction of the Slaves should be exempt from Military Service.   I say

overseers, not owners of slaves, because as a general rule, slaves have been managed by overseers; and but few owners have manifested the industry, skill and energy, necessary to successful Agriculture.

The safety of the Confederate States demands the exemption of overseers, for two important reasons. First, because without them slaves will not labor in a manner to secure subsistence for the armies in the field, the support of families at home, and to ensure the revenue necessary to the Confederate and State Governments. Secondly, If left without the control of overseers to whom they have been accustomed to yield obedience, the result will probably be, insubordination and insurrection.

A more effectual auxiliary to the Emancipation Scheme of Lincoln, and for the subjugation of the South, could not, in my humble judgment be devised, than an Act of Congress (if it shall be respected by the States) which would entrust the Agriculture, and the lives of families, to the slaves unrestrained by the presence, authority and skill of overseers.

As a matter of policy, owners and overseers on plantations where cotton shall be planted, might be subjected to military service; but, on plantations where labor is exclusively directed to the raising of grain, meat &c for subsistence, overseers should be exempt from Military Service.

In a time of profound peace, when not the slightest anticipation of war could have reasonably existed, the General Assembly of this State in its wisdom (the result of experience) enacted a law requiring a white person (either the owner or an overseer) to reside on the plantation where slaves lived, for their proper control and management. A copy of the last act on the subject is herewith enclosed. If the Slaves are left without proper management, they will not only fail to make the crops, but will destroy the Stock, necessary to the very existence of the country.

Convinced of the truth of the allegations herein made, as the
Governor of the State, in the maintenance of its laws and for the
General Welfare of the Confederate States, I feel it my duty to protest
against the enforcement of the Conscript Act in its application to
overseers, where necessary to the management and direction of Slaves;
and more especially on plantations where the labor is devoted to
securing the means of subsistence necessary to maintain our armies and
protect our people from starvation.   I have the honor to be Very
Respectfully

John Milton[26]

HLS

Confederate military setbacks in the summer of 1863—notably the
surrender of Vicksburg, Mississippi, and the costly defeat at Gettysburg, Pennsylvania—caused slaveholders to fear for the worst.
With the Union army now in control of the entire Mississippi River,
slaveholders transferred (or "refugeed," as the process was called)
tens of thousands of slaves to the interior rather than lose them to
the Yankees. The large-scale removals undermined slave discipline
and placed enormous burdens upon the resources of interior regions. Such desperate times called for desperate measures, a
planter in eastern Mississippi advised President Jefferson Davis,
including, if need be, the induction of slave men into the Confederate army.

Louisville Miss   July 20th/63

Dear Sir   Visburg is gone and as a consequence Mississippi is gone
and in the opinion of allmost every one here the Confederacy is gone.   I
can myself see but one chance, but one course to pursue to save it, and I
fear it is now too late for even that to check the tide that is overwhelming

us.   It is simply by your own authority, and without waiting for congress
to give you authority, to call out every able bodied *Negro* man from the
age of sixteen to fifty years old.   They will go readily and cheerfully.
The owners would gladly give them up and afford every facility in
getting them off.   On every road leading from the western Country
there is a constant stream of negroes running into Ala & Georgia & the
Carolinas.   They will destroy all the food in those states like an army of
locusts.   This if nothing else would starve us into subjection in a few
months   It is precisly what our enemy want.   Take our nego men away
and thereby relieve us of a dangerous element.   Force the young white
men, who are running off with them, into the army and we, the old men
will take care of the negro women and children and make corn.   Act
promptly   the negro men will all go to the enemy if not taken to our
own army   I believe fully half of them had rather go into our ranks
than the Yankees   They want to be in the frollick & they will be one
way or the other.   Away with all squeamesness about employing negroes
in civilized warfare.   Our enemies are doing it as rappidly as they can
and we are left no other alternative.—   If you knew with what pleasure
I would send off every negro man I have tomorrow morning you would
not dismiss this hastily.   I am only one of the masses and what I say I
believe nearly every slave holder in the South would say and do.   With
the highest considerations of respect I am verry truly youre friend.

ALS   O G Eiland[27]

Nine days later, a slaveholder in Georgia also urged upon President
Davis the expedient of employing black soldiers. "The patriotic
men of the south have given up all their sons," he argued, "and why
not give up their negroes?" "The enemy has marched his black sol-

diers down upon us, and many of them the property of those
against whom they are sent to fight,—let us meet him upon his own
principle."[28]

Other Confederates had no thought of turning slaves into soldiers
but instead proposed their systematic mobilization in auxiliary military roles. A slaveholder in Alabama who was willing to contribute
his own slaves for this purpose warned the secretary of war that if
the Confederacy failed to draft slave men to support its armies,
they would end up fighting for the Yankees.

Montgomery Ala   July 23 /63
Dear Sir   Permit me to make a suggestion, which seems to me will
strengthen our military arm and enable us to strike a more effective
blow in the cause of our country—   I understand that it requires about
one fourth of the men in the army to *wait* on the others, in attending
upon wagons, and other things necessary for the movements of the main
body.   I think this could be supplied by negroes and thereby release a
large force of white men to do the fighting.   It would require a small
number of whites to act as superintendents & directors, but the number
would be comparitively small, whilst the work would be as effectively
done   I am willing as a slaveholder to contribute one fourth or more of
my fellow force for this purpose, & I think it would be generally
responded to.   Some might grumble but the majority would prefer any
sacrifice rather than subjugation—   By drafting the requisite number
of negroes promptly & placing them in the army as teamsters, nurses &
for bringing the wounded to the rear, such a number of men may be
released as would enable us to keep back the enemy from ravaging the
country and *possibly* to drive him beyond our limits—   If you do not do

this, they are taken by the enemy and placed not only in similar positions but also armed and placed in their ranks as fighting men— Negroes are easily influenced by those around them and when placed in our army would make it a matter of pride to remain loyal & true to our cause, but when left in contact with the enemy they are imposed upon by their teachings and are enticed away by them,   As an evidence of the truth of my position, see how few of those who have been carried as servants into the army have deserted, and they too come from a class which would be most likely to do so—   I hope you will excuse me for making these suggestions.   I am actuated solely by a desire to benefit my country—   Very Respectfully

W C Bibb

[*In the margin*] The negroes, refugees, would supply the deficit of labour if any, necessary to produce food for the country[29]

ALS

At the Confederate War Department, Bibb's proposal received a favorable hearing from officials convinced that slaves should have been used to perform the army's "heavy work" from the beginning. "The sacrosanctity of slave property in this war has operated most injuriously to the Confederacy," lamented the assistant secretary of war. The secretary of war commended Bibb's ideas to President Davis but expressed skepticism about effecting them. Systematic use of slaves as military laborers, he explained, "could only be obtained by additional Legislation, unless by the voluntary action of slave owners, which I fear is not to be expected."[30]

With the "sacrosanctity of slave property" impeding the mobilization of slaves, many Confederates demanded the conscription of black men who were free. Not only did the freemen lack powerful owners who might object, but they also exercised an unsettling in-

fluence on the slaves. A civil officer in western North Carolina, a region infested with unionists and deserters from the rebel army, advised Secretary of State Judah P. Benjamin that the conscription
of black freemen would add to Confederate strength while neutral-
izing a dangerous class.

Marion, N.C.   August 4th/63.

Hon. Mr. Benjamin: Your Honor will pardon the intrusion of a
communication from an inferior source, upon your time and patience.

I am the District Collector of the Confederate Taxes, for McDowell,
Mitchell and Yancy Counties in Northcarolina, and I have discovered
that the people here apprehend great fears, that when the Conscripts all
are called out, the *Free Negroes* will cause an insurrection among the
Slaves.   There are, probably, nearly or quite as many Free Negroes in
some of the Western Counties of N. Carolina as slaves; and already have
some of these Free Negroes made their boast, that when the Conscripts
were all gone, they would be Cols. and Captains in these localities.

One Free boy has gone so far as to say that he already had 50 negroes
at his command, who could be called out at any hour.

Is there no law or authority lodged in your hands, that can call these
Free Negroes into camps and make them *fight* for the country?   If it is
not Constititional to do so, could not the Congress of the Confederate
States so change the Constitution as to make these people liable to
Conscription as well as the whites?

I trust Sir, if anything can be done, it will be done speedily.

The Union men and deserters have united in portions of my District,
and every pass upon the Blue Ridge from Virginia to S.C. are guarded
by the tories;* and here are hundreds of strong, well-developed Free

---

*Southern unionists, especially those who opposed the Confederacy by
active measures.

Negroes lounging about and endeavoring to poison the minds of the slaves.

I believe several Regiments of Free Negroes could be mustered in N.C; and if the whole South were *raked* for these people, an army little inferior in numbers at least, to that afforded by any *two* States, could be collected.

Again, I must ask your Honor's pardon for *presuming* even to address you upon this subject. But being a *true* Southern man, amidst many *tories*, I could not refrain.

I remain, Honored Sir, Your obedient servant,

ALS   R. L. Abernethy[31]

> If some slaveholders advocated more extensive military use of black men, others objected to Confederate requisitions. Fearing that their slaves would escape from military superintendents or be damaged by hard work and poor living conditions, many owners refused to forward them when requested to do so. Others complied but surreptitiously enabled their slaves to return home after only a short stint of labor on Confederate defenses. To the consternation of both owners and military employers, slaves found other allies as well, including Confederate soldiers who were willing to help them for a price. The engineer in charge of fortifications on Sullivans Island, near Charleston, reported to departmental headquarters that such subversive activities were depleting his labor force. He enclosed a letter he had received from two slaveholders.

Charleston [*S.C.*]   Augt 25th 1863

Gen[l] According to instructions to discharge the negroes only on demand, I have required it generally to be made positive, which are very freely made and some of the owners even venting themselves to charge

"breaches of faith and contract on the part of the Gov. State
&c." demands are becoming very numerous. together with the
runaways will soon materially reduce the present force in numbers, and
large parties of them have been caught and returned, in possession of
passes of all descriptions. many, the negroes state are given them by
Soldiers, for pay and other considerations. And no doubt some of them
come down with their owners passes to return home in their pockets. as
they have been found with them in their possession. The boats also
permit perfect freedom of transportation to the negroes, with or without
passes. I enclose a sample.* Total [*laborers*] received since 10" July
about 3900, effective force 2500. I have the honor to be very
respectfully Your obt svt.

Wm H. Echols[32]

ALS

[*Enclosure*]   Mayesville [*S.C.*]   August 24th 1863
Dear Sir   We have good reason to believe that you have some traitor in
your camp on Sulivans Island, who are giving our negroes forged Tickets
or at least Such is the testimony of the negroes, that have
returned   they report that Tickets are given by one of the guard with
instructions to tare it up as soon as they past over the bridge   they
report that they pay 75 cents for each ticket which goes to shew that the
object in part is to make money & no doubt another object is to leave the
fortification in an unfinished State,   the precident is a very bad one, and
will no doubt cause dissatisfaction amongst those that are still in your
employ   it is reported that there is at least 30 hands that have
returned in this clandestin manner contrary to the wishes of their
owners)   You will please do as good a part by those who remain with

---

*The sample is a barely literate, undated pass to "Permit Boy to pass
home."

you as the nature of your Situation will Admit   I hope will be able to
keep the enemy at bay until you get such ordinance in your possession as
will batter down the Iron Clads of the enemy   We remain yours Truly

Wm Harris

C. T. Rembert[33]

HLSr

> Two months later, in response to complaints that Confederate sol-
> diers were selling passes to slave laborers, General P. G. T. Beau-
> regard, commander of the Department of South Carolina, Georgia,
> and Florida, prohibited "trafic of any kind whatsoever between en-
> listed men and slaves engaged at work on fortifications."[34]

> As federal forces threatened larger expanses of the South, Confed-
> erate commanders ordered the evacuation of slaves from endan-
> gered areas to prevent them from falling into Union hands. In a let-
> ter sent to each of his highest-ranking subordinates, General E.
> Kirby Smith, commander of Confederate forces west of the Missis-
> sippi River, emphasized that it was a question of removing slaves
> now or fighting them later.

Shreveport La   Sept 4th 1863

General,   The policy of our enemy in arming and organizing negro
regiments, is being pushed to formidable proportions.   Our plantations
are made his recruiting stations, and unless some check can be devised,
a strong and powerful force will be formed which will receive large
additions as he advances on our territory

More than 1000 recruits, in some cases organized on the plantations
and forced into the ranks, were made in the recent raid on Monroe.
When we fall back, as little as possible should be left for the enemy.

Able bodied male negroes and transportation should be carried back in
advance of our troops.   Facilities should be given, and our friends and
planters instructed, in positions exposed to the enemy, that it is the wish
of the Dept Commander that, without awaiting his approval they
remove to safe localities, their able bodied slaves and transportation

Every sound male black left for the enemy becomes a soldier whom we
have afterwards to fight.   This is a difficult subject and must be
handled cautiously, but I believe it will be wisdom to carry out the above
policy to the extent of our abilities   I am General respectfully Your obt
servt

HLeSr   (signed)   E Kirby Smith[35]

> Instead of securing slave property, relocation frequently became
> the occasion for its loss. Slaveholders and Confederate officials of-
> ten evacuated only the most valuable slaves, leaving behind the
> young and the old. Slaves hated these frightening removals and the
> resulting separation from family and friends. Many of them fled at
> the first hint of transfer. A Mississippi planter warned the secre-
> tary of war that a shotgun migration ordered by Confederate au-
> thorities would fail to accomplish its purpose.

Washington County   Miss   November 3ᵈ 1863
Dear Sir   I was told to day that you had commissioned A. M. Paxton
Esq as Major for the express purpose of coming into the Island formed
by the Yazoo and Miss Rivers, to remove all of the able bodied men and
women, mules and stock of every description, leaving only the old
decrepid men and women and the children— The reason assigned by
you was, that by doing so, it would prevent the Yankees from getting

them and thus weaken them to that extent— If you were here upon the spot you would see the utter impracticability of accomplishing it— Instead of weakening the Yankees the very first lot of negroes taken by surrounding the quarters, which would be the only way to secure even one lot, there would be a stampede of all the balance, who would take every mule with them to the Yankees— Some three months since Mr J. W. Vick had his quarter surrounded and his men all taken to the hills— Since that time the negroes have been very shy of our Soldiers and only within the last month all the negro men on the Creek laid out for about ten days while they were in here collecting cattle— The report came before them that they were taking all the men for the army and the consequence was all the men laid out for over a week and many were scared off entirely to the Yankees— There are over one hundred and ninety negroes on this place, I have never thought or talked about moving them, and had not lost one by running off until the scare about a month ago when four men and a woman left— I am the only one as far as my acquaintance extends who had not either attempted to or were preparing to move and every one who did so lost nearly if not all of the men and many of the women and children— I believe every negro on this place will go the Yankees before they would go to the hills, and at same time think they have made up their minds to stay at home and wait the issue of events if they are permitted to do so— I believe it utterly impossible for major Paxton to be successful in such a measure, but the result will be the running off the negroes now on the plantations and the mules they would steal and the making of bad citizens of good ones, who will view the measure as intolerable oppression— There were many persons who ran with the residue of their negroes to the hills, who found it impossible to live and either have or are returning to their homes— I write to you because I can make myself known to you, when I tell you,

that I am the brother of Mrs Martha Stanard the widow of Robt C.
Stanard both of whom I know esteemed you as a friend— I have not
the value of one dollar interested in the measure and if you want
disinterested testimony I have given it to you and you can take it for
what it is worth   Yours truly

Jon'a Pearce[36]

ALS

Denying that he had ordered an evacuation, the secretary of war
nevertheless insisted that "when there was a probability that the enemy would either seduce or force the able bodied male negroes into
their Armies they should be removed by our Forces." "Is it not the
duty of the Confederate Gov^{t}," he asked, ". . . instead of allowing
the male slave to be converted into armed soldiers agst us to preserve
them as useful laborers for their owners & the Confederacy?"[37]

In parts of the Confederacy near Union-held territory, slaveholders
tightened discipline and kept careful watch over their slaves to
forestall flight. A patrol guard and a pack of hounds strengthened
the hand of Duplin County, North Carolina, slaveholders—at least
until members of the patrol were drafted into the Confederate
army. A slaveholder asked President Jefferson Davis to return the
patrol to its former duties.

Kenansville N.C.   25th Novr 1863.

His excellency Pres^{t} Davis,   A perfect stranger presumes to address you
in behalf of his Countrymen.

Some time during the past year, the Govr of this State ordered a detail
of Patrol guard for this County, amounting to twenty men; and
immediately thereafter, the Citizens made up a fund & purchased a pack

of Hounds at heavy cost to accompany them; and I have *no* fears of contradiction, when I say they have been of *great* service in preventing escapes of Slaves, & also preventing desertions &c.

The Govr issued his order to the Col of the County, and he made his appointments under my advisement (as Chair^n of Co. C^t) as also of other Citizens which he relied upon for Counsel: The appointment I think was a *good* one; and (by no means reflecting on our respectable troops in this County,) I must be pardoned for saying that the said Patrol have been "the ounce of preventive in place of the pound of Cure" We are here not far distant from the Yankee lines; and you well Know a good watch should be Kept. Since the organization of this Company, there has been *no* attempt of escapes by the Slaves *but one*, (save in the Raid in July) and the whole number of negroes (save one, & he was shot & killed *near* the Yankee lines) were Captured & returned to their owners through this Company.

I have just heard, that the said Company has been disbanded, and the members of the Company conscripted. I hope it is not so. But if such be the order, I hope your Excellency will reverse the order, & commission the said Company to attend to their former duties. Ours is almost a defenceless section, and this Guard we consider a *very valuable* outpost. It secures us from escapes & deserters; and is also an important Courier establishment to the army; they quartering & manouvering on or near the line of separation &.c.

I repeat my request that your Excellency will continue the protection to this section by Continuing the Patrol Organization mentioned. With much respect &c. I have the honor to be Your Obe^t Servt &.c.

ALS   Jere Pearsall[38]

Ranking the army's need for men above the slaveholders' difficulty in controlling their slaves, Confederate officials denied Pearsall's request.[39]

———◆———

Some slaves who escaped their owners were too far from Union-held territory to seek sanctuary there. Other runaways simply preferred to remain close to their old homes, forging their own freedom in the swamps and forests. Such slaves sometimes formed bands that survived for months or even years.* They raided nearby plantations for supplies and employed their wits and daring to evade capture. A Confederate officer described to departmental headquarters his pursuit of such fugitive slaves through the rivers and marshes of Florida's gulf coast.

Christal River Flor[ida]. September 8" 1863

In my report to you of 1st inst I stated that I had suceeded in capturing the boat and had the negroes cut off so as there would not be much doubt in my getting the negroes . . . † raid on Mr Kings plantation. on the morning of the second day I took their trail from where I fired on them the evening previous. they led off towards the mouth of Withlacoochee River, edgeing the Coast as near as they could for tide creeks &c. about 4 ock in the evening we discovered one in a cedar tree looking out, on an Island they discovered us about the same time, we being in the open marsh. here they seem to have seperated only two being together. after chasing them about two miles through the saw Grass we came up in gun shot of them. we began to fire at them, and they returned the fire very cool and deliberately but we

---

*See, for example, above, pp. 51–52.

†Letter torn at fold; two or three words missing.

soon got in close range of them and killed them.   one of these negroes
was recognized by some of my men as belonging to Mr. Everett, who
lives near hear, which ran away from him about nine months ago.   he
was styled Captain of the party, as I learned from the negroes
recaptured of Mr Kings.   myself and men being completely tired down
for the want of water, we had to go back and camp until next morning
when we took the trail and followed on the third day.   about the same
time in the eveing of the third day, we came up with two more, and after
a Similar chase of the second day, we succeeded in Killing both of
them.   from here I never could strike the trail of any more of them, but
I am under the impression that we killed or wounded the other three the
first day.   I could not get any information from either of the four that
was killed, as they were killed dead.

The only information that I have been able to get is from an old negro
man of Mr Kings who ran away from them the first day and came back
home.   he says that [they] . . . * [left] Sea Horse Key at the same
time [that] boat did destined for Homasassa, but as yet they have not
reached there.   he also states that a Gun-boat had gone up the Suwanee
River and as soon as it returned it was to come up this River.

Night before last my picket Guard heard several guns down the River
in the direction of shell Island.   it may be them, but I think if they go up
either River their destiny will be as these has been.   I am Captain Very
Respectfully Your obt Sevt

ALS
                                          Samuel E. Hope[40]

As federal forces intensified their recruitment of black soldiers,
Confederate military commanders demanded that slaves be removed from areas subject to recruiting raids, especially the no-

---

*Letter torn at fold; approximately three words missing.

man's-land between Union and Confederate lines. Slaveholders, however, saw much to lose in any attempt at forcible relocation. When the secretary of war asked the Virginia House of Delegates to sanction such measures, the chairman of its Committee on Confederate Relations reported strenuous objections. The proposed evacuation would almost certainly fail, his colleagues believed. And even if it succeeded, the evacuated slaves would spread to their counterparts in the interior the poison of insubordination they had imbibed from the Yankees.

[*Richmond, Va.*]   January 13 1864

Sir   Your communication, to me, of the   inviting attention of the Legislature to the policy of withdrawing all able bodied male slaves from within the enemies' lines, and without our own, liable to seizure by them, through the intervention of our own forces, was referred to the Committee of Confederate Relations, and has received from them the attention its importance demands.   They have considered the subject in both the aspects in which you presented it viz: The saving the property of our citizens, and the defeating of the enemy's design of recruiting a black force within the limits indicated, and have invited and obtained the expression of the views of a large number of the member[s] of the House, representing the counties more immediately interested, as to the effects likely to be produced by the adoption of the policy suggested.   They concur, I believe without exception in believing it would be attended with very serious mischiefs, and with very partial compensating good.   They represent that within the enemies lines the number of slaves left at their homes, fit for military service, is now very limited—forcibly or voluntarily the great bulk of them of that description having already gone to the enemy: That the few remaining are retained, generally, by strong local, or family, attachments, but none by any motive which would not yield to the aversion they entertain to be forced away from their homes within our

lines, and employed on our public works.   That they are so scattered, that
but a very small proportion could be captured, if any, by a military raiding
party before they would fly to the woods, or to the enemy, soon to be
followed by their families, whose labor and assistance is now so invaluable
to the loyal whites (chiefly females and children) still remaining in the
enemies lines would be attended with the most deplorable consequences.
That many of those citizens would be left in great extremity for support if
they remained, or exposed to great loss and suffering, if they removed,
besides, by coming further into the interior, increasing the existing
pressure on our already overtaxed means of subsistence.   The fear was
also expressed by some of the gentlemen who favored the Committee with
their views, that the loss of their still remaining slaves, occasioned by such
an intervention of the Government, might lead, however injustifiably, to
alienating from our cause persons now friendly to it.   The effects, on the
slaves of the interior, of bringing amongst them, so far as the measure
should prove successful, those who had become imbued by the enemy
with ideas and habits, but little consistent with the obedience and
subordination proper to their condition, and necessary to the peace and
safety of the whites, was strongly urged as dissuading from the adoption
of the policy under consideration.   In respect to the consequences of such
a measure as applied to the district's, between our lines, and those of the
enemy, the gentlemen representing them thought the effects would be
similar to those above presented.   While in them a plan might be adopted,
no doubt, attended with more success for getting possession of the slaves
than in the other case, yet they believe large numbers would attempt
successfully to escape to the enemy, while it would be the signal for the
immediate stampede into the enemys camps of all the slaves within their
lines.   There was no difference of opinion as to the general opposition of
the owners to the plan, nor as to its resulting in a greater loss of slave
property to the state than would ensue by leaving the owners to pursue

the best measures in their power to save them as exigencies might
recommend. Not considering that the communication received from you
was intended so much to indicate a line of policy determined on, as to
invite a conference, and comparison of views, with those most interested
in it, in regard to its expediency, the committee have instructed me to
lay before you the facts and views herein communicated for your
consideration, before adopting any conclusions, or taking any definite
action, on the subject.   They should probably say, however, that they so
far feel the force of them as to be disinclined to recommend to the favor
of the House the policy of a forcible withdrawal of the slaves from the
Quarters of the state embraced by your suggestion, by the military
intervention of the Confederate Government.
                                             . . . .
                                             Wyndham Robertson[41]

ALS

Confederate military claims on slave labor helped spread demoralization throughout Southern society—in remote rural settlements
as well as state capitals, among poor farmers as well as wealthy
planters. Complaining about policies that favored plantation counties over impoverished yeoman counties, farmers in eastern Alabama emphasized that the enlistment of soldiers and the impressment of slaves had depleted the local agricultural labor force. The
results included widespread destitution, inadequate supplies to relieve the poor, growing disaffection with the Confederate cause,
and even riots by angry women. Forty-six men asked President Jefferson Davis to spare their community from renewed impressment
and its consequences.

                    Wesabulga   Randolph Co   Ala   May 6[th] 1864
   To his Excellency Jefferson Davis   The undersigned citizens &
Slaveholders of the county of Randolph & State of Alabama would

respectfully represent to your Excellency That Col Blount impressing
ag[en]t of Slaves Stationed at Mobile Ala; has recently ordered an
impressment of 33 1/3 per cent of the able bodied Slaves of this County;
when in adjoining counties where the Slave population is greater only
from 5 to 10 per cent have been taken— This we think to be unjust, &
not in accordance with the intentions of the act. We think that an
uniform rate should be levied in the whole State; or so much of it as is
now within our lines; So that the burden Should fall uniformly on
all; But he appears to order an arbitrary number from each county
without refferance to the number of Slaves in the County. He thus
levies a percentage which is uniform in the county, but does not bear any
proportion to the levies in adjoining Counties— He also counts *in* all
the women that are within the ages of 17 to 50 & takes one third of the
total number in men between the ages of 17 to 50.

Randolph is a poor & mountainous County with the largest population
of any in the State. There are only 300 negroes (women & men) within
the prescribed ages in the county & he takes one Hundred Seventy
five per cent of the White Males are now in the Service; leaving the great
majority of their wives & children to be Supported by the
remainder There are numbers of widows & orphans of the Soldiers
who have perished by the casualities of war to be also Supported by
public funds—

The County does not in ordinary times produce more than a
Sufficiency of food for its population; last year there was a deficit of over
40000 bushels; of corn about one half of which has been provided from
the tax in Kind;* the ballance has to be purchased in the Canebrake;

---

*Under the "tax-in-kind," adopted in April 1863, Confederate
authorities collected 10 percent of specified crops and livestock
directly from producers. Some of the impressed grain was distributed
as poor relief.

transported a distance of 125 miles on R.R, & hauled thence in waggons from 30 to 50 miles to reach the various points of distribution in the county—

There are now on the rolls of the Probate court, 1600 indigent families to be Supported; they average 5 to each family; making a grand total of 8000 persons   Deaths from Starvation have absolutely occurred; notwithstanding the utmost efforts that we have been able to make; & now many of the women & children are seeking & feeding upon the bran from the mills

Women riots have taken place in Several parts of the County in which Govt wheat & corn has been seized to prevent Starvation of themselves & families;   Where it will end unless relief is afforded we cannot tell

We have entered into these details that your Excellency may See the deplorable condition of things in this County, & aid us if in your power & the exigencies of the Service permit—

To take the Negroes *now* from the fields when the crop is just planted & ready for cultivation would inevitably cause the loss of a portion of the crops So essential to feed the County   we have appealed to Col Blount asking that the impressment be delayed or abandoned; but without effect & we now appeal to your Excellency as our last resource under God to give us Such measure of assistance as you can.   If you refuse us—we must Submit & take our [chance]—do our duty & trust to Almighty Providence for the result   under all the circumstances we therefore pray your Excellency.

That Randolph County be exempt from the operations of the impressment act. If, however the Case is so urgent & the hands are so essential to save Mobile; then we ask that the impressment be delayed until fall when the crops are gathered;   In case neither of these prayers can be granted we pray that the rate be made uniform in the Whole

State—& that *we* be not punished for our poverty— we would Humbly
Suggest to your Excellency that there are large numbers of negroes
about our towns & cities (used for the pleasure of their owners; or idling
about; a curse to the community—*consumers not producers*) that we
think might be exhausted before the agricultural labour of the county is
interfered with.

Hoping that your Excellency may favourably consider our humble
prayer—we remain as ever your Excellencies devoted Servants

HLS   [*46 signatures*][42]

> The surrender of Atlanta to Union general William T. Sherman in
> early September, 1864, pushed many white Southerners to consid-
> er measures previously dismissed as unthinkable, notably the con-
> scription of slave men into the Confederate army. The time for hes-
> itation had passed, an alarmed Georgian warned President Jeffer-
> son Davis.

Greenville Merriwether Co Ga Septr 16th '64
Mr President. Is it not time now to enlist the negroes? I have been in
favor of it ever since the enemy commenced it, & have feared no effort
would be made on our side until it was too late. It is now our only
resource to augment the army.— My plan is to conscribe them & force
them into the army, all between Sixteen & fifty-five, upon the condition,
if necessary, of freedom after the war. I have not been alarmed until
now. I assure you Sir. that if the question were put to the people of this
state whether to continue the war or return to the union, a large
majority would vote for a return— I am almost inclined to believe that
they would do it if *emancipation* was the *condition*. It occurs to me if

you will call congress together & pass a bill to raise a negro force of two or even one hundred thousand, it would have a good effect upon the election at the North,* if nothing more—

Has Congress & the authorities ever had this subject under consideration? I learn our army is falling back to Macon! In a very short time every able bodied negro in the abandoned section will either be a Soldier in the yankee army or employed in some way to contribute to our destruction. It seems to me this subject is well worthy your consideration if it is not now too late to do anything— I fear it is— Sir I am seriously alarmed! The cries of Starving women & children will make cowards of us all.— The policy of Sherman is to crowd our people together in the lower part of the State until want drives us to terms.

By Christmas he will have an army of fifty thousand negroes in his army— ought we not to hold on to all the territory we can until the drafting season is over— Their large bounties & the promise of freedom, will put all our negroes into their army   Your &c

ALS   F. Kendall[43]

> During the Confederacy's desperate final months, the deteriora-
> tion of slave discipline, especially in areas near Union-held territo-
> ry, enabled many slaves to leave their owners at will. Under such

---

*The impending presidential election, in which Abraham Lincoln, candidate of the National Union (Republican) Party, was opposed by former general George B. McClellan, candidate of the Democratic Party. The Democratic platform pledged to preserve "the rights of the States unimpaired" (presumably including slavery) and called for the cessation of hostilities and resolution of the conflict by "peaceable means," whereas the Republicans endorsed a constitutional amendment abolishing slavery and promised to continue the war until the Confederates surrendered unconditionally. (James M. McPherson, *Battle Cry of Freedom: The Civil War Era* [New York, 1988], pp. 716, 772.)

circumstances, efforts to impress black laborers to support the rebel army resulted only in loss of the slaves. Slaveholders south of Petersburg, Virginia, asked President Jefferson Davis to suspend plans for impressment in their county.

Coman's Well   Sussex Co[*un*]ty V^a October 13 1864

Dear Sir   A report has reached us that the Government is about to make another requisition on this County for Slaves for the Publick works,   We most respectfully represent to your Excellency the State of things in this County   The County of Sussex adjoins that of Prince George which last County you are aware is occupied by the enemy, There is no barier to prevent the escape of our Slavs who choose to go to the enemy,   they may pass directly into Prince George Coty, or cross the Blk water,   they are going constantly,   Any attempt of the Gov^t to enforce a draft of negroes in this county or even a report to that effect (if it reaches the negroes) will have the effect in our deliberate opinion to cause a stampede among those of the men who are not now disposed to go or are hesitating to do so,   We believe that for every man the Gov^t would obtain by such a measure the Enemy would add ten or twenty to his ranks to Say nothing of the imposibility of gathering the crops & seeding wheat,   Some of us will find it almost imposible to Save our Crops by the Small force left and all of us have suffered more or less,

We hope the Gov^t will at least Suspend the requisition (if any was intended for this County) until it can obtain information as to the truth of our Statement,   we are personally unknown to you, but well known to Hon John R Chambliss, Hon Robert Whitfield & Hon Thos S Gholson,   none of these Gentlemen are in the County at this time

We Submit that the County of Sussex has on three or four occasions promptly responded to the requisitions of the Gov^t for hands for the

publick works, but in the present ticklish Situation of things, such a
requisition would be of no benefit to the Gov^t, but tend to Strenghten the
enemy, and bring disaster and ruin to many of the Citizens,   With the
best wishes for the triumph of the Cause in which you are so ardently
and industriously engaged, we ask your attention to this and remain
Your obedient Servants

Wm D. Taylor   James. D. Howle

Nathaniel. R. Peebles   Henry Harrison

HLS   J. B. Freeman[44]

The Sussex County slaveholders' fears were confirmed by events in
neighboring Southampton, where renewed impressment proved "altogether futile," causing nearly 200 slaves to flee to the Yankees.[45]

Numerous slaves who were held securely within the Confederacy
nevertheless found opportunities to aid the Union cause. Alonzo
Jackson, during the war a slave in Georgetown, on the South Carolina coast, described for a postwar commission the assistance he
had rendered Northern soldiers who escaped from the prisoner-of-
war stockade at Florence, in the interior of the state. Jackson's testimony also recounted the suspicion with which he had been regarded by Confederate authorities and their unsuccessful attempts
at intimidation.

State of South Carolina   Georgetown County   Georgetown
March 17th 1873—

. . . .

To question 1, he says— "My name is Alonzo Jackson—   I was born a

slave, in the state of Virginia—and am 64 years of age— I reside at
Georgetown state of South Carolina and am a Livery stable keeper by
occupation— To question 2 he says— I have lived all the time at
Georgetown since 1823—and from that time was a slave until made free
by the war when the US. Forces came to Georgetown in February
1865— When the war began in 1861, I belonged to Mr Joseph B.
Pyatt who lived on his own plantation about 2 miles from Georgetown
(he lives there now) For 18. years just before the war I hired all my
time from my master and continued to do so all the time I was a slave—
I paid every year $140— for my time and supported myself and family
from my own earnings—working only for whom I chose— When the
war began I was employed as "hostler" (in the same livery stable which I
now keep on my own account) I was then receiving $25. pr month for
my wages—and had been receiving the same wages at same place for
about 18. years continuously I had in 1861—a wife—one child and 2
nieces to support— My wife earned money as pastry cook &
Laundress— My child and 2 neices were small children— I remained,
employed as stated, until February 1864—when I hired a flat boat at
Georgetown and did freighting business on the "SamPitt" "Black" "Pee
dee" & "Waccamaw" rivers— I continued about a year in this business,
all the time on my own account, until the US. Soldiers came to
Georgetown in Feby 1865 when I left the flat boat and was employed as
a laborer at Georgetown by citizens until the end of the war— I
received all my wages from the livery stable except during the last year I
worked there— The rebel soldiers plundered the stable so that we
could not do business— The last year I was at the stable during the
war I divided the earnings of the stable with my employer— my share
was only enough to feed my family— I had 2 horses of my own at the
stable, all the time during, and for about 4 or 5 years before the war,

while I was employed there— I received extra pay whenever my horses
were used and earned some money in this way— I owned a house and
lot at Georgetown when the war began— I have lived in the house all
the time since then—

. . . .

To question 3. he says— Yes I went twice to "North Island" in
"Winyaw bay" (about 10 miles from Georgetown) during the 3rd year of
the war with Union soldiers who had escaped from the rebel "stockade"
at Florence— I went with them to show them the way to the [*Union*]
gun boats— I went out of the rebel lines to do so, and returned without
being discovered— I took the soldiers in a boat and landed them on
"North Island" which was then in possession only of Union forces—
About one month after Georgetown was occupied by Union forces during
the last year of the war I went about 10. miles out of the Union lines, to
a plantation on "Black river" for a boat load of rice—with a flat boat—
I was hired to do so by a citizen of Georgetown, I had a permit from the
US. Provost Marshal to do so— I got the rice and brought it to
Georgetown— The rebels came very near catching me, they fired at
me, and I heard them threaten me— They said they would "kill me for
taking provisions to the yankees." They were separated from me by the
river and did not catch me— I never went through either lines at any
other times during the war

. . . .

To question 26, he says Yes— About 6 months after the war began—a
constable at Georgetown named "Gasquay" (a white man) came one day
to the livery stable where I was employed and told me he had been sent
to me by the Confederate Provost Marshal (Dr Parker) to order me to
assist in hanging 3 colored men at the jail in Georgetown— I knew at
the time that the 3 men were to be hung for attempting to escape to the

blockading fleet—but did not know either of the 3 men— I had not had
anything to do with their attempt to escape and had not been accused of
knowing anything about it— I believed that I had been ordered to
assist in the hanging because I was suspected of being on the side of the
Yankees— (The rebels tried colored people very often in this way, to
frighten them) I replied to the constable that I was busy and could
not go— The constable was angry and said I must go— I insisted
that I was busy and could not go— I gave no other reason for refusing
to assist in the hanging, and did not say anything about the hanging—
I deceived the constable by saying that I had to go to Gen'l Trapiers
plantation (2 miles distant) for Gen'l Trapier—and in order to make
him believe me, I got on my horse and went there— The Constable said
"if you don't look pretty sharp, you will be hung next"— At the time I
went to Black river for rice in the flat boat, (after Union Army came to
Georgetown) with permission and pass from US. Provost Marshal—(as
stated) The rebels who fired at and tried to catch me told me they would
sink my boat and hang me because I was taking provisions to
Georgetown for the Yankees. I do not know of any other threats that
were made to me in person, on account of my Union sentiments. To
question 27. he says No. except when I was at the livery stable during
the war— I was employed by a free colored man named Augustus
Carr—who owned the livery stable— The rebel soldiers came so often
to the stable with their horses and treated us so badly that as stated we
had to give up the business— They used to feed their horses without
paying anything and if we asked for any pay they would sometimes draw
pistols on us, threatening to shoot us— They behaved so unkindly
towards us that we could not do business— My employer lost a great
deal of money by their conduct and for this reason could not pay me my
last years wages at the stable—and has never done so— I am now

renting the same stable from him and what he owes me for back wages
will be deducted from the rent I pay him— I have already had the
stable for one year at $200— and have paid no rent— I expect to pay
rent after I have occupied the stable long enough to get my back
wages— He owed me about $500. one year ago— I was not injured in
any other way on account of my Union sentiments— To question 28.
he says— No. except giving food to Union soldiers when they came to
my house— They sometimes asked for food and sometimes took it
without asking I never refused them— To question 29. he says.
Yes— About 8 months before Georgetown was occupied by Union
soldiers—while I was in the freighting business on my flat boat on
"Mingo creek" (up "Black river") about 30 or 40 miles from Georgetown
by water, 3 white men came near the boat which was at the bank of the
river— I was on the boat with only one person a colored man (in my
employ named "Henry") As soon as the 3 white men saw we were
colored men they came to the boat and said "we are Yankee soldiers, and
have escaped from the rebel "stockade" at Florence, we are your
friends can't you do something for us we are nearly perished" As
soon as I saw them, before they spoke, I knew they were Yankee
soldiers—by their clothing. They were all private soldiers—so they told
me— I invited them to come on the boat and told them I would hurry
and cook food for them, which I did and gave it to them in my boat—
As soon as they entered the boat I shoved off from land and anchored in
the creek about 60. ft from shore— I was loading cord wood in my boat
when the soldiers came and had completed my load within about 4.
cords— I did not wait to take it all—fearing that, some one else might
come and catch the Yankees— Neither of the 3 soldiers ordered me to
take them in the boat, or made any threats— They did not go in the
boat or secure it in any way so that I could not leave in it— They only

entered the boat after they had told me who they were (as stated) and
when I invited them— They were very weak—and had no weapons—
They had no shoes on— It was then winter weather, and cold— The 3
Yankees did not suggest anything for me to do for them except to feed
them—and wanted to get to the gun boats— They did not know where
the gun boats were— I did—and I told them I would take them where
they could get to the gun boats unmolested. The soldiers did not pay or
give me anything—or promise anything to me at any time—and I have
never received anything for any service rendered to any Union
soldiers— They did not threaten me or use any violence— they were
very friendly and glad to get into such good hands— They showed that
they felt very grateful— I hid the 3 soldiers in my flat boat and started
at once down the river towards Georgetown as soon as the tide
allowed— In about 3 days time we came to "North Island" (about 12
miles from Georgetown) which I then knew was in possession of the
Union forces— I did not pass Georgetown by day light for fear of being
stopped by the rebels who had "pickets" all along the shore to stop all
boats from going below— In the night I floated with the ebb tide
(without being seen) to "North Island"— I got there in the night and
landed the 3 soldiers in my small boat— I showed them the direction to
cross the Island so as to get to the gun boats— I knew there were many
of the gun boat people on the shore there at that time— I saw the 3
soldiers go as I directed— I never saw or heard from any of the 3
soldiers afterwards—but through a colored man named "Miller" (who
was on the shore near the gunboats) learned that the 3 soldiers had got
to the fleet— "Miller" told me this about 2 weeks after I took the 3
soldiers— he saw them and described them so that I was certain he
had seen the same 3 soldiers safe in the protection of the gun boats—
About 2 Months after this occurrence—I brought 2 other Yankee

soldiers (one a corporal) to "North Island" from the same place in
"Mingo creek"   The circumstances were nearly the same except that
when I saw the soldiers I called to them saying there was "no danger"—
for they were running away in a swamp—   They came nearer and asked
me if I was a friend to them that, they were Yankee soldiers who had
escaped from rebel prison—   I replied that "I was as good a friend as
ever they had in their lives"!   Then they came on my boat where I fed
and delivered them (as before described) on "North Island"   In
February 1865 while I was at "Mingo creek" as before I found 4. other
Yankee soldiers there who also said they had escaped from Florence—
I fed and took them towards "North Island" but told them it might not
be necessary as the Yankees were then probably at Georgetown—
When we came near Georgetown I found out that this was true—and
landed the 4 soldiers there—   I never asked or received anything or the
promise of anything for what I gave or did for any Yankee soldiers
during the war—   While they were in my boat I kept them hidden
away—   I know I would have been killed if the rebels had found out that
I had Yankees on my boat—   I cannot remember that I ever did
anything else to aid any Union soldiers—   I never had a chance to do
anything else—or I would have done it!

                            · · · ·

To question 40. he says—   I sympathized with the Union cause—   "I
knew what I needed most and looked that way certain"!   I wanted to be
free—and wanted my race to be free—   I knew this could not be if the
rebels had a government of their own—   All the time during, and before
the war, I felt as I do now that, the Union people were the best friends of
the colored people—   I always rejoiced over Union victories—   I talked
with a few white men at Georgetown and with such colored men as I
could trust, in favor of the Union all the time during the war, but I knew

my life would be taken if it was known how I really felt about the war—
To question 41. he says. Yes.   I was all the time anxious for the success
of the Yankees—   I never did or said anything to help the rebels and
never wished for the success of any rebel soldiers—   I did what I could
for the Yankees and wanted to do more!   I was always ready and willing
to do what I could even at the risk of my own life—   I could every time
have avoided bringing the Yankee soldiers to "North Island" and could
have caused their arrest if I had wished to do so, on my way to "North
Island"—

· · · ·

HDS   Alonzo Jackson[46]

Two captured Union officers who slipped their guards in Charleston,
South Carolina, also received the protection and aid of black people, slave and free. Unlike the enlisted men assisted by Alonzo Jackson, however, the two officers found allies among the white popu-
lace as well. The willingness of white Southerners to abet the escape of Union prisoners exposed growing disaffection—and even
disloyalty—within the Confederacy. The Union officers recounted
their saga to the provost marshal general of the federal Department of the South.

Hilton Head S.C.   December 7th 1864
Sir   Agreeably to your request the undersigned have the honor to
present to you the following brief summary of their observations in and
escape from the Southern States
    On the 5th October, the officers confined in Roper Hospital Charleston
S.C. received orders to prepare for a removal,   we, together with Lieut

Millward A[*ide*]. D[*e*]. C[*amp*] to Gen' Scammon, having provided
ourselves with rebel uniforms (while in route to the depôt, walked
deliberately out of the ranks.   Knowing no one in the city we relied upon
the negroes & the same day, we related to one Thos Brown (Col'[*ore*]d
Barber) who we were, & asked assistance—   Said Brown, who seemed
proud of speaking of his being a Black Republican—placed us in charge
of his son who the same night procured for us a hiding place among
some friends of his (colored) where we remained at least one month.
We, a short time after our escape, heard of one Mr. Riels (German) who
was hiding away the other officers—   This gentleman provided us with
money & used all endeavors to get us away.   Having procured 5 negroes
and about on the 2[7]" Oct. we made the attempt to run out of the
harbor, from the foot of Hazel St.   As we were about starting, a Lieut
with 7 men—suddenly appeared and without speaking fired at the men
collected on the wharf wounding the Lieut. in charge and capturing the
negroes—   We, in the obscurity of the night, crawled away and hid in an
empty building—   Being compelled to leave our quarters we got
separated from Lt. Milward who we have since learned was recaptured
on Sullivans Islan

Being introduced to a Mr. Christmen (German) we in conjunction
with Capt. Telford & a private made an attempt together with a Mr
O'Conner (Citizen) to leave by the route by which we subsequently
escaped.

But Capt[n] Telford whilst presenting his pass at the bridge in the
Ashley river was recognized by the guard (who had previously guarded
us) & he Mr O'Connor, & private Sweeney were lodged in Charleston jail
after being stripped of watches & all money in their purses. Mr
O'Connor though a British Subject being heavily ironed

Becoming acquainted with a Mr. N. Sherhumer, formerly a U.S.

soldier who took us to his house gave us clothes, money &c.   Here in the
room of a Mr. Whittaker, we stayed till Nov. 29"   On that day passes
being procured for us by Mr Whittaker & Mr. Riels, we under the
guidance of Towles priv. 32nd Ga. arrived by the cars at his (Towles)
house & with Mr. Whittaker & 5 deserters from Castle Pinckney arrived
via Toogoods creek & the Edisto river in our lines landing on board the
U.S. Sloop o War, the "St. Lewis".   This route, leaving the cars at New
Road, distant from Charleston 22 miles & marching easterly to Towles'
house by the Toogoods Crk, has been open a long time.   Its known to the
Union men in Charleston & to some officers & men of the 32nd Ga. who
are paid by Towles for their connivance.   We stayed in Charleston two
months, relying all that time on the negroes for safety—who we found
remarkably intelligent, thoroughly comprehending their own *Status* in
the Rebellion.   The Germans also rendered us every assistance.   Indeed
without them we could not have escaped.   As a general rule the foreign
born population (Chiefly Germans) are loyal.   They have a Union
Association to which 1400 belong who, as a member told us, carry one of
these—suiting the action to the word and showing a revolver.   They say
they're ready at any time with security of protection to co-operate with
our forces upon an attack.

    They [*the Confederates*] have about 5000, troops in & around
Charleston—   The yellow fever carried off several officers & men whilst
hid away in the City.   We both of us had it.

    There's a general depression prevailing among the soldiers and
civilians,   they move about like melancholy shadows, [&] there's no
doubt that if the middle & poor classes dare express their sentiments,
that they would declare themselves ready to return to their proper
allegiance.   All that has been said about the sufferings of our prisoners,
particularly enlisted men, does not, cannot depict their sufferings—

Let one fact suffice.   A negro told us that when they were on the race course*—they actually allayed their thirst with *urine*   We have the honor to be sir, in haste Very Respectfully Your Obdt. Servant

(Signed)   Alured Larke

HLcSr
(Signed)   R. H. Day[47]

> Nothing more fully presaged the Confederacy's impending collapse than the debate over enlisting slaves as soldiers. In November 1864, President Davis proposed their enlistment, while evading the question of whether and when they would be freed. Observing that slaves could hardly be expected to fight without an assurance of freedom, other Confederate leaders urged emancipation upon enlistment. Still, opposition to black soldiers remained intense in February 1865, when General Robert E. Lee endorsed the idea. To strengthen his position, Lee invited soldiers in the Army of Northern Virginia to register their opinions about the advisability of recruiting slaves and their willingness to fight alongside black soldiers. With only fourteen dissenting votes, the 325 officers and enlisted men of one regiment adopted the following resolutions.

Hd Qrs 18th V[a] Infantry [*near Petersburg, Va.*]   Feb: 20th 1865
Resolved 1st   That the 18th V[a] Infantry, reposing the most implicit, & unlimited confidence in the wisdom, skill & patriotism of our beloved General in Chief [*Robert E. Lee*], will cheerfully acquiesce in the arming of any portion of our slaves for the defence of our Common Country whenever in his opinion this grave action on the part of Congress becomes necessary in order to successfully resist the further progress of a devastating & remorseless foe—*provided* that such armed slaves shall

---

*The Confederates held Union prisoners of war at the fairground on the outskirts of Charleston.

form a separate & distinct Corps, & shall not be incorporated with our
skeleton Regts—

Resolved 2nd   That believing that freedom is not a boon to the negroe
we are in favor of offering freedom to those only who elect it—[48]

HD

> Despite the desperate military situation, the Confederate Congress
> continued to vacillate on the question of enlisting slaves. Finally, on
> March 13, 1865, less than a month before Lee's surrender at Ap-
> pomattox, the legislators reluctantly authorized President Davis to
> call upon owners to volunteer their slaves for service in the army.[49]
> Although it came too late to influence the course of military events,
> the Confederate decision to employ black soldiers confirmed that
> slavery was doomed. The slaves' conviction that the war portended
> their freedom had proved as true in the Confederacy as it was in
> the Union.

CHAPTER

LIFE AND LABOR WITHIN UNION LINES

ROM THE MOMENT THE FIRST FUGITIVE SLAVES
arrived in Union camps, federal authorities had to deal with
intertwined questions of labor and welfare. The able-bodied men
could be put to use working for the Union. Many of the runaways,
however, were women, children, and old and disabled people who
were physically unsuited for strenuous military labor. Federal officials had to decide whether the army should provide for them and,
if so, how and to what extent.

Deemed a "problem" by federal authorities, former slaves within Union lines confronted problems of their own. Camps full of
armed soldiers, some of whom objected to the very presence of
black people, could be dangerous places. Freedmen and women
were vulnerable to abuse: forced labor, overwork, nonpayment of
wages, inadequate food and clothing, even physical assault. Nevertheless, the former slaves made the most of the opportunities afforded by life within Union lines. Relying on their wits and their
readiness to work, most freedpeople supported themselves and
their families, some quite handsomely. They attended schools and

churches sponsored by Northern churches and freedmen's aid societies or established by their own efforts. As military laborers, they contributed greatly to the Union war effort, fostering a conviction that their service entitled them to respect and fair treatment at the hands of the government.

———•———

Harboring and employing fugitive slaves raised especially complicated problems early in the war, before the North had committed itself to emancipation. For one thing, acceptance of "contrabands" and their employment as military laborers contradicted the Lincoln administration's pledge not to interfere with slavery. For another, the precise legal status of the contrabands was far from clear. Were they slave, free, or some ill-defined intermediate category? Other questions also troubled officials in Washington and commanders in the field. Should ex-slaves be compensated the same as other military laborers? Who should foot the bill for the support of contrabands who were not employed by the army but were being housed and fed at its expense? Among the first officers to confront these issues was General John E. Wool, who assumed command at Fortress Monroe, a federal outpost in southeastern Virginia, in the summer of 1861. Wool instituted an arrangement in which black men employed by the army drew rations and were credited with wages. Of those wages, however, the men received only a fraction; the government applied most of their earnings to the support of the women, children, and old or disabled men.

Fort Monroe [*Va.*].   November 1st 1861

General Orders Nº 34   The following pay and allowances will constitute the valuation of the labor of the Contrabands at work in the Engineer, Ordnance, Quartermaster, Commissary, and Medical Departments at this post to be paid as hereinafter mentioned,

Class 1st   Negro men over 18 years of age and able-bodied ten dollars per month, one Ration and the necessary amount of Clothing,

Class 2nd. Negro boys from 12 to 18 years of age and sickly and infirm negro men, five (5) per month, one ration and the necessary amount of Clothing,

The Quartermaster will furnish all the Clothing. The departments employing these men, will furnish the subsistence specified above, and as an incentive to good behaviour, (to be witheld at the discretion, of the Chiefs of the departments, respectively) each individual of the 1^s Class, will receive, two (2) dollars per month; and each individual of the 2nd Class one (1) dollar per month for their own use. The remainder of the money valuation of their labor, will be turned over to the Quartermaster, who will deduct from it the cost of the Clothing issued to them,   the balance will constitute a fund to be expended by the Quartermaster under the direction of the Commanding Officer of the department for the support of the women and children, and those that are unable to work,

For any unusal amount of labor performed they may recieve extra pay, varying in amount from (50) fifty cents to one (1) dollar, this to be paid by the departments, employing them, to the men themselves, and to be for their own use.

Should any man be prevented from working on account of sickness for six consecutive days, or ten days in any one month, one half of the money valuation will be paid,   For being prevented from laboring for a longer period than ten days in any one month all pay and allowances cease,   By command of Maj Genl Wool[1]

HD

Lacking legal title to freedom, dependent on the Union army for protection, and presented with few alternative means of earning a living, the former slaves who performed military labor at Fortress

Monroe were vulnerable to abuse. The terms under which the army employed and provided for fugitive slaves outraged Lewis C. Lockwood, an antislavery clergyman who had come to southeastern Virginia to minister to the contrabands. Writing to Henry Wilson, a U.S. senator from his home state of Massachusetts, Lockwood condemned the army's exaction of forced, uncompensated labor, questioned federal policies that upheld slavery, and demanded a congressional investigation.

Seminary near Fortress Monroe Va   Jan 29 /62

Respected Sir,   I wrote you, as you remember, by Mr Coan, a few weeks ago concerning the desirableness of a Committee of Investigation to search into the affairs of the Colored Refugees at Fortress Monroe.   I was told that it was seen reported in a paper that you had moved the appointment of such a Committee.   Will you please inform me soon whether one has been appointed.   With this request I will respectfully present other urgent reasons for such appointment

Contrabandism at Fortress Monroe is but another name for one of the worst forms of practical oppression—government slavery.   Old Pharaoh slavery was government slavery, and Uncle Sam's slavery is a Counterpart—the subordinate officials of the latter vieing with the taskmasters of the former in bad preeminence.   And Genl Wool, through fear, acts the Gallio,* ignoring as far as possible all responsibility in reference to the delicate matter.   Masters who are owners or who have been brought up with their slaves [*have an interest in them*]; but what do government officers generally care how they treat

---

*A Roman governor in Corinth during the apostle Paul's sojourn there. When Jews complained that Paul's proselytizing in their synagogue was "contrary to the law," Gallio refused to intervene, insisting that because the question involved religious and not civil law he would "be no judge of such matters." (Acts 18:12–17.)

these poor waifs, who have been cast upon their heartless protection.

But by what constitutional right does government treat these persons as slaves? Certainly not on the basis of the Fugitive Slave law, whose provisions are of a specific character, and give sanction to no such treatment. And by what military right does government become a great practical slaveholder? Was it not enough to throw the shield over state slavery? Must general government adopt the accursed system and reduce it to practical working to carry on the war or pay its expenses? Yet such is the repulsive unconstitutional fact. If a man was a slave by the laws of Virginia, his slave status is recognized by government; if free, his free status. The free colored man is allowed to work for himself; or if he work for government, he is paid fair wages,—some, a dollar a day. A few of the slaves are allowed to work for themselves, and they are making a good livelihood for themselves and families; & if all were allowed to do so—or were employed by government as freemen—there would be no want Among them. But most of the slaves are compelled to work for government for a miserable pittance. Up to two months ago they had worked for nothing but quarters and rations. Since that time they have been partially supplied with clothing—costing on an average $4 per man. And in many instances they have received one or two dollars a month cash for the past two months. Some—an engineer Corps, at work on the rail-road, who were promised the pay of freemen by Genl Wool, and whose labor, according to the estimate of the Assistant Engineer, Mr Goddard, was valued at from one to two dollars a day, have recieved but one dollar cash for five & six months' work & but little clothing. Genl Wool told me that from the earnings of these slaves a surplus fund of $7000. has been accumulated. Yet, under the direction of Quarter Master Tallmadge, Sergeant Smith has lately reduced the rations, given out, in Camp Hamilton, to the families of

these laborers and to the disabled, from 500 to 60.   And some of the
men, not willing to see their families Suffer, have withdrawn from
government service.   And the Sergeant has been putting them in the
Guard-house, whipping and forcing them back into the government
gang.   In some instances these slaves have been knocked down senseless
with shovels and clubs—

But I have just begun to trace the long catalogue of enormities,
committed in the name of Union, freedom and justice under the Stars
and Stripes.   Yours with great respect

Lewis. C. Lockwood

P.S.   I have sent duplicates of this to Senators Sumner, Hale,
Fessenden & Wade; And Representatives Lovejoy and Van Wyck.—

L. C. L.

Addenda—   About 70 of the slaves are worked on the Sabbath and
on an average three nights in the week, sometimes till 10 & 2 o'clock,
and sometimes till morning, and then compelled to work on through the
day.   For this extra work they get 50 cts for Sabbath & 50 cts for 3
nights' work; but in that case they do not receive the one or two dollars a
month given to others.—

P.S.   I understand that Genl Wool is to appoint a commission to which
our mission will be accountable—   I hope it will not be another "High
Commission".

ALS

L. C. L[2]

In February 1862, the commission appointed by General Wool confirmed allegations of fraud and the abuse of military laborers. It also criticized Wool's labor and welfare policies, recommended that

the wages of black laborers be paid directly to the workers, and urged the appointment of a superintendent of contrabands. General Wool adopted the recommendations.[3]

Unlike the contrabands at Fortress Monroe, who had left their homes to enter Union lines, former slaves in the South Carolina Sea Islands gained de facto freedom on their home ground when their owners fled before a federal invasion in November 1861. Given the opportunity, they remained on the plantations and worked for themselves rather than venture into the unknown realm of Union army camps. War Department officials in Washington, who had expected an abundant and willing supply of military laborers on the islands, were surprised to learn that soldiers were doing most of the army's work. General Thomas W. Sherman, a commander of the invading force, tried to explain why.

Port Royal (S.C.)   December 15" 1861.

Sir: For the information of the proper authorities, and for fear lest the Government may be disappointed in the amount of labor to be gathered here from the Contrabands I have the honor to report that from the hordes of negroes left on the plantations, but about 320 have thus far come in and offered their services.   Of these the Quarter-Master has but about sixty able bodied male hands—the rest being decrepid, and women and children.   Several of the 320 have run off.   Every inducement has been held out to them to come in and labor for wages, and money distributed among those who have labored.   The reasons for this apparent failure thus far appear to be these:

1st   They are naturally slothful and indolent, and have always been accustomed to the lash, an aid we do not make use of.

2nd   They appear to be so overjoyed with the change of their condition that their minds are unsettled to any plan.

3^{d} Their present ease and comfort on the plantations as long as their provisions will last, will induce most of them to remain there untill compelled to seek our lines for subsistence.

Although comparitively few have thus far come in it is therefore probable that in time many will, and if they are to be received and taken care some provision should be made to cover them. They are a prolific race, and it will be found that for every able-bodied male, there will be five to six females, children and decrepid.

It is really a question for the Government to decide what is to be done with the Contrabands. Very Respectfully Your Ob't. Sv't.

T. W. Sherman

P.S. Besides those who have come in there are many still on the plantations employed in gathering cotton. T. W. S^{4}

HLS

In the Union-occupied parts of eastern North Carolina, as at Fortress Monroe, Virginia, virtually every able-bodied black man could find employment with the army. Prospects were more limited for women, children, and elderly or disabled people, who were of little use to military authorities. A few women worked as servants, laundresses, and hospital attendants; others pieced together a livelihood as best they could, often by pooling their earnings with those of other household members. Vincent Colyer, a Northern missionary who served as "superintendent of the poor" in eastern North Carolina during the spring and summer of 1862, later recounted to a War Department commission the various ways in which the former slaves under his charge had assisted the Union army and supported themselves.

New-York [*N.Y.*]   May 25th 1863.

. . . .

My first order from Genl Burnside under this appointment, was to
employ as many negro men as I could get up to the number of five
thousand to offer them eight dollers a month. one ration of clothes.
They were to work on the building of forts.   This order remained
standing on my book,s up to the day I left the Departement with
General, July 6th [*1862*] without our ever being able to fill it   Up to the
time I left there were not over twenty five hundred able bodied men
within our lines, so that it will be readily understood why the negroes
were mover [*never*] a burden on our hands.

   The truth was we never could get enough of them, and although for a
little while there were a few more at Roanoke Island then were wanted
there—after the cost [*fort?*] was completed.

   They were brough to Newbern as it was known.

   There were all in the department 10.000.   of them 2500 were men
2500 women and Children.

   They were at the following places.

   At Newbern and vicinity 7.500   At Roanoke Island and posts
adjacent 1.000.   At Washington, Hatteras, Carolina and Beaufort
1.500.

   In the four months that I had charge of them. the men built three first
class earth work forts; Fort Totten at Newbern. a large work. Fort
Burnside on the upper end of Roanok [Il—] & [Fort?] at Washington
N.C.   These three forts were our chief reliance for defence against the
rebels. in case of an attack. have since been sucesfully used for that
purpuse by our forces under Major Genl Foster.

   The negroes loaded and discharged cargoes. for about three hunderd
vessels. served regularly as crews on about forty steamers. and acted as

permanent gangs of laborers in all the Quatermasters. Commissary and Ordnance offices of the department.

A number of the men were good carpenters. blacksmiths coopers &c. and did effective work in their [. . .] at bridge building ship joining &c   The large railroad bridge across the Trent was built chiefly by them. as was also the bridge across Bateholors & other creeks. & the docks at Roanoke Island & elsewhere   Upwards of fifty volunteers of the best & most courageous were kept constantly employed on the perilous. but most important duty of spies. scouts and guides.   In the work they were invaluable and almost indispensable.   They frequently went from thirty to three hundred miles within the enemy's lines; visiting his principle camps and most important posts and bringing us back important reliable information.

They visited Kingston Goldsboro. Trenton Onslow Swansboro, Tarboro of points on the Roanoke river; after these errands barely escaping with their lives.   They were pursued on several occasions by blood hounds   two or three of them were taken prisoners; one of these was shot; the fate of the others not known.   The pay they received for this work was small but satisfactory.   They seemed to think their lives were well spent, if necessary in giving rest, security, and success, to the Union troops, whom they regarded as their deliverers.   They usually knelt in solemn prayer before they left, & on their return, from that hazardous duty.

. . . .

The women and children supported themselves with but little aid from the government by washing, ironing. cooking, making pies, cakes &c. for the troops   The few women that were employed by the government in the hospitals received 4$ a month, clothes and one ration.

Those in the neighborhood of Newbern were ordered to report at my
office as soon as they arrived within our lines.   They obtained quarters
in the out-houses, kitcheons and poorer classes of dwellings, deserted by
the citizens on the taking of Newbern.   They attended our free schools &
churches regularly and with great earnestness.   They were peaceable,
orderly, cleanly, & industrious.   There was seldom a quarrel known
among them.   They consider it a duty to work for the U.S. government
& though they could in many cases have made more money at other
conditions; there was a public opinion among them that tabooed any one
that refuses to work for the Government.   The churches & schools
established for their benefit, with no cost to the government,* were of
great value in building up this public opinion among them.

As I have previously related, that the men frequently led foraging
parties, to places where supplies necessary for the department were
obtained.   In this way boat-loads of prime [*pine?*] and oak wood for the
hospitals. Government officers. a steam boat load of cotton bales for the
protection of the gunboats and with forage for the same, number of
horses and mules for the Quarter Master Department.   Small sheep
were obtained at no other cost than the small wages of the men.
Without doubt property far exceeding in value all that was ever paid to
the blacks, was thus obtained for the Government.   Under my
appointment as Superintendent of the Poor, from Major Genl. Burnside.
I had to attend to the suffering poor whites as well as blacks.   There
were 18.00 [*1,800*] men, women, & children of the poor whites. who felt
compelled to call for provisions at my office.

· · · ·

---

*The schools and churches were supported by Northern religious and
charitable organizations.

On an avarage in most articles of *sixteen* times as much, was called for by the poor whites, as was wanted by the poor blacks.

Work was offered to both. to the whites 12.$ month

  "   "   "   "   "   "   "   Blacks $8.   "

· · · ·

HLeSr   Vincent Colyer[5]

> Raised in a world shaped by slavery, former slaves within Union lines encountered Northerners with fundamentally different ideas and experiences. Notions about labor that most Yankees took for granted—among them the payment of wages, the necessity of prompt and steady endeavor, the employer's right to discharge unwanted workers, and the laborer's right to change employers—were alien to most freedpeople. In describing to the chief of engineers how he had organized ex-slave workers on the defenses at Fort Clinch, Florida, a Union officer revealed assumptions regarding work and welfare that many Northerners brought South.

Fort Clinch   Florida   12th August 1862.

General   I have the honor to report, that ever since my return here from Hilton Head S.C. whence I last addressed you I have been engaged in arranging and rearranging the Working parties and preparing the Monthly returns.

There is so much sickness among the men, that I have not refused a discharge to any who ask it since I am able to put the Work in a state of present defence with those remaining, and high priced mechanics are not profitable and will not be until the middle or last of September.

I had thought you might disapprove, my curtailing the length of the working day and therefore determined on my return, to add an hour to it; but I find that two men have been sunstruck and among the soldiers have appeared several similar cases.   I have therefore allowed the day-length to remain at eight hours.

I have had but little time as yet to look at the drawings, but shall proceed immediately to their study.   I have confined my attention to preparing the Fort so that we may hold it from a land attack.

It has been necessary to reconstruct the labor arrangement.

Under the old system (before the war) Slaves were hired of their masters at a *price per month* Without deduction for loss of time by sickness.   Since the war, Slaves have come in on us and have been set to work, not so much because they were desirable men as because they must be supported.   As Gen. Hunter and the Quartermasters are able and willing to perform that duty, it seems to me proper, that I should drop the system.   Indeed unless especially instructed otherwise, I don't see how I can employ a man unless I need him for the work in hand. For this work, I need the best men—no cripples or laggards.

I have therefore determined not to issue rations to families;—but to employ good men at fair wages and leave the support of families to the proper pillars thereof.

To this end, my payroll is reconstructed and instead of a host of sick—lame and lazy at 15¢, 25¢, 40¢ 30¢ & 50¢ with rations for themselves and families working a day or two and then "loafing" a day or two or pretending sick, I have good laborers at 75¢ a day and one ration.   If they are late at roll-call they lose a "quarter."   If they are absent a day without good cause or if they are not up to the mark in their work they are discharged.   I find the result thus far to be a fewer number of names on the roll, but a larger number of day's work and a better looking body of men about my work.

Every black laborer has a number on his cap; and a time-keeper at every quarter of a day finds out the position of each man on his roll.

In the present condition of things, it becomes necessary to allow the commissary to sell some stores from his goods to the families of our men.

· · · ·

ALS   Alfred F. Sears.[6]

With the passage of the Second Confiscation Act and the Militia Act in the summer of 1862, the federal government pledged protection to all fugitive slaves in Union-occupied territory and encouraged the employment of those capable of military labor.* But the promise of protection was often mocked by hostile Union soldiers, who turned their overwhelming power against the freedpeople in their midst. Nor did employment by the army guarantee either compensation or decent treatment to the workers and their families. Writing to the commander of the Department of the Missouri, three officers at Helena, Arkansas, described the abuse suffered by the former slaves.

Helena Arkansas   Dec 29th 1862

General   The undersigned Chaplains and Surgeons of the army of the Eastern District of Arkansas would respectfully call your attention to the Statements & Suggestions following

The Contrabands within our lines are experiencing hardships oppression & neglect the removal of which calls loudly for the intervention of authority.   We daily see & deplore the evil and leave it to your wisdom to devise a remedy.   In a great degree the contrabands are left entirely to the mercy and rapacity of the unprincipled part of our

---

*For a discussion of the two laws, see above, pp. 59–60.

army (excepting only the limited jurisdiction of cap^t Richmond)* with no
person clothed with Specific authority to look after & protect them.
Among their list of grievances we mention these:

Some who have been paid by individuals for cotton or for labor have
been waylaid by soldiers, robbed, and in several instances fired upon, as
well as robbed, and in no case that we can now recal have the plunderers
been brought to justice—

The wives of some have been molested by soldiers to gratify thier
licentious lust, and thier husbands murdered in endeavering to defend
them, and yet the guilty parties, though known, were not arrested.
Some who have wives and families are required to work on the
Fortifications, or to unload Government Stores, and receive only their
meals at the Public table, while their families, whatever provision is
intended for them, are, as a matter of fact, left in a helpless & starving
condition

Many of the contrabands have been employed, & received in numerous
instances, from officers & privates, only counterfeit money or nothing at
all for their services.   One man was employed as a teamster by the
Government & he died in the service (the government indebted to him
nearly fifty dollars) leaving an orphan child eight years old, & there is no
apparent provision made to draw the money, or to care for the orphan
child.   The negro hospital here has become notorious for filth, neglect,
mortality & brutal whipping, so that the contrabands have lost all hope
of kind treatment there, & would almost as soon go to their graves as to
their hospital.   These grievances reported to us by persons in whom we
have confidence, & some of which we know to be true, are but a few of
the many wrongs of which they complain—   For the sake of humanity,
for the sake of christianity, for the good name of our army, for the honor

---

*Captain Richmond was in charge of black military laborers.

of our country, cannot something be done to prevent this oppression & to stop its demoralizing influences upon the Soldiers themselves? Some have suggested that the matter be laid befor the [*War*] Department at Washington, in the hope that they will clothe an agent with authority, to register all the names of the contrabands, who will have a benevolent regard for their welfare, though whom all details of fatigue & working parties shall be made though whom rations may be drawn & money paid, & who shall be empowered to organize schools, & to make all needfull Regulations for the comfort & improvement of the condition of the contrabands; whose accounts shall be open at all times for inspection, and who shall make stated reports to the Department— All which is respectfully submitted

Samuel Sawyer
committee   Pearl P Ingall
J. G. Forman[7]

HLSr

Probably as a result of the petition, Chaplain Sawyer was appointed superintendent of contrabands at Helena and Chaplain Forman became his assistant.

Exploitative working arrangements and physical privation were not confined to Helena. Freedpeople throughout the Union-occupied South often toiled harder and longer under federal officers and soldiers than they had under slave owners and overseers—and received inferior food, clothing, and shelter to boot. Such hard usage took a heavy toll in disease and death. A Northern officer at Kenner, Louisiana, not far from New Orleans, described the living and working conditions of former slaves assigned to repair the levees.

Kenners [*La.*].   Jan'y 27. 1863

Lieut J H Metcalf A[*cting*] A[*ssistant*] A[*djutant*] G[*eneral*].   The order of Col Nickerson, directing me to report the state of the Hospital and Quarters of the Contrabands at this place, was received this PM.

I had intended either to have made a written or verbal report this week.

Last Monday (the 19th) I took Doct Sangar through the Hospital and Quarters to show him the condition I had found them.

He stated he should make a report of affairs to Gen Sherman

When I took charge here I found a lot of clothing on hand.   Lieut Hopkins, whom I relieved, stated he had delivered but few articles. And advised me there was no necessity for my doing so.

The following day I visited the Quarters &c which I found in a very bad state.   There were about 12 or 15 sick in Hospital.

They had a few old blankets and a little hay for bedding— some had nothing but the bare boards.   The building is an old house formerly used as one of the negro Quarters on the plantation.   It has a chimney, with a fire place on each side of it, in the center, but in the top there was a large hole, and the sides have cracks between the boards, consequently the rain and wind have free access.

Doct Norcom of this place is the surgeon.   He visits them every second day and oftener if called upon.   He informs me that he has urged upon those in command the necessity of procuring suitable clothing and blankets, especially for the sick, but without success.   He says he has been able to aid the sick but little, although he has sufficient medicine at his command, owing to the want of a suitable building and clothing for them.   The chimney was in one corner at first, and of but little use towards warming the room untill he had negros detailed to make one in the center.   It was a month before it was completed owing to the overseers taking the men off to work on the levees.

The sick are in charge of a mulatto man who understands administering medicine.   As rations they have one lb rice and 1/4 d[*itt*]o of sugar each per day.

The Quarters are an old barn—three building made by the negros out of fence materials, and some dozen old tents.

Excepting the first named none have any windows, or chimneys.   The only way for the smoke to escape is by the door, or through the cracks between the boards.   But few have fireplaces, the only method of heating being by fires built on the ground.   Bunks of rough boards are built around the sides.   The only bedding consists of a few quilts and blankets with a little hay.

The reason the negros gave for their filthy condition was that they had no time to clean up in.   On inquiry I found they have worked from sunrise till dark, Sundays included, since last Sept.   Many have worked three months without losing a single day.   I directed some of the old men to clean the Quarters which in a degree has been done.   Capt Page* gave me permission to allow them Sundays which I did last Sunday for the first time, and also gave a liberal ration of soap which they all very much needed.

The men were in a shocking condition in regards clothing   Many were entirely barefooted, and others nearly so—Others with no shirts, and a majority without pants excepting in the most ragged state.   In this condition they worked daily on the Levees.

Hardly an article of clothing had been issued, excepting about 75 pairs of shoes, and not a single blanket.

I immediately issued all the clothing on hand consisting of about 120

*Captain Edward Page, Jr., the local provost marshal, whose duties
included the enforcement of military regulations pertaining to slaves
and former slaves.

jackets, shirts, hats and pants   There were no shoes on hand   To make them in any way comfortable there is wanted about 150 suits of clothing— 150 prs of shoes and 150 blankets.   Capt Page informed me a week since that he had drawn on Q[*uarter*] M[*aster*] Crowel for them. I have not seen or heard since from him

   The rations are given out every day.   Either Sergeant Hagerthy or myself have attending to issuing them in order to be sure that the proper persons receive them.

   Many of the women are in even a worse condition than the men as regards clothing.   From 5 to 16 work daily on the levee,   more would if they had shoes   Their rations we issue once a week.   They receive 2 qts of meal and 2 lbs pork for a week.

   Yesterday we issued to 248 men—19 sick and 74 women, Total 341 The total number of deaths has been 78.   None have died since I have been here

   I will in a few days make another report.   Yours Respectfully

Charles L Stevens

Capt Page has a patrol of *citizens, armed,* between Fellsons and Judge Rost's to prevent negro's from coming down by there without a pass.   I have been informed several have been stopped.[8]

ALS

> "*My cattle at home are better cared for than these unfortunate persons,*" remarked Colonel Frank S. Nickerson, the officer who had requested Stevens' report.[9]

To reduce contact between former slaves and soldiers and to simplify the employment, relief, and protection of black refugees, many Union commanders established "contraband camps" with specially appointed superintendents, usually army chaplains. During the winter of 1862–63, the region under the command of General Ulysses S. Grant included contraband camps at Corinth, Mississippi; Lake Providence, Louisiana; Cairo, Illinois; and Memphis, Lagrange, Bolivar, Grand Junction, and Jackson, in western Tennessee. By spring, they had received more than 22,000 people.[10] Residents of these makeshift settlements struggled to make the most of their first home in freedom. Assisted by the superintendents of contrabands and agents of Northern aid societies, they reunited their families, established schools and churches, and began to reorder their lives.

A questionnaire circulated to local superintendents during February and March, 1863, by Chaplain John Eaton, Jr., general superintendent of contrabands in Grant's Department of the Tennessee, elicited replies that not only revealed the superintendents' own presuppositions about the ex-slaves, but also documented the gritty reality of life in the contraband camps and the aspirations of people in transit from slavery to freedom. Eaton compiled the superintendents' responses for a report to Grant's headquarters.

April 29, 1863.   Memphis [*Tenn.*].

. . . .

Answers to Interrogatories.

Interrogatory 1st What of their clothing, when they entered and since?

Answers.

Corinth   Very poor, with exceptions.   Some came dressed in suits borrowed from those over them.   Now, good by their own earnings, & by donations.

Cairo   Was very poor, many of them having hardly enough to cover their nakedness.   A few well dressed, & clothes for future use.

Grand Junction[#]   Of those coming earliest, much worn; of those later, most needy— since supplied by Government, & donations from loyal States.

[*Footnote in manuscript*] #After being at Grand Junction a month, taken away by General Order, I left Lt. McClarren in charge, who in turn was succeeded by Chaplain Grant.   The answers for Grand Junction were furnished by Assistants David L. Jones and W. G. Sargent, continuously there; from all other points by Superintendents, as per table.

Holly Springs and Memphis*   Very poor— supplied since by Govermnt and donations.

Memphis   Included in the above   Chaplain J. R. Locke first in charge at Memphis.

Bolivar   Very indifferent

La Grange   In nearly every instance, very destitute.

Providence   Many, not enough to cover their nakedness;— few, to make themselves comfortable;— clothing arriving from the North.

INTERROGATORY 2^D Have they been sheltered by tents, houses, or cabins?

ANSWERS.

Corinth   First tents; finally, chiefly by cabins, built by themselves.

Cairo.   Old barracks.

Grand Junction.   Houses, and old tents.

Holly Springs & Memphis.   "   "   "   "   & in some cases no shelter.

Memphis.   Tents.   Building log cabins.

Bolivar.   Board cabins.

La Grange   Old houses, then tents.

Lake Providence.   Deserted houses.

．　．　．　．

---

*A contraband camp at Holly Springs, in northern Mississippi, had
  been abandoned when Confederate forces seized the post in December
  1862; its residents were moved to Memphis.

INTERROGATORY 5ᵀᴴ   What of the property brought in by them, its amount and disposition?

ANSWERS.

Corinth. Horses, mules, wagons, cotton, oxen, &c., estimated at $3000—all turned over to Quartermaster.

Cairo. None whatever.

Grand Junction   Oxen, yokes, chains, wagons, mules, horses;—generally, in poor condition; used for employing and caring for contrabands, as per order.   Much taken from them by officers and soldiers.

Holly Springs & Memphis.   15 horses and mules—15 pairs oxen.   12 pairs turned over to U.S. Quartermaster.   Otherwise used for benefit of freedmen.

Memphis.   Included in the above, and brought by Chaplain Locke on removal of freedmen from Holly Springs.

Bolivar.   Teams; large number turned over to Quartermaster.   Value not known— part used in camp.

La Grange   Two ox-teams.   They were allowed to sell them.

Providence.   Turned over to Quartermaster.

Interrogatory 6ᵗʰ   What of hospitals in connection with your camp; their management, & character of diseases treated?

ANSWERS.

Corinth. Surgeon Humphrey treated diseases in hospital   Surgeon MᶜCord in camp.   Those in hospitals visited twice a day; those in camp, once a day.   In camp, we have a bathing trough to wash all the dirty & filthy, when necessary.   Surgeons, both kind & faithful.   Health of camp improving.   *Diseases*—Pneumonia, rapid in its progress, sometimes terminating fatally in twelve hours after the attack; typhoid and congestive fevers, of a low grade; measles, sometimes terminating in gangrene of the feet, requiring amputation.

Cairo. Three hospitals—male, female, and pest house. Measles, pneumonia, small pox. Two surgeons.

Grand Junction. About 50 sick in hospital—balance treated in quarters. Diseases as above.

Holly Springs & Memphis. Diseases—Diarrhoea & pneumonia.

Memphis. Hopital not under charge of Superintendent. Its condition wretched in the extreme. Lack of medicines, of utensils, of vaccine matter. No report of admissions, of diseases, of deaths, or discharges. No attention to sick in camp by surgeon. Sent assistants out of my own office, having some Knowledge of medicine, but surgeon refused vaccine matter & medicines. Improvement at date. *Diseases*— Pnuemonia, fevers, small pox. . . .

Bolivar. One hospital. Not more than 10 or 12 inmates at a time. *Diseases*—Pnuemonia & measles.

La Grange. Hospital under Dr. Welsh— common diseases; mostly pneamonia. Pest Hospital well managed by Dr. Wilson.

Providence. Difficulty in obtaining surgeons & medicines. One surgeon.

Interrogatory 7th   The situation of your camps with respect to town and troops—how guarded and regulated?

Answers.

Corinth. Location good—half mile from any troops—wood plenty— abundant water from deep well dug in camp, costing $50—paid from their own earnings. Cabins, nearly 100, from [*form*] three sides of a square. Church & Commissary buildings occupy the fourth   Grounds ditched & regularly policed. Until about Feb'y 1[st], was guarded by a

company of white soldiers; since by blacks, organized under authority of
Gen. Dodge, drilled & managed by two soldiers.   Black guards have
lea[r]ned readily, & discharged their duty with the highest degree of
satisfaction to camp and garrison commanders.

Cairo.   Location of camp grounds, low, wet & unpleasant.   Only
guards, freedmen— have rendered efficient service

Grand Junction.   Two camps near troops— no guards since first
patrol was removed, until lately.   As a consequence, the freedmen
suffered robbery and all manner of violence dictated by the passions of
the abandoned among the soldiery.

Holly Springs and Memphis.   As far as possible, separate from
troops.   Freedmen arranged in families; to some extent, their own
guards.

Memphis.   Camp two miles from town—on high bluff, easily drained;
water from river; in the midst of wood.   No soldiers near, except guard
of eight from convalescent camp.   One man regulates camp—another
directs the working men, who are divided into squads of eleven;—the
most intelligent selected as leader.   Each three or four of squads are
under a white foreman, who directs and credits their work, notes and
supplies their necessities.

Bolivar.   One & half miles from town— guarded in part by soldiers,
and part by colored police.

La Grange   Near depot— troops all around.

Providence.   In the midst of town and troops— great evils resulting.

INTERROGATORY 8TH   What coöperation or opposition from the army?
ANSWERS.

Corinth.   Now, no opposition from the army or any of its members,
but their highest approbation.

Cairo. No coöperation— little opposition.

Grand Junction. No coöperation— any amount of opposition;— in some cases, unable to procure suitable rations, quarters or guards.

Holly Springs and Memphis. No opposition; always coöperation from Gen Grant & Commanders at Holly Springs & Memphis.

Memphis. From the commander of the Post, every reasonable facility. Sometimes embarrassment in obtaining Quartermaster supplies. Many soldiers and some officers manifest only bitterness and contempt, resulting, among the abandoned, in the violence and abuse of these helpless people, in addition to the injuries heaped upon them by the vicious & disloyal in the community.

Bolivar. None of either worthy of note.

La Grange. All favors possible, especially from Col. Loomis, Commander of Post:

Providence. Little coöperation— considerable interference.

INTERROGATORY 9TH What of the work done for individuals or Government, by men, by women?

ANSWERS

Corinth. All men, except the infirm, & few for camp, employed. All women, save those having large families or small children;— generally reported industrious & faithful, when half [*decently?*] treated. Many have worked from 2 to 12 months, and never received a cent or rag yet as reward—alike as private servants & Government employees.

Cairo. Many in Quartermaster's Department and Post Hospitals. Cannot give definite numbers.

Grand Junction. All men, but the feeble, employed by Government, or individuals, or in camp; have cut wood & lumber, handled goods, erected defences. 160 went to Vicksburg.— many in Quartermaster &

Commissary Departments. Women & children pick cotton for Government and private individuals.

H. Springs & Memphis. Large amount for each.

Memphis. Average able-bodied men for the month 85. Erecting cabins,—preparing camp,— many have been turned over to different Departments, sometimes most grossly abused—as, for instance, worked all day in water, drenched, nearly frozen, and then driven to tents for shelter, to sheds for sleep, without covering, and almost without fire and food, they have come back to die by scores. Wages seldom paid—none in hospitals. The services of a large number have been stolen outright.

Bolivar. None for individuals— large amount for Government— building fortifications, cutting wood, rolling logs, running sawmills, and in Quartermaster's Department and Hospitals. No general system of pay.

Providence. Digging canal— picking cotton.

. . . .

INTERROGATORY 11   What, if any, means of instruction?
ANSWERS.

Corinth. No school. About 100 books, from which they are taught incidentally, besides Sabbath services, & talks by the Superintendent.

Cairo. School taught eleven weeks gratuitously by Job Hadley, wife & niece.

Grand Junction. None, save incidentally.

Holly Springs & Memphis. Very little religious instruction.

Memphis. School taught two months before the designation of any Superintendent here. gratuitously, by Miss L. Humphrey, of Chicago, See Report. School-house soon to be built.

Bolivar. Many taught to read by Mr. Richards, carpenter.

La Grange.   None but incidental and occasional divine service

Providence;   "   "   "   "   "   "   "

INTERROGATORY 12.   What of the motives which induced those under your care to change their relations to their masters?

ANSWERS.

Corinth.   Can't answer short of 100 pages.   Bad treatment—hard times—lack of the comforts of life—prospect of being driven South; the more intelligent, because they wished to be free.   Generally speak kindly of their masters; none wish to return; many would die first.   All delighted with the prospect of freedom, yet all have been kept constantly at some kind of work.

Cairo.   All have a repulsive idea of going back into slavery, but would prefer going back to their old places, if they could be free there.

Grand Junction   Cruel treatment, or being pressed into the rebel service, or driven South, or because they were bewildered by the presence of our army.

Holly Springs & Memphis.   Universal desire to obtain their freedom.

Memphis.   Destitution at their old homes, or the running away of their masters, or the fear of being driven South, or simply because others came away.   Many chose to be free, and so abandoned their masters.

Bolivar.   Fear of going South, or severe treatment, or desire for liberty

La Grange.   Most have a tolerably well developed idea of freedom, and long to enjoy it.

Providence.   As above—   very many abandoned by their masters.

INTERROGATORY 13   What of their intelligence?

Corinth. Far more intelligent than I supposed. Some are men of fine intelligence and correct views.

Cairo. Their common intelligence is good—much better than we had supposed.

Grand Junction. Exhibit intelligence greater than has been attributed to their race; very shrewd in escaping from their masters and in shirking work, if so disposed.

Holly Springs & Memphis. House servants much more intelligent than field hands. All learn rapidly—are intuitive, not reflective—need line upon line

Memphis. Higher than I had expected— keen & bright when they wish to understand;—stupid and idiotic when they do not.

Bolivar. Better than many suppose; good as any could expect under the circumstances.

La Grange. As good as that of men, women & children anywhere, of any color, who cannot read.

INTERROGATORY 14   What of their notions of liberty?
ANSWERS.

Corinth. Many, if not most, have correct notions— believe they must work— anxious for pay— put no value upon money in spending it.

Cairo. Indefinite; anticipate having it as the result of the war.

Grand Junction   Ideas of liberty are freedom from restraint and labor— need instruction.

Holly Springs and Memphis. Generally correct. They say they have no rights, nor own anything except as their master permits; but being freed, can make their own money and protect their families.

Memphis. A slander to say their notion of liberty is idleness— that is their laziness.   Their notions of liberty have no more to do with their love of ease in the black than in the white race.

Bolivar.   Varies.   Don't seem to realize that labor is attendant on liberty.

La Grange   No answer.

Providence   No answer.

INTERROGATORY 15   What of their notions of property?

ANSWERS.

Corinth.   Beyond the possession of a little kitchen plunder, they seem generally to have but little idea.   Many are dishonest—the result of a system which compels them to steal from their masters.   Have met many who have a high sense of honor, and are strictly honest.

Cairo.   Wholly childlike.   Having had nothing to provide for, they have no ripeness of judgment in regard to accumulating.

Grand Junction   Entirely undeveloped

Holly Springs and Memphis.   Generally strong desire to make money or get property;— when theirs, they use it much as whites do.   Many have been laying up their money for months, preparing to leave their masters.

La Grange.   Good enough.

INTERROGATORY 16.   What of their notions of honesty?

ANSWERS.

CORINTH.   Included in answer to Inter. 15.

Cairo.   Have little idea of honesty.

Grand Junction.   Large proportion act upon the principle of getting what they can by any means, while others are perfectly honest.

Holly Springs and Memphis.   They do not consider it dishonest to take from their masters. I[*n?*] making them feel that I have placed confidence in them, I have seldom been disappointed.

Memphis. I verily believe that their habits in this particular have not been so thoroughly prostituted by the influence of all the centuries of their degradation in slavery as have those of our patriot soldiery, in two years of war.

Bolivar   Most seem to be honest; many prove to be otherwise.

La Grange   Equal to soldiers.

INTERROGATORY 17. What of their disposition to labor?
ANSWERS.

Corinth. So far as I have tested it, better than I anticipated. Willing to work for money, except in waiting on the sick. One hundred and fifty hands gathered 500 acres of cotton in less than three weeks— much of which time was bad weather. The owner admitted it was done quicker than it could have been done with slaves. When detailed for service, they generally remained till honorably discharged, even when badly treated. I am well satisfied, from careful calculations, that the freedmen of this Camp and District have netted the Government, over and above all their expenses, including rations, tents, &c., at least $3000 per month, independent of what the women do, & all the property brought through our lines from the rebels.

Cairo. Willing to labor, when they can have proper motives.

Grand Junction. Have manifested considerable disposition to escape labor, having had no sufficient motives to work.

Holly Springs and Memphis. With few exceptions, generally willing, even without pay. Paid regularly, they are much more prompt.

Memphis. Among men, better than among women. Hold out to them the inducements,—benefit to themselves and friends,—essential to the industry of any race, and they would at once be diligent and industrious.

Bolivar.   Generally good— would be improved by the idea of pay.

La Grange.   No report.

Providence   "   "

INTERROGATORY 18   What of their religious notions and practices?

ANSWERS.

Corinth.   Very religious— always orthodox— mostly Methodists, Baptists & Presbyterians.   Notwithstanding their peculiar notions, when any one dies, they often pray & sing all night.

Cairo   Naturally religiously inclined.   During my six months' connection with them, I have not heard over ten colored men swear. Their religious meetings are both solemn and interesting.

Grand Junction.   During the cold months, no house for church. Their religious notions & practices have failed of any marked manifestation.   Show a strong religious inclination.

Holly Springs and Memphis.   Great majority religious—Baptists or Methodists.   Their notions of the leading doctrines of the Bible are remarkably correct.   Justification, repentance, faith, holiness, heaven, hell; are not troubled, like educated white men, with unbelief.

Memphis.   Notions of doctrine better than to be expected.   Practices not always in accordance with their notions, as is also true of other colors.   Have been taught to make their religion one of feeling, not necessarily affecting their living.   If one finds himself susceptible to religious excitement or sentiment, he is a religious man, though at the same time, he may lie, steal, drink, and commit adultery.

Bolivar.   Exceeding those of the whites in the army.

La Grange.   Good, but full of superstition.

Providence. Not answered.

INTERROGATORY 19   What of their marital notions & practices.
ANSWERS.

Corinth. All wrong. All entering our camps who have been living or desire to live together as husband and wife are required to be married in the proper manner, and a certificate of the same is given. This regulation has done much to promote the good order of the camp.

Cairo. Their idea of the marriage relations and obligations is very low.

Grand Junction   Most of them have no idea of the sacredness of the marriage tie, declaring that marriage, as it exists among the whites, has been impossible for them. In other cases, the marriage relation exists in all its sacredness without legal sanction.

Holly Springs and Memphis. The greater number have lived together as husband and wife, by mutual consent. In many cases, strongly attached and faithful, though having no legal marriage.

Memphis. They know what marriage is among the whites, but have yielded to the sad necessity of their case. Generally, I believe the men to be faithful to the women with whom they live, and the women to reward their faith with like truth. Free and married, they will maintain the marital relations as sacredly as any other race.

Bolivar. Have had no opportunity for correct notions and practices.

La Grange. Loose & by example.

Providence. No answer.

INTERROGATORY 20   What is your opinion of the possibility of arming the negro?

ANSWERS.

Corinth. I can see but one answer. That the negro is better than the white man, I do not see; nor do I, why we should fight for our country and exempt him. I do not doubt he will make a good soldier, especially for Southern climates. Blacks have made better guards for our camps than whites. Most of the officers & men in this Division are in favor of arming the negro at once, believing it will be the best means of ending the war.

Cairo. Should be at once armed. Many of them are bold—willing to fight, and are capable of rendering good service as soldiers.

Grand Junction. Have had no experience in this matter, but find they will unhesitatingly follow into any danger, so long as their leader exhibits no sign of fear. I am confident, that with competent and brave white officers, they will make the best of soldiers.

Holly Springs and Memphis. I believe in giving them their freedom by their swords. Policy and humanity say, Arm the negro. History affords all the necessary precedents for liberating slaves and arming them as soldiers, to fight in defence of their country. Blacks fought in the Revolutionary struggle, and in the war of 1812. Let them fight in the war for their own liberty.

Memphis. Yes, arm him! It will do him worlds of good. He will know then he has rights, and dare maintain them—a grand step towards manhood. Arm him! For our country needs soldiers. These men will make good soldiers. Arm him!—for the rebels need enemies, & heaven knows the blacks have reason to be that. Once armed and drilled, the black man will be an enemy the rebels will neither love nor despise. Arm him, & let the world see the black man on a vast scale returning good for evil, helping with blood and life the cause of the race which hated, oppressed & scorned him.

Bolivar. When the pickets at this place were attacked of a night,

their coolness and readiness for the fight convinced me of their fitness
for soldiers.

La Grange. Arm them at once. We can hurt the rebels more by the
use of the negro than by any other means in our power. Arm him—use
him; do it speedily. Why leave him to labor for our enemy, & thus keep
up the strife? Arm him—he is a man—he will fight—he can save the
Union. I pledge you & the world they will make good soldiers.

. . . .

HLcSr   (Signed)   John Eaton, Jr.[11]

Federal authorities seldom hesitated to impress workers when it
was impossible or inconvenient to obtain them by other means.
Many black men became military laborers at gunpoint. When
shorthanded quartermasters in Washington, D.C.—the chief supply center of the army in the East—found themselves unable to obtain enough workers locally, they tried to hire black men in coastal
Virginia and North Carolina. But hardly any were willing to leave
their homes and families to accept employment in Washington.
Most of them were already working for the government, for civilian
employers, or for themselves. The frustrated quartermasters therefore sought permission to recruit laborers by *"forcible persuasion,"*
and Secretary of War Edwin M. Stanton soon agreed.[12] A letter to
Stanton by a Northern minister described the result.

Washington D.C.   July 11th/63

Dear Sir. In complyance with a suggestion just received at your Office I
proceed to make the following statement of facts.

1st I am a missionary among the Contrabands at Fortress Monroe &

vicinity.   My present location is at Norfolk, Va.

2^d   I have no intention of *interfering in the least* with any military order, but simply to state facts, & make a few requests.

3^d   On Saturday July 4th an order was received at Norfolk, from the War Department, by way of Fortress Monroe, which was understood by the authorities at the two places to require them to *impress* all ablebodied colored men in the two places to the Number of 1000 or 1500 & send them to Washington to work in the Quartermaster's Department. The authorities commenced executing said order at the Fort & Hampton on the 4th, & at Norfolk on Sund. the 5th Inst.   In executing said order the following events transpired.

(a) In the afternoon a large congregation of colored people were assembled at the Colored Methodist Church for divine worship.   As the Minister closed his sermon, the soldiers entered the house, called out a large number of men, & marched them to the Dock & put them under guard.

Others were taken in the streets.   Some of them were allowed to go home during the night & change their clothing; others say they had not such opportunity.   Some were brought away without shoes, & some without coats; many without any change whatever.

(b) There were a large number of contrabands on Craney Island. Some of them had been at work on Government fortifications in the vicinity of Suffolk & Portsmouth, *but had not received their pay.* Soldiers went to the Island & told the men to go up to Norfolk in the Boat & get their pay.   They went without bidding their families good bye, & without any extra clothing, & were not allowed to return.   Their families do not know where they the men are gone

(c) I beg leave to call attention to a few individual cases.   The men brought up are in two divisions called on the List of Trasportation

"From Norfolk,' & "From Hampton." Among those from *Norfolk*, are the following.

John Jordan, has worked on Fortifications & otherwise *twelve months* & received but *86 cents*. Cannot he, & others in similar circumstances, have assurance from the War Department of pay *for past services*, as well as for the future. It will do much to quiet their apprehensions & render them contented.

Nelson Sprewell says he has a rupture & is unfit for Service.

Cornelius Smith says he has free papers, at home place.

Richard Stewart says he was born free & has free papers at some place.

Nelson Wiley is an old man, drove a carriage all his life.

Among the men "From Hampton" I mention the following: Philip Bright, Edward Bright   Henry Tabb, Emanuel Savage, Miles Hope, Willson Hope, Joseph Hope, Ned Whitehouse, Carl Holloway, Charles Smith, Thomas Needham, Jacob Sanders, Francis Garrar, & Anthony Armsted.   Except the last two names, & these men have rented farms, purchased teams, seed corn & fencing, & have good crops well under way. They were taken away from their families & farms, & leave no one to care for them.   To appearance they will loose every thing.   *Their all is invested in their farms*.

Anthony Armstead is a shoemaker & left a sick family with none to care for them.

W^m R Johnson is an old man 62 years of age, conducted Gen Butler to "*Big Bethel*," two years ago; Has served in the Hospital much of the time since, but has *received no pay*.

Henry Minor, is 63 years old, was free born & has free papers which he was obliged to leave in the vicinity of Whitehouse only the day previous to being taken up at Hampton.

George Parker, has a store & goods worth about $100. from which he was taken without notice, & left no one to care for them.

Thomas Risby is a School Teacher, was taken without notice

Lewis Roberson left a team & hogs worth $50. with none to care for them.

Merrit Morris is Ruptured & had been discharged by Lieut Sage as unfit for service.

In view of these facts I would respectfully inquire.

1st Cannot those men who came without proper clothing be supplied?

2^d Can the men whom I have specified by name all, or any part of them, be discharged & sent to their homes?

3^d Can arrangements be made by which the families of these men can draw a part of their wages, *at their request, each month*, at Fortress Monroe or Norfolk?

4th Would it be proper for you to give me an official statement for the benefit of their friends, specifying what wages these men will receive per month, about what time they will be allowed to return home, & what they will be required to perform while here?

5th If some of these men think best to send for their families, will they be allowed to come & make this their home?

6th Will you give me permission to visit these men before my return & tell them the results of my interview with you?   I am Very Respectfully Yours,

ALS   Asa Prescott.[13]

Although the War Department instructed the Union commander in eastern Virginia to respond to "the allegation that many contrabands have been employed on public works . . . and have not been paid for their services," it ignored the other issues raised by Prescott.[14]

———•———

The impressment of men from eastern Virginia did little to relieve the labor shortage in Washington. Quartermasters in the capital therefore tried to obtain laborers who were engaged elsewhere in the city. One officer proposed to the chief quartermaster of the Washington Depot that many of the menial tasks performed by black men in Washington's military hospitals might be assigned to convalescing patients, freeing some of the former for service at the depot. His enumeration of the duties of the black workers unintentionally revealed just how vital they were to the hospitals' operations.

Washington, D.C.,   July 31" *1863*

General: I have the honor to report, that in accordance with your instructions of the 28" inst. I have examined into the manner in which the contrabands, reported by Lt. N. W. Carroll, are employed, and respectfully submit the following as the result of such investigation.

At Columbian Hospital there are Eleven (11) men. employed, as follows. (6). Six. Policeing ditching and draining (2) Carrying water & Cleaning floors (2) Two Sawing wood for Hospital Kitchens (1) Surgeon's Waiter & Ostler

At Carver Hospital Twenty nine men are employed, as follows. (22) Twenty two. Policeing. Ditching and Draining (2) Two. Sawing wood for Wash House & Laundry. (1) One. Washing Sinks (4) Four, Hauling water for Officers Mess, Stewards Mess & Cooking purposes, removing Slops from wards, Cook House &c,

At Harewood Hospital Forty nine (49) men are employed as

follows.   (2) Asst. Cooks. One for Contrabands and One for Clerks
Mess,   (3) Assistants to Hospital Bakers,   (2) Taking Care of
Ambulance Horses,   (36) Policeing and improving grounds,
(1) Grinding Coffee &c. at Hospt. Commissary   (3) Sawing wood.
Carrying water and hanging out Clothes at Laundry   (2) Sawing wood
for Wards and Bake House.

At Finley Hospital Thirty Seven (37) men are employed, as follows—
(1) One, Assisting Mason   (1) One Assisting Carpenter   (1) One
Assisting Gardner   (8) Eight, Cleaning Spittoons, Sinks & Wards.   (1)
One, Ostler for Surgeon's and Ambulance Horses.   (2) Two, Pumping
Water for, and making fires in Laundry   (20) Twenty, Policeing &
improving grounds.   (3) Three Sawing wood for Surgeon, Clerks, and
Laundry.

At Emory Hospital Thirty eight (38) men are employed as follows
(3) Chopping wood and making fires in Hospital and Laundry
(1) Waiter at Surgeons Quarters,   (1) Ostler   (1) Waiter at
Commissary building   (1) Waiter at Dispensary   (31) Policeing and
improving grounds,

At Lincoln Hospital Fifty One (51) men are employed, as follows,
(3) Pumping Water for Hospital.   (5) Cleaning Sinks & Quarters
(1) Teamster   (2) Cooks   (40) Policeing and improving grounds

At Armory Square Hospital Twenty Six 26. men are employed   (1)
One. As Teamster and (25) Twenty five in Policeing Grounds &c.

At Campbell Hospital Twelve (12) men are employed in Policeing and
improving the grounds

At Camp Hayti, There are Fifty Six (56) men employed as follows
(18) Scavengers   (3) Cooks for Contraband messes   (36) Laborers,
burrying Horses, night soil &c.

I am informed by Lt. N. W. Carroll that no definite instructions have been given him in regard to the kinds of work for which these men should be employed at Hospitals. The Contrabands have, in most cases, been detailed by the Military Governor, and the Surgeons have considered themselves as having entire control of the men when so detailed and, as above stated, have used them as waiters, Ostlers, for hanging out clothes &c.

I would respectfully recommend that definite instructions be given to Lt. Carroll, with authority to enable him to carry out such instructions, he having been detailed by the Military Governor to take charge of these Contrabands.

The force at the Hospitals could be reduced at least one third, and in my opinion, might be wholly dispensed with, by having the work they now do, done by convalescents. All the scavenger work at the Hospitals is now done by the Camp Hayti Scavengers. I have the honor to be, General, Very Respectfly Your obd Servt,

HLS

E. E. Camp[15]

A medical officer disputed Camp's assertion that convalescing soldiers could or would supplant black laborers at such tasks as "cleansing cesspools, scrubbing privies and policing the grounds in their immediate vicinity, whitewashing, and hauling wood and water." "Some of these duties require strong, vigorous men," he argued, "and others are so repugnant to the soldiers, that they will not even imperfectly, perform them except under the fear of punishment."[16]

Employment with the Union army gave black workers formal channels through which to present grievances and fostered a conviction that they were entitled to a hearing. A group of black men em-

ployed by the army's Subsistence Department, all of whom had
been free before the war, criticized the policy whereby all black military laborers in Washington and in Alexandria, Virginia, had $5
deducted from their monthly wages for the relief of destitute former slaves. The assessment, the freemen complained, not only reduced their earnings at a time when the cost of living had soared,
but also unfairly taxed one class of black people for the benefit of
another. Two petitions to their military supervisor having failed,
they addressed a third directly to the secretary of war.

Alexandria [*Va.*]   Aug 31st 1863

Dear Sir,   we a potion of the free people of Alexandria Virginia, that has
been imployed in Lieut Co^l Bell Commissary in this place ever since the
commencement of the war, and has laboured hard though all wheathers,
night and day, sundies included, and we hope that you will pardon us for
these liberties in writing to your honour for the porpose of asking you to
add a little more to our wages as, L, Co^l, George Bell says it is with you
to raise our wages or not,   when we first went to the commissary to
word, our pay was $30, per month,   after one or two months they was
curtailed to $25 per month with which we made out to get along
with,   since the first of December 1862 we has been curtailed to $20 per
month so said to be for the benefit of the contrabands, and the men that
is in the employment is provided for by the government, houses to live
in, provission for them selves and families, and even wood a coal to cook
with; and has all the attention, and we the free men has to pay a tax of
$5 per month for they benefit, and have to support our selves and
families, and provide for them in every respect with the exceptions of our
own rations, and we have tried to get along without saying any thing,
but sir every thing is so high that you know your self sir that our $20
will not go any whare,   it is true that the government, has agreat

expence, and it is nomore then wright, that the contrabands employed in the government, service should be curtailed in wages for the surport of they fellow men, but we free people I dont think sir has any rite to pay a tax for the benefit of the contrabands any more then white labours of our class, which we have on our works, which they receive they 25 dollars and Co¹ Bell has some favourite men whom he pays 25 dollars to and others has to get along the best they can, and undergo deprivation, so we embraced this opportunity of laying the case before you and if you thinks [it] right, sir, then we made our selves satisfied, but we believe that you will do all for us you can in the case, as we believe sir that you is a gentlemen that works on the squar.   we remain your obedient servants,

HD   Colord labours of Alexandria va Commissary Dept[17]

The secretary of war considered the petition, but refused to repeal the deduction.

Few grievances of black military laborers elicited more heartfelt protests than impressment. For black people who were free before the war, involuntary labor constituted a violation of accustomed rights; for those newly freed, it smacked of slavery. At Beaufort, North Carolina, impressed workers fired off an indignant petition to General Benjamin F. Butler, the principal Union commander of the area.

Beaufort   N. Carolina   Nᵒᵛ 20ᵗʰ 1863
the undersigned Colored Citizens of the town of Beaufort in behaf of the Colord population of this Commuinty in view of the manner in which

their Brotheren on oppressed by the military authurities in this Vicenity
Respeckfuley pitision you are at the Head of this military Department
for a redress of grievunces

Your [politiness] [*petitioners*] disire to make known to you that they
and there brothern to the President of the United States are
undiscriminately inpressed by the authorities to labor upon the Public
woorks without compensation   that in Consequence of this System of
fource labor they Have no means of paying Rents and otherwise
Providing for ther families

Your pitisioners disire futher to Express ther Entire Willingness to
Contribute to the Cause of the union in anyway consistant with there
cause as Freemen and the Rights of their families

Anything that can Be don By You to relieve us from the Burden which
wee are nou Labooring will Be Highly appriciated By Your Pitistior[ers]

And your pititioners Will Ever pray   Yours Respeckfully & Soforth

[*17 signatures*]

HDSr   and fifty outher[18]

The petition apparently received no reply whatsoever.

———•—————

Amid rapidly changing wartime conditions, former slaves often experienced a variety of work routines in a short span of time. Robert
Houston of Arkansas certainly did. He was by turns a slave on a
plantation, a fugitive from Confederate labor impressment, a laborer on a federal gunboat, an independent woodcutter, and a
Union soldier. In the course of testifying before a postwar commission to establish his ownership of cordwood seized by a Union
steamer (and hence his entitlement to compensation), Houston recounted his wartime odyssey.

[*Helena, Ark.*]   6— day of June 1873

   I was borne a Slave in Buckinham Co— Va.—   I was brought to
Memphis Tenn. at the beginning of the war by a negro trader named
A M Boyd with 40 or 50 other slaves—   From here Mr Boyd sent me
with the others to Chico Co— Ark— to work on his Plantation—   This
was in the winter of 1861—before the fireing on Fort Sumpter.—   Then
I was put to work on Mr Boyds Plantation with the others makeing
corn.—   After a time the Yankees took Memphis and the Gun & other
Boats were passing up & down the river.—   the Confederate Authorities
made a requizition on Boyd my Master for a large number of Slaves to
work in breast works.—   Boyds Father in Law—in charge would send
only one—then went to Lake Village and made a Speech against the
order saying it was death to put the negroes to work in the swamps
   The requisition was repeated and demand for all his slaves when Mr
Hedspeth—in charge told all of us Slaves to put out to the woods and he
would send us provissions till we could get to the Yankees—and he had
to leave the country—   We stayed in the woods about three weeks then
made our way to the Miss— river and got taken on [*the Union*] Marine
Fleet and hired to work at $60. per Month.—for two Months.   A few
days before the two months were up I was taken with the small Pox—
when I was put off on Island 76—   There were a good many here
cutting wood.   When I got able to work I was seperated from the
others—and told by one seeming to have control to go by myself on the
other side of a Slew and I might have all the wood I could cut & sell.   I
then built me a Shanty on that ground & went on cutting as I was
able.—   I remained here for a long time or till I cut & hawled out—to
the river 150 cords—intending when I made enough to go to farming.
When this much cut and put up then came the Federal Steam Boat
South Western and took all of us men and wood here to Helena and

swore us into the Army service— This steamer took this lot of wood at
different times as she was forageing up & down the river.— When
called upon I went into the Union Service very willingly, having by this
time learnt something of the principles & object of the war. From my
first information of the war my actions feelings and Sympathies have all
the time been for the Success and maintainance of the Union Cause &
all the time willing and desireous to fight or do any thing else in my
power, in that behalf— I never done any thing to my knowledge to aid,
assist or countenence the rebellion and could never be induced to go in
that direction.

The way I got at the quantity of wood taken was this— When cut I
ranked it all up and measured with a four foot stick except 25 cords or
about that laying as it was cut which I do not charge for— There was
125 cords so put up and this steamer South Western got all of it   also
sent teams in the woods & took the 25 cords Scattered.— At this time
Steam Boats were paying for this kind of wood $3^{50} per cord for
wood:—& I consider this worth that much   I asked the officer for pay
when they commenced takeing it— It was Lieut— Hadlock— He
consulted with other officers—then come back and said part would be
paid when we get to Helena. and asked how much I expected for it   I
told him $3^{50} the same as others got.— then he gave me a receipt for
it,   At Helena he said I must wait for the Pay Master to come— Then
when I enlisted, he was not permitted to pay—must wait till mustered
out & take it with Bounty money— After I was mustered out I made
unsuccessful attempts for pay till finally the receipt was worne out and
lost[19]

HD

Houston had submitted a claim for $562.50, but the commission-
ers rejected his contention that he had owned the wood. Instead,
they maintained, he had "[d]oubtless" been a wage laborer, whose
"interest" in the wood was "about $1.00 per cord." He was award-
ed $125.[20]

Former slaves living within Union lines were subject to military restrictions, and official orders could have a profound effect on their
daily lives. Louisa Jane Barker, the wife of a Northern chaplain,
described the fate of a small settlement of black families that had
received an officer's permission to locate between Fort Albany, in
northern Virginia, and a nearby contraband camp. Relying on his
assurances, the freedpeople built houses, supported themselves,
and planned for the future. But an order from higher authority
dashed their hopes.

[Washington, D.C.? January? 1864]

Mrs Louisa Jane Barker (wife of Chaplain Barker (1st Mass Heavy
Artillery

I know the spot of ground which was assigned by Lieut Shepard to the
colord people to build their cottages upon.   A little village had collected
there.   I made frequent visits among them to ascertain their wants,
plans occupations &c   Their freedom had been taken mostly under the
Presidents [*Emancipation*] proclamation of January 1st 1863   Since
that time they had not only supported themselves, and their families,
but saved money enough to build the little shanties they then occupied
They expressed great reluctance to enter the contraband camp, because
they felt more independent in supporting themselves, and families, after
the manner of white laborers.

I think they were proud of their past success— The first help they

required was education— Every head of a family eagerly entered into
my proposition to start a school for their children   They gave their
names to be responsible for tuition at any rate I might decide upon to be
paid monthly— A well educated mulatto woman engaged to take the
school as soon as a building could be procured   I interested some
gentlemen of Boston in my plan, and had obtained the promise of a
contribution of a part, if not the whole of a school house, when the whole
project was thwarted by a sudden order for a second removal of this
village outside of the Rifle pits or into the Contraband Camp.   This
order created great unhappiness amongst them—

I enquired of the most intelligent negro whether any complaint had
been made to him as to the new settlement— He had not heard of any
just ground of complaint from any one— several groundless complaints
had been mad: there was no truth in them.

About ten days after this conversation a body of soldiers entered the
village claiming to have been sent by Genl Augur with peremptory
orders "to clear out this village."   This order was executed so literally
that even a dying child was ordered out of the house— The
grandmother who had taken care of it since its mothers death begged
leave to stay until the child died, but she was refused

The men who were absent at work, came home at night to find empty
houses, and their families gone, they knew not whither!— Some of
them came to Lieut Shepard to enquire for their lost wives and
children—

In tears and indignation they protested against a tyranny worse than
their past experiences of slavery— One man said "I am going back to
my old master— I never saw hard times till since I called myself a
freeman—

I have never seen any of the sixteen families composing this

settlement since the conversation above alluded to; and I regret to find
that I have lost the list of their names—[21]

HD

> Self-organized settlements of former slaves sprang up throughout
> the Union-occupied South. Poverty and the unpredictable events of
> war made life difficult, but residents of such settlements neverthe-
> less struggled to maintain their hard-worn independence. In early
> 1864, an assistant to the military superintendent of freedmen in
> Arkansas reported upon his visit to a wood yard established by pri-
> vate contractors on the banks of the Mississippi River and a nearby
> shantytown that was home to 180 people.

Helena Ark   Feb 5th 1864

. . . .

Their cabins consist of an incongruous assemblage of miserable huts no
attempt haveing been made towards introduceing any system whatever
Their floors are on or quite near the ground   they have no windows
and are only lighted by holes in the roofs   consequently in rainy
weather most of their Scanty Bedding is wet their floors are damp and
no wonder that from this little community they have already furnished
one hundred and sixteen subjects for the Graveyard notwithstanding
quite a number had been sent off sick

And in addition to other inconveniences a recruiting officer or as they
termed them (De Pressers) came among them, and carried away twenty
of the Best men leaveing some families without any men to assist them

Some of those women thus left alone with little children seemed
discouraged whilst others were quite cheerful   I will give a single
instance   one Martha Thompson eighteen years old had a small Babe

when asked where her husband was replied he run away the first chance
and joined the union army   The next question asked was how she come
there   she replied her brother come with her but that the pressers took
him   I enquired how she made a liveing   she replied that she left her
baby with a neighbor and then went and piled cord wood   she seemed
cheerful and determined

I met with but few Cases of Sickness in camp

The people invariably said Messrs Love & Hugus [*the contractors*] had
measured the wood that they cut and corded fairly and had paid them
promtly every saturday night if they wished for their pay   they also
said that there had been at all times provisions on hand for sale but
some of them complained of the prices that they had to pay Beef 12 cts
pr lb   pork 12 cts pr lb   flour 7 cts pr lb   meal 6 cts pr lb and some of
the people complained of the prices of Clotheing   Shoes $3.75 c[*ents*]
pr pair   Blankets $5.00 a piece   common coarse coats $12.00
pants $7.00   Shirts $3.00   As to the distribution of those donated
goods I was careful when makeing the Registration to make a minute of
the wants of the most destitute and sickly and if I could have had a room
and some one to have assisted me I would have adopted the ticket
System but haveing but little room and no assistance I made amongst
the needy as near an equal distribut[ion] as I could make   Then I gave
out as rewards for industry the ballance on hand with the exception of
a few articles for Small Boys that was not needed which I have returned

Most of the clothing was very thankfully received indeed but I heard
of one woman expressing dissatisfaction with the Smallness of the
donation

Those people had at one time begun a meeting house but after so
many of the men were pressed they abandoned the undertakeing but
they still have some religious meetings have hopes of happiness after

death and all of them believe that President Lincoln is their friend

There is no Physician here to administer medicine to the sick neither is there any preparations being made for a school nor have those people had any Rations issued to them from the goverment   they have relied solely upon their own industry for a support

The price paid for cutting and cording wood is one dollar pr cord   other hands are paid for loading the waggons and 12: cts pr cord is paid for cording at the River after it is halled

.   .   .   .

ALS   A W Harlan[22]

> Many former slaves in the Union-occupied South sought indepen-
> dence not in rural settlements but in cities and towns. Urban life
> offered numerous attractions: a variety of employment possibili-
> ties, especially for skilled workers and for domestic servants and
> laundresses; ready access to churches, schools, mutual-aid soci-
> eties, and other institutions; and the protection of federal gar-
> risons, which often included black troops. Natchez, Mississippi,
> was one of many Southern cities that became crowded with former
> slaves from the countryside. The presence of large numbers of
> masterless black people offended not only former slaveholders but
> also some Union military authorities. Ostensibly to reduce the
> threat of epidemic disease, Major A.W. Kelly, the "health officer" at
> Natchez, forbade any former slave to live or work outside the con-
> trol of a white employer, on pain of forced relocation to a contra-
> band camp. His policy received the approval of the post comman-
> der, General James M. Tuttle.

Health Office, NATCHEZ, MISS.,   March 19th, 1864.

TO PRESERVE THE GENERAL HEALTH of the troops stationed in the City of Natchez, and of the inhabitants, and to guard against the origination here, and the introduction of pestilential diseases the

ensuing summer and autumn, it imperatively requires the *prompt,
vigorous* and *steady* enforcement of the Sanitary Regulations heretofore
prescribed in this City.

It is of the first and greatest importance and necessity that all causes
tending to the engendering and dissemination of pestilential diseases
here, so soon as their existence is known, shall be at once abated, or
removed so far as practicable.   It is to be apprehended that serious
danger to the health of this City will result from the congregation within
its limits of the large numbers of *idle* negroes which now throng the
streets, lanes and alleys, and over-crowd every hovel.   *Lazy* and
profligate, unused to caring for themselves; thriftless for the present,
and recklessly improvident of the future, the most of them loaf idly
about the streets and alleys, prowling in secret places, and lounge lazily
in crowded hovels, which soon become dens of noisome filth, the hot
beds, fit to engender and rapidly disseminate the most *loathsome* and
malignant diseases.

To prevent these evil effects it *is hereby ordered* that after the first day
of April, 1864, no contraband shall be allowed to remain in the city of
Natchez, who is not employed by some *responsible white person* in some
legitimate business, and who does not reside at the domicil of his or her
employer; and no contraband will be allowed to hire any premises in this
city for any purpose whatever, and no other person will be allowed to hire
such premises for the purpose of evading this order, nor allowed to hire
or harbor any contraband who cannot satisfy the Health Officer that he
or she needs the services of said contraband in some legitimate
employment.   All contrabands remaining in the city in contravention of
this order after April 1st, will be removed to the contraband
encampment.

The word contraband is hereby defined to mean all persons formerly slaves who are not now in the employ of their former owners.

Any evasion of this order will be punished more severely than the direct infraction of it, and all persons renting buildings to contrabands will be held responsible.

Persons drawing rations from U.S. Government are not supposed to need many *hired* servants. The number allowed to each family will be determined by the undersigned.

By order of A. W. KELLY,

Surgeon and Health Officer.

Approved: J. M. Tuttle, Brig. Gen. Commanding District.[23]

PDSr

Kelly's order resulted in the expulsion of hundreds of men, women, and children, prompting outraged protests by other black residents of Natchez and by Northerners in and outside the army. The city's superintendent of freedmen complained that the order was "put in force against many people of color for which it was not really intended—the draymen Hackmen and other tradesmen in the city." He maintained that "some distinction ought to be made between the worthless and vagrant and those as capable of supporting and caring for themselves as thier *former* masters." But Kelly refused to make exceptions.[24] A delegation that included several local agents of Northern freedmen's aid societies appealed to General Tuttle, insisting that the former slaves deserved better at the hands of a government committed to their freedom. A newspaper in Iowa—where Tuttle, a Democrat, had been defeated in the 1863 election for governor—printed the appeal and reported the exchange that followed.

[*?, Iowa*] May 5 [*1864*]

. . . .

General Tuttle issued an order that all free persons must hire themselves to white masters, or be banished the city. The Northern agents and missionaries at that place presented the following protest:

NATCHEZ, Miss., April 1, 1864.

General Tuttle:

SIR: The undersigned citizens of Natchez would respectfully ask you to modify the recent order of the Health Officer of this city, because of the manifold and manifest evils arising from its execution, as it is now carried out. It certainly cannot be the interest or policy of the Government of the United States at this time to alienate the colored people from it and make them its enemies. The colored soldier in the field hearing that his mother or his wife has been driven from her quiet and comfortable home, simply because she supported herself and was not dependent upon some white person, may feel less inclined to hazard his life in the cause of his country now struggling for *its life*, and many doubt whether the pledges made by the Government to him have been fulfilled. And it seems strange just now, when the Government is fighting for the principles of universal liberty, that a distinction should be made in this district in favor of those who have been slaveholders, and against well-doing and self-supporting freedmen.

In the execution of the order referred to, the most flagrant wrongs have been inflicted upon the better class of the freed people. An old woman who has lived fifty years in this city, and was not disturbed before, was driven at the point of the bayonet to the camp. Mothers who having young infants and attending to lawful business were arrested, and were not allowed to see their babes. Many persons in the employment of respectable white citizens, were driven from their houses, and no time allowed them to obtain certificates of being employed. Many others who had paid their taxes and rents in advance, and who had official and personal security of protection and safety, were suddenly turned out of their neat and comfortable houses, without any time allowed them to arrange their affairs, and driven away to the camp, without shelter or clothing for the night. Parents were driven away from their young children, and children coming out of school were driven away by soldiers without the knowledge of their parents. These wrongs have been inflicted upon a people already sufficiently oppressed and injured, and upon many of them because

they are not in a state of servitude, whilst it is the evident policy and
design of the Government to liberate and elevate them.

Signed by.

James Wallace, Missionary of the Reformed Presbyterian Church.

J. C. H. Feris, Missionary of the Reformed Presbyterian Church to
Freedmen.

S. G. Wright, Missionary American Association, N.Y.

H. A. McKelvey, Northwestern Freedmen's Aid Commission,
Chicago.

J. B. Weeks, Northwestern Freedmen's Aid Commission, Chicago.

J. G. Thorn, Agent Western Freedmen's Aid Commission,
Cincinnati, Ohio, and Acting Agent National Freedmen's Relief
Association, N.Y., and Western Sanitary Commission.

William G. Thompson, M.D., Assistant Surgeon, Freedmen.

After the general had read this paper, he said to them who presented
it, "You appear to think that colored men have a great many more rights
than white men." To which it was replied, "We did not; that we had
never dreamed of them having more rights than white men, but we
simply believed that a colored man or woman who decently and
comfortably supported himself or herself in lawful employment, might
be permitted to remain in the city." He then referred the paper to Dr.
Kelly.[25]

PD

The episode did not end there. In mid-May 1864, the House of
Representatives—at the behest of a Republican congressman from
Iowa—instructed the Joint Committee on the Conduct of the War
to investigate General Tuttle's actions. In June, amid well-founded
allegations that he had abused his official position for personal
gain, Tuttle resigned his commission.[26]

Despite the hardships of life under Union occupation, liberated
slaves never lost sight of the new possibilities opened by their war-
born emancipation. Among these was the opportunity to obtain legal marriages and thereby affirm the integrity of their families,
which, under slavery, had always been at risk. In a report to the adjutant general of the army, the chaplain of a black regiment in
Arkansas confirmed the importance of marriage to the freedpeople
and described their conviction that wartime emancipation was less
an end than a beginning.

Little Rock   Ark   Feb 28th 1865

The movements of the 54th during the month has interfered to some
extent with our Sabbath services; and has also, rendered it impracticable
to continue the day school.   On reaching this post from, Ft Smith, the
Reg[t] was divided, and five companies sent out towards Brownsville, to
guard the Rail Road.   These have been ordered back to Little Rock and
the ten companies, are now camped, on the north side of the river, doing
guard, & provost, duty in & around Little Rock: As soon as a building
can be procured, I design to open a day school for such as are disposed
to attend.

Weddings, just now, are very popular, and abundant among the
Colored People.   They have just learned, of the Special Order No' 15. of
Gen Thomas* by which, they may not only be lawfully married, but have
their Marriage Certificates, *Recorded*; in a *book furnished by the
Government*.   This is most desirable; and the order, was very opportune;
as these people were constantly loosing their certificates.   Those who
were captured from the "Chepewa"; at Ivy's Ford, on the 17th of

---

*Adjutant General Lorenzo Thomas's order authorized "[a]ny ordained
minister of the Gospel, accredited by the General Superintendent of
Freedmen, . . . to solemnize the rites of marriage among the
Freedmen." (*Black Military Experience*, p. 712n.)

January, by Col Brooks, had their Marriage Certificates, taken from
them; and destroyed; and then were roundly cursed, for having such
papers in their posession.   I have married, during the month, at this
Post; Twenty five couples; mostly, those, who have families; & have been
living together for years.   I try to dissuade single men, who are soldiers,
from marrying, till their time of enlistment is out: as that course seems
to me, to be most judicious.

The Colord People here, generally consider, this war not only; their
exodus, from bondage; but the road, to Responsibility; Competency; and
an honorable Citizenship—   God grant that their hopes and
expectations may be fully realized.   Most Respectfully

ALS   A. B. Randall[27]

> The approach of Northern victory broadened the former slaves' ex-
> pectations of freedom and intensified their dissatisfaction with the
> inequities of life within Union lines. Little more than a month be-
> fore the Confederate surrender, black men living in a contraband
> camp on Roanoke Island, North Carolina, met to air a variety
> of grievances, including actions taken by the camp's military su-
> perintendent, Captain Horace James, and his assistant, Holland
> Streeter. Their petitions, the first to President Lincoln and the sec-
> ond to Secretary of War Stanton, were written in several fragments
> whose intended order is not clear; they were probably drafted by
> Richard Boyle, a black schoolteacher who journeyed to Washington
> to present them in person.

Roanoke Island N.C   march 9th 1865.
M[r] President Dear Sir   We Colored men of this Island held a meeting
to consult over the affairs of our present conditions and our rights and

we find that our arms are so Short that we cant doe any thing with in our Selves So we Concluded the best thing we could do was to apply to you or Some of your cabinets   we are told and also we have read that you have declared all the Colored people free bothe men and woman that is in the Union lines and if that be so we want to know where our wrights is or are we to be Stamp down or troden under feet by our Superintendent which he is the very man that we look to for assistents,   in the first place his Proclamation was that no able boded man was to draw any rations except he was at work for the Government   we all agreed to that and was willing to doe as we had done for $10,00 per month and our rations though we Seldom ever get the mony

   the next thing he said that he wanted us to work and get our living as White men and not apply to the Government and that is vry thing we want to doe, but after we do this we cant satisfie him   Soon as he Sees we are trying to Support our Selves without the aid of the Government he comes and make a Call for the men, that is not working for the Government to Goe away and if we are not willing to Goe he orders the Guards to take us by the point of the bayonet, and we have no power to help it   we know it is wright and are willing to doe any thing that the President or our head Commanders want us to doe but we are not willing to be pull and haul a bout so much by those head men as we have been for the last two years and we may say Get nothing for it,   last fall a large number of we men was Conscript and sent up to the front and all of them has never return   Some Got Kill Some died and When they taken them they treated us mean and our owners ever did   they taken us just like we had been dum beast

   We Colored people on Roanok Island are willing to Submit to any thing that we know the President or his cabinet Say because we have Got since

enough to believe it is our duty to doe every thing we Can doe to aid M[r]
Lyncoln and the Government but we are not willing to work as we have
done for Chaplain James and be Troden under foot and Get nothing for
it   we have work faithful Since we have been on the Island   we have
built our log houses   we have Cultivate our acre of Ground and have
Tried to be less exspence to the Government as we Possible Could be
and we are yet Trying to help the Government all we Can for our
lives   those head men have done every thing to us that our masters
have done except by and Sell us and now they are Trying to Starve the
woman & children to death cutting off they ration   they have Got so
now that they wont Give them no meat to eat, every ration day beef & a
little fish and befor the Ten days is out they are going from one to
another Trying to borrow a little meal to last until ration day   M[r]
Streeter will just order one barrell of meet for his fish men and the others
he Gives nothing but beaf but we thank the Lord for that if we no it is the
President or the Secretarys orders   this is what want to know whoes
orders it is,   one of our minister children was fool to ration house and
Sent off and his father working three days in every week for his ration

                    Roanoke Island N.C   march 9th 1865
    we have appeal to General Butler and Gen[l] Butler wrote to Capt
James to do Better and Capt James has promies to do Better and
instead of doing better he has done worst and now we appeal to you
which is the last resort and only help we have got, feeling that we are
entily friendless,   on the Island there numrous of Soldiers wives and
they Can hardly get any rations and some of them are almost starving
    we dont exspect to have the same wrights as white men doe   we
know that are in a millitary country and we exspect to obey the rules and
orders of our authories and doe as they say doe, any thing in

reason   we thank God and thank our President all of his aids for what
has been done for us but we are not satisfide with our Supertendent nor
the treatement we receives   now we want you to send us answer what
to depen upon   let it be good or bad and we will be Satisfide
Respectifully yours

HL   Roanoke Island N.C.[28]

                              Roanoke Island N.C   March 9th 1865
    we want to know from the Secretary of War has the Rev Chaplain
James which is our Superintendent of negros affairs has any wright to
take our boy Children from us and from the School and Send them to
newbern to work to pay for they ration without they parent Consint   if
he has we thinks it very hard indeed   he essued a Proclamation that no
boys Should have any rations at 14 years old   well we thought was very
hard that we had to find our boy Children to Goe to School hard as times
are, but rather then they Should Goe without learning we thought we
would try and doe it and say no more a bout it and the first thing we
knowed M[r] Stereeter the Gentlemen that ration the Contrabands had
Gone a round to all the White School-Teachers and told them to Give the
boys orders to goe and get they ration on a Cirtain day   so the negros
as we are Call are use to the Cesesh plots Suspicion the Game they was
Going to play and a Greate many never Sent they Children. So Some
twenty or twenty-five went and M[r] Streeter Give them they rations and
the Guard march them down to the head quarters and put them on
board the boat and carried them to newbern   here is woman here on
the Island which their husbands are in the army just had one little boy
to help them to cut & lug wood & to Goe arrand for them   Chaplain
James has taken them and sent them away   Some of these little ones

he sent off wasen oer 12 years olds.   the mothers of Some went to Chaplain and Grieved and beg for the little boys but he would not let them have them   we want to know if the Prisident done essued any ration for School boys   if he dont then we are satisfide   we have men on the Island that Can Support the boys to Goe to School but here are Poor woman are not able to do it So the orphans must Goe without they learning   that all we can say a bout the matter

the next is Concerning of our White Soldiers   they Come to our Church and we treat them with all the Politeness that we can and Some of them treats us as though we were beast and we cant help our Selves   Some of them brings Pop Crackers and Christmas devils and throws a mong the woman and if we Say any thing to them they will talk about mobin us.   we report them to the Capt he will Say you must find out Which ones it was and that we cant do but we think very hard it   they put the pistols to our ministers breast because he Spoke to them about they behavour in the Church,   the next is Capt James told us When he got the mill built he would let us have plank to buil our houses   we negroes went to work and cut and hewd the timber and built the mill under the northern men derection and now he Charges us 3 and 4 dollars a hundred for plank and if we Carry 3 logs to the mill he takes 2 and Gives us one.   that is he has the logs haul and takes one for hauling and one for Sawing and we thinks that is to much Without he paid us better then he does.   and the next thing is he wont allow a man any ration While he is trying to buil him Self a house. to live in and how are negroes to live at that rate   we Cant See no way to live under Such laws, Without Some Altiration

Roanoke Island N.C.   March 9th 1865

here is men here that has been working for the last three year and has

not been paid for it.   they, work on the forts and Cut spiles and drove
them and done any thing that they was told to do   Capt James Came
on the Island Jan. 1864 and told they men that he had made all the
matters wright a bout they back pay and now says he I want all of you
men that has due bills to carry them to Mr Bonnell at head quarters and
all them has not got no paper to show for they work I will make them
Swear and kiss the Bibel   and the men done just as he told them and
he told us that he had made out the rolls and sent them up to
Washington City and now he says that money is all dead   So we are
very well Satisfide just So we know that he has never received it for our
head men has fool us so much just because they think that we are
igorant we have lost all Confidince in them.   so all we wants is a Chance
and we can Get a living like White men   we are praying to God every
day for the war to Stop So we wont be beholding to the Government for
Something to Eat   Yours Respectfully

HL   Roanoke Island.[29]

The petitioners' complaints went unaddressed.

———•———

At the end of the war, black soldiers stationed near Petersburg, Virginia, wrote to the commissioner of the Freedmen's Bureau to
protest the suffering of their wives, children, and parents on
Roanoke Island. Enlisted under promises that their families would
be fed and sheltered while they served the Union, the soldiers bitterly arraigned the government for failing to keep its word.

[*City Point?, Va.   May or June 1865*]

Genl   We the soldiers of the 36 U.S. Col[*ored*] Reg[t] Humbly petition to
you to alter the Affairs at Roanoke Island.   We have served in the US
Army faithfully and don our duty to our Country, for which we thank
God (that we had the opportunity) but at the same time our family's are
suffering at Roanoke Island N.C.

1   When we were enlisted in the service we were prommised that our
wifes and family's should receive rations from goverment.   The rations
for our wifes and family's have been (and are now cut down) to one half
the regular ration.   Consequently three or four days out of every ten
days, thee have nothing to eat.   at the same time our ration's are stolen
from the ration house by Mr Streeter the Ass[t] Sup[t] at the Island (and
others) and sold while our family's are suffering for some thing to eat.

2nd   Mr Steeter the Ass[t] Sup[t] of Negro aff's at Roanoke Island is a
througher Cooper head* a man who says that he is no part of a
Abolitionist. takes no care of the colored people and has no Simpathy
with the colored people.   A man who kicks our wives and children out of
the ration house or commissary, he takes no notice of their actual
suffering and sells the rations and allows it to be sold, and our family's
suffer for something to eat.

3rd   Captn James the Suptn in Charge has been told of these facts
and has taken no notice of them.   so has Coln Lahaman the
Commander in Charge of Roanoke, but no notice is taken of it, because
it comes from Contrabands or Freedmen   the cause of much suffering
is that Captn James has not paid the Colored people for their work for
near a year and at the same time cuts the ration's off to one half so the
people have neither provisions or money to buy it with.   There are men
on the Island that have been wounded at Dutch Gap Canal, working

---

*I.e., "copperhead," a Northerner who supported or sympathized with
the Confederacy.

there, and some discharged soldiers, men that were wounded in the service of the U.S. Army, and returned home to Roanoke that Cannot get any rations and are not able to work,   some soldiers are sick in Hospitals that have never been paid a cent and their familys are suffering and their children going crying without anything to eat.

4th our familys have no protection   the white soldiers break into our houses act as they please steal our chickens rob our gardens and if any one defends their-Selves against them they are taken to the gard house for it.   so our familys have no protection when Mr Streeter is here to protect them and will not do it.

5th.   Genl we the soldiers of the 36 U.S. Co Troops having familys at Roanoke Island humbly petition you to favour us by removeing Mr Streeter the present Asst Supt at Roanoke Island under Captn James.

Genl prehaps you think the Statements against Mr Streeter too strong, but we can prove them.

Genl order Chaplain Green to Washington to report the true state of things at Roanoke Island.   Chaplain Green is an asst Supt at Roanoke Island, with Mr Holland Streeter and he can prove the facts.   and there are plenty of white men here that can prove them also, and many more thing's not mentioned   Signed in behalf of humanity

Richard Etheredge

Wm Benson[30]

HLS

The wartime experience of many black military laborers broadened their horizons. Those who accompanied armies on the march saw a world beyond their home plantations and farms. But that very mobility could make it difficult for them to document their employment and, consequently, to receive their pay. Four women, whose duties in military hospitals had taken them to Georgia, Tennessee, and Alabama, discovered as much. Months after their discharge, one of them recounted their travels before an official of the Freedmen's Bureau to whom they had applied for assistance in claiming unpaid wages.

[*Chattanooga, Tenn. February 27, 1866*]

Statement of Anna Irwin Washerwoman in Genl Field Hospital D[*epartment of the*]. C[*umberland*]

Commenced work at Rasacca Geo. in the month of April 1864— remained there about two months— then went to Big Shanty Stopped there four days— went to Cartersvill stayed ther four days— then went to Marietta stayed there about three weeks— then went to Vining station stayed there about two Months   then went to Atlanta & stayed there about two months.   then came to Chattanooga Tenn   All the time under the charge of surgeon Woodruff   When we came to Chattanooga were turned over to surgeon E. L. Bissell.   then went to Huntsvill AL.   left there on Christmas day 1864   then went to Bulls Gap Tenn remained there one month   then went to Nashvill where we remained untill we were mustered out.—   was to recieve four dollars pr week.   Anna acted as foreman and was to recieve $5.00 pr week.   they have recieve but $44^{00}.   Stewart Johnson & John Hardenberg took the money and made away.   The other claimants names are Laura Irwin Rhoda Willis and Milly Humphries

The above named persons were discharged at Nashvill Tenn June 16th 1865 by virtue of special orders No 3 Gen Field Hospital, by E. L. Bissell   Surg 5 Conn. Vols in charge[31]

HD

The Freedmen's Bureau agent forwarded Irwin's statement to the surgeon general in Washington, noting that he was in receipt of "[d]aily applications . . . for settlement of similar claims many of which bear evidence of fraud haveing been practiced on the Negro by persons connected with the army." The surgeon general's office could find no records pertaining to the women's employment and declared it "impossible to take any action."[32]

Workers constructing a stockade at Alexandria, Virginia.
(National Archives)

Workers refurbishing wharf for Union supplies. (National Archives)

Former slaves employed as servants by Union officers near Petersburg,
Virginia, August 1864. (Library of Congress)

Burial detail at Cold Harbor, Virginia. (National Archives)

Laundresses at Yorktown, Virginia. (National Archives)

Teamsters near Bermuda Hundred, Virginia. (National Archives)

Former slaves planting sweet potatoes, Edisto Island, South Carolina, 1862.
(New-York Historical Society)

Working for the Union army:
driving cattle; washing for the troops; chopping wood
and cooking; repairing railroads.
(Vincent Colyer, *Brief Report of the Services Rendered by
the Freedpeople . . . in North Carolina* [1864])

Contraband camp at Hampton, Virginia. (*Harper's Weekly*,
September 30, 1865)

Former slaves selling goods to Union soldiers, Beaufort, South Carolina.
(*Frank Leslie's Illustrated Newspaper*, February 1, 1862)

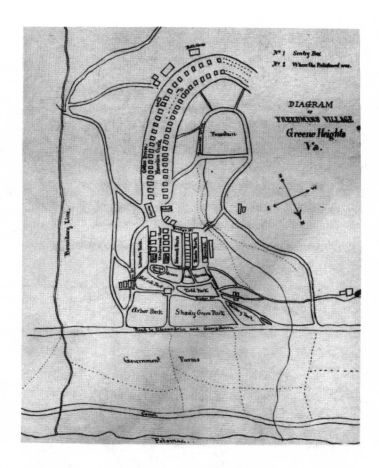

Freedman's Village, a contraband camp on the estate of Confederate general
Robert E. Lee, Arlington, Virginia, 1864. (National Archives)

Women and children, Spotsylvania Court House, Virginia, May 14, 1864.
(Pencil drawing by Edwin Forbes, Library of Congress)

Women and children near Alexandria, Virginia. (Private collection,
courtesy of Michael Musick)

REGULATIONS!

1st. The Inspector of Plantations will be present at each pay day, keep a correct account of the amount of money paid each hand, together with a full and complete record of every transaction in his office.

2d. Settle all difficulties between employer and employee, arising under lease.

3d. See that proper quality and quantity of Rations are issued, and proper amount and quality of clothing is issued to employees.

4th. Inspect the plantation and report if it is cultivated according to lease.

5th. Report all derilictions of duty on part of employer or employee, promptly to this office.

TO GOVERN HANDS.

1st. All hands to be in the field within one half hour after bell rings.

2d. Each hand two hours late in the field, without proper excuse, shall be docked one half day's labor for each two hours so absent.

3d. No hand shall be allowed to leave a plantation without a pass from the manager, and no hand allowed to leave the parish without a pass from Inspector of Plantations, endorsed by Provost Marshal. Every hand found off the plantation, without a proper pass, will be docked one day's work for each offence.

4th. Half hour shall be allowed for breakfast each day, and two hours each day for dinner.

5th. No hand shall be allowed to roam at will over plantations in the night, and any hand found out of his or her quarters after 9 o'clock, each night, without proper excuse, shall be fined one half day's work.

6th. No hand shall be allowed to ride on horses or mules belonging to the plantation without proper permission from lessee or overseer, and each and every person guilty of such offence shall forfeit the amount of two days' work.

7th. No hand shall be allowed to keep any horse, mule, hog, pigs, or cattle on any plantation on which he may labor, the value of those now owned by any negro or negroes, on any leased plantation, shall be assessed by the parish Inspector of Plantations, and either purchased by the lessee, or permitted to be sold by owner.

In case of questions materially affecting the interests of either party to a lease, the Inspector of Plantations shall forward a certified statement of the case to the Superintendent of Plantations for his decision. Any party deeming himself aggrieved by any decision of the Inspector of Plantations of the parish, may appeal the same to the Superintendent of Plantations, or to the Provost Marshal of the Parish, as he may deem proper, whose decision in the case shall be final, he first notifying the Superintendent of such appeal.

8th. No hand cultivating any part or parcel of ground under the permission of the Major General Commanding, shall be allowed to plant any Cotton or Sugar Cane upon the land so cultivated by him upon his own account, but shall devote his time and land to the raising of corn or vegetables.

No hand shall be hired on any of the leased or private plantations without a written permission from last employer, or from the Inspector of Plantations of the Parish.

9th. Hands leaving Plantations without proper authority, wherever found shall be forced to return, and employers of said hands fined according to the offence for each hand so employed by the Provost Marshal of the Parish.

BY ORDER OF
S. W. COZZENS,
Superintendent of Plantations.

Labor regulations for leased plantations, Louisiana, 1864.
(National Archives)

CHAPTER

IV.

FREE LABOR
IN THE MIDST
OF WAR

EMANCIPATION IN THE UNION-OCCUPIED SOUTH undid familiar ways of living and working; not knowing exactly what would take the place of slavery, former slaves and former slaveholders struggled to shape the emerging order as best they could. Former slaves sought to liquidate the last remnants of their owners' rule and place their freedom on a foundation of economic independence. But because they were liberated without land or other productive resources, most had nothing with which to provide for themselves and their families except their ability to work. Former slaveholders, for their part, fought to regain control over laborers they once had owned. Into their midst came Northern entrepreneurs, ministers, and teachers, all of whom were determined to remake the South in the image of the North. A many-sided contest ensued, refereed by federal authorities who, in the course of waging war and administering occupied territory, oversaw the construction of a new labor system on the ruins of the old.

The free-labor arrangements that emerged were improvised responses to pressing necessities, not systematic designs for the future. Federal officials, military and civilian, sought first to provide subsistence and employment to former slaves who were not needed by the army—women, children, and the old or disabled—and thereby reduce expenditures for relief. They also hoped to restore production of cotton, sugar, and other valuable commodities, which would yield revenue for the Union's depleted treasury. Seeking to replace slavery with labor relations similar to those in the North, they forbade whipping, required employers to pay wages, and placed other restrictions on both employers and laborers. But the federal intervention that ended slavery also opened new contests over free labor. Conflict arose over the terms and conditions of labor, including the extent of discipline and supervision, the amount and form of compensation, and access to land and other means of making a living.

Although confined to the relatively narrow bounds of Union-occupied territory, the free-labor regimes initiated during the war established important precedents. Tens of thousands of former slaves and former slaveholders entered the postwar world with experience in free labor. In many ways, reconstruction in the defeated Confederacy would begin where wartime measures left off.

In early 1862, a small band of Northern abolitionists arrived in the Sea Islands along the coast of South Carolina to supervise the labor and education of the region's slaves. The slaveholders of the islands, who ranked among the wealthiest in the South, had fled in November 1861, when federal forces invaded the region. Their slaves remained behind and were working the plantations on their own. But treasury officials pronounced the estates "abandoned" and appointed the Northern abolitionists to manage them for the government. Although the new superintendents lacked agricultural experience, they were eager to demonstrate the superiority of free labor and confident that the former slaves would cooperate enthusiastically. Many of them found the task more difficult than they had foreseen. In a letter to Edward Atkinson, secretary of the Boston society that was partly underwriting the free-labor "experiment," Edward S. Philbrick, one of the Northern superintendents, described the trials of managing a plantation in a war zone, including

the disruptive presence of Union soldiers, interference by treasury
agents, difficulty obtaining supplies, and, not least, laborers who
had their own notions of how their work should be organized.

Coffins Point   St. Helena I. [*S.C.*]   April 12th 1862

Copy

Dear Ned

.   .   .   .

I will now give you a sort of diary to show how life is spent here.

Apl. 3^d   68 hands in the potato field planting sweet potatoes,
swinging their hoes in unison timed by a jolly song, words
undistinguishable.   They work with a good will, and plant about 13
acres during the day.   I walk over to the Fripp's Pine Grove plantation
& find the people planting corn, teach school after task is done 3 to 5
P.M. in loft of Cotton House, benches supplied from "Praise house" that
is, chapel, and carried back to same after school every day, the chapel
being too small for school house.   I find an old sulky with shafts and
body supplied by a negro carpenter who says the wheels and frame
belong to the Gov^t but thinks his work in saving the pieces & rebuilding
sulky worth $4.   I pay the same and take possession of sulky, riding
home with an old sore-backed horse and a harness consisting mostly of
old hemp.

April 4th   Spend most of the forenoon making my sulky harness by
sewing together sundry bits of leather picked up at different times, &
take out the bits of string with which it was held together.   Mr. Gannett
gives out a few garments to some worthy women; the other women make
a terrible fuss because they don't all get some.   Their husbands leave
their work and come down on me in a posse & say their wives deserve as
much as any (& I dare say they do)   All hands agree to wait till we can
get clothing or cloth enough to give each family a piece.   They dislike

this made-up clothing & the first thing they do is to make it over to suit their wants.   They have always made all their clothes and their mistress' [&] masters' too except the best suit, so our Northern ladies get no thanks for their sewing.

Sat^y Apl. 5.   The people on Coffin's hesitate about working Saturdays.   I tell them they must work or I shall report them to Massa Lincoln as too lazy to be free.   The best part go into the field grumbling about "no clothes, no tobacco, no molasses, no bacon, no salt, no shoes, no medicine &c." which is all very true and unanswerable.   I can only say the war has shut up all these things and we can't get them in the North as we used to, but I would do my best to get a little.

I take my sulky and *new* harness and drive off to spend the night with Dr. Wakefield on my way to church to-morrow, stopping at Fripp's as I go along & teaching school.

Sunday April 6th Ride on to the brick church and meet there about 500 negroes from all about the island in their best dresses, of which a good part are very ragged.   Meet Mr. Pierce* and a lot of our companions.   Mr P. says he has no authority to offer any definite pay per acre for cotton planting & I mustn't show favors to my people.   I am content with the latter rule, but think it too bad that the people who are so distracted by camp labor† at $10. per month, should not have a definite promise for their plantation work.   I know if the leasing system had been adopted they would have had this stimulus from the contractors, who know how to use such motives to good advantage.‡

---

*Edward L. Pierce, the treasury agent who was in charge of the plantation superintendents.

†I.e., military labor.

‡Philbrick advocated a system under which the government would lease the plantations to Northern entrepreneurs rather than operate them directly.

After church I ride on three miles to get some sugar at Mr. Eustis's
where our rations have been waiting nearly a week for conveyance.
Have a nice dinner and chat with Mr. Eustis & Mr. Hooper & start back
about 5 P.M. flies biting like fun; take a bucket of rice & 4 bottles
molasses between my feet, and a candle box full of sugar, salt, & bread
tied on behind.   Twelve miles of fine sandy road give my rations an
ample supply of grit especially the bread, & my tired horse can't be
induced to go over 2 1/2 miles an hour.   For the last three miles I walk
by his side with my blanket wrapped about me to keep warm.   Splendid
moonlight.

April 7th All hands at work in the new Cotton field for the first time
this year, working well.   Men women and children swinging some 65
heavy hoes, without shoes.   The wife of the driver* (we have two drivers
on this plantation) who left to seek his fortune among the soldiers last
week, comes to me & complains that she does not get her allowance of
"clabber" (i.e. bonny clapper or milk).   I tell her she mustn't expect to
get the allowance of a driver's wife now her husband is not here, but
must be content with an equal share of milk with all the women.   She
mutters a good deal but the other women only laugh at her as if to say
"that's right."

Steamer Flora comes to our wharf about noon after Cotton.   All
hands at work loading and hauling to wharf the rest of the day.

Apl. 8   All the men at work loading Cotton.   I stroll out through the
woods to the cotton field expecting to find the women at work, but find
none.   On inquiring find Col. Nobles† told them to come & get some

---

*The "driver" was a slave responsible for supervising and disciplining field hands.
  Drivers and their families often received privileges not accorded other slaves.

†William H. Nobles, a former army officer who was one of several treasury
  agents in charge of collecting "abandoned" property, including the previous
  year's cotton crop.

sugar after the steamer was loaded and they thought best to hang about
the steamer till noon.   The bbl. [*barrel*] sugar is then carried up to
house and sold to them for money, each taking what they can pay for.   I
find Col. N. & both Salisburys in the house removing all the best
furniture from the house.   I told Col. N. that Col. Reynolds had
promised Mr. Pierce and myself that this furniture should not be
removed, that Mr. P. expected to put some more folks on this part of the
island and that no other furniture could be found hereabouts fit to use,
& I protested against the removal of any of it.   Col. N. replied that he
knew nothing about any understanding about it and that he had a
requisition from Gen. Hunter for some furniture and this was the only
place he knew of to get it.   He went on abusing me and Mr. Pierce
exhausting a choice supply of epithets in presence of his agents and
some of the negroes and ended by saying I had told so many lies about
him he didn't believe a word I said about the furniture and he should
accordingly take it and did so.   I go to the Fripp's Point plantation in
P.M.   Find the people had quit work in middle of forenoon, tasks only
half done.   Men were all here helping load Cotton & women left to work
alone—so (of course) got quarelling, felt discouraged about pay, &
declared they wouldn't work on Cotton without the usual supply of
clothes.   I called them all up and had a grand pow-wow   I first heard
their complaints, & then told them the usual facts about the difficulty of
getting clothing &c. during the war, told how much they had at stake in
their own welfare and that of millions of other negroes, and that if they
failed to show now that they could work as hard without the whip as
they used to work with it, that the Govt would be disgusted with them &
believe all the stories their masters told us about their laziness &c. &c.
hinting that if they didn't raise Cotton enough to pay for all the
comforts they wanted the people of the north would say "these islands

are not worth keeping, let's take our soldier's away & let the Secesh
come back." I told them I had just bought some salt at Beaufort with
my own money, meaning to give them a quart all round, but that if they
behaved lazy I shouldn't try to do much more for them. They all broke
out at this with "Thank you massa" thank you a thousand times! "We
will work. You shan't call us lazy. We will never work again for old
massa & his whip. We only wanted to know if we were sure of our pay, it
is so hard living without clothes a whole year, & we get sick putting sea
water in our hominy, & haven't had our salt for so many months." A
good many promised to make up the unfinished tasks, of the morning, &
I called the children together for school, leaving all in good humor. The
Driver tells me that Massa Washington Fripp, the brother of his old
owner has just been shot near Charleston for refusing to enlist. He was
told this by a negro just escaped from the main[*land*]. He says "our
massa didn't like this war: he told other white people it was all wrong &
that the Yankees were sure to beat. He would have stayed here with us
but didn't dare to, the other white folks would have killed him. He told
us before he went off when the Yankees took Hilton Head that we must
stay here and work as we used to, & that if we went to the main[*land*] as
the [*Confederate*] soldiers told us, we should all starve, so we hid in the
woods till the soldiers gone, & then came back here and went to work sir,
getting ready to plant corn as massa told us, & if you had only come a
month earlier sir, we could have planted as much cotton as ever sir, but
now it is too late to list* much ground, & we can't plant much." I told
him to plant all he could & I would do all I could for the comfort of the
people. The Flora goes off in P.M. with all the rest of Coffin's Cotton,
about 58000 lbs. in all when clean ginned.

Apl. 9th   Violent thunder storm in morning, leaving the air clean &

---

*I.e., prepare for planting by making ridges and furrows.

cool,   about 10 A.M. it clears up & the people go to work.   The Flora
having unloaded at Beaufort comes back to Fripp's point about 2 P.M. &
commences to load their Cotton, calling people away from their work in
the field.

Apl. 10th   All the men from Coffin's go to Fripp's to help load cotton
at daylight; our Driver goes over about 8 A.M. & finds the Cotton all
loaded & steamer leaving.   Men come back hungry and won't work in
field to-day.   Women get uneasy without them & quit early.   I paddle
across to Fripp's Point in a canoe & teach School, paddling back about
sunset.   The team I had sent to Mr. Eustis's for salt comes back with it
& our rations for April, also letters from home up to March 27th   Also
hear that two boxes clothing have arrived at Eustis's for Mr. Gannett, &
I order mule cart sent for them to-morrow   Mr. Salisbury informs me
he wants a scow crew of 4 good men for several days excursion to the
further side of Morgan island to collect cotton.   This being an extra
piece of civility on his part to *tell me* he wanted the men before taking
them I put it down to his credit.   I don't like to let the men go, for we
are already short by 24 smart young hands of the usual number here,
leaving scarce any but women, children and old men to plant; but I have
no authority to say no and so assent.

Apl. 11th   People all start for the Cotton field in good humor.   Driver
is called off by Mr. Salisbury to furnish him with the crew: while he is
absent from field, the people, mostly women and children, say among
themselves "Here are 24 of our husbands and brothers gone to work for
their own selves,* what's the use of our workg for our Driver or massa.
Let's go work for ourselves too and away they scatter, the greater part
go to work listing Cotton ground in detached patches, scattered all over

---

*The men were earning wages working in Union army camps or
collecting abandoned cotton.

300 acres, in a most republican spirit, but not in a way to be encouraged at present.   Some go catching crabs, some go planting corn on their own hook.   All leave the field early.   I go out and find the Driver utterly discouraged, says it's no use bothering with such people, & he goes to planting in his own patch too.   Now this would do well enough in a more advanced state of civilization, but just now it must be treated as chaos & insubordination, for under such a system, the non-workers, old folks, &c. would starve.   I walk about among some of them & tell them this day's work will count them nothing on my book, & that if they don't work as the driver tells them, I shall never give them any salt, or clothing or anything else.   Visiting Fripp's plantation in P.M. I find all in good order, corn & potatoes all planted & about 15 acres cotton land ready for planting.

April 12.   Go out with the people early and see them go to work cheerfully, planting cotton seed.   About 20 acres ready on this plantation, which they will plant to-day.   I find one man a little saucy to the driver & give him a lecture, sending him about his work.   I find my hint about the *salt* has taken effect, & the people appear to work willingly and cheerfully.   In fact they are the most docile and easily managed people in the world, & I can only admire the amount of patience exhibited under such untoward circumstances.   This plantation shows more demoralization than any other on the island I am told.   The reason is plain enough.   The 79th N.Y. [*Infantry*] were quartered here for some time, making a slaughter house of this building where we now live, killing some 80 head of cattle, eating lots of their sweet potatoes & leaving barely enough for seed.   The soldiers hired the men for cooks, & told them they were free to do as they pleased now, they need never mind a driver any more, that each of them was good as a driver &c. telling them to go to work each on his own patch, & raise what

corn they wanted.   Now this may have been meant well enough, but it
had a most chaotic effect.   Men should be careful how they disorganize
labor if they don't substitute a better organization in the place of that
they pull down.   They ought to have seen that with a rude childlike
people like these, any independant individual action was not to be
expected to succeed except in isolated cases.   They neglected to tell
them that they must plant cotton to pay for clothes, & every other
comfort which they expected to receive except corn & potatoes.   The
natural disgust for cotton labor was left to brood till we arrived, &
nothing but corn ground was prepared except on Mr. Eustis's who came
before.   Thanks to the natural good sense of the negroes, they prepared
a good deal of land for corn on their own responsibility with no orders
from any one but their drivers.   I think I may be able to plant 100 acres
cotton here and 50 or 60 on each of the Fripp plantations, but can't
promise.   I hope that the cloth for summer clothes will be forthcoming.
I gave a list of the articles furnished by Coffin every 6 mos. to Mr. Pierce
a month ago, & Mr. Gannett sent a copy to Mr. Emerson some 2 weeks
since.   I enclose another copy for you.   Mr Pierce thinks northern
benevolence will supply it.   But I think the Government *ought* to.   It is
a good large pile when applied to 8000 people.

.   .   .   .

Considering the fact that a limited amt. of clothing has already been
supplied both from northern contributions and purchases by negroes
with money earned about camps, & by selling eggs chickens &c, the
whole of the above amt. would not be required now, but they will
doubtless earn enough by the Cotton labor to pay for the whole, & we
mean to give out clothing when we get enough to go round, at a low
price, charging it to them on account of their Cotton labor as I do the
salt, of which I have bought enough to give a quart all round on my 3

plantations once.   I suppose Mr. Gannett reports all about the schools, so I say nothing.   He teaches 3 daily & I teach one, when not interrupted by other duties.   He is working harder than he ought to do when the weather gets hot, but is probably none the worse for it now.   I shall endeavor to hold him back bye & bye.   We enjoy excellent health. Let us hear from you how matters look at your point of view.   Truly yrs,

HLcSr   (Signed)   E. S. Philbrick[1]

In the Sea Islands, virtually all the planters had abandoned their estates at the approach of Union forces, but in the sugar-growing region of southern Louisiana many planters remained at home af-ter federal occupation, asserted their loyalty to the Union, and de-manded that federal authorities uphold their right to their slaves. As a result, slaves in southern Louisiana usually had to run away to obtain freedom. By the fall of 1862, thousands had fled to New Orleans and the army camps on its outskirts. Their escape enraged planters, who needed workers for the forthcoming harvest. It also worried General Benjamin F. Butler, the federal commander in the region. He sought not only to appease unionist planters, but also to reduce the army's heavy outlays for the relief of destitute civilians. In consultation with planters, Butler devised an arrangement whereby military officials would provide laborers from among the runaway slaves to planters who agreed to pay them wages. The agreement prohibited corporal punishment and limited the planters' prerogatives in other ways, but promised that the Union army would enforce discipline. Although it left unsettled whether the laborers were legally free, the agreement nevertheless marked a significant break with slavery.

[*New Orleans, La.   late October?, 1862*]
Memorandum
of an arrangement entered into between the Planters, loyal citizens of

the United States, in the Parishes of St. Bernard and Plaquemines, in
the State of Louisiana, and the Civil and Military authorities of the
United States in said State.

Whereas many of the persons held to service and labor have left their
masters and claimants and have come to the city of New Orleans and to
the Camps of the army of the Gulf, and are claiming to be emancipated
and free,   And whereas these men and women are in a destitute
condition,   And whereas it is clearly the duty, by Law, as well as in
humanity of the United States to provide them with food and clothing,
and to employ them in some useful occupation,

And whereas it is necessary that the crop of cane and cereals, now
growing and approaching maturity in said Parishes shall be preserved
and the Levees repaired and strengthened against floods;

And whereas the Planters claim that these persons are still held to
service and labor, and of right ought to labor for their masters, and the
ruin of their crops and plantations will happen if deprived of such
services,

And whereas these conflicting rights and claims cannot immediately
be determined by any tribunals now existing in the State of Louisiana;

In order therefore to preserve the rights of all parties, as well those of
the Planters as of the persons, claimed as held to service and labor and
claiming their freedom, and those of the United States, and to preserve
the crops and property of loyal citizens of the United States and to
provide profitable employment at the rate of compensation fixed by act
of Congress for those persons who have come within the lines of the
army of the United States,*

---

*The Militia Act of July 1862 set the wages of black military laborers
at $10 per month, $3 of which could take the form of clothing.
(*Statutes at Large*, vol. 12, pp. 597–600.)

It is agreed and determined that the United States will employ all the persons heretofore held to labor on the several plantations in the Parishes of St. Bernard and Plaquemines belonging to loyal citizens as they have heretofore been employed and as nearly as may be under the charge of the Loyal Planters and overseers of said Parishes and other necessary directions.

The United States will authorize or provide suitable guards and patrols to preserve order and prevent crime in the said Parishes.

The Planters shall pay for the services of each able-bodied male persons Ten (10) Dollars per month, three (3) of which may be expended for necessary clothing, and for each woman   dollars, and for each child above the age of ten (10) years and under the age of sixteen (16) years the sum of   dollars, all the persons above the age of sixteen years being considered as men and women for the purpose of labor.

Planters shall furnish suitable and proper food for each of these laborers and take care of them and furnish proper medicines in case of sickness,

The Planters shall also suitably provide for all the persons incapacitated by sickness or age, for labor bearing the relation of Parent child or wife of the laborer so laboring for him.

Ten hours each day shall be a day's labor, and any extra hours during which the laborer may be called by the necessities of the occasion to work shall be reckoned as so much towards another days labor,   Twenty six days of ten hours each shall be deemed a month's labor except in the month of December, when twenty shall make a month's labor,   It shall be the duty of the overseer to keep a true and exact account of the time of labor of each person and any wrong or inaccuracy therein shall forfeit a months pay to the person so wronged.

No cruel or corporal punishment shall be inflicted by any one upon the

persons so laboring or upon his or her relatives, but any insubordination
or refusal to perform suitable labor or other crime or offence shall be at
once reported to the Provost Marshal, for the district and punishment
suitable for the offence shall be inflicted under his orders preferably
imprisonment in darkness on bread and water.

This arrangement to continue at the pleasure of the United States.

If any Planter of the Parishes of St. Bernard or Plaquemines refuse
to enter into this arrangement or remains a disloyal citizen, the persons
claimed & to be held to service, by him may hire themselves to any loyal
Planter or the United States may elect to carry on his plantations by
their own agents and other persons than those thus claimed may be
hired by any planter at his election.   It is expressly understood and
agreed that this arrangement shall not be held to effect, after its
termination, the legal rights of either master or slave; but that the
question of freedom or slavery are to be determined by considerations
wholly outside of the provisions of this contract, provided always that
the abuse of any master or overseer of any person laboring under the
provisions of this contract shall after trial and adjudication by the
military or other courts emancipate the person so abused.[2]

HD

Former slaves in southern Louisiana expected more from freedom
than wage labor under close supervision. When conflicts arose between laborers and their employers, Union soldiers often partici-
pated in settling them. Newly recruited black soldiers, many of
whom had themselves been slaves, commonly allied with the plantation workers. A Northerner who was managing a sugar estate
complained to General Butler's successor about the treatment he

had received from black soldiers and three of their officers, Captain
Hannibal Carter, Lieutenant George F. Watson, and Lieutenant
Frank L. Trask, who were freemen of African descent.*

Raceland Plantation [*Lafourche Parish, La.*] Jan. 5 1863

Sir— As manager of this Plantation I desire to mak complaint against
Capt. Carter, Lieut. Watson, & Trask, of Co. C. 2nd Reg. La. N[*ative*].
G[*uard*]. for interfering with work on this place

Having come to this Country as guid to Gen Weitzels Brigade and then
by the Generals advice and concent I have undertaken to save if possible a
part of the Sugar crop that was spoiling in the field. After making
satisfactory arangements with the owners of the place I employed hands
at $15 per month for good men and others in proportion to what they
could do   On the 10th of last Nov. I commenced with every prospect of
success all the hands working well and seemed Satisfied and
contented   Capt Carter was Camped on the Rail Road near my
place   his men was allowed to go upon the place as they pleased   some
eight or ten H[*ogs*]h[*ea*]ds of Sugar was taken from the place   Theas
Soldiers was so much with my hands that very little work could be
done   I asked the Officers repeatedly to keep their men away that the
work might go on   they promised to do so but have since acknowledged
themselves unable to controul their men   I was arrested taken to the
Camp where they threatened to shoot me and then let me go wieth no
punishment nor did they charge me with any crime; and I do not know
what the arrest was made for.   I suppose it was to show the hands that
they the Soldiers was masters and, that obediance was due them, and not
me.   They tell my hands that there is no necesity of their doing any work

*Black freemen held commissioned office in several regiments of
Louisiana Native Guards that were incorporated into Union ranks in
August 1862. (See below, pp. 437–38.)

that the Government will feed and care for them whether they work or
not; and language to this effect is repeated to them every day   They try
every means to excite the hands to insubordination by telling them that I
am a Rebel and calling me other names to profane or obscean to be
repeated here,   Thay have threatened my life four or five times cocking
and caping their muskets pointing them at my head and declairing with
an oath that thay would blow out my brains, and when I go to the Camp
to complain to the Officer the threats are repeated   Many shoots have
been fired at me in the night   I saw the flash of their guns and heared
the balls whisel   theas Soldiers were about here with their muskets a
short time befoe the fireing and I suppose it was them that did it

I believe thay intend to take my life when thay can do it and eccape
punishment   Many of my hands (the wimen) spend most of the day
time in the Camps and return with a gang of Soldiers at evening to
carous the night away.   Thay have so demorlized the hands that I was
obliged to stop the [*sugar*] Mill at a lose of not less than two thousund
Dollars in spoiled Cane and Lost fuel.   I have now been under arrest for
two days by orders of Lieut. Watson for Assault & Battery   I have
asked for a tryal but have not had it nor do I expect it soon as Lieut
Watson has gon to New Orleans   I have not been informend where or
when the aleged crime was commited.   I do not know that I have given
them cause for offence unless my desire to be let alone is one and they
have never asked a favor of me that I have not granted if it was in my
power to do so   I cannot go ahead with the work on this place unless I
can controul the labor I pay for

Sir As a Loyal Citizen of the State of Illinois I respectfully clame that
protection due the Subjects of the United States   Respectfully yours
Truly

ALS   J. A. Pickens[3]

Captain Carter gave a different account of events at Raceland plantation. Before Pickens arrived, Carter had persuaded "a number" of slaves to remain at work; had placed a guard on the plantation, at the owner's request, after the overseer was "threatened by some of the hands"; and had ordered the slaves to return sugar and furniture taken for their own use. Soldiers in his company who made unauthorized visits to the plantation or threatened Pickens had been punished. Far from advising plantation hands not to work, Carter and his fellow officers had "endeavored to impress upon their minds the neccessity of labor." The shutting down of the sugar mill he attributed not to interference by his soldiers but to "lack of hands"; "numbers [had] left on account of cruel treatment," and "sickness [had] so thinned [Pickens's] forces that it was not possible to continue." The cause of Pickens's arrest, Carter explained, was his abuse of women workers on the plantation; among other misdeeds, he had evicted "a woman with her suckling babe only because she was a soldiers wife."[4]

Former slaves throughout the Union-occupied South aspired to farm on their own, without the intrusion of a plantation owner, overseer, or government agent. Very few got the opportunity. Freedpeople on one abandoned plantation in southern Louisiana received permission from a nearby federal officer to work the estate, only to have another claimant challenge their right to do so. They appealed to the provost marshal general of the Union army's Department of the Gulf.

Camp Hoyt   Terre Bonne [*La.*]   April 5th/63.

Sir   We the undersigned Negroes residing on Major Potts Plantation Parish Terre Bonne La. respectfully submit to you the following statement;

Captain Goodrich Provost Marshal at Thibodeaux told us to go on and cultivate the land on the Plantation, and do something for

ourselves, until the Government could do something for us and gave
orders for all the Stray Mules belonging to the plantation to be brought
in, so that we could work the land, and we understood that we were to be
protected in our labor— We have about 60 Arpents* of land broken up
a large portion of which is already planted, and the balance ready for
planting. Now a Mr Wright comes on the plantation with Authority
from the Government to work it and claims the result of our labor—
We have had a hard struggle to get along and we feel it hard now that we
have succeeded in making ourselves in a measure independent, to have
to [*turn*] it all over to someone else.

We have at present on the place about 14 men, 23 women 10 of whom
are old and with Children, 24 Small Children & Babies. Under the
circumstances we think it but just that we should be allowed to work the
land already broken up and planted on equal shares with the
Government.

We therefore ask your aid and assistance in having secured to us what
was promised us by Provost Marshal Cap't Goodrich—and the
posession of the property we [*have?*] and land acquired by our labor.

Henry Norvall	Littleton Saunders,
Claiborn Thomas,	Thos Essex,
Thornton Boller,	Phil Sergeant,
Thos Mathews,	Parker Williams,
Jefferson Rounds,	Nelson McClenny,[5]

HLSr

A Union officer attested to the accomplishments of the freedpeople
on the Potts plantation.

---

*Approximately 50 acres. (An arpent is an old French unit of
measurement equal to .85 acre.)

Terre Bonne   Louisiana   April 5 1863,

At the request of some of the contrabands on the plantation of Major Potts I have visited the plantation & certify to the following facts.

1. They appear to be of unusual respectability & bear a good character, giving all the evidences of neat, thrifty & industrious laborers,

2. They have broken up & partially planted with corn as nearly as I can compute about sixty arpents of land and have acquired some corn & cotton seed sufficient I should judge for planting this ground.

3 From what I can learn they have thus far received no aid from the government but have supported themselves creditably by their own exertions & labor—although a very large proportion are aged men, women & young children.

ADS   *Charles C Nott.*[6]

As a result of their petition and Nott's support, the freedpeople retained control of the estate. In August, an agent of the Treasury Department reported that they had worked "without the assistance of any white man; they have made sufficient Corn for their own use and some to sell" and enough cane to produce as many as fifty hogsheads of sugar. "The Negroes," he continued, "are contented and happy and larger returns will be found from the management of this place than any one I have seen managed by inexperienced Govm't agents or Soldiers."[7]

Northerners in the Union-occupied South generally saw no contradiction between doing good for the former slaves and doing well for themselves. As a plantation superintendent in the South Carolina Sea Islands, Edward Philbrick had chafed under the restrictions of working for the government. Northern businessmen, he believed, could introduce former slaves to the system of free labor far more ef-

fectively, while making a profit in the bargain. With wartime short-
ages pushing the price of cotton to record heights, many Northern
capitalists were eager to invest in Southern cotton-planting.

In early 1863, having resigned his position as a plantation superintendent, Philbrick and a consortium of investors purchased
eleven Sea-Island plantations from the government. In a single
stroke, Philbrick became the largest planter in the Union-occupied
islands; as manager of the consortium's holdings, he presided over
8,000 acres and more than 900 laborers. Later that year, in a letter
to a War Department commission, Philbrick set forth the principles that had guided his efforts to reorganize labor. As he described
his operations, he unwittingly revealed numerous ways in which
the demands and aspirations of the freedpeople had forced him to
modify those principles.

13 India St   Boston [*Mass.*]   August 17th 1863
· · · ·

As it may be of interest to you to hear of the attempts already made in
detail towards the re-organization of labor which have come under my
notice I will attempt a short history of our expenses [*experiences*] in that
work.

Having to deal with large numbers of laborers and large areas of land,
where the old organization had melted away, from the sudden removal of
its only stamina [*stimulus*] the, lash. we found the people timid Even to
suspicion, & little inclined to believe what we had to say to them by way
of advice.   The white race had they far been known to them as a sort of
natural Enemy, against which it behoved Every man to be on his guard,
and it was only after a *personal acquaintance with* the character of their
individual Employers that they could be induced to believe Enough of
our promises to feel any confidence in our disposition to *pay* for their
labor.   In this state it was nearly impossible to Employ them to labor

regularly by the day or Month with any satisfactory result   Their
previous life had been such as to Educate them most thoroughly in the
art of shirking & had faild to give the labor that pride in the faithful
performance, which can arise only from self respect and requited
labor   When at work by the day. some few of the older and more
faithful hands began by doing a fair days work as re[quired] of
all   The young and careless ones. found of play, and less serious in
their intentions invariably began by shirking, and continued by a serious
of daily Experiments to test the minimum of labor which would be
accepted by their Employers as a days work.

The faithful ones soon followed their Example, not wishing to furnish
more labor for their money than did the lazy ones.

The result was soon found to be the Entire failure to accomplish
anything regular or definite.   An attempt was then made to fix a
standard for a days work, and to record Every day, by means of the
reports of the black foreman; the Exact amount of work done by Each
hand.

Here a new trouble arose in the lack of organization and the difficulty
of creating any.

All systems of day wages presuppose an independent, unprejudiced
foreman who Enjoys the confidence of the laborers and who controls the
time and manner doing the work; he must also keep a record of the
amount of work done by Each laborer and be responsible to his
Employer for the correct preformance of the work.

The black drivers appointed by the former masters. had always been
in the habit of doing this duty, reporting to the overseer Every night all
cases of dilinquency, which were duly punished by the lash.

But the position of this driver was purely artificial.

Selected from among the crowed from whom he was distinguished

only by a slightly superior animal Energy and mental Endowment, but
not by any peculiar Education he was sustained in his authority merely
the power of the owner represented by the lash.

Now that this power had vanished. the driver had lost his prestige and
in place of it was the object of hatred and jealousy among the crowed,
almost every one of whom had old scores to settle with him.   His
authority was a cypher, and he could not be relied upon to render an
account of the work done daily by the several hands simply because
Each hand had been at work when & how it pleased him, or her to
go.   In the absence of any men, who Enjoyed the confidence of those
people to a degree to enable any authority to be used, after trying a
change of foremen with little success, we cast about us for some means
by which the result of each mans labor could be made to show for itself
in the crop to be judge of at the amount produced.   The Eagerness with
which this proposal was sezed by the negroes themselves was an Earnest
of its success.

The planting had already been done by working in the old fashioned
"gang" but the field was readily divided in such lots or patches as could
be managed by single families, and a share of the field assigned to Each
for the season in such proportions as they desired.   The responsibility of
the crop was thus thrown upon Each family separately, to the Extent of
its patch in the field and a price per lb was offerd for the cotton.

But the daily wants of the people could not wait for the harvest of the
crop, without some help.   Some partial payments must be made which
[*while*] the crop was growing in order to keep up the interest in the work
inspired confidence in their current wants.   It was Evident that all
payments of this sort must be made with great caution in order that
they might be proportioned, as nearly as possible to the amount of labor
actually performed   To secure this end, the field were mapped so that

riding over them I could always tell on whose patch, I happened to stand at any moment.

Occasional Examinations were made of the state of the crop & the thoroughness of the cultivation   For every hoeing 50 cents per acre was paid, the payment being made monthly as nearly as possible.

The success of this system has Exceeded our hopes   The division of the land into these temporary allotment gives the laborers a proprietary interest in the crop & he feels as if working for himself.   The more Efficnt and endustrious soon showed the Effects of their industry by the superior condition of their crops.

Their care and attention soon gave evidence, that they understood the details of cultivation and needed no help on that subject which we could afford.

They took an evident pride in the condition of their crops.   The more industrious soon ridiculed the lazier, for the neglected appearance of their fields and view [vied] with each other in the excellence of the cultivation.

The above experience relates to those cases, where large numbers of laborers fell under the management of a limited number of employers.   In cases where small proprietors begin by working in the field themselves, with a few negroes, or by spending the greater part of the time in the immediate supervision of the labor. I have no doubt that the negroes could be advantageously hired by the day or month.

Such a course, by keeping the control of the work, in the hands of white men, who have a larger share of forethought and energy than the negroes, besides acquired knowledge would conduce to the misprovement [improvement] of their methods of culture; the introduction of new manners, implements &c.   Still the system which our circumstances forced us to adopt, i.e. the tempory allotments of land to separate families, certainly tends to the advancement of the laborer, by developing in him a degree of self-reliance forethought and industry and may in the end be attained, with many of the good results which would be gained, by a more intelligent supervision, and control.

As the welfare of the negroes and the value of their services may be greatly enhanced, by such rudiments of education, as can readily be given them, any system of government, which looks to the permanent good of the community, will provide for this.   The children learn, and a small number of the adults with great eagerness.   There are now five teachers at work, upon the estates which I bought, their salary, being charged to the [general?] expenses of the work.   At some future time the people will perhaps provide for the education at their own expense, but during the present state of society, some provision should be made for furnishing such privileges, either at the expense of the Govt or the proprietors of the soil.   Very respectfully Your obedient Servant

HLcSr   Edw. S. Philbrick.[8]

If most freedpeople strove to achieve independence through self-directed cultivation of land, some sought opportunities in Union-occupied towns and cities. The presence of federal troops and the influx of civilians from the surrounding countryside created new customers for artisans, tradesmen, and small-scale merchants. These petty proprietors included a number of former slaves, among them Samuel Larkin, a freedman from Alabama who had followed the Union army into Tennessee. In 1863, Larkin used $500 of his hard-earned wages (including earnings from military labor) to establish a freight-hauling business in Nashville, a major military post. His independent status was undermined in August of that year, when Northern soldiers seized his horses and wagons for the use of the army. Denied payment for his property at that time, Larkin sought compensation from a federal commission established after the war.

[*Nashville, Tenn.   February 9, 1872*]

Samuel Larkin Claimant

vs

The Government of the United States

Samuel Larkin aged 31 years being duly sworn and examined by his Attorny A. W. Wills stated as follows:

Am a colored man.   I live in Davidson County. Ten miles from Nashville on the Lebanon Turnpike—have lived there, and about two miles from there since 1864—   Before the War I lived in Huntsville Ala. and came to Nashville Tenn. with Col. Chapins Regiment (Union) in 1862. and remained with the Regiment several months.   I then settled in Nashville. and had with me about five hundred Dollars. that I had made by working. which money I invested in horses.   I bought three horses one mule. and a blind horse. which animals I worked in teams hauling different stores &c. for merchants and others in Nashville Tenn. and did an express business.   I kept my stock in a stable on Vine St. near Church.   Sometime in the month of August 1863, my three horses, mule and blind horse—were working as usual. two of the horses in one wagon. two in another. and the mule in a dray. when a squad of Soldiers under charge of an Officer took them all. wagons and dray included. drove them to a Government Wagon yard on corner of Broad and Spruce Sts. Nashville Tenn. when one of my drivers came to me. (I was then working on Cedar St. Nashville) and told me the Government Troops had taken all my stock.   I immediately went to the Wagon yard on corner of Broad & Spruce Sts. and found my wagons. and the Blind horse—   they had taken the other three horses and the mule on toward the Camps on Franklin Turnpike.   I followed on out, and met the Officer and Soldiers who had my stock with others. and I asked the Officer to return me my Stock.   he asked if I could point them out.   I said yes. and did so— He then said he could not return them. that he had orders to press all serviceable stock he could find. for the use of the Government, but that I would be paid in full for all my Stock.   Upon finding that I could not get my Stock, I returned to the aforesaid Wagon Yard and my blind horse. with the two Wagons was returned to me. but I never got back the three horses and mule. nor did I ever get pay for the same— I saw my three horses and mule. many times afterward. being driven in Government teams. and used by the Government.

. . . .

his
Samuel $\times$ Larkin[9]
mark

HDSr

Larkin had submitted a claim for \$400; he was awarded \$350.[10]

Whereas some former slaves purchased property after becoming free, others brought property with them into Union lines when they escaped from slavery. Such goods included not only personal effects like clothing and bedding, but also tools, wagons, and livestock. But in the absence of strong evidence to the contrary, federal authorities generally assumed that such items belonged to the fugitives' owners and were therefore subject to seizure by the army. This practice dismayed the freedpeople, who had expected to use the property for their own betterment. General John P. Hawkins, commander of the District of Northeastern Louisiana, sympathized with their position and made an ingenious argument on their behalf to the departmental commander.

Goodrichs Landing [*La.*]   Oct. 9. 1863.

General,   A nice and peculiar question has come up in this District as to the rights of a negro, coming into our lines from the country occupied by the enemy, to the property he may bring with him such as mules oxen or wagons,   When the case has been brought up before me I have decided the right of property in favor of the negro.   President Lincolns [*Emancipation*] Proclamation gives legal freedom to the slaves,   The masters in the lines of the enemy deprive them. of this right and attempt to hold them contrary to law,   I hold it no crime that the slave should attempt to escape this wrong and in so doing has a right to make use of the facilities that might assist him in his escape by taking horse, mule or any thing else of his masters that might help him to get away,   We have a distinguished precedent for this when the children of Israel went out fugitive slaves from the Egyptians,   Again, I think the negro should hold the property as his own which he has secured by his energy and effort, and that it is a very small thing on the part of a Government that should be magnanimous towards such persons to take it away from him,   By letting the property remain in their possission, they will be enabled next year to cultivate a few acres of ground and the Gov,ment be relieved of their support,   By taking it away they or their families are made paupers for perhaps all time to come,   The immediate gain to Gov,ment by the seizure is very small compared with the great loss to them,   As the wealth of a Gov,ment consists in the prosperity of its Citizens, and as these people have been declared Citizens of the United States nothing is gained to Gov,ment by interfering with the individual prosperity of any one of them,   Many of them now use their property to make a living,   when planting season comes they will be able to do a great deal better if they have half a chance,   I am willing to run this District without instructions, without troubling the Department

Commander on delicate questions that may arise, and would not write now only that General Thomas intends to refer the matter to Dept. H^d Qrs. for decision and I wished to present my views of the question. I am Genl, Very Respectfully Your Obdt, Servt,

ALS   John P. Hawkins[11]

> General William T. Sherman, Hawkins's commander, was not persuaded. "The negro on his becoming free," Sherman ruled, "has no right to the property of his former owner, unless by special gift. All property belonging to their former Masters brought within our lines by negroes should be taken charge of at once by the Government."[12]

In the spring of 1863, after Union troops took control of the west bank of the Mississippi River, opposite Vicksburg, federal commissioners began leasing abandoned cotton plantations to Northern investors and to a handful of freedmen who were judged competent to manage a plantation on their own. The lessees agreed to hire former slaves who had gathered at military posts and in contraband camps, paying them wages and providing food and clothing for both the workers and their dependents. But the Northerners, drawn south by the prospect of bonanza profits, often failed to fulfill their obligations. To make matters worse, planting proceeded in the midst of a military campaign. Confederate raiders killed dozens of laborers and lessees, reenslaved hundreds of freedpeople, and disrupted work on the cotton crop. Instructed in mid-September to inspect "the Condition of the Contrabands in [the district,] including those under the care of Government Agents[,] the floating population & those in the employment of Government Lessees,"[13] Major Julian E. Bryant made the following report to the headquarters of the District of Northeastern Louisiana.

Goodrich's Landing   Dist. N.E. La.   October 10th 1863.
Captain: I have the honor to make the following report of my tour of
duty up to the present time, as Inspecting Officer to enquire into the
condition of the Contrabands in this District, as required by S[*pecial*].
O[*rders*]. No. 14 from District Head Quarters.

In my report I have divided the contrabands into three classes.   1st,
those on plantations controlled by Government Lessees: 2nd: those on
what are called Infirmary Farms, and in camps controlled by
Government Agents, and 3rd: the floating population, including those in
the temporary employ of Government Contractors for wood, etc,

The estimates I have made of the numbers of Contrabands on
plantations & in camps the number of deaths, and the amount of crops
and stock on the places may not be perfectly correct, as I had in most
cases to depend on the statements of negroes and interested parties,
modified by my own Judgement.   I regret to state that in no case have I
found a strict compliance with the terms of their contracts on the part of
Lessees of plantations, and in too many an utter disregard of even the
commonest principles of humanity and the rights of individuals, in their
treatment of the contrabands.   Generally the negro has been treated by
those employing him, as a mere brute, from whom the greatest amount
of labor should be gained at the least possible expense: and not as a free
citizen with personal rights and immunities.   No schools have been
established, with one or two exceptions, and those have been taught by
intelligent negroes who were on the plantations and who were unfit for
other labor.   Almost nothing has been done to raise the negro to a
higher level, or to convince him that our Government is in earnest in its
declarations that he is a free man with all a freeman's rights and
privileges.   In this District during the past summer he has been in a far
more servile and pitiable condition than when a slave under his master.

Some it is true have a false idea of their freedom and its responsibilities, thinking that it releases them from all restraint, and are consequently roving the country stealing and committing depredations on property: but it has been demonstrated that the majority, if stimulated by the right kind of treatment, proper wages, and a prospect of bettering their condition, would labor faithfully and steadily: while some show a capacity for management an energy and executive ability that would do credit, to men of better education and a whiter skin. The contrabands in the District are generally much in want of clothing, and unless it is furnished before winter they will suffer much from its want. Many who had a supply in the spring have been robbed of it or had it burned in their quarters. I have in my report given the condition of the contrabands on each plantation & camp.

Contrabands on "Infirmary Farms"

These are plantations on which were placed by the Government Commissioners, aged and infirm contrabands and their families, who could not be disposed of on the leased plantations. Two of these known as the Savage and Front Raliegh plantations are situated on the river a mile & a mile and a half respectively below Goodrich's Landing: the others known as the Richardson Blackman, Stone, Hardison and Carry plantations, are situated west of the "telegraph road" leading from Goodrich Landing to Millikens Bend. The majority of these contrabands depend on Government for subsistence, which they draw weekly from the Commissary for Contrabands" at Goodrich Landing.

The ration issued, consists of bacon, flour, salt and rye coffee, and occasionally rice, beans and sugar. Some of these contrabands have planted cotton, corn, potatoes and other vegitables, which have generally yeilded fine crops: but no system seems to have been adopted to compel them to support themselves, and therefore many well able to work are idle. What crops there are, on these places, are due solely to the exertions of a few individuals.   In some cases Government has furnished mules.   The remainder of the stock on these places has been collected from the abandoned plantations in the vicinity.   A portion of the negroes are earning a good living by the sale of vegitables, by day's work, and by cutting wood.

The health on these places is generally good at present: but there has been a great deal of sickness and mortality amongst them during the past summer.   The supply of medicines has been very limited.   On the "Savage" farm, a hospital is established for Contrabands, and also a pest house for small pox cases.   The Surgeon in charge Dr H. H. Littlefield has been there but a short time: but his hospital shows evidence of great improvement in cleanliness and system.   Medical supplies and hospital stores are greatly needed.

On one farm, the "Savage," there is a school of about twenty children taught by a lame negro, which is the only instance of any effort being made for the mental improvment of the children on these farms.

Only an approximate estimate can be made of the numbers on the farms, the number of deaths, or the amount of the crops.

Below is given the estimate which I have made of the persons and crops on these farms.

Total number of Contrabands:	1057
" " of Field hands	304
" " " Sick	95
" " Deaths	300
No of acres of Cotton	189
" " " Corn	245
" " " Potatoes and Other Vegitables	52

No. of Mules	26
" " Cattle	42
" " Hogs	15.

Contrabands on Leased Plantations.

The "Bell Plantation" leased by Cha's Hays and Co. is situated about three miles below Goodrich Landing on the river. The Lessees have been absent from the plantation for nearly three months. Since July 1st but little has been furnished for the comfort of the contrabands employed. Rations have been limited, and recently the negro in charge, has purchased rations from his own means to supply the hands. But few medicines were on the place, and the contrabands had applied to and recieved medical assistance from the army surgeons at Goodrich's Landing. No clothing has been furnished, although the blacks are much in need of it and no school established. The sickness of the Lessee Mr Hayes may be a partial excuse for the neglect of the colored people on the place. The total number of contrabands, is ninety (90). No. of field hands, sixty (60). No. of deaths during the season, twenty three (23). No. of acres of cotton four hundred (400). No. of mules sixty (60): of cattle thirty (30). of hogs thirteen (13).

Since my first visit to this place the Lessees have returned, and the negroes are better provided for than before.

The plantation leased by Mr Newman, the owner, is the next below on the river. The care of the contrabands is quite good although the full ration required has not been issued, although perhaps that lack may have been compensated for by the issue of vegetables etc, which have been furnished them. No school has been organized for the children. The number of contrabands on the place is one hundred & thirteen (113). No. of field hands forty four (44). No of sick five (5): No. of death during the season, eleven (11).   No of acres of cotton one hundred & seventy (170): of corn fifty (50).   No. of mules thirty five (35), of cattle twelve (12).   The Lessee complains of the want of power to make the negroes work.

The plantation known as the (Back) Raliegh place is situated one and a half miles below Goodrich's Landing and the same distance back from the river.   The contrabands here are in good condition in regard to health.   The ration furnished is meal, salt and fresh meat.   A little rice, flour, sugar and coffee has been kept for issue and sale.   There is no school.   A small quantity of clothing has been furnished, and a few have recieved wages.   Medicines have been furnished in good quantities. The number of persons on the place is about one hundred and fifty (150)   Number of field hands seventy two (72).   No of deaths during the past season fifteen (15).   No. of acres of cotton four hundred (400). of corn thirty (30).   No of mules forty (40) of cattle ten (10).   The crop of cotton is being gathered in by the field hands.   Since the first visit to the place, I find that *no rations* are issued to persons unfit for work.   The Henderson place, situated about half way between Goodrich Landing and Milliken's Bend, on the river, and leased by J. Williams & Co. shows the evidence of good management, and of consideration for the wants of those employed.

Rations of meal, flour, meat, molasses, grits and beans are issued: and coffee, sugar etc are kept on hand for sale at reasonable prices to the contrabands.   Money has been paid when called for in sums of from two to twenty dollars.   The Lessees intend the purchase of at Memphis or St Louis as soon as the cotton crop can be forwarded.   The number of persons on the place is two hundred and twenty (220).   No. of field hands one hundred and eighty eight (188).   No. of acres of cotton six hundred (600)   No. of bales. three hundred (300)   No. of mules thirty two (32).

The Harris' places leased by John Dunham, adjoins the Henderson place below. The contrabands on this place I found badly cared for and discontented. Meal and a little salt pork is issued to them and they are allowed the privilege of killing cattle and hogs on the plantations and in the woods. There are on the places two hundred, and eleven persons unfit for work, old, infirm, or maimed or children, who have to be supported, and only seventy (70) field hands, The number of deaths has been, during the past season, sixty three (63), No. of acres of cotton four hundred (400). No of bales of cotton three hundred (300). There is no school on the place, & the place has evidently been badly managed, The negroes are allowed to prowl around nights and steal mules, hogs and cattle, from the neighboring plantations.

The Harding place, three miles back from Millikens Bend has been abandoned since this Lessee Mr Walker was taken prisoner by the rebels in June last. A few contrabands, about thirty in number, have returned there and have commenced picking the cotton, of which it is estimated there will be two hundred bales. No attention has been paid to these negroes by any one. They have been living on fresh meat killed in the woods, and on the corn obtained on the place— It is reported that the cotton crop is claimed by Mr Dunham Lessee of the Harris places.

The "Compromise" and "Parham" places leased by Farmer and Dunlap: the "Orkney & Buckner places leased by J. W. Green lying back from Millikens Bend have been neglected by the Lessees during the summer: but they have returned within a few days to secure what crops there are on the places. I could not learn that any rations had been issued to the negroes since the fore part of summer. The negroes have subsisted mainly on the corn and meat obtained from the country around.

The "Outpost" plantation a part of which is leased by Duke & Hotchkiss is situated two miles back from Goodrich Landing. The treatment of the negro in the main seems to be good.   The ration issued is mainly salt meat, meal & molasses,   Sugar, flour and Tobacco are kept for sale to the hands at reasonable prices, though at an advance on first cost.   The crops are small.   The cotton may average one half bale per acre—

The portion of the place leased by Sancho, Humphrey, and Jackson, seems to be quite well managed.   About sixty (60) persons are in thier employ, thirty (30) of whom are field hands   They are well fed, and most of them have a supply of vegitables raised on the place.   No wages have been paid by either of the lessees, on this plantation.   The negroes have depended for medical attendance, on the army surgeons   A school has been established, taught by a black man, in which the children seem to make good progress in reading.   The number of deaths on the whole place during the season has been about forty (40).   The colored Lessees will make about two hundred bales of cotton, and have eighty (80) acres of corn.

The plantations leased in the name of R. V. Montague, & Montague and Clary, known as the Wilton, Buckner, Albion, Steam boat, Mound and Keene Richards places, I found, with the exception of the two latter in an entirely neglected condition.   The Lessees had paid but little attention to them since the raid made by the rebels on the 28th day of June last.   At that time all the quarters and gins on the places were burned with the exception of those on the Wilton place, and the negroes captured or driven from the plantations and scattered.   Many of them came to Goodrich Landing and were there furnished with rations from the Government.   At the time of visiting the plantations I found on the Wilton place about one hundred contrabands who had returned, and on the Buckner Albion and Steam boat places fifty more, all in a most neglected condition.   The quarters were very filthy and there was much consequent sickness. The exposure of these people after being driven from their quarters, caused a great deal of sickness and death. But five barrels of meat had been furnished since last June, no other rations. No wages have been paid and no clothing furnished. Nothing even has been paid for the labor done in gathering in the old crop of cotton which was picked last spring.

The contrabands have evidently been totally neglected, and the terms of the contract disregarded by the Lessees. About four thousand acres of cotton were planted on these places, which will yield probably from three to five hundred bales. Two places originally leased by R. V. Montague and Clary, the Mound & Keene Richards places, have been subleased by a Mr Campbell, who now has charge of them. The contrabands on these places seem much better cared for than on the others, are all at work and quite well supplied with rations. The number of contrabands on these places is one hundred and seventeen (117) of field hands ninety seven (97). No school is established, and no medicines furnished. About three hundred and fifty acres of cotton are being gathered. The number of mules on the place is twenty (20): of cattle twenty (20). The plantations leased by H. B. Tibbetts & L. Dent, Lewis Dent, and Ledbetter and Dent, known as the "Benjamin," "Concord" "Bodine," and "Benton" places, situated near and above Transylvania Landing, suffered much by the raids made upon them last summer by the rebels: but I found that many of the negroes who then left had returned, and were living in temporary quarters, prepared for them; the quarters on most of the places having been burnt down. The hands are kept employed, were paid one months wages in the spring, and are now paid one dollar per hundred pounds for picking cotton. Shoes and a few other articles of clothing have been furnished them during the season. A good supply of rations is furnished and the negroes seem contented, and are humanely treated.   There are nearly four hundred (400) persons on these places: one hundred and sixty (160) of whom are field hands.   Quite a number are sick from exposure and diseases contracted during the summer while they were driven from their quarters.   Between three and four hundred bales of cotton will be made on these places, this season.   The corn crop will be very light.

The plantations leased by [Deweese?], Alexander & Smith known as the "Noland" Bledsoe, Nutt & Neely places are situated near the Omega Landing above Milliken's Bend.   On these places are about one hundred and eighty contrabands.   The ration issued to them is mainly meal and salt meat: occasionally molasses is issued.   The rice, beans and hominy required by contract is but rarely furnished.   No food of a better kind for the use of the sick is issued or even kept for sale: and but little medicine is furnished.   A little clothing has been furnshed them at exorbitant prices.   From eight hundred to one thousand bales of cotton will be made on these places, an amount which would fully justify the Lesses in a liberal and humane treatment of those employed.   The contrabands are much in need of clothing & unless it is furnished soon, they will suffer for the want of it.

Some other plantations, the "Dr Noland—" & "Holly Grove" places, have been entirely abandoned, and have no crops worth gathering.

ALS   Julian E. Bryant[14]

> General John P. Hawkins, who had appointed Bryant to inspect
> the leased plantations, forwarded the report with an endorsement
> calling for fundamental reform.

Goodrichs Landing [*La.*]   Oct. 14, 1863
Respectfully forwarded to Dept H^d Qrs with the recommendation that

the report be forwarded to Washington for the information of the
Sec[*retar*]y of War.   The report does not half show the hardships and ill
treatment the free negroes are subjected to and if better policy for them
cannot be introduced, and humanity, is a matter of consideration we had
better call back their former masters and let them take charge of them.
If a proper policy is adopted they will become good industrious Citizens,
but the present treatment will make vagabonds of them and is doing it
just the same as it would make of white people.   If the vacant lands here
can be divided into farms of from 80 to 200 acres and the farmers of the
north invited down to farm for one year every farmer would make a
moderate fortune the first season and the labor of the negro be in the
market and in demand for what it is worth and the competition would
insure his proper treatment.   As it is now and will be under the system
of large leases a monopoly controls the labor and treatment,   any one
who has seen the emigration to California to dig for gold can know how
the people of the west would flock here to cultivate for one year,   the
banks of the Miss. River would be thickly populated in three months
with a loyal people and the profits to them would be greater than ever
realized from the California or Pikes Peak gold mines

John P. Hawkins[15]

AES

Federal authorities oversaw free labor not only in Union-occupied
plantation regions of the lower South, but also in parts of the upper
South. Beginning in early 1863, military officials took control of
abandoned estates between the York and James rivers, in southeastern Virginia, and on the south side of the James, near Norfolk.
In these areas of tobacco and grain farming, as many black people
had worked on small farms as on large plantations. Superintendents of contrabands designated several dozen properties "government farms" to be worked by freedpeople formerly crowded into con-

traband camps. Because so many men had enlisted in the Union army or were employed at military labor, women and children great-ly predominated on the government farms. Most of the freedpeople worked under overseers and received as wages a portion of the crop they produced; some, however, rented land and farmed it on their own. In testimony before a War Department commission, Francis W. Bird, a prominent Northern abolitionist, recounted his recent tour of southeastern Virginia. He underscored both the obstacles facing the former slaves and the success some had nevertheless en-joyed in providing for themselves.

[Washington, D.C.?   December 24, 1863]
Testimony of Hon. F. W. Bird

Question   I understand Mr Bird that you have lately had an opportunity of observing the Freedmen in Eastern Virginia and I would like to know the result of your observations.

Answer   I have lately visited the Department of Virginia with a view to a particular examination of the condition of the Freedmen employed upon the Government Farms.   I first visited those near Hampton in charge of Capt. Chas. B. Wilder assistant superintendent of Freedmen. These freedmen are fugitives partly from the peninsular in the vicinity of Richmond, but, mostly from the neighborhood of Norfolk and Suffolk and the adjacent portions of North Carolina.   They commenced their labors on the farm late in the season and under very great disadvantages. A large portion of the ground was not ploughed at all until April Whereas the ploughing season in that section commences in January. They experienced considerable loss also from the failure of the crops, owing to drought.   A large portion of the seed they were obliged to replant from the first planting being so late, and a large portion of the crop imperfectly ripened.   Some of these laborers were of the large number who were herded upon Craney Island* in the winter and spring, where very many of them contracted disease unfitting them for active labor.

Q   Were these people men women and children?

A   Yes. It is also to be borne in mind that very few able bodied men are now employed upon these farms, nearly all of that class having been drawn either into the army or employed in other labor for the Government. Notwithstanding these drawbacks I think it is safe to say, that on all these farms the laborers have raised crops abundantly sufficient to support themselves and their families until the next harvest.

A portion of the farms are worked "to halves" as it is called, for the Government—the Government furnishing seed agricultural implements and horses and recieving one third or one half of the produce; another portion of the freedmen have managed entirely on their own account. I did not take accurate statistics of many of the Farms; and I was the less anxious to do this as the Superindents will very soon make reports in full of the results of the season. The facts in the cases of which I took notes are in entire accordance with the results upon the other farms, so far as I learned.

Here is the case of a farm carried on by Gibberty Davis—an old man 70 or 80 years of age. His wife is free. His master is a Captain in the rebel service. He is the only one remaining on the farm out of a gang of thirty slaves   He has cultivated with the assistance of two boys who are free thirty acres on which they have raised, besides supporting themselves 250 Bushels of corn and 150 pounds of cotton. They were obliged to replant nearly the whole of the corn. Mr Davis said he should have had four or five hundred pounds of cotton but for the early frost. The corn is worth 90 cts pr bushel and the cotton perhaps 60¢ pr pound;

---

*A contraband camp near Norfolk.

showing that he has now more than enough left to support himself and family until the next crop.

Another is the farm of Wm Jones consisting of 400 acres where seventy four slaves were formerly employed, of whom only ten are left. The master is in the Rebel Army.   They have raised 1000 bushels of shelled corn and 145 Bbls. of Sweet Potatoes.   They all have families and have raised enough to carry them all through the season; and they all said they had lived better than they ever did under their masters. This last was a Government Farm; the other was not.   These two cases are fair specimens of all that I saw and are I believe fair specimens of the whole.

I found a very bad state of things at what is known as the tobacco drying house where several hundred of the Freedmen last taken from Craney Island were crowded together very closely with nothing to do— all infirm old men and women and children—with great liability to fire, which would almost inevitably prove particularly if occurring in the night, very destructive to life.   They seem to be there from necessity, for the present as the Superintendent has found it impossible to provide huts for them rapidly enough to prevent this crowding.   Capt Wilder is doing every thing in his power to provide huts and to encourage the freedmen in building huts for themselves, for separate livings.   In some cases where the men are employed at a distance by the Government, they gather in villages in large numbers as at Hampton where the ruins of the houses of the First Families of Virginia are now covered with the cabins of their former Slaves, many of them built out of the same material as their masters houses.—   Where it has been practicable they have been assisted in building cabins with a view to giving to each family a seperate allotment of ten acres for their own cultivation.   Their collection in villages has been discouraged except in special cases.

Some five or six miles from Hampton, Capt Wilder has just started a Steam Saw Mill, which has been dumped down in the forest and is set at work in the open air turning out some five thousand feet of boards per day, which are furnished to the freedmen for their cabins.

With the exception of the state of things at the tobacco drying house, the condition of the freedmen of this district is as good as could be expected; wonderfully improved since my visit there a year and a half ago. This improvement is due to the change of policy in their treatment. Then they were treated as men who had no rights that white men were bound to respect; now they are beginning to comprehend that if they behave like men, they will be treated like men. Only one thing is needed and that they crave above all other boons; and that is the right to own the soil.

I also visited several of the farms in the vicinity of Norfolk under the charge of Capt. Orlando Brown, Assistant Superintendent of Freedmen. Most of these are carried on "to halves" for the Government.

The Poindexter Farm.

This farm is under a white overseer—a native of Norfolk. He has four men on the farm, all married. They have raised 730 bushels of shelled corn, forty bushells of sweet potatoes, and have sold about $300 worth of Milk. The Government furnished seed, utensils and teams.

The Baxter Farm.

I next visited the Baxter Farm, consisting of 3000 acres, which was formerly owned by Oscar F. Baxter, a surgeon in the Federal navy, now a surgeon in the Rebel army. He had as Jack Herring told us "jam by" (nearly) forty slaves. I give the results of the labor on this farm, as furnished by the assistant Superintendent. The place is known as Woodlawn. The whole number of freedmen on the farm is 70 of whom thirty eight are able bodied. Three hundred acres have been cultivated and there are now on hand 5090 bushels of corn

Jack Herring, one of Dr Baxter's late slaves, has cultivated, this last season, about thirty acres of this farm. He has done all the work himself, except what he hired. He had a little money of his own in the spring and his "boss" when he ran away left him corn enough for seed. He has raised 500 bushells of shelled corn. He has bought his team with his own money, and has one cow and twenty pigs. I was struck with the difference between the results of this poor freedmans labor and those of the Poindexter Farm. This latter as I have said was managed by a white native of Norfolk; and yet every thing about the place was slovenly and slip-shod. The overseer seemed hardly able to take care of himself and I have no doubt the men would have done better without him than with him. Certainly they would have done very much better, if they had had one intelligent negroe for their overseer instead of him.

The Wise Farm.

I also visited the place known as "Rolleston" which was occupied by [*Confederate*] Gen Wise for two years before the Rebellion. The results of the season on this farm are given from the figures furnished by the Assistant Superintendent.— The whole number of freed people on the farm of all ages, is 61. Of these the number of able bodied men is five stout boys and men over 15, four. Boys under fifteen, five. Able bodied women, fifteen. Girls under fifteen who work occasionally, seven. Leaving the number aged and young unfit to work, twenty five.— Two hundred and fifty acres of land were cultivated. The amount of produce sent off or on hand was, potatoes 100 Barrells, corn 2100 bushels.

It should be observed to the credit of the experiment, how small the proportion of able-bodied men is to the non-producers on these farms, to the infirm and the women and children, whom they have had to support. With the exception of Herrings place one half of the crops on these farms belongs to the Government; and in all cases so far as I could understand this half more than pays for all the materials furnished by the Government

Another fact must be borne in mind, that all the teams used on these farms, in both districts, are condemned horses.* Capt. Brown is doing his best to furnish all the freedmen with huts and cabins of their own. He has been very much embarrassed by the want of land which was safe from Guerrillas, and by the want of houses for the freedmen. He has now several hundred built and is well prepared to commence operations early in the ensueing season. The same difficulty was experienced here as on the other side, in consequence of the late planting; but they are now already commencing their ploughing, and unless something extraordinary happens, will show much better results another year.

I was very much struck with the view from the mansion house on the Baxter Farm. Stretching around the outskirts of the farm for a mile or more are the huts of the freedmen at a distance of ten or twenty rods apart; the plan being for each family to have an allotment of its own of ten acres thus laying the foundation of an industrious and self supporting peasantry who at the same time will be able to work for the owner of the central farm. All that is needed to establish there a truly loyal and prosperous community is that the men and women who have watered the soil with their tears and blood, should be allowed to own it when they have earned it by their own labor. They regard it a great boon that they are allowed to own their share of the crops, the boon will be infinitely greater when they are allowed to own the soil.

The schools in both districts are represented to be in a very flourishing condition. I visited only those in Norfolk, and am entirely

---

*I.e, horses judged unfit for military use.

safe in saying from my own experience in the management of schools and from the testimony of teachers that they have made at least as great progress as white children could have made in the same condition of life and under simular discouraging circumstances.

Q   How far do these people show a disposition to re-establish their old family relations?

A   Their opinions of conjugal fidelity are very loose.

Q   How is it in regard to parental instincts?

A   The fathers I should think are indifferent—much more so than the mothers.   I am not prepared to state very positively from my own enquiries except from those I made of the superintendents and teachers. They all say, that the men are very much inclined when they get tired of their wives to change them and think it is hard if they cannot.

Q   How far do the Government Superintendents rely upon the intelligence of the negroes to direct their farming operations, in comparison with what they would if they were employing Irish or other laborers?

A   I think quite as much, particularly where they find slaves on the farms where they have lived.

Q   Do they trust them with the care of cattle, seeds, tools &c?

A   I think so entirely.   I heard no complaints of dishonesty or untrustworthiness.

Q   How far do these men show any thrift or economy in the management of what they get—their rations, seeds, tools, and things of that kind?

A   I dont think that question can be answered intelligently because the crops have not been sold yet and the proceeds have not been placed in the freedmen's hands.   They have just had their living out of their farms and are waiting for the reports of the Assistant Supt. soon to be made up, when there will be a division of the produce.

Q From what you have seen of these people, how far do you think they would succeed in taking care of themselves if not placed under white supervision, but put on the land, and aided in the outset with seeds and tools?

A That is a hard question to answer. I don't see why a great many of them would not do as well as Gibberty Davis or Jack Herring has done.

Q Would they be inclined to try that experiment?

A A portion of them would have confidence enough to do it—perhaps as large a portion as would be the case among the poor whites but the majority, perhaps, would rather work under superintendence.

Q How far are they thrifty with what little money they do get?

A I only know from the testimony of the superintendents, that they are thrifty and economical, and save their money and deposit it.

Q Are they apt to spend money in drink?

A No.

Q Do you find any instances of quarrelling among them?

A No, they don't seem to need any police.

Q Are any of them trusted with arms?

A They have on the Baxter Farm a squad of men who drill an hour a day. It was found that the Government being short of troops, was unable to protect them from guerillas, and a few weeks ago, Capt Brown organized this squad and placed twenty five muskets in their hands. I saw them drill. They are very proud of a musket and will do better service in taking care of guerillas than white soldiers. Capt. Brown says he would altogether prefer for a scouting party to hunt for guerillas, black soldiers to white.

. . . .16

HDf

Conflict between laborers and employers simmered on plantations and farms throughout the Union-occupied South, occasionally boiling over in violent confrontation. Fannie Bisland, the wife of a secessionist planter in southern Louisiana, was a party to one such episode. Her husband's plantation, Aragon, had been seized by federal authorities and operated by Northern lessees during 1863, but she contracted with the government to lease it for 1864. Her attempt to install an overseer on the estate sparked a showdown involving not only workers on Aragon—many of whom had lived on the plantation as slaves—but also freedpeople on Hope Farm, a nearby plantation owned by her brother-in-law. In a letter to her mother, Bisland described the explosive events.

Terre Bonne [*La.*]   Jan. 12th [*1864*]

My dearest Ma   Mrs. Winder is here and intends to leave this morning for home,   she advises me to write to you and let her send the letter to the city, about trying to get some servants for me there.   There is no disposition among my house servants to return,   they have taken a house near Houma and of course so long as they can live in that way they are not going to return to me.   None of the people in the quarter are willing to work for me either,   indeed, before this reaches you, you will probably hear of the *rebellion* on the place about Mr. Grey's (the overseer) coming there.   On Sunday he sent his baggage down ahead of him and towards evening came himself in the buggy.   He stopped here for a few moments and I told him I thought he would have a good deal of trouble before he could bring them straight, but never dreaming of the trouble he did have.   He says, when he came in sight of the plantation, the bell commenced ringing furiously, and by the time he crossed the bridge every man, woman and child on the plantation had collected around the overseer's house.   Before he quite reached the house, one of the men seized the bridle and told him he should not set foot in that house, that the quarter belonged to them and no d——— white man should live there.   He tried to speak to them but they shut him up immediately and told him they did not want to hear a word from him. That he should not come on the place unless he could show a written order from Gen. Banks* and if Gen. Banks himself said that he was to come there, he should not live down there but must live at the house with *Mrs. Bisland*.   Mrs. Bisland had no right to come there and give orders. &c &c.   They said too much for me to begin to tell you what they did'nt say.   He says every man woman and child were talking at the same time,   one man told him if he went to live in that house they would burn powder and lead round it all night.   When he started off, he told them his baggage would have to stay there all night as the mules would not pull it any further,   they at first refused to let it stay there but at last consented to let it remain there till morning, under the cane shed.   Mr. May (the guard) was here when Mr Grey came up and told his story,   he was very much excited and started off to Thibodiaux to get a squad of soldiers to come down and arrest some of the ring-leaders.   He has not yet returned but we look for him to day,   if a severe example is set in this instance; something may be done,   if not all the white people will have to leave and give the parish up to the negroes.   Mr. May seemed to be very much impressed with the necessity of doing something with them.   Tell Uncle, I think he ought to come *here* from the city and stay until things get quiet.   I forgot to mention that as soon as Mr. Grey left Aragon to return, that two negroes rode past him on their way to Hope Farm, and just before he reached there, the bell commenced ringing there and such shouting and rejoicing that we could hear it, way up here.   This shows a concerted movement between the two places.—   I

---

*Nathaniel P. Banks, the principal Union commander in southern
  Louisiana.

wish you would get me a washerwoman and cook, if you can.   I am more
determined than ever to take charge down there since this affair, and if
the government will support me in it I will do so,   Mr. Grey says he is
going there if they kill him in the attempt.   The whole parish is
interested in putting this down.   I have five rooms cleaned and ready to
go into and the house looks very well, so that if I could get some one to
cook and wash for me I think I could move very soon.   You might try
and get a good old negro woman for cook, but I should prefer a white
woman for a washerwoman.   However you can exercise your own
judgment about it.   Try to get them as reasonably as you can.   I dont
like to incur this expense but dont know how I can avoid it, and after all
I dont know but what it will be almost as cheap, as I wont have to clothe
them.   I think Uncle had better report this case to the authorities in the
city, for they have made similar threats on several places; that no
overseer or white man shall come on the places.   I would write more but
Mrs. Winder is waiting.   All well but the weather is still as bad as can
be.   Do bring me a letter from John when you return.   Yours as ever.

ALS   Fannie[17]

By early 1864, free labor was encroaching upon slavery even in
Union-occupied areas like Tennessee, where slavery remained legal
because of the state's exemption from the Emancipation Proclamation. Knowing that they could flee to Union camps or to the city of
Nashville and there obtain both freedom and employment, slaves in
middle Tennessee pressed their owners for the elimination of old restrictions and the establishment of new privileges, including compensation for their labor. More and more slaveholders found themselves forced to negotiate with their slaves or risk losing them altogether. In a memorandum to the adjutant general of the army, a
middle-Tennessee unionist described the bargains that had been
struck in his neighborhood.

[*Murfreesboro, Tenn.   January 1864*]

Planters in the County of Rutherford with the view of securing the services of there slaves—or in other words to conciliate & prevent them from running away—have promised to give them 10 cts p^r lb for all the cotton they may produce & take care of & support them as they have before done—

Other planters are hiring their own Slaves. agreeing to give them $70.00 p^r year and cloath & support them—requiring them to work as they have usually done—

Others. say to their slaves to go on as usual. and they will see they are as well off as those employed by the Goverment. or others

A common farm hand can easily cultivate—8 acres of Land—6 in Cotton & 2 acers in Corn

One Horse or mule can tend 20 Acres

200^{lbs} of Ginn'd Cotton per Acre is a good average Crop—

5 Bbls of Corn. or 25 Bushels is a fair average Crop—[18]

HD

By 1864, freedpeople in the South Carolina Sea Islands had had two years' experience with free labor under Yankee auspices. Having learned all too well the limitations of wage-work, they aspired more than ever to an independence based upon control over land and other productive resources. When the federal government sold many of the islands' plantations in February of that year, scores of the freedpeople on those plantations managed to transform their aspiration into reality. But former slaves whose home plantations had been purchased by Edward Philbrick the previous year* feared that their chances of obtaining land were slipping away. In a petition to President Lincoln, they accused Philbrick of treachery and

---

*For Philbrick's purchase of Sea-Island plantations in 1863, see above, pp. 259–60.

complained about abusive treatment by one of his managers. They also asked why the government had sold so much land to outsiders like Philbrick when lifelong residents like themselves were willing and able to purchase.

St Helena Island   S.C.   Mar 1st 1864

Sir   Wee the undersigned. beleaveing wee are unfarely delt with, Are led to lay before you, these, our greaveiences first; then our petetion. And wee here beeg, though it may be long, You will beare kindly with; Reade & answere uss, And as now so, henceforth, our prayrs shall asscende to the Throan of God, for your future success on Earth. & Tryumph in Heaven.

For what wee have receaved from God, through you, wee will attempt to thank you,   wee can only bow our selves, and with silent lips feel our utter inability to say one word, the semblence of thanks.   Trusting this our Petetion in the hands of Allmighty God, and your kindness, wee now say, Let there be what success may in stor for you and your Armies,   Wither our freedom is for ever or a day, wither as Slaves or Freemen, wee shall ever, carry you & your kindness to us in our hearts,   may Heaven bless. you.

Our greaveincess

Mr Edward Philbrick. (A Northern Man) has bought up All our former Masters Lands under falls pretences;

To wit

He promis'd to buey in, at public sale, with our consent all the Lands on the following Plantations,

Mr Coffin's Place, Mr. Coffin's Cherrie Hill, Maulbuery Hill place. Big House place. Corner place. Dr Fuller's place, Pollawanney place, Mary Jinkins'es place. Hamelton Frip place, Morgan Island, & John

Johntson's place, of Ladies Island.

Before bueying he promised to sell to us again any ammount of the Land at $1.00 one Dollar pr Acre wee wish'd to purchas, Said sail was to be made when ever the Government sold the balance of its Land to the People resideing thereon,

On the 18th day of last month sailes of Publick Lands began in Beaufort, & what doo wee see to day, on all the Plantations our Breathern are bueying thr Land. getting redy to plant ther cropps and build ther Houses, which they will owne for ever

Wee hav gon to Mr Philbrick & Ask'd him to sell us our Land, and get for an answere he will not sell us one foot, & if he does sell to any one he will charge $10.00 Ten Dollars pr Acre. Wee have work'd for Mr Philbrick the whole year faithfully, and hav received nothing comparatively, not enough to sustaine life if wee depended entirely uppon our wages, he has Stors here chargeing feerefull prices for every nessary of life, and at last the People have become discouraged, all most heart broken.

He will not sell us our Land neither pay us to work for him; And if wee wish to work for others where wee might make something, he turns us out of our Houses, he says wee shall not live-on his plantation unless wee work for him, If wee go to Genl Saxton he tells us if Mr Phlbrick sees fit he will sell us the Land according to agreement If not then wee must go on Government Land where wee can buey as much as wee please, But, the Tax Commissioners say they cannot sell to us unless wee are living on the Plantations now selling, Wee go to the Sup^t Genl of the Island; Mr Tomlinson, he says work For Mr Phibrick for what ever wages he sees fit to pay if wee do not Mr Philbrick may drive us off the Land and wee shall not taks our Houes with us, He says, 'Mr Philbrick bought everything Houses Lands & all.

Why did Goverment sell all our Masters Land's to Mr Philbrick for so trifling a sume;   we are all redy & willing of truth anxious to buey all our Masters Land, & every thing upon them; and pay far more than he did for them

Wee will not attempt to lay all our greaveinces before you as t'will take much to long   we will only mention one cas which exceedes anything done in our Masters time   Charl's Ware an agent of Mr Philbrick's turn'd the cloths of a Colard Girl over her head turned her over a Barrel, & whipd her with a Leathern Strap   She had been confined* but two days before & allthough the case was reported to Mr Tomlinson Sup^t. Genl the Agent still retains his place,   Thiss is shamefull,   wee blush [*to*] write or send it you but the truth must be told,   But you may ask what wee would have done,

If possible wee Pray for either one of theese two things.

Petetion

1st Either let Mr Philbrick be compeeld to live up to his promises with us, and sell us as much Land as wee want for our owne Homes at a reasonabele price, giving us cleare deeds for the same.

2nd Otherwise wee pray Goverment to repurchas the Land of Mr Philbrick and then let us farm it giveing one half of all that is rais'd to the Goverment   wee would much rather this and will furnish everything ourselves and will warrent there will be but few feet of Ground Idle.   As Mr Philbrick has broken his part of the contract is Government bound to keep thers?

And wee will her mention, that many of us told Mr Philbrick not to buey the Land as wee wanted it our selves.

3rd And wee furthermore beeg that an Agent may be sent us, who will see not wrong; but right done us one who will deal justly by us,   Wee doo

---

*I.e., had given birth.

not want a Master or owner Neither a driver with his Whip   wee want a Friend

Trusting this may be lookd upon kindly beeging a immediate answer that wee may know what to doo Wee are with very great respect your most Humble & Obdt Srvt's

HLSr

[19 signatures][19]

For former slaves in the Mississippi Valley, ownership of land was not a possibility in 1864. Although the federal government controlled thousands of acres belonging to rebel planters, none of the necessary legal steps had been taken to permit its sale. Instead, the land was leased out, mostly to Northerners. Although a few hundred freedpeople became small-scale lessees, most former slaves lacked the necessary capital and thus had little choice but to work for wages. In a report to Adjutant General Lorenzo Thomas, Colonel Samuel Thomas, who had jurisdiction over the freedpeople on both sides of the Mississippi River between Vicksburg and Natchez, described the condition and prospects of the lessees and laborers in his war-torn district and offered his own opinions about the proper path to free labor.

Vicksburg Miss   June 15th 1864

Genl: In making out a report of the Provost Marshal business of the Department. I find it almost impossible to get at the figures necessary, as the Assistant Provost Marshals* have been so engaged with the duties around them that they have not had time to furnish me with the facts.   Their duties were new to them, and it required all the ability they could bring to bear upon the affairs of their districts to remedy the confusion existing at the time of their appointment.   Their duties were

*Colonel Thomas's subordinates, who were called provost marshals of freedmen.

not fully defined, and for some time they were not aware of what they really were.   Planters gave them but little assistance, and often refused to comply with their request.   The planting district under my supervision, extending from Lake Providence. La. to Natchez Miss was divided into eight sub-districts and a Lieutenant assigned to each district as Assistant Provost Marshal.   They entered upon their duties April 15th and have been actively engaged ever since.   By the removal of the troops two of the districts have been abandoned and the Provost Marshals relieved.   Some of the sub-districts are necessarily so large that it is almost impossible for one man to attend to the business; but we have every man engaged that can be spared for the work

The planting region that is in cotton, is a line of plantations near the Mississippi, from Lake Providence to Natchez, seldom over three miles from the river.   Most of them have been leased to Northern men by Agents of the Treasury Department, and are cultivated by freedmen that have come within our lines since our occupation of this country   They are cultivated on the basis of General Orders No. 9. of the Secretary of War, by Adjutant General Thomas.*   I make the following report from the Assistant Provost Marshals Reports, sent to me monthly:

Washington County Miss.

There were a large number of plantations leased in this county. during the spring; but lack of protection has forced all who were loyal, to

---

*The order, issued in March 1864, regulated the treatment, pay, and
living conditions of plantation laborers in the Mississippi Valley. It set
minimum monthly wages at $10 for men and $7 for women (with
smaller sums for children and other less able workers) and required the
employer to furnish food, clothing, and shelter in addition to the wages.
It also limited the workday to ten hours in summer and nine hours in
winter, prohibited whipping, required laborers to remain at work until
the end of the year, and forbade them to leave their place of employment
without permission. (*Wartime Genesis: Lower South*, pp. 802–8.)

leave.   There are several thousand acres of cotton planted in this county, but by citizens who are on good terms with the leaders of the bands of rebels which infest the country, or in such small quantities that it does not attract their attention.   The Provost Marshal does not visit the county, as it would be unsafe.   During the spring, large numbers of people were sent to the plantations; but since that time they have nearly all returned, and found employment in safer localities   The freedmen while there, run great risk of being carried off into slavery again; and after their return were unwilling to go to plantations at all for fear of the same result.

Goodrichs Landing, and Millikens Bend.

This district extends from Lake Providence to Vicksburg on the Louisiana side of the river, with a few plantations in Issaquena Co., Miss.   There are fifty-one plantations embraced in this district 30970 acres of cotton planted.   They furnish employment for 4456 hands and have in the aggregate of people 7720.   It will be seen from this, that nearly three-fifths of the freedmen are working hands.   There is a population of 200 white men in the capacity of superintendents clerks &c.   A large portion of this district was cultivated last year, and furnished but few obstacles to the Northern Planter.   There are but few Southern men in the district, and what are left are becoming reconciled to the new order of things, and are joining hands with the new men. Military protection for this district has been granted and but small loss has been sustained by the planters from the incursion of rebel bands. This section is one of the finest cotton-growing regions of the South; and from all appearances will prove as fruitful under the free labor exertions of Northern men as it ever did under the lash of the Southern slave driver

A great many cases of difficulties between the employer and employee are constantly referred to the Provost Marshal and keep two men busy

hearing the complaints and adjusting their difficulties. This duty is
laborious and requires great firmness on the part of the officer, to use
the proper discrimination in the various cases that come before him.
The records in the offices of the Assistant Provost Marshals in this
district, show a report of 122 cases that have been brought before them
and disposed of. The amount of fines imposed is large but as it has not
all been collected, no report has been received. For the want of a proper
place to confine criminals brought before them there has been some
complaint of their leniency; but I am satisfied the interests of all parties
have been weighed in their actions. The planters have complied with
"Orders No. 9." and "Regulations for Leasing Abandoned Plantations,"*
and seem to manifest a willingness to comply with every rule or order
that is for the good of the government or the freedmen employed by
them. The plantations in this district are large—1000 acres being the
average size. Yet the lessees have not been able to get more than 600
acres planted. The cotton of this district will compare favorably with
that of any along the river; and I believe the hands are as well fed and
clothed as laborers elsewhere. There are a large number of negro
lessees in this district who have leased from the Government and are
doing well. The Government is supplying them with food, and doing
what can be done under existing orders, to aid them   They are, as a
body, industrious, economical and determined in their efforts to sustain
themselves

I should like before leaving this report, to mention the names of
several planters who are making extra exertions to make a good field of
cotton on liberal principles, dealing honestly with their freedmen
laborers; but to any one visiting the field of labor such a planter is easily

---

*Issued in January 1864 by the Treasury Department, the regulations
governed the leasing of plantations and the employment of plantation
laborers. (*Wartime Genesis: Lower South*, pp. 774–78.)

distinguished, by the fine condition of his cotton, the cleanliness of his
plantation and gardens, the cheerfulness of his hands and their
willingness to do anything they can for him.

Warren County Miss.

In this county from the Yazoo River to the Big Black there are thirty-
three plantations; 11874 acres of cotton under cultivation; 1280 hands
employed; and 2396 people in the aggregate.   A large portion of this is
by the owners of the land, in connection with Northern men who furnish
the supplies.   Vicksburg furnishing a good market for vegetables, a
large amount of land is devoted to the culture of such vegetables as can
be sold in the market.   There are a large number of colored lessees in
this county: but we have no returns from them, and can make no
estimate of how much they are cultivating.   This county being upland
and very uneven it has not presented so many inducements for the
culture of cotton, as the neighboring river bottoms.   Those who have
planted in this county have received good protection from the military
authorities: as there has been until quite recently, a military post on the
Big Black which made the county comparatively safe.   The freedmen
are healthy, contented and as a general thing, well treated by the lessees
who employ them.

Davis Bend.

This Bend, containing about 8000 acres of land, is securely protected
by three companies of soldiers stationed at the neck which connects it
with the main land.   There are only two lessees here, who are
cultivating about 3000 acres of land.   They employ about 250 hands
and have in their quarters fully 1000 people.

. . . .

Two thousand acres are cultivated by negro lessees, supplied with
material by the Government, and under the control of the

Superintendent of Freedmen. The enterprise promises success. These lessees are as far advanced with their work, are as industrious, and have as good a prospect of succeeding as the white lessees around them

St Joseph

This is a colony located in the bend of Lake St Joseph, about 30 miles below Vicksburg. It was organized by Professor Winchell and J. A. Hawley, and commenced work about the 1st of March. They have met serious obstacles from the very beginning, and have had to contend with obstacles that would have disheartened less resolute men. Their plantations have been raided twice and two of their number murdered under the most brutal circumstances: yet they manifest a determination to face the storm, and carry out their project of raising cotton. They are more exposed than any other body of cotton planters and farther from help in case of trouble. They merit great praise for the determined manner in which they have battled for their possessions and deserve success

There are eight plantations under cultivation; 6047 acres planted in cotton, furnishing employment for 666 hands, and a home for 1400 people in the aggregate. They need more hands in order to succeed; but find trouble in getting them to go, owing to their exposed condition. They are men of experience and judgment, who have brought correct business principles to bear upon their work. There would not be a necessity for near as many Provost Marshals, if all the planters came here imbued with the same principles.

Waterproof

At this place there were troops stationed during the months of March and April which led lessees to lease plantations in the vicinity and commence the work of planting. About the last of April the troops were moved to Vidalia, La., and the planters were left at the mercy of the

guerrillas.   Six plantations were leased by Northern men, who bought
stock and provisions and commenced work.   Other places in the vicinity
were carried on by their owners; but they only planted such an amount
of land, as they thought the guerrillas would allow them to cultivate.
After the troops left, the Northern lessees deserted their places and
abandoned the enterprise; but not until they had been raided and robbed
of everything they had invested.   The Southern men who were at work
are still there, and will be allowed to raise enough to support their
families.   There is but little cotton planted from this place up to Lake
St Joseph, and but few freedmen; what few there are being old men and
women who still stay around the old plantation quarters, too harmless to
attract the attention of either party.

Natchez Miss.

This district extends from Marengo to Ashley, in Concordia Parish,
La., on both sides of the river.   On the Mississippi side there is but little
done, as there is not protection sufficient outside the city limits, to
insure planters in making investments.   There are a number of
freedmen on nearly every plantation in the district, whether it be
abandoned or not; as they manage to raise a little garden, and live on
what may be left by their former masters.

In Concordia Parish. La. along the Mississippi river from Marengo to
Ashley, there is a tier of 34 plantations with 22590 acres of cotton under
cultivation.   They furnish employment for 2390 freedmen, with a
population of 4312 people.   The freedmen of this district are mostly
made up of the original hands that have worked the plantations they are
on, for years.   This fact makes them work better and more contentedly,
as they have the little community commonly known as "fellow servants"
all together, as they have lived for years

Planters have not enough freedmen to cultivate what they have

planted; and as the competition for hands increases, wages for their
work go up, and actually settle the troublesome question of what wages
shall be paid. A planter must pay well and punctually, or he will not get
laborers to do his work

Early in the spring preparations were made for planting extensively;
but the vigilance of the guerrillas has confined them to the narrow limits
of what the military authorities can protect. The desolating influences
of a large army, that have made a perfect waste of most of the cotton
country above here, did not reach this district. The plantations are
some of the finest in the South, being in fine order at the beginning of
the year. Dwelling houses, negro quarters, fences, steam gins and sawmills—all in good repair and ready for use.

Several raids have been made, and a large number of mules, horses
and wagons carried off, besides valuable material that will cripple the
planters losing it very much. During the week ending June 15th nine
steam gins have been burned in the lower end of the district by the
guerrillas, who seem to be determined to do what they can to thwart the
project of raising cotton. Perhaps one-half of the plantations being
worked in this district are not abandoned, but have been leased from the
owners who have some share in the crop. The cotton was planted early,
looks well, and as a general thing has been well cultivated. The
combination of Yankee skill, and Southern experience will work a great
improvement in raising cotton in this Valley.

Recapitulation

Number of plantations 162; number of acres of cotton in the whole
district under my supervision 74.981; number of hands employed,
9.192; number of freed people living on the plantations. in the
aggregate, 17319; number of white men engaged as superintendents,
clerks, &c., 397.

Number of freedmen lessees, 180; acres in cultivation 5,870; hands
employed exclusive of lessees. 380; people supported by lessees including
hands employed, 1.280. This does not include many small pieces of
ground being cultivated by one or two freedmen, who have no claim to
their lands, except to occupy what they find abandoned, for their own
use.

The above estimates of land under cultivation are made from the old
calculation of the number of acres in the plantations that are being
worked   The constant changing of hands would make some variation
from the above calculation; but the statement is as near correct as it is
possible for me to get it.

Conclusion.

I find that the planters have not executed the form of contract
between themselves and their hands. prescribed by this office, and by
Orders No. 9, of the Secretary of War,* owing to the fact that they have
had to change hands several times since they commenced work; and the
labor of making these contracts has been so great, that my office has not
had time to execute the part assigned to it, of furnishing the blanks and
visiting the plantations to see the contracts executed.   To remedy this as
far as practicable, my Assistant Provost Marshals are required to visit
every plantation in their districts once a week, and examine into the
condition of the people and hear all complaints that may be made of
neglect or failure of either party to fulfill his part of what is understood
to be the regulation.   The duty is arduous and perplexing.   Nearly
every form of complaint comes before them; and as far as I have received
reports, the decisions of the Provost Marshals have been satisfactory to
all parties.   The wages of the freedmen for half the time worked have
been paid up to June 1st, which gives satisfaction to all, except a few who

---

*See above, p. 295n.

are not contented in any position, and who, through stupidity, or a
desire to be finding fault, complain of the wages not being paid, and tell
hard stories of their treatment, which are not founded on facts.   I find a
desire among a considerable portion of the hands to change about; and
to justify their desire, they invent stories, which if taken by themselves,
would reflect upon the planters, and lead to the belief that serious
abuses existed among them.   I do not think this is the case.   As a
general thing, I find the planters as upright and just a body of men as
can be found anywhere.   I will venture the assertion that they will
compare favorably with any body of business men of the same number.
With a few exceptions they have treated their hands justly and
humanely in all the transactions that have come to light and seem to do
all they can to inculcate manliness and self-reliance on their laborers,
rendering their labor dignified and respectable   That the laborer is
going to receive a large amount of money for his year's work is not
claimed by any one.   I cannot see how this would help him in gaining the
place that some enthusiastic people would have him hurried into
immediately.   The best we can do is, to place his labor on an equal
footing with white labor, and neither endow him with a fortune, nor open
up his road to jump at once to ease or affluence, that he does not know
how to use or enjoy.   Guard him against imposition, give him his just
dues at the end of each month, and if there is one able to carry on
business for himself so construct rules as to assist him, and let him work
his way up.   Our country has enough to bear without undertaking the
enormous task of starting out each freedman with a competency for the
rest of his life.   They are free but they must labor for the food they eat.
and the clothes they wear.   Capital does now, and will for some time to
come carry on great enterprises; and a large portion of the human
family, both white and black, must labor for this capital at regulated

wages, without any direct interest in the result of the enterprise.

One of the terrors of the planting system has been the guerrillas, who lurked in swamps and canebrakes near the river, ready at any moment to pounce upon the planter, and destroy the fruits of his labor. The loss of life has not been great, as I find that there have been only eleven Northern, and seven Southern men killed while engaged in cultivating plantations since Jan'y 1st 1864.

The planting season this year has been very dry. The oldest planters claim that it is an exception. Planters were late in getting arrangements made to start their plantations, owing to the different changes in the policy of the Government about leasing them. Great dissatisfaction existed in the beginning, and many went home disgusted with their efforts to obtain information as to the course that was to be pursued by the Government. Expectations were encouraged at one time, that there would be protection furnished; but military operations might demand the withdrawal of the troops, and the planters would be left at the mercy of the rebels. Most of the plantations were entirely destitute of everything except buildings and many were without these in adequate numbers to shelter their laborers. Forage, mules, provisions and tools must come from the North, and be brought through all the tortuous routine of trade regulations. Planters commenced planting cotton about the 1st of April and continued to the 1st of June. The largest amount of seed went into the ground the last week of April. and the 1st week of May. The ground was very dry during the months of April and May. making it almost impossible to prepare it for the seed. Seed planted during this dry weather did not come up very well; and what did come up remained at a stand still for some time after peering through the ground. Planters all replanted, and some even commenced anew, and put in a new crop about the last of May. The continued rains

during the first part of June have brought this planting up, and it looks
well.   All have a good stand of cotton, although very uneven in height.
It was difficult to get good seed, as all that could be procured was two
years old, and had been subject to the wet weather which had rotted and
made it unfit for use.   At this time, (June 20th) most of the cotton has
been worked over once.   The lack of hands is being severely felt.   There
is not a plantation but what could take more hands, and actually needs
more, to cultivate the crops properly.   As a whole, the planters gained
nothing by planting early crops this season.   While they were losing for
lack of rain to bring their cotton out of the ground they were gaining in
being sure that the floods in the Mississippi would not sweep through the
breaks in the levee and destroy their crops   This must be a serious
drawback the next season, if the levee is not repaired.   I have the honor
to be. Your obedient Servant

ALS   Sam[l] Thomas[20]

As they enforced labor discipline in the occupied South, Northern
officials drew upon their own notions of proper modes of work and
appropriate behavior by manual laborers. Disturbed by former
slaves' traveling about, fishing, or doing odd jobs instead of working steadily for a single employer, a newly appointed superintendent of contrabands in the South Carolina Sea Islands proposed
remedies derived from Northern practices.

Contraband Office   Beaufort S.C.   August 25 '64
Colonel: In accordance with a request made by you at this office some
days since concerning measures to be instituted to lessen the number of
idle & dissolute persons hanging about the central Posts of the

Department & traveling to & from between them, desiring my opinion thoughtfully made up as to what measures would be best, I write this note, at a somewhat late day on account of sickness. I write with some delicacy withal inasmuch as it would seem to come from an office which would give the weight of an extended experience touching the matter, whereas the person who has acquired the experience & has manifested a well-tried ability withal is absent on furlough home. However, having had considerable experience in dealing with the people & having thought much of what their best interests demand I will write what I think.

Had I the control of the negroes the first thing I would endeavor to do, & the thing I think of most importance to be done, is to Keep all the people possible on the farms or plantations at *honest steady* labor. As one great means to this end, I would make it as difficult as possible for them to get to the centres of population.— Young women particularly flock back & forth by scores to Hilton Head, to Beaufort, to the country simply to while away their time, or constantly to seek some new excitement, or what is worse to live by lasciviousness. This class of persons is as great a curse to the soldier as to themselves. All persons in town or at posts should be peremptorily sent to the country if they have not *steady* employment. There are numbers who would wash or hire themselves out just enough to answer the order, but that should not suffice. This getting a precarious livelihood by doing a little at this thing, & a little at that is the very curse of the people. So far as possible they should be compelled to *steady labor*. Hence I would allow no peddling around camps whatsoever. Fishing I would discourage as much as possible unless a man made a livelihood of it. All rationing* I would stop utterly, & introduce the poor house system, feeding none on any pretense who would not go to the place provided for all paupers to

---

*I.e., government issues of food to individuals.

live.   This wo'd cut off rations by 3/4 their present amount.   Then to be
fed by the public would soon come to be a disgrace as it should be.   All
persons out of the poor house & running from place to place to beg a
living I would treat as vagabonds, & also all persons, whether in town or
on plantations, white or black, who lived without occupation should
either go to the poor house or be put in a place where they *must work*—a
work house or chain gang, & if women where they could wash iron &
scrub for the benefit of the public.   Under a military order those at
present charged with the care of negroes would cheerfully labor to carry
out such suggestions, and after the system was well instituted their
labors would be made less by it—   Some one must take care of the poor
but the diminution in expense of rations would well nigh pay for it & I
doubt if a new officer would be needed.   At any rate there is not the
least doubt in my mind that a military order should be made *stringent* to
take care of the floating Negro population, nor that it sho'd be made
very much more difficult to get into centers of population by greatl
restricting passes.   Very Respectfully

ALS   A. S. Hitchcock[21]

The provost marshal general of the Department of the South forwarded Hitchcock's letter to the departmental commander, prais-
ing it as "a well considered and sensible document." On the
grounds that the freedpeople's boats opened opportunities for
"communication with the enemy," he recommended that they be
prohibited except by special permit. Adopting that recommendation, the department commander issued an order that resulted in
the confiscation of dozens of boats and angry protests by the freedpeople and their allies. One Northern plantation manager warned
that the loss of their boats "[would] greatly distress many hundreds of poor men and families, whose dependance for food is
chiefly fish, oysters, &c, and great numbers thus live who are unfit

for the heavy labor of cultivating the land." The military governor
of the region concurred. "[T]housands of these poor people live by
fishing," he wrote, "and taking away their boats, takes away their
living."[22]

In most nonplantation regions of the Union-occupied South, military authorities exercised little direct supervision over agricultural
labor. Former slaves and former slaveholders therefore had considerable latitude in negotiating new working arrangements. Alfred
Scruggs, set free as a result of the federal occupation of northern
Alabama in 1862, thereafter made his own bargains and, together
with his wife, earned a comfortable livelihood. By farming rented
land, doing job work, and washing and ironing, the couple accumulated two mules, a horse, and some cattle—all of which were seized
or slaughtered by Union soldiers. Years later, in seeking compensation from a federal commission, Scruggs explained how they had
acquired the property.

[*Huntsville, Ala.   July 31, 1872*]
Deposition of Alfred Scruggs, Colored,
In answer to the First General Interrogatory, the Deponent says:
My name is Alfred Scruggs, *my age* 45 *years, my residence* Near
Huntsville, *in the State of* Alabama, *and my occupation a* Farmer; *I am
the claimant, and have a beneficial interest in the claim.*

To the 2nd he says:

Near Huntsville Alabama,   In 1861 I came from Arkansas to
Huntsville.   In 1862 or until June I was hired by consent of my Master
James H Scruggs to Col David Kelley.   In June 1862 I was turned loose
by my old master to make a living for my self—   When I was turned
loose I went to hauling wood to Huntsville.   The team belonged to my
old master,   My old master gave me the use of the team if I would feed
and take care of.   I used the team until the Yankee soldiers took them

from me in the latter part of the summer 1862.   In 1863 I had my own
team.   I rented about forty acres of land from Mrs Patteson, near
Huntsville and raised a crop of cotton and corn that year.   I also
haulued wood during the time I was not in my crop,   During the year
1864 I farmed on Mr Ed Spotswoods place four miles of Huntsville.   I
had about twenty five acres in corn,   I hauled wood and everything that
I could get to do.   I did not use my own team that year or all of that
year,   In the early part of the year 1865 I was preparing to farm on Mr
Nash Malones place

· · · ·

To the 43rd he says:

I was a slave.   I was free when we was declared free, but my master
turned me loose in 1862   Hauling working and making money in any
way I could in an honorable manner.   I bought this property.   I cant tell
the exact date.   I bought my property about the end of 1862. or about
1863,   I worked and made the money in 1862 by hauling and jobbing
with my fingers: and my wife washing and ironing is the way I made the
money which I paid for the property in my claim.   James H Scruggs
was my former master.   I am not in his employment.   I do not live on
his land,   Do not live on land purchased from him,   I do not owe him,
he owes me.   No one saveing me has any interest in this claim.

· · · ·

his

HDSr   Alfred ✕ Scruggs.[23]

mark

Scruggs had submitted a claim for $381; he was awarded $340.[24]

In Savannah, Georgia, on the evening of January 12, 1865, was assembled one of the most remarkable gatherings of the Civil War era. Twenty black ministers and lay leaders joined Secretary of War Edwin M. Stanton and General William T. Sherman at the general's headquarters. They had been summoned to consider the future of the thousands of slaves freed by the scourging march of Sherman's army. A Northern newspaper reported the proceedings.

[*New York, N.Y. February 13, 1865*]

· · · ·

MINUTES OF AN INTERVIEW BETWEEN THE COLORED MINISTERS AND CHURCH OFFICERS AT SAVANNAH WITH THE SECRETARY OF WAR AND MAJOR-GEN. SHERMAN.

HEADQUARTERS OF MAJ.-GEN. SHERMAN,
CITY OF SAVANNAH, GA., Jan., 12, 1865—8 P.M. }

On the evening of Thursday, the 12th day of January, 1865, the following persons of African descent met by appointment to hold an interview with Edwin M. Stanton, Secretary of War, and Major-Gen. Sherman, to have a conference upon matters relating to the freedmen of the State of Georgia, to-wit:

One: William J. Campbell, aged 51 years, born in Savannah, slave until 1849, and then liberated by will of his mistress, Mrs. May Maxwell. For ten years pastor of the 1st Baptist Church of Savannah, numbering about 1,800 members. Average congregation, 1,900. The church property belonging to the congregation. Trustees white. Worth $18,000.

Two: John Cox, aged fifty-eight years, born in Savannah; slave until 1849, when he bought his freedom for $1,100. Pastor of the 2d African Baptist Church. In the ministry fifteen years. Congregation 1,222 persons. Church property worth $10,000, belonging to the congregation.

Three: Ulysses L. Houston, aged forty-one years, born in Grahamsville, S.C.; slave until the Union army entered Savannah. Owned by Moses Henderson, Savannah, and pastor of Third African Baptist Church. Congregation numbering 400. Church property worth $5,000; belongs to congregation. In the ministry about eight years.

Four: William Bentley, aged 72 years, born in Savannah, slave until 25 years of age, when his master, John Waters, emancipated him by will. Pastor of Andrew's Chapel, Methodist Episcopal Church—only one of that denomination in Savannah; congregation numbering 360 members; church property worth about $20,000, and is owned by the congregation; been in the ministry about twenty years; a member of Georgia Conference.

Five: Charles Bradwell, aged 40 years, born in Liberty County, Ga.; slave until 1851; emancipated by will of his master, J. L. Bradwell. Local preacher in charge of the Methodist Episcopal congregation (Andrew's Chapel) in the absence of the minister; in the ministry 10 years.

Six: William Gaines, aged 41 years; born in Wills Co., Ga. Slave until the Union forces freed me. Owned by Robert Toombs, formerly United States Senator, and his brother, Gabriel Toombs, local preacher of the M.E. Church (Andrew's Chapel.) In the ministry 16 years.

Seven: James Hill, aged 52 years; born in Bryan Co., Ga. Slave up to the time the Union army came in. Owned by H. F. Willings, of Savannah. In the ministry 16 years.

Eight: Glasgon Taylor, aged 72 years, born in Wilkes County, Ga. Slave until the Union army came; owned by A. P. Wetter. Is a local preacher of the M.E. Church (Andrew's Chapel.) In the ministry 35 years.

Nine: Garrison Frazier, aged 67 years, born in Granville County, N.C. Slave until eight years ago, when he bought himself and wife, paying $1,000 in gold and silver. Is an ordained minister in the Baptist Church, but, his health failing, has now charge of no congregation. Has been in the ministry 35 years.

Ten: James Mills, aged 56 years, born in Savannah; free-born, and is a licensed preacher of the first Baptist Church. Has been eight years in the ministry.

Eleven: Abraham Burke, aged 48 years, born in Bryan County, Ga. Slave until 20 years ago, when he bought himself for $800. Has been in the ministry about 10 years.

Twelve: Arthur Wardell, aged 44 years, born in Liberty County, Ga. Slave until freed by the Union army. Owned by A. A. Solomons, Savannah, and is a licensed minister in the Baptist Church. Has been in the ministry 6 years.

Thirteen: Alexander Harris, aged 47 years, born in Savannah; free born. Licensed minister of Third African Baptist Church. Licensed about one month ago.

Fourteen: Andrew Neal, aged 61 years, born in Savannah, slave until the Union army liberated him. Owned by Mr. Wm. Gibbons, and has been deacon in the Third Baptist Church for 10 years.

Fifteen: Jas. Porter, aged 39 years, born in Charleston, South Carolina; free-born, his mother having purchased her freedom. Is lay-reader and president of the board of wardens and vestry of St. Stephen's Protestant Episcopal Colored Church in Savannah. Has been in communion 9 years. The congregation numbers about 200 persons. The church property is worth about $10,000, and is owned by the congregation.

Sixteen: Adolphus Delmotte, aged 28 years, born in Savannah; free

born.   Is a licensed minister of the Missionary Baptist Church of
Milledgeville.   Congregation numbering about 300 or 400 persons.
Has been in the ministry about two years.

Seventeen: Jacob Godfrey, aged 57 years, born in Marion, S.C.
Slave until the Union army freed me; owned by James E. Godfrey—
Methodist preacher now in the Rebel army.   Is a class-leader and
steward of Andrew's Chapel since 1836.

Eighteen: John Johnson, aged 51 years, born in Bryan County,
Georgia.   Slave up to the time the Union army came here; owned by
W. W. Lincoln of Savannah.   Is class-leader and treasurer of Andrew's
Chapel for sixteen years.

Nineteen: Robt. N. Taylor, aged 51 years, born in Wilkes Co., Ga.
Slave to the time the Union army came.   Was owned by Augustus P.
Welter, Savannah, and is class-leader in Andrew's Chapel for nine years.

Twenty: Jas. Lynch, aged 26 years, born in Baltimore, Md.; free-
born.   Is presiding elder of the M.E. Church and missionary to the
department of the South.   Has been seven years in the ministry and two
years in the South.

Garrison Frazier being chosen by the persons present to express their
common sentiments upon the matters of inquiry, makes answers to
inquiries as follows:

First: State what your understanding is in regard to the acts of
Congress and President Lincoln's [*Emancipation*] proclamation,
touching the condition of the colored people in the Rebel States.

Answer—So far as I understand President Lincoln's proclamation to
the Rebellious States, it is, that if they would lay down their arms and
submit to the laws of the United States before the first of January, 1863,
all should be well; but if they did not, then all the slaves in the Rebel
States should be free henceforth and forever.   That is what I understood.

Second—State what you understand by Slavery and the freedom that
was to be given by the President's proclamation.

Answer—Slavery is, receiving by *irresistible power* the work of
another man, and not by his *consent*.   The freedom, as I understand it,
promised by the proclamation, is taking us from under the yoke of
bondage, and placing us where we could reap the fruit of our own labor,
take care of ourselves and assist the Government in maintaining our
freedom.

Third: State in what manner you think you can take care of
yourselves, and how can you best assist the Government in maintaining
your freedom.

Answer: The way we can best take care of ourselves is to have land,
and turn it and till it by our own labor—that is, by the labor of the
women and children and old men; and we can soon maintain ourselves
and have something to spare.   And to assist the Government, the young
men should enlist in the service of the Government, and serve in such
manner as they may be wanted.   (The Rebels told us that they piled
them up and made batteries of them, and sold them to Cuba; but we
don't believe that.)   We want to be placed on land until we are able to
buy it and make it our own.

Fourth: State in what manner you would rather live—whether
scattered among the whites or in colonies by yourselves.

Answer: I would prefer to live by ourselves, for there is a prejudice
against us in the South that will take years to get over; but I do not
know that I can answer for my brethren.   [Mr. Lynch says he thinks
they should not be separated, but live together.   All the other persons
present, being questioned one by one, answer that they agree with
Brother Frazier.]*

---

*Brackets in the original.

Fifth: Do you think that there is intelligence enough among the slaves of the South to maintain themselves under the Government of the United States and the equal protection of its laws, and maintain good and peaceable relations among yourselves and with your neighbors?

Answer—I think there is sufficient intelligence among us to do so.

Sixth—State what is the feeling of the black population of the South toward the Government of the United States; what is the understanding in respect to the present war—its causes and object, and their disposition to aid either side.   State fully your views.

Answer—I think you will find there are thousands that are willing to make any sacrifice to assist the Government of the United States, while there are also many that are not willing to take up arms.   I do not suppose there are a dozen men that are opposed to the Government.   I understand, as to the war, that the South is the aggressor.   President Lincoln was elected President by a majority of the United States, which guaranteed him the right of holding the office and exercising that right over the whole United States.   The South, without knowing what he would do, rebelled.   The war was commenced by the Rebels before he came into office.   The object of the war was not at first to give the slaves their freedom, but the sole object of the war was at first to bring the rebellious States back into the Union and their loyalty to the laws of the United States.   Afterward, knowing the value set on the slaves by the Rebels, the President thought that his proclamation would stimulate them to lay down their arms, reduce them to obedience, and help to bring back the Rebel States; and their not doing so has now made the freedom of the slaves a part of the war.   It is my opinion that there is not a man in this city that could be started to help the Rebels one inch, for that would be suicide.   There were two black men left with the Rebels because they had taken an active part for the Rebels, and thought something might befall them if they stayed behind; but there is not another man.   If the prayers that have gone up for the Union army could be read out, you would not get through them these two weeks.

Seventh: State whether the sentiments you now express are those only of the colored people in the city; or do they extend to the colored population through the country? and what are your means of knowing the sentiments of those living in the country?

Answer: I think the sentiments are the same among the colored people of the State.   My opinion is formed by personal communication in the course of my ministry, and also from the thousands that followed the Union army, leaving their homes and undergoing suffering.   I did not think there would be so many; the number surpassed my expectation.

Eighth: If the Rebel leaders were to arm the slaves, what would be its effect?

Answer: I think they would fight as long as they were before the bayonet, and just as soon as soon as they could get away, they would desert, in my opinion.

Ninth: What, in your opinion, is the feeling of the colored people about enlisting and serving as soldiers of the United States? and what kind of military service do they prefer?

Answer: A large number have gone as soldiers to Port Royal [*S.C.*] to be drilled and put in the service; and I think there are thousands of the young men that would enlist.   There is something about them that perhaps is wrong.   They have suffered so long from the Rebels that they want to shoulder the musket.   Others want to go into the Quartermaster's or Commissary's service.

Tenth: Do you understand the mode of enlistments of colored persons in the Rebel States by State agents under the Act of Congress?* If yea, state what your understanding is.

Answer: My understanding is, that colored persons enlisted by State agents are enlisted as substitutes, and give credit to the States, and do not swell the army, because every black man enlisted by a State agent leaves a white man at home; and, also, that larger bounties are given or promised by State agents than are given by the States. The great object should be to push through this Rebellion the shortest way, and there seems to be something wanting in the enlistment by State agents, for it don't strengthen the army, but takes one away for every colored man enlisted.

Eleventh: State what, in your opinion, is the best way to enlist colored men for soldiers.

Answer: I think, sir, that all compulsory operations should be put a stop to. The ministers would talk to them, and the young men would enlist. It is my opinion that it would be far better for the State agents to stay at home, and the enlistments to be made for the United States under the direction of Gen. Sherman.

In the absence of Gen. Sherman, the following question was asked:

Twelfth: State what is the feeling of the colored people in regard to Gen. Sherman; and how far do they regard his sentiments and actions as friendly to their rights and interests, or otherwise?

Answer: We looked upon Gen. Sherman prior to his arrival as a man in the Providence of God specially set apart to accomplish this work, and we unanimously feel inexpressible gratitude to him, looking upon him as

---

*A law adopted in July 1864 permitted agents from Northern states to recruit soldiers among black men in the Confederate states, crediting them against the draft quotas of the Northern states. (*Statutes at Large*, vol. 13, pp. 379–81.)

a man that should be honored for the faithful performance of his duty. Some of us called upon him immediately upon his arrival, and it is probable he would not meet the Secretary with more courtesy than he met us.   His conduct and deportment toward us characterized him as a friend and a gentleman.   We have confidence in Gen. Sherman, and think that what concerns us could not be under better hands.   This is our opinion now from the short acquaintance and interest we have had. (Mr. Lynch states that with his limited acquaintance with Gen. Sherman, he is unwilling to express an opinion.   All others present declare their agreement with Mr. Frazier about Gen. Sherman.)

Some conversation upon general subjects relating to Gen. Sherman's march then ensued, of which no note was taken.

. . . .25

PD

Four days after the meeting, General Sherman issued Special Field Order 15, which set aside a large expanse of coastal land, stretching from Charleston, South Carolina, to northern Florida, "for the settlement of the negroes now made free by the acts of war and the proclamation of the President of the United States." Each family would be allotted "forty acres of tillable ground . . . in the possession of which land the military authorities will afford them protection, until such time as they can protect themselves, or until Congress shall regulate their title."[26]

Criticism of federal free-labor policies came from various quarters and rested on conflicting premises. Whereas Southern planters complained that the prohibition of whipping left them without effective means to discipline their workers, many black people—particularly those who had long enjoyed free status—resented military regulations that required agricultural laborers to enter year-long contracts and restricted their freedom of movement. Near the end of the war, black freemen in New Orleans called a mass meeting to protest such provisions of the labor system established by General Nathaniel P. Banks and continued by his successor, General Stephen A. Hurlbut. Military restrictions, the freemen maintained in a petition to Hurlbut, might have been necessary earlier in the war, but now they posed obstacles to a "complete freedom" in which laborers made their own bargains without outside interference.

New Orleans [*La.*]   March 21st 1865

General   At a mass meeting of the colored Citizens of New-Orleans, held at the Economy Hall on Friday March 17th 1865. The following resolutions, were passed unanimously. And the undersigned were appointed to forward a copy of the resolutions to you, for your consideration.

Resolutions

Whereas: The labor system established by Maj. General Banks— which does not pratically differ from slavery, except by the interdiction from selling and whipping to death, the laborers. were only intended by its promoter to be a temporary one.

Whereas: Some enlargement of the liberties of the laborers was contemplated to gradually take place, and were really to be introduced unless Emancipation be a by-word. and the boon of freedom a falsehood intended to deceive the world. and.

Whereas: An abridgment of the liberties of the black, will have for effect, the strengthening of the hands, of the enemies of our beloved country, who have been asserting for several years, that the emancipation movement at the North, was a shame [*sham*], that the United States government was not in earnest, on the abolition question, and did not intend to treat the negro better than the southern slaveocrats do. thereby damaging before the world, the honor and the social cause of the American Union, and

Whereas: There is no pratical liberty for the laborers, without the right of contracting freely, and voluntarily, on the terms of labor and

Whereas: The right of traveling is guaranteed by the National Constitution, to all Citizens, and any particular restriction put upon any particular class of Americans, on account of color, is unconstitutional. and

Whereas: Equal taxation, and reciprocal obligations between all classes of citizens, are the natural consequences of equality before the law. and have become the recognized principles of all liberal governments: and

Whereas: Congress has discountenanced the growing interference, with the rights and privileges of the Freedmen, by refusing during two successive sessions, the proposed organization of a Freedmen's Central Bureau and

Whereas: A liberal policy can only be conceived and carried out by men of liberal spirit and progressive tendencies. Be it therefore

Resolved: That the right of the employee to freely agree and contract, according to his best judgment, with his employer, for the term of labor, is the unquestionable attribute of every freeman.

Resolved: That as freinds of freedom, equal rights, and liberty, we enter our protest against every restriction put on the traveling facilities on account of color.

Resolved: That we denounce, to the world, the attempts, and wishes of the former slaveowners to transform, the boon of Liberty, solemnly offered to the American Slaves into a disguised bondage.

Resolved: That while we are prepared for any sacrifice dictated by philanthropy and patriotism, we earnestly protest, against any tax imposed on account of color.*

Resolved: That it is highly important to institute, in this city a tribunal of Arbitrators composed partly of Freedmen, to decide in the simplest, but in the most equitable way the cases of appeal, from the decisions rendered, on matter of labor, by the Provost-Marshals—of the parishes.

Resolved: That we consider the existence of a Bureau of Free-labor† as inconsistent with freedom, and we pledge ourselves, to use our most active efforts, to have it abolished by the proper authorities, in order to make room for complete freedom.

Resolved: That new ideas want new men, that the past has shown, that we cannot expect any decided progress, in the conduct of labor, so long as superintendant Thomas W. Conway remains at the head of the Bureau of free Labor of Louisiana.

Resolved: That it is shall be the duty, of the Officers, of this meeting to respectfully transmit the above preambles and resolutions, to the Commanding General of the Department of the Gulf, and to have published in the New-Orleans Tribune in French and English, and in the liberal press throughout the North.

---

*At issue was a poll tax recently levied by General Hurlbut to defray the costs of military supervision of plantation labor and relief of destitute freedpeople. Planters were to pay $2 for each laborer aged eighteen to fifty, and each laborer was to pay $1. Hurlbut had also announced his intention to collect $1 "from all colored persons not on plantations, so that the active labor of this race may contribute to the support of their own helpless and disabled." (*Wartime Genesis: Lower South*, p. 593.)

†The Bureau of Free Labor, a military agency established by General Banks in 1863, enforced orders regarding plantation labor in southern Louisiana.

General

You will please give an answer to this communication at your earliest convenience.

The undersigned can be addressed at No 82 Baronne street.   We are General Respectfully Your Obedient Servants

James H. Ingraham.

Committee[27]

D[r] A. W. Lewis

> Hurlbut's reply insisted that federal military policies were necessary to protect former slaves and questioned whether the experience and interests of the freemen entitled them to speak for the newly freed.

New Orleans [*La.*]   March 23" 1865.

Gentlemen,   Your Communication of 21" March has been considered by me.

It consists of Preambles that do not state facts and resolutions that are based upon false views.   I hope you have been led into these misstatements by error rather than wilfully, although I can scarcely believe you could have been so singularly misinformed.

If instead of assembling in Mass meetings and wasting your time in high sounding Resolutions you would devote Yourselves to assisting in the physical and moral improvement of the Freedmen you would do some practical good.   As it is you do not in any respect represent the "Emancipated Freedmen of Louisiana," nor are you doing their cause any good.   The Mass Meeting which you claim to represent was not composed of "Freedmen" but of the Free Colored People of New Orleans, free by the Old Laws of the State, and some at least of them in the old system themselves slave holders.

Between them and the "slaves" there was always and is now bitterness of feeling. You are striving for social equality, they for personal freedom. The first is not a thing that can be reached by laws and orders but can only come from the social tastes prejudices or inclinations of the people where you live; the Second is the Creature of Law and can be secured by the sanctions of Law.

Your Statement that the condition of the Freedmen is but little better than slavery is notoriously untrue, and I believe you know it.

I believe that you have wilfully inserted in your resolutions for publication statements that you must know to be baseless.

The Freedmen is paid for his labor,   The slave is not.

The Freedman's wife and family are his—   The Slave's are not.

Free Education is given to the Freedman and his children. To the slave it is forbidden.

The Freedman can bring suits and be a witness—   The slave cannot.

These things you know to be true and yet your falsify and deny these great facts.

You know further perfectly well that without some supervision on the part of the United States these Freedmen would be cheated of their labor, induced into contracts that would ruin them and even if fair contracts were made would be uncertain as to their fulfilment. You know this because you have seen it, because you have reported it, because you have ask for the assistance of Military officers to remedy it.

You also know that as a Rule these payments have been Enforced by the military authorities rigorously and that many a hard working man now has his money that otherwise would have been robbed of his dues.

These results can only be obtained by control and supervision of the contracts by the Government officers.   There must be some tribunal to ascertain and secure these rights.   Freedmen may make contracts as they please, but the contract must be approved and registered and will be so done unless manisfestly unfair to the Laborer.

This is provided for in General Orders Nº 23*   If they do not make such contract they can adopt that made by the terms of the order.

They cannot be allowed to lie around doing nothing, because then they become paupers and thieves and fall upon the Government for support.

The Freedmen and the Planters are charged a Capitation Tax, Two Dollars to the Planter, one to the hand to aid in supporting the disabled and helpless.

I have never heard of an undustrious working man who objected to it.

Are you willing with your knowledge of Society here to have the military officers withdraw all control and leave these questions of Labor of Freedom and of rights to such Civil authority as exists in this State.

You well know that you are not? for I receive constant complaints from you in relation to invasion and neglect of your rights.

Your cannot do away with the effects of two centuries of wrong upon White and Black in a day or a year,   you must take time and slow processes of Education to root out such prejudices and habits of thought.

It is more than probable that an entire generation must grow up under new auspices before all this ill effect can be done away.

You must wait and work.   Not call meetings and pass resolutions but work faithfully and slowly to educate the public mind both of whites and

---

*The order, issued by General Hurlbut on March 11, governed plantation labor for the 1865 crop season. (*Wartime Genesis: Lower South*, pp. 591–94.)

blacks, for the future.

It is true that this system prescribed in order of General Banks, and continued by me is temporary to be succeeded in its turn by other step of progress.

Whenever the time comes in which the Freedman can safely appeal to society and the Civil Courts for his rights when invaded, this military supervision will cease.   I do not believe that this time has yet come.

No one will rejoice more than I when it shall come.

Until then under some form or other their paramount rights of living and of Education will be secured to them under the best plan that experience shall devise. and under such control as to officers as the United States may determine.

I differ Entirely from you as to Mr Conway and consider his services valuable and therefore retain him.

I consider your proposal of a mixed Tribunal of arbitration impracticable and decline to establish it.

I shall however forward your Communication and this reply to the Secretary at War to be laid before proper authorities.

Of course I shall be glad to have your assistance as far as it may go in advancing the condition of the Laborers, but in as much as you are not responsible for your acts and I am for mine, I shall not change a system adopted without facts and reasons satisfactory to my mind.   Very Respectfully

HLcS   S A Hurlbut[28]

Labor agreements negotiated informally between former slave-holders and their former slaves were inherently unstable. Even when both parties acted in good faith, they often arrived at conflicting interpretations of their respective rights and obligations. And not everyone acted in good faith, as the former slaves of Thomas Abernathy discovered. Two months after the end of the war, they made an affidavit before a military officer in hopes of forcing Abernathy to clarify the terms of their employment and to make good his promise of payment for the previous year's work.

Freedmen Camp   Tunnel Hill Tenn.   June 19" 1865

Joseph Abernathy & Hustin Abernathy (Colored) being Duly Sworn Deposeth and Says

I   That on the 1^s day of April 1865 Thomas E. Abernathy proposed to me that if I would take the hands that foremaly belonged to Said Thomas E. Abernathy and make him a good crop that he would give us the half of all raised on Said Thomas E Abernathy farm   that each one of you Shall make an equal division of your half of all products raised

II   We was to put in (40) Fourty acres of cotton and (50) Fifty acres of corn (6) Six acres of Sorgum and (2) two of potatoes also Some cabbage all of wich we complied within good faith on our Side

III   At the time of making this contract with Said Thomas E. Abernathy he did not live on his place but had abandon it for the space of (6) Six months prier to Said contract   after he returned to Said farm he told me that he could not give us the half of all produce raised on Said farm as he had agreed to do but I will make a new contract with you   I will give one third instead of one half of all products raised on said farm to wich we upon our part agreed to take in good faith   One week after that time he Said he would not give the One third that we did not have in crop Sufficient to justify him in giving us any portion of Said crop raised on Said farm   he then said that he wanted ten (10) more acres of corn put in to wich proposition we agreed provided he would give us the third as in accordiance with his Second bargain to wich he

replied that he would not give us any portion of the crop   he then Said
that he was going to employ a new man to attend to his business as
overseer who turned out to be Mr John Howard from
Pennsylvania   Mr Howard after taking charge of Said farm told us
that Mr Abernathy told him that he had made a bargain with us and
that we was to have One third of all the products raised upon Said farm
but that he could not now comply with his bargain   Then we asked him
what he would give   Mr Howard replied that Mr Thomas E Abernathy
Says that he will hire you and pay you $15^{00} Fifteen Dollars per month
but your clothing provision and Doctor Bill must come out of Said $15^{00}
Fifteen Dollars per month

IV   And if you will not hire on those terms you Shall all leave the
place   after we Studied the mater over we Came to the Conclusion on
account of our wives & Children that we would make this our third
bargain with Thomas E. Abernathy wich we d[id] in good faith upon our
part   One week after this last contract was made he told us that he
would not give us $15^{00} Fifteen Dollars per month   again we asked
him what will you give us when the Said Thomas E Abernathy replied I
will not tell you what I will give you   I will gi[ve] you just what I please
and no more

V   In 1864 we bargained & agreed with Said Thomas E Abernathy to
raise a crop on Said farm on the following terms   he told us to go on
and raise all the cotton that we wanted to raise that he did not want any
cotton for hisself that if he had any raised the yankees would take it
from him   all that he wanted was (5) five acres of corn raised by us for
him to wich we agreed   Said Thomas E Abernathy after Came to the
Conclusion that he wanted Some cotton raised for his own use and
benefit   we asked him how much cotton he wanted planted   Thomas
E. Abernathy Said plant me (4) Four acres of cotton Seperate from

yours is all that I ask of you   we planted him his (4) Four acres of
cotton raised picked gined and baled Seperate & apart from that raised
as our own   after we had gined & baled our own he marked it in his
own name   he told us that he was obliged to do that as we was not
allowed to Sell any cotton   we had (5) Fife bales of cotton averaging
(500) Five hundred pounds each wich Said Thomas E. Abernathy tuck
to Nashville Tenn. and disposed of   Said Thomas E Abernathy kept all
the proceeds accruing from Said Sales of Said Cotton with the exception
of $150 One hundred and Fifty Dollars wich we received in goods   we
also raised in 1864 about (800) Eight hundred bushels of Corn wich
Said Thomas E. Abernathy did take possession of use and make way
with for his own private use and benefit also would not allow us to use
any of it unless we paid him for it

    VI   We farthers testify and Say that of our own free will and accord
gathered and delivered to Said Thomas E. Abernathy in person at Mrs
Mary Rivers Residence where Said Thomas E Abernathy went to after
he had abandon his own plantation the (5) Five acres of corn that we
raised for Said Thomas E Abernathy in 1864[29]

HD

> The freedmen's affidavit was eventually referred to officials of the
> Freedmen's Bureau, a War Department agency created by Con-
> gress in March 1865 to oversee the transition from slavery to free-
> dom. After investigating the case, the bureau officials ordered
> Thomas Abernathy to make "a written contract with the freedmen
> on his farm . . . by the terms of which the freedmen shall receive
> one third of the crop raised during [1865]." They also negotiated a
> settlement whereby each of five freedmen received $68.67 as his
> share of the proceeds from the cotton raised in 1864.[30]

For some former slaves, the return of peace jeopardized gains made
during the war. When William Bonner abandoned his southern-
Tennessee farm in 1863, his slaves remained behind and supported
themselves by their own labor. Bonner's return shortly before February 1865, when the state abolished slavery, threatened their
hard-won self-sufficiency. A sympathetic white neighbor described
their plight to General Clinton B. Fisk, the head of the Freedmen's
Bureau in Tennessee.

[*Fayetteville, Tenn.*]   (Augst 8th 1865)

Gen[l]   I am called upon by some very worthy and deserving Freedmen
to make a statement of their grieveances to the end that your advise &
directions may be obtained by which they can govern themselves and to
plead that an agent may be sent for their protection at your earliest
convenience

The grievances of which they complain are as follows, that their
former master Dr W[m] Bonner abandoned them with all his other
property in this county in June 1863 by taking what he could transport
and going South in advance of our Army commanded by Genl
Rosecrans   they were left with just such means of support as could
not be moved   there were a few hogs left on the farm which were
subsequently taken from them thereby throwing them entirely upon
their own resourses.   Since then they have worked and lived   his Dr
Bonners Daughter Mrs Lamb in the mean time has been taking from
time to time such of their products as she thought proper for her own
use with out compensation untill last winter when he returned and
reassumed his authority over his possessions

When by the act of the Loyal people of the state they were made free
he first ordered them off his land.   they were preparing to comply when
he proposed to them that if they would remain and go to work he would

make such arrangements as would be satisfactory to them and to the mutual interest of both parties, since which time they have frequently called on him to have the terms definitly understood but have as often failed in getting a satisfactory answer, from what they can learn from himself and their fellow Freedmen his object is to defraud them of the present crop and if they will not submit to the old slave policy to drive them off the land   he has told them and reiterates that if they do not submit that not one of them will be allowed to remain on his land all of which they have great cause to fear without the benign influence of your authority is thrown around them as a wall of defence and a sure refuge in this their time of trouble   for the past Three years they have furnished all the salt they used and the last two have supported themselves entirely and this present year they have stocked the farm with what horses that has been used in making the crop paid the smiths bill and every expence not costing him one cent expence and now to loose it all under the circumstances they cannot they will not believe you will allow

     The complainants of the foregoing represents three families numbering 14 souls   they have managed to procure by purchase and otherwise about 70 head of Hogs Large and small and now William Bonner Sr tells them that they will not be allowed to have or to raise hogs or stock of any kind on the farm that is all his   they have also about 55 acres of corn and also about 30 acres of cotton with a very flattering prospect of a fine yield and with the fear of loseing their labor before them they will be very unesy untill they can hear from you   your attention to the foregoing is earnestly solicited and will place them and myself under obligations to your kindness   there is one other matter to which they desire me to call your attention and it is to know whether they are entitled to any remuneration for their services for last

year. they have had read in their hearing your Circular* and it gives
entire satisfaction   they make but one expression and that is
unanimously in its favor and with an agent within reach they would be-
entirely Content   and another matter they are anxious about the next
year for homes   they wish to know whether an oppertunity will be
afforded within the year to procure a home out of those abandoned
lands   there are enough of such lands to accommodate all the
freedmen and some for refugees   I think from my recollection there are
over Twenty thousand acres that are abandon,d under the Law†   I have
the Honor to be your Obt Serv't

ALS   William French[31]

---

*Circular 2, issued by General Fisk on July 24, 1865, summarized the
objectives of his agency: "promotion of productive industry,"
settlement of former slaves "in homes of their own, with the guarantee
of their absolute freedom and their right to justice before the law . . .
[and] the dissemination of virtuous intelligence." The circular forbade
"[c]ompulsory, unpaid labor," encouraged freedpeople to work "for an
interest in the crop," and pledged that "Special efforts" would be
made to settle them on confiscated or abandoned land. (*Wartime
Genesis: Upper South*, doc. 127n.)

†The law of March 3, 1865, that created the Freedmen's Bureau
authorized its commissioner to "set apart, for the use of loyal refugees
and freedmen," land in the Confederate states that had been
abandoned by its owners or confiscated by the federal government.
(*Statutes at Large*, vol. 13, pp. 507–9.)

CHAPTER

V.

SLAVERY WITHIN THE UNION

ITH THE EMANCIPATION PROCLAMATION TARGET-
ing slavery for destruction in the rebellious states, federal
officials found it harder and harder to clarify the status of slavery
in the loyal slave states—whether for slaves, for slaveholders, or
for the Union military. The escape of slaves to federal forces in
Maryland, Missouri, and Kentucky thrust the issue on officers of
the Union army and navy, and fugitives proved inconveniently
adept at manipulating federal laws to secure their freedom. By
their persistence and ingenuity, the runaways forced their liberty
onto the nation's agenda alongside that of slaves in the Confederacy; they also quickened the government's will to use in the border
states the authority Congress had granted in July 1862 to recruit
"persons of African descent" for military service. Recruitment of
slaves condemned slavery to death, leading Maryland and Missouri
to abolish it on their own and dooming Kentucky to a futile effort to
revive the rotting corpse. Slaves in all three states paid a heavy
price to see the corpse laid to rest, however, for nowhere did slaveholders yield peacefully.

A Union commander in southern Maryland attempted to sort out
the requirements of various federal laws regarding slaves and their
owners: the March 1862 article of war, which forbade members of
the armed forces to return fugitives to those claiming to own them;
the Second Confiscation Act of July 1862, which declared free the
slaves of owners who supported the rebellion, forbade military personnel to judge the validity of claims to runaway slaves, and authorized the employment of persons of African descent to suppress the
rebellion; and the Militia Act of July 1862, which provided freedom
for slaves employed by Union forces. In a circular to his troops, he
set forth in complex array the circumstances under which runaway
slaves ought and ought not to be welcomed and the rules governing
their expulsion.

Pt Lookout, Md   Mch 30, 1863

(Copy)

(Circular)

The Brigadier General Commanding directs that there shall be no
interference with the slave population by the troops within his command
except for certain specific purposes hereinafter named.   Military Camps
shall not be used as places of public resort or for idlers, and All those
coming there, except on important business, or to give information,
should be denied admittance,   Such as have business will be conducted
to the proper Officers of the Camp,   Information will be sought for from
all sources and rewards in money, with protection from danger from
giving information may be promised to all, White and Black.   Any one
suffering from having given information will be protected, without or
within the Camp, as may be necessary.   Commanding Officers will
generally be sustained in the protection afforded by them, but will be
held responsible that there be just grounds for such protection.   All
cases of the kind, should be immediately reported to Head Quarters.

All informants—where the information leads to a capture—will be remunerated, and with a view to this, their names should be taken, by the Officer to whom the information is given and reported. Negroes entering the Camps clandestinely, must be placed without the lines, but in no case *delivered*—either *directly* or *indirectly*—to their Masters, Nor should they be placed without the lines, when their masters or others seeking them are in the Neighborhood of the Camps. All vessels lying at the wharves where there are Troops will be considered within the lines. No distinction will be made as to the departure from the Shores of the Potomac of any persons, on account of color, and all orders heretofore issued or Regulations made by any officer making such distinction, either directly or by inference are hereby declared null and void   All negroes coming from the Western Shore of the Potomac* will be received and protected. With a view to prevent negroes from being used in the illicit trade,† all negroes leaving should be interrogated, as to whether their departure is voluntary. If it shall not appear to be voluntary, they will be detained and protected.

All Commanding Officers, Quartermasters &c, are cautioned not to employ negroes in the Public Service, unless they be free or refugees from the Western Shore, but when once so employed, they will—in accordance with the act of Congress relating to the subject—be forever thereafter protected   By order of Brigadier Gen'l Lockwood[1]

HDc

Already unsettled by the abolition of slavery in the neighboring District of Columbia, slaveholders in Maryland suffered a further blow in June 1863 when the War Department authorized the en-

---

*I.e., from Virginia.

†I.e., illegal trade with the Confederacy.

listment of the state's freemen of African descent. Slaveholders
feared that recruitment of the free would lead inevitably to recruitment of slaves. Events quickly proved them right. Colonel William
Birney, the officer in charge of enlistment, found a ready supply of
potential recruits among slaves consigned by their owners to public
jails and private slave pens in Maryland, where they had been sent
either for safekeeping or to evade emancipation in the District of
Columbia. Birney's superior, General Robert C. Schenck, ordered
him to release from imprisonment slaves belonging to the Confederate general J. E. B. Stuart and other "Rebels and Rebel sympathizers" and to enlist the able-bodied men.[2] Birney reported to
Schenck's headquarters the results of his mission.

Baltimore [*Md.*], July 27, 1863.

Sir, I have the honor to report that immediately on the receipt of
Special Order No. 202, of this date, I proceeded to Camlin's Slave Pen in
Pratt Street, accompanied by Lieut. Sykes and Sergeant Southworth. I
considered any guard unnecessary.

The part of the prison in which slaves are confined is a brick-paved
yard about twenty five feet in width by forty in length, closed in on all
sides. The front wall is a high brick one; the other sides are occupied by
the cells or prisons two or three stories in height. The yard is not
covered in. It is paved with brick. A few benches, a hydrant,
numerous wash tubs and clothes lines covered with drying clothes were
the only objects in it. In this place, I found 26 men 1 boy 29 women and
3 infants. Sixteen of the men were shackled together, by couples, at the
ancles with heavy irons and one had his legs chained together by
ingeniously contrived locks connected by chains suspended to his waist.
I sent for a blacksmith and had the shackles and chains removed.

The following statement exhibits the names of the prisoners, names &
residence of their owners and the periods for which they have been held
in confinement:

Names.	Belongs to	Residence	Period of imprison.	Loyalty.
1. Charles Dorsey,	Thos. Worthington,	Baltimore Co.,	10 d.	Dis.
2. William Sims,	Nancy Counter,	Prince George Co.	17 months.	Disl.
3. Samuel Davis,	Wm. H. Cleggett,	" "	4 mo.	Disl.
	Mr. Cleggett is said to have two sons in rebel army.			
4. John Francis Toodles	Jas. Mulligan,	Prince Geo. Co.	16 mo.	Dis.
	This man has been confined in all about three years.			
5. Henry Toodles,	Emanuel Wade,	Baltimore,	14 mos.	Dis.
6. Henry Wilson,	Geo. Ranniker,	Balt. Co.	1 mo.	Dis.
7. James Dent,	Alfred Osborne	Prince Geo. Co.,	22 mos.	Dis.
8. Geo. Hammond,	Reese Hammond,	Ann Ar. Co.	24 mo.	Dis.
9. Charles Foote,	Thos. Ristar,	Lime Kiln Bot. Balt. Co.	15 m.	Dis.
10. Michael Fletcher	Chas. Hill,	Prince Geo. Co.	14 m.	Dis.

. . . .

These all expressed their desire to enlist in the service of the United States and were conducted to the Recruiting Office on Camden Street to be examined by the Surgeon.

In regard to the slaves of General Stewart, of the rebel army, I could not execute the order, they being confined in the Baltimore City Jail, and not in Camlin's Slave Pen.

The women are in number:

1. Betsey Ward,	Dr. Snyder,	Georgetown,	23 m.	?
2. Virginia West,	Mr. Cleggett,	Prince Geo. Co.	7 m.	D
3. Ellen J. Roberson,	Eriah Hassett,	Washington,	15 mo.	?
4. Lena Harrod,	Dr. Lewis Makel,	Georgetown,	15 m.	?
5. Rachel Harrod (,6 yr. old)	" "	"	15 m.	?
6. Sophia Simmons,	Wm B. Hill,	Malbern,	12 m.	?
7. Martha Wells,	"	"	12 m.	?
8. Susan Collins,	Hammond Dorsey,	Ellicott's Mills,	24 m.	Dis.
9. Willie (child of Susan, & 4 mos. old)		" born in prison.		
10. Martha Clark,	Thos. E. Berry,	Prince Geo. Co.	12 mos.	Dis.

. . . .*

---

*The omitted passages are the remainder of lists totaling twenty-seven men and thirty-two women and children. Forty of the slaves had been confined longer than a year; three had been in jail for over two years. Two children had been born in prison, and one two-year-old child was listed as having been jailed, with his mother, for twenty-three months.

These unfortunates were all liberated in accordance with your order.
It appears from their statements that this slave pen has been used
chiefly for the purpose of holding persons in evasion of the laws of
Congress, entitled to their freedom in the District of Columbia and
persons claimed as slaves by rebels or rebel sympathizers.   Respectfully
Submitted,

ALS   William Birney[3]

> Among Maryland's people of African descent, the free were nearly
> as numerous as the slaves, and nonslaveholders, who relied on the
> labor of the free, far outnumbered slaveholders. Nonslaveholders
> complained that the restriction of recruitment to freemen would
> bring slaveholders an undeserved windfall. William T. Chambers,
> a civilian agent recruiting on Maryland's Eastern Shore, laid the
> nonslaveholders' case before the secretary of war.

Centreville, Queen Anns Co., Md.   Augst 22[d] 1863

Dear Sir: While I believe in the wisdom, and justness of intention on
the part of the Government in all its efforts to put down the rebellion,
you will allow me to call your attention to one thing which is very unjust,
unfair, and which bears very hard on a large majority of the loyal men of
Maryland, viz. the drafting and recruiting free colored men and leaving
out the slaves.

In this (Queen Anns) County, nearly all the slave holders are disloyal
men and are doing all they can against the Government, while nearly all
of the non-slaveholders are loyal and true men to the Government.   By
taking away the free colored men, you take away the labour from the
very men who are doing their utmost to sustain the Government, and

give every advantage to the men who oppose the Government. It ought not to be so. In nearly every case between master and slave, the slave is the only loyal man and anxious to fight for the country, but is prohibited from doing so. Can you not remove the barrier so that all the slaves who wish to, may join the army also? Under existing laws, the disloyal men of this county will be benefitted rather than hurt by the draft. If they happen to be drafted they will either pay the three hundred dollars, commutation money, or put in substitutes, and soon more than get their money back by the exorbitant prices they will demand for the hire of their slaves. But if you will allow the slaves to go, you strike a deeper blow against the rebellion than can be given in any other way.

Sincerely hoping that you will give the matter due consideration, and speedily order the recruiting of slaves, I am, with great respect, your humble and obedient servant.

ALS   William T. Chambers[4]

Civil authorities devised ingenious methods to obstruct the enlistment of freemen. Reasoning that, once hired to an employer, freemen became slaves for the period of their hire and were therefore not eligible to volunteer for the army, local officials arrested both recruiters and recruits.[5] While authorities were using the machinery of the law, local citizens terrorized the families of enlistees. Colonel William Birney described the state of affairs in Maryland to the War Department's Bureau of Colored Troops.

Baltimore [*Md.*],   August 26, 1863.

Sir, The scheme to obstruct and arrest the enlistment of U.S. Colored Troops in Maryland is prosecuted with activity by a few political

schemers; while I have had every reason to believe that the great
majority of loyal men in the state are ready to favor and promote the
measure.   The arrest of my agent, J. P. Creager, acted as was
anticipated: it intimidated the people of color, giving them the
impression that the United States was powerless to protect them against
their enemies in this state.   That act alone caused me to lose between
one and two hundred recruits who were ready to come to the rendezvous
at Baltimore.   It perplexed and disheartened the many respectable
gentlemen who had, in different parts of the state, volunteered to aid me
in gathering in the men willing to enlist.   Nearly all of them have since
been deterred by menaces from the further prosecution of the work; and
the business of recruiting is going on but slowly.   Encouraged by their
success, the enemies of the enlistment of U.S. Colored Troops have
within the last week resorted to the most inhuman outrages against the
families of free men of color who have enlisted: the cornfields of these
poor people have been thrown open, their cows have been driven away
and some of the families have been mercilessly turned out of their
homes.   I shall immediately take measures to lay before you in an
authentic shape the facts of some of these outrages designed to
intimidate the men of color from enlisting.

I have the honor at this time to bring to the notice of the Brevet
Brigadier General Commanding the acts in Queen Ann's County of the
opponents of colored enlistment.   On or about the 19th inst., John
Singer, a free man of color, was arrested, when on the point of leaving
for Baltimore with the avowed intention of joining the U.S. Colored
Troops, on a pretended writ, of which I annex a copy.   Such a writ, I am
advised by counsel learned in the law, is not known to the law of Maryland.
The men who were concerned in this arrest avow their intention to
prevent enlistments by issuing the writ in all similar cases.   I therefore

request that Louis Hergremather, Clement McConner and Charles Chambers may be at once arrested and brought to trial for obstructing enlistments in the Army of the United States.   Your obedient servant,

ALS   William Birney[6]

[*Enclosure*]   [*Queen Annes Co., Md.*]   18th day of August. 1863. The State of Maryland To Clement M[c]Connor.   greeting   Whereas, application has this day been made to me by Charles Chambers, agent of H. S. Mitchell, that John Singer a free Negro after hiring himself to said H. S. Mitchell has left his house, and quit the service of said H. S. Mitchell before the expiration of the time the said hiring was to terminate without reasonable and proper cause.

You are therefore hereby commanded immediately to apprehend the said John Singer and bring him before me the subscriber on the 19th day of inst. ensuing the date hereof, or some other justice of the peace of Queen Ann's Co. in case of my absence, resignation or death, to be dealt with according to law.

HDeSr   (Signed)   Louis Hergremather, J.P.[7]

Identifying enlistment as a route to freedom, slave men volunteered despite their exclusion under the War Department's guidelines. And according to charges lodged by slaveholders, recruiting parties not only welcomed but actively encouraged them. Even as authorities and worried citizens tried to safeguard slavery by obstructing the authorized enlistment of freemen, the unauthorized enlistment of slaves was placing the goal out of reach. In a letter to Postmaster General Montgomery Blair, Governor Augustus W. Bradford denounced the unauthorized enlistment and pleaded that slaveholders might be spared what they considered the greatest provocation of all: the presence in their midst of "a Regiment of negroes."

Baltimore [*Md.*]   Sep. 11 1863

My Dear Judge.   Whilst the progress of our army every where just now
is calculated to fill us with joy & hope I can not enjoy it as I would like,
witnessing as I do the excitement and alarm existing here from what
may almost be called the kidnapping of our slaves.   It sometimes really
almost seems that there is a determination somewhere to get up if
possible, something of a Civil War in Maryld. just as we are about to
subdue it every where else.   I went to Washington two weeks ago on this
subject and regretted that you were absent.   I had an earnest
Conversation with the President and Mr Stanton,* but I fear to little
purpose, for though they both declared that the enlistment of slaves had
not been determined on and no one had been authorized to enlist them,
the practice not only continues but seems from what I see and hear to be
every day increasing.   They are being sent over from the Eastern Shore
by scores and some of the best & most loyal men are among the
sufferers.

   I will not trouble you with many details, but refer only to the last
Committee which waited on me yesterday.—   They were four
Gentlemen from St Michaels District in Talbot County, represented to
me as of undoubted loyalty.   The District itself, as perhaps you know, is
notorious throughout the Shore for its early and inflexible loyalty.   They
said that a few days ago they went on board the Steamer when she was
about to leave her landing, to see if their Slaves were not on board.
They found a large number of slaves from the County huddled together
in the Bow of the Boat armed with uplifted Clubs prepared to resist any
close inspection.   One of these gentlemen—and in his relation he was
very calm & dispassionate—approached the officer having them in
charge & told him that he had come merely to ascertain whether his
Slave was among those on board—and respectfully asked to be allowed

---

*Secretary of War Edwin M. Stanton.

merely to see whether he was there told him at same time that if he
found him, he had no idea of demanding him, or interfering with the
officer's possession of him or interfering in the slightest manner with his
purpose.   That he merely wanted to be able to identify his negro, that
he might have some proof of his being taken by the Government in case
it should think proper to pay for such— *And this request was denied.*—
Now my dear Judge is it not almost a mockery to talk of paying loyal
owners any thing, if the Contraband Camps are closed against them,
and their negroes after being taken by the recruiting officers are at the
very threshold of their own homes suffered to crouch together, conceal
themselves from the possibility of identification, to club off their owners
who make any such attempt, and then carried off before their face to—
no one knows where?

I understand that the President & Secretary of War will say that such
recruiting is unauthorized— Then why in God's name permit it?   It
seems to me to be most obviously due not only to the Citizen but to the
Government itself that some open and positive stand should be taken on
the subject and that nothing should be suffered to be done indirectly
that is not directly ordered.   Let the practice be openly recognized or
openly repudiated.— And let such recruiting either be expressly
ordered or positively forbidden— I write to you with freedom on this
subject and as to a Marylander understanding our Condition and
capable of appreciating the effects of such proceedings in such a
community— I beseech you to stop them, if it be possible.   You can
hardly estimate the damage we are Suffering.— These complaints
come not from the Secessionists or the Democrats—they are
comparatively quiet, and I doubt not are Chuckling in their hearts over
the practice, But our most loyal men, men who are willing and anxious
to sustain the Government—Aye to sustain the Republican party sooner

than again put themselves in the grasp of the Democracy.— But I tell
you, and mark my prediction—if these practices are not speedily
stopped we are given over in spite of all we can do, once more to the
Democratic rule.— As things are now going nothing but Bayonets at
the breast of the people can prevent it.

I have gone farther into the matter than I intended.— if you can by
any possibility have a stop put to this slave enlistment—let me beg you
to do it.

I sat down to write you chiefly about a Supplemental matter.—
These gentlemen whom I saw last evening said to me: "We have come to
you Governor at this time not so much to get pay for our slaves—if the
Government stands in need of them let it have them; but we have come
earnestly to entreat that a *negro regiment* which they threaten to bring
down from Baltimore and quarter in our neighbourhood may not be
allowed to come. Our people are in a state of utter Consternation at the
propect of such a thing.— Whilst we are willing that the Government
shall take from us any thing it needs, for God's sake let it not suffer us
to be pillaged by a Regiment of negroes."

I give you Judge the language as nearly as I can of one of the
Committee—a plain straightforward, sensible, loyal Farmer. I wish you
could have heard him. And can not this poor boon at least be granted?
Can not this Regiment be kept here where it is? or must it without the
shadow of necessity be sent across the Bay only further to inflame,
terrify and disgust our Citizens? Truly this would seem to be adding
insult to injury.— Will you my dear Sir, see the President and if you
can do nothing else, keep at least this negro Regiment at home. Yours
very Truly

ALS   A W Bradford[8]

Although the slaveholders' complaints moved President Lincoln to suspend the enlistment of black men in Maryland, military necessity argued for continued access to such convenient manpower. Recruitment resumed in early October under a new policy, announced by the War Department in General Order 329, which became the model for recruitment in Missouri as well. The new policy extended recruitment to slaves whose owners consented (with compensation for unionist owners) and even to slaves whose owners objected if, after a thirty-day grace period, not enough recruits could be obtained among freemen and the slaves of consenting owners. Armed recruiting parties of black soldiers roved the countryside, protecting recruits from retaliation and provoking a fresh spate of complaints. When Lincoln protested to the Union commander in Maryland that the black troops were "frightening quiet people," he was informed that the only "disorder" attending their presence had been the murder of a federal officer by two secessionists. He responded: "It seems to me we could send white men to recruit better than to send negroes, and thus inaugerate homicides on punctilio."[9] In late October, a group of slaveholders asked the help of Reverdy Johnson, one of Maryland's U.S. senators, in getting the soldiers removed.

Upper Ma[r]lboro [*Md.*].   Wednesday, Oct 28. 1863

Dear Sir   Your letters to Major Lee gave us great relief.   But the negro troops have *not* been withdrawn.   The promise made to you last friday has not been kept.   They are still harassing us, plundering us, abducting our negroes.   So far from being withdrawn the field or their raid upon is much extended; now all way up the Patuxent.   Yesterday a steamboat of them came up to Hill's landing, the head of navigation of the river, opposite this place.   The negroes in the fields refusing their persuasions to go with them, they threaten them, that they will return to-morrow, thursday, and carry them off by force.   We beg your prompt and urgent interposition.   Judge Blair, we trust, will aid you.   The

officer of the adjutant general's department, whom he told our
deputation in Washington, last Wednesday, would be despatched that
day to the Patuxent, never came at all.   Very truly, your friends and obt.
sevts

Thos Clagett Jr	C C Mapson
Thos. Hodgkin	W^m. B. Hill
Shelby Clark	J. F. Lee
R. H. Sasscer	Saml. H. Berry[10]

> In an endorsement refuting the slaveholders' charges, Colonel Bir-
> ney insisted that black people were virtually the only unionists to
> be found in the area.

Newtown, Md.   Nov. 8 /63.

The authors of the within letter are reckless in their statements.   I
intend to recruit up the Patuxent but never have done so.   Above
Benedict, where my stockade camp is located, there never has been a
recruiting station or party.   The "steamboat of them" (negro troops)
contained *three* colored soldiers placed on board to prevent slaveholders
from burning the boat.   There was one officer on board.   The object of
the trip was to observe the landings, with a view to future recruiting
under order No. 329 and to give the regular pilot of the boat the
advantage of the instruction of a Patuxent river pilot who accompanied
him.   There was no *"harrassing," "plundering"* or "abducting," terms
which I understand Senator Johnson's correspondents to apply to the
Government recruiting of Colored Troops for the defence of the country.

The threats to return next day and "carry them off by force" are the
coinage of Messers Hodgkin and his associates.   The officer & men on

the boat fully understood they were *not* to return next day. The boat
has never returned there nor has there since that date been a colored
soldier or an officer of the U.S. Colored Troops up the Patuxent above
Benedict for any purpose whatever.

The Western Shore* slave owners are more unscrupulous than the
same class elsewhere. Two of them killed my Lieutenant, the
unfortunate and noble-hearted White, others helped off the murderers,
nearly all of them justified the murder; and now, we have strong grounds
for suspecting that four of my soldiers, who have died suddenly—after
an hour's convulsions—have been poisoned by the emissaries of these
men.

When there is sufficient loyalty and public virtue on the Western
Shore to make it unpopular to run the blockade or to harbor rebel
officers and spies, it will be time enough for its inhabitants to claim
peculiar privileges from Government and to oppose the increase of the
U.S. Army. At present, nearly all the loyal men here are among the
class which I have been sent here to recruit.

AES   William Birney[11]

> Responding to another complaint, Birney curtly refuted the charge
> that he and his recruiters were forcing unwilling men to enlist. At
> the same time, he pinpointed what he considered the chief motive of
> those slaves who remained with their owners.

Camp Stanton [*Md.*],   Jan. 28, 1864.

No slaves whatever have been mustered by me against their will; and
no free persons. Every person prior to muster has full opportunity to

---

*The portion of Maryland on the western shore of Chesapeake Bay.

say whether or not he will enter the service or not.   I do not keep my recruits under guard.

Slaveholders have frequently offered me their slaves, provided I would take them by force.   I have uniformly declined having any thing to do with forcing them, although if the slaveholders had brought the men to me, I should have taken them, the orders recognising their right to enlist them.

Nine owners out of ten will insist upon it that their slaves are much attached to them and would not leave them unless enticed or forced away. My conviction is that this is a delusion.   I have yet to see a slave of this kind.   If their families could be cared for or taken with them, the whole slave population of Maryland would make its exodus to Washington.

AES   Wm Birney[12]

With freedom beckoning in the District of Columbia and recruitment dissipating what remained of owners' authority, many Maryland slaveholders became indifferent to the fate of slavery. Proponents of emancipation gained the upper hand in state politics, and in April 1864, a constitutional convention opened with a mandate to abolish slavery. The prospect of freedom under a new constitution removed the major motive for slaves to enlist. Answering charges that recruiters were resorting to force, Colonel Samuel M. Bowman, who had succeeded Birney, expressed the opinion that recruitment had reached its limit in Maryland.

Balt[*imore*]. M^d   May 11" 1864

Sir: I have the honor to submit the following report in regard to the allegations of Saml. T. Redgrave and others

The officer referred to was. Capt Reed. 19th USC.T.   He says, he lay with his boat at Annapolis three days, and gave his name to all who inquired of him.   He says further, that he was informed the negroes in the district referred to, had been told not to enlist, that they would be sold to Government for breast works &c and that he directed many of them to be brought up so he could see them, and talk to them personally some friendly citizens assisting; that after seeing them and disabusing their minds of needless fear, they cheerfully enlisted.   It is my custom to talk to the men before I muster them in, and in no instance have I finally mustered a recruit who expressed the least unwillingness

It is my opinion that Negro recruiting in Maryland is hurtful; negroes by force of circumstances and the costoms of the county have heretofore performed all the labor, and able bodied negroes between 20 & 45 have become exceedingly scarce, and whenever the U.S. gets a soldier, sombody's plow stands still; or sombody has lost a slave or servant of somekind

The only way to prevent these outrages is to stop recruiting entirely   I have the honor to be Very Respy Your Obedt Servant

HLS   S. M. Bowman[13]

Witnessing the collapse of slavery and aware that a constitutional convention was debating emancipation, some slaves mistakenly concluded that freedom was already theirs by law. A woman in northern Maryland, perplexed at being still treated as a slave, demanded that the president himself clarify her status.

Belair [*Md.*]   Aug 25th 1864

Mr president   It is my Desire to be free. to go to see my people on the eastern shore.   my mistress wont let me   you will please let me know if we are free. and what i can do.   I write to you for advice.   please send me word this week. or as soon as possible and oblidge.

ALS   Annie Davis[14]

Although Lincoln did not answer, the voters of Maryland soon did.
In October they ratified a new state constitution abolishing slavery;
it took effect on November 1.

In Missouri, as in Maryland, slaves probed federal regulations for
loopholes that might afford them freedom. They gained an ally
during General Samuel R. Curtis's command of the Department of
the Missouri, between September 1862 and the spring of 1863. His
General Order 35, issued in December 1862, gave practical force
to the Second Confiscation Act. The order required provost marshals to "protect the freedom and persons" of those emancipated
by the act and to provide them with certificates—in effect, free
papers—declaring them "entitled to the protection of all officers
of the United States."[15] General Curtis's identification with the antislavery faction in Missouri and the hostility of Governor Hamilton R. Gamble and most slaveholding unionists prompted Lincoln
to replace Curtis with General John M. Schofield in May 1863.
But the slaves had already learned how to turn the rules to their
advantage. A group of slaveholders complained to Governor Gamble that fugitives seeking to bolster claims for sanctuary deliberately misled soldiers about their owners' loyalty.

Lexington [*Mo.*]   June 4. 1863

Dear Sir   We the undersigned Union men Citizens of Lafayette
County in the State of Missouri, would earnestly state to your
Excellency, that under the order of F. A. Dick Lt. Col. & Provost
Marshall General Department of the Missouri, purporting to be "By
command of Major General Curtis, dated St Louis 24th December 1862
and numbered General Orders N° 35, we have been made to suffer great
inconvenience as well as loss of property—

Our servants have been induced to run away and come to the Post at
Lexington; and we have in vain endeavored to get them—   We go to the

Post Commander and though our loyalty is unquestioned, we have been unable to reclaim our negroes— We see them in camp or around the Camp, the Commander will not do anything: but his soldiers in many cases are standing by, ready to aid the negroes in resisting their masters; These negroes are most of them armed; they have been furnished with tents and with rations— It is no matter what proof the master offers, the negroes say that they be long to secessionists, and the officers believe them— We suppose that there are now or were on yesterday at least 150 negroes at the College and around it at Lexington—and not one can be obtained by the owner, no matter how loyal he may be— Apply by force of legal process and the soldiers will pay no regard to civil officers or civil process— Now Governor, what can we do?— The Military will obey Dick's order; but have no respect for the advice or orders of the President and the Attorney General— These self-constituted Judges, Military Judges, will decide and confiscate our slaves and little subordinate Provost Marshalls under the order of Mr. Dick will gravely confiscate the best Union man's servant; give him a pass and imprison his master, if he resent this injury by retaking his servant. Such has been the practice at this Post heretofore— We ask your Excellency since we have a new Commander here, and a new Provost Marshall, that you will see Major General Schofield & have so much of said order N° 35 above mentioned rescinded or abrogated as relates to the confiscation of our negroes & other property by the mere Military arbitrament of Provost Marshalls— Have articles or paragraphs XIII, XIV up to XVIII either rescinded or altered, so that we may be safe in our property— We ask nothing for the disloyal men of our Country— Still we think the Courts & not the Military should confiscate the property, after trial & hearing in open Court—

The President's [*Emancipation*] Proclamation of 1st Jany '63 does
not embrace Missouri. Why should the radicals enforce it here—at the
point of the bayonet? This is grievous, a crying evil and calls loudly for
redress— We therefore desire you as our Chief Magistrate to do
something for us in this business— Genl Schofield will do what is right,
we doubt not, especially if you Governor will call his attention to it—
We ask a repeal of this abolition order; this military license to steal our
negroes— We will not be understood to cast censure on the present
Provost Marshall & the Commander now at this Post, they but obey
Dick's order & Genl Loan's instructions as we beleive— Very
respectfully your obt servts

| | John F. Ryland | Henry C Chiles |
| HLS | Eldridge Burden | L W Smallwood[16] |

In July, General Schofield countermanded the system of certificates of freedom issued by provost marshals, ordering that the
claims of slaves be handed over to civil authorities for individual
adjudication.

While General Schofield was trimming the free-paper system, a
state convention attempted to halt the erosion of slavery by executing a tactical retreat: it passed an ordinance providing for eventual
emancipation, but so gradually that the process would not begin
until 1870 and would not end until the turn of the century. Slaves
cared little for the loyal slaveholders' needs, which the ordinance
was designed to protect. Nonslaveholders cared not much more,
gladly hiring runaways to ease their own shortage of labor. And
even as the convention was attempting to shore up the wobbling ed-
ifice of slavery, Union recruiting parties were mining its foundation. In June, E. P. Cayce informed his father, M. P. Cayce, a dele-
gate at the convention then under way, that recruiters were jeopar-
dizing local farmers' supply of labor.

Farmington M°   June 19, 1863

My Dear Pa   I have just returned from the Harvest Field where I have been making a pretty good shocker.   We are getting along very well indeed considering all the drawbacks we have had to encounter.   We have almost finished the two smaller fields & will begin on the large field of Mediterranean tomorrow.   There has been considerable excitement here among the negroes, owing to the fact that a recruiting party from the 3ᵈ Mo Cavalry are here endeavouring to raise men for the black brigade: They seem to be by no means particular however; either as it regards sex, or age, as they are willing to take men, women & children, the oldest & the youngest alike.   I fully expected to awake and find all of ours preparing to leave me this morning.   Night before last several of the men came to the Cabins, collected the Negroes together and lectured them for several hours, the consequence was that they (the negroes) could not resist the glowing pictures presented to them, & they had all about come to the conclusion to leave in a body.   Seven or Eight of the men dined with me yesterday & requested me have all of the Negroes brought in from the Farm & that he (the Lieut) would make a plain statement to them in my presence of what was wanted of them & what duties they were expected to perform, and all that volunteered might go and all that refused should remain.   I agreed to this, preferring an open statement to secret persuasion.   We did so, but as soon as the negroes found that they were required to fight & be separated from their families, they did not desire to go.   This spokesman happened to be the same man who had lectured them the night before.   And the Negroes say that he used very different arguments—in my presence, from those which he presented the night before.   Dick Glenday was the only one, that was willing to volunteer, & his courage failed him this evening. This morning all went back to Harvesting.   The soldiers have not gone yet: a large portion have gone to Big River for Recruits.   If they will lett our negroes alone the will remain at home satisfied.   But there is no telling what they may do—if constantly plied with the most seductive persuasions.   They have about stripped Cooks Settlement & Fredericktown of negroes—   The crops are rotting in the Fields for want of Harvest hands—   Farmers are offering 3 dollars per day; but they cannot be got.

But I must close, as it is growing late.   I will write to you again tomorrow.   I have heard nothing of the stolen mare—   The children are getting well very rapidly.   All join me in love—   Yours Affectly

ALS   E. P. Cayce[17]

> Governor Gamble seconded Cayce's charges, calling the conduct of the recruiters "most intolerable." The colonel from whose regiment the recruiters had operated reported that they had acted in his absence; their methods he condemned as "lawlessness, that can not be surpassed."[18]
>
> Still, the objections of slaveholders failed to deter slaves eager to enlist, and recruiters disregarded General Schofield's guidelines limiting recruitment to freemen and the slaves of disloyal owners. Nor did the gradual emancipation ordinance staunch the hemorrhage of slave workers. A month after his son wrote to him about the damage recruitment was doing, M. C. Cayce sought General Schofield's help in denying fugitives access to government posts and in tightening the owners' hold on slaves still in their possession.

Farmington M⁰   July 31. 1863

Sir.   Since the adjournment of the State Convention I have been frequently questioned by Loyal owners of Slaves, respecting the probability of their being able to reclaim fugitives from labor now at the various Military Posts; and also, whether the services of those they still retain possession of will not be rendered more secure by our Government during the term of years granted by the Convention.   I have understood, & have hazarded the opinion that a gradual scheme of Emancipation, similar to ours, would meet with favor from President Lincoln, & that as soon as feasible, as much security would be granted to loyal owners, in the possession of their property—as the present condition of Affairs will admit of.

So far as my knowledge extends, the Slave owners of this district gave a cheerful acquiescence to the Emancipation Act, hoping that this might be the occasion of ensuring the possession of their Slaves until free labor could be obtained, which cannot now be done.   They, however, continue to lose their slaves as rapidly as before this act was passed.   In this vicinity several Negro Men have left their owners, and the Women & Children are preparing to go also: Indeed, it is expected that in a short time there will be an extensive stampede among them.

It would not be proper in me, Sir, to offer advice in the management of the affairs of our State.   But I would venture to express the belief that if our Government could with propriety exclude Slaves from entering military Posts or Camps, & forbid their passage on Rail Roads, that it would give confidence to many loyal & law abiding Citizens, and also serve to induce a greater respect for the Emancipation ordnance, from those whom it most narrowly concerns.   With high consideration & respect I am your obedient Servant

ALS   M. P. Cayce[19]

Calculating owners tried to protect their investment by removing their slaves to Kentucky, where neither emancipation nor the prospect of enlistment yet threatened slave property. Army officers

in Louisville estimated in November 1863 that "thousands" of
slaves had been moved from Missouri to Kentucky.[20] Jason Chamberlin, the owner of Fanny Ann Flood and her husband, did not
await the outcome of the state convention's deliberations; he forced
the couple to accompany him to Kentucky in May 1863. After the
war, Fanny Flood recounted Chamberlin's murder of her husband
the September after they reached Kentucky.

State of Kentucky   County of Jefferson   7th of Mch. 1866

Fanny Ann Flood, colored, being duly sworn, declares

I am 35 years of age.   I reside on Jefferson St, at D[r] Hughes's,
between 1st and 2nd.   I am a widow.

My husbands name was Peter Flood.   I married him in Shelby Co.
Ky, about eleven years since   We then belonged, both of us, to Jason
Chamberlin a farmer, near Middletown.   My Owner carried us to
Georgetown, in Pettus Co, Missouri;   Immediately after reaching there
he hired us out to James Mitchel, a preacher in Saline Co—about thirty
miles from Georgetown.   We remained about two years with M[r]
Michel—   M[r] Chamberlin then carried us to Pettus Co and sold us, by
private bargain, to one George Rothwell a surgeon.   D[r] Rothwell kept us
eight years.   He then lived in Longwood, Pettus Co,   He is now in
Booneville, M[o].

One day the D[r] came to me and said "Fanny, I want you & Peter to
stay here, and take care of my family,   I cannot stay here,
constant,   He talked as if he was afraid of the soldiers killing him, if
they Caught him.   He said he would come now and then to see us & how
things were getting on.   We lived twelve miles from M[r] Chamberlin.   I
only saw him once during these eight years after he sold us.   I on that
occasion went to see him.   The Doctor was a widower.   He had four
children.   I did the work inside, had full charge of it—   My husband did

the whole outside work.

One morning Mr Chamberlin came to the Doctor's house. He told me & my husband, that we had to go with him to Kentucky; that he had not been paid for us by the D^r. My husband objected to leaving so suddenly—and without the consent of the doctor—but Chamberlin forced us to come off at once— He would not give me time to pack or take my own few personal things. He said he was in a great hurry, and would pay me for them—but he has not done so yet.

We left Sedalia on a Wednesday and arrived here next Friday. He took us at once to Middletown. We remained with him until next Tuesday when he took us to Mrs Chamberlins on the Bardstown pike & about three miles from Louisville. This was in May two years ago. We remained with the widow Chamberlin until next October, (1863,)

While we were at the widow Chamberlin's my husband was wishful to return to Missouri. He told me so often. One day he left me, he did not tell me whereto. In about a month afts he came to see me. On a Sunday. He told me he had been across the [*Ohio*] river, and was working for the Gov^t He came about ten AM and left about 3 P.M. He told me he would come to see me in about two or three weeks again. He gave me $5.

Next day, Monday, Mr Chamberlin heard of my husband having been to see me, and also where he was working.

Next Wednesday, a gent^n who boarded with Mrs Chamberlin, named Major Kemp, read from a newspaper, that my husband was dead, that he had been put in gaol, and that Mr Chamberlin had whipped him to death in the jail. Major Kemp told myself so. He said "Fanny I have bad news to tell you, Your husband was whipped to death"— That Chamberlin had went, or sent, and got him. Mrs Chamberlin told me that Chamberlin allowed he did not wish to punish him to death, but only to give him a severe whipping.

About a week before Christmas Mr. Chamberlin came to the widow's   He sent for me.   I found him in his buggy, at the front of the house.   He asked me how I was, & then went into the house.   While he was in the house I went to him and asked him for help   The widow, & her aunt Mrs Hall, were present.   He asked me what help I wanted.   I told him all the other servants in the house received help from their owners & I asked him to give me some.   He said I had good clothes & he reckoned I got plenty to eat & he did not see what more I wanted.   He told me if I was "not satisfied, to pick up my duds, and leave",—and he would "get me and serve me as he "did Peter."   After he left Mrs Chamberlin (the widow) came to me and said she would give me something as my owner would not.

Mr Chamberlin was rough to us, after he took us from Missouri.

My husband was a man of good health.   I never knew him to be sick a moment, except when we lived in Missouri   I saw him have a chill once or twice there.   He had none after we returned to Kentucky   He was a strong, very strong man.   He was rather younger than me   We had five children: four of them are living.   Three of them are now with me. My oldest, a boy, works out.

her

Fanny Ann ✕ Flood[21]

mark

HDSr

In another affidavit, a white witness attested that Peter Flood had been imprisoned as a runaway and, while in prison, beaten to death by Chamberlin and Chamberlin's son-in-law. Rejecting a jury's verdict that the beating had caused Flood's death, the county coroner convened a new inquest. Two surgeons "made a Poste Mortom on the body—but could not determin the real cause of death," according to the coroner, and the second inquest resulted in a verdict of death "from some cause unknown to the Jury."[22]

The pretense of limited recruitment in Missouri ended in November 1863. In his General Order 135, General Schofield announced a new policy: enlistment of any able-bodied man of African descent, slave or free, regardless of the owner's loyalty or consent, with freedom for slave enlistees and compensation for loyal owners.[23] Like slaves in Maryland, slaves in Missouri sought to enlist for one reason above all: to gain freedom for themselves and their families. And like owners in Maryland, those in Missouri opposed such enlistment for the same reason. They gained leverage when General Schofield and his successor, General William S. Rosecrans, banned mobile recruiting parties. As Aaron Mitchell, a slave in northeastern Missouri, made clear in an affidavit concerning the murder of a fellow fugitive, slaves wishing to enlist had to weigh the risk of being captured by armed patrols before they could reach the recruiting station.

[*Louisiana, Mo.*]   Janry 4" 1864.

Aaron Mitchell, colored man, belongs to Thomas Waugh, Says

I was present last October, about the 8" or 10", when Alfred a colored man of James Stewart was Shot.   Alfred, myself, Mrs Beasley's Henry and a girl named Malvina had Started to Hannibal a few days before to Enlist.   We were arrested near Frankford, by George Tate, Joseph Brown, Robert Huff and John Cash taken to Frankford, kept there all night, and the next day we were taken back to our homes near Prairieville.   They took Henry home to Mrs. Beasly and whipped him. They then took me and Alfred to Stewarts, and whipped us both.   I was first taken home to Mr Waugh's & learning that Mr Waugh was at

Stewarts, they took me there. Just before we got to the house I heard a pistol fired   I was about 200 yards off when I heard it. When I got there, I saw Alfred lying in a little ice house in the yard. He was dead. He had been Shot through the heart, the ball coming to the Skin on his back. Ja[s] Stewart, Henry Pollord, James Calvin Mr. Gee, the overseer, W[m] Richardson, Tho[s] Waugh, Samel Richardson, Walker Johnson, Geo Tate, and Bob Huff were standing, looking at him.[24]

HD

In an earlier investigation of the same incident, another army officer learned that after Alfred had been severely whipped, "the owner (who I am informed is a widow woman) offered to give any one five dollars who would kill the negro, whereupon one of the party steped forward and drew his Revolver and Shot him through the heart, killing the boy almost instantly."[25]

———•———

Slave men who made good their escape generally had to leave their families behind, at the mercy of owners who tried to prevent the soldiers from communicating with their wives and children, let alone attending to their needs. The wife of a slave who had enlisted in a Missouri regiment warned her husband against sending money in care of her owner, for fear he would intercept it.

Paris Mo   Jany 19, 1864

My Dear Husband   I r'ecd your letter dated Jan'y 9th also one dated Jany 1st but have got no one till now to write for me. You do not know how bad I am treated. They are treating me worse and worse every day. Our child cries for you. Send me some money as soon as you can for me and my child are almost naked. My cloth is yet in the loom and there is

no telling when it will be out.   Do not send any of your letters to
Hogsett especially those having money in them as Hogsett will keep the
money.   George Combs went to Hannibal soon after you did so I did not
get that money from him.   Do the best you can and do not fret too much
for me for it wont be long before I will be free and then all we make will
be ours.   Your affectionate wife

Ann

P.S.   Sind our little girl a string of beads in your next letter to remember
you by.   Ann[26]

HLSr

[*Endorsement*]   Andy if you send me any more letters for your wife do
not send them in the care of any one.   Just direct them plainly to James
A Carney Paris Monroe County Mo.   Do not write too often   Once a
month will be plenty and when you write do not write as though you had
recd any letters for if you do your wife will not be so apt to get them.
Hogsett has forbid her coming to my house so we cannot read them to
her privately.   If you send any money I will give that to her myself.
Yrs &c   Jas A Carney

> The vulnerability of their families to reprisals by their owners dis-
> couraged many men from volunteering and angered those already
> in the army. Soldiers convalescing in a military hospital near
> St. Louis threatened owners with the armed might of the federal
> military;* other soldiers made forays into the countryside to free
> their families. Some sought and received support from their offi-
> cers. Lieutenant William P. Deming relayed to General William A.
> Pile, who supervised the recruitment of black soldiers in Missouri,
> his men's complaints that owners were punishing their wives and
> children by assigning them heavy work normally done by the men.

---

*See below, pp. 481–82, and *Destruction of Slavery*, pp. 483–85.

Benton Barracks Mo Feb 1ˢᵗ 1864

Sir,   Complaint has been made to me, by Martin Patterson, of Co. "H,"
2ᵈ Missouri Vols of A[*frican*]. D[*escent*]. that he has direct and reliable
information from home that his family is receiving ill treatment from
James Patterson their master, of Fayette, Howard Co. Mo

He says, that his wife is compelled to do out door work,—such as chop
wood, husk corn &c. and that one of his children has been suffered to
freeze, and has sinc died

Further complaint has been made by Wᵐ Brooks that his wife and
children are receiving ill treatment from Jack Sutter their master, of
Fayette, Howard Co. Mo.   He says that they are required to do the
same work that he formerly had to do, such as chopping wood, splitting
rails &c

The said Martin Patterson and Wᵐ Brooks request that permission be
granted to remove their families to Jefferson City   Yours Respectfuly
ALS   William P Deming[27]

In a petition to General Rosecrans, more than one hundred citizens
of a county in northeastern Missouri detailed the methods by which
local slaveholders sought to prevent slaves from enlisting.

[*Louisiana, Mo.   February 1864*]

TO MAJOR GENERAL W. S. ROSECRANS. COMMANDING
DEPARTMENT OF THE MISSOURI.   The subscribers citizens of the
city of Louisiana and vicinity, in Pike County, Missouri respectfully beg
to call your attention to certain abuses, existing in our county and we
doubt not elsewhere, and which we believe grow out of, Either a want of

perspicuity in existing orders and consequent misconstruction of those orders, or from a want of disposition to execute them.

Some two or three months since Leiut Jefferson A Mayhall 3rd M[*issouri*]. S[*tate*]. M[*ilitia*]. was appointed Asst. Pro. Marshall at this place, with orders to recruit Negros under General Order N° 135,* and at once entered earnestly on his duties. It soon became apparent that from many sections of the County, the Negros failed to come in, as was alleged by the few that did come in, because they were prevented by their owners, in some cases by actual violence, others by threats of violence, in others by the locking up the clothing, and in some cases by the owners promising rewards or bounties to them not to Enlist. These facts being communicated to the Pro. Mar General, the Order Dated Dec 19th 1863 (a copy of which is herewith handed) was sent to him. In compliance with this order, he sent out his small guard to make inquiry as to the facts, and to notify the Negroes of their right to Enlist without hindrance. A large number did come immediately and enlisted, proving conclusively and for some of the reasons assigned, they had been prevented. Many Women and children the families of those who had Enlisted, escaped from their owners, and came into this place in the most deplorable condition, many of them in a condition of almost *Nudity* at the coldest season during the present Winter, and found temporary shelter and employment among the Loyal Citizens of this place.

Again Lieut Mayhall the Asst Pro Marshall here receives an order from the Provost Marshall General, (of which we hand copy herewith dated January 22nd 1864) prohibiting the sending out of men for the purpose contemplated by the former order, but directing him to send out and notify such persons as were necessary to prove the fact of

---

*The order authorized the recruitment of any able-bodied black man, slave or free, with or without the owner's consent. (See above, p. 359.)

obstructions to Negroes coming in to Enlist &c. We beg to submit, that, in Missouri the testimony of Negroes is not to be received under any circumstances, and it is not probable that any white person would be permitted to witness any such obstructions, except those implicated.

Again, the copy of letter from H. V. P. Block to Pro Mar General (herewith dated January 15. 1864) was forwarded by that officer with his order of January 22 to the Asst Pro Marshall here. Mr. Block asserts in the above named letter "that Col Marsh" (Pro Marshal General) *"told me I could offer any under my control any inducement I choose to remain"* By sending the copy of that letter, we presume the Pro. Mar. General avows the truth of this statement. We submit whether this be not an open violation of the Law and orders, which prohibits any person from dissuading men from voluntering in the United States service.

We understood the object of General Order N°. 135. to be to obtain recruits and that every reasonable means of giving information to the Negroes of their right to Enlist without molestation, the pay to be given them, and the acquirement of their freedom &c were not only the right of the Asst Pro Marshal here, but his duty. The effect of the last order from the Pro. Mar. General, has been to suspend Enlistments of Negroes altogether.

We earnestly desire the Enlistment of all of them that will do so, but they will not do so, if their families are to be abused, beaten, seized and driven to their former homes in the night and deprived of reasonable food & clothing because of their Enlistment These sceines have been enacted here in our streets by day and night during the past two weeks by the owners of the women and children, families of recruits, that have come here for shelter scarce one of these owners ever having made a pretense of loyalty

We do not desire to add to the perplexities of your position. We therefore earnestly hope that such clear and specific orders as to the duties of recruiting officers may be given, that they may not be mistaken. That the provisions of general order N°. 135 may be conducted and carried out in good faith, as we suppose it was intended, to secure the Enlistment of all who desired. We beg further that if, under the Law, the families of recruits are to be protected from violence in consequence of the Enlistment of their Husbands and Fathers it may be so stated in clear and unequivoical terms. If those families are entitled to freedom on the enlistment of the recruits, or only at the end of his term of service, that this also may be decided, so as to put an end, so far as may be, to all disquiet among the Negroes. That if the families of recruits are to be surrendered up to their owners notwithstanding all the brutal treatment they may receive, that this also may be fully stated, so there shall be no misapprehension on the subject. Attempts of Negroes to reach recruiting stations for the purpose of Enlistment, prior to the issuing of order N°. 135, have resulted, in one instance at least, in this county, in the deliberate shooting of one of them, no notice of which was ever taken by inquest or otherwise by the parties having knowledge of it, until the guilty party had ample time to make his escape. We think it is time indeed to put an end to such brutality.

We beg to state that we believe our Asst Pro. Marshal Lieut Mayhall has endeavoured to execute his orders, to the utmost of his ability, so far as it was possible to do so from their apparently conflicting character. We have the Honor to be very respectfully, Your fellow Citizens.

HDS   [*132 signatures*][28]

Declaring that the abuse of soldiers' families had "almost suspended enlistment," a federal recruiter told a member of the state's congressional delegation in February 1864 that there was only one
remedy: *"emancipation immediate and unconditional."*[29]

As the fabric of slave society unraveled in Missouri, recruitment
gained reluctant converts among owners who had already lost control of their slave men. In one southeastern county, an obliging
provost marshal honored a request from slaveholders who wanted
him to forcibly enlist slaves who had "left them and gone to work
for them Selves."[30] In a petition to General Rosecrans, nearly 200
state legislators proposed that forcible enlistment be adopted as official policy.

Jefferson City [*Mo.*] Feb 13th 1864

Sir   The undersigned members of the General Assembly of Missouri:
would respectfully call your attention, to the fact: that, a large number
of negros have left their masters or owners, and are now wandering
about: many of them out of employment, and in a destitute condition:
and likely to become a nusiance to the neighborhoods in which they have
located.

Believing it but right, and just, that such as are able, who have left
their owners, and have not enlisted, should be compelled to do so at once.
We would therefore respectfully ask, that such steps be taken, as will
force every colored man who is suitable for service, and who has left his
owner, *to enlist*

HDS   [*178 signatures*][31]

At the same time that owners sought forcible enlistment of slave
men, they forcibly evicted slave women and dependents. Reporting
on one such incident and knowing that others would follow, a Union

officer asked for instructions from the provost marshal general of the Department of the Missouri, Colonel John P. Sanderson.

Fulton M^{o} March 28th 1864

Colonel.   The wife of a colored recruit came into my Office to night and says she has been severely beaten and driven from home by her master and owner.   She has a child some two years old with her, and says she left two larger ones at home,   She desires to be sent forward with her husband; says she is willing to work and expects to do so at home or elsewhere; that her master told her never to return to him; that his men were all gone, and that he could not, and would not support the women. What is proper for me to do in such cases?   I know many such will occur.   Several persons have asked me the question. "What are we to do with the women and children"?   the men are in the army; we cannot raise enough for them to eat.   I am well convinced that threats are made, that in case the men go away, the women will be turned out of door.   The owner of the woman refered to, is an aged man, a most inveterate rebel, and has, or did have when the war commenced, four sons in the rebel army.   I am Colonel Very Respectfully Your Obedient Servant

ALS   Hiram Cornell[32]

Colonel Sanderson characterized Cornell's request as "one of dozen's of similar applications of like character."[33]

———•———

One development that owners did not resign themselves to was the transformation of slaves into men and women who contracted their own labor and collected its reward. As an officer in the Missouri

State Militia advised Colonel Sanderson, laws prohibiting the hire of slaves without their owners' consent remained on the statute books, a potent weapon for intimidating would-be employers.

Marshall Mo   April 15th 1864

Col.   We have quite a number of Negro men around here: who have left their masters.   The farmers about here are anxious to procure all the labor they can possibly get, but are deterred from hiring these negroes for fear of being Indicted by the Grand Jury.   Their masters will not come & take them away. but object to any ones hiring them.   Our county needs all the labor this year she can possibly get: Let the farmers procure all the labor possible and the crops this year will fall far short of any previous year;   Please let me Know at your earliest convenience what can be done in the matter & oblige.   Yours very Resptfly &c

ALS   B H Wilson[34]

Sanderson referred Wilson's letter to the departmental commander, insisting that "humanity imperatively demands the announcement of some definite policy or mode of action in these cases."[35]

Employers of former slaves risked criminal indictment or civil lawsuits; their employees risked personal attack. Using threats and force to drive away former slaves whom their neighbors had hired, a party of men in northern Missouri declared that "free negros shall not be permitted to stay in this Community."[36] But neither threats, legal action, nor outright violence stopped slaves from trying to reap the fruits of their own labor.   As the needs of farming pressed against a diminished supply of able-bodied men, slaves found that they could command high wages.   Many refused to work unless their owners offered them wages or shares of the crop. A local provost marshal complained to his superior that the wages available for farm hands had shut off the supply of willing recruits.

Lexington Mo   Aug 3ʳᵈ 1864

Capt   I wish to Make Some inquiries in refference to recruiting negroes.   There is a great many here that have left their masters and they are either loafering about town or at work for themselves.   I have made all the effort that can be made to recruit them, unless they are forced in they will not go in the army.   Wages is high and demand for hands keep the negroes out of the Army.   Is there any way by which these negroes can be recruited.   It seems that neither master nor Slave is willing to enlist.   If the master would Say recruit the Slave I woul recruit him.   But there Seems to be in the minds of the most of the Slave-holders in this Section that all is not lost yet.   The time is a comming in their estimation when they will have the power and they will get all their negroes back and be able to keep them at home   Yours Respectfully

ALS   J M Gavin[37]

While federal recruiters in Missouri, like their counterparts in Maryland, were concluding that recruitment of black men had reached its limit, many Missouri citizens, like their counterparts in Maryland, were concluding that slavery had reached its limit as well. With nearly 40 percent of the state's black men of military age in the federal army, with slaves at home refusing to work unless paid for their effort, and with Confederate sympathizers either exiled or disfranchised, voters decided in the fall elections of 1864 to acknowledge the end of slavery. On January 11, 1865, a state constitutional convention abolished slavery in Missouri immediately and without compensation to owners.

No sooner had slavery been abolished in Maryland and Missouri than slaveholders and other citizens in both states placed a large question mark over the newly won freedom. In Maryland, armed marauders terrorized the freedpeople and slaveholders persuaded complaisant courts to bind their former slaves' children to them as apprentices. The judges who bound former slaves as apprentices and the parties to whom apprentices were bound insisted that apprenticeship served the interests of the children, whose parents were unable to care for them. Witnesses to the proceedings, however, charged that the children were old enough to earn their own wages and that former owners withdrew many of them from jobs that had been arranged by their parents. Thomas B. Davis, keeper of a lighthouse near Annapolis, recounted to the emancipationist judge Hugh L. Bond the devices by which local citizens tried to nullify the former slaves' freedom. Davis deemed it prudent to offer an assurance at the same time that his concern was disinterested, rather than "a fathers interest, manifested in young darkies."

                                     Sandy Point [*Md.*]   Novr 6th 1864

Sir   i wish to impose A few moments on your Valuable time By Speaking to you after this maner   I Have bein Living or Rather Staying on the Bay Shore about Seven miles N. East From annapolis in the midts of a people Whose Hearts is Black in treason and a more fearless peopel for Boldly Expressing it Lives not outside of the Hosts that Bare Arms in upholding it

Since we the people have Proclaimed that Maryland Should Be free the Most Bitter Hatred has bein Manifested against the poor Devils that Have Just Escaped from beneath there Lash   there actions Since Tusday Last* Indicates to me that there is all Ready Orginized Bands Prowling apon Horse Back around the Country armed with Revolvers

---

*November 1, the day the state constitution abolishing slavery took effect.

and Horse Whips threatning to Shoot every Negroe that gives Back the
first word after they Lacerate his flesh with the Whip   i have bein told
By Several Pearsons that a man By the name of Nick Phips on Last
Wesnsday the first Sun That Rose apon the [wrech] in hes fredom after
years of Bondage took in the Seller of Tom Boons the Post Master of St
Margrets a negroe Woman stript her and with a Cow Hyde Lasarated
her flesh untill the Blood ozed from every cut and She with in a Month of
giveing Burth to a child   She appeared Before Court with the Blood
Still Streaming from her   To Cover his guilt he ivents a Charge   She
is thrown in prson and he goes free   the Same parties caught a Man
By the name of Foster Eight Miles from annapolis hand cuffed him and
Drove him before them and they on Horse With Such Rapidity that
when he got to Severen Ferry he fell apon the Beach Exausted Covered
with foam   and this Man was Born free   this mans offence was [*to
say*] that he nor no wife of his Should be Treated in that maner without
avenging it.   What i have bein trying to get at is this   Sam[1]
Richardson has taken to annapolis four Childern of one of his
Slaves   apon the face of the Mothers Ojections in court he has had
them Bound to him after She stating that all the cloth they had on were
By her after Night   there is a woman down heare By the name
Yewel   She is allso Demanding of the wiman She has turned without a
stich of winters clothing all there childen to be bound to her When she
cannot get Bread for her Self   On friday there was upwards of hundred
young Neagroes on the ferry with there old Masters draged away
forseble from there parents for the purpose of Haveing them Bound
    a number of other cases i could cite that i Will Not Bother you with
    In the Name of Humanity is there no Redress for those poor ignorant
down troden Wreches.   Is this or is it not Involuntarey Slavery   you
may juge what for peopels they are for ever cent worth i purchase i have

to get in Baltimore   they will neather Lend give nor Sell me any thing
not even a ho[r]se to go for a Doctr if my wife to be confined
unfortunatly that acurs every Eleven or Twelve Month'ˢ   I would not
stay heare if i could possible get away   unkel Sam has got me stuck
down heare on three hundred and fifty a year   you may Juge how
much i save out of that   there is five Rooms in the house and each one
you can pick up three or four Children   I am the only union man
within ten miles of my Residence   you may guess the feelings of my
neighbours towards me   Some folks in Baltimoe to see this Letter
would hint that it was a fathers interest, manifested in young darkies
but it not so   every one of them are Jett Black and every knot of wool
that groes on there Heads Both ends groes in there Schull   therefore
there is no anglow Saxon in them   Yours [&c]

ALS   Thoˢ B Davis[38]

A black clergyman in Baltimore told an army officer about an owner who apparently hoped to avoid emancipation altogether.

                                Balt[*imore, Md.*]   Nᵒᵛ 11th, 1864.
Dear Sir   You will please excuse me for troubling you but feeling much
interest for my people, and being informed that you are to see that
justice is to be done to them has prompted me to send this letter to
you   I have been informed that a Mʳ Amos living on N. Charles st one
door this side of Reed ˢᵗ has still several slaves which he still holds.   I
went there a few days ago and saw them there myself.   Such has been his
wife's System, that no one has ever been permited ever to see them   Mʳ
Amos is a noted rebel sympathizer, and if his, and his friend—Dr.
Doulan's houses Monument ˢᵗ were examined much rebel information

would be obtained.   praying that this communication may be strictly personal and that you will use all your influence in behalf of the oppressed. I have the honour to be Your's most Obedient

Justitia

Wm *A. Willyams*

PS.   You will please use my signature *Justitia* if you may have occasion to use my information   *W^m A Willyams*[39]

ALS

> When a former slave from southern Maryland learned that her for-
> mer owner regarded her children's apprenticeship as the price of
> her own freedom, she took their recovery into her own hands. In re-
> claiming property she had been forced to leave behind, however, she
> asked the help of military authorities.

Bal^{to} [*Md.*]   Novr 14"/64

Statement of Jane Kamper

Slave of Wm Townsend of Talbot County Md.

I was the slave of Wm Townsend of Talbot county & told Mr. Townsend of my having become free & desired my master to give my children & my bedclothes   he told me that I was free but that my Children Should be bound to me [*him*].   he locked my Children up so that I could not find them   I afterwards got my children by stealth & brought them to Baltimore.   I desire to regain possession of my bed clothes & furniture.

My Master pursued me to the Boat to get possession of my children but I hid them on the boat

her

Jane × Kamper (f[*ree*] n[*egro*])[40]

mark

HDSr

On December 2, General Lew Wallace, the principal commander
in Maryland, sent General Henry H. Lockwood to the state's Eastern Shore to "break up the practice" of involuntary apprenticeship.[41] But no sooner had Lockwood begun to execute the orders
than pressure from Washington compelled Wallace to countermand
them. Because apprenticeship enjoyed the sanction of state law,
federal officials were reluctant to end it by force. In a letter to Wallace's headquarters, Lockwood reported how the apprenticeship
system worked and to whose benefit.

Baltimore [*Md.*], December 15th. 1864.

Colonel: I have the honor to report, that in compliance with Your
instructions of December 2[d]— I proceeded to the lower counties of the
Eastern Shore and put forth a circular, of which I enclose copy,* that I
posted the same and in some cases executed it.— I found, that the
binding-out had been very general and began as early as October last;
masters having manumitted their slaves under 21 years of age for that
purpose. I found, that the spirit of the apprentice law had been very
generally disregarded, no attention being paid to whether parents could
or could not support or to their wishes as to binding out. They were
told, that they must select masters, willing or unwilling. In some cases
the apprentices were at the time at hired service at good wages,—some
10- to 12$ per month. That many parents had rented small farms,
expecting to have the labor of their childern;— that many poor tenants
had made their arrangements to use this labor and are disappointed by
the course pursued; That the apprenticing works advantageously only
for the rich slave holder—generally *disloyal*—and disadvantageously for
the poor white tenant and colored man. I could burden this report with
cases, but deem it unnecessary, peticularly as I have not the names at

---

*The circular publicized Wallace's order and announced Lockwood's
intention of carrying it out. (*Wartime Genesis: Upper South*, doc. 150.)

hand.   The feeling among our friends in Somerset and Worcester seemed to be, that the law, executed in its proper spirit is a good one, but that, as these gross abuses have attended it, something should be done.

Having on my arrival at Salisbury on Sunday last learned of Your Counter-instructions of the 8th inst.—I came to this City. . . .

I have not deemed it necessary to post any counter circulars.   With Respect Your Obedt. Servt

HLS   Henry H Lockwood[42]

The postwar statement of a freedman, two of whose children were earning wages for their former owner's benefit, refuted the common justification that the apprenticed children would otherwise be destitute.

Washington, D.C.   Aug. 24, 1865.

Danl. Chase of the City of Washington, being duty sworn states:

That he was formerly the slave of Virgil Gant, of Prince Frederick, Calvert Co. Md.,   that when he left said Virgil Gant, in 1863, he left with him his five children, viz. Rachael Ann, aged 8, Hanson, 7— Sias & David (twins) 6— & Caroline, 3 years, who, about the time of the passage of the emancipation act, were bound by the Orphans Court of Calvert Co. to the said Virgil Gant; & further—that the said Gant has hired out to Mr. Danl. Bowen—the boy Hanson, & "Sias," to Mr. Thos. Hutchins—he (Gant) to receive their wages: that he went to Mr. Gants house in Prince Frederick, the 19" inst. and asked for his children, he wishing to bring them to Washington.   He was refused possession of them: he further states that the children were bound without the Knowledge or consent of either himself or his wife—, the mother of the

children: that his wife, Mina, the mother of the children went after
them in Decembr 1864, as soon as she heard they were free, but was
refused possession of them by Mr. Gant.

his

(Signed)   Danl. ✕ Chase[43]

mark

HDcSr

> Writing on behalf of a freedwoman who had been jailed for encour-
> aging her son to leave his master, a white resident of southern
> Maryland warned a federal official that the mistreatment of the
> former slaves threatened to drive them from the state.

Prince Frederick [*Md.*]   September 14' 1865

General Howard or those having charge of freedmen. at Washington
DC.   I have been Called upon by Rindy M Allen the barrer of
this.   [she] [. . .] me to state to you her condition and situation in
regard to her children. whis is as follows.

She has a boy which she had hired last Christmas for which she was
drawing wages. besides the boy was Clothed and fed,   but it seems some
time after the boy was hired out by his mother. that Ira Young her
former master complains to the orphans Court and the said Court
bound the boy to him (young)   the boy stayed with his employer about
a month.   Young then replevys* the boy. and the Justice or something
in shape of a human being called a Justice of the peace decided that the
boy was the property of young, notwithstanding it was proved on trial
that the boy was hired out by his mother and she geting wages for

---

*I.e., recovers under a writ of replevin, a legal action to regain property
wrongfully taken.

him. this man young treats the boy wors than a dog out to treated. he
neither feeds or cloths the boy   he does not get half enougth to eat and
no cloths but what his mother gives him.

Some time ago the boy left young and it was some weeks before he
could find him but he found him at last. and on last Sunday young with
two others found out where the boy was at and carred him home again
and whiped him—the boy in an unhuman manner and still has him yet,.
and I have stated in a former letter it is no use to appeal to the law here
to have Justice done. in any Casese where a Colored person is to have or
ought to have thre rights under the law. nor Can will it ever be any use
as long as we have the officers of the that we now have. I sugusted in a
former letter an establishment of a milatary court which is the only way
that Justice can be done here now. as I before stated that the Colord
people in this County. Can and would do very well if they Can have what
they ought to have. that is to get there children un bound. or restored to
them and have the privilege of hireing them or working them themselvs.
in order that they can help now to surport there parrents in order that
they may not be come a burthen opon the goverment. but if this state
of thing is suffred to be Contued—some of them will be Compelled to
leave ther native place for other quatrs and thus be come a burthen on
the Goverment when they might home here in native place and be a use
to themselves and to a great many white people whou will hire them and
gave them good wages. and so all would be benefited. the Colord people
ask of me to say that they ask the favor to interfare in ther behalf or
appoint some person to do so. in order that they may be settled and
know what to do. It may be that some person have or may state that
what is stated here by me is not so. but all I ask is an examination and
you will find what I have stated is not as bad as it is. it is to hoped that
some thing will be done to have this matter investigated   as I before

stated any information wanted Concerning this affar Can be had by addressing Joseph Hall at this place

I forgot to state that this woman rindy is now. held to bail for court to be trid in about tow weeks for persuading this boy to leave young. which she never did but I would not be surprised if she will be Convicted be cause she probly may not be able to have justice done her. when she is not even gilty of any offence   so you may know how justice is adminsterd here in this den of treason   yours truly

Joseph Hall

Please ansur this[44]

ALS

> Slaveholders in Missouri who expected the state constitutional con-
> vention to abolish slavery were less interested in holding on to for-
> mer slaves than in shedding responsibility for them, as a provost
> marshal in northeastern Missouri explained to his superior.

Hannibal Mo   Jan. 12th 1865—

Sir— I find that many of the Citizens of my Sub: Dist: especially the disloyal element—are anticipating the action of the state convention and send their negroes adrift at such time as it suits them—and it is working very badly indeed up here— The negro men have left their masters some time since—and those now on hand are principally women & children—and they being found rather unprofitable, and expensive— are turned loose upon the people to support— Their former owners make no provision for them, save hauling them to within a convenient distance of some military post, and set them out with orders to never return home—telling them they are free.   There has one case come to my knowledge where the sons of an old man—drove the negroes off from

the place—because the old man began to show signs of recognizing five
of his servants as half brothers & sisters to his children lawfully
begotten— I have in two instances ordered that the former owners
shall take care of these helpless negroes until some other provision is
made for them—and I think some action should be taken to let the
rebels generally know that they shall not shirk in this manner.   They, I
think, fear the convention will resolve—that they shall take care of their
helpless negroes on hand, until they get large enough to take care of
themselves—

. . . .

ALS   John F. Tyler—[45]

> Wittingly or unwittingly, Lincoln's administration sometimes lent
> its favor to border-state secessionists against loyal black people. In
> November 1864, Lincoln ordered that Colonel John H. Waring, who
> had been imprisoned for traitorous activities, be released and per-
> mitted to reclaim his confiscated estate in southern Maryland. Dur-
> ing Waring's imprisonment, General Henry H. Lockwood had au-
> thorized Patrick Scott, a black carpenter, to look after the buildings
> and stock and to raise a crop to compensate himself for his work.
> Upon his return to reclaim the property, Waring drove Scott from
> the premises and seized the crop. A white unionist of the vicinity,
> who braved ostracism by his neighbors to champion Scott's cause,
> asked a friend in Baltimore to help Scott claim what was due him.

[*Prince George's County, Md.*]   January 24th 1865
My Dear Sir & Friend   I arived hom on satterday the 21st instant
arfter a bad dayes travel   it raind & hailed & frosed as it fell all the
way hom from Washington & I had to wride outside with the driver to
Marlborough & had to walk hom through rain & snow & hale   I was

very wet when I got hom & I took a very bad cole & hav felt bad ever
cince but I found my famely all well,   I must say to you that I found
when I got hom from what I can lern a grate dele of pregedus agance me
groing out my renting my place to Partrick scoot   I fine that most
every Bodey is agance the pore fellow it all groing out his being on
Warrings place & I think that warring is the cose of it   he wonts all
that Partrick made thare   he has taken from Partrick the kees of the
corn houses & he is bringing up charges agance him about taking things
of the place & selling them   Mr Warring & his friends are seeking &
finding out every thing thay can agance him & I dont know what will be
the result   I hav imployed him to work my place & I would like very
much for the leading athoretys to deside what intrust Partrick has
thare   if aney I think that Govement aught to proteck him in it becose
the govement put him thare to take care of the propety & toled him to
make what he could to pay himself for his troble   Now Mr Warring
wonts to know what has becom of his poltrey & utentials & all of the
little things left on the place   those things was not put under Partrick
charge but the farm & houses & Fenceing was & you know that partrick
took care of what was put under his charge & toled him to pay himself of
the place   from what I can lern thay are trying to [reape] up all those
charges agance him   I beleave the fellow is truly honis & would state
all of the facts in the case   I wish you would asertane what he is entitel
to   he made a crop of corn last year at his on exspence & I think it
would be a hard case if Govement will not alow him apart of what was
rased as he rased it by his on laber & by hiering laber   I wish you could
so arange the mater so as partrick can get his writes & get the govement
to cend thare wagones down & buy his share of corn & take it of & cend
men with the wagons clothd with proper athorety to settel the bisness
betwen Partrick & Mr Warring & ortherise those offercers to investergate

the mater properly as Partrick is a black man & you very well know that
a bleck man has no chance in this contrey & I think as Partrick has bin
in the Govement imploy & imployed by them I think it is thare dutey to
protect him   if he is entitel to aney thing he aught to have it & thay
aught to see he gets it   I hope you will make som inquire about it & if
he is entitel to a part of the corn & hay & other provendor sell it to
Govement & cend them down for the corn & hay & cend men clothd with
athorety to investegate the mater & take it away & pay him for it   you
are autherrise to sell his corn & hay & other provendor such as shuckes &
foder   Partrick thinkes he made som 450 or 500 Barrels of corn & he
has som 5 or 6 stacks of good timethey hay & a grate maney shuckes & if
Govement thinkes he is entitel to aney thay can say how much & thay
can cend teames down to take all of it at once   if thinges are alowed to
go on as thay are at this time I think Partrick will be in a bad way & as
he has a letter from Generl Lockwood & athorety a wretin one two from
Govement thay aught to protect him & see that he getes his
writes   hoping you will attend to the mater for him & ceape me out of
the scrape as I am now very unpoperlor withe the peopel

W, N, B,

As I had not room to write you all I wonted to write you I am compeld
to troble you with a few lines more   now if you can get the Govement to
cend you down with other offercers tò investegate the mater I would be
glad as you are acquanted with maney of the facts in the case & farther
if shuch a investigation was to be made down in this contrey it mite
alarm som of those hot headed Rebes & do som good   it would be of
benefit to the few that are loyal her & you know thare is few of them   I
am one & I hope I will not be her long   as sune as you & T. B. Burch
can get me a place I shall leave   I dont hardly leave my home unless I
leave it for a distance   I hav no friends her but my famely & tharefor I

cant fine aney consolation aney whare elce   it seames to me that every
thing is glume & despare with me   I think it worst now than ever it has
bin & it will continue to grow worst I think

Now my Dear Friend if you will put yourself to som troble to help me
out in getting away from her & also in getting Partricks rights I will ever
be under obligations to you & I am shure Partrick will feale the same
towards you

when you com down you must be shure to call & see me as me &
famely will be glad to see you   give my best regardes to your famely &
to T. B Burch if you meate with him & all inquiring friends

I hope you will write sune & cend the Papers of scoot & your opinion
what he can do   Partrick looks up to me as his only friend & I am
looking up to you as my only friend to advise me about what aught to be
dun   Yours Respectfuly

ALS   Wm N. Burch[46]

In February Joseph Holt, the judge advocate general of the army,
ruled that Scott's right to the crop was "such that the Government
could not, without breach of faith, deprive him thereof" and expressed certainty that in "granting mercy and pardon to a criminal," the president had not intended to "commit for [Waring's]
benefit an act of bad faith and injustice." Holt recommended that
Lincoln's order restoring Waring's estate be amended to exclude
Scott's crop and that military authorities compel Waring to return
the crop if he had already appropriated it. The government took no
action, however, to secure Scott's rights.[47]

In Missouri, enemies of emancipation and of the freed men and
women turned to direct action. Beginning in late February, 1865,
bushwhackers posted notices in the countryside near Columbia,

warning, according to a witness, "that all blacks were to leave in 10
Days, or be killed." The hanging of one person drove the rest into
town, where the safety of numbers carried with it the danger of epidemic disease.[48] Warning that a "reign of terror" had defeated local farmers' efforts to hire freed men and women or rent land to
them, the president of a university in Columbia recommended to
the district commander a show of military force.

Columbia, Mo   Mch 8 1865

Dear Sir,   I shall be obliged to make brief reply to the communication
with which you have honoured me, bearing date, Mch 4th inst.   I
propose to investigate the matter further, and report again.

The *main fact* touching the freedmen of Boone, is as you understand
it.   Those that remain in the County are, for the most part, congregated
in Columbia; and in crowded quarters, with precarious support.
Measles have been epidemic among them, and a good deal of fatality has
occurred, from the force of the disease, and the exposure to which they
have been subject.   The picture has been overdrawn, by such as are
disposed to disparage the ordinance of freedom.   A coloured man, on
whose judgment and truthfulness I rely, informs me that the deaths
have been about *twenty five* in number; and he added that a like
mortality, scattered over the county, would have passed without special
remark.   But that want and suffering have been aggravated by the
congregating of these people in town, is undoubted.

When the army was first opened to the Africans, recruiting was out of
favor *here*, and there was an exodus of the men of military age to
Jefferson, Mexico, and other recruiting posts; and some women followed
husbands and brothers.   The result up to this time has been, that the
county is depleted of its male coloured population, largely; and of negro
men, the number here in Columbia is no greater now than before the

rebellion.   The crowd consists of women and children.

The farmers generally, throughout the county, would, I think, have preferred to provide these people work and support, on the farms; with or without special contracts for remuneration.   Many are now ready to hire men and women for wages.—   Many offer to let out their farms and farming stock to the freedmen on equal shares;—   Others sell off their stock, and offer the *land* for cultivation—the tenant taking two thirds of the produce.   There is a general disposition among former owners, to accept our altered social condition as a necessity; and, it is my belief, that arrangements would very readily be made for the absorption of the present surplus of black population in Columbia, throughout the County, were it not for the reign of terror, which makes the town less dangerous, for black and white, than the country.   Within a few weeks, notices have been posted up in various places, warning black men and women that their lives were in peril, if found in the country, and several murders of colored people have followed in execution of the threat.   This fact has caused the final influx of this people into town, and has broken up arrangements which were being made for the return of our previous surplus to the country.   This brings us to the very pith of our trouble—to wit, the *rebellion in the brush,* which calls for military force in its suppression, just as distinctly as does the rebellion in Richmond.   Civil power is just as inadequate a remedy, in this case, as in that.   When *this case* shall have been successfully treated by the military power, so that no seed of rebellion be left to germinate in North Missouri I think we shall be able to dispose of the African, peaceably and successfully.   Culture will bring out their moral as well as intellectual capabilities;—and their gentle and confiding nature will make them the *best peasantry in the world*; ill replaced by the sweepings of Europe.   This is my theory; and if my cooperation were worth anything to you, I would very cheerfully offer it, in the work of developing, benefiting, and protecting this section of the human race.   They are on our hands, & their best good is the problem we have to solve.

. . . .

ALS   J. H. Lathrop[49]

Later that month, the district commander reported that his "hands & heart [were] full" dealing with refugees from the terror. "I blush for my race," he wrote, "when I discover the wicked barbarity of the late Masters & Mistresses."[50]

Bushwhackers dealt summarily with the former slaves, but ordinary citizens had to tread warily with well-placed landowners whose favor they required. A farmer or farm laborer addressed a courteous protest to a neighbor who had introduced a black settler into the area, possibly as a renter or hired hand.

[*southwest Missouri?, spring? 1865*]

Mr. Campbell Sir   I am Ablede [*obliged*] to go to town to day and I Cant help you   Mr Campbell Sir thare appears to be sum dissatisfaction about that niger setler on this side of the Creek   it appears that all the nabers is opposes to it   as we have had no nigers on this Sid of the Creek I think it would be beter for him to go back on his own Side   I am afraid it will Cass others to setel herere   that we had beter keep them out when we have them out

Mr Campbell Sir I Send this to you not to rase any hard feeling

ALS   James Martin[51]

When the War Department authorized the enlistment of slaves in
Missouri and Maryland, it spared Kentucky for fear of upsetting
the state's precarious unionism. Slaves in Kentucky seeking freedom through enlistment could achieve their goal only by escaping
to recruiting stations across the state line. In lieu of recruitment
for armed service, federal officers in Kentucky impressed a limited
number of slaves for military labor, with compensation to their
owners. Some owners voluntarily hired their slaves to the army, intending to collect the wages themselves. Such an arrangement
backfired on slaveholders near the town of Lebanon, however, when
an army officer—ostensibly by mistake—transferred the hired
slaves to Tennessee. There, to their owners' frustration, they collected their own wages. Moreover, under the March 1862 article of
war and the Second Confiscation Act, they could not be retrieved
across the state line unless they went voluntarily. The owners of the
slaves complained indignantly to Governor Thomas E. Bramlette.

Lebanon Ky   Febry 24th 1864

To his Excellency Gov. Bramlette   The undersigned citizens of Marion
County respectfully state to your Excelancy that on the last days of
December they hired to James Wright of Lebanon Several of their
Slaves as Teamsters for the Government servace with the distinct
understanding and agreement that they were to be engaged at the Post
of Lebanon Ky and in no case to be taken out of the state of Ky   Said
Hiring was made after an Advertisement calling for Teamsters by Cap[t]
Geaubert Quartermaster at this place promising $30. per month to
them or their masters if slaves.   Under these circumstances they hired
their slaves to M[r] Wright who had the promise of the position of wagon
master in the Train,   He had had at this post that position hertofore
and had some of our Servants ane we were pleased with his management.
They would further state that on the 26 day of January 1864 all the
Teamsters hired by Wright and ours with them were transfered to
Nashville Tenn. and taken there with M[r] Wright as wagon master and

with them was transfered the 26 days they were employed here.   Since
they arrived at Nashville Said negroes have been paid themselves, the
Quartermaster Donalson there ignoring our claims and refusing to
make any difference with teamsters Black or white.   They also
understand that said negroes will not be returned to us at the end of the
time for which they were hired which will be the 1st April next, unless the
negroes are willing to return   The undersigned would respectfully
state to your Excellancy, that they think they are entitled to have the
hire of their slaves and to have them returned to them on the 1st April
next and that the United States Authorities on a proper statement of the
case would give the necessary orders to secure us justice   we earnestly
request your aid and assistance in the pemasises   Whatever may be
done for our benefit we desire to go also for the benefit of our neighbours
who had Slaves to go off with Mr Wright.   Mr Wright is now Devision
Quartermaster 1st Brig. 1st Devision 11. A[*rmy*]. C[*orps*].

Hervey. McElrey   John Lancaster

HLS   Sam. Spalding   R M. Spalding[52]

The governor relayed the slaveholders' complaint to the commander of the District of Kentucky, who forwarded it through military
channels. While disavowing prior knowledge that the disputed
teamsters were slaves, the quartermaster who had received them
insisted that he had no choice but to pay them. When the question
reached General William T. Sherman, he declared it "a matter for
the War Dept. and not for a military officer, who deals with men
and not Constitutional or legal questions."[53]

Kentucky's immunity to the recruitment of slaves could not last in-
definitely. Enrollment of slaves in anticipation of a draft began in
February 1864, with enlistment deferred only if white volunteers

satisfied the state's draft quota. In the state's westernmost counties, administered for military reasons as a separate jurisdiction,
the army began enlisting slaves at Paducah. That initiative emboldened a nonslaveholding unionist to propose to his congressman
that the effort be extended.

                                            Smithland [*Ky.*]   February 1864
Dear Sir   Dr. F A McNeil Chaplain of the Post at Paducah and W. H.
Shook Esq, the Special Confidential Agent of the Treasury Department,
informed me as well as other prominent men who are glad to be called
your Constituents that Col. R. D. Cunningham of Paducah has
mustered in about 200 colored men in his Regiment, according to the
order of the Hon E. M. Stanton.   But he complains that the Order only
Extends at Paducah and Vicinity.   And he told Mr Shook of Caseyville
that if he had sufficent Authority he would come up to this Rank *Seceesh
Hole* and get some recruits
    Now, my dear Sir I ask if the order of Sec[*re*]t[*ary*] Stanton is good
for the Government, in Paducah why is it not Equally so in Smithland
and in fact all through the 1st Congresion District— Of course such
nigger union men as Blunt, Hodge, H. F. Givens Dr. Saunders and
B Barner of this town will cry out and say it is a great violation of the
C O N S T I T U T I O N of K*ai*ntucky. While in thier hearts
they sigh for Jeff. Davis and his hellish crew, to win, so as to save thier
niggers— But—Sir the true unconditional Union me[*n*], who had the
honer, to work for your Election, will now, Stand up for you, and we wish
you to assist us in having the order Extended, through the 1st District
of Ky. Embracing 14 counties 7 on the East, & 7 on the West side of the
Tennessee River
    Mr Shook further informed me confidentially that the Kentucky
Conservative Copperheads had made up a purse, and hired some weak

kneeded, Union man to go on to Washington & Endeavor to have the
order of Sec[re]t[ary]. Stantons, *revoked*, so that no more Negroes,
should be mustered or conscripted in Kentucky— Now as your friend
and the friend of the Government I ask is it not right that Rebel
Sympathizers negroes, should be taken to put Down this infernal
rebellion and restore the Government to its former Dignity & power.
Therefore I would respectfully request you to assist the true Union men
of your district in having the order of Sec[re]t[ary]. Stanton to Extend
over this whole Congressional District, as I am informed there are many
men anxious to recruit Colored Regiments, if they can get the Authority
to do so   I am very Respectfully Your Obt Sevt

ALS   J. L Seaton[54]

General Stephen G. Burbridge, the commander of the District
of Kentucky and a slaveholding Kentuckian himself, did his best
to ease recruitment into operation without offending slaveholders.
He limited eligibility to freemen, of whom there were few in the
state, and to slaves at the "request" of their owners. Because he
forbade armed mobile recruiting squads, the thousands of slaves
who thronged to recruitment centers without awaiting their owners' permission had to brave the armed fury of local citizens and
militia. As a retrospective report by a provost marshal made clear,
armed menace followed the men even into camp and threatened recruiters as well as recruits.

[*Lebanon, Ky. June 15, 1865*]

. . . .

The History of Colored Volunteer Recruiting.

The enrolment of colored persons under the act amending enrolment
Act approved February 24th 1864 had just been finished, when Brig.

Genl. Burbridge, then in command of the Dist. of Ky. issued Genl.
Order. No 34 Hd. Qrs. Dist. Ky. Series 1864 authorizing the recruiting
of free negroes and of slaves at the "request" of their owners.   This
order was more vehemently opposed, if possible, than the law
authorizing the enrolment of colored persons.   Provost Marshals and
their deputies were constantly denounced; the people were arroused by
the seditious speeches of such men as *Wolford* and Lt Gov. *Jacob:*, and
those men who shewed favors to the executors of the law were banished
from society.   The President was denounced as a "tyrant" the
Government as a "tyranny," and Prov. Mar's as the "petty instruments
in the hands of a despot."   Of course, as was forseen, slave-holders
refused to give their slaves permission to enlist in the army.   These
slaves, however, flocked to my Hd. Qrs. begged to be recruited, and
returned to their masters to be met with torrents of abuse, and the
merciless lash.

(1) On the 10^(th) day of May 1864 seventeen (17) colored men from
Green Co. Ky. presented themselves at my Hd. Qrs. for enlistment.   They
were kindly received, furnished with passes home, and with notes to their
owners asking that the negroes be permitted to enlist.   A mob of young
men of Lebanon followed these black men from town, seized them and
whipped them most unmercifully with cow-hides.   Further than this they
declared that "negro enlistments should not take place in Lebanon".
Upon my arresting them I was threatened with a mob.

(2) About the same time a colored man presented himself to a Deputy
Prov. Mar. in Adair Co. to be enlisted.   He was seized by the young men
of the place, tied to a tree and subjected to the most unmerciful beating.

(3) A colored man, while *en route* to my Head Quarters in order to
enlist was seized in Taylor Co, badly whipped, and consigned to jail as a
runaway.

(4) Negro men were chased and killed in Nelson Co, for attempting to enlist.

(5) In Green Co. violent speeches were made, the Depty Prov. Mar. threatened, and negroes knocked down when they spoke of enlisting.

(6) In Spencer Co. the D[*eputy*]. P[*rovost*]. M[*arshal*]. was severely beaten with clubbed guns, and chased from his home for attempting to do his duty.

(7) In LaRue Co, a Special Agent was caught, stripped, tied to a tree and cow-hided for enlisting slaves.

It became absolutely necessary for the protection of the slave to enlist him without the consent of the owner. Those who knew the *animus* of Ky slaveholders, soon saw that mild measures would do no good, and that indeed, leniency to the slaveholder was death to the slave, and punishment to the loyal man.

Slaves had already began to leave the state for the purpose of enlisting in Indiana and Tennessee. The poor man saw that the determined opposition of the slaveholder would prevent the filling of the state's quota with colored recruits, and he, therefore, became loud in his calls for the removal of those restrictions which were running off Kentuckians to fill the quotas of other states. Just as the draft under call of February and March 1864 was about to be executed, the people became frightened, and cried out "enlist the negro—dont draft—" Therefore on the 13th day of May 1864 the Prov. Mar. Genl. of Ky directed me "to receive all negroes who may offer themselves regardless of the wishes of the owner."

It is not possible to depict the anger of the slaveholder or to repeat his denunciations, upon the publication of this order. So thoroughly infuriated were many of the people that public sentiment justified *M*ᶜ*Cann*, an Irish laborer in cutting off the left ears of two colored boys who were attempting to reach my Hd. Qrs. to enlist.   Not less than eight negroes were killed in Nelson Co, for leaving their masters with the intention of volunteering.   About this time Ex-Col *Wolford* and Lt Gov. R. T. *Jacob* visited the southern part of Ky, for the purpose of making speeches.   These speeches were simply seditious, and so infuriated the people that the Board of Enrolment could not have remained in Lebanon but for the presence of Federal bayonets.

The 13th Ky. Cavalry was ordered to Lebanon about the 7th of June 1864.   Many of the members of this regiment had been particularly active in preventing colored enlistments in Adair Co, and its Colonel had been under arrest for permitting an enrolling officer to be run from his camp in Cumberland Co Ky.   When it arrived in Lebanon it announced that "negroes should not be enlisted."   A negro man was forced from my camp for recruits, in my absence from my office, and upon attempting to escape the guard over him, was shot at.   Maj. *Hu[s]t*, Lt *Cunningham*, Lt. *Shipman*, and others of this regiment denounced me, threatened to retake the negro man from camp with their regiment, and were so violent in their demonstrations that I ordered Lt *Horten* Comdg' Co. "B" 23. V[*eteran*]. R[*eserve*]. C[*orps*]., then on duty at my Hd. Qrs to prepare to protect the recruits.   An attempt was made in the afternoon of the 19th of June to assassinate me by shooting at me from a hotel window.   Disaffected citizens secretly gave aid and assistance to this seditious and badly disciplined regiment.   Negroes did not dare to present themselves in the town of Lebanon and of course all recruiting ceased, during the time this regt, was stationed at my Hd. Qrs.

My experience in this connection was the experience of all of my employees.   Every possible indignity was offered them, while the members of the Board of Enrolment were constantly insulted.   It is fortunate for me that I can say that not one of the employees of this office refused or failed to do his duty when so thoroughly tried.

The treatment of the slaves in Ky, during the summer of 1864, the indignities offered the executors of the law of the land; the denunciations of the President and the machination of slave holders for the benefit of treason during the same time, admirably exemplified the barbarities of slavery.

. . . .

HDS
Jam^s M. Fidler[55]

Despite the obstacles, slaves besieged recruiting centers in such numbers that the provost marshals could not keep up with the influx. Greedy for the manpower so close at hand, the War Department overrode Burbridge's conciliatory policy. Lorenzo Thomas, adjutant general of the army, established eight centers within Kentucky for the organization of black regiments and ordered that squads of newly recruited black soldiers fan out over the countryside to protect slave volunteers.[56] Such squads further subverted the already weakening authority of the slaveholders.

While slavery was losing hold in Maryland and Missouri, it remained the law in Kentucky, and slaveholders showed little restraint in dealing with those subject to their authority. Some slaves, aged and infirm, gained a backhanded freedom when spiteful owners left them to fend for themselves. Others, family members hoping for protection from the army their men had agreed to serve, followed enlistees to camps within Kentucky and across the state line. Hundreds took refuge at Camp Nelson, near Lexington. In November 1864, after months of futile efforts to forbid entry to new refugees and remove those already there, the army expelled the women, children, and old people from Camp Nelson. In an affidavit sworn before military authorities, a soldier protested the expulsion of his wife and ailing daughter, whose owner had already threatened them with retribution for giving aid to Union forces.

Camp Nelson Ky. Dec. [*15,*] 1864.

Personally appeared before me. E. B W. Restieaux Capt and A[*ssistant*]. Q[*uarter*]. M[*aster*]. John Burnside—a man of color who being sworn upon oath says— I am a soldier in Company K. 124 Regt. U.S.C.T. I am a married man. My wife and children belonged to William Royster of Garrard County Ky. Royster had a son John who was with [*Confederate General John H.*] Morgan during his raid into Kentucky in June 1863. He got separated from Morgan's command and went home. The Provost Marshal instituted a search for him at two different times He was not found. My family were charged with giving the information which led to the measures of the Provost Marshal. William Royster told me that my wife had been trying to ruin him for the last two years and if he found that this—meaning the information went out through the black family—meaning my family— he would scatter them to the four winds of heaven. This was said about the last of September 1864. In consequence of this threat my family were in constant dread, and desired to find protection and employment from the Government. At that time I had been employed at Camp Nelson and was not enlisted. A few days afterward I was sick at my mothers. I sent my sister to see Col. Sedgwick* and inquire if my family might come to Camp, and if they might, would they be protected: She returned the same night and informed me that Col. Sedgwick said tell him (me) to bring them in and I, Col Sedgwick, will protect them. Before, I was unwilling that they should come but on receiving the promised protection of Col. Sedgwick. I told them to come. While my wife and family were in Camp they never received any money or provision from the government but earned their living with hard work

On Friday afternoon Nov. 28. [*25*] 1864 the Provost guard ordered

---

*Thomas D. Sedgwick was in charge of the organization of black troops at Camp Nelson.

my wife and family out of Camp.   The guard had a wagon into which my wife and family were forced to go and were then driven out the lines

They were driven to a wood belonging to Mr. Simpson about seven miles from Camp and there thrown out without any protection or any home.   While they were in the wood it rained hard and my family were exposed to the storm.   My eldest daughter had been sick for some time and was then slowly recovering.   and further this deponent saith not.

HDeSr   John Burnside[57]

A Northern missionary, challenging the idea that the family members gathered in Camp Nelson had been a charge upon government resources, denounced the callousness with which they had been expelled.

Camp Nelson Ky   Dec. 16" 1864

Personally appeared before me E B W Restieaux Capt and A[ssistant]. Q[uarter]. M[aster]. Abisha Scofield who being duly sworn upon oath says.   I am a clergyman of the congregational denomination and have been laboring among the Freedmen at Camp Nelson Ky. under the auspices of the American Missionary association since the 20th of Sept 1864.   The families of the colored solders who were in Camp lived in cabins and huts erected by the colored solders or at the expense of the women.   During my labors among them I have witnessed about fifty of these huts and cabins erected and the material of which they were constructed was unserviceable to the Government.   I have had extensive dealing with these people and from my observation I believe that they supported themselves by washing cooking and &c.

Until the 22nd of last November I never heard any objection made by

the military authorities of the Post to the women and children of colored
soldiers residing within the limits of the camp.   On Tuesday the 22nd of
November last the huts and cabins in which the families of the colored
soldiers lived were torn down and the inhabitants were placed in
Government wagons and driven outside the lines.   The weather at the
time was the coldest of the season.   The wind was blowing quite sharp
and the women and children were thinly clad and mostly without shoes.
They were not all driven out on one day but their expulsion occupied
about three days.

When they were driven out I did not know where they were to be taken
and on the following Sabbath Nov 27" I went in search of the exiles.   I
found them in Nicholasville about six miles from Camp scattered in
various places.   Some were in an old Store house, some were straying
along and lying down in the highway and all appeared to be suffering
from exposure to the weather.   I gave them some food.   I received the
provisions from Capt T. E. Hall A[*ssistant*]. Q[*uarter*]. M[*aster*].

The food was absolutely needed.   On Monday Nov. 28 I saw and
conversed with about sixteen women and children who had walked from
Nicholasville in the hopes of getting into Camp.   The guard refused
them admittance.   I told the guard that the order by which the women
and children were expelled had been countermanded.   The guard told
me that he had strict orders not to admit them   They were not
admitted.   Among the number was a young woman who was quite sick
and while I was conversing with the guard she lay on the ground.   A day
or two after this they were allowed to return to Camp.   They were then
very destitute most all complaining of being unwell.   Children trembling
with cold and wearied with fatigue.   Since that time they have been
crowded in a school room in Camp and their condition has been most
abject and miserable, whereas they were pretty comfortable before they

were driven out.   While out of Camp they incurred disease and are now
suffering from the effects of this exposure   As a clergyman I have no
hesitation in pronouncing the treatment to which these poor people have
been subjected as exceedingly demoralizing in its effects in addition to
the physical suffering it entailed.   And further this deponent saith not

HDcSr   (Signed)   Abisha Scofield[58]

> The vocal opposition of Northern missionaries and sympathetic of-
> ficers forced the government to readmit the banished women and
> children, although not before the expulsions had caused suffering
> and at least one death.*

> Although erosion was clearly under way, support for slavery re-
> mained strong. In a letter to a member of Kentucky's congression-
> al delegation, a white unionist identified military recruitment as
> the best way to rid the state of slavery.

Irvine Kentucky   Decr. 5th 1864

Sir: The result of the Nov. Election in Ky.,† demonstrates the fact to
my mind that the people of Kentucky are so wedded to the Institution of
Slavery, that they will never make any disposition of it or adopt any
system of Emancipation until it is uprooted and rendered worthless by
some power capable of consumating such an object.   This can easily be

---

*See below, pp. 493–95.

†The presidential election in which Abraham Lincoln had been
 reelected. In Kentucky, an overwhelming majority of voters had cast
 their ballots for George McClellan, the Democratic candidate.

done, and promote the best interest of the Gov. in the mientime, by enlisting into the Federal service every able bodied male slave in the state   This once accomplished; the Masters would soon be found trying to releave themselves of the duty (burthen they call it) of maintaining the Slave women and children and thus the Abolition of Slavery in Kentucky would soon be accomplished.   I am satisfied that a large majority of your Constituants would rejoice to learn that such a line of policy had been adopted by the Administration at Washington.

It may be claimed by the opponents of the Administration, that, such a policy would be oppressive.   Let them claim it.   No milk and Cider policy will be attended with success.   If we would be successfull in our undertaking we must adopt and closely persue a rigorous and determined policy, adopting such measures and employing such means as will most certainly accomplish the object in view.   I am truly your friend and Obedient Servant—

ALS   H. C. Lilly[59]

Voluntary enlistment had stalled in Kentucky by late 1864. Forays by "substitute brokers" who kidnapped men to satisfy repeated drafts, forcible impressment of men who had escaped from owners without enlisting, and mistreatment of enlistees and their families by federal officers all discouraged potential volunteers. In any case, few eligible men remained in areas near recruitment centers, and owners began offering wages and crop shares to persuade slaves to remain at work. Nevertheless, a soldier scornfully denied that he had begged his former master to get him released from military service, as the former master had insisted in a statement to federal officials.

State of Ky.   Co of Henderson   30th day of May 1865

Charles Green, Corp[oral] "D" Co. 120 U.S.C.I. being duly sworn deposeth and sayeth: that on or about the 20th day of January 1865, some colored soldiers came to the residence of E. H. Green, in the Co. of Hopkins State of Ky. and found me at a pond back of the house. asked me if I wished to enlist in the service.   I replied "No Sir."   They then said well come up town (meaning Nebo) and see the Colonel meaning Lt Col. Glenn.   They then took me up to Lt Col. Glenn, who told me to fall into line which I did.   He then brought me to town and put us in quarters with the other men.   When Col. Glenn wanted me to enlist he had me brought up to his office.   I told him I did not want to enlist.   Lt Col. Glenn asked me "What in hell was the reason," I did not want to go. He then turned around to the Sergeant who stood by and told him to "take this damned nigger to the jail," that "I was but a damed Secesh nigger anyway."   I then replied, "Well rather than go in jail I will join. I was mustered at Louisville by Capt Womack.   I made no objection to being mustered in.   I do not want now to be mustered out.   I am perfectly satisfied.   On or about the 18" of May 1865, E. H. Green asked me how I was getting along, and was I satisfied   I replied I was very well satisfied   Mr Green then replied I am glad.   I never went to Mr Green or anyone else and with tears in my eyes beseech him to see justice done me.   I never cried to anyone but my mother.   I would not take five hundred dollars and go back to E. H. Green as a slave

his

HDSr   Charles ✕ Green[60]

mark

On March 3, 1865, a new inducement stimulated enlistment afresh: a joint resolution of Congress providing freedom for the wives and children of soldiers and future recruits. The commander of the Department of Kentucky, General John M. Palmer, publicized the joint resolution in printed circulars and at church meetings. His General Order 10, issued on March 12, invited slave men to "coin freedom for themselves and posterity" by joining the army and pledged that military authorities would enforce that freedom.[61] Thousands answered the call during the next few weeks. By the end of the war, almost 60 percent of Kentucky's black men of military age had joined the Union army, the largest proportion of any slave state. But the freedom mandated by Congress proved elusive to one soldier's widow.

Camp Nelson Ky   25" March 1865

Personally appeared before me J M Kelley Notary Public in and for the County of Jessamine State of Kentucky Patsey Leach a woman of color who being duly sworn according to law doth depose and say—

I am a widow and belonged to Warren Wiley of Woodford County Ky. My husband Julius Leach was a member of Co. D. 5" U.S. C[*olored*]. Cavalry and was killed at the Salt Works Va. about six months ago. When he enlisted sometime in the fall of 1864 he belonged to Sarah Martin Scott County Ky.   He had only been about a month in the service when he was killed.   I was living with aforesaid Wiley when he died. He knew of my husbands enlisting before I did but never said any thing to me about it.   From that time he treated me more cruelly than ever whipping me frequently without any cause and insulting me on every occasion.   About three weeks after my husband enlisted a Company of Colored Soldiers passed our house and I was there in the garden and looked at them as they passed.   My master had been watching me and when the soldiers had gone I went into the kitchen.   My master followed

me and Knocked me to the floor senseless saying as he did so, "You have
been looking at them darned Nigger Soldiers"   When I recovered my
senses he beat me with a cowhide   When my husband was Killed my
master whipped me severely saying my husband had gone into the army
to fight against white folks and he my master would let me know that I
was foolish to let my husband go he would "take it out of my back," he
would "Kill me by picemeal" and he hoped "that the last one of the
nigger soldiers would be Killed"   He whipped me twice after that using
similar expressions   The last whipping he gave me he took me into the
Kitchen tied my hands tore all my clothes off until I was entirely naked,
bent me down, placed my head between his Knees, then whipped me
most unmercifully until my back was lacerated all over, the blood oozing
out in several places so that I could not wear my underclothes without
their becoming saturated with blood.   The marks are still visible on my
back.   On this and other occasions my master whipped me for no other
cause than my husband having enlisted.   When he had whipped me he
said "never mind God dam you when I am done with you tomorrow you
never will live no more."   I knew he would carry out his threats so that
night about 10 o'clock I took my babe and travelled to Arnolds Depot
where I took the Cars to Lexington   I have five children, I left them
all with my master except the youngest and I want to get them but I
dare not go near my master knowing he would whip me again.   My
master is a Rebel Sympathizer and often sends Boxes of Goods to Rebel
prisoners.   And further Deponent saith not.

Her

Signed   Patsey   Leach[62]

mark

HDeSr

To the anger and frustration of their owners, some slaves chose to assert their freedom at home rather than in the army. One master sought to have his "boy"—at forty-nine, somewhat past military age—forcibly enlisted for military duty.

Lexington [*Ky.*]   April 1st 1865

Kind Sir: I have a black Boy, or rather, a mulatto, who has refused to serve me any longer, and affirms that he is as free as I am.   Said Boy has done me only one days work since Christmas.   He is 49 years old, about five feet ten in., high; and a very stout, able bodied Boy.   I wish to enlist him into the service; and being some distance from home, and anxious to join my family, I will be under lasting obligations to you; if you will instruct your recruting officer, Porteus P. Bielby (at Lexington) immediately to have him arrested and enlisted.

    Said Boy is in the vicinity of Hutchison's station nine miles from Lexington on the Covington R.R.   Yours very Respectfully,

ALS   I. N. Steele[63]

Joint resolution of Congress or no, soldiers and their families found it difficult to coin freedom while Kentucky law continued to coin slavery. In late March, 1865, a state circuit judge held the joint resolution unconstitutional. The judge ruled in favor of an owner who, citing a state law making it illegal to hire a slave without the owner's consent, sued the employer of his former slave, the wife of a Union soldier.[64] That decision paved the way for similar suits by former owners against the employers of freed women and children. Wondering how to intervene, a Union officer sought General Palmer's advice.

Maysville, Ky.,   April 25 *1865*

Sir   The civil authorities are doing all in their power to annul Genl.
Order No. 10 Head Quarters Dept. Ky.* by permitting cases to be tried,
where parties have employed the wives and children of colored soldiers
made free under the provisions of said *order*, and the courts here have in
one instance given damages to the amount of one thousand dollars
($1000.00)   There are in this city about fifty (50) wives and children
of soldirs who are employed by parties who wish to keep them but cannot
as they are liable to a heavy fine for doing so under the *state decisions*.
These parties ask, of me, protection.   How shall I give it.   Shall I arrest
the party who brings suit. The officer who serves the *writ*, the Jury who
give damages, or the Judge who charges the Jury to find damages

The effect of these decissions is to drive every person from the State
who claim freedom under the order.   I am Genl. Very Respectfully Your
Obedient Servt.

ALS   W. A. Gage[65]

In late April, General Palmer issued a circular extending military
protection to persons claiming freedom under the joint resolution.[66]

———•———

The end of the Civil War did not mean the end of slavery in Kentucky. Indeed, the more obvious the disintegration of slavery became, the more vindictively owners and state officials enforced its
remaining forms. Writing to the judge of the Louisville City Court,
General Palmer, a lawyer himself, denounced the jailing of a slave
because his owner could no longer control him.

*For a summary of the order, see above, p. 400.

Louisville. Ky.   June 3. 1865.

Sir: Your letter of yesterday's date, addressed to Capt. E. B. Harlan. Assistant Adjutant General, in which you state that "Jacob Hardin, represented to the court to be a slave, was committed to the workhouse until his master should give bail that he would not be suffered to go at large and hire himself out as a free man," was this morning laid before me.

It is no part of the duty of the military authorities, under ordinary circumstances, to interfere with the action of the courts of the State, or to obstruct the operations of the local laws, but it is their clear and positive duty to protect the people from forcible wrongs, whether inflicted under the forms of law or otherwise.

I beg to assure you that I do not question the integrity of the Judge whose sentence is under consideration, though I express the opinion that it is wholly without and unsupported by any existing law.   "When the reason of the law ceases, the law itself ceases," is a rule founded in reason, and is recognized by all courts.

The particular law, which must be referred to to support this order, was enacted by the Legislature of Kentucky in support of slavery. According to the policy of the State, then recognized as correct, it was the duty and it was then in the power of masters to prevent their slaves from going at large and hiring themselves as free persons, while the slave himself had no interest in the question.

This state of things has, however, ceased.   During the last four years, from causes familiar to every one, masters were not, in a majority of cases, able to give protection to their slaves.   It was not their duty, then, even according to the theory of the law itself, to restrain them; and now, when the bonds of slavery are relaxed, if not totally broken, it is not in the power of masters to prevent slaves from going at large and hiring themselves as free men.

This highly penal law, which demands impossible acts from the owners of slaves, must, therefore, be held to have ceased to exist, as much as if repealed by Legislative authority.

There is, however, another thing to be said, which demonstrates the correctness of that conclusion. Masters have ceased to provide for or control those who are nominally their slaves. According to the theory of this obsolete law, these were his duties. He has neglected them, yet, by a strange perversion of justice, the slave is selected as the object of punishment. This man Hardin, now before me, has upon his limbs marks made by iron fetters placed upon him only because his master has failed to obey this law. Nor is this the only enormity presented by the case. Hardin is ordered to be kept in the workhouse, as you inform me, not for a period so fixed as to terminate, not until he does some act, but until the master, over whom he can have no influence or control, and who has, now that slaves are valueless, no interest in him, shall voluntairly give bail that he shall never again go at large or hire himself as a free man.

For anything Hardin himself can do, his confinement must be perpetual.

I forward you herewith my order made upon a consideration of the whole case.* Very Respectfully,

HLcS

John M Palmer[67]

Fearing that President Andrew Johnson might lift martial law, which Lincoln had imposed in July 1864, a delegation of black men traveled to Washington to acquaint the new president with the state of affairs in Kentucky and present him with their petition.

---

*Presumably an order for Hardin's release; it has not been found.

[*Washington, D.C.   late June, 1865*]

M[r] President   Haveing been delegated by the Colored People of
Kentuckey to wait upon you and State their greiveances and the terrible
uncertainty of their future, we beg to do so in as respectfull and concise
a manner as Posible—

First then, we would call your attention to the fact that Kentuckey is
the only Spot within all the bounds of these United States, where the
People of colour Have No rights *whatever* Either in Law or in fact—and
were the Strong arm of Millitary Power no longer to curb her—Her
Jails and workhouses would Groan with the Numbers of our people
immured within their walls—

Her Stattutes are disgraced by laws in regard to us, too barbarous
Even for a community of Savages to Have Perpetrated.   Not one of
those laws have Even yet become obsolete,   all Have been Executed
Promptly and Rigoursly up to the time the government intervened—and
will be again Executed in the Most remorseless Manner and with four
fold the Venom and Malignanty they were Ever Heretofore Enforced—
the Very Moment the Government ceases to Shield us with the broad
aegeis of her Power—

Not only that—but the brutal instincts of the Mob So Long
restrained will Set no bounds to its ferocity but like an uncaged wild
beast will rage fiercely among us—Evidence of which is the fact that a
member of the present common council of the city of Louisville who
when formerly Provost Marshall of that city caused his guards to carry
bull whips and upon meeting colored men, women or children in the
Public High ways any time after dark to surround them and flay them
alive in the public Streets) is allready a petitioner to Gen[l] Palmer to
remove the Millitary Restrictions that he and others May again renew
the brutaleties that Shocked Humanity during that Sad Period—

therefore to Prevent all the Horrible calamities that would befall us and to shut out all the terrors that So fiercely Menace us in the immediate future—we Most Humbly Petition and Pray you that you will Not Remove Marshall Law from the State of Kentuckey Nor her Noble Millitary commander under whose Protection we have allmost learned to Realise the Blessings of a Home under the Safeguard and Sanction of law for in him and him alone do we find our Safety— we would Most Respectfully call your attention to a few of the laws that bear Most cruelly upon us—

1st we have No Oath

2nd we have no right of domicil

3rd we have no right of Locomotion

4th we have no right of Self defence

5th a Stattute law of Kentuckey makes it a penal crime with imprisonment in the Penitentiary for one year for any free man of colour under any Sircumstances whatever to pass into a free State Even although but for a Moment   any free man Not a Native found within her Borders is Subject to the Same penalty and for the Second offence Shall be sold a slave for life—

the State of Kentuckey Has contributed of her colored Sons over thirty thousand Soldiers who have illustrated their courage and devotion on Many battle fields and Have Poured out their blood Lavishly in defence of their Country and their Country's flag and we confidently hope this Blood will be carried to our credit in any Political Settlement of our Native State— yet if the government Should give up the State to the control of her civil authorities there is not one of these Soldiers who will Not Suffer all the grinding oppression of her most inhuman laws if not in their own persons yet in the persons of their wives their children and their mothers—

Therefore your Excellency We Most Earnestly Petition and pray you
that you will give us Some security for the future or if that be
impracticable at least give us timely warning that we may fly to other
States where law and Christian Sentiment will Protect us and our little
ones from Violence and wrong.

Chas A Roxborough   Jerre Meninettee

R M Johnson   Henry H. White

Thomas James   Wm F. Butler[68]

HLS

Martial law continued until October 1865.

———•———

Although slaveholders in the defeated Confederacy had perforce to
confront a future without slavery, those in Kentucky continued to
dream of restoration. In pleading that President Johnson curb the
military authorities who were undermining slavery, one slaveholding Kentuckian gave voice to long-held assumptions that had silently underpinned the slaveholders' view of the world.

Craborchard [*Ky.*],   July 24th 1865.

My Dear Sir;   As you are at the head of a Government that admits of
petitions and grievances, you will excuse this letter, which is intended
more for your own good, for the honor of the nation, and for the
harmony of the people and their good will towards yourself, than from
anything I can expect from it.   And now the simple question whether,
(under the constitution of the U. States, the laws of Congress which
authorized us to take our property from any state in the union, and
under the constitution and the laws of Kentucky), my Tom belongs to me

or to some unknown power under your individual influence; will bring
my grievance and the complaint of Kentucky fairly and squarely up
before your mind.   Tom and I have lived together as mutual friends for
fifty years, without a hard thought or a harsh word passing.   I gave him
a good home, boarded him free of charge, nursed him when sick, clothed
and fed his family and paid his debts, while Tom, on his part, seeing his
family healthy and happy and protected from the wants of the world by
a kind Master, Guardien, Friend or whatever you may see proper to call
it, did his duty cheerfully.   But now Tom comes to me with what he calls
free papers from Camp Nelson* and a pass to go where he pleases and to
do what he pleases; and yet he is unhinged and unhappy, feeling that he
is by his new master turned out upon the world with all its cares and
troubles, without a home and without a protector   He has seen those I
myself set free, call upon me in times of distress, to help them to pay
thier debts and to bury them, and knwing that his acceptance of those
papers divorced him from me, he under no circumstancs would ever
again have a right to call upon me.   Thousands of such cases occur daily
and hourly throughout Kentucky, where whole families, even sucking
infants are taken off and exposed by thier mothers, and I only mention
Tom's case, that like the Dred-Scot case, may represent all others.   Tom
was worth nothing to me, and in his case I have no feeling but pitty for
him, but have a deep and abiding sense of feeling for the insecurity of all
property, for if our constitutional rights can be invaded with impunity in
one case or in one species of property, it may in all.   Had I a pet-bird,
worth nothing, taken from me and kept by force of arms, it would
involve a principle alarming to every man in the community   If the

*Under General Orders 32 and 49, issued in May and July, 1865,
General Palmer had authorized provost marshals to issue passes
permitting freedom of movement to black people in search of
employment. Slaves interpreted these passes as certificates of
freedom. (*Destruction of Slavery*, pp. 619–21.)

signeture of Tom Dick and Harry can free every man woman and child in Kentucky, as it is now doing, why disturb the nation and spend the people's money in a struggle for a Constitutional Amendment?*

We profess before foreign nations to be living under a written Constitution, a Divine and sacred instrument which protects life liberty and property, and it cannot then be by your approbation that the best of its citizens are, by arbitrary arrests and consequent death, with other acts, as above named, deprived of life liberty and property, and that in the face of Heaven and in open day! I then though an humble citizen, hold it as my privilege and feel it my duty to appeal to you, as our *Legitimate* (and I say) *Good* President, to save our count[r]y from the charge of infamy and the reccords of eternal disgrace. Did I believe that you knew of what is now going on in Kentucky, I certainly would not write you, for though we poor fellows in the west, have as good a right to humbly and respectfully address you, as the imperious and dogmatic down easters have to call upon you by committees; yet I view them both, when seeking office or aiming at party preponderance, as insolent and anoying to one already over taxed with the cares of the nation. And Honored Sir, let me here impress it upon you, that I have no object aside from the honor of the Administration and the well being of our common country. I know that you have fought too hard against rebellion to now place yourself in rebellion against the Government of the united states; for, you know, the Administration is not the Government, as in that case, we should have no stable Government, but every four years a new one, and the dictation of a single man would overrule the constitution and make it a misnomer and a rediculous farce. Then I again, most

---

*The proposed amendment to the Constitution abolishing slavery throughout the United States. Congress had adopted the amendment in late January 1865 and sent it to the states for ratification; several states had already ratified, but Kentucky had thus far refused to do so.

respectfully assure you, that being unwilling for millions of your subjects to secretly feel in thier hearts that our Administration is in rebellion against the Government and laws of the land, as a friend, I will do all in my power to correct such unfortunate impression.   I know there is a party, at Wasington, who would be willing to see the Administration take from the states who created it, all their inherent and reserved rights, and thus place it as certainly in rebellion against its Maker, as is the man who defies Heaven, a rebel against the God who made him,   Thus with my views of the limited powers of the Administration, I have looked on with alarm and disgust at the scenes now acting in Kentucky.   Though the Constitution of Kentucky forbids free blacks remaining in the state, they are bid, by Camp Nelson papers, to remain in it: and again, the laws of the State orders that no public conveyance shall take a slave off, without the consent of the Master, yet those papers order all conveyances to take them off.   And now, if this is not a violation of the laws of Kentucky, a grievous wrong to her people and a gross insult to her National dignity; we may next strip our backs for the lash and sink in contempt with all mankind, who *like yourself*, have a high sense of personal honor and of state rights   You would not—you could not respect craven and degraded Kentucky, were she too recreant to make her wrongs known to you.

I, this moment, hear that this high-handed and sudden breaking up of all our domestic relations and leaving our crops to perish for want of help, has been checked by your kind and just order, and were it sure, I would throw my pen down and cry long live Andrew Johnson, and long live the Government which he has cemented by just and kindly acts, but I fear you have not yet known our condition.   Not having had time to supply the place of the blacks, we are forced to suffer   On yesterday morning, there was hardly a servant to be found in our town.   The man

with a sickly wife had his cow to milk and the breakfast to get, while
many an old and infirm widow, whose only son has fallen in the federal
service, has now had the servant she reared with tenderness and care to
be a support in her old days, taken from her, by that government she has
given her all to support, and she left sadly and alone a begger upon the
world. A fanatic and radical brute might say this is all right, for people
should do their own work; but if by the order of any man or set of men,
Washington should be suddenly deprived of all help, and Mr S. or any
other member of your Cabinet had to get up and milk the cow and get
their breakfast; circumstances would as quickly alter the case as they
did with the farmer and the lawyer in the Fable of the ox and the cow.
We feel that we as certainly own our slave property as any other, and any
power which may rench it from us without consent or compensation is
unjust; and be assured that he who submits to it, submits as does the
traviller his purse to the highway robber, because the knife is across his
throat—as has been beautifully expressed by my Friend Joseph Holt,
your able Judge advocate, when speaking upon this very subject of state
rights and domestic institutions. I am, myself, an emancipationist, and
have written a work upon that subject, but my moral sense and my
judgement of right have led all my efforts to do justice to the Master and
to better the condition of the Slave. By the destinies of Providence and
the original action of the Northern states, the blacks have been placed
amongst us, and we cannot help it, nor can they help it; but all who know
human nature know this—that an unprepared for and violent breaking
up of all domestic control and turning loose four millions of beings upon
the world, who never thought or acted for themselves any more than
children have done under the guidance of their parents, is not a remedy,
but a grievous evil to both black and white. Were you to witness the
scenes I have, you would shudder at the sight— Old and young, blind

and lame, with heavy packs, crowd the highways and the by ways, rushing on through heat and dust for free papers and as certainly to ultimate distruction, as presses the Pilgrim Hindoo on his path to perish by the hand of the god he worships.   The unrestrained Abolitionist, whose only feeling is envy and malice to the whites and whose selfish heart would not give a dime for the purchase or freedom of a slave, is to be the death of the African race in America

But as I set out to give you some idea of the state of things in Kentucky I will on with the work.   The servants being seduced from their happy homes by the pledge of free papers at Camp Nelson, assemble in such numbers as to render their condition uncomfortable and unhealthy; so much so that the fatality amongst those deluded creaturs has been sadly and notoriously great.   Mothers becoming wearied with the toil of their children and scarce of food often neglect them till they perish, while others throw them into the ponds around camp Nelson, from which many have been taken   Disease of every kind, *Private* and public, seems to be rife in thier ranks, and the time is fast coming when, if not checked, the loafing vagrants and filthy lepers will die off like sheep with the rot.   The worst feature about this Camp Nelson business is, that the blacks have taken up the idea that their free papers is to enable them to live the remainder of their lives without work, and that the Government will support them, at the expense and labor of the white man: in short, they feel that by the aid of the military, they can defy the decrees of Heaven itself which bid them get their living in the sweat of their face—   Yes and there is another unfortunate sequel of this pass manufactory; those servants who return home, do not do it with the view of living in harmony with their old Master, but to taunt him with their free papers and threaten him with military power; a thing illy calculated to reconcile our people with the

Administration or gain friends to the Constitutional amendment, as you
will find, by the result of the Kentucky election.*

I have lived long (75 years) and been much through the world and
found that an open hand and kind heart was worth all the weapons I
could buckle about me, and in your case you are safer and more beloved
than a million of bayonets would make you.   A Government sustained
by standing armies and ruinous taxation is not worth the cost, and
cannot last, while one governed by even handed justice and cemented by
fraternal love will last through ceaseless ages.   It is now in your power
to do more than any man on earth can do, and to immortalize your name
in the pages of history.   Clamor as much as the present, but short lived
faction may, for standing armies, for office and for blood, heed them not,
but rise manfully above their din like the towering mountain above the
thunders brawl, and show to them and to the world that you are without
envy malice or revenge against your erring subjects, but that you are the
Saviour of your country and like the Saviour of the world have a heart
for those who cry for mercy, even his persecurtors and the thief upon the
cross.   Such endearing loveliness such Divine forgiveness will command
the respect of all mankind and make friends of enemies.   The foulest
fanatic in the radical ranks knows that he could not whip a wife a ~~child~~
man of honor or neighbour into a love for him, and in spite of his
vengeful heart and sorded grasp, would have more respect for a
conciliatory than a cruel course   Therefore heed not their Moloch†
howl, but gain the hearts of the people, discharge your armies, tell the

---

*A reference to the impending election of August 1865, at which U.S.
representatives would be selected, as well as many state officers. The
chief issue of the election was whether Kentucky should ratify the
proposed amendment to the U.S. Constitution abolishing slavery.

†A god referred to in the Old Testament, whose worship featured the
ritual sacrifice of children by their parents.

idle negroes they must support themselves, pay our myriad debt, redeem the currency and sustain the credit and the honor of the nation—

I have done, and now if there be anything offensive or unbecoming in my hurried address, I shall be exceedingly sorry, and as a good subject ask for pardon.   I am a Quaker and had intended to address you Brother Andrew, for we are all Brothers and should not be offended at any familiarity intended for the good of all so I have made free to advise with you upon some subjects,   I will farther say to you, that I am one who would be unwilling to see our poor black Breathern driven from their native land; but think they should remain amongst us, where the climate suits them, where their labor is wanted and where they can get good wages and feel at home.   There is, *at present*, much bad feeling between the races in Kentucky, owing mainly to the premature and daring interference, as before related, with our domestic institutions. The blacks are not to blame, but the whites who *seduce* them from home *in more ways than one*, and make them insolent and refractory.   Your authority however will soon settle all things down satisfactorily.   A captain in your servic stationed at Camp Nelson, told us here, a few days ago, that the authorities there were giving seventy-five dollars a head for cows to give milk to the idle blacks who would not work—   This he did not approbate, nor will the people of the U. States, *who pay the tax*, approbate it.   Just proclaim to the blacks and to your Agents, that they must go to work and support themselves, and all will soon go like clock work, for the blacks will then want a home and the whites want their services.   This would be humanity to the tender infants many of whom are daily dieing for want of care, and it would give to the infirm a home, where they might again be taken into favor and receive the blessings of friendship and kindness in their dieing moments.   I do not wish to bore you, but while on this subject will say, that I recogniz the white man, the black man and the red man, and all human beings on earth, as of the one great family, and for the brute force of one over the other, I have a deeply abiding and religious abhorrence; consequently feel more rational kindness for our coloured breathern than any abolitionist in the north, for their envious and levelling spirit seems to be against their white breathern and spending nothing and careing nothing of what becomes of the blacks.   Thousands of dollars may be taken out of the pocket of a white brother in Kentucky, and they will chuckle over it—ah, and take but one dollar out of theirs by the same authority, and they would cry robbery. robbery!

Thus you will see that I am not promted by any designing or party spirit, but that my efforts are for peace peace and prosperity to all; and now knowing God to be my judge, who will approbate what I have said, I have a hope that you will forgive any seeming impropriety in this my appeal to you.   Most respectfully and sincerely, your adviser well wisher and Friend

C. Graham, M.D.

. . . .69

ALS

Slaveholders lacked the power to revitalize slavery, but they enjoyed ample means to hinder the efforts of slaves and former slaves to establish new lives in freedom. Agents of the Freedmen's Bureau, which Congress created in March 1865 to superintend the transition to freedom, faced a sticky task in Kentucky, where many of their charges remained legally enslaved. Colonel Hubert A. McCaleb, the bureau superintendent in Louisville, ran head-on into the technicalities of Kentucky's slave code when he tried to compel the owners of a hotel to pay wages due a black employee.

Louisville Ky   Sept 11th 1865

Gentlemen   Wilson Hail—a colored refugee. being duly sworn. states
that he contracted with your steward to work for you at Twenty-five
($25[00]) Dollars per month, that under this contract he worked for you
from the 10th day of July 1865 until the present time.   He states
further that you paid him for July and that his former master has
notified you not to pay him for August.   The boy is a "refugee"* and as
such is entitled to his wages.   You will pay the boy Wilson for his labor
and refer parties claiming his earnings to this office.   Very Respectfully
HLS   H A M[c]Caleb[70]

Louisville Ky   September 11th 1865

Dear Sir   The colored man "Wilson" referred to in your order of this
date makes a true statement that he was hired by the Stewart of the
Hotel and that he was paid the amount of his earnings in the month of
July.—   He should also have stated to *You*, as he has to us, that he is a
slave man—The *property* of H Hale of *Simpson Co. Kentucky*; that said
Hale has heretofore allowed him a portion of his wages—That he Wilson
is not now willing to divide his wages with Hale, and claims the whole
amount.—

We would respectfully represent that about the first of the present
month we received a verbal message from Hale, notifying us that Wilson
is his slave, and that he will hold us liable to him for the wages of Wilson

Under the Laws of the State of Kentucky, *now in force* there seems to
be no doubt of our liability to owners of the hire of their slaves.—   We
desire to pay the money to the proper person, and avoid the responsibility

---

*McCaleb reasoned that, having left his master, Hail had become a
refugee and thus fell within the jurisdiction of the Freedmen's Bureau,
whose full name was Bureau of Refugees, Freedmen, and Abandoned
Lands. (*Wartime Genesis: Upper South*, doc. 239.)

of paying both Owner and Slave—and therefore request that the subject be referred to Maj. Gen[l.] O. O. Howard, Chief of Freedman's Bureau Washington City—and that Your order be suspended until his decission be had,

Please submit to the General Your order and this letter   Yours very truly

ALS   Kean, Steele & Co[71]

> General Clinton B. Fisk, the Freedmen's Bureau assistant commissioner for Tennessee and Kentucky, ordered McCaleb to enforce the hotel's contracts with "persons who are under the jurisdiction of this Bureau" and to see that Wilson Hail received his wages.[72] But, pressed to say exactly which persons fell under the bureau's jurisdiction—for example, did they include slaves who had left their masters under General Palmer's "free papers"?—Fisk threw up his hands and awaited instructions from Washington. "I can not see how I can run a *Freed*mens Bureau for *Slaves*," he complained.[73]

> General Palmer took the occasion of a complaint from the mayor of Paris, Kentucky, to lecture the mayor and his constituents about the need to let go of slavery and accept responsibility for its baneful consequences. Palmer's letter, which was clearly intended as a public pronouncement, duly appeared in the public press.

Louisville. Ky.,   August 22, 1865.

Sir: I reply to your letter of the 19" inst which reached me to day.

I cannot sympathize with the citizens of Paris if you correctly represent them when you say, "The great desideratum is to rid ourselves

of a population that will not labor but simply exist as a nuisance—
Where they go or to whom they are sent is a matter of little moment to
us, so that they be constrained to active honest labor and we releived of a
burden." Such views and feelings of and toward a race born in your
midst with just such habits of industry and morals as you have taught
them are not very creditable to your humanity, or to the system to which
these people have been subjected.

I trust however that you do the good people of the rich and refined
city of Paris an unintentional injustice, and that they will be found
willing to endure their share of the burdens of a system which they have
supported with so much zeal and which has created the vagrancy and
vice from which they now suffer.

I assure you that I would be glad to be able to suggest some speedy
and effectual remedy for the evils you describe which would meet your
approbation, but I am certain that no such remedy is possible. Your
people expect or desire what can never be accomplished. They seem to
hope that after enjoying the unpaid and extorted labor of the colored
people for generations, after having denied them all means of mental
and moral elevation and improvement, enforced them to that condition
that their earnings are in the hands of their late masters, and the
negroes for that reason utterly destitute, some one or some people will
be found who are willing to "relieve them of a burden" and eagerly
accept a population which you say "Will not labor but simply exist as a
nuisance." Any such expectation is chimerical. The people of Paris
will be compelled in a great measure to bear this evil themselves, and if
they care as little for the welfare and happiness of their late bondmen, as
might be inferred from your language, but few persons can be found who
will much care how heavily it presses them.

I do not think that any plan can be devised which will realize all you
desire.

Under present circumstances there is but one course which can rid
the people of Paris of their present embarrassment, and in that alone
can they have the cooperation of the Military Authorities of Kentucky.
This plan includes several distinct things to be done.

1st The colored people to whom you allude must be relieved of all
doubts and anxieties with respect to their status.   They must be assured
of freedom.   They cannot and will not understand that they are free as
long as men who have heretofore owned them deny it.   My assurances
which are sincerely given to them that all are in fact free though fortified
and strengthened by the declared opinion of the present able and
patriotic Governor of the Commonwealth, and by many of the most
distinguished citizens are neutralized by the claims of men once their
masters, and whom they have been accustomed to fear and obey.   The
clear, precise and unreserved admission of the fact of freedom is one
indispensable preliminary condition to the success of any plan which
may be presented for the relief of the races from the evils they inflict
upon each other.

2^d You must abandon the scheme of expelling them from the state.
The idea of expulsion is morally unjust, and politically tyranical and in
the highest degree oppressive.   These furnish sufficient reasons for
abandoning it, but what will have more weight with many is that it is
impracticable.   You may by injustice which will degrade and injure you
and by the petty oppressions which are now possible compel a few
negroes to leave the state of Kentucky; You may in this way compel the
most sensative and intelligent to abandon their birth place and seek
homes in other states amongst strangers, but the old and helpless, the
stolid and worthless will endure all and stay with you and burden you.
The political economists of Kentucky will begin to enquire soon whether
it is a paying policy to give to the adjoining states all of the most

valuable portion of your colored population, retaining for yourselves only the aged, the maimed the halt and the blind.   The policy of persecution will result in this, as certain as it is persisted in.

3^d You must gain or regain, if that form of expression is preferred, the confidence of the colored people.   You have not that confidence now.   whether you desire it or not, need not be discussed.   The unreserved admission of their right to freedom and of their right to live where they were born and have toiled will go far toward reassuring them of your purpose to be just, and if to this you will add that perfect protection in life, liberty and property which you demand for yourselves, and which is secured to you by the laws, the work will be complete.   A few years of unrestrained industry will give to the largest portion of the colored population improved habits of industry, morality and usefullness and put them in possession of the material results which are sure to follow industry and thrift.

To cling to the shadow of slavery and that is all they left, is to hug vagrancy amongst the negroes and discontent and disappointment to your bosoms.   Slavery never can be reestablished: To struggle for its reestablishment, is injurious to both races.   the weakest suffers most now, but "time makes all things even."

In conclusion I will gladly cooperate with the authorities of the city of Paris in every effort to rid the people of the burdens of which you complain, which is based upon the following leading principles.

1st The free admission of the right of the colored people to the enjoyment of their personal freedom.

2^d Their perfect right to remain in Kentucky, or to emigrate if they prefer emigration, and I will render such assistance to those who are able to support themselves, and desire to go to some other state as may be in my power.   I will not encourage or aid the helpless to go out of the state; their support is properly the duty of your own people; I will not assist in throwing it upon others. I have the honor, to be, Very Respectfully,

HLcS
John M Palmer[74]

Neither in Paris nor elsewhere were white Kentuckians prepared to surrender gracefully. Not until December 1865—when the Thirteenth Amendment was ratified without Kentucky's concurrence— did slavery officially end.

As time ran out for slaveholders, they vented special rancor against returning veterans who had been their slaves. A soldier who, armed with an order from General Palmer, attempted to move his wife from the home of her former owner promptly landed in jail. The soldier's company commander recounted the episode to the commander of the regiment, who added his own endorsement.

Battery Rodgers, Va— November 15th 1865—

Sir: I have the honor to make the following statement, relating to Serg't Tho[s] M[c]Dougal of Co. "F" 107th U.S.C.I. who received a Furlough of thirty days on the 1st of October 1865, to visit his family in Ky.; and would respectfully request that it be forwarded to the proper authorities in order that *justice* may be done in his case.

After reaching Louisville Ky. Serg't M[c]Dougal got an order from Gen'l Palmer,—in charge of the Freedman's Bureau of Kentucky,—to move his family to Louisville— His wife is living with her old master Hillary Johnson, Judge of the county of Larue Ky, and living in the town of Hodgensville.   he is an old rebel and one of some note in that County.— Serg't M[c]Dougal was arrested by Johnson soon after reaching Hodgensville, his order taken from him and he lodged in the

County jail, where he has been confined since October 24th 1865, on account of trying to free his family from bondage.

The above is a true statement of the case at it has reached me.

Serg't McDougal is a superior Non-com. Officer and his services are much needed in this Company. I am sir, very respectfully, Your obedient servant,

ALS   F. B. Clark[75]

[*Endorsement*]   Hd Qrs 107th U.S. C[*olored*] Inf'y   Fort Corcoran V^a. Nov 21st 1865   Respectfully forwarded.   Quite a number of instances have occurred where men of this Regiment have been incarcerated in prison upon the most frivolous pretences.   The Regiment was organized in Kentucky; and when the men return home to provide for their families they are often shamefully treated by their former masters.   Especially is such the case in the interior districts of the state, where the disloyal element strongly preponderates, and where it is impossible for colored soldiers to obtain justice from magistrates who despise the Federal uniform—particularly so when worn by their former slaves.   I would respectfully request that some action be taken to have Sergt McDougall released, so that he can return to his regt as soon as practicable   D. M. Sells. Lt. Co^l. Comdg

Forwarded through military channels, Captain Clark's letter eventually reached General Palmer, in Kentucky, who endorsed it as follows.

Louisville [*Ky.*]   Nov 30 1865
Respectfully returned to Col C W Foster A[*ssistant*] A[*djutant*] G[*eneral*] with the remark that the case of Sergeant McDougal

illustrates in an eminent degree the peculiar ideas of loyalty honesty, and justice which animates certain of the judicial officers of Kentucky   The facts as I have ascertained them are substantially as follows.   McDougal went to the house of Johnson who is county Judge of Larue County Ky and formerly owned McDougals wife and demanded her   Johnson refused to give her up without my order which was promptly given   He then removed his family from Johnsons house and in doing so inadvertently took with them the clothes of some other colored child of the value of 75. cts as I am advised   When these clothes were demanded of him he said "There they are take them   I knew nothing about them supposed they belonged to my children" which I am assured by respectable people is true.   Judge Johnson however had him arrested for larceny brought before himself and committed him to jail in default of bail   (The Judge it is reported takes the astute distinction that though the act of Congress may free the wives and children of soldiers "it does not divest the owner of the title to the clothes they wear")   I at once took steps to investigate the case found the facts as before stated with the additional fact that a loyal man had become McDougals bail and the court just at hand   As the soldier was in civil custody upon colorable process authorised for a scandalous purpose in a rascally way I determined to wait the action of the Court trusting that justice would be done   The court met on last Monday— The result of its action will be promptly reported

I may add that the colored soldiers who return to this state are persecuted and outraged in many ways.

AES   John M Palmer[76]

In January 1866, General Palmer reported that a grand jury failed to indict McDougal, who had been reunited with his family.[77]

Slave into soldier: Private Hubbard Pryor of
Georgia before and after his enlistment in the
44th U.S. Colored Infantry, 1864.
(National Archives)

Freemen into soldiers: Sergeant Lewis H. Douglass (left) and Private Charles R. Douglass (right) of the 54th Massachusetts Infantry, sons of Frederick Douglass. (Moorland-Spingarn Research Center, Howard University)

Flag of the 22d U.S. Colored Infantry. (Photography Collections, University of Maryland Baltimore County)

Insignia from the flag of the 3rd U.S. Colored Infantry.

{429}

Battery A, 2d U.S. Colored Light Artillery, Department of the
Cumberland. (Chicago Historical Society)

A hero's welcome for returning black veterans, 1866.
(Pencil drawing by A. R. Waud, Library of Congress)

Marriage ceremony of a black soldier and a freedwoman at Vicksburg, Mississippi. (*Harper's Weekly*, June 30, 1866)

Soldiers of the 1st Louisiana Native Guard standing picket. (*Frank Leslie's Illustrated Newspaper*, March 7, 1863)

Assault by the 54th Massachusetts Infantry on Fort Wagner,
South Carolina, July 18, 1863. (Private collection)

Black soldiers liberating slaves in North Carolina.
(*Harper's Weekly*, January 23, 1864)

Privates and noncommissioned officers at Fort Stevens, Washington, D.C. (Library of Congress)

Black soldiers, many holding books, with their teachers, probably in South Carolina. (Library of Congress)

Company F 13th U S Colored Infantry
Exchange Barraks
Nashville Tenn October 8th 1865

Sir

I have the honor to call your attention
To the neccesity of having a school for
The benefit of our regement We have never
Had an institutions of that sort and we
Stand deeply inneed of instruction the
majority of us having been slaves We
Wish to have some benefit of education
To make of ourselves capable of buisness
In the future We have established a litterary
Association which flaurished previous to our
March to Nashville We wish to become a
People cupable of self support as we are
Capable of being Soldiers my home is in
tucky Where Prejudice reigns like the
Mountain Oak and I do lack that cultivation
of mind that would have an attendency
To cast a cloud over my future After have
been in the United states service I had
a leave of abscence a few weeks ago on
A furlough and it made my heart ache to
see my race of people there neglected
And ill treated on the account of the lack
of Education being incapoble of putting
Their Complaints or applications in writing
For the want of Education totally ignorant
Of the Great Good Workings of the
Government in our behalf We as soldiers
Have our officers Who are a protection
To teach how to act and to do

A black sergeant requests a school for his regiment. (See p. 518)

Virginia soldiers request discharge to care for their families.
(See pp. 533–35)

CHAPTER

VI.

SOLDIERS
AND CITIZENS

SEEING MILITARY SERVICE AS A MEANS TO EMANCI-
pation and equality, black men in both the North and the
South pressed for an opportunity to join the Union army. Initially,
they met opposition from most of the Northern public and rebuff
from the Lincoln administration, but fast-moving events forced a
reconsideration. By the end of 1862, black regiments in Louisiana
and South Carolina—originally raised by local commanders on
their own authority—had received the sanction of the War Department. The Emancipation Proclamation opened the door to large-
scale enlistment. First in the North, then in Union-occupied parts
of the Confederacy, and finally in the border states, black men
thronged federal recruiting centers. By the end of the war, nearly
180,000 had served, about one-fifth of the nation's black men of
military age.

Black soldiers sped the transformation of the Union army into
an army of liberation. The act of enlistment itself freed the slaves
who became soldiers. Eventually their families also gained title to
freedom. Once under arms, black soldiers liberated tens of thou-

sands of slaves. The military service of black men had profound im-
plications for all black Americans, helping to free the enslaved and
enlarge the liberty of the free.

For black soldiers, service in the federal army was a complex experience, mixing tragedy with triumph and frustration with fulfill-
ment. Fighting for the Union did not eliminate the inequities of
American life; in many ways, it reflected them. Whereas some black
men eagerly volunteered to join the army, others entered at the
point of a bayonet. Once enlisted, black soldiers were organized into separate regiments, paid less than white soldiers, assigned to
hard labor more often than combat, denied the opportunity to serve
as commissioned officers, and frequently ill-used by their white officers. On balance, however, service in the army bequeathed a positive legacy to black soldiers. It broadened their knowledge of the
world and dramatically countered the debasement of slavery. Many
soldiers learned to read and write in regimental schools. Fighting
and dying for the Union advanced their claims to the rights and
privileges of full citizenship. Battling the Confederates on the field
and fighting discrimination within the Union army politicized not
only the soldiers, but also their families and friends, breeding a
confidence that would serve them well after the war. As black soldiers fought to destroy slavery, they also laid the foundation for a
new world of freedom.

The Emancipation Proclamation provided that black men would
"be received into the armed service of the United States to garrison
forts, positions, stations, and other places, and to man vessels of all
sorts."[1] It did not specify the terms and conditions under which
they would serve. The governor of Massachusetts assured George
T. Downing, a black businessman and prominent abolitionist, that
black soldiers would stand on an equal footing with white soldiers.

Boston [*Mass.*],　March 23. 1863.

Dear Sir: In reply to your inquiries made as to the position of colored
men who may be enlisted and mustered into the volunteer service of the

United States, I would say, that their position, in respect to pay, equipments, bounty, or aid and protection, when so mustered, will be precisely the same, in every particular, as that of any and all other volunteers.

I desire further to state to you, that when I was in Washington, on one occasion, in an interview with Mr Stanton, the Secretary of War, he stated in the most emphatic manner, that he would never consent that free colored men should be accepted into the service to serve as soldiers in the South until he should be assured that the Government of the United States was prepared to guarantee and defend, to the last dollar and the last man, to these men, all the rights, privileges and immunities that are given, by the laws of civilized warfare, to other soldiers. Their present acceptance and muster-in, as soldiers, pledges the honor of the Nation in the same degree and to the same rights with all other troops. They will be soldiers of the Union—nothing less and nothing different. I believe they will earn for themselves an honorable fame, vindicating their race and redeeming their future from disaspersions of the past. I am yours truly,

HLcSr

John A. Andrew.[2]

Promises of equal treatment were broken time and again, exposing the limits of the Union's commitment to equality. The exclusion of black men from the commissioned ranks—lieutenant and higher— was a case in point. At the end of 1862, Union troops in southern Louisiana included several "Native Guard" regiments composed of freemen of African descent, most of whose officers were also free men of color. A few companies had served in the militia under the Confederacy, but when federal troops occupied New Orleans they declared their allegiance to the Union. In August 1862, General Benjamin F. Butler incorporated them into his command and began recruiting to augment their ranks. Butler's successor, General Nathaniel P. Banks, accepted the regiments but not their officers;

he considered them unfit to hold commissioned rank. Early in 1863, Banks began forcing them to resign, and within months all but a handful had complied. Demobilized but not demoralized, they reiterated their desire to serve the Union. Invoking their long tradition of military service, including valorous conduct during the War of 1812, they urged Banks to reconsider his position.

New Orleans [*La.*]   April 7th *1863*

Sir   we the undersigned in part resigned officers of the Third (3rd) reg^t La vol native guards and others desiring to assist in putting down this wicked rebelion. And in restoring peace to our once peaceful country. And wishing to share with you the dangers of the battle field and serve our country under you as our forefathers did under [*Andrew*] Jackson in eighteen hundred and fourteen and fifteen—On part of the ex officers we hereby volunteer our services to recruit A regiment of infantry for the United Satates army—   The commanding Genl may think that we will have the same difficulties to surmount that we had before resigning. But sir give us A commander who will appreciate us as men and soldiers, And we will be willing to surmount all outer difficulties   We hope allso if we are permitted to go into the service again we will be allowed to share the dangers of the battle field and not be Kept for men who will not fight   If the world doubts our fighting give us A chance and we will show then what we can do—   We transmit this for your perusal and await your just conclusion. And hope that you will grant our request We remain respectfuly your obedient servants

Adolph. J. Gla	James. E. Moore
Samuel. Lauence	William. Hardin
Joseph G Parker	William. Moore
Joseph. W. Howard	Charles. A. Allen
Charles. W. Gibbons	Danl W. Smith J^{r3}

ALS

To refute persistent charges that they would not fight, black soldiers were eager to prove themselves under fire. In three bloody battles during mid-1863—Port Hudson (Louisiana) in May, Milliken's Bend (Louisiana) in June, and Fort Wagner (South Carolina) in July—they silenced the doubters. Their conduct not only sealed the federal government's commitment to enlisting as many black soldiers as possible, but also guaranteed them a role in the front line. Furthermore, participation in combat established the soldiers' claim upon the nation. In a letter to the chief recruiter of black troops in southern Louisiana, a Union officer reported the bravery of the black soldiers at Port Hudson, many of whom had until recently been slaves.

Baton Rouge [*La.*]   May 29th/63.

General.   feeling deeply interested in the cause which you have espoused, I take the liberty to transmit the following, concerning the colored Troops engaged in the recent battles at Port Hudson.

I arrived here the evening of the 26th Inst, was mustered and reported to Maj. Tucker for duty—

During the night I heard heavy connonadeing at Port Hudson.   Early next morning I obtained permission and went to the front. But was so much detained, I did not reach our lines until the fighting for the day had nearly ceased—   There being no renewal of the engagement the following day—I engaged in removing and administering to the wounded, gathering meantime as much information as possible concerning the battle and the conduct of our Troops.   My anxiety was to learn all I could concerning the Bravery of the Colored Reg. engaged, for their good conduct and bravery would add to your undertakings and make more popular the movement.   Not that I am afraid to meet unpopular doctrins, for I am not. But that we may show our full strength. the cause should be one of general sanction.

I have ever believed, from my idea of those traits of character which I deemed necessary to make a good soldier, together with their history, that in them we should find those characteristics necessary, for an effictive army.   And I rejoice to learn, in the late engagements the fact is established beyond a doubt.

The following is (in substance) a statement personally made to me, by 1st Lt. Co. F. 1st R[egiment]. La. Native Guard who was wounded during the engagement.

"We went into action about 6. A.M. and was under fire most of the time until sunset.

The very first thing after forming line of battle we were ordered to charge— My Co. was apparrently brave. Yet they are mostly contrabands,* and I must say I entertained some fears as to their pluck. But I have now none— The moment the order was given, they entered upon its execution.   Valiantly did the heroic decendants of Africa move forward cool as if Marshaled for dress parade, under a most murderous fire from the enemies guns, until we reached the main ditch which surrounds the Fort.   finding it impassible we retreated under orders to the woods and deployed as skirmishers— In the charge we lost our Capt. and Colored sergeant, the latter fell wraped in the flag he had so gallantly borne— Alone we held our position until 12. o'clock when we were relieved—

At two o'clock P.M. we were again ordered to the front where we made two separate charges each in the face of a heavy fire from the enemies Battery of seven guns—whose destructive fire would have confuse and almost disorganized the bravest troops.   But these men did not swerve, or show cowardice.   I have been in several engagements, and I never before beheld such coolness and darring—

---

*I.e., former slaves.

Their gallantry entitles them to a special praise.   And I already
observe, the sneers of others are being tempered into eulogy—"

It is pleasant to learn these things, and it must be indeed gratifying to
the General to know that his army will be composed of men of almost
unequaled coolness & bravery—

The men of our Reg. are very ready in learning the drills, and the
officers have every confidence in their becoming excellent soldiers.

Assureing you that I will always, both as an officer of the U.S. Army
and as a man, endeavor to faithfully & fully discharge the duties of my
office, I am happy to Subscribe Myself, Very Respectfully, Your Most
Obt. Servt,

ALS   Elias D. Strunke[4]

At Milliken's Bend, another post on the Mississippi River, untested
black soldiers joined a white regiment in hand-to-hand combat with
Confederate troops who had vowed to show the black men and their
officers no mercy. The commander of the District of Northeastern
Louisiana described the battle to his superiors.

                                       Young's Point, La.,   June 12", 1863.
Colonel: I have the honor to report, that in accordance with
instructions recieved from me, Colonel Leib, Commanding 9" La.
A[frican]. D[escent]. made a reconnaisance in the direction of
Richmond, on June the 6th starting from Milliken's Bend at 2 A.M.   He
was preceeded by two Companies of the 10" Illinois Cavalry,
Commanded by Captain Anderson, whom he overtook three miles from
the Bend.   It was agreed between them that the Captain should take the
left side of Walnut Bayou, and pursue it as far as Mrs. Ame's
Plantation, while Colonel Leib proceeded along the Main Richmond

road to the Railroad Depot, three (3) miles from Richmond, where he
encountered the enemies Pickets and advance, which he drove in with
but little opposition, but anticipating the enemy in strong force, retired
slowly toward the Bend.   When about half way back, a squad of our
Cavalry came dashing up in his rear, hotly pursued by the enemy.—
Colonel Leib immediately formed his regiment across an open field, and
with one volley, dispersed the approaching enemy.   Expecting the enemy
would contest the passage of the Bridge over Walnut Bayou, Colonel
Leib fell back over the bridge, and from thence to Milliken's Bend, from
whence he sent a Messenger informing me of the success of the
expedition, and reported the enemy to be advancing.   I immediately
started the 23" Iowa Vol. Inft. to their assistance, and Admiral Porter
ordered the Gun-Boat "Choctow" to that Point.

At three (3) o'clock the following morning the enemy made their
appearance, in strong force, on the Main Richmond road, driving the
Pickets before them.   The enemy advanced upon the left of our line—
throwing out no skirmishers—Marching in close column, by division,
with a strong Cavalry force on his right flank.   Our forces—consisting
of the 23^d Iowa Vol. Inft. and the African Brigade, in all, 1061 men—
opened upon the enemy when within musket-shot range, which made
them waver and recoil; a number running in confusion to the rear, the
balance, pushing on with intrepidity, soon reached the Levee, when they
were ordered to "charge," with cries of "No Quarters!"   The African
Regiments being inexperienced in use of arms—some of them having
been drilled but a few days, and the guns being very inferior—the enemy
succeeded in getting upon our works before more than one or two volleys
were fired at them.   Here ensued a most terrible hand to hand conflict,
of several minutes duration, our men using the bayonet freely and
clubbing their guns with fierce obstinacy, contesting every inch of

ground, until the enemy succeeded in flanking them and poured a murderous enfilading fire along our lines—directing their fire chiefly to the officers, who fell in numbers. Not 'till they were overpowered, and forced by superior numbers, did our men fall back behind the bank of the river, at the same time pouring volley after volley into the ranks of the advancing enemy

The Gun-Boat now got into position and fired a broad-side into the enemy, who immediately disappeared behind the Levee, but all the time keeping up a fire upon our men

The enemy at this time appeared to be extending his line to the extreme right, but was held in check by two Companies of the 11" La. Inft. A[frican]. D[escent]., which had been posted behind cotton bales and part of the old Levee. In this position the fight continued until near noon, when the enemy suddenly withdrew. Our men seeing this movement, advanced upon the retreating column, firing volley after volley at them, while they remained within gun-shot. The Gun-Boat "Lexington" then paid her compliments to the "flying foe," in several well directed shots, scattering them in all directions. I here desire to express my thanks to the officers and men of the Gun-Boats "Choctaw" and "Lexington" for their efficient services in the time of need. Their names will long be remembered by the officers and men of the "African Brigade," for their valuable assistance on that dark and bloody field.

The officers and men deserve the highest praise for their gallant conduct, and especially Colonel Glasgow of the 23^d Iowa, and his brave men, and also Colonel Leib, of the 9" La., A[frican]. D[escent]., who by his gallantry and daring, inspired his men to deeds of valor, until he fell, seriously, though not dangerously wounded. I regret to state that Col. Chamberlain, of the 11" La. A[frican] .D[escent]., conducted himself in a very unsoldierlike manner.

The enemy consisted of one (1) Brigade, numbering about 2,500, in command of General McCullough, and two hundred Cavalry. The enemies loss is estimated at about 150 killed, and 300 wounded. It is impossible to get anything near the loss of the enemy, as they carried killed and wounded off in ambulances. Among their killed is Colonel Allen, 16" Texas.

Enclosed please find tabular statements of killed, wounded and missing—in all 652. Nearly all the missing Blacks will probably return, as they were badly scattered

The enemy, under General Hawes, advanced upon Youngs Point whilst the battle was going on at Milliken's Bend, but several well-directed shots from the Gun-Boat's compelled them to retire.

Submitting the foregoing, I remain Yours Respectfully,

                                        Elias S. Dennis[5]

HLS

Paying rueful tribute to the black soldiers who fought at Milliken's Bend, a Confederate officer reported that they had resisted "with considerable obstinacy, while the white or true Yankee portion ran like whipped curs."[6]

Among those who questioned the ability of black soldiers to fight were high-ranking Northern officers, including General Quincy A. Gillmore, who commanded the Department of the South. But the performance of the 54th Massachusetts Infantry in the ill-fated—and, some thought, ill-advised—assault on Fort Wagner, South Carolina, in July 1863 changed many minds. Several months after the battle, Nathaniel Paige, a correspondent for the *New-York Tribune* who had witnessed the engagement, testified before a War Department commission about its effect on prevailing prejudices.

[*New Orleans, La. February? 1864*]
. . . .

Gen. Gilmore had little confidence in negro troops when he assumed
command of the Department; Col. Turner was Chief of Staff; Maj.
Smith was assistant Adjutant General; his generals were Terry,
Seymour, Strong, Vogdes, Stevenson, Gordon and Wilde; the colored
troops were in Strong's brigade; the bombardment of Fort Wagner
commenced at 11 A.M. from the iron-clad fleet and all the shore
batteries; the action continued until about an hour before sunset, with
occasional replies from Wagner and Sumter; Gen. Seymour had
command; Gen. Gilmore with his staff, the leading colonels, and the
correspondents of the press, were on the observatory, 2 1/2 miles from
Sumter and 1 3/4 from Wagner.   An hour before sunset, Gen. Gilmore
(who had been most of the time on the observatory) came down and
asked Gen. Seymour (who was lying on the ground) if he thought the
fort could be taken by assault.   Gen. Seymour replied: "I can run right
over it.   I can camp my whole command there in one night."   Said Gen.
Gilmore: "Very well.   If you think you can take it you have permission
to make the assualt.   How do you intend to organize your command?"
Gen. Seymour answered: "Well, I guess we will let Strong lead and put
those d—d niggers from Massachusetts in the advance; we may as well
get rid of them, one time as another.   But," said he, "I would give more
for my old company of regulars than for the whole d—d crowd of
volunteers."   Gen. Gilmore laughed, but ordered the movement to take
place.   Gen. Seymour's command were soon formed in line of battle on
the beach in front of the town; 1 3/4 miles from Wagner.   The division
was organized by placing Gen. Strong in advance, Col. Putnam second
and Gen. Stevenson in reserve.   The whole column moved together up to
a house about a mile from Fort Wagner, in open daylight and in full view

of the enemy from all the forts; there all halted but the brigade of Gen. Strong; he marched up at double quick towards the fort, under a most terrific fire from Forts Gregg and Sumter and all the James Island batteries, losing on the way 150 killed and wounded. The first brigade assaulted at dusk, the 54th Massachusetts in the front. Col. Shaw was shot just as he mounted the parapet of the fort. Notwithstanding the loss of their Colonel, the regiment pushed forward, and more than one-half succeeded in reaching the inside of the fort. Three standard bearers were shot, but the flag was held by the regiment until their retreat. The regiment went into action commanded by their Colonel and a full staff of officers; it came out led by Second Lieut Higginson—a nephew of Col. H—he being the highest officer left to command, all ranking being either killed or wounded. Gen. Strong's brigade was led out by Maj. Plimpton of the 3d New Hampshire. Gen. Strong received a mortal wound almost at the commencement of the action; Col. Shaw was killed, and all the other colonels severely wounded. The 1st brigade having been repulsed with such severe loss, the second brigade was then ordered to move. Col. Putnam led his brigade gallantly; carried the flag of the 7th New Hampshire into the fort, which he held for half an hour without being reinforced. The enemy succeeded in bringing to bear against him ten or twelve brass howitzers, loaded with grape and canister, when the slaughter became so terrible that he was forced to retire, after having lost nearly all his officers. About fifty of the 54th Massachusetts were taken prisoners; none have been exchanged; I believe all reports as to the harsh treatment of our colored prisoners are untrue; I have reason to think that they are treated as prisoners of war. Gen. Gilmore and staff ridiculed negro troops; the evident purpose in putting the negroes in advance was to dispose of the idea that the negroes could fight; Major Smith advised Gen. Gilmore to put the negroes at the head of the assaulting party and get rid of them. On the

previous week Gen. Terry had made favorable mention of the 54th
Massachusetts for gallantry on James Island. Many of Gen. Terry's
officers spoke of them unfavorably before and favorably since the action
referred to. The regiment is now at Morris Island; numbers four
hundred men; is in Col. Littlefield's brigade and is commanded by Major
Hallowell. Gen. Seymour was not in the advance at Fort Wagner, but
early in the action received a very slight wound in his heel, not drawing
blood, immediately after which he retired to the south end of Morris
Island and remained there all night; next morning he congratulated the
remaining officers upon their escape, and charged the failure of the
assault upon the d—d negroes from Massachusetts. He is now an
ardent admirer of negro troops. These facts are personally known to
me, and I am willing to swear to their truth.

. . . .[7]

HD

The participation of black soldiers in combat engendered fear
about the treatment they would receive if captured by the enemy.
The fear was well-founded, for Confederate authorities from the
first refused to recognize armed black men in Union uniforms as legitimate soldiers. Instead, they regarded them as slaves in insurrection and their white officers as instigators of slave rebellion. At
first, local Confederate commanders decided the fate of captured
black soldiers and their officers, often executing them on the spot.
In December 1862, however, President Jefferson Davis ordered the
soldiers delivered to civil authorities in "the respective [Confeder-
ate] States to which they belong to be dealt with according to the
laws of said States"; their officers were also to be remanded to state
authorities.[8] Under state laws, the soldiers faced punishments
ranging from reenslavement or sale into slavery to execution, and
officers convicted of inciting slave insurrection were subject to execution or imprisonment. Confederate policy toward black prisoners
of war infuriated many Northerners, but the Lincoln administration was slow to respond. Union General David Hunter, who had

initiated the recruitment of black soldiers in coastal South Carolina and Georgia,* therefore took matters into his own hands. Flout-
ing military protocol to address President Davis directly, he warned
that mistreatment of black soldiers or their officers would be met
with swift retaliation.

HILTON HEAD, Port Royal, S.C.,   April 23rd 1863.

The United States flag must protect all its defenders, white, black or
yellow.   Several negroes in the employ of the Government, in the
Western Department, have been cruelly murdered by your authorities,
and others sold into slavery.   Every outrage of this kind against the
laws of war and humanity, which may take place in this Department,
shall be followed by the immediate execution of the Rebel of highest rank
in my possession; man for man, these executions will certainly take
place, for every one murdered, or sold into a slavery worse than death.
On your authorities will rest the responsibility of having inaugurated
this barbarous policy, and you will be held responsible, in this world and
in the world to come, for all the blood thus shed.

In the month of August last you declared all those engaged in arming
the negroes to fight for their country, to be felons, and directed the
immediate execution of all such, as should be captured.†   I have given

---

*See above, pp. 56–59.

†On August 21, 1862, the Confederate War Department issued an
  order condemning General Hunter and General John W. Phelps (a
  Union officer in Louisiana) as "outlaws" for "hav[ing] organized and
  armed negro slaves for military service against their masters"; it
  directed that, should any officer engaged in organizing slaves for
  armed service be captured, "he shall not be regarded as a prisoner of
  war, but held in close confinement for execution as a felon." (U.S. War
  Department, *The War of the Rebellion: A Compilation of the Official
  Records of the Union and Confederate Armies*, 128 vols. [Washington,
  1880–1901], ser. 1, vol. 14, p. 599.)

you long enough to reflect on your folly.   I now give you notice, that
unless this order is immediately revoked, I will at once cause the
execution of every rebel officer, and every rebel slaveholder in my
possession.   This sad state of things may be kindly ordered by an all
wise Providence, to induce the good people of the North to act earnestly,
and to realize that they are at war.   Thousands of lives may thus be
saved.

The poor negro is fighting for liberty in its truest sense; and M^r
[*Thomas*] Jefferson has beautifully said,—"in such a war, there is no
attribute of the Almighty, which will induce him to fight on the side of
the oppressor."

You say you are fighting for liberty.   Yes you are fighting for liberty:
liberty to keep four millions of your fellow-beings in ignorance and
degradation;—liberty to separate parents and children, husband and
wife, brother and sister;—liberty to steal the products of their labor,
exacted with many a cruel lash and bitter tear,—liberty to seduce their
wives and daughters, and to sell your own children into bondage;—
liberty to kill these children with impunity, when the murder cannot be
proven by one of pure white blood.   This is the kind of liberty—the
liberty to do wrong—which Satan, Chief of the fallen Angels, was
contending for when he was cast into Hell.   I have the honor to be, very
respectfully, Your mo[*st*]. ob[*edient*]. serv[*ant*].

HDcS

D. Hunter[9]

Shortly after the battle of Fort Wagner, the mother of a soldier in
the 54th Massachusetts Infantry urged President Lincoln to guarantee the proper treatment of captured black soldiers. In measured
but heartfelt words she defined the president's responsibilities to
the soldiers and their families and demanded that he fulfill them.

Buffalo [*N.Y.*]   July 31 1863

Excellent Sir   My good friend says I must write to you and she will
send it   My son went in the 54th regiment.   I am a colored woman and
my son was strong and able as any to fight for his country and the
colored people have as much to fight for as any.   My father was a Slave
and escaped from Louisiana before I was born morn forty years
agone   I have but poor edication but I never went to schol, but I know
just as well as any what is right between man and man.   Now I know it
is right that a colored man should go and fight for his country, and so
ought to a white man.   I know that a colored man ought to run no
greater risques than a white, his pay is no greater his obligation to fight
is the same.   So why should not our enemies be compelled to treat him
the same, Made to do it.

My son fought at Fort Wagoner but thank God he was not taken
prisoner, as many were   I thought of this thing before I let my boy go
but then they said M^r. Lincoln will never let them sell our colored
soldiers for slaves,   if they do he will get them back quck   he will
rettallyate and stop it.   Now Mr Lincoln dont you think you oght to stop
this thing and make them do the same by the colored men   they have
lived in idleness all their lives on stolen labor and made savages of the
colored people, but they now are so furious because they are proving
themselves to be men, such as have come away and got some edication.
It must not be so.   You must put the rebels to work in State prisons to
making shoes and things, if they sell our colored soldiers, till they let
them all go.   And give their wounded the same treatment.   it would
seem cruel, but their no other way, and a just man must do hard things
sometimes, that shew him to be a great man.   They tell me some do you
will take back the Proclamation,   don't do it.   When you are dead and
in Heaven, in a thousand years that action of yours will make the Angels

sing your praises I know it.   Ought one man to own another, law for or
not,   who made the law, surely the poor slave did not.   so it is wicked,
and a horrible Outrage, there is no sense in it,   because a man has lived
by robbing all his life and his father before him, should he complain
because the stolen things found on him are taken.   Robbing the colored
people of their labor is but a small part of the robbery   their souls are
almost taken, they are made bruits of often.   You know all about this

   Will you see that the colored men fighting now, are fairly treated.
You ought to do this, and do it at once, Not let the thing run
along   meet it quickly and manfully, and stop this, mean cowardly
cruelty.   We poor oppressed ones, appeal to you, and ask fair play.
Yours for Christs sake

Hannah Johnson.

[*In another handwriting*]   Hon. Mr. Lincoln   The above speaks for
itself   Carrie Coburn[10]

ALS

> Unbeknown to Hannah Johnson, Lincoln had only the previous
> day promised to retaliate against Confederate prisoners if captured
> black soldiers were denied the rights of prisoners of war. Through-
> out the North, recruiters attempting to enlist black men made ef-
> fective use of Lincoln's threat.

COLORED SOLDIERS!

EQUAL STATE RIGHTS!

AND MONTHLY PAY WITH WHITE MEN!!

On the 1st day of January, 1863, the President of the United States proclaimed

FREEDOM TO OVER

THREE MILLIONS OF SLAVES!

This decree is to be enforced by all the power of the Nation.   On the 21st of July last he issued
the following order:—

PROTECTION OF COLORED TROOPS.

"WAR DEPARTMENT, ADJUTANT GENERAL'S OFFICE,
WASHINGTON, July 21.

" *General Order, No. 233.*

"The following order of the President is published for the information and government of all concerned:—

EXECUTIVE MANSION, WASHINGTON, July 30.

"'It is the duty of every Government to give protection to its citizens, of whatever class, color, or condition, and especially to those who are duly organized as soldiers in the public service. The law of nations, and the usages and customs of war, as carried on by civilized powers, permit no distinction as to color in the treatment of prisoners of war as public enemies. To sell or enslave any captured person on account of his color, is a relapse into barbarism, and a crime against the civilization of the age.

"'The Government of the United States will give the same protection to all its soldiers, and if the enemy shall sell or enslave any one because of his color, the offence shall be punished by retaliation upon the enemy's prisoners in our possession. It is, therefore, ordered, for every soldier of the United States, killed in violation of the laws of war, a rebel soldier shall be executed; and for every one enslaved by the enemy, or sold into slavery, a rebel soldier shall be placed at hard labor on the public works, and continued at such labor until the other shall be released and receive the treatment due to prisoners of war.

"'ABRAHAM LINCOLN.''

"'By order of the Secretary of War.

"'E. D. TOWNSEND, Assistant Adjutant General.''

That the President is in earnest the rebels soon began to find out, as witness the following order from his Secretary of War:—

"WAR DEPARTMENT, WASHINGTON CITY, August 3, 1863.

"SIR:—Your letter of the 3d inst., calling the attention of this Department to the cases of Orin H. Brown, William H. Johnston, and Wm. Wilson, three colored men captured on the gunboat Isaac Smith, has received consideration. This Department has directed that three rebel prisoners of South Carolina, if there be any such in our possession, and if not, three others, be confined in close custody and held as hostages for Brown, Johnston, and Wilson, and that the fact be communicated to the rebel authorities at Richmond.

"Very respectfully your obedient servant,

"EDWIN M. STANTON, Secretary of War.

"The Hon. GIDEON WELLES, Secretary of the Navy."

And retaliation will be our practice now—man for man—to the bitter end.

7

When black soldiers went to war, they did so for reasons that differed from those of many Northerners. In two documents found in
a street in New Orleans, an anonymous "Colored man" insisted
that saving the Union was a hollow objective unless accompanied
by the destruction of slavery. He further maintained that discrimination within the Union army and the continuing legality of slavery
in southern Louisiana—a region exempted from the Emancipation
Proclamation—made it difficult for people of African descent to
identify their interests fully with those of the Union.

[*New Orleans, La. September? 1863*]

the president Shall be Commander in Chief of the Army and navy of
the united States and of the militia of the Several States when called
into the actual Service of the united States

Let See if Slavery was any value   what m^r Yancy* Say the number
of Slaves in the Southern States estimated 3,500,000 and the were
worth $1200,000 000 in gold which would be a bout $1800,000,000 in
Green Backs Eighteen hundred million Dollars   the Collored
population is not educated but what Great responciblity has been
placeed on them   the have been Steam boat pilots ingenears and Black
Smiths Coopers Carpenters Shoe makers Drivers on plantations Sugar
makers porters on Steam boats and at hotels Dineing Servant Porters in
Commision houses Grocery Stores Public weighers Carrige Drivers
preachers of the Gospel the best Soldiers the united States Can Raise
but the tel lies Sometimes and So dos all negro traders   the get Drunk
and lawiers and merchants Generals and Governors and all Clases   the
black men has wives and Sweet harts Jest like the white men   Some
white men has Collored wives and Sweet hearts   god made all   it is
not a City rule for Collored people to ride in the white peoples cars but

*William Lowndes Yancey of Alabama, a prominent secessionist.

the bed togeather   God mad all   the must all Die

it is retten that a man can not Serve two master But it Seems that the Collored population has got two a rebel master and a union master   the both want our Servises   one wants us to make Cotton and Sugar And the Sell it and keep the money   the union masters wants us to fight the battles under white officers and the injoy both money and the union   black Soldiers And white officers will not play togeathe much longer   the Constitution is if any man rebells against those united States his property Shall be confescated and Slaves declared and henceforth Set free forever   when theire is a insurection or rebllion against these united States the Constitution gives the president of the united States full power to arm as many soldiers of African decent as he deems nescesisary to Surpress the Rebellion and officers Should be black or white According to their abillitys   the Collored man Should guard Stations Garison forts and mand vessels according to his Compasitys

A well regulated militia being necessary to the cecurity of a free State the right of the people to keep and Bear arms Shall not be infringed

we are to Support the Constitution but no religious test Shall ever be required as a qualification to Any office or public trust under the united States   the excitement of the wars is mostly keep up from the Churches   the Say god is fighting the battle but it is the people   But the will find that god fought our battle once   the way to have peace is to distroy the enemy   As long as theire is a Slave their will be rebles Against the Government of the united States   So we must look out our white officers may be union men but Slave holders at heart   the Are allways on hand when theire is money but Look out for them in the battle feild   liberty is what we want and nothing Shorter

our Southern friend tells that the are fighting for negros and will have

them   our union friends Says the are not fighting to free the
negroes   we are fighting for the union and free navigation of the
Mississippi river   very well let the white fight for what the want and we
negroes fight for what we want   there are three things to fight for and
two races of people divided into three Classes   one wants negro Slaves
the other the union the other Liberty   So liberty must take the day
nothing Shorter   we are the Blackest and the bravest race   the
president Says there is a wide Difference Between the black Race and
the white race   But we Say that white corn and yellow will mix by the
taussels but the black and white Race must mix by the roots as the are
so well mixed and has no tausels—freedom and liberty is the word with
the Collered people

We the people of the united States in order to form a more perfect
union Establish Justice insure domestick tranquillity provide for the
common defence promote the general wellfare and secure the blessings
of liberty to ourselves and our posterity do ordain and establish this
Constitution for the united States of America

My Dear union masters and reble masters or friends   How are we
Slave Population to take hold of a musket under white officers which a
great part of them has been in the reble army and the meet to hold a war
Consels all to them Selves   Dear Sir I heard a federal officer Say after
the fall of Port hudson to a Collored Soldier we will not want any more
negro Soldiers   go home to your master   i my Self went to a union
lawyer on Some Buiness   the first question are you free or
Slave   Before the fall of porthudson the white Preachers told us we
were all free as any white man and in Less time than a month after you
weare taking us up and puting in the lockups and Cotton presses giving
us nothing to eat nor nothing Sleep on And haveing negro traders for
recruting officers Drawing his Sword over us like we were dogs   By

those means you will Soon have the union north   if any union man can
deny this i will write no more   i am for the union and liberty to all men
or nothing Shorter   treason against the united States Shall consist
only in Levying ware against them or in adhering to theire enemies
giving them aid and Comfort   no person Shall be convicted of treason
unless on the testimoney of two witnesses to the Same overt Act or
Confession in open Court   the Congress Shall Have power to declare
punishment of treason but no attainder of treason Shall work
Corruption of blood or forfeiture Except during the life of the person
attained

Now let us see whether the Colored population will be turn back in to
Slavery and the union lost or not   on the 4" of last July it was Said to
the colored population that the were all free and on the 4" of August
locked up in Cotton presses like Horses or hogs By reble watchmen and
Saying to us Gen banks Says you are All free why do you not go to him
and get passes   And one half of the recruiting officers is rebles taken
the oath to get a living and would Sink the Government into ashes   the
Scrptures says the enemy must Suffer death before we can Have
peace   the fall of porthudson and vicksburg is nothing   the rebles
must fall or the union must fall   Sure the Southern men Says the are
not fighting for money the are fighting for negros   the northern men
Say the did not com South to free the negroes but to Save the
union   very well for that much   what is the colored men fighting
for   if the makes us free we are happy to hear it And when we are free
men and a people we will fight for our rights and liberty   we care
nothing about the union   we heave been in it Slaves over two hundred
And fifty years   we have made the contry and So far Saved the union
and if we heave to fight for our rights let us fight under Colored officers
for we are the men that will kill the Enemies of the Government   pleas
let me continue

Art 173   the Slave is entirely Subject to the will of his master Who
may Correct and Chastise him though not with unusal Rigor nor So as
to maim or mutilate him or to expose him to the danger of loss of life or
to cause his death

Art 174   the Slave is incapable of making any kind of Contract
Except those which relate to own emancipation

Art 175   All that a Slave possesses belongs to his master   he
Possesses nothing of his own excep his peculium that is to Say the Sum
of money or movable estate which his master chooses He Should possess

Art 176   the can transmit nothing by Succession or otherwise but the
Succession of free persons related to them which the would have
Inherited had the been free may pass through them to such of their
descendants as may have acquired their liberty before the Succession
opened

A part of the Civil Code of louisiana

the united States Shall guarantee to every State in this union a
republican form of government and Shall protect each of them a gainst
invaison and on Aplication of the legislature. or of the executive when
the legislature. can not be convened against Domestic violence

now is the united States government and constitution free or a local
Goverment   if it is free let us colored population muster in to ams and
garison forts guard Station and mand vessels and then we will know
wheather we are free people or not   then we will know wheather you
want to make brest works of us or not or make us fools ornot   I heard
one of most Ables and distingush lawiers Say that the Colored
population was all free and Had as much liberty in the union as he
had   in four or five days after I went to him to get him to atend Some
buiness for me he Said to me Are you free or Slave   Sir Said i am free
By your own speeches   was you born free   no Sir Said i   we have

been made fools of from the time Butlers fleet landed hear but I have
remained At my old Stand and will untill i See what i am dowing   I
know very well that the white union men cannot put down the rebeles for
them that was not rebles Soon will be   i am Sory that I am not able to
write good   may the union forever Stand with peace and liberty to All
good people

HD   A Colored man[12]

                              [*New Orleans, La.   September? 1863*]
     the President Shall at Stated times receive for his Services a
Compensation which Shall neither be increased or diminished During
the period for which he Shall have Been Elected and he Shall not receive
within that period Any other emolument from the united States or any
of them   Before he enters on the execution of his office he Shall take
the following oath or Afirmation   I do Solemnly Sweare (or Affirm)
that I will faithfully execute the office of president of the united States
and will to the best of my Ability. preserve Protect and defend the
Constitution of the united States   the president Shall be commander
in chief of the Army and navy of the united States and of the miltia of
the Several States when called Into actual Service of the united States
     when the president ordered three hundred thousand Colored Soldiers
to be mustered into the united States Army on the first Day of last April
if So the rebles would have fell like the Surrender of vicksburg and
porthudson
     Declare freedom at onc and give us Somting to fight for   Black
Soldiers Black officers and all white rebles will Soon run them in or out
of the union
     the writer was born in 18.18 feb 16"

HD   one of the union Colored friends[13]

As the "Colored man" knew, black soldiers could not always rely upon their professed friends in the North. Disregarding promises of equal treatment, the government often employed black soldiers as little more than uniformed drudges. Many white soldiers and officers simply assumed that black soldiers would and should do the dirty work. Colonel James C. Beecher, a member of a prominent antislavery family and the commander of a regiment of former slaves from North Carolina, protested to his brigade commander the harmful effects of such assignments.

Folly Island [*S.C.*] Sept. 13th 1863.

General   It is reported to me on good authority that men of my command ordered to Morris Island on fatigue duty, are put to work laying out and policing camps of white soldiers on that Island.   I am informed that to day a detachment of 60 men properly officered, having been ordered to report to a Major Butts of some New York Regiment were set to work levelling ground for the Regimental Camp, digging wells &c pitching tents and the like.

Since the commencement of the war I have never before known such duty imposed upon any Regiment; it being (unless I am greatly in error) the custom of New York and other Regiments to pitch their own tents and lay out their own camps a privilege, by the way, which my men have had little time to enjoy by reason of constant detail on fatigue.

As you are aware—the fatigue duty of my regiment has been incessant and trying—so that my sick list has increased from 4 or 5 to nearly 200 in a little over one month; and I respectfully protest against the imposition of labors which by no principle of custom or right devolve upon my command.   I respectfully protest against this particular imposition because of its injurious influence upon the men in another respect.

They have been slaves and are just learning to be men   It is a draw-back that they are regarded as, and called "d—d Niggers" by so-called "gentleman" in uniform of U.S. Officers, but when they are set to menial work doing for white regiments what those Regiments are entitled to do for themselves, it simply throws them back where they were before and reduces them to the position of slaves again.

I therefore request that you will entertain this my protest; and, if you find no objection to the matter or manner of the same, will forward it through the proper Channel to the General Commanding the Department—   If these men do their duty in the trenches, and in the field, I do not believe that he will make them hewers of wood and drawers of water for those who do no more.   I am General Very Respectfully Yours

HLcSr

James C. Beecher[14]

Favorable endorsements by Beecher's superiors—one of whom, however, found the complaint "wanting in proper respect"—result-ed in orders prohibiting the use of black soldiers "to prepare camps and perform menial duties for white troops" in the Department of the South.[15] Similar protests by black soldiers and their officers in other commands eventually led the adjutant general of the army, in June 1864, to order that black troops "only be required to take their fair share of fatigue duty, with the white troops."[16]

Of all the inequities black soldiers endured, the most galling result-ed from the Militia Act of July 1862. Primarily intended to govern the mobilization of fugitive slaves as military laborers, the law au-thorized the president to employ "persons of African descent" at $10 per month ($3 of which could be deducted for clothing).[17] It

was not immediately apparent that these provisions would apply to
black soldiers. Until the summer of 1863, all Union privates—
black and white—collected $13 per month (plus an allotment of
clothing or its equivalent cash value of $3.50); noncommissioned
and commissioned officers drew higher amounts. But in June of
that year, the army began paying all black soldiers—whether
freemen or ex-slaves, and regardless of rank—in conformity with
the Militia Act. That decision ignited a firestorm of protest that
raged for a full year. Writing directly to the president, a freeborn
corporal in the 54th Massachusetts Infantry eloquently stated his
comrades' case for equal pay; he emphasized in particular the injustice of applying to Northern freemen a law meant for former
slaves.

Morris Island [*S.C.*].   Sept 28th 1863.

Your Excelency will pardon the presumtion of an humble individual
like myself, in addressing you. but the earnest Solicitation of my
Comrades in Arms, besides the genuine interest felt by myself in the
matter is my excuse, for placing before the Executive head of the Nation
our Common Grievance: On the 6th of the last Month, the Paymaster of
the department, informed us, that if we would decide to recieve the sum
of $10 (ten dollars) per month, he would come and pay us that sum, but,
that, on the sitting of Congress, the Regt would, in his opinion, be
allowed the other 3 (three.)   He did not give us any guarantee that this
would be, as he hoped, certainly *he* had no authority for making any
such guarantee, and we can not supose him acting in any way interested.
Now the main question is. Are we *Soldiers*, or are we LABOURERS.   We
are fully armed, and equipped, have done all the various Duties,
pertaining to a Soldiers life, have conducted ourselves, to the complete
satisfaction of General Officers, who, were if any, prejudiced *against* us,
but who now accord us all the encouragement, and honour due us: have

shared the perils, and Labour, of Reducing the first stronghold, that
flaunted a Traitor Flag: and more, Mr President. Today, the Anglo
Saxon Mother, Wife, or Sister, are not alone, in tears for departed Sons,
Husbands, and Brothers. The patient Trusting Decendants of Africs
Clime, have dyed the ground with blood, in defense of the Union, and
Democracy. Men too your Excellency, who know in a measure, the
cruelties of the Iron heel of oppression, which in years gone by, the very
Power, their blood is now being spilled to maintain, ever ground them to
the dust. But When the war trumpet sounded o'er the land, when men
knew not the Friend from the Traitor, the Black man laid his life at the
Altar of the Nation,—and he was refused. When the arms of the
Union, were beaten, in the first year of the War, And the Executive
called more food. for its ravaging maw, again the black man begged, the
privelege of Aiding his Country in her need, to be again refused, And
now, he is in the War: and how has he conducted himself? Let their
dusky forms, rise up, out the mires of James Island, and give the
answer. Let the rich mould around Wagners parapets be upturned, and
there will be found an Eloquent answer. Obedient and patient, and
Solid as a wall are they. all we lack, is a paler hue, and a better
acquaintance with the Alphabet. Now Your Excellency, We have done a
Soldiers Duty. Why cant we have a Soldiers pay? You caution the
Rebel Chieftain, that the United States, knows, no distinction, in her
Soldiers: She insists on having all her Soldiers, of whatever, creed or
Color, to be treated, according to the usages of War. Now if the United
States exacts uniformity of treatment of her Soldiers, from the
Insurgents, would it not be well, and consistent, to set the example
herself, by paying all her *Soldiers* alike? We of this Regt. were not
enlisted under any "contraband" act. But we do not wish to be
understood, as rating our Service, of more Value to the Government,

than the service of the exslave, Their Service *is* undoubtedly worth much to the Nation, but Congress made express, provision touching their case, as slaves freed by military necessity, and assuming the Government, to be their temporary Gaurdian:— Not so with us— Freemen by birth, and consequently, having the advantage of *thinking*, and acting for ourselves, so far as the Laws would allow us. We do not consider ourselves fit subjects for the Contraband act. We appeal to You, Sir: as the Executive of the Nation, to have us Justly Dealt with. The Regt, do pray, that they be assured their service will be fairly appreciated, by paying them as american SOLDIERS, not as menial hierlings. Black men You may well know, are poor, three dollars per month, for a year, will suply their needy Wives, and little ones, with fuel. If you, as chief Magistrate of the Nation, will assure us, of our whole pay. We are content, our Patriotism, our enthusiasm will have a new impetus, to exert our energy more and more to aid Our Country. Not that our hearts ever flagged, in Devotion, spite the evident apathy displayed in our behalf, but We feel as though, our Country spurned us, now we are sworn to serve her.

Please give this a moments attention

ALS

James Henry Gooding[18]

Corporal Gooding hinted at the hardship endured by black soldiers' families in the free states, but the families of their comrades from the border states, where slavery was still legal, suffered even greater trials. Many wives, children, and parents of border-state soldiers remained in the custody of slaveholders embittered by the men's enlistment. Martha Glover of Missouri described to her husband the burdens she had borne since he joined the army.

Mexico Mo   Dec 30th 1863

My Dear Husband   I have received your last kind letter a few days ago
and was much pleased to hear from you once more.   It seems like a long
time since you left me.   I have had nothing but trouble since you left.
You recollect what I told you how they would do after you was gone.   they
abuse me because you went & say they will not take care of our children
& do nothing but quarrel with me all the time and beat me scandalously
the day before yesterday—   Oh I never thought you would give me so
much trouble as I have got to bear now.   You ought not to left me in the
fix I am in & all these little helpless children to take care of.   I was
invited to a party to night but I could not go   I am in too much trouble
to want to go to parties.   the children talk about you all the time.   I
wish you could get a furlough & come to see us once more.   We want to
see you worse than we ever did before.   Remember all I told you about
how they would do me after you left—for they do worse than they ever
did & I do not know what will become of me & my poor little
children.   Oh I wish you had staid with me & not gone till I could go
with you for I do nothing but grieve all the time about you.   write & tell
me when you are coming.

    Tell Isaac that his mother come & got his clothes   she was so sorry
he went.   You need not tell me to beg any more married men to go.   I
see too much trouble to try to get any more into trouble too—   Write to
me & do not forget me & my children—   farewell my dear husband from
your wife

ALS   Martha[19]

Martha Glover's troubles had only begun. Six weeks later, her master attempted to safeguard his valuable human property by transporting her and three of her children to Kentucky. But the superintendent of black recruitment in Missouri foiled the plan.[20]

Although the tribulations of black soldiers' families remained, for the most part, private, the abuse of captured soldiers claimed the attention of the Northern public. In a notorious episode, on April 12, 1864, Confederate troops commanded by General Nathan Bedford Forrest captured the federal garrison at Fort Pillow, Tennessee, and then slaughtered scores of Union soldiers who had already surrendered, most of whom were black. The atrocity sparked a congressional investigation and demands that President Lincoln make good his threat of retaliation. Failure to do so, a black New Yorker warned the secretary of war, would alienate black Americans from the Union cause.

New York [*N.Y.*] April 18th 1864

Sir: Some Sixty or Seventy thousand of my down trodden and despised brethren now wear the uniform of the United States and are bearing the gun and sword in protecting the life of this once great nation   with this in view I am emboldened to address a few words to you in their behalf if not in behalf of the government itself.   Jeff Davis issued a threat that black men fighting for the U.S. should not be treated as prisoners of war and the President issued a proclamation threatening retaliation.   Since then black soldiers have been murdered again and again yet where is there an instance of retaliation.   To be sure there has been a sort of secrecy about many of these slaughters of colored troops that prevented an official declaration to be made but there is now an open and bold murder,   an act following the proclaimed threat made in cold blood gives the government an opportunity to show the world whether the rebels or the U.S. have the strongest power.   If the murder of the colored troops at Fort Pillow is not followed by prompt action on the part of our government. it may as well disband *all its colored troops* for no soldiers whom the goverment will not protect can be depended upon   Now Sir if you will permit a colored man to give not exactly advice to your excellency but the expression of his fellow colored men so as to give them heart and courage to believe in their goverment you can do so by a prompt retaliation. Let the same no. of rebel soldiers, privates and officers be selected from those now in confinement as prisoners of war captured at the west and let them be surrounded by two or three regiments of colored troops who may be allowed to open fire upon them in squads of 50 or 100, with howitzers loaded with grape. The whole civilized world will approve of this necessary military execution and the rebels will learn that the U.S. Govt. is not to be trifled with and the black men will feel not a spirit of revenge for have they not often taken the rebels prisoners even their old masters without indulging in a fiendish spirit of revenge or exultation. Do this sir *promptly and without notice to the rebels at Richmond* when the *execution has* been made then an official declaration or explanation may be made. If the threat is made first or notice given to the rebels they will set apart the same no. for execution. Even that mild copperhead Reverdy Johnston avowed in a speech in the Senate that this govt. could only be satisfied with man for man as an act of retaliation. This request or suggestion is not made in a spirit of vindicativeness but simply in the interest of my poor suffering confiding fellow negros who are even now assembling at Annapolis [*Md.*] and other points to reinforce the army of the Union Act first in this matter afterward explain or threaten the act tells the threat or demand is regarded as idle. I am Sir with great respect Your humble Servant.

<small>ALS</small> Theodore Hodgkins[21]

> Discussions between President Lincoln and his cabinet about responding to the Fort Pillow massacre resulted in a decision to retaliate only against actual offenders from Forrest's command, should

any be captured, but to warn the Confederate government that a number of captured Southern officers would be held as hostages against such actions in the future. The policy, however, was not put into effect.[22]

———————◆———————

The smaller pay received by black soldiers not only demonstrated a double standard based on color, but also caused hardship for their families. Payday inequities cut in other directions as well. Federal authorities held all black soldiers to the restrictions of the Militia Act but often paid higher wages to black military laborers, for whom the law was originally intended. William J. Brown, a free-born sergeant in a regiment composed mostly of former slaves, conveyed his comrades' resentment to the secretary of war.

Fort Halleck   Columbus—Ky.   Aprile 27th 1864

I Sir by way of Introduction was made 1^(st.) Sergeant of *Co*. C which was then denominated as *2^(nd) Tenn* Heavey Artillery now as 3^(d) United States Heavey Artillery, as I wish to state to you, the facts which can be Relied, upon as I am fully able to prove if necessary   I may say to you this *Reg*. is a *coloured* one of Southern Birth consequently have no Education,   not so with my self   I was Freeborn and Educated to some extent which makes me know   we know that we have never had our Just Rights, by the Officers who command us,   the white officers of other *Reg*. here persuaded me to Join when there were no *Reg*. of coloured here to Join so I consented and being the first to sign my name in this *Reg*.   They promiced to pay us the same wages as was paid the whites & Rations & clothing the same   they have given us clothing & Rations sufficient for the time but have not paid us our Money according to promice   the white privates tell us we Should get the same pay as they do but none of us has yet   we never have been paid more than

Seven Dollars per Month   they now say that is all we are allowd by the
Govornment of the United States   Many of these people have Families
to support and no other means of doing it than what they get in this way.
Such of those that are not able Bodied men are employed on
Govornment work and are paid Ten Dollars per Month   We who belong
to this *Reg.* have done more work than they on Fatigue and other wise
the very Labour that was appointed for them   we have had to toil day
and night when necessity demands it,   I may say to you at the presant
our Regimental officers are nearly played out   they have been Turned
out and their places have not been furnished with other
commanders   now *Hon.* Secretary of war I wish to ask you not only for
my own Satisfaction but at the Request of my *Reg.* is Seven Dollars per
month all we Soldiers are to get or may we Expect in the final settlement
to get our full Rights as was promiced us at the first

   If we are to Recieve as much as White Soldiers or the Regular thirteen
Dollars per Month then we Shall be Satisfied and on the field of Battle
we will prove that we were worthy of what we claim for our Rights

   With this Statement I may close by Requesting your Answer to this
for the many Anxious and disappointed men of this *Reg.*   I am Sir your
obedient Servant

ALS   W^m. J. Brown[23]

   The appointment of black men to military positions that entailed
   authority over white men was unacceptable to federal officials,
   white soldiers, and the Northern public. The cashiering of the
   Louisiana black officers in 1863* reflected that hostility, and until
   early 1865 the War Department steadfastly refused to commission
   black men as line officers, no matter what their qualifications.
   They nevertheless continued to press for commissions, if not as

*See above, pp. 437–38.

captains and lieutenants then as chaplains and surgeons. And because the latter positions did not involve battlefield command, the War Department received such applications with somewhat more favor. The former slave of a prominent secessionist sought the endorsement of Secretary of State William H. Seward for his appointment to a chaplaincy.

Camp Casey   Washington City [*D.C.*]   May 18th 1864
dear sir   please parden me for troubling you with business that is not Immediately connected with your office, yet it being justice to myself & of interest to my comrads in the military service of the government, I hope your honor will at once pardon me for the liberty I take in writing you such a letter.   You will judge from past correspondence whilst in Canada that I was anxious to serve my country to the best of my humble ability.   I have recruited colored men for every colored regiment raised in the north forsaken my church in ohio & canvassed the intire north & west urging my people to inlist & have succeded in every instant at various times were told that I would have the chaplaincy of some one of the colored Regiment.   I nearly recruited half the men in the 28th U.S. Colored Infrantry Regiment raised in Indiana   Gov O. P. Morton of Ind promised to give me the office *but* could not as it was transfered from the volunteer serv to that of the regular Army.   my officers have me acting as a chaplain but no man seeke my commission.   I pray you will see me justified after having done as much as I have in raising such troops.   I refer you to Gov Andrew of Mass Todd of ohio Morton of Ind Seymore of New York & Spridge of Rhode I—   I also joined the regt as a private to be with my boys & should I fail to get my commission I shall willingly serve my time out, but I know you can get me my commission if any other gentleman in the world can & at the same time feel quite certain that should you vail to give my humble plea due consideration no

other will.   I pray you will aid me sprining from so humble an origin as
myself namely that of being the body servant of Robert Toombs.   please
let your humble servant hear from you as soon as possible.   May heaven
Bless you & family in all your future pursuits   I am dear sir your very
humble servant

ALS
                                                            Garland. H. White[24]

> White was commissioned a chaplain, thanks in part, no doubt, to a
> favorable word from Seward.

> No matter what their rank, black soldiers—like white ones—trea-
> sured their memories of home and family. Stealing a quiet moment
> before going on picket duty, Private Ruphus Wright described a re-
> cent battle to his wife.

                                        wilson Creek Va May 25th 1864

dear wife   I take the pleasant opportunity of writeing to you a fiew
lines to inform you of the Late Battle we have had   we was a fight on
Tuesday five hours   we whipp the rebls out   we Killed $200 &
captured many Prisener   out of our Regiment we lost 13 Thirteen
Sergent Stephensen killed & priate out of Company H & about 8 or 10
wounded   we was in line Wednesday for a battele But the rebels did
not Appear   we expect an Attack every hour   give my love to all & to
my sisters give my love   to Miss Emerline tell John Skinner is well &
sends much love to her.   Joseph H Grinnel is well & he is as brave a
lion   all the Boys sends there love them   give my love to Miss
Missenger   You must excuse my short Letter   we are most getting
ready to go on Picket   No more from your Husband

ALS
                                                            Ruphus Wright[25]

From above the fray, other observers sustained Private Wright's assessment of the black soldiers' performance. The adjutant general
of the army, who was in charge of recruiting black troops in the
Mississippi Valley, sang their praises to the chairman of the Senate
Committee on Military Affairs. In so doing, he added his voice to
the growing chorus calling for equal pay.

Washington [*D.C.*],   May 30, 1864.

Dear Sir: On several occasions when on the Mississippi river I
contemplated writing to you respecting the colored troops, and to
suggest that as they have been fully tested as soldiers their pay should
be raised to that of white troops, and I desire now to give my testimony
in their behalf.   You are aware that I have been engaged in the
organization of freedmen for over a year, and have necessarily been
thrown in constant contact with them.

The negro in a state of slavery is brought up by the master from early
childhood to strict obedience, and to obey implicitly the dictates of the
white man, and they are thus led to believe that they are an inferior
race.   Now, when organized into troops, they carry this habit of
obedience with them; and their officers being entirely white men, the
negro promptly obeys his orders.   A regiment is thus rapidly brought
into a state of discipline.   They are a religious people, another high
quality for making good soldiers.   They are a musical people, and thus
readily learn to march and accurately perform their maneuvers.   They
take pride in being elevated as soldiers, and keep themselves neat and
clean, as well as their camp graounds.   This I know from personal
inspection, and from the reports of my special inspectors, two of my
staff being constantly on inspecting duty.

They have proved a most important addition to our forces, enabling
the generals in active operations to take a large force of white troops

into the field; and now brigades of blacks are placed with the whites.
The forts erected at the important points on the river are nearly all
garrisoned by blacks—artillery regiments raised for the purpose—say
at Paducah and Columbus, Kentucky; Memphis, Tennessee; Vicksburg
and Natchez, Mississippi, and most of the works around New Orleans.
Experience proves that they manage heavy guns very well.   Their
fighting qualities have also been fully tested a number of times, and I am
yet to hear of the first case where they did not fully stand up to their
work.   I passed over the ground where the first Louisiana made the
gallant charge at Port Hudson, by far the stronger part of the rebel
works.   The wonder is that so many made their escape.*   At Milliken's
Bend, where I had three incomplete regiments, one without arms until
the day previous to the attack; greatly superior numbers of rebels
charged furiously up to the very breast-works.   The negroes met the
enemy on the ramparts, and both sides freely used the bayonet, a most
rare occurrence in warfare, as one or other party gives way before
coming in contact with the steel.   The rebels were defeated with heavy
loss.†   The bridge at Moscow, on the line of railroad from Memphis to
Corinth, was defended by one small regiment of blacks.   A cavalry
attack of three times their number was made, the blacks defeating them
in the three charges made by the rebels.   They fought them hours, until
our cavalry came up, when the defeat was made complete, many of the
rebel dead being left on the field.   A cavalry force of one hundred and
fifty attacked three hundred rebel cavalry near the Big Black with signal
success, a number of prisoners being taken and marched to
Vicksburg.   Forrest attacked Paducah with seven thousand five
hundred.   The garrison was between five and six hundred; nearly four

---

*For an account of the battle of Port Hudson, see above, pp. 439–41.

†For an account of the battle of Milliken's Bend, see above, pp. 441–44.

hundred were colored trops, very recently raised.   What troops could
have done better?   So, too, they fought well at Fort Pillow until
overpowered by greatly superior numbers.

   The above enumerated cases seem to me sufficient to demonstate the
value of the colored troops.   I make no mention of the cases on the
Atlantic coast with which you are perfectly familiar.* I have the honor to
be, Very respectfully, Your obedient servant,

TLcSr   L. Thomas[26]

> Such assessments cast unflattering light upon the government's
> failure to grant its soldiers equal pay for equal service, and black
> soldiers added fiery illumination of their own. Since July 1863, the
> men of the 54th and 55th Massachusetts Infantry had refused to
> accept unequal compensation. They also rejected as a matter of
> principle an offer by the state legislature to make up the difference.
> Their forthright stand came at considerable cost, often including
> the impoverishment of their families. A year after they opened
> their protest, believing that the government had still not acted to
> correct the injustice, members of the 55th Massachusetts peti-
> tioned President Lincoln for immediate discharge and settlement
> of accounts.

                    Folly island   South Carolina   July 16th 18.64
Sir   We The Members of Co D of the 55th Massechusetts vols Call the
attention of your Excellency to our case
   1st   First We wase enlisted under the act of Congress of July 18.61
Placing the officers non Commissioned officers & Privates of the
volunteer forces in all Respects as to Pay on the footing of Similar Corps

---

   *The best-known case was the assault on Fort Wagner, South Carolina;
   see above, pp. 444–47.

of the Regular Army   2nd We Have Been in the Field now thirteen
months & a Great many yet longer   We Have Recieved no Pay & Have
Been offered only seven Dollars Pr month Which the Paymaster Has
said was all He Had ever Been authorized to Pay Colored Troops   this
was not acording to our enlistment   Consequently We Refused the
Money   the Commonwealth of Massechusetts then Passed an act to
make up all Deficienceys which the general Government Refused To Pay
But this We Could not Recieve as The Troops in the general service are
not Paid Partly By Government & Partly By State   3rd that to us
money is no object   we came to fight For Liberty justice & Equality.
These are gifts we Prise more Highly than Gold   For these We Left
our Homes our Famileys Friends & Relatives most Dear to take as it
ware our Lives in our Hands To Do Battle for God & Liberty

    4th after the elaps of over thirteen months spent cheerfully &
willingly Doing our Duty most faithfuly in the Trenches Fatiegue Duty
in camp and conspicious valor & endurence in Battle as our Past History
will Show

    P 5th therefore we Deem these sufficient Reasons for Demanding
our Pay from the Date of our inlistment & our imediate Discharge
Having Been enlisted under False Prentence as the Past History of the
Company will Prove

    6th Be it further Resolved that if imediate steps are not takened to
Relieve us we will Resort to more stringent mesures

    We have the Honor to Remin your Obedint Servants   The members
of Co D

HLS   [74 signatures]^{27}

In fact, responding at last to demands for equal pay, Congress had on June 15 increased the compensation of black privates to $13 per month (the same as white privates) and provided that higher-ranking black soldiers receive the same pay as their white counterparts. For men who had been free before the war, the change was retroactive to the time of their enlistment; for those who had been slaves, to January 1, 1864.[28]

———◆———

Even after the new legislation, some soldiers went without pay because of bureaucratic inefficiency. A letter written by Thomas Sipple and attested to by three of his comrades informed President Lincoln about the effects of unpaid wages and other broken promises on enlisted men and their families.

New Orleans   Louisiana   Camp Parpit   [*August*] 1864 My Dear and Worthy Friend MR. President.   I thake this oppertunity of interducing my self to you By wrteing thes fiew Lines To let you know that you have Proven A friend to me and to all our Race   And now i stand in the Defence of the Country myself Ready and Willing to oBay all orders & demands that has A tendency to put Down this Rebelion In military Life or Civel Life.   I Enlisted at Almira state of N. York, shemoung County Under *Mr* C. W. Cawing Provose Marshall And [*when*] I Enlisted he told me i would get 13 Dollars Per. Mounth or more if White Soldiers got it   he expected the wages would Raise And i would get my pay every 2 Months   hear i am in the survice 7 months And have Not Recived Eney Monthly Pay   I have a wife and 3 Children Neither one of them Able to thake Care of Themselfs and my wife is sick   And she has sent to me for money   And i have No way of geting Eney money to send to her Because i cant Get my Pay.   And it gos very hard with me to think my family should be At home A suffering have money earnt and cant not get it   And I Dont know when i will Be Able to Releave my suffering Family   And another thing when I Enlisted I was promised A furlow and I have Not had it   Please MR Lincom Dont think I Am Blameing you for it   I Dident think you knew Eney thing About it   And I Dident know eney Other Course to thake To obtain what I think is Right   I invested my money in Percuring A house an home for my wife and Children   And she write to me she has to work and can not surport the Children with out my Aid   When I was At home i could earn from 26 to 28 Dollars A Month   When I Enlisted it told i was to have the same Bounty Clothing and Ration as the Soldier and 325 Dollars wich the 25 Dollars i Never got   I Dont Beleave the Goverment wants me eney how   In fact i mean the New York 20th Regiment   The Reason why i say so is Because we are treated Like A Parcels of Rebs   I Do not say the Goverment is useing us so   I [*do not*] Believe the Government knows Eney thing About how we are treated   we came out to be true union soldiers the Grandsons of Mother Africa Never to Flinch from Duty   Please Not to thinks I Am finding fault with the rules of the Goverment   If this Be the rules i am willing to Abide by them   I wonce Before was a Slave 25 years   I made escape 1855   Came In to York state from Maryland   And i Enlisted in the survice got up By the union Legue Club   And we ware Promised All satisfaction Needful   But it seem to Be A failure   We Are not treated Like we are soldiers in coleague Atall   we are Deprived of the most importances things we Need in health and sickness Both That surficint Food And quality   As for The sick it is A shocking thing to Look into thire conditions   Death must Be thire Doom when once they have to go to the Hospital   Never Return Again   such is the medical Assistance of the 20th Rig n.y   your sarvent under Arms sincerely

George Rodgers

Thomas Sipple   Wilmington Delaware.

Samuel Sampson

[*In another handwriting*]   Mr President   I Surtify that this I is jest
what mr Rodgers sais and my other frend mr Sipele   Nimrod
Rowley   Elmira Chemong CO. N.Y.

[*In the original handwriting*]   Pease excuse your Needy Petishners   We
most heartly wish you the intire victory over All Your Enemys.   And A
spedy sucsess To the Commander-in Chief of the Army And Navy   And
may Peace Forever Reighn[29]

HLS

> Some 36,000 black soldiers died in the service of their country dur-
> ing the Civil War. Disease claimed eleven men for each one who suc-
> cumbed to battlefield wounds. Contributing to the high incidence of
> disease was the presumption by federal authorities that people of
> African descent were physiologically adapted to tropical climates
> and peculiarly suited to duty in unhealthy settings. The assign-
> ment of many black soldiers to endless rounds of arduous fatigue
> duty further endangered their health. An unsigned letter, whose
> handwriting matches that of the preceding document, described to
> an unnamed official the toll that hard labor and short rations were
> taking on his regiment.

New Orleans   Camp Parpit   Louisiana   [*August*] 1864
My Dear Friend and x Pre   I thake up my Pen to Address you A fiew
simpels And facts   We so called the 20th u.s. Colored troops we was
got up in the state of New York so said By A grant of the President.   we
Dont think he know wether we are white or Black   we have not Bin
Organized yet And A grate meney Brought Away without Being
Musterd in, and we are treated in a Different maner to what others

Rigiments is Both Northern men or southern Raised
Rigiment   Instead of the musket It is the spad and the Whelbarrow
and the Axe   cuting in one of the most horable swamps in Louisiana
stinking and misery   Men are Call to go on thes fatiuges wen sum of
them are scarc Able to get Along the Day Before on the sick List And
Prehaps weeks to And By this treatment meney are thowen Back in
sickness wich thay very seldom get over.   we had when we Left New
York over A thousand strong   now we scarce rise Nine hundred the
total is said to Be   we lost 1.60 men who have Left thire homes friends
and Relation And Come Down hear to Lose thire Lives in For the
Country thy Dwll in or stayd in   the Colored man is like A lost
sheep   Meney of them old and young was Brave And Active. But has
Bin hurrided By and ignominious Death into Eternity.   But I hope God
will Presearve the Rest Now in existance to Get Justice and Rights   we
have to Do our Duty or Die and no help for us   It is true the Country
is in A hard strugle   But we All must Remember Mercy and Justice
Grate and small.   it is Devine.   we All Listed for so much Bounty
Clothing and Ration And 13 Dollars A month.   And the most has fallen
short in all thes Things   we havent Recived A cent of Pay Since we Bin
in the field.   Instead of them Coming to us Like men with our 13
Dollars thay come with only seven Dollars A month wich only A fiew
tuck it   we stand in Need of Money very much indeed And think it is
no more than Just an Right we should have it   And Another thing we
are Cut short of our Ration in A most Shocking maner.   I wont Relate
All now But we Are Nerly Deprived of All Comforts of Life   Hardly
have Anough Bread to Keep us From starving   six or 8 ounces of it to
Do A Soldier 24 hours on Gaurd or eney other Labor and About the
Same in Meat and Coffee   sum times No meat for 2 Days   soup meat
Licqour with very Little seazing the Boys calls hot water or meat tea for

Diner   It is A hard thing to be Keept in such a state of misery
Continuly   It is spoken Dont musel the ox that treads out the
corn.   Remember we are men standing in Readiness to face thous vile
traitors an Rebeles who are trying to Bring your Peaceable homes to
Destruction.   And how can we stand them in A weak and starving
Condition[30]

HL

> Black soldiers who fell in battle earned special honor, especially in
> the eyes of their comrades. A soldier from Maryland consoled the
> mother of a friend who had died in combat.

                                Near Petersburge [*Va.*]   August 19th 1864
Dear Madam   I receave A letter from You A few day Ago inquir in
regard to the Fait of Your Son   I am sarry to have to inform You that
thear is no dobt of his Death   he Died A Brave Death in Trying to
Save the Colors of Rige[*ment*] in that Dreadful Battil   Billys Death
was unevesally [*mourned*] by all but by non greatter then by my
self   ever sins we have bin in the Army we have bin amoung the moust
intimoat Friend   wen every our Rige[*ment*] wen into Camp he sertan
to be at my Tent and meney happy moment we seen to gether Talking
about Home and the Probability of our Living to get Home to See each
other Family and Friend   But Providence has will other wise and You
must Bow to His will   You and His Wife Sister and all Have my
deepust Simppathy and trust will be well all in this Trying moment
   You Inquired about Mr Young   He wen to the Hospetol and I can
not give You eney other information in regard to Him
   Billys thing that You requested to inquired about I can git no informa

of as in the bustil of the Battil every thing was Lost

 Give my Respects to Samual Jackson and Family not forgeting Your
self and Family   I remain Your Friend

ALS G. H. Freeman[31]

Drawing strength from both the Union's commitment to emancipation and its march toward victory, a black soldier from Missouri assured first his daughters and then the woman who owned one of
them that the federal army would do the Lord's work, and that he
would be there when it did. The moment of liberation was at hand.

[*Benton Barracks Hospital, St. Louis, Mo., September 3, 1864*]

My Children   I take my pen in hand to rite you A few lines to let you
know that I have not forgot you and that I want to see you as bad as
ever   now my Dear Children I want you to be contented with whatever
may be your lots   be assured that I will have you if it cost me my
life   on the 28th of the mounth. 8 hundred White and 8 hundred
blacke solders expects to start up the rivore to Glasgow and above there
thats to be jeneraled by a jeneral that will give me both of you   when
they Come I expect to be with, them and expect to get you both in
return.   Dont be uneasy my children   I expect to have you.   If Diggs
dont give you up this Government will and I feel confident that I will get
you   Your Miss Kaitty said that I tried to steal you   But I'll let her
know that god never intended for man to steal his own flesh and
blood.   If I had no cofidence in God I could have confidence in
her   But as it is If I ever had any Confidence in her I have none now
and never expect to have   And I want her to remember if she meets me

with ten thousand soldiers she [will?] meet her enemy   I once [*thought*] that I had some respect for them but now my respects is worn out and have no sympathy for Slaveholders.   And as for her cristianantty I expect the Devil has Such in hell   You tell her from me that She is the frist Christian that I ever hard say that aman could Steal his own child especially out of human bondage

You can tell her that She can hold to you as long as she can   I never would expect to ask her again to let you come to me because I know that the devil has got her hot set againsts that that is write   now my Dear children I am a going to close my letter to you   Give my love to all enquiring friends   tell them all that we are well and want to see them very much and Corra and Mary receive the greater part of it you sefves   and dont think hard of us not sending you any thing   I you father have a plenty for you when I see you   Spott & Noah sends their love to both of you   Oh! My Dear children how I do want to see you

HL   [*Spotswood Rice*][32]

[*Benton Barracks Hospital, St. Louis, Mo.,   September 3, 1864*]

I received a leteter from Cariline telling me that you say I tried to steal to plunder my child away from you   now I want you to understand that mary is my Child and she is a God given rite of my own and you may hold on to hear as long as you can but I want you to remembor this one thing that the longor you keep my Child from me the longor you will have to burn in hell and the qwicer youll get their   for we are now makeing up a bout one thoughsand blacke troops to Come up tharough and wont to come through Glasgow and when we come wo be to Copperhood rabbels and to the Slaveholding rebbels for we dont expect to leave them there root neor branch   but we thinke how ever that we that have Children in the hands of you devels we will trie your

[vertues?] the day that we enter Glasgow   I want you to understand
kittey diggs that where ever you and I meets we are enmays to each
orthere   I offered once to pay you forty dollers for my own Child but I
am glad now that you did not accept it   Just hold on now as long as
you can and the worse it will be for you   you never in you life befor I
came down hear did you give Children any thing not eny thing whatever
not even a dollers worth of expencs   now you call my children your
pro[*per*]ty   not so with me   my Children is my own and I expect to
get them and when I get ready to come after mary I will have bout a
powrer and autherity to bring hear away and to exacute vengencens on
them that holds my Child   you will then know how to talke to me   I
will assure that and you will know how to talk rite too   I want you now
to just hold on to hear if you want to   iff your conchosence tells thats
the road go that road and what it will brig you to kittey diggs   I have
no fears about geting mary out of your hands   this whole Government
gives chear to me and you cannot help your self

ALS   Spotswood Rice[33]

Like Private Rice, many slaves-turned-soldiers took "chear" from
their new status. As slaves, they had been subject to the personal
power of their owners, with no means to appeal arbitrary or violent
acts. As soldiers, they belonged to a bureaucracy ruled by imper-
sonal laws to which officers and enlisted men were equally accountable. Although orders proceeded from superior to subordinate, men
with grievances had access to formal channels of redress. Moreover,
soldiers accused of violating army regulations or particular orders
were subject to a regular process of court-martial. In principle,
court-martial procedures provided a framework in which every
case—whether it involved a private or a general, a black soldier or
a white one—could be tried impartially. In practice, military justice
was not always impartial, and even when it was, it often imposed

severe penalties for minor infractions. Many a black soldier discovered that the law of the army, though fundamentally different in
character from the law of slavery, could be every bit as harsh. A
sergeant from Louisiana asked President Lincoln to reverse his
conviction for disobedience of orders, breach of arrest, and muti-
nous conduct.

Fort Barrancas   Florida   Oc^t 7 1864

To. The. Honerable Abrham Lincon   I your Partishener W^m D Mayo
1st Sarg^t C^o D. 86 cullard Infentry of L.A. will now state to you the
condishons I am in being confined in the Provost Guard House under
the sentanc of A Genl Cort Marshal held hear on the 8^{inst} of Aug
last   this centence being to serve a turm of one year and 9 months
hard Labour without pay on Tortugas Island   the charges bein against
me is 1st disobediants of Orders which I can prove I am not guilty of by
over 25 of the same Reg^t charge 2nd Breach of Arest which I plead
guilty to under those surmstances,   thare was a Private John Vier
suffering punishment in the way of Riding a Wooden Horse*   the word
came to me that he had falen from the horse dead   I was excited and
Humanity hurid me to his asistince at once not remembering that I was
under arest untill My Capt ordred me back to my quarters which I
returned to amediatly   charge 3^d Mutinus conduct in that I W^m D
Mayo gathered some 6 or 8 men and said I would not serve under Capt
Miller any longer which they faild to prove and which I can say before
God and Man I never uterd   one thing more I will draw your attention
to is I was denied the privaleges of having some 25 witesness who I
could of Prooved my entire inocences by and alowed but 2 only   thare
being two comishend Officers against me I was suposed of course to be

---

*A punishment in which the offender was compelled to sit astride a
wooden rail without touching the ground, often for hours.

guilty.   under this unlawfull and unjust punishment I can. but Apeal to
your Honner for Justice in this case   in a pucenarury [*pecuniary*]
point of view I say nothing however I will say one thing.   I am getting
towards 50 years of age and my Wife is over fifty and Goverment will
hav to suport while I am reely willing and able to as enny good Loyal
man can   I hav ben always ben faithfull and don My Duty as a
Souldier should and concequencely I want Justice don me in return by
hir   when I was sent to the Guard house I was deprived of My own
private property   I had the Army Regulations that I bought and paid
for with my own money, and charged me with reading that which a
Nigar had no buisness to know.   now Dear Sir I Apeal to a Greate Man
a man that is governing this Nation to govern the Justice and
punishment that is delt out to one of its Faithfull subjects   I Remain
Your Obediant Servent

ALS   W^m. D. Mayo[34]

> The army's judge advocate general recommended against pardon-
> ing Mayo.[35]

— • —

> Six months after he was imprisoned for desertion, Warren Hamel-
> ton, a young soldier from Louisiana, appealed his conviction on the
> grounds that the government had failed to fulfill its own obliga-
> tions to him. As a result, he was unable to support his mother. Un-
> der these circumstances, he maintained, his desertion was justified.
> A fellow inmate penned Hamelton's letter to the secretary of war.

Fort Jefferson   Tortugas Fla.   May 1865

Sir   I have the honor to respectfully request that I may be released
from imprisonment   I have ben in imprisonment six months and over.
and if I should remain here six years. I could not be more sory of having
done rong then I am know. althou I though mysalfe somewhat justified
doing what I have done, at the time.   I persume you honor has been
enform in what manner of treatment the 73. U.S.C.T. has ben subject to
doing the short-period of the first years servise.   when I enlisted I had
no other entention then perform my duty faithfully as a soldier. and
would fermily have done so if we had not ben treatted in such ill manner
and was subject to all kinds of missrepresentations.   My crme was
(dissertion)   not wishing to justify mysalf althou I though[t] at the
time that one breack of enlissment was quite sufficient to justify another
perticulurly when it was transacted on the part of the gov.   Althou most
of us are free men and was before the war yet the most of us have
nothing more then is required to support our family from day to day as
we labor for it.   althou I am now but seventeen years old I have my old
mother to support and as such expectted that the gov. or its agents in
this department would comply with its agreement I could have
something to support my relitives.   I persume your honor has been
enformed that Gel Buttler promas my regt $13.00 per month $58.00
Bounty and I suppose his promasses should have been kept   if a genl
promas or assureance is paid no respect to how much less could there be
expectted of a poor soldier (pri[vate].)   I do not wish to justify my[self]
in and act of dissertion for I dont think it write wrere a soldier can get a
redress to his grevences other wise but we tried every way and could not
get no redress   after having been some 8. moth in servise when pay day
came we were in dept to the gov. at the rate thay ware to settle with
us.   I hope you will comply with my request   should you require my

cerviseses any longer into U.S. servise I am willing to act in any capasity your honor may see fit to have me to perform   Very Respectfully Your obt servt

ALS
    Warren D. Hamelton[36]

> Private Samuel Roosa, a black soldier from New York who was completing a sentence in military prison, appealed to President Lincoln on behalf of Private Jack Morris, who had been sentenced to two years' imprisonment, without pay, for leaving his post and stealing a can of fruit. Emphasizing Morris's long and faithful service and the burden that his sentence placed upon his family, Roosa argued that Morris's illiteracy and his ignorance of written regulations—circumstances attributable to his prior condition as a slave—should have been considered at his trial.

Fort Jefferson   Turtugas Fla.   Jenuary 24th 1864 [*1865*]

Sir   I have the honor to respectfully call your attention to a few remarks which I hope may receive your libral consideration.

I am a prisener here at fort Jefferson turtugas fla.   I was sentence here for the short period of six months   I will not mention the injustice I received at the discretion of my court martrial. for I have but such short period to remain here that I deem it hardly nessessary to enter into the merits of the case.   but I shall speek inbehalf of a great number of poor but patriocic colored soldirees who have become victoms to a cruel ponishment for little arror.   I will attemp to state in bref the circumstences connected with the case of Jack Morris of Co. "F" 73th U.S. Colored Infy. who enterd the U.S. servise on the 27th day Sept 1862 and was errested on the 27th day of June 1864. and sentencd. on about

the 20th day October 1864 at Morganza. having served some two years
allmost fathfully without even as much as being once ponish in the
lease.   He was trie and held to answer the charge of leveing his
post   he had often been told by his officers he said not to leve his post
the consequence of which he know not   he having call siveral times for
the corporal of the guard but without responce   with respects to you
sir It being case of necesity he thought that it would not be a killing
circumstance as much as he did not go out sight and hearing of his
post   he was absent but five minits and when he returned the corpral
ask him where he had been   he told him after which he was poot
immediately under arrest. and received a sentence of two years hard
labor at this post   he is a man of famely and has not had no pay sinc he
has been in servise but once and then he received but few months pay at
seven dollars per month which of couse couldnot efford his famely much
releaf.   I am well awere that every breach of military regulations which
officers or soldiers are guilty of is ponishable at the discretion of a
propper court martrial but I do say and appeal to your honor that there
aut to be a liberal consideration and allowance made for ignorence   the
person refered to enfect most all of the colored troop recruted in this
department with few excepttion are egnorent men who know nothing
more then the duties of hard labor and as slaves was held for that
perpose and where not permtted to even as much as hendle there
masters book. much less having the privelage of reading or even allow
the use of a small elementry speling book and of corse are as total
egnorent of the regulations as a poor while efrican is of gramer or
elgebra.   I appeal to your honor and most respectfuly request in the
name of him who has at his command the destination of all nations that
his sentence may be repreved.   he says he dont mind the ponishment
that he is receiving here but he would like to be where his serviseses may

be of some use to the contry and the proceeds of which may be used for
the support of his famely which is in great need of it   in this
department it is different from the most of the military post   the
famely of the (colored) soldiers perticularly the poor who are depending
upon there husband for support   the most of the inhabitince perticular
the welthey portion are so prejudice against the famely of colored
soldiers in the US servise that thay wont even give them employment for
no prise to sustain if posible the old hipocrittical idea that free colored
people wont work and of cours the soldiers families have to suffer   in
other states infact in most of the northern states there is releaf fonds
but here there is none, and if the only support are taken away by death
or any other cause thay must suffer and that severely. for I have been
and eye witness to a grate many cases not only deprved of there homes
on the a/sc^t [*account*] of little means to pay there house rent but laught
at abused by passe[*r*]s by insulting words such as (now you see what the
yenkees will do for you had you not better stay with your masters.)   the
soldier seeing his famely subject to such crual ponishment and ill
treetment does feel some what discuraged when he is ill treeted by thoes
who is his only relience is for justice and his present existence for I have
never have saw a more solom lot a priseners then I saw here from like
circumstances   (all thay have to say that the yankes treat me more
woser then the rabs)   for my part I cant complane   I have had evry
respect shown me since I have been in the servise with but few
exceptions   I even was allowed while under arrest as a freehold cittizon
of the state of New York to cast my vote on a ritten form for that
perpose* for the first time for the candidate of my choise and as we hale
the election of the fondor of the proclamation of emencipation we as

*Unlike all the Southern states and many Northern ones, New York
permitted black men to vote, provided they met a discriminatory
property qualification.

poor priseners with undanted patriocism to the cause of our contry look
foward towards washing[*ton*] to here something in behalf of poor
priseners   we know that your four years of administration has been as
berdensome as it has victorious and no dought you have but lettle time
to listen to the grate many pleas that comes through such scorce   we
do feal as union soldiers that we may ask with that positive assureanc
that we will be herd   all we can say that we are sory that we have
become victoms to a millitary crime and do senserely repent and ask to
be forgiven   we cant do no more   where we to remain here 5 years we
should be know less sory then we are know.   Very respectfully your
humble & obt servt

ALS   Samuel Roosa[37]

> President Lincoln referred Roosa's appeal to the judge advocate
> general, who reported that Morris had pleaded guilty to theft and
> been proven guilty of leaving his post; his sentence was "warranted
> by the circumstances."[38]

—————— ❖ ——————

> Nothing eradicated the prejudices of white soldiers as effectively as
> black soldiers performing well under fire. And nothing inspired
> black soldiers to fight as desperately as the fear that capture meant
> certain death. General James S. Brisbin, who supervised the re-
> cruitment of black soldiers in Kentucky, described to his superiors
> how the "jeers and taunts" of white soldiers were silenced by their
> black comrades' bravery.

Lexington Ky   Oct 20 /64

General   I have the honor to forward herewith a report of the
operations of a detachment of the 5th U.S. Colored Cavalry during the
late operations in Western Virginia against the Salt Works.

After the main body of the forces had moved, Gen'l Burbridge Comdg District was informed I had some mounted recruits belonging to the 5th. U.S. Colored Cavalry, then organizing at Camp Nelson and he at once directed me to send them forward.

They were mounted on horses that had been only partly recruited* and that had been drawn with the intention of using them only for the purpose of drilling. Six hundred of the best horses were picked out, mounted and Col Jas. F. Wade 6th. U.S.C. Cav'y was ordered to take command of the Detachment.

The Detachment came up with the main body at Prestonburg Ky and was assigned to the Brigade Commanded by Colonel R. W. Ratliff 12th O[hio]. V. Cav.

On the march the Colored Soldiers as well as their white Officers were made the subject of much ridicule and many insulting remarks by the White Troops and in some instances petty outrages such as the pulling off the Caps of Colored Soldiers, stealing their horses etc was practiced by the White Soldiers. These insults as well as the jeers and taunts that they would not fight were borne by the Colored Soldiers patiently or punished with dignity by their Officers but in no instance did I hear Colored soldiers make any reply to insulting language used toward [them] by the White Troops.

On the 2ᵈ of October the forces reached the vicinity of the Salt Works and finding the enemy in force preparations were made for battle. Col Ratliffs Brigade was assigned to the left of the line and the Brigade dismounted was disposed as follows. 5ᵗʰ U.S.C. Cav. on the left. 12ᵗʰ O[hio]. V.C. in the centre and 11ᵗʰ Mich. Cav. on the right. The point to be attacked was the side of a high mountain, the Rebels being posted about half way up behind rifle pits made of logs and stones to the height

*I.e., disabled or diseased horses that had been only partly rehabilitated.

of three feet.   All being in readiness the Brigade moved to the attack. The Rebels opened upon them a terrific fire but the line pressed steadily forward up the steep side of the mountain until they found themselves within fifty yards of the Enemy.   Here Col. Wade ordered his force to charge and the Negroes rushed upon the works with a yell and after a desperate struggle carried the entire line killing and wounding a large number of the enemy and capturing some prisoners   There were four hundred black soldiers engaged in the battle. one hundred having been left behind sick and with broken down horses on the march, and one hundred having been left in the Valley to hold horses.   Out of the four hundred engaged, one hundred and fourteen men and four officers fell killed or wounded.   Of this fight I can only say that men could not have behaved more bravely.   I have seen white troops fight in twenty-seven battles and I never saw any fight better.   At dusk the Colored Troops were withdrawn from the enemies works, which they had held for over two hours, with scarcely a round of ammunition in their Cartridge Boxes.

On the return of the forces those who had scoffed at the Colored Troops on the march out were silent.

Nearly all the wounded were brought off though we had not an Ambulance in the command.   The negro soldiers preferred present suffering to being murdered at the hands of a cruel enemy.   I saw one man riding with his arm off another shot through the lungs and another shot through both hips.

Such of the Colored Soldiers as fell into the hands of the Enemy during the battle were brutally murdered.   The Negroes did not retaliate but treated the Rebel wounded with great kindness, carrying them water in their canteens and doing all they could to alleviate the sufferings of those whom the fortunes of war had placed in their hands.

Col. Wade handled his command with skill bravery and good
judgement, evincing his capacity to command a much larger force.   I
am General Very Respectfully Your Obedt. Servant

HLS   James S Brisbin[39]

> While black soldiers anxiously awaited each test of arms, their fam-
> ilies contemplated the injury or death of a loved one. Apprehensive
> about her son's safety as well as her own survival, the elderly moth-
> er of a Pennsylvania soldier petitioned President Lincoln for his re-
> lease from the army.

Carlisles [*Pa.*]   nov 21 1864

Mr abarham lincon   I wont to knw sir if you please wether I can have
my son relest from the arme   he is all the subport I have now   his
father is Dead and his brother that wase all the help that I had   he has
bean wonded twise   he has not had nothing to send me yet   now I am
old and my head is blossaming for the grave and if you dou I hope the
lord will bless you and me   if you please answer as soon as you can if
you please   tha say that you will simpethise withe the poor   thear
wase awhite jentel man told me to write to you   Mrs jane Welcom if
you please answer it to

he be long to the eight rigmat co a u st colard troops   mart welcom
is his name   he is a sarjent

AL   [*Jane Welcome*][40]

> President Lincoln forwarded Welcome's letter to the Bureau of
> Colored Troops, which informed her that "the interests of the ser-
> vice will not permit that your request be granted."[41]

The enlistment of black soldiers did not always entail separation
from their families. In Union-occupied parts of the Confederacy,
parents, wives, and children often lived in contraband camps near
the soldiers' bivouacs, enjoying a measure of security by virtue of
these arrangements. But in Missouri and Kentucky, where slavery
remained legal, federal commanders refused food and protection to
the families of black soldiers, on the grounds that their owners
were responsible for their support. Many owners, however, repudiated the obligation and drove away the soldiers' kinfolk to fend for
themselves. Joseph Miller, a soldier from Kentucky, described the
ordeal of his family.

Camp Nelson Ky   November 26, 1864

Personally appered before me E. B W Restieaux Capt. and Asst.
Quartermaster Joseph Miller a man of color who being duly sworn upon
oath says

I was a slave of George Miller of Lincoln County Ky.   I have always
resided in Kentucky and am now a Soldier in the service of the United
States.   I belong to Company I 124 U.S. C[*olored*]. Inft now Stationed
at Camp Nelson Ky.   When I came to Camp for the purpose of enlisting
about the middle of October 1864 my wife and children came with me
because my master said that if I enlisted he would not maintain them
and I knew they would be abused by him when I left.   I had then four
children ages respectively ten nine seven and four years.   On my
presenting myself as a recruit I was told by the Lieut. in command to
take my family into a tent within the limits of the Camp.   My wife and
family occupied this tent by the express permission of the
aforementioned Officer and never received any notice to leave until
Tuesday November 22" when a mounted guard gave my wife notice that
she and her children must leave Camp before early morning.   This was

about six O'clock at night.   My little boy about seven years of age had
been very sick and was slowly recovering   My wife had no place to go
and so remained until morning.   About eight Oclock Wednesday
morning November 23" a mounted guard came to my tent and ordered
my wife and children out of Camp   The morning was bitter cold.   It
was freezing hard.   I was certain that it would kill my sick child to take
him out in the cold.   I told the man in charge of the guard that it would
be the death of my boy   I told him that my wife and children had no
place to go and I told him that I was a soldier of the United States.   He
told me that it did not make any difference.   he had orders to take all
out of Camp.   He told my wife and family that if they did not get up
into the wagon which he had he would shoot the last one of them.   On
being thus threatened my wife and children went into the wagon   My
wife carried her sick child in her arms.   When they left the tent the wind
was blowing hard and cold and having had to leave much of our clothing
when we left our master, my wife with her little one was poorly clad.   I
followed them as far as the lines.   I had no Knowledge where they were
taking them.   At night I went in search of my family.   I found them at
Nicholasville about six miles from Camp.   They were in an old meeting
house belonging to the colored people.   The building was very cold
having only one fire.   My wife and children could not get near the fire,
because of the number of colored people huddled together by the
soldiers.   I found my wife and children shivering with cold and famished
with hunger   They had not recieved a morsel of food during the whole
day.   My boy was dead.   He died directly after getting down from the
wagon.   I Know he was Killed by exposure to the inclement weather   I
had to return to camp that night so I left my family in the meeting house
and walked back.   I had walked there.   I travelled in all twelve
miles   Next morning I walked to Nicholasville.   I dug a grave myself

and buried my own child.   I left my family in the Meeting house—where they still remain   And further this deponent saith not

his

(Signed)   Joseph   Miller[42]

mark

HDcSr

Another Kentucky soldier unsuccessfully sought a discharge so that he could provide for his wife and children, whose owner would not maintain them.

Taylors Barrecks [*Louisville, Ky.*]   December 4th 1864
Mr Abrham Lincoln   I have one recest to make to you that is I ask you to dis Charge me for I have a wife and she has four Children   thay have a hard master one that loves the South hangs with it   he dos not giv them a rage nor havnot for too yars   I have found* all   he says let old Abe Giv them Close   if I had them I raise them up but I am here and if you will free me and hir and heir Children with me I Can take Cair of them

She lives with David Sparks in Oldham Co Ky

My Woman is named Malindia Jann my daughter Adline Clyte and Malindia Eler and Cleman Tine and Natthanel Washington and my name is George Washington   heir in Taylors Barrecks and my famaly suferring   I have sent forty dollars worth to them cence I have bin heir and that is all I have and I have not drawn any thing cence I have bin heir   I am forty eight years   my woman thirty three   I ask this to your oner to a blige yours &c   your un Grateful Servent

George Washington[43]

ALS

---

*I.e., provided.

Recounting his regiment's battlefield success, a black sergeant stationed in Florida felt confident that the general who had supervised recruitment in his home state would grant him a "Small favor."

Barrancas Fla.   Dec 27. 1864

Sir   I beg you the granterfurction of a Small favor   will you ples to Cross the Mississippia River at Bayou Sar La. with your Command & jest on the hill one mile from the little town you will finde A plantation Called Mrs Marther. H. Turnbuill & take a way my Farther & mother & my brothers wife with all their Childern & U take them up at your He^d Quarters. & write to me   Sir the ar ther & I will amejeately Send after them.   I wishes the Childern all in School.   it is beter for them then to be their Surveing a mistes.   Sir it isent mor then three or four Hours trubel   I have bain trying evry sence I have bin in the servis it is goin on ner 3. years & Could never get no one to so do for me   now I thinks it will be don for you is my Gen.   I wishes evry day you would send after us.   our Regt. ar doing all the hard fightin her   we have disapointe the Rebes & surprizeed theme in all. importan pointes   they says they wishes to Captuer the 82nd Regt that they woul murdar them all   they Calls our Reg^t the Bluebellied Eagles   Sir my Farthers Name Adam Harris   he will Call them all to gether. & tel him to take Cousan Janes Childarn with hime

Joseph. J. Harris

Sir I will remain Ob your Soldiar in the U.S.A.[44]

ALS

During the waning months of the war, efforts to inaugurate political reconstruction prompted intense debate about slavery and freedom, loyalty and treason, and the rights of citizens. Active in that

debate were Americans of African descent, who argued that their
services to the nation had entitled them not only to freedom but also to civil and political rights. Black Tennesseans petitioned a convention of white unionists that was considering reorganization of
the state government and the abolition of slavery. Among the many
arguments they advanced for the fitness of black men to exercise
the suffrage and other privileges of citizenship, they especially emphasized the role of black soldiers in saving the Union. In the
months and years to come, this theme would reappear in countless
demands by former slaves for full citizenship.

                                     [Nashville, Tenn.,   January 9, 1865]
To the Union Convention of Tennessee Assembled in the Capitol at
Nashville, January 9th, 1865:

We the undersigned petitioners, American citizens of African
descent, natives and residents of Tennessee, and devoted friends of the
great National cause, do most respectfully ask a patient hearing of
your honorable body in regard to matters deeply affecting the future
condition of our unfortunate and long suffering race.

First of all, however, we would say that words are too weak to tell how
profoundly grateful we are to the Federal Government for the good work
of freedom which it is gradually carrying forward; and for the
Emancipation Proclamation which has set free all the slaves in some of
the rebellious States, as well as many of the slaves in Tennessee.

After two hundred years of bondage and suffering a returning sense
of justice has awakened the great body of the American people to make
amends for the unprovoked wrongs committed against us for over two
hundred years.

Your petitioners would ask you to complete the work begun by the
nation at large, and abolish the last vestige of slavery by the express
words of your organic law.

Many masters in Tennessee whose slaves have left them, will certainly make every effort to bring them back to bondage after the reorganization of the State government, unless slavery be expressly abolished by the Constitution.

We hold that freedom is the natural right of all men, which they themselves have no more right to give or barter away, than they have to sell their honor, their wives, or their children.

We claim to be men belonging to the great human family, descended from one great God, who is the common Father of all, and who bestowed on all races and tribes the priceless right of freedom.   Of this right, for no offence of ours, we have long been cruelly deprived, and the common voice of the wise and good of all countries, has remonstrated against our enslavement, as one of the greatest crimes in all history.

We claim freedom, as our natural right, and ask that in harmony and co-operation with the nation at large, you should cut up by the roots the system of slavery, which is not only a wrong to us, but the source of all the evil which at present afflicts the State.   For slavery, corrupt itself, corrupted nearly all, also, around it, so that it has influenced nearly all the slave States to rebel against the Federal Government, in order to set up a government of pirates under which slavery might be perpetrated.

In the contest between the nation and slavery, our unfortunate people have sided, by instinct, with the former.   We have little fortune to devote to the national cause, for a hard fate has hitherto forced us to live in poverty, but we do devote to its success, our hopes, our toils, our whole heart, our sacred honor, and our lives.   We will work, pray, live, and, if need be, die for the Union, as cheerfully as ever a white patriot died for his country.   The color of our skin does not lesson in the least degree, our love either for God or for the land of our birth.

We are proud to point your honorable body to the fact, that so far as our knowledge extends, not a negro traitor has made his appearance since the beginning of this wicked rebellion.

Whether freeman or slaves the colored race in this country have always looked upon the United States as the Promised Land of Universal freedom, and no earthly temptation has been strong enough to induce us to rebel against it. We love the Union by an instinct which is stronger than any argument or appeal which can be used against it. It is the attachment of a child to its parent.

Devoted as we are to the principles of justice, of love to all men, and of equal rights on which our Government is based, and which make it the hope of the world. We know the burdens of citizenship, and are ready to bear them. We know the duties of the good citizen, and are ready to perform them cheerfully, and would ask to be put in a position in which we can discharge them more effectually. We do not ask for the privilege of citizenship, wishing to shun the obligations imposed by it.

Near 200,000 of our brethren are to-day performing military duty in the ranks of the Union army. Thousands of them have already died in battle, or perished by a cruel martyrdom for the sake of the Union, and we are ready and willing to sacrifice more. But what higher order of citizen is there than the soldier? or who has a greater trust confided to his hands? If we are called on to do military duty against the rebel armies in the field, why should we be denied the privilege of voting against rebel citizens at the ballot-box? The latter is as necessary to save the Government as the former.

The colored man will vote by instinct with the Union party, just as uniformly as he fights with the Union army.

This is not a new question in Tennessee. From 1796 to 1835, a period of thirty-nine years, free colored men voted at all her elections without question. Her leading politicians and statesmen asked for and

obtained the suffrages of colored voters, and were not ashamed of it.
Such men as *Andrew Jackson,* President of the United States, Hon.
Felix Grundy, John Bell, Hon. *Hugh L. White, Cave Johnson,* and
Ephraim H. Foster, members of the United States Senate and of the
Cabinet, *Gen. William Carroll, Samuel Houston,* Aaron V. Brown, and,
in fact, all the politicians and candidates of all parties in Tennessee
solicited colored free men for their votes at every election.

Nor was Tennessee alone in this respect, for the same privileges was
granted to colored free men in North Carolina, to-day the most loyal of
all the rebellious States, without ever producing any evil consequences.

If colored men have been faithful and true to the Government of the
United States in spite of the Fugitive Slave Law, and the cruel policy
often pursued toward them, will they not be more devoted to it now than
ever, since it has granted them that liberty which they desired above all
things? Surely, if colored men voted without harm to the State, while
their brethren were in bondage, they will be much more devoted and
watchful over her interests when elevated to the rank of freemen and
voters. If they are good law-abiding citizens, praying for its prosperity,
rejoicing in its progress, paying its taxes, fighting its battles, making its
farms, mines, work-shops and commerce more productive, why deny
them the right to have a voice in the election of its rulers?

This is a democracy—a government of the people. It should aim to
make every man, without regard to the color of his skin, the amount of
his wealth, or the character of his religious faith, feel personally
interested in its welfare. Every man who lives under the Government
should feel that it is his property, his treasure, the bulwark and defence
of himself and his family, his pearl of great price, which he must
preserve, protect, and defend faithfully at all times, on all occasions, in
every possible manner.

This is not a Democratic Government if a numerous, law-abiding, industrious, and useful class of citizens, born and bred on the soil, are to be treated as aliens and enemies, as an inferior degraded class, who must have no voice in the Government which they support, protect and defend, with all their heart, soul, mind, and body, both in peace and war.

This Government is based on the teachings of the Bible, which prescribes the same rules of action for all members of the human family, whether their complexion be white, yellow, red or black. God no where in his revealed word, makes an invidious and degrading distinction against his children, because of their color. And happy is that nation which makes the Bible its rule of action, and obeys principle, not prejudice.

Let no man oppose this doctrine because it is opposed to his old prejudices. The nation is fighting for its life, and cannot afford to be controlled by prejudice. Had prejudice prevailed instead of principle, not a single colored soldier would have been in the Union army to-day. But principle and justice triumphed, and now near 200,000 colored patriots stand under the folds of the national flag, and brave their breasts to the bullets of the rebels. As we are in the battlefield, so we swear before heaven, by all that is dear to men, to be at the ballot-box faithful and true to the Union.

The possibility that the negro suffrage proposition may shock popular prejudice at first sight, is not a conclusive argument against its wisdom and policy. No proposition ever met with more furious or general opposition than the one to enlist colored soldiers in the United States army. The opponents of the measure exclaimed on all hands that the negro was a coward; that he would not fight; that one white man, with a whip in his hand could put to flight a regiment of them; that the experiment would end in the utter rout and ruin of the Federal army.

Yet the colored man has fought so well, on almost every occasion, that the rebel government is prevented, only by its fears and distrust of being able to force him to fight for slavery as well as he fights against it, from putting half a million of negroes into its ranks.

The Government has asked the colored man to fight for its preservation and gladly has he done it. It can afford to trust him with a vote as safely as it trusted him with a bayonet.

How boundless would be the love of the colored citizen, how intense and passionate his zeal and devotion to the government, how enthusiastic and how lasting would be his gratitude, if his white brethren were to take him by the hand and say, "You have been ever loyal to our government; henceforward be voters." Again, the granting of this privilege would stimulate the colored man to greater exertion to make himself an intelligent, respected, useful citizen. His pride of character would be appealed to this way most successfully; he would send his children to school, that they might become educated and intelligent members of society. It used to be thought that ignorant negroes were the most valuable, but this belief probably originated from the fact that it is almost impossible to retain an educated, intelligent man in bondage. Certainly, if the free colored man be educated, and his morals enlightened and improved, he will be a far better member of society, and less liable to transgress its laws. It is the brutal, degraded, ignorant man who is usually the criminal.

One other matter we would urge on your honorable body. At present we can have only partial protection from the courts. The testimony of twenty of the most intelligent, honorable, colored loyalists cannot convict a white traitor of a treasonable action. A white rebel might sell powder and lead to a rebel soldier in the presence of twenty colored soldiers, and yet their evidence would be worthless so far as the courts are concerned, and the rebel would escape. A colored man may have served for years faithfully in the army, and yet his testimony in court would be rejected, while that of a white man who had served in the rebel army would be received.

If this order of things continue, our people are destined to a malignant persecution at the hands of rebels and their former rebellious masters, whose hatred they may have incurred, without precedent even in the South. Every rebel soldier or citizen whose arrest in the perpetration of crime they may have effected, every white traitor whom they may have brought to justice, will torment and persecute them and set justice at defiance, because the courts will not receive negro testimony, which will generally be the only possible testimony in such cases. A rebel may murder his former slave and defy justice, because he committed the deed in the presence of half a dozen respectable colored citizens. He may have the dwelling of his former slave burned over his head, and turn his wife and children out of doors, and defy the law, for no colored man can appear against him. Is this the fruit of freedom, and the reward of our services in the field? Was it for this that colored soldiers fell by hundreds before Nashville, fighting under the flag of the Union? Is it for this that we have guided Union officers and soldiers, when escaping from the cruel and deadly prisons of the South through forests and swamps, at the risk of our own lives, for we knew that to us detection would be death? Is it for this that we have concealed multitudes of Union refugees in caves and cane-brakes, when flying from the conscription officers and tracked by bloodhounds, and divided with them our last morsal of food? Will you declare in your revised constitution that a pardoned traitor may appear in court and his testimony be heard, but that no colored loyalist shall be believed even upon oath? If this should be so, then will our last state be worse than

our first, and we can look for no relief on this side of the grave.   Has not
the colored man fought, bled and died for the Union, under a thousand
great disadvantages and discouragements?   Has his fidelity ever had a
shadow of suspicion cast upon it, in any matter of responsibility confided
to his hands?

There have been white traitors in multitudes in Tennessee, but where,
we ask, is the black traitor?   Can you forget how the colored man has
fought at Fort Morgan, at Milliken's Bend, at Fort Pillow, before
Petersburg, and your own city of Nashville?

When has the colored citizen, in this rebellion been tried and found
wanting?

In conclusion, we would point to the fact that the States where the
largest measure of justice and civil rights has been granted to the
colored man, both as to suffrage and his oath in court, are among the
most rich, intelligent, enlightened and prosperous.   Massachusetts,
illustrious for her statesmen and her commercial and manufacturing
enterprises and thrift, whose noble liberality has relieved so many loyal
refugees and other sufferers of Tennessee, allows her colored citizens to
vote, and is ever jealous of their rights.   She has never had reason to
repent the day when she gave them the right of voting.

Had the southern states followed her example the present rebellion
never would have desolated their borders.

Several other Northern States permit negro suffrage, nor have bad
effects ever resulted from it.   It may be safely affirmed that Tennessee
was quite as safe and prosperous during the 39 years while she allowed
negro suffrage, as she has been since she abolished it.

In this great and fearful struggle of the nation with a wicked
rebellion, we are anxious to perform the full measure of our duty both as
citizens and soldiers to the Union cause we consecrate ourselves, and our

families, with all that we have on earth. Our souls burn with love for the great government of freedom and equal rights. Our white brethren have no cause for distrust as regards our fidelity, for neither death nor life, nor angels, nor principalities, nor powers, nor things present, nor things to come, nor height, nor depth, nor any other creature, shall be able to separate us from the love of the Union.

Praying that the great God, who is the common Father of us all, by whose help the land must be delivered from present evil, and before whom we must all stand at last to be judged by the rule of eternal justice, and not by passion and prejudice, may enlighten your minds and enable you to act with wisdom, justice, and magnanimity, we remain your faithful friends in all the perils and dangers which threaten our beloved country.

[59 signatures]

PD   And many other colored citizens of Nashville[45]

The convention adopted an amendment to the state constitution abolishing slavery, which was ratified on February 22, 1865. The delegates took no action to extend the rights of suffrage or testimony to black Tennesseans.

Aaron Oats, a soldier from Kentucky, believed that his service to the Union entitled him to assistance in liberating his family. In a letter to the secretary of war, Oats enclosed two letters he had received, one from his wife and the other from her owner; both were in the same handwriting, presumably that of the master.

U.S. Gen. Hospital, Hampten, V.A.   January 26th 1865

Sir. I the under-Sined, Respectfully ask for the liberation of my Wife and children now residing in the State of Ky. Boone County.

I enclose two letters Received from there   one is supposed to be from my Wife   the other is from a man claiming to be my Wifs master by the name of Jerry, *Smith.* You can see by the contents of his letter forbidding me not to write, Saying that he only gave her to me on my good conduct Of which he Says I have not fullfiled   it is not necessary for me to say anymore   you can see his letter,—

And as I am a *Soldier.* willing to loose my life for my Country and the liberty of my fellow man I hope that you will please be So Kind as to attend to this   please lett me know, or send me your Reply and oblige your humble Servent,   yours very Respectfully

ALS   Aaron Oats[46]

[*First enclosure*]   [*Union, Ky.*]   December the 22 64

Dar husban   I receive your letter dated December the 7 64 which gave me much pleasure to hear that you ar alive and well   I mus state that I and mother and the children ar all well hopping thet these few lines may still find you well still   I am at home and far as well as usial   I shall content myself and wait for the time to come as you thought you could not get a ferlough   I must state that there is another one was Born sence you left but I suppose you heard of it   if you have not I will tell you hernane is effis tell   [pood?] as they call him can run half as fast as you can and fat asever   your sisters ar all well   Johns mother states that, she wish that John would right and if he wont Right when you right again send all the perticklers About him whether he is live ordead.

N.B   you stated in your letter that you sent me too letters and your picture but I never receivd either

so I must conclude my short letter by saing that I send my love to you all and keep the Best part for your self   so no more till death

HLSr   Lucrethia[47]

[*Second enclosure*]   [*Union, Ky. January 10, 1865*]

When your letter came to hand it was red and answerd and when I
went to put it in the office ther was another at hand Equal as insolent as
the other so I concluded to send you a few lines apon my own
responsibelity and, not to wright any more with out you will have some
Respect for me   ~~if you dont they will not be red nor answered~~   my
darkes has too much Sence to be foold in such away   ther has been
agreat menny woman and children have left and returned back
again   one instant in my nabohood   Henry corben's mandy you nod
her   dan had encoyd her and six children over in cincinnati out on
walnut hill and there she and three children starved to death   the
oldest that could travel came home and got his master to bring them
home to keep them from starvation and too of the youngest had ate flesh
of ther fingers   N B Lucretia dont belong to you   I only gave her to
you for wife dureing good behaviour and you have violated your
plede,   my darkes olways tells me when they want to leve me   they will
tell me   they say that if they ar to be deliberated they want it don
honorable

this lettere was rote the 22 of December but taken it back to answer
you my self I neglected to put it in the office till now this being the 10 of
January 1865   But my darkes is as well now as they wer then and
doing better than when you was hear   now, they ar wated on   when
you was hear they had you to wait on   so no more

HL   [*Jerry Smith*][48]

For thousands of ex-slave soldiers like Aaron Oats, military service
was a dramatic counter to the degradation of slavery. In a report to
the Bureau of Colored Troops, the white chaplain of a Louisiana
regiment surveyed the changes he had witnessed among his men.

Vicksburg, Miss.,   Feb. 1st 1865.

Sir: Agreeably to orders and my own duty, I have the honor to forward
my report for the month ending 31st Jan. 1865.

The ninth day of the current month is the first anniversary of my
entrance into military service.   The present thus is a favorable time to
make comparisons, and to note the progress which has been made.   In
reporting from month to month, it frequently happens, that the progress
made in the regiment is not very apparent.   But when we compute time
by the year and not by the month, the change is vast and apparent to all.

During the past year, great progress has been made in a military
aspect.   This fact is evident to an observer at dress parade, and in the
increased attention bestowed upon the minor duties of daily routine.
The men are not only more manly, but far more soldierly.   Their guns
are uniformly cleaner, their brass brighter, their personal cleanliness
and general appearance has vastly improved.

The improvement in an educational view is also very marked.   One
year ago, but a few, not more than fifteen in the regiment knew the
alphabet thoroughly.   But now the converse is true.   The teacher, who
is now employed in the regiment, has been connected with it for three
months, and during that time, she has found but *one* person who does
not know the alphabet.

In the religious life of the regiment, there has been great change; here
even where we would least expect it; for history testifies to the reluctance
with which any race give up their religious forms and customs, or their
language.   The haughty Norman strove, in vain, for years, to supplant
the religion and language of the ancient Britons.   But here we find a
people, so tractable, with such unlimited confidence in their liberators,
as to yield up set forms of expression, religious customs and manners,
familiar from infancy for those of *another race*.   This is due to no

instruction given on these points, nor any effort to make a change.   It simply shows the necessary tendency of the human mind to grow into the likeness of those with whom we are brought in contact.   These colored people are easily moulded and shaped by the stronger minds which press upon theirs, and which command them.

During the year past, a deep and abiding foundation has been laid for a vast change in moral sentiment, in No. 15 Special Orders, Sec[*re*]t[*ary*]. of War legalizing marriages among the Freedmen.*   A revolution is rapidly going on among them in reference to the sacred nature and binding obligations of marriage.   One more measure in this direction is greatly needed,—a court with power to grant divorces, on legal and scriptural grounds.   The demand is urgent, that evil consequences may be avoided.   One instance has come to my knowledge, in my own regiment, where a divorce should be granted, and that for reasons expressly stated in Scripture.   It would be well and safe to apply to such persons the doctrine held by the christian church, during all ages, on this subject.

As I have witnessed the progress of freedom for the past year,—when slavery was abolished and forever prohibited in all the territories,— when the negro was admitted to equal rights in United States Courts as parties to suits and as witnesses,—as "the Statute book was cleansed of every support of slavery,"—as state after state has declared emancipation,—as I now witness how christian men and women are following our loyal and conquoring armies with the agencies of mental and moral instruction, to fit and prepare the freedmen for the duties of a new and higher life, every chamber of my heart is filled with rejoicing. Such tidings are grateful to our ears.   My response, and that of my

---

*The order authorized "[a]ny ordained minister of the Gospel,"
accredited by proper military authority, to perform such marriages.
(*Black Military Experience*, p. 712n.)

fellow officers to such legislation, is, the colored race is worthy of
it. Respectfully Submitted.

ALS   C. W. Buckley[49]

> In the border states, the continued legality of slavery affected every
> aspect of black soldiers' military service. Even after emancipation
> had won the day in Maryland and Missouri, slaveholders in Ken-
> tucky continued to fight tenaciously to keep freedom at bay. As a
> result, enlistment in the Union army remained the only road to lib-
> erty for Kentucky's slaves. When Congress adopted a joint resolu-
> tion in March 1865 freeing the wife, children, and mother of every
> black soldier, slaves in Kentucky responded with a renewed surge of
> enlistments.* Angry owners threatened volunteers and their fami-
> lies with violence, while local police and slave patrols redoubled ef-
> forts to obstruct the flight of slaves to recruitment centers. A sol-
> dier recounted how he and his wife had been foiled in their first at-
> tempt to escape.

                          Camp Nelson Ky   March 29, 1865
    Personally appeared before me J M Kelley Notary Public in and for
the County of Jessamine State of Kentucky William Jones a man of
color who being duly sworn according to law doth depose and say—I am
a soldier in the 124th U.S. C[*olored*]. Infty.   Before enlisting I belonged
to Newton Craig   Scott County Ky   My wife belonged to the same
man.   Desiring to enlist and thus free my wife and serve the
Government during the balance of my days I ran away from my master
in company with my wife on Saturday March 11th between nine and ten
Oclock at night.   Our clothes were packed up and some money we had
saved from our earnings we carried with us.   On our way to Camp
Nelson we arrived at Lexington about Three Oclock next morning

---

*See above, p. 400.

Sunday March 12" 1865 where we were accosted by the Capt of the
night watch James Cannon, who asked us where we were going.   I told
him I was going to see my daughter   He said I was a damned liar, that
I was going to Camp Nelson.   I then told him that I was going to Camp
whereupon he arrested us, took us to the Watch House where he
searched us and took our money from us taking Fifty eight (58) dollars
from me and eight (8) dollars from my wife.   I told him that the money
was my own that I desired to have it,   He told me that he would send it
with the man who would take us back to our master and when we got
there we should have it.   I said I would rather die than go back to
master who said he would kill any of his niggers who went to Camp.
Cannon made no reply but locked us up in the Watch house where he
kept us all that day and night and on Monday morning March 13" 1865
he sent us back to our master in charge of an armed watchman whose
name I believe was Harry Smith.   When we arrived at my masters
master was away from home and Smith delivered us to our mistress.   I
asked Smith to give me my money.   He said Cannon had given him none
but had kept the whole to himself.   I ran away from home that day
before master came home.   I have never received a cent of the money
which Cannon took from me.   I have three sons and one son-in-law now
in the service of the United States.   I want to get my money back.   And
further Deponent saith not

HDcSr

his

(Signed) William   Jones[50]

mark

The surrender of the principal Confederate armies in April 1865
ended the Civil War but not the military service of black soldiers.
Although some black men were mustered out soon after the war
was over, most were not. Indeed, because Union regiments with the

longest service were generally the first to be disbanded and most black regiments had not been organized until relatively late in the war, the postwar army had a higher proportion of black soldiers than the wartime army. That circumstance troubled some federal officials, and they welcomed the opportunity to ship many of the black troops to the Mexican border to counter the threat posed by the emperor Maximilian. For the soldiers, the increased distance from home and the harsh environment of the Texas frontier only magnified other injustices. As a soldier from Pennsylvania informed Secretary of War Stanton, overbearing officers made the assignment all the more objectionable.

Camp Near Brownsville. Texas   On the Riogrande River
July the 20th A.D. (1865)

Sir   i Seat myself to Rite you a few lines to inform you of my Health Wich is Good at Present and I hope When these few Badly Written lines Reach you they Will find you in the Best of Health.   Sir last night there was about a Dozen of my fellow Soldiers Desired to have Worship as they usualy have Been Doing, and no one interrupted them Untill last Night.   and there Was a lieutenant By the Name of Stacy.   he told them if they Wanted to Pray they must Go out on the Perade Ground about a half amile from camp   i am not a member of the church But i Do not like to See the Peopple of God Disturbed   they Pray for all in artharity their families &c   Sir Do you think it is Right, that they Should be molested.   Sir we have Some new men in our Regt. that we Got Since Richmond was Taken and they Dont understand how to Drill as Well as the old Soldiers and the officers Will Smote them over the Head with all theire might and they even Beat the older Soldiers, Who have Proved themselves on the Different Battle fields. Petersburgh July 30 /64 and many other Places.   Do you think it is right that we Should Be thus used.   When we joined the 9th A[*rmy*]. C[*orps*]. at annoppolis

M.D. in 64, Gen. Burnside Rode through our Camp and told us that he
wanted us to Be Good Soldiers for he had Some Work for us to
Do   last Summer While we was in his Corps, there was not a man
Struck With a Sword.   But as Soon as we was transferred into the 25th
Corps there Was men tied up* So high that they lost the use of their
arms.   Capt Brown just Believes in Beating men with there Swords also
Capt Wright and Capt Dill went to the extent to Break his Sword over a
mans Back   if a Private Soldier Goes to Colonel he Gets no
Satisfaction.   there is men who has Been in Bondage   we cant expect
them to Do as well as a man that has Been free.   when we was on the
Boat Capt Dill, Struck a Private and kicked him, and the Soldier
Defened the Blows of[f] So as to keep the capt. from knocking him
Down the hatch way.   they Put hand Cuffes on him and they have had
them on him evry Since we Strted from City Point Va.   there is a Dozen
Pair of them in the Reg[t]   will you Please to intercede for us.   Mr
Staunan Do you Remember a colored man By the Name of Jacob Prisby
who lived in Stubenville Ohio.   i Dont Doubt But what he has Done
some Work for you Before the War   I live with his Brother Peter
Prisby in Washington Co. Pa. Just 2 miles from Stubenville ohio   I
mus close   From

ALS   Simon Prisby[51]

Black soldiers in the postwar army of occupation assumed special
responsibility for protecting the lives and liberty of the freedpeople
among whom they were stationed. A sergeant from Michigan complained to the military commander in South Carolina when a post
commander failed to render justice to a freedman who had appealed to him.

---

*In a common military punishment, an offender was suspended by his
thumbs, usually such that his feet barely touched the ground.

Collumbia S.C   August 7th /65

Dear Sir   With Due Respect to you, after Coming to this pleasant City and Getting somewhat acquainted I find the freedmen are Shamefuly abused   for instance one Andrew Lee a Collord man Come in from the Country to Report some White men for Going into his house and Breaking open his trunks with a pretinse of searching for a hog that they Claimed to have lost.   The Said Andrew Lee Went General Horton Commanding Post and Entered Complaint   after hearing Andrew Lees Complaint he General Horton told Lee to Go off and that he General Horton had ought to put Lee in the Guard house and that those men had a Wright to search his house   This is a queer state of things Brought about to allow those Miscreants to plunder houses Without Some officer or Written authority   Sir I am only a sergeant and of Course Should be as silent as posible But in this I Could not hold my temper After fighting to get wrights that White men might Respect By Virtue of the Law   Sir I Would further say to you try and Give those things Due Considderation   No More But Remain Yours With Respect and true friend to the Union

ALS   E S Robison^{52}

White Southerners resented the presence of black soldiers, for nothing more vividly demonstrated their own humiliation and defeat. Resentment sometimes boiled over into brutal attacks. Two policemen in Memphis vented their anger against a sergeant who refused to be cowed by threats.

Memphis, Tenn.,   [*September 11*] 1865

Sergt Joe. Brown. Co. D. 3^{d} US [*Colored Artillery*] (H[*eav*]y) states I was sitting in my own door on Sunday night the 10" of Sept., about dark. And a policeman who lives opposite to me on corner Brown-Avenue and Causey Streets Named Sweatt. said to me I wish I could get a chance to kill all the Damned Nigger Soldiers. and I said you cant kill me— he then stepped back a few paces and ran up and struck me with his *club*, on the head— at that time another Policeman came up and he struck me several times. and they thru me down and stamped me in the back while lying on the ground. My shirt was torn off and I was badly bruised. The man who I rent of saw this and knows the Policeman— Thy tried to take me to the station House and [*I*] told them I would not go—and about this time the Patrol came along and took me to *Irving Block*.—

I had commited no offence at the time the Policeman came for which to be arrested. I was sitting in the door with this man Tom talking quitly.[53]

HD

> Even after the war, physically taxing duties and exposure to the elements continued to take a toll on black soldiers. A high incidence of sickness was only one of many hardships endured by a veteran unit from Maryland, as described in an unsigned letter to Secretary of War Stanton.

New Berne *N.C.*   October 2nd 1865

Kind & Hornorible Sir   i am Veary Happy that it is my good Fourchan & i am Sorry Dear Sir that i hafto availe myselfe of this Sorrowfull opportunity but i Reealy thought that when i came out into the Servus that We Would be Honestly Dealte with but i find Since i have come out that there has bin a Vase Differrances & a Conciderble Change in my officers   We came out in 1[8]63 as Valent hearted men for the Sacke of

our Surffring Courntury & Since that Time things has chings a Round.
We have Never Refuces of Douing any Duty that We war call on to Dou
& when Ever We war orded to go we always Whent Like men but Mr
E. M. Stanton we Never bin Treated as men Since we have bin out in the
field   We have bin cut Down to Only 75 men out of one 1000 Strong
but we have Never bin forchenent as to Ever be call off of the field. & We
are now in a Veary Hard & a Dreadfull condishion   for the Last three
months we have bin a Surffring in a Tearrable condision   Ever Since
we have bin a Laying hear at this awlffull & Deserble & Forceaken Place
We have bin a Surffring in the wors Kind of a manner.   We havent a 150
men for Duty & the officers are a Reporting 400 men for Duty & they
cant Raies a Relefe of guard   We have men that bin on Duty now for
Near Two months havent bin Releve from guard & when we Put men on
guard in Town we hafto Leve them there for a Weeke at a Time & i Know
that it tis not milertary to Keepe men on guard Longer 48 Hours at the
Longes.   & we have bin a careing has high as five & Six men to the
Hospital a in a Day   & Day a after We have bin a Douing the Likes & i
Supose as Long as we Shall Stay hear in this forcaken Plasce we Shall
contineua to So to Doue it.   We have come out Like men & we Expected
to be Treeated as men but we have bin Treeated more Like Dogs then
men.   Sir alow me to Say that i hope that the Time Shall Soon come
when Shall all be Eacklize as men hear   our Hospital is full of sick
men & our camp is a Laying one halfe of the men that are in campe ar
Cripples & Still they are Reporting 400 men for Duty.   & they are Even
Puting the fiffers & Drummars on guard.   i have Read the Reagulations
Enough to Know that it is Rong but i Supose that because we are
colored that they think that we Dont no any Better   & the officers have
wa[i]ters & they Send them to the companys for there Rations & i Dont
think in my Small judgment that a officer has any Right to Send his

wa[i]ter to the company for Rations   if he is not able to Bord him he
would better Dou without any.   & if thare is any Reagulation in this;
Kind of Buisness then i will Sey that i arnt United States Soldier nor
Dont Know any thing army Reagulations.   if we Ever Expect to be a
Pepple & if we Dont Reply to some one of a thourety we Shall for Ever
be Troden Down under foot of man.   We have made Two Sutlars* Rich
Since We have bin out in the Servus   We would Like to Know if it
Lawfull for us to Set Up or to Reastablish Some three Specturlaters &
to Set them upe for Buisniss. by them a Seialing there goods at Duble
Prices Which we have bin a Paying Double Priceses for things from our
Sutlars Ever Since we have had them.   Where we Lay now a Person
cant go a Houndred yeards from camp without geting into a
Swamp   We are Surounded with Ponds chills & fevers & Deseasses of
Every Kind & i hope that it whont be but a Short Time befor We Shall be
Remove from hear or Some thing Don for us for the Better.   Even our
chaplain who Should be ar Best freind & to Lookeout for our wellfear
has Even gone intou Buisness of Spectulation & in my Small Judgment i
think that it would be Prudent to Dischage them all Let go Back to
Where they come from Worke foor there Liveing as they heartofor have
Don for all they are after is a makeing money   it tis not the Love for
there counntary that they whant Stay for but it only for the money
    Pleass to Excuse bad writing & also mistakes   Hoping to hear from
you Sir i have the Hornor to be Repectifully Your o.b. Serviant   this is
from Two of the Old 1863 Soldiers to which you have our warmest & well
wishess   this is from the Camp of 4ᵗʰ Regᵗ U.S.C.T.⁵⁴

HL

---

*I.e., sutlers, civilian merchants who were authorized to set up shops at
army posts and sell goods to soldiers.

Education provided a means to escape being "Troden Down under foot of man." In a letter to an official of the Freedmen's Bureau, a federal agency established in March 1865 to oversee the transition from slavery to freedom, a black sergeant from Kentucky emphasized the importance of education to his people.

Nashville Tenn   October 8th 1865

Sir   I have the honor to call your attention To the neccesity of having a school for The benefit of our regement   We have never Had an institutiong of that sort and we Stand deeply inneed of instruction the majority of us having been slaves   We Wish to have some benefit of education To make of ourselves capable of buisness In the future   We have estableshed a literary Association which flourished previous to our March to Nashville   We wish to become a People capable of self support as we are Capable of being soldiers   my home is in Kentucky Where Prejudice reigns like the Mountain Oak and I do lack that cultivation of mind that would have an attendency To cast a cloud over my future life after have been in the United States service   I had a leave of abscence a few weeks a go on A furlough and it made my heart ache to see my race of people there neglected And ill treated on the account of the lack of Education being incapable of putting Thier complaints or applications in writing   For the want of Education totally ignorant Of the Great Good Workings of the Government in our behalf   We as soldiers Have our officers Who are our protection To teach how us to act and to do   But Sir What we want is a general system of education In our regiment for our moral and literary elevation   these being our motives We have the Honor of calling your very high Consideration   Respectfully Submitted as Your Most humble serv[t]

ALS   John Sweeny[55]

Sweeny's request fell on receptive ears. The letter is endorsed: "Will send Teacher as soon as possible."[56]

———————◆———————

Black soldiers demonstrated an interest in education not only within their own ranks, but also in the communities where they served. When former slaves in a northeastern Mississippi town sought to establish a school, they enlisted the aid of two noncommissioned officers.

Okolona Miss   Oct 25 1865,

Regtl Orders No 137   Sergt Eli Helen and Corporal Joseph Ingram Co K having been selected by the Colored Citizens of Okolona and vicinity as collecting agents for the fund to establish a school for colored children, are hereby granted permission to visit Okolona in the execution of their duties as such

This order to continue in force during their good behavior   By order of Col John S Bishop[57]

HD

Former slaveholders despised black soldiers for the same reason that former slaves welcomed them. To men and women who had owned slaves, armed black men in positions of authority embodied the world turned upside down. Soldiers defending freedpeople or even advising them of their rights appeared to former slaveholders as dangerous provocateurs. A Mississippi planter warned three state legislators of the disaster that loomed unless the "Negro Soldiery" was removed.

Panola [*Miss.*].   Oct 22[d], 1865

Gentlemen.   I wish to call your attention to a serious & growing evil, with the hope that you will give it your earliest attention, that something

may be done to remove it from our midst— The Negro Soldiery here
are constantly telling our negroes, that for the next year, The Goverment
will give them lands, provisions, Stock & all things necessary to carry on
business for themselves,—& are constantly advising them not to make
contracts with white persons, for the next year.— Strange to say the
negroes believe such stories in spite of facts to the contrary told them by
their ~~masters~~ employers.— The consequence is they are becoming
careless, & impudent more & more, for they are told by the soldiers that
they are as good as the whites & that they have come here for their
protection & that they shall not be hurt.— furthermore I have good
cause to believe that our negroes are told that when the soldiers are
withdrawn, that the whites will endeavor to enslave them again—& that
they are urged to begin at an early day, perhaps about Christmas, a
massacre of the whites, in order to ensure their freedom, & that if the
whites are got out the way here, that then they will have no further
apprehension—& that this Country will then be given to them by the
northern people forever as an inheritance.—& Gentlemen to ignorant
persons situated as the negro is such arguments seem quite plausible.—
In truth the people of the South are in very great danger, more so than
many suppose— I have been born & reared in the midst of negroes. I
know their nature well, & have never, yet been deceived in my estimate of
them. I am no alarmist, but I tell you most seriously that the whole
south is resting upon a volcano—& that if the negro troops are not
removed from our mids pretty Soon—that trouble of the direst kind will
befal us— They will stimulate the negroes to insurrection & will then
lend them a helping hand— It is well Known here that our negroes
through the country are well supplied with fire arms, muskets, Double
Barrel, shot Guns & Pistols,—& furthermore, it would be well if they are
free to prohibit the use of fire arms until they had proved themselves to

be good citizens in their altered state.— Gentlemen I do not write you
these views hastily.— I have well considered them, & they appear more
& more convincing day by day— I have talked with many of our
citizens upon this matter— they appear anxious & say something
ought to be done—but no one feels disposed to move in the matter.—
Get the negro Soldiery removed from our midst & no danger will
follow—our negroes will be quiet, will hire for another year.—& will do
their duty in many cases very well— Let the Soldiery remain—& our
negroes will refuse to hire will grow more & more insolent & will without
a doubt—(relying upon the help of the Soldiery which they will be sure
to get) will endeavor by universal Massacre to turn this fair land into
another Hayti.*— Our only hope of escape from the evils above
enumerated & many others, is to get the negro troops removed from the
State. Cannot it be done?— I think with Such men as Gov Sharkey—
& others like him making application to the President to that effect, that
the South can be Saved from Anarchy & bloodshed— Please to enlist
youselves with Dr Mosely in this matter, for much indeed depends upon
it for the weal or woe of our selves our wives & our little ones— I
remain Your friend, truly &c

E. G. Baker

P.S. Esq Ballard has just told me that a squad of colored Soldiers met
him near his house this morning & without any provocation—his not
even speaking a word—they called him a damned old rebel & threatened
to kill, him; they did the same to Wiley Baker a few minutes before using
the most vulgar abusive language to him— they have several times
arrested citizens walking about the streets of a night attending to their
own business—their camp being down near the old mill,— they are

---

*In 1791, slaves in the French colony of Saint-Domingue revolted
against their owners, killing or exiling all of them, and eventually
establishing an independent republic (Haiti).

generally drunk when they act So—but the Lt who commands them
when complained to merely says that he does not authorise them to do so
& there the matter ends— they are also killing up the hogs robbing
potatoe, patches,—parading (mustering) up & down the streets in the
most offensive manner.— If things go on this way much longer there
will be a collison between the citizens & the black rascals let the
consequences be what they may— Please to give the matter of their
removal from our midst your earliest & most serious attention—& you
will have the most lastings feelings of gratitude for your efforts in behalf
of the whole country—Your friend—B.[58]

ALS

Transmitting Baker's letter to the Union commander in Northern
Mississippi, Governor Benjamin G. Humphreys advised that "unless some measures are taken to disarm [the freedmen] a collision
between the races may be speedily looked for. . . . That the colored troops are the cause of the mischief is not doubted."[59]

The ex-slaves' enemies in Mississippi were already taking steps to
disarm them and further restrict their freedom. In late 1865, the
state legislature enacted laws that acknowledged emancipation but
severely limited the former slaves' liberty and legal rights. Meanwhile, ex-Confederates terrorized freedpeople under the pretext of
averting a rumored insurrection. Hampered by a shortage of
troops, the Mississippi branch of the Freedmen's Bureau under
Colonel Samuel Thomas could barely begin to respond. In a letter
to the bureau's national commissioner, a black private assigned to
Thomas's office described the freedpeople's predicament and proposed a solution.

Vicksburg. Miss. De^c 16th 1865.

Sir   Suffer me to address you a few lines in reguard to the colered
people in this State,   from all I can learn and see, I think the colered
people are in a great many ways being outraged beyound
humanity,   houses have been tourn down from over the heades of
women and Children—and the old Negroes after they have worked there
till they are 70 or 80 yers of age drive them off in the cold to frieze and
starve to death.

One Woman come to (Col) Thomas, the coldest day that has been this
winter and said that she and her eight children lay out last night, and
come near friezing after She had paid some wrent on the house   Some
are being knocked down for saying they are free, while a great many are
being worked just as they ust to be when Slaves, without any
compensation,   Report came in town this morning that two colered
women was found dead side the Jackson road with their throats cot
lying side by side,   I see an account in the Vicksburg. Journal where the
(col[*ored*]) peple was having a party where they formily had one. and got
into a fuss and a gun was fired and passed into a house.   they was
forbidden not to have any more but did not heed.   The result was the
house was fired and a guard placed at the door   one man attemped to
come out but was shot and throed back and burned   five was consumed
in the flames, while the balance saught refuge in a church and it was
fired and burned.   The Rebbles are going a bout in many places through
the State and robbing the colered peple of arms money and all they have
and in many places killing.

So, General, to make short of a long story I think the safety of this
country depenes upon giving the Colered man all the rights of a white
man, and especialy the Rebs. and let him know that their is power
enough in the arm of the Govenment to give Justice, to all her loyal
citizens—

They talk of taking the armes a way from (col[ored]) people and
arresting them and put them on farmes next month* and if they go at
that I think there will be trouble and in all probability a great many lives
lost.   They have been accusing the colered peple of an insorection which
is a lie, in order that they might get arms to carrie out their wicked
designs—

for to my own knowledge I have seen them buying arms and
munitions ever since the lins have been opened and carring them to the
country.   In view of these things I would suggust to you if it is not
incompatible with the public interest to pass some laws that will give
protection to the colered men and meet out Justice to traters in arms.

For you have whiped them and tried them and found out that they will
not do to be depended upon,   now if you have any true harted men send
them down here to carrie out your wishes through the Bureau in
reguarde to the freedmen.   if not get Congress to stick in a few
competent colered men as they did in the army and the thing will all go
right,   A trouble now with the colered peple on account of Rebs. after
they have rendered the Government such great survice through the
rebellion would spoil the whole thing—and it is what the Rebles would
like to bring a bout, and they are doing all they can to prevent free labor,
and reasstablish a kind of secondary slavery   Now believe me as a
colered man that is a friend to law and order, I blive without the
intervention of the General governmt in the protection of the (col[ored])
popble that there will be trouble in *Miss.* before spring   please excuse
this for I could not have said less and done the subject Justice.   infact I
could say more, but a hint to the wise is soficient   If you wish to drop

---

*A recently adopted state law required that all black men and women
 find a white employer by the second week of January, failing which
 they would be arrested as vagrants and forced to labor for whoever
 paid their fines.

me a line Direct Calvin. Holly. *Vick* Miss Box 2$^{\rm d}$ yours Most
Respectfully,

ALS   Calvin. Holly., colered[60]

> For black soldiers in the Union army of occupation, encounters
> with impoverished and abused freedpeople reminded them of the
> travail of their own loved ones. Although legally free, the families of
> black soldiers remained vulnerable, especially when their husbands
> and fathers were stationed far from home. Former slaveholders not
> only lashed out with punishments reminiscent of slavery, but also
> employed modes of harassment that derived from freedom. Among
> the latter was eviction, as the wife of one black soldier informed her
> husband.

Roseland Plantation [*La.*]   July 16$^{\rm th}$ 1865

My Dear Husband   I received a letter from you week before last and
was glad to hear that you were well and happy.

This is the fifth letter I have written you and I have received only
one— Please write as often as you can as I am always anxious to hear
from you.   I and the children are all well—but I am in a great deal of
trouble as Master John Humphries has come home from the Rebel army
and taken charge of the place and says he is going to turn us all out on
the Levee unless we pay him (8.00) Eight Dollars a month for house
rent— Now I have no money of any account and I am not able to get
enough to pay so much rent, and I want you to get a furlough as soon as
you can and come home and find a place for us to live in.   and besides
Amelia is very sick and wants you to come home and see her if
possible   she has been sick with the fever now over two weeks and is
getting very low— Your mother and all the rest of your folks are well

and all send their regards & want to see you as soon as you can manage
to come— My mother sends her compliments & hopes to see you soon

My children are going to school, but I find it very hard to feed them
all, and if you can not come I hope you will send me something to help
me get along

I get all the work I can and am doing the best I can to get along, but if
they turn me out I dont know what I shall do— However I will try &
keep the children along until you come or send me some assistance

Thank God we are all well, and I hope we may always be so   Give my
regards to all the boys.   Come home as soon as you can, and cherish me
as ever   Your Aff wife

HLSr   Emily Waters[61]

> An officer of the company in which Waters's husband was serving
> reported her case to the head of the Louisiana branch of the Freed-
> men's Bureau, explaining that eviction was a widespread occur-
> rence.

                         Fort St. Philip.   La.   Aug. 1st, 1865.

Sir.   I am an officer in a co. of 140 men.—have been with them
continually Since their organization as a Co., and most of the time the
Sole officer with them.   Feeling an interest in the advancement and
prosperity of the colored race and always sympathizing with them in
their trials and Sufferings, which are now very great, owing to the
peculiar condition of the country, and their people, those under my
immediate charge have learned to look to me for consolation in regard to
many matters not Strictly military.   I always do what I can but
frequently that is nothing at all.   One of the most frequent complaints

brought to me is the mistreatment of Soldiers wives, and in Some cases their ejectment for non-payment of rent by *returned rebels* who seem to be resuming their old positions all over the country. This of course is inhuman as well as contrary to Genl. Orders. No. 99. H^d Qrs. Dept. of the Gulf. June 30th, 1865, which declares that the families of Soldiers in the Service of the Gov't. either on land or water, Shall not be ejected for rent past due, and no collections of rent forced until further orders. This is a very humane provision but owing to the ignorance of many colored persons it is *very* often violated. Those who know of the provision do not know how to go to work to receive their rights under it, frequently, and when they do attempt it they are often snubbed by those who they feel a right to expect as their friends. Truly, the colored race are passing through an ordeal that will test every virtue they possess, and it will not be astonishing if, in many cases they fail to meet the expectation of an uncharitable world.

My object in writing you this letter is to call your attention to a Mr. John Humphrey, who I am told is a returned rebel officer, now living on Roseland Plantation, St. Charles Parish, who is Said to have made innumerable threats and at least one attempt to put out the family of one of my Soldiers.—*for non-payment of rent.*— I gave the man a furlough and he got home Just in time to find a *Provost Guard* at his house for the purpose of ousting his wife and children. These look like Strange proceedings viewed at this distance with my understanding of the law. The fact is, persecution is the order of the day amongst these returned rebels, against the colored race in general, and Soldiers families *in particular*. And I am grieved to Say that many wearing the U.S. uniform are too easily bought body and Soul over to the evil designs and purposes of these same individuals. It seems to me that your Bureau and its agents are the "forlorn hope" of the colored people.—

These rebels Strongly object to these agents, and declare that they will only keep up a confusion and disturbance, continually.   That means that they do not intend to manifest the "good faith" for which Genl. Howard* hopes, but intend to take Such a course with the colored people as will *oblige* the interference of the agents of your Bureau.

These are my views, although I owe you an apology for expressing them at Such length.   If it pleases you I shall be glad to lay the frequent cases which arise in my Co. before you, as I know your voice is very potent   With great respect I am Your Most Obt. Servt.

ALS   Hugh P. Beach.[62]

> On behalf of comrades from Missouri and Tennessee, an anony-
> mous black soldier outlined to the secretary of war the men's solici-
> tude for their families, as well as their dissatisfaction with routine
> duties and disdain for a particularly obnoxious officer.

                                        Chattanooga Ten.   August th 22 1865

Sir   I have the honor of Reporting Sevral condishtion to you about difference Circumstance   the Colored Men of these 44th & 16th & 18th there Wives is Scatered abut over world without pertioction in Suffernce condishtion & there Husband is here & have not seen there Faimlys for 2 years & more   we would be under ten thousand obligations to you if pervid Some plain for Our benfit   the greats Duites that is performed at this Place is Poleasing Ground   Some of us has not heard from our Wivies for 2 & a half [*years*] & Some of theses Familys I am very sure that is worse then I Repersent them to be   the all says the would be

---

*Oliver O. Howard, commissioner of the Freedmen's Bureau.

willing to fight there Enemy but at the present time is no fighting on this side of the Rior Grand   the says that dont want to go their whilce thire Familys is in a Suffernce condishtion but to Fight in the U.S.A. the all say the will do it without Truble   the think under the present [*circumstances*] of their Familys the ought to be permitt to go & see after Familys   I was late from Mo. & Ka. & anoumber of them that I saw all most Thread less & Shoeless without food & no home to go   sevral of there Masters Run them off & as fur as I can see the hole Race will fall back if the U.S. Goverment dont pervid for them Some way or ruther   the is noumbers of them here at this place suffering for the want of Husband Care   the Ration is giving to them dose not degree very well with Childern   recording to there Enlistments there times is out for the war is over   the Enlist 3 years or during [*the war*]   well the war is over   the is some talk of consolidating Regiments   Some of the Officers says if the men will Stack ther Arms* the will Stand at the head of there Companys until the fall   I glorys in there Spunk   I am a friend to the U.S. Goverment but [*not*] to Col. L. Johnson of the 44th U.S.C.I   please reply to this   Col Johnson if he Don't look out he will git apple cart tumbled   he has been kicking some of the Boys but the say the will stop that or stop his life & I am will to report the case before hand   I am very respectful and & &

these three Regiments that I Speak of has a very notion to Stack there Armys because there times of Enliting is out   the say the Enlited 3 years or during the War & the war is over & there times is out.[63]

HL

---

*Stacking arms signified collective refusal to perform duties and was tantamount to mutiny.

At times the white officers of black regiments exhibited as little respect for the family connections of their men as slaveholders did for
the family connections of their slaves. A black soldier stationed in
northern Alabama protested to the commander of the military division that his regimental officers prevented the wives of the enlisted
men from visiting camp, while boarding their own wives within its
limits.

Bridgeport Ala   N 19th 1865

Dear Ser   We are here at this place under the cormand of Colonel
luster   genel I rite you thes few lines to let you know the condishon
that we are living   we are guarded there night and day no even
permitted to go to the spring after a drink of water onley by
companys   wether Corprel Sargent they hav all got in to such a
comfuse ment they say they will not stand it any longger   I say to you
less than ten days there will be over half the men gon from the regment
if they is not treatted better   they keep they bys hand cuf evver day
and night and I cant see what it is for   if they do any thing to be hand
cuff for we wold not exspec any thing eles   mens wifes comes here to
see them and he will not alow them to come in to they lines uur the men
to go out to see them after the comg over hundred miles   but evver
offiscer here that has a wife is got her here in camps & one mans wif feel
jest as near to him as anurther   a colard man think jest as much of his
wife as a white man dus of his   if he is black they keep us hemd up
here in side the guarde line and if our wife comes they hav to stand out
side & he in side and talk a cross they lines   that is as near as they can
come   they treat this hold reg ment like it was prisners   we volenterd
and come in to the servest to portec this govverment and also to be
portected our selves at the same time but the way colonel luster is
treating us it dont seem like to me that he thinks we are human

I rite these few lines to you to see if we cant get some releaf   yours
truly a friend

ALS   George Buck Hanon[64]

> When he was ordered to respond to Buckhanon's charges, the regi-
> mental commander cast aspersions upon his men's attachment to
> the women they regarded as their wives. He also defended the
> stringent disciplinary measures of which Buckhanon complained.

Bridgeport Ala   Decr 14th/65

General   I have the honor to acknowledge the receipt of a
communication addressed to the Major Genl com^{dg}, professing to be
signed and written by "George Buchhanon 40th U.S.C.I."

Altho' no such man can be found in the rolls of the regiment nor any
name approximating to it, neither can any man be found to father the
document, yet in obedience to the order contained in your endorsement,
I subjoin the following statement.

The sum & substance of the complaint set forth against me seems to
resolve into this, that I am endeavoring to maintain discipline in a
regiment of U.S. troops committed to my care, and that I prevent the
camp of the said regiment from becoming a brothel on a gigantic
scale.   To this I plead guilty.

The marital relationship is but little understood by the colored race,
and, if possible still less respected.

I have from time to time caused a careful inquiry to be made by
company commander's with the view to ascertain the number of men
who are married by any process known to civilization, or even those who
by long cohabitation might be looked on as possessing some faint notions

of constancy and decency. Even with this lax view not more than one in four who claim to have wives can support that claim.

In fact the larger proportion of the enlisted men change their so called wives as often as the regiment changes stations.

The immorality developed after last pay day required a strong effort to repress it. Large herds of colored prostitutes flocked to Bridgeport from both ends of the line, but the guard regulations not suiting them, the greater proportion soon left for "fresh fields & pastures new."

It is just within the bounds of possiblity that some virtuous wives may have been amongst the number so excluded from camp, but I gravely doubt it.

The Revnd John Poucher, Chaplain of my regiment is doing his best to correct the vices so prevalent amongst colored soldiers, but the habits of licentiousness not only permitted but greatly encouraged by the former owners of these men are hard to eradicate.

The charge of guarding parties going for water is partly true. Water has to be brought from a considerable distance, the road to it lies thro' the line of stores erected here for the express purpose of robbing soldiers, the proprietors of which having laid in a stock of whisky in anticipation of pay-day did, both on and on the day after that day, make nearly the entire regiment drunk.

I was compelled to adopt severe measures with store keepers and soldiers, since which there has been no trouble on that subject.

It is also true that I keep some of the men hand-cuffed, and only regret I cannot have some of them shot. Deserters who have twice escaped and who are constantly trying to escape, men who draw their bayonets on officers, and who stab their comrades are I think fit subjects for irons whilst awaiting trial.

On the subject of leave from camp &c I submit the following rules.

All men not on duty may leave camp without passes between company drill and dinner roll call or from 10 A.M. to 12. M, and again from 12.30 to 1.30 P.M, making in all three hours daily.   I have a vivid recollection of the time when I did not spend that time from my regiment in one year, and think that three hours daily is sufficent for these men of tender and domestic feelings to enjoy in the bosoms of their families.

   Prowling over the country between tattoo & reveille is entirely stopped, in fact it never existed, and that is of course the time the badly disposed men want to commit outrages.   I have the honor to be, General, Very respectfully, Your obed^t Servt

ALS   F. W. Lister[65]

The soldiers' fears for the well-being of their families increased in proportion to their distance from home. Already dissatisfied with garrison life on the Texas frontier, men in a Virginia regiment became desperate to leave the service after receiving discouraging news from their loved ones. In a letter to an unnamed official in Washington, they offered to buy their way out of their enlistments in order to return home to care for their families.

                         Brazos Santiago   Texas,   Dec 1865
Sir   here is my Compliment & wishes to be pertectd by the War Department

   1st U S Colred Cavalry   sir Wee present to you our sufering at present Concerning our Famileys wich wee are now informed that Commisserys has been Closed a gainst them as though wee were rebeling a gainst U S. and has Came to be a great Wonder & a great

Contemplation a mung the men of this regt and wee would be happay to find some one to pertect us in thes Case   Wee have been on Dayley fetig from the Last of Juli up to this Day without a forlough or any comfort what ever & our wifes sends Letters stateing thir suferage saying that they are without wood without wrashions without money and no one to pertect them   Wee have Done the best that wee can do and trys to obey orders and would pleassed to know the Cause of our Dishonorble in treatment   Wee have been exspecting to be musered out of the Army.   Why because wee knew the men wich wee have taken for our friends was acquinted with what Liberty. wee have been granted up to this time and for that cause wee thought that it would please any good hearted man to turn us out of servis to the pertecttion of our be loved wifes   and if there be any man North or south Let him say to Day what shell be our pertecttion for this Day wee Disiaer to know.

here wee have come in as U S. Soldiers and are treated as Slaves   never was wee any more treated Like slaves then wee are now in our Lives   I well remember before the Closeing of the war that men who was fighting a gainst the U S. how thir wifes were pertected and if our wifes were half pertected as they were wee would be happy men.   Wee are said to be U S Soldiers and behold wee are U S Slaves   Wee are now well acquinted with earley riseing and Late bed time and such things wit wich has been don here of Late is a shame to. be. don before the men of the south

Wee had rather pay for our next years serviss and be turned out then to stay in and no pertecttion granted to our wife

Sir wee would be verey much pleased to be Dis banded from the field and if the War Department Can not spar us or spar the time. wee. will. pay them for one years. servis. in the beside what soldiering wee have done   Wee onely wish the pertecttion of our wifes and as we has been all ways been so acomodated with the Law for any thing that wee do young [*wrong*] wee now wish to be comodated for what wee have done right   and if I have said any thing young I pray to be exc[*used*].   your obeient U S Servts

    also wee cant get a forlough unless paying $60 Dollars and wee thinks verey hard of it[66]

HL

Soldiers in a South Carolina regiment addressed similar complaints to their departmental commander.

                    Morris Island   So Ca   January 13 1866
My Dear Respictfully Friend General Sickels   it is with much Honor we take to write to you about the Circumstances of our case   now Genl do if you please Cir to this lookin to this [for us].   now General the Biggest Majority of our mens never had a Home Science this late wor Commence between the States   the Greatist majority of them had Runaway from they Rebels master & leave they wives & old mother & old Father & all they parent   jest Run away from they Rebels master in the years 1862. & 1863 & come Right in under the Bondage of Soldiers life living & according to agreement & promised we was expected to get out at the Closing of the wor, & then go back over the Rebels lands to look & seek for our wives & mother & Father

    But General now to see that the wor is over & our Enlisment is out the Greatist majority of by two months & the General characters of our Regiment we do not think that the our Goverment have knowit   for Instant I think if he had know the General characters of our Regt he would let us go at the Closing of this [*war*]   for instant look & see that

we never was freed yet   Run Right out of Slavery in to Soldiery & we
hadent nothing atoll & our wifes & mother most all of them is aperishing
all about where we leave them or abbout the Country & we hear on
morris Island Perishing sometime for something to Eate   Half of our
money got to use up in the Regtal Sutler for somthing to Eate & we all
are perrishing   our self & our Parent & wives all are Suffering

& do General if you Please do see & Enterceed & see if you cannot do
any good to get us out of this if you please cir   for all other Colored
Soldiers that had a Home & is well situated at Home is go back but we
that never had a Comford Home we is heer yet & we will have to buy our
lands & places & by the time we get out of this all the Goverment cheap.
Property & all the lands that would be sold cheap will be gone & we will
have a Hard struggle to get along in the U S   & then all the Southern
white Peoples will have us for alaughin & game after for our Braverist
that we did to Run away from them & come asoldiers   they will be glad
to see that we would not have but very little money & we would not have
any land, atoll for all the cheap in things are going now   So do Gen you
is the only one that we know could do any good for us beside forwarded
to Washington.   So Please if you can do any good for us do it in the
name of god   it is a mejority of men of the 33 Regt USCT[67]

HL

> Even after they had left the service and returned home, black sol-
> diers faced a formidable task in protecting themselves and their
> kin. The wife of a discharged soldier paid a high price for his asso-
> ciation with the Union army, as she related to an agent of the
> Freedmen's Bureau.

[*Griffin, Ga.*]   Sept. 25, 1866

Rhoda Ann Childs came into this office and made the following statement:

"Myself and husband were under contract with Mrs. Amelia Childs of Henry County, and worked from Jan. 1, 1866, until the crops were laid by, or in other words until the main work of the year was done, without difficulty.   Then, (the fashion being prevalent among the planters) we were called upon one night, and my husband was demanded; I Said he was not there.   They then asked where he was.   I Said he was gone to the water mellon patch.   They then Seized me and took me Some distance from the house, where they 'bucked' me down across a log, Stripped my clothes over my head, one of the men Standing astride my neck, and beat me across my posterior, two men holding my legs.   In this manner I was beaten until they were tired.   Then they turned me parallel with the log, laying my neck on a limb which projected from the log, and one man placing his foot upon my neck, beat me again on my hip and thigh.   Then I was thrown upon the ground on my back, one of the men Stood upon my breast, while two others took hold of my feet and stretched My limbs as far apart as they could, while the man Standing upon my breast applied the Strap to my private parts until fatigued into stopping, and I was more dead than alive.   Then a man, Supposed to be an ex-confederate Soldier, as he was on crutches, fell upon me and ravished me.   During the whipping one of the men ran his pistol into me, and Said he had a hell of a mind to pull the trigger, and Swore they ought to Shoot me, as my husband had been in the 'God damned Yankee Army,' and Swore they meant to kill every black Son-of-a-bitch they could find that had ever fought against them.   They then went back to the house, Seized my two daughters and beat them, demanding their father's pistol, and upon failure to get that, they entered the house and took Such articles of clothing as Suited their fancy, and decamped.   There were concerned in this affair eight men, none of which could be recognized for certain.

her

Roda Ann × Childs[68]

mark

HDSr

More than a year after the war ended, Kentucky soldiers on the Mexican border compared their service to the Union with the shoddy treatment they and their families had endured and challenged their commander-in-chief to make good the nation's promises to them.

White Ranch [*Tex.*]   July 3rd 1866

Dear President   I have the honer to address the as followes   the few remarks i wish to say and to inform you of is this   the Condition of our familys in Kentucky and the Condition of our self   we Kentuckians are men that Came out in this great and noble cause   we did come out like men   we have stood up to geather with Comrades and have proved not only to the people but to the world that we have been faithfull and prompt to all dutys   we have fulfilled all posts that we have been put and then as for a Regiment Commander to treat the soldiers so mean as we have been treated i think it is out of the question   My President and vice i think as a dutyfull as the 116th Regiment of U.S. Coloured Infantry have not had no more quarters shown them then what as been i dont think it is right for i think that there are not the tenth part of quarters shown us that is intended for us for if our officers and field officers would take the Law as it is given to them and use it they have

not the power to use such ill treatment   Mr President and vice we learn
by the papers that the sum of three Hundred dollars that was promised
us when we inlisted in the service we would not get it   but if the
Govener should turn out the men of our standing barehanded i would
like to know how you would expect for us to live ear after   we are a
nation that was poor and had nothing when we came to the service   we
had neather house nor money no place to put our familys   now these
poor nation of colour have spent the best part of his days in
slavery   now then what must we do   must we turn out to steal to get
a start   we left our wifes and Children no place for them to lay there
heads   we left them not counted on Eaqual footing as the white
people   they where looked on like dogs and we left them with a willing
mind to exicute our duty in the army of the United States war to eather
to make us a nation of people eather in this generation or the next to
come   now Mr President i wish you to ansure this letter and let us
know we are to do as this Regiment is labouring under a great mistake
untill you let us know what we are to do and you will releive our mind a
great deal and we will remain your affectionate Brother Soldier
Direct to

1est Sargint Wm White

1 "   Do   Mc Meail

2 "   Do   Taylor

[Corpor]arl Thomass[69]

HLSr

NOTES

INTRODUCTION

1. See p. 349.
2. See pp. 461–63.
3. *Black Military Experience*, p. 804.
4. See pp. 450–51.
5. See pp. 512–13.
6. See p. 496.
7. See pp. 480–82.
8. See pp. 370–72.
9. *Black Military Experience*, p. 111n.
10. Rebbeca Barrat to My Dear Son, 27 Nov. [1863?], service record of William B. Barrett, 74th USCI, Carded Records, Volunteer Organizations: Civil War, series 519, Records of the Adjutant General's Office, Record Group 94, National Archives.
11. See pp. 533–35.
12. *Wartime Genesis: Lower South*, p. 246.
13. See pp. 461–63.

CHAPTER 1

1. Wm. H. Lee to J. Davis, 4 May 1861, *Black Military Experience*, p. 282.
2. John J. Cheatham to Hon. L. P. Walker, 4 May 1861, *Black Military Experience*, pp. 282–83.
3. Thomas T. Gantt to Brig. Genl. W. S. Harney, 14 May 1861, *Destruction of Slavery*, p. 413.
4. Brigadier General [William S. Harney] to Thomas T. Gantt, Esq., 14 May 1861, *Destruction of Slavery*, pp. 413–14.
5. Benj. F. Butler to Lieutenant Genl. Scott, 27 May 1861, *Destruction of Slavery*, pp. 70–71.
6. *Destruction of Slavery*, p. 72.
7. Benjamin F. Butler, *Private and Official Correspondence of Gen. Benjamin F. Butler during the Period of the Civil War*,

5 vols. (Norwood, Mass., 1917), vol. 1, pp. 185–88.
8. *Statutes at Large*, vol. 12, p. 319.
9. Bvt. Brig. Gen. [Charles H. Howard] to Hon. John P. C. Shanks, [20 Nov.] 1867, *Destruction of Slavery*, pp. 347–48.
10. General Orders No. 16, Head Quarters, Corps of Observation, 23 Sept. 1861, *Destruction of Slavery*, pp. 348–49.
11. Brig. Genl. A. McD. McCook to Genl. W. T. Sherman, 5 Nov. 1861, *Destruction of Slavery*, pp. 519–20.
12. Brig. Genl. W. T. Sherman to Brig. Genl. McCook, 8 Nov. 1861, *Destruction of Slavery*, p. 520.
13. Tho. H. Hicks to Hon. S. Cameron, 18 Nov. 1861, *Destruction of Slavery*, pp. 352–53.
14. General Orders, No. 3,

Head Quarters,
Department of the
Missouri, 20 Nov. 1861,
Destruction of Slavery,
p. 417.

15. Wm. A. Jones to Hon. S.
Cameron, 27 Nov. 1861,
Black Military Experience,
pp. 80–81.

16. John A. Andrew to Hon.
Simon Cameron, 7 Dec.
1861, *Destruction of
Slavery*, pp. 353–54.

17. Unsigned excerpt, 28 Nov.
1861, *Destruction of
Slavery*, p. 354.

18. *Destruction of Slavery*,
p. 354n.

19. *Destruction of Slavery*,
p. 202n.

20. Proclamation of Brigr.
Genl. J. W. Phelps to the
Loyal Citizens of the
South-West, 4 Dec. 1861,
Destruction of Slavery,
pp. 199–201.

21. H. Willis to Freind
Camron, 5 Dec. 1861,
Destruction of Slavery,
p. 269.

22. *Destruction of Slavery*,
pp. 420–21.

23. Major Geo. E. Waring, Jr.
to Acting Maj. Gen.
Asboth, 19 Dec. 1861,
Destruction of Slavery,
pp. 421–22.

24. *Destruction of Slavery*,
p. 423.

25. John Boston to Mrs.
Elizabeth Boston,
12 Jan. 1862, *Destruction
of Slavery*, pp. 357–58.

26. Maj. Genl. Geo. B.
McClellan to Hon. Edwin
Stanton, 21 Jan. 1862,
A-587 1862, Letters
Received, series 12,
Records of the Adjutant
General's Office, Record
Group 94, National
Archives.

27. Jno. H. Bayne et al. to
Hon. E. M. Stanton,
10 Mar. 1862, *Destruction
of Slavery*, pp. 360–61.

28. Affidavit of A. J. Smoot,
1 Mar. 1862, *Destruction
of Slavery*, pp. 361–62.

29. *Destruction of Slavery*,
p. 362n.

30. Brig. Genl. A. E. Burnside
to Hon. E. M. Stanton,
21 Mar. 1862,
Destruction of Slavery,
pp. 80–81.

31. *Destruction of Slavery*,
p. 81n.

32. *Statutes at Large*, vol. 12,
p. 354.

33. A[ssistant]. A[djutant].
G[eneral]. E. P. Halsted to
Col. J. D. Shaul, 6 Apr.
1862, *Destruction of
Slavery*, pp. 178–79.

34. Joint Resolution by the
Washington, D.C., City
Council, Apr. 1862,
Destruction of Slavery,
p. 178.

35. *Statutes at Large*, vol. 12,
pp. 376–78.

36. Joseph Enoch Williams et
al. to the Honorable the
Senate and House of
Representatives, [Apr.
1862], *Wartime Genesis:
Upper South*, doc. 51.

37. Affidavit of Grandison
Briscoe, 6 Feb. 1864,
Destruction of Slavery,
p. 365.

38. L. H. Minor to Sir, 2 May
[1862], *Destruction of
Slavery*, pp. 698–99.

39. *Destruction of Slavery*,
p. 276n.

40. Brig. Gen. O. M. Mitchel
to E. M. Stanton, 4 May
1862, *Destruction of
Slavery*, p. 275.

41. Edwin M. Stanton to
General O. M. Mitchel,
5 May 1862, *Destruction of
Slavery*, pp. 275–76.

42. *Destruction of Slavery*,
pp. 397–98, 415–16.

43. Proclamation by Abraham
Lincoln, 19 May 1862,
Destruction of Slavery,
pp. 123–25.

44. Capt. Edward Page, Jr., to
Major Genl. Benj. F.
Butler, 27 May 1862, as
extracted in Capt. P.
Haggerty to Brig. Genl. J.
W. Phelps, 28 May 1862,
Destruction of Slavery,
pp. 208–9.

45. *Destruction of Slavery*,
p. 209.

46. Testimony of Corporal
Octave Johnson before the
American Freedmen's
Inquiry Commission,
[Feb.? 1864], *Destruction
of Slavery*, p. 217.

47. Lieut. W. T. Truxtun to
Flag Officer S. F. Du
Pont, 13 June 1862,
Destruction of Slavery,
pp. 125–27.

48. [General David Hunter]
to Edwin M. Stanton, 23
June 1862, *Black Military
Experience*, pp. 50–53.

49. *Statutes at Large*, vol. 12,
pp. 589–92.

50. *Statutes at Large*, vol. 12,
pp. 597–600.

51. Testimony of Samuel
Elliot before the Southern
Claims Commission, [17
July 1873], *Destruction of
Slavery*, pp. 146–50.

52. R. Q. Mallard et al. to
Brigadier General Mercer,
[1 Aug. 1862], *Destruction
of Slavery*, pp. 795–98.

53. *Destruction of Slavery*,
p. 798n.

54. Samuel J. Kirkwood to
General [Henry W.
Halleck], 5 Aug. 1862,
Black Military Experience,
pp. 85–86.

55. Maj. Genl. W. T. Sherman
to Thomas Hunton, Esq.,
24 Aug. 1862, *Destruction
of Slavery*, pp. 292–94.

56. *Statutes at Large*, vol. 12,
pp. 1267–68.

57. John C. P. Wederstrandt
to Brig. Genl. Shepley, 19
Sept. 1862, *Destruction of
Slavery*, pp. 219–20.

58. S. D. Atkins to Miller, 2
Nov. 1862, *Destruction of
Slavery*, pp. 528–29.

59. Clipping from an
unidentified Cleveland,
Ohio, newspaper, [Nov.?
1862], *Destruction of
Slavery*, pp. 531–33.

60. Captain Charles S. Rogers
to General Granger, [24?
Nov. 1862], *Destruction of
Slavery*, pp. 534–35.

61. Col. Smith D. Atkins to Capt. B. H. Polk, 25 Nov. 1862, *Destruction of Slavery*, p. 535.

62. *Destruction of Slavery*, p. 570.

63. Col. M. Mundy to His Excellency Abraham Lincoln, 27 Nov. 1862, *Destruction of Slavery*, pp. 546–47.

64. Pre. Soniat to General, 20 Dec. 1862, *Destruction of Slavery*, p. 231.

65. J. M. Marshall and Henry Clay to Gen. N. P. Bank, 22 Dec. 1862, *Destruction of Slavery*, p. 235.

CHAPTER 2

1. *Statutes at Large*, vol. 12, pp. 1268–69.

2. Adj't. Pleas. Smith to A.A.G. J. Thompson, 8 Jan. 1863, *Destruction of Slavery*, p. 300.

3. *Destruction of Slavery*, p. 300n.

4. *Destruction of Slavery*, p. 88n.

5. Mil. Gov. Edw. Stanly to Major Genl. Foster, 20 Jan. 1863, *Destruction of Slavery*, pp. 87–88.

6. Brig. Gen. Wm. Sooy Smith to Lieut. Col. Binmore, 27 Mar. 1863, *Destruction of Slavery*, p. 303.

7. Circular, 24 Apr. 1863, *Destruction of Slavery*, p. 244.

8. Genl. in Chf. H. W. Halleck to Major Genl. U. S. Grant, 31 Mar. 1863, *Black Military Experience*, pp. 143–44.

9. Affidavit of Amy Moore, [14? Aug. 1865], *Destruction of Slavery*, p. 567. For legal papers regarding the arrest and sale of Moore and her family, see *Destruction of Slavery*, pp. 568–70.

10. F. W. Kellogg to Maj. Gen'l. Burnside, 4 May 1863, *Destruction of Slavery*, pp. 577–78.

11. *Destruction of Slavery*, pp. 573–74.

12. *Destruction of Slavery*, pp. 591–92.

13. Testimony of Capt. C. B. Wilder before the American Freedmen's Inquiry Commission, 9 May 1863, *Destruction of Slavery*, pp. 88–90.

14. H. Styles, "Report Dick Robinsons Plantation," 18 Aug. 1863, *Wartime Genesis: Lower South*, p. 460.

15. Capt. Geo. G. Davis to Brig. Gen. James Bowen, 21 Aug. 1863, *Black Military Experience*, p. 157.

16. Affidavit of Archy Vaughn, 13 Sept. 1865, *Destruction of Slavery*, p. 323.

17. Maj. Gen. S. R. Curtis to General, 13 Mar. 1864, *Destruction of Slavery*, pp. 480–81.

18. Brig. Genl. Edwd. A. Wild to Maj. Robert S. Davis, 12 May 1864, *Destruction of Slavery*, pp. 95–97.

19. Statement of Mrs. Laura A. Moody, 25 May 1864, *Destruction of Slavery*, pp. 379–80.

20. Brig. Gen'l. E. B. Tyler to Lieut. Col. S. B. Lawrence, 15 June 1864, *Destruction of Slavery*, pp. 380–81.

21. *Destruction of Slavery*, pp. 381, 381n.

22. John Q. A. Dennis to Hon. Stan, 26 July 1864, *Destruction of Slavery*, p. 386.

23. Brig. Gen. Edwd. A. Wild to Brig. Gen. G. F. Shepley, 1 Sept. 1864, *Destruction of Slavery*, pp. 98–99.

24. Testimony of Nancy Johnson before the Southern Claims Commission, [22 Mar. 1873], *Destruction of Slavery*, pp. 150–54.

25. *Destruction of Slavery*, p. 154n.

26. Governor John Milton to Hon. James A. Seddon, 17 Feb. 1863, *Destruction of Slavery*, pp. 746–47.

27. O. G. Eiland to President Davis, 20 July 1863, *Black Military Experience*, pp. 284–85.

28. *Black Military Experience*, pp. 285–86.

29. W. C. Bibb to Hon. James A. Seddon, 23 July 1863, *Destruction of Slavery*, pp. 704–5.

30. *Destruction of Slavery*, p. 705.

31. R. L. Abernethy to Hon. Mr. Benjamin, 4 Aug. 1863, *Destruction of Slavery*, pp. 763–64.

32. Maj. Wm. H. Echols to Brigr. Genl. Thomas Jordan, 25 Aug. 1863, *Destruction of Slavery*, pp. 802–3.

33. Wm. Harris and C. T. Rembert to Sir, 24 Aug. 1863, *Destruction of Slavery*, p. 803.

34. *Destruction of Slavery*, p. 803n.

35. Lt. Gen. E. Kirby Smith to Maj. Genl. Price, 4 Sept. 1863, *Destruction of Slavery*, p. 772. The same letter was sent to General Richard Taylor.

36. Jon'a. Pearce to Honl. Jas. A. Seddon, 3 Nov. 1863, *Destruction of Slavery*, pp. 775–76.

37. *Destruction of Slavery*, p. 776.

38. Jere Pearsall to Prest. Davis, 25 Nov. 1863, *Destruction of Slavery*, pp. 94–95.

39. *Destruction of Slavery*, p. 95n.

40. Capt. Samuel E. Hope to Capt. W. Call, 8 Sept. 1863, *Destruction of Slavery*, pp. 805–6.

41. Wyndham Robertson to Hon. James A. Seddon, 13 Jan. 1864, *Destruction of Slavery*, pp. 778–79.

42. Wm. N. Harris et al. to his Excellency Jefferson Davis, 6 May 1864, *Destruction of Slavery*, pp. 756–58.

43. F. Kendall to Mr.
President, 16 Sept. 1864,
Black Military Experience,
pp. 286–87.
44. Wm. D. Taylor et al. to His
Excellency Jefferson
Davis, 13 Oct. 1864,
Destruction of Slavery,
pp. 807–8.
45. *Destruction of Slavery*,
p. 808n.
46. Testimony of Alonzo
Jackson before the
Southern Claims
Commission, 17 Mar.
1873, *Destruction of
Slavery*, pp. 813–18.
47. Capt. Alured Larke and
Capt. R. H. Day to the
Provost Marshal, 7 Dec.
1864, *Destruction of
Slavery*, pp. 809–10.
48. Resolutions of the 18th Va.
Infantry, 20 Feb. 1865,
Black Military Experience,
pp. 297–98.
49. Robert F. Durden,
*The Gray and the Black:
The Confederaie Debate
on Emancipation* (Baton
Rouge, La., 1972),
chaps. 8–9.

CHAPTER 3
1. General Orders No. 34,
Head Quarters Dept. of
Va. &c, 1 Nov. 1861,
*Wartime Genesis: Upper
South*, doc. 2.
2. Lewis C. Lockwood to
Hon. Senator Wilson, 29
Jan. 1862, *Wartime
Genesis: Upper South*,
doc. 3.
3. For the report, see
*Wartime Genesis: Upper
South*, doc. 4; for Wool's
action on its
recommendations, doc. 4n.
4. Brig. Genl. T. W. Sherman
to Genl. L. Thomas, 15
Dec. 1861, *Wartime
Genesis: Lower South*,
pp. 118–19.
5. Vincent Colyer to Hon.
Rob. Dale Owen (American
Freedmen's Inquiry
Commission), 25 May
1863, *Wartime Genesis:
Upper South*, doc. 7.

6. Capt. Alfred F. Sears to
Brig. Gen. Jos. G. Totten,
12 Aug. 1862, *Wartime
Genesis: Lower South*,
pp. 211–12.
7. Samuel Sawyer et al. to
Maj. Gen. Curtis, 29 Dec.
1862, *Wartime Genesis:
Lower South*, pp. 675–76.
8. Lieut. Charles L. Stevens
to Lieut. J. H. Metcalf, 27
Jan. 1863, *Wartime
Genesis: Lower South*,
pp. 410–12.
9. *Wartime Genesis: Lower
South*, p. 412.
10. *Wartime Genesis: Lower
South*, pp. 684–86.
11. Chaplain John Eaton, Jr.,
to Lt. Col. Jno. A.
Rawlins, 29 Apr. 1863,
*Wartime Genesis: Lower
South*, pp. 684–97.
Interrogatory numbers and
italicized place names
appearing in the margin of
the manuscript have been
inserted into the body of
the text.
12. *Wartime Genesis: Upper
South*, doc. 19.
13. Asa Prescott to Hon. E. M.
Stanton, 11 July 1863,
*Wartime Genesis: Upper
South*, doc. 20.
14. *Wartime Genesis: Upper
South*, doc. 20n.
15. Capt. E. E. Camp to Brig.
Genl. D. H. Rucker, 31
July 1863, *Wartime
Genesis: Upper South*,
doc. 65A.
16. *Wartime Genesis: Upper
South*, doc. 65B.
17. Colord labours of
Alexandria va Commissary
Dept to Honorble
Secretary Stanton, 31
Aug. 1863, *Wartime
Genesis: Upper South*,
doc. 66.
18. Rober Henry et al. to Maj.
Genl. B. F. Butler, 20
Nov. 1863, *Wartime
Genesis: Upper South*,
doc. 25.
19. Testimony of Robert
Houston before the
Southern Claims
Commission, 6 June 1873,

*Wartime Genesis: Lower
South*, pp. 737–38.
20. *Wartime Genesis: Lower
South*, p. 739n.
21. Testimony of Mrs. Louisa
Jane Barker, [Jan.?
1864], *Wartime Genesis:
Upper South*, doc. 68.
22. A. W. Harlan to Maj. W.
G. Sargent, 5 Feb. 1864,
*Wartime Genesis: Lower
South*, pp. 786–89.
23. Order, Health Office,
Natchez, Miss., 19 Mar.
1864, *Wartime Genesis:
Lower South*, pp. 814–15.
24. *Wartime Genesis: Lower
South*, pp. 815–16.
25. Clipping from an
unidentified [Iowa]
newspaper, 5 May [1864],
*Wartime Genesis: Lower
South*, pp. 817–18.
26. *Wartime Genesis: Lower
South*, pp. 819n.
27. Chaplain A. B. Randall to
Brig. Genl. L. Thomas, 28
Feb. 1865, *Black Military
Experience*, p. 712.
28. Roanoke Island N.C. to
Mr. President, 9 Mar.
1865, *Wartime Genesis:
Upper South*, doc. 47A.
29. Roanoke Island to
[Secretary of War], 9 Mar.
1865, *Wartime Genesis:
Upper South*, doc. 47A.
30. Sergt. Richard Etheredge
and Wm. Benson to Genl.
Howard, [May or June
1865], *Black Military
Experience*, pp. 729–30.
31. Statement of Anna Irwin,
[27 Feb. 1866], *Wartime
Genesis: Upper South*,
doc. 124.
32. *Wartime Genesis: Upper
South*, doc. 124n.

CHAPTER 4
1. E. S. Philbrick to Ned
[Edward Atkinson],
12 Apr. 1862, *Wartime
Genesis: Lower South*,
pp. 182–88.
2. Agreement between the
planters of St. Bernard
and Plaquemines parishes
and the United States,

[late Oct.? 1862], *Wartime Genesis: Lower South,* pp. 383–85.

3. J. A. Pickens to Major General Banks, 5 Jan. 1863, *Wartime Genesis: Lower South,* pp. 405–7.

4. *Wartime Genesis: Lower South,* p. 407n.

5. Henry Norvall et al. to Brig. Gen'l Bowen, 5 Apr. 1863, *Wartime Genesis: Lower South,* pp. 438–39.

6. Statement of Col. Charles C. Nott, 5 Apr. 1863, *Wartime Genesis: Lower South,* p. 439.

7. *Wartime Genesis: Lower South,* pp. 439–40n.

8. Edw. S. Philbrick to Robert Dale Owen et al. (American Freedmen's Inquiry Commission), 17 Aug. 1863, *Wartime Genesis: Lower South,* pp. 255–59.

9. Testimony of Samuel Larkin before the Southern Claims Commission, 9 Feb. 1872, *Wartime Genesis: Upper South,* doc. 97.

10. *Wartime Genesis: Upper South,* doc. 97n.

11. Brig. Genl. John P. Hawkins to Brig. Genl. J. A. Rawlins, 9 Oct. 1863, *Wartime Genesis: Lower South,* p. 725.

12. *Wartime Genesis: Lower South,* p. 726.

13. *Wartime Genesis: Lower South,* p. 735n.

14. Major Julian E. Bryant to Captain, 10 Oct. 1863, *Wartime Genesis: Lower South,* pp. 728–34.

15. Endorsement of Brig. Genl. John P. Hawkins, 14 Oct. 1863, *Wartime Genesis: Lower South,* pp. 734–35.

16. Testimony of Hon. F. W. Bird before the American Freedmen's Inquiry Commission, [24 Dec. 1863], *Wartime Genesis: Upper South,* doc. 28.

17. Fannie to My dearest Ma, 12 Jan. [1864], *Wartime Genesis: Lower South,* pp. 489–91.

18. [William Bosson], memorandum on terms of employment, [Jan. 1864], *Wartime Genesis: Upper South,* doc. 107.

19. John H. Major et al. to his Exelency Abraham Lincoln, 1 Mar. 1864, *Wartime Genesis: Lower South,* pp. 297–99.

20. Col. Saml. Thomas to Brig. Genl. L. Thomas, 15 June 1864, *Wartime Genesis: Lower South,* pp. 834–41.

21. A. S. Hitchcock to Col. Hall, 25 Aug. 1864, *Wartime Genesis: Lower South,* pp. 316–17.

22. *Wartime Genesis: Lower South,* pp. 317–20, 321n.

23. Testimony of Alfred Scruggs before the Southern Claims Commission, [31 July 1872], *Wartime Genesis: Upper South,* doc. 112.

24. *Wartime Genesis: Upper South,* doc. 112n.

25. Clipping from *New-York Daily Tribune,* [13 Feb. 1865], *Wartime Genesis: Lower South,* pp. 332–37.

26. *Wartime Genesis: Lower South,* pp. 338–40.

27. James H. Ingraham and Dr. A. W. Lewis to Major General S. A. Hurlburt, 21 Mar. 1865, *Wartime Genesis: Lower South,* pp. 594–96.

28. M.G. Comd'g. S. A. Hurlbut to James H. Ingraham and Dr. A. W. Lewis, 23 Mar. 1865, *Wartime Genesis: Lower South,* pp. 596–98.

29. Affidavit of Joseph Abernathy and Hustin Abernathy, 19 June 1865, *Wartime Genesis: Upper South,* doc. 125.

30. *Wartime Genesis: Upper South,* doc. 125n.

31. William French to Brig. Genl. Clinton B. Fisk, 8 Aug. 1865, *Wartime Genesis: Upper South,* doc. 127.

CHAPTER 5

1. Circular, Head Quarters First Separate Brigade, 8th Army Corps, 30 Mar. 1863, *Destruction of Slavery,* pp. 371–72.

2. *Black Military Experience,* pp. 199–200n.

3. Colonel William Birney to Lt. Col. Wm. H. Chesebrough, 27 July 1863, *Black Military Experience,* pp. 198–99.

4. William T. Chambers to Hon. Edwin M. Stanton, 22 Aug. 1863, *Black Military Experience,* pp. 205–6.

5. *Black Military Experience,* p. 206n.

6. Colonel William Birney to Capt. C. W. Foster, 26 Aug. 1863, *Black Military Experience,* pp. 206–7.

7. Writ for apprehension of John Singer, 18 Aug. 1863, *Black Military Experience,* p. 207.

8. A. W. Bradford to Hon. M. Blair, 11 Sept. 1863, *Black Military Experience,* pp. 208–10.

9. *Black Military Experience,* p. 215n.

10. Thos. Claggett Jr. et al. to Hon. Reverdy Johnson, 28 Oct. 1863, *Black Military Experience,* pp. 213–14.

11. Endorsement by Colonel William Birney, 8 Nov. 1863, *Black Military Experience,* pp. 214–15.

12. Endorsement by Brig. General Wm. Birney, 28 Jan. 1864, *Black Military Experience,* p. 215.

13. Col. S. M. Bowman to Lt. Col. Lawrence, 11 May 1864, *Black Military Experience,* pp. 222–23.

14. Annie Davis to Mr. president, 25 Aug. 1864, *Destruction of Slavery,* p. 384.

15. *Destruction of Slavery,* pp. 441–44.

16. John F. Ryland et al. to His Excellency Governor Gamble, 4 June 1863,

Destruction of Slavery, pp. 457–58.

17. E. P. Cayce to Mr. M. P. Cayce, 19 June 1863, *Black Military Experience*, pp. 226–27.

18. *Black Military Experience*, p. 228.

19. M. P. Cayce to Maj. Gen. Schofield, 31 July 1863, *Destruction of Slavery*, p. 460.

20. *Destruction of Slavery*, p. 592.

21. Affidavit of Fanny Ann Flood, 7 Mar. 1866, *Destruction of Slavery*, pp. 587–89.

22. *Destruction of Slavery*, pp. 589–91.

23. *Black Military Experience*, p. 188.

24. Affidavit of Aaron Mitchell, 4 Jan. 1864, *Black Military Experience*, pp. 237–38.

25. *Black Military Experience*, p. 238n.

26. Ann to My Dear Husband, 19 Jan. 1864, *Black Military Experience*, pp. 686–87.

27. 1st Lieut. William P. Deming to Brig. Genl. Pile, 1 Feb. 1864, *Black Military Experience*, pp. 242–43.

28. Wm. Fuller et al. to Major General W. S. Rosecrans, [Feb. 1864], *Black Military Experience*, pp. 238–40.

29. *Black Military Experience*, pp. 248–49.

30. *Black Military Experience*, p. 250n.

31. Robert Bailey Jnr. et al. to Maj. Genl. Rosencrantz, 13 Feb. 1864, *Black Military Experience*, p. 250.

32. Capt. Hiram Cornell to Col. J. P. Sanderson, 28 Mar. 1864, *Black Military Experience*, p. 688.

33. *Black Military Experience*, p. 688n.

34. Captain B. H. Wilson to Col. J. P. Sanderson, 15

Apr. 1864, *Wartime Genesis: Upper South*, doc. 184.

35. *Wartime Genesis: Upper South*, doc. 184.

36. *Wartime Genesis: Upper South*, doc. 186.

37. Lieut. J. M. Gavin to Capt. R. L. Ferguson, 3 Aug. 1864, *Black Military Experience*, pp. 250–51.

38. Thos. B. Davis to Hon. J. Lanox Bond, 6 Nov. 1864, *Wartime Genesis: Upper South*, doc. 141.

39. Wm. A. Willyams to Major Wm. M. Este, 11 Nov. 1864, *Wartime Genesis: Upper South*, doc. 144.

40. Statement of Jane Kamper, 14 Nov. 1864, *Wartime Genesis: Upper South*, doc. 146.

41. *Wartime Genesis: Upper South*, doc. 148.

42. Brigadier-General Henry H. Lockwood to Lieut. Col. S. B. Lawrence, 15 Dec. 1864, *Wartime Genesis: Upper South*, doc. 154.

43. Affidavit of Danl. Chase, 24 Aug. 1865, *Wartime Genesis: Upper South*, doc. 158B.

44. Joseph Hall to General Howard or those having charge of freedmen at Washington D.C., 14 Sept. 1865, *Wartime Genesis: Upper South*, doc. 159A.

45. Col. John F. Tyler to Col. J. H. Baker, 12 Jan. 1865, *Wartime Genesis: Upper South*, doc. 192.

46. Wm. N. Burch to Cpt. Wm. H. Hogarth, 24 Jan. 1865, *Wartime Genesis: Upper South*, doc. 156B.

47. *Wartime Genesis: Upper South*, doc. 156An.

48. *Wartime Genesis: Upper South*, doc. 195.

49. J. H. Lathrop to Gen. Clinton B. Fisk, 8 Mar. 1865, *Wartime Genesis: Upper South*, doc. 196.

50. *Destruction of Slavery*, p. 489.

51. James Martin to Mr.

Campbell, [spring? 1865], *Wartime Genesis: Upper South*, doc. 198.

52. Hervey McElrey et al. to his Excellency Gov. Bramlette, 24 Feb. 1864, *Destruction of Slavery*, pp. 595–96.

53. *Destruction of Slavery*, p. 597.

54. J. L. Seaton to Hon. Lush. Anderson, Feb. 1864, *Black Military Experience*, p. 255. The local post commander and five citizens appended their signatures to the letter, with statements of concurrence in its sentiments.

55. Captain Jams. M. Fidler, historical report, [15 June 1865], *Black Military Experience*, pp. 256–59.

56. *Black Military Experience*, pp. 193–94.

57. Affidavit of John Burnside, 15 Dec. 1864, *Wartime Genesis: Upper South*, doc. 225C.

58. Affidavit of Abisha Schofield, 16 Dec. 1864, *Black Military Experience*, pp. 715–16.

59. H. C. Lilly to Hon. W. H. Randall, 5 Dec. 1864, *Black Military Experience*, p. 271.

60. Affidavit of Charles Green, 30 May 1865, *Black Military Experience*, p. 274.

61. *Black Military Experience*, p. 275.

62. Affidavit of Patsey Leach, 25 Mar. 1865, *Black Military Experience*, pp. 268–69.

63. I. N. Steele to Bt. Brig. Gen. J. S. Brisbin, 1 Apr. 1865, *Destruction of Slavery*, p. 616.

64. *Destruction of Slavery*, pp. 617–18.

65. Lieut. Col. W. A. Gage to Maj. Genl. J. M. Palmer, 25 Apr. 1865, *Black Military Experience*, p. 277.

66. *Destruction of Slavery*, p. 619n.

67. Major General John M. Palmer to Judge Geo. W. Johnston, 3 June 1865, *Destruction of Slavery*, pp. 622–23.

68. Chas. A. Roxborough et al. to Mr. President, [late June, 1865], *Destruction of Slavery*, pp. 624–26.

69. C. Graham, M.D. to Hon. Andrew Johnson, 24 July 1865, *Destruction of Slavery*, pp. 626–31.

70. Lieut. Col. H. A. McCaleb to Messrs. Steel, Kane and Judd, 11 Sept. 1865, *Wartime Genesis: Upper South*, doc. 239.

71. Kean, Steele & Co. to Lt. Col. H. A. McCalebs, 11 Sept. 1865, *Wartime Genesis: Upper South*, doc. 239.

72. *Wartime Genesis: Upper South*, doc. 239n.

73. *Destruction of Slavery*, pp. 656–57.

74. Major General John M. Palmer to B. F. Bullen, 22 Aug. 1865, *Destruction of Slavery*, pp. 639–41.

75. Capt. F. B. Clark to Lieut. E. T. Lamberton, 15 Nov. 1865, *Black Military Experience*, pp. 750–51.

76. Endorsement of Maj. Genl. John M. Palmer, 30 Nov. 1865, *Black Military Experience*, p. 751.

77. *Black Military Experience*, p. 751n.

CHAPTER 6

1. *Statutes at Large*, vol. 12, pp. 1268–69.

2. John A. Andrew to George T. Downing, 23 Mar. 1863, *Black Military Experience*, pp. 88–89.

3. Adolph J. Gla et al. to Majr. Genl. N. P. Banks, 7 Apr. 1863, *Black Military Experience*, p. 329.

4. Capt. Elias D. Strunke to Brig. Genl. D. Ullman, 29 May 1863, *Black Military Experience*, pp. 528–29.

5. Brig. Genl. Elias S. Dennis to Colonel John A. Rawlins, 12 June 1863, *Black Military Experience*, pp. 532–34.

6. *Black Military Experience*, p. 518.

7. Testimony of Nathaniel Paige before the American Freedmen's Inquiry Commission, [Feb.? 1864], *Black Military Experience*, pp. 534–36.

8. U.S. War Department, *The War of the Rebellion: A Compilation of the Official Records of the Union and Confederate Armies*, 128 vols. (Washington, 1880–1901), ser. 2, vol. 5, p. 797.

9. Major Gen. D. Hunter to Jefferson Davis, 23 Apr. 1863, *Black Military Experience*, pp. 573–74.

10. Hannah Johnson to Hon. Mr. Lincoln, 31 July 1863, *Black Military Experience*, pp. 582–83.

11. Recruitment broadside, [1863], *Black Military Experience*, p. 103.

12. Statement of A Colored man, [Sept.? 1863], *Black Military Experience*, pp. 153–56.

13. Statement of one of the union Colored friends, [Sept.? 1863], *Black Military Experience*, pp. 156–57.

14. Col. James C. Beecher to Brig. Genl. Edward A. Wild, 13 Sept. 1863, *Black Military Experience*, p. 493.

15. *Black Military Experience*, p. 494.

16. *Black Military Experience*, pp. 500–501.

17. *Statutes at Large*, vol. 12, pp. 597–600.

18. Corporal James Henry Gooding to Abraham Lincoln, 28 Sept. 1863, *Black Military Experience*, pp. 385–86.

19. Martha to My Dear Husband [Richard Glover], 30 Dec. 1863,

Black Military Experience, p. 244.

20. *Black Military Experience*, pp. 245–46.

21. Theodore Hodgkins to Hon. E. M. Stanton, 18 Apr. 1864, *Black Military Experience*, pp. 587–88.

22. James M. McPherson, *Battle Cry of Freedom: The Civil War Era* (New York, 1988), p. 794.

23. Wm. J. Brown to Honourable Secretary of War, 27 Apr. 1864, *Black Military Experience*, pp. 377–78.

24. Acting Chaplain Garland H. White to Hon. Wm. H. Seward, 18 May 1864, *Black Military Experience*, pp. 348–49.

25. Ruphus Wright to dear wife, 25 May 1864, *Black Military Experience*, p. 663.

26. Adjutant General L. Thomas to Hon. H. Wilson, 30 May 1864, *Black Military Experience*, pp. 530–31.

27. Sergt. John F. Shorter et al. to the President of the United States, 16 July 1864, *Black Military Experience*, pp. 401–2.

28. *Statutes at Large*, vol. 13, pp. 129–30.

29. George Rodgers et al. to Mr. President, [Aug.] 1864, *Black Military Experience*, pp. 680–81.

30. Unsigned to My Dear Friend and x Pre., [Aug.] 1864, *Black Military Experience*, pp. 501–2.

31. G. H. Freeman to Madam, 19 Aug. 1864, *Black Military Experience*, "pp. 600–601.

32. [Private Spotswood Rice] to My Children, [3 Sept. 1864], *Black Military Experience*, p. 689.

33. Spotswood Rice to Kittey diggs, [3 Sept. 1864], *Black Military Experience*, p. 690.

34. 1st Sargt. Wm. D. Mayo to the Honerable Abrham

Lincon, 7 Oct. 1864, *Black Military Experience,* pp. 452–53.

35. *Black Military Experience,* p. 454n.

36. Warren D. Hamelton to Hon. E. M. Stanton, May 1865, *Black Military Experience,* p. 384.

37. Samuel Roosa to Abraham Lincoln, 24 Jan. 1864 [1865], *Black Military Experience,* pp. 477–79.

38. *Black Military Experience,* p. 479.

39. Col. James S. Brisbin to Brig. Gen. L. Thomas, 20 Oct. 1864, *Black Military Experience,* pp. 557–58.

40. [Jane Welcome] to abarham lincon, 21 Nov. 1864, *Black Military Experience,* p. 664.

41. *Black Military Experience,* p. 665n.

42. Affidavit of Joseph Miller, 26 Nov. 1864, *Black Military Experience,* pp. 269–71.

43. George Washington to Mr. Abrham Lincoln, 4 Dec. 1864, *Destruction of Slavery,* p. 608.

44. 1st Sgt. Joseph J. Harris to Gen. Ullman, 27 Dec. 1864, *Black Military Experience,* pp. 691–92.

45. Unidentified newspaper clipping of Andrew Tait et al. to the Union Convention of Tennessee, 9 Jan. 1865, *Black Military Experience,* pp. 811–16.

46. Private Aaron Oats to Hon. Ed. M. Stanton, 26 Jan. 1865, *Black Military Experience,* pp. 692–93.

47. Lucrethia to Dar husban [Aaron Oats], 22 Dec. 1864, *Black Military Experience,* p. 693.

48. [Jerry Smith] to Aaron Utz, 10 Jan. 1865, *Black Military Experience,* pp. 693–94.

49. Chaplain C. W. Buckley to Lt. Austin R. Mills, 1 Feb. 1865, *Black Military Experience,* pp. 623–24.

50. Affidavit of William Jones, 29 Mar. 1865, *Black Military Experience,* p. 276.

51. Simon Prisby to Honerable E. M. Staunton, 20 July 1865, *Black Military Experience,* pp. 424–25.

52. Sergt. E. S. Robison to Major General Q. A. Gilmore, 7 Aug. 1865, *Black Military Experience,* p. 742.

53. Statement by Sergt. Joe Brown, [11 Sept.] 1865, *Black Military Experience,* pp. 743–44.

54. Unsigned to Mr. Edwin M. Stanton, 2 Oct. 1865, *Black Military Experience,* pp. 654–55.

55. 1st Sergeant John Sweeny to Brigadier General Fisk, 8 Oct. 1865, *Black Military Experience,* p. 615.

56. *Black Military Experience,* p. 615n.

57. Regtl. Orders No. 137, Head Quarters 108" U.S.C.I., 25 Oct. 1865, *Black Military Experience,* p. 749.

58. E. G. Baker to Messrs. Irby & Ellis & Mosely, 22 Oct. 1865, *Black Military Experience,* pp. 747–49.

59. *Black Military Experience,* p. 749n.

60. Privt. Calvin Holly to Major General O. O. Howard, 16 Dec. 1865, *Black Military Experience,* pp. 754–56.

61. Emily Waters to My Dear Husband, 16 July 1865, *Black Military Experience,* p. 698.

62. 2nd Lieut. Hugh P. Beach to Mr. Thomas W. Conway, 1 Aug. 1865, *Black Military Experience,* pp. 699–700.

63. Unsigned to Mr. E. M. Santon, 22 Aug. 1865, *Black Military Experience,* pp. 773–74.

64. George Buck Hanon to Genel thoms, 19 Nov. 1865, *Black Military Experience,* p. 713.

65. Col. F. W. Lister to Brigr. Genl. W. D. Whipple, 14 Dec. 1865, *Black Military Experience,* pp. 713–15.

66. Unsigned to Sir, Dec. 1865, *Black Military Experience,* pp. 725–27.

67. Unsigned to General Sickels, 13 Jan. 1866, *Black Military Experience,* pp. 777–78.

68. Affidavit of Roda Ann Childs, 25 Sept. 1866, *Black Military Experience,* p. 807.

69. Sargint Wm. White et al. to Dear President, 3 July 1866, *Black Military Experience,* pp. 763–64.

suggestions for

FURTHER READING

Few events have been subjected to such close inspection as the American Civil War. A small but growing proportion of the resulting scholarship deals with emancipation and its consequences. This brief guide provides a point of entry, focusing on books that are readily available in bookstores and libraries; those available in paperback are preceded by an asterisk.

Anyone interested in the transformation of slaves into free people must, sooner or later, turn to W. E. B. Du Bois's monumental *Black Reconstruction in America: An Essay toward a History of the Part Which Black Folk Played in the Attempt to Reconstruct Democracy in America, 1860–1880* (1935). Although superseded in many particulars by more than a half century of research, it remains the seedbed of modern scholarship. One of the first historians to place black people at the center of the war for the Union was Benjamin Quarles; his *The Negro in the Civil War* (1953) is still a good place to begin.

The words of black people—slave and free—are interwoven with thoughtful commentary by James M. McPherson in *The Negro's Civil War: How American Negroes Felt and Acted during the War for the Union* (1965). *The Destruction of Slavery*, ed. Ira Berlin, Barbara J. Fields, Thavolia Glymph, Joseph P. Reidy, and Leslie S. Rowland (1985), which is series 1, volume 1 of *Freedom: A Documentary History of Emancipation, 1861–1867*, uses documents and interpretive essays to demonstrate that slaves were the agents of their own emancipation. Leon F. Litwack, *Been in the Storm So Long: The Aftermath of Slavery* (1979), is a richly textured portrayal of the ways in which slaves attained and gave meaning to their freedom during and after the war. Two recent surveys, James M. McPherson's crisply written *Battle Cry of Freedom: The Civil War Era* (1988) and Eric Foner's magisterial *Reconstruction: America's Unfinished Revolution, 1863–1877* (1988), incorporate the best recent scholarship on emancipation and add insights of their own. The authors of the present volume offer a brief treatment of wartime emancipation in *Slaves No More: Three Essays on Emancipation and the Civil War* (1992).

John Hope Franklin, *The Emancipation Proclamation* (1963), considers the legal and political context of emancipation. Constitutional as well as political questions are skillfully analyzed in Herman Belz, *A New Birth of Freedom: The Republican Party and Freedmen's Rights, 1861–1866* (1976).

Historians have given special attention to the role of black soldiers. Dudley Taylor Cornish, *The Sable Arm: Negro Troops in the Union Army, 1861–1865* (1956), outlines the story, and Joseph T. Glatthaar, *Forged in Battle: The Civil War Alliance of Black Soldiers and White Officers* (1990), considers the soldiers' relationship with their officers. *The Black Military Experience*, ed. Ira Berlin, Joseph P. Reidy, and Leslie S. Rowland (1982), series 2 of *Freedom: A Documentary History of Emanci-*

pation, presents documents by and about black soldiers, along with interpretive essays. Among the most articulate soldiers was James Henry Gooding of Massachusetts, whose letters to his hometown newspaper have been collected in *On the Altar of Freedom: A Black Soldier's Civil War Letters from the Front*, ed. Virginia Matzke Adams (1991). The soldiers may also be viewed through the eyes of one of their most enthusiastic and perceptive officers in Thomas Wentworth Higginson's classic memoir, *Army Life in a Black Regiment* (1870; reprint, 1984).

Less has been written about black people who did not wear a Union uniform. A groundbreaking attempt to depict the lives of slaves and freedpeople within both Union and Confederate lines is Bell I. Wiley's *Southern Negroes, 1861–1865* (1938; revised, 1953). Louis S. Gerteis, *From Contraband to Freedman: Federal Policy toward Southern Blacks, 1861–1865* (1973), critically examines federal labor and welfare measures in the Union-occupied South. Documents and interpretive essays about the former slaves' wartime experiences within Union lines are presented in *The Wartime Genesis of Free Labor: The Lower South*, ed. Ira Berlin, Thavolia Glymph, Steven F. Miller, Joseph P. Reidy, Leslie S. Rowland, and Julie Saville (1990), and *The Wartime Genesis of Free Labor: The Upper South*, ed. Ira Berlin, Steven F. Miller, Joseph P. Reidy, and Leslie S. Rowland (forthcoming, 1993)—series 1, volumes 2 and 3 of *Freedom: A Documentary History of Emancipation*. For a unique account by a slave who escaped to Union lines and subsequently served as laundress, teacher, and nurse with a regiment of black soldiers, see Susie King Taylor, *Reminiscences of My Life in Camp with the 33d United States Colored Troops, Late 1st S.C. Volunteers* (1902), reprinted as *A Black Woman's Civil War Memoirs*, ed. Patricia W. Romero and Willie Lee Rose (1988).

Much can be learned about former slaves within Union lines from the military officers who supervised them and from the teachers, clergymen, and other Northerners who ministered to them. John Eaton, *Grant, Lincoln and the Freedmen: Reminiscences of the Civil War, with Special Reference to the Work for the Contrabands and Freedmen of the Mississippi Valley* (1907; reprint, 1969), is an example of the former. Examples of the latter include Elizabeth Ware Pearson, ed., *Letters from Port Royal Written at the Time of the Civil War* (1906; reprint, 1969); Rupert Sargent Holland, ed., *Letters and Diary of Laura M. Towne Written from the Sea Islands of South Carolina, 1862–1884* (1912); Elizabeth Hyde Botume, *First Days amongst the Contrabands* (1893; reprint, 1968); and Henry L. Swint, ed., *Dear Ones at Home: Letters from Contraband Camps* (1966).

The events that transformed slaves into freedpeople were equally wrenching for their owners and other white Southerners. James L. Roark, *Masters without Slaves: Southern Planters in the Civil War and Reconstruction* (1977), views the death of the master class with sensitivity but without sentimentality. The effect of the deterioration of slavery and other wartime events on civilian morale in the Confederacy is an important theme of Paul D. Escott, *After Secession: Jefferson Davis and the Failure of Confederate Nationalism* (1978). Documents pertaining to the Confederate debate over the status of black people, including the eleventh-hour attempt to enlist black men into the rebel army, are presented in Robert F. Durden, *The Gray and the Black: The Confederate Debate on Emancipation* (1972). The interaction among former slaveholders, former slaves, and Yankee entrepreneurs eager to spread the gospel of free labor is examined with wit and insight in Lawrence N. Powell, *New Masters: Northern Planters during the Civil War and Reconstruction* (1980).

The best studies of emancipation in particular states and localities offer insights that transcend their geographical bounds. In a class by itself is Willie Lee Rose, *Rehearsal for Reconstruction: The Port Royal Experiment* (1964), a history that reads like a novel. Emancipation and free labor under Union military supervision are the subjects of C. Peter Ripley, *Slaves and Freedmen in Civil War Louisiana* (1976). Clarence L. Mohr, **On the Threshold of Freedom: Masters and Slaves in Civil War Georgia* (1986), considers the collapse of slavery in a state that remained largely behind Confederate lines, and Wayne K. Durrill, *War of Another Kind: A Southern Community in the Great Rebellion* (1990), examines a section of North Carolina that lay in the no-man's-land between the two belligerents. A model study of the tortuous road to freedom in one of the Union's own slave states is Barbara Jeanne Fields, **Slavery and Freedom on the Middle Ground: Maryland during the Nineteenth Century* (1985).

Northern abolitionists, black and white, had a special perspective on emancipation in the South. A standard work that has held up well is James M. McPherson, *The Struggle for Equality: Abolitionists and the Negro in the Civil War and Reconstruction* (1964). An impressive five-volume collection of documents by black abolitionists has been edited by C. Peter Ripley, Roy E. Finkenbine, Michael F. Hembree, Donald Yacovone, and others; the final volume of *The Black Abolitionist Papers* (1992) concerns the Civil War years. The writings of two black Northerners who traveled south during the war are also revealing: **Thomas Morris Chester, Black Civil War Correspondent: His Dispatches from the Virginia Front*, ed. R. J. M. Blackett (1989), and **The Journal of Charlotte Forten: A Free Negro in the Slave Era*, ed. Ray Allen Billington (1953; reprint, 1981).

INDEX

Abernathy, Hustin: affidavit of, 326–28
Abernathy, Joseph: affidavit of, 326–28
Abernathy, Thomas E., 326–28
Abernethy, R. L.: letter from, 136–37
Agricultural labor, 278–86, 294–305; composition of work force, 248, 258–59, 272–77, 279, 282–83, 296; discipline of, 240, 246–47, 249, 253–54, 260–64, 273, 296–97; disrupted by black enlistment, 349, 352–54; federal policy on, 241–42; hours of work, 253; and law of slavery, 252–54, 368, 402–3; military policy on, 251–54, 294–95, 305–7, 322–24; military policy on, criticized by free blacks, 319–22; military policy on, criticized by Union general, 277–78; organization of, 259–64; privately

negotiated arrangements, 289–90, 308–9, 325–30, 368–69, 384, 398; privately negotiated arrangements, disrupted by apprenticeship, 374, 376–78; supervised by Northern abolitionists, 242–51; Treasury policy on, 240; wages for, 244, 253, 263, 273, 276, 280, 290, 302–3, 326–28; *see also* Agricultural laborers; Overseers; Planters; Slavery
Agricultural laborers, 235, 260–64, 268–86, 290–305, 325–31; abused by employers, 257, 293; attacks on, 268, 275–76, 368; and black soldiers, 254–57, 520–21; education of, 251, 263–64, 269, 271, 275; medical care of, 272; nonpayment of, 276; and overseers, 287–89; as quasi soldiers, 286; taxation of, 321n., 324; threatened by guerrillas, 382–85; and Union soldiers, 249–50;

see also Agricultural labor; Slaves
Alabama: agricultural labor in, 308–9; black soldiers in, 530–33; destitution and relief in, 148–51; former slaves from, reenslaved in Kentucky, 103–7; fugitive slaves in, 44–45; impressment of slaves in, 148–51; land in, occupied by former slaves, 308–9; military laborers in, 230; nonslaveholder in, advocates Confederate enlistment of black soldiers, 4; refugeeing to, 133; slaveholder in, advocates impressment of slaves for military labor, 134–35; slavery in, undermined by Union occupation, 308; slaves in, expect freedom, 4; *see also* Huntsville AL
Alexandria VA: former slaves near, 239; military laborers in, 206–8, 232
Alexandria VA, free blacks in:

letter from, 207–8

Alfred (fugitive slave): murdered by order of owner, 359–60

Allen, Charles A.: letter from, 438

Allen, Rindy M. See Smothers, Derinda

American Freedmen's Inquiry Commission, xxxi; letters to, 175–78, 260–64; testimony before, 51–52, 107–10, 279–86, 445–47

American Missionary Association, 395

Amos (Mr.): holds former slaves in bondage, 372–73

Anderson, Lucien: letter to, 388–89

Andrew, John A., 469; letters from, 19–20, 436–37; pledges equal treatment of black soldiers, 436–37

Anonymous (black civilian): statements by, 453–58

Anonymous (black soldiers): letters from, 477–79, 515–17, 528–29, 533–36

Anonymous (former slaves): letters from, 222–27

Anonymous (white soldier): letter from, 20–21

Antietam MD: battle at, xxx, 71

Apprenticeship, 370–71, 373–78; military policy on, 374–75

Arkansas: black soldiers in, 221–22; emancipation in, by state constitution, xxxii; enlistment of black soldiers in, 214–15; families of black soldiers in, 214–15; former slaves from, reenslaved in Kentucky, 105–7; land in, occupied by former slaves, 214–16; relief in, 215; see also Helena AR; Mississippi Valley

Arlington VA: contraband camp at, 238

Armstead, Anthony, 202

Army, U.S. See Black soldiers; Enlistment of black soldiers; Volunteers, U.S.; name of particular officer

Article of War (1862), xxix, 35–36, 334, 386

Asboth, Alexander S.: letter to, 27–29

Atkins, Smith D.: letters from, 74–75, 80–81; newspaper story about, 76–79; policy on fugitive slaves, 74–81

Atkinson, Edward, 242; letter to, 243–51

Augur, Christopher C.: orders eviction of former slaves, 213

Auguste (slave), 72–73

Baggs, David, 124–26

Bailey, Robert, Jr.: petition from, 366

Baker, E. G.: letter from, 519–22; seeks removal of black soldiers, 519–22

Baker, J. H.: letter to, 378–79

Baker, Wiley, 521

Banks, Nathaniel P., 325, 456; free blacks criticize labor policy of, 319–22; letters to, 84–85, 255–56, 438; policy on black officers, 437–38; and recruitment of black soldiers, 101

Barker, Louisa Jane: testimony by, 212–14

Barteau, Clark R., 97

Bayne, John H.: letter from, 31–33

Beach, Hugh P.: letter from, 526–28; protests abuse of black soldiers' families, 526–28

Beaufort NC: fugitive slaves in, 175; military laborers in, 208–9

Beaufort SC: marketing in, by former slaves, 237

Beauregard, P. G. T.: prohibits contact between Confederate soldiers and slave military laborers, 139

Beecher, James C.: letter from, 459–60; protests discriminatory treatment of black soldiers, 459–60

Bell, George, 207–8

Bell, John, 500

Benjamin, Judah P.: letter to, 136–37

Benson, William: letter from, 228–29

Bentley, William, 311

Bermuda Hundred VA: military laborers near, 235

Berry, Samuel H.: letter from, 345–46

Bibb, W. C.: letter from, 134–35

Big Black River MS: battle at, 472

Binmore, Henry: letter to, 99

Bird, Francis W.: testimony by, 279–86

Birney, William, 121; endorsements by, 346–48; enlists black soldiers, 336–38; letters from, 336–41; liberates jailed slaves, 336–38

Bishop, John S.: order by, 519

Bisland, Fannie A.: letter from, 287–89

Bissell, Evelyn L., 230

Black officers. See Black soldiers, as commissioned officers

Black soldiers, 56–59, 84, 425–32; and agricultural laborers, 254–57, 520–21; animosity of white Southerners toward, 514–15, 519–22, 536–37; attacked by policemen, 514–15; camp life of, 479; in combat, xxxi, 431, 439–47, 470–73, 479–80, 489–92, 496; as commissioned officers, 437–38, 468–70; discipline and punishment of, 483, 486–88, 513, 529–33; discriminatory treatment of, 436, 453–63, 467–68, 473–74, 476–79, 485, 516–17, 534, 538–39; education of, 432, 436, 487, 508, 518–19; federal policy on, 436–37; and former slaveholders, 422–24; and former slaves, 94, 513–14, 518–25; as garrison forces, 472; health of, 459, 477–79, 515–17; jailed by civil authorities, 422–24; as laborers, 459–60, 468, 477–79; as liberators, 93, 111–12, 122–23, 431, 435–36, 480–82, 496; marriages of, 221–22, 430, 509; medical care of, 476; and military justice,

482–89; military policy on duties of, 460; motivations of, 438, 453–58, 462–63, 474, 480–82, 510, 515–16, 518, 528–530, 535, 538; nonpayment of, 229, 475–78; number enlisted, 435; in postwar army of occupation, 511–36, 538–59; as prisoners of war, xxx–xxxii, 446–52, 465–67, 491; protest treatment of families by Union authorities, 533–35; religion of, 480–81, 508, 512; seek discharge to care for families, 533–36; significance of, to black community, 436, 456, 497, 499, 501–4; and slaveholders, 480–82, 507; struggle for equal pay, 461–63, 467–68, 473–75; as veterans, 429, 536; wages of, xxxii, 460–63, 467–68, 471, 473–75, 478, 485, 487; and white officers, 454–56, 460, 483, 512–17, 529–33, 538; and white soldiers, 489–91; see also Enlistment of black soldiers; Families of black soldiers; Native Guard (Louisiana); Volunteers,U.S.

Blair, Montgomery, 345; letter to, 341–44

Bolivar TN: contraband camp at, 186–200; military laborers at, 192

Boller, Thornton: letter from, 257–58

Bond, Hugh L.: letter to, 370–72

Bonner, William, 329–30

Border states, 6, 12–13, 46; black soldiers from, 510; families of black soldiers in, 463; fugitive slaves in, 333; Lincoln urges gradual emancipation in, xxix–xxx, 47–48; not subject to Emancipation Proclamation, 95, 333; reject gradual emancipation, xxix; slavery in, undermined by black enlistment, 333; see also Kentucky; Maryland; Missouri

Bosson, William: memorandum by, 290

Boston, Elizabeth: letter to, 29–30

Boston, John: letter from, 29–30

Bowen, James: letters to, 111–12, 257–58

Bowman, Samuel M.: letter from, 348–49

Boyd, A. M., 210

Boyle, Richard: letters from, 222–27

Bradford, Augustus W.: letter from, 341–44

Bradwell, Charles, 311

Bramlette, Thomas E.: letter to, 386–87

Bright, Edward, 202

Bright, Philip, 202

Brisbin, James S.: letter from, 489–92; letter to, 402

Briscoe, Grandison: affidavit of, 42–43

Brooks, William: protests abuse of family, 362

Brown, Aaron V., 500

Brown, Joe: statement by, 514–15

Brown, Orlando, 282, 284, 286

Brown, William J.: letter from, 467–68; protests unequal pay, 467–68

Bryant, Julian E., 268; letter from, 269–77

Buckhanon, George: letter from, 530–31; protests treatment of black soldiers' wives, 530–31

Buckley, C. W.: letter from, 508–10

Bull Run VA: battle at, xxviii, 11

Bullen, B. F.: letter to, 418–22

Burbridge, Stephen G.: policy on enlisting black soldiers, 389–90, 393

Burch, William N.: letter from, 379–82

Burden, Eldridge: letter from, 350–52

Bureau of Colored Troops, xxxi, 492; letter to, 508–10

Bureau of Free Labor (Louisiana), 321

Bureau of Refugees, Freedmen, and Abandoned Lands. See Freedmen's Bureau

Burke, Abraham, 312

Burnside, Ambrose E., 513; letter from, 34–35; letter to, 105–6; policy on fugitive slaves, 32, 34–45; policy on military labor, 175; voids reenslavement of former slaves, 107

Burnside, John: affidavit of, 394–95

Butler, Benjamin F., 51, 224; leasing policy of, 254; letter from, 9–10; letters to, 49–50, 208–9; policy on agricultural labor, 251–54; policy on enlisting black soldiers, xxx, 437; policy on fugitive slaves, xxviii, 8–11; policy on military labor, 8–10; relief policy of, 8–10; slavery policy of, 254

Butler, William F.: petition from, 406–8

Cairo IL: contraband camp at, 186–200; military laborers at, 191

Cameron, Simon, 57–58; advocates emancipation and enlistment of black soldiers, xxviii, 26n.; letters to, 15–20, 26–27; policy on fugitive slaves, 10; slavery policy of, 21

Camp, E. E.: letter from, 204–6

Camp Nelson KY: contraband camp at, 393–97, 413, 493–95; enlistment of black soldiers at, 510–11; families of black soldiers evicted from, 393–97, 493–95; free papers issued at, 409, 411, 413; military laborers at, 394

Camp Parapet LA: fugitive slaves at, 48–52

Campbell, (Mr.) (landowner): letter to, 385

Campbell, (Mr.) (plantation lessee), 276

Campbell, William J., 310

Carney, James A.: endorsement by, 361

Carroll, N. W., 204–6

Carroll, William, 500

Carter, Hannibal, 255–57

Cayce, E. P.: letter from, 353–54

Cayce, M. P.: letter from, 354–55; letter to, 353–54

Central America: emigration to, 38–41

Chamberlin, Jason: murders fugitive slave, 357–59; removes slaves from Missouri to Kentucky, 356–57

Chambers, William T.: advocates enlistment of slaves, 338–39; letter from, 338–39

Charleston SC: black soldiers in, 93; German immigrants in, assist Union prisoners, 161–63; slaves and free blacks in, assist Union prisoners, 161–63; union association in, 163

Chase, Daniel: affidavit of, 375–76

Cheatham, John J.: letter from, 5

Chesebrough, William H.: letter to, 336–38

Childs, Roda Ann: affidavit of, 537–38; rape of, 537–38

Chiles, Henry C.: letter from, 350–52

Choctow (Union gunboat), 442–43

Ciles, Bartlet, 113

Clagett, Thomas, Jr.: letter from, 345–46

Clark, F. B.: letter from, 422–23

Clark, Shelby: letter from, 345–46

Clay, Henry: letter from, 85

Clopton, William H.: whipped by former slaves, 115–16

Coburn, Carrie, 451

Cold Harbor VA: military laborers at, 234

Colonization abroad: advocated by free blacks, 38–42; congressional policy on, xxix, 38; presidential policy on, xxix–xxx

Colored troops. See Black soldiers; Enlistment of black soldiers; Native Guard

(Louisiana); Volunteers, U.S.

Columbia MO: health in, 383

Colyer, Vincent, 174; letter from, 175–78

Confiscation acts: 1861 act, xxviii, 11, 19; 1862 act, xxix–xxx, 59–60, 67, 76, 180, 334, 350, 386

Congress, C.S.A.: conscription policy of, xxx; policy on enlisting black soldiers, xxxiii, 165

Congress, U.S., 59; colonization policy of, xxix, 38; emancipation policy of, xxviii–xxx, xxxii–xxxiii, 11, 38, 39n., 48, 59–60, 400, 402, 510; Joint Committee on the Conduct of the War, 220; land policy of, xxix–xxx, 331; petitions to, 37–41; policy on enlisting black soldiers, 60, 317, 333; policy on families of black soldiers, xxxiii, 400, 510; policy on fugitive slaves, xxviii–xxx, 35–36; policy on military labor, xxx, 60; policy on wages of black soldiers, xxxii, 475; questions Hunter's enlistment of black soldiers, 56–57; Senate Committee on Military Affairs, 471; slavery policy of, xxviii, 6

Conscription (Confederate): congressional policy on, xxx; proposal to exempt overseers from, 130–32

Contraband camps, 185–200, 210, 222–29, 237–38, 268–72, 280–81, 393–97, 413; education in, 192–93, 225–26; guarded by former slaves, 190, 199–200; housing in, 187; labor in, 191–92, 196–97, 224, 226, 270–71, 394–95; medical care in, 188–89, 271; religion in, 197; residents of, abused by Union soldiers, 190–91, 226; residents of, evicted by Union authorities, 393–97, 493–95; see also Relief

Contraband relief societies. See Freedmen's aid societies

Contrabands. See Agricultural laborers; Contraband camps; Fugitive slaves;

Military laborers; Urban laborers

Conway, Thomas W., 321, 325; letter to, 526–27

Corinth MS: contraband camp at, 186–200; fugitive slaves at, 96–97; military laborers at, 191

Cornell, Hiram: letter from, 367

Cox, John, 310

Cox, Samuel: murders recaptured fugitive slave, 11–12

Cozzens, Samuel W.: labor regulations by, 240

Craig, Newton, 510–11

Craney Island VA: contraband camp on, 280–81; impressment of military laborers on, 201

Creager, J. P.: arrested for recruiting black soldiers, 340

Curtis, Samuel R.: emancipation policy of, 350–52; letter from, 113–15; letter to, 180–82

Davis, Annie: letter from, 349

Davis Bend MS, 298–99

Davis, George G.: letter from, 111–12

Davis, Gibberty, 280–81

Davis, Jefferson, xxvii, xxxiii, 90, 133, 135; letters to, 4, 132–33, 142–43, 148–54, 448–49; policy on black prisoners of war, xxx, 447, 465; proposes enlistment of black soldiers, 164

Davis, Robert S.: letter to, 115–16

Davis, Thomas B.: letter from, 370–72

Day, Robert H.: letter from, 161–64

Delmotte, Adolphus, 312–13

Deming, William P., 361; letter from, 362

Dennis, Elias S.: describes battle at Milliken's Bend LA, 441–44; letter from, 441–44

Dennis, John Q. A.: letter from, 120–21

Dent, Lewis, 276
Deweese, Alexander & Smith (plantation lessees), 277
Diggs, Kittey, 480–81; letter to, 481–82
Direct Tax Act (1862), xxix; land sales under, 290–93
District of Columbia: black soldiers in, 432; emancipation in, 335–36, 338, 348; emancipation in, by federal law, xxix, 37–38; free blacks in, 38–42; fugitive slaves in, 36, 42; military labor in, 200; military laborers in, 204–6
Dix, John A.: policy on fugitive slaves, 32; slavery policy of, 16
Dodge, Grenville M., 190
Doubleday, Abner: policy on fugitive slaves, 36
Douglass, Charles R.: photograph of, 427
Douglass, Frederick, 427
Douglass, Lewis H.: photograph of, 426
Dove, W. T., 37–38
Dow, Neal: issues free papers to slaves, 71–73
Downing, George T.: letter to, 436–37
Du Pont, Samuel F.: letter to, 52–56
Duke & Hotchkiss (plantation lessees), 274
Dunham, John, 274
Dunlop, Robert P.: letter from, 31–33
Dutch Gap VA: military laborers at, 228–29
Duvall, George W.: letter from, 31–33

Eaton, John, Jr., 186; letter from, 186–200
Echols, William H.: letter from, 137–39; letter to, 138–39
Edenton NC: military laborers liberate slaves in, 98
Edisto Island SC: agricultural laborers on, 235
Education: of black soldiers, 432, 436, 487, 508, 518–19; in contraband camps, 192–93, 225–26; desire of

former slaves for, 121, 213; of former slaves, 167–68, 177, 284–85, 519, 526; on plantations, 251, 263–64, 269, 271, 275
Eiland, O. G.: letter from, 132–33
Elliot, Samuel: testimony by, 60–61
Ellis, (Mr.) (Mississippi legislator): letter to, 519–22
Emancipation politics, xxviii–xxxiii, 3–4, 152n., 348, 352, 369, 397–98, 410, 413–14, 422, 497–505; former slaves' understanding of, 313–17; see also Reconstruction politics
Emancipation Proclamation, xxx–xxxi, 4, 71, 75, 84–85, 94–97, 103, 107, 109, 333, 450–51, 488, 497; and enlistment of black soldiers, 435–36; not applicable to border states, 95, 106, 352; parts of Confederacy exempted from, xxxi, 95, 98–100, 453
Emigration. See Colonization abroad; Migration
Enlistment of black soldiers, xxxi–xxxii, 111–12, 139–40, 145–46, 210–11, 316–17, 347–48, 352–54, 362–65, 369, 383, 386–93, 400–401, 435, 437–38, 510; Confederate policy on, 448; congressional policy on, 60, 317, 333; federal policy on, 101–3; by impressment, 214–15, 348–49, 398–99; military policy on, xxviii–xxxii, 26n., 56–59, 335–38, 345, 362–65, 389–91, 393, 400; obstructed by civil officials, 339–41, 510–11; opposition to, by slaveholding unionists, 341–47; opposition to, within Union army, 392; presidential policy on, xxxi, 345; recruitment broadside for, 452; support for, by black men, 435; support for, by black religious leaders, 314, 316–17; support for, by nonslaveholders, 338–39, 388–89, 391, 397–98;

support for, in Northern states, 67–68; support for, within Union army, 198–200; see also Black soldiers; Families of black soldiers; Volunteers, U.S.
Enlistment of black soldiers (Confederate): advocated by Jefferson Davis, 164; advocated by nonslaveholder, 4; advocated by Robert E. Lee, 164; advocated by slaveholders, 5, 132–34, 151–52; congressional policy on, xxxiii, 165; proposal to conscript free blacks, 135–37; support for, in Confederate army, 164–65
Essex, Thomas: letter from, 257–58
Este, William M.: letter to, 372–73
Etheredge, Richard: letter from, 228–29

Families of black soldiers, 112, 214–15, 348, 363–65, 429–30, 470, 479–80, 496, 505–7; abused by former owners, 525–28; abused by slaveholders, 360–62, 364–67, 400–401, 463–64, 495; abused by Union soldiers, 229; abused by white Southerners, 536–38; condition of, after Civil War, 525–29, 533–36, 538–39; employers of, sued by slaveholders, 402–3; evicted by employers, 257; evicted by former owners, 525–28; evicted by Union authorities, 219, 393–97, 493–95; freed by joint resolution of Congress, xxxiii, 400, 510; held as slaves after Civil War, 422–24; military policy on, 227–29, 362–66, 393–97, 400, 403, 493–95, 509; and soldiers' pay, 463, 473, 475–76, 484–85, 487–88, 492, 495; treatment of, by Union authorities, 224–29, 530–33
Families of military laborers, 42–43, 97–98, 117–20, 122–23, 171–72, 201–3,

209, 281; evicted by Union authorities, 212–14; treatment of, by Union authorities, 181

Family life of former slaves: assessed by Northerners, 198, 285

Ferguson, R. L.: letter to, 369

Feris, J. C. H.: letter from, 219–20

Fidler, James M.: report by, 389–93

Fisk, Clinton B., 418; circular by, 331; letters to, 329–31, 383–85, 518

Fleming, Thomas W.: letter from, 61–66

Flood, Fanny Ann: affidavit of, 356–58

Flood, Peter: murdered by owner, 357–59

Florida: fugitive slaves in, 144–45; governor of, 130–32; Hunter declares emancipation in, xxix, 46–47; land in, set apart for former slaves, xxxiii, 318; see also Fort Barrancas FL; Fort Clinch FL; Fort Jefferson FL

Forman, Jacob G., 182; letter from, 180–82

Forrest, Nathan B., 472–73; and massacre of captured black soldiers, xxxii, 465–66

Fort Albany VA: settlement of former slaves near, 212–14

Fort Barrancas FL: prisoner at, 483–84

Fort Clinch FL: fugitive slaves at, 179; military labor at, 178–80

Fort Jefferson FL: prisoners at, 485–89

Fort Pillow TN: battle at, 473; massacre at, xxxii, 465–67

Fort Sumter SC: attack on, xxviii

Fort Wagner SC: battle at, xxxi, 431, 439, 444–47, 449–50

Fortress Monroe VA: fugitive slaves at, xxviii, 8–11, 88, 107–10; military labor at, 168–72; relief at, 168–69

Foster, Charles W.: letter to, 339–41

Foster, Ephraim H., 500

Foster, John G.: letter to, 98; policy on fugitive slaves, 32

Frazier, Garrison, 312; answers questions on slavery and freedom, 313–18

Free blacks, 310–13; assist Union prisoners, 161–63; in Confederacy, 135–37, 157–58; and Confederate soldiers, 157; criticize military policy on agricultural labor, 319–22; emigration of, from United States, 38, 40n.; enlistment of, 336, 338–41; families of, attacks on, 340; impressment of, as military laborers, 202–3; Northern, 18–19, 450–51; protest taxation, 207–8; seek to enlist in Union army, 18–19; as soldiers, xxx, 437–38, 461–63, 467–68, 473, 475, 485, 486–89, 512–13; support colonization, 38–42; as voters before Civil War, 488, 499–500, 504

Freedman's Village VA, 238

Freedmen's aid societies, 168, 177n., 186; agents of, 218–20

Freedmen's Bureau, xxxiii, 230, 331n., 416–18, 422, 518–19, 522, 526–28, 536; oversees labor settlement, 328

Freeman, G. H.: letter from, 479–80

Freeman, J. B.: letter from, 153–54

Frémont, John C.: emancipation order by, xxviii, 46

French, William: letter from, 329–31

Fripp, Washington, 247

Fugitive slaves, 8–11, 13–15, 26–27, 29–30, 35, 60–66, 68–71, 73–79, 86–91, 93, 152–54, 167, 179, 247, 251–52, 279, 333, 350, 354–55, 413; attacked by slaveholders, 122–23; bands of, in woods and swamps, 51–52, 144–45; captured by Confederate soldiers,

96–97; Confederate policy on, 96–97; congressional policy on, xxviii–xxx, 35–36, 59–60; criticism of military policy on, 26–27; employed by Confederate soldiers, 43–44; executed by Confederate authorities, 156–57; execution of, proposed by slaveholders, 61–66; federal policy on, 19, 180, 334; as guides and spies, 36, 105–6, 176, 334–35; as liberators, 96–98, 107–10, 113–15; military policy on, xxviii, 8–11, 13–15, 17–18, 27–29, 31–32, 36, 44–46, 48–49, 68–71, 75–78, 80–81, 99–100, 168, 182, 334–35, 350–52; military policy on, criticized by Northern missionary, 170–72; ownership of personal property by, 266–67; patterns of flight of, 98–99, 107–10; punishment of, 11–12, 42–43, 112–15, 357–60, 365, 390–92; pursued by Confederate soldiers, 144–45; pursued by owners, 15–16, 30, 74, 76–81, 142–43; reenslavement of, 103–7; return to owner, 507; returned to owners, 7–8, 11–12, 19–21, 28–29, 109–10, 511; and Union soldiers, 12, 15–16, 30–34, 44–45, 79–80, 82–83, 102, 180–82, 351; values of, assessed by Northerners, 193–98; whip former owner, 115–16; see also Slaves

Fuller, William: petition from, 362–65

Gage, W. A.: letter from, 403

Gaines, William, 311

Gamble, Hamilton R., 350, 354; letter to, 350–52

Gannett, William C., 243, 248, 250

Gant, Virgil: hires out apprentices, 375–76

Gantt, Thomas T.: letter from, 6–7; letter to, 7–8

Garrar, Francis, 202

Gavin, J. M.: letter from, 369

Georgia: black soldiers from, 425; families of black soldiers in, 537–38; free blacks in, 310–13; fugitive slaves in, 60–66, 89, 156–57; Hunter declares emancipation in, xxix, 46–47; land in, set apart for former slaves, xxxiii, 318; military laborers in, 229–30; refugeeing to, 133; slaveholders in, advocate Confederate enlistment of black soldiers, 5, 133–34, 151–52; slaveholders in, fear slave insurrection, 5; slavery in, 123–29; slaves in, assist Confederate deserters, 124; slaves in, assist Union prisoners, 124; slaves in, expect freedom, 5; *see also* Savannah GA

German immigrants: assist Union prisoners, 161–63

Gettysburg PA: battle at, xxxi, 132

Gibbons, Charles W.: letter from, 438

Gillmore, Quincy A., 75; doubts abilities of black soldiers, 444–46; letter to, 514; policy on fugitive slaves, 78

Gla, Adolph J.: letter from, 438

Glenn, John: impresses black soldier, 399

Glover, Martha: letter from, 464

Glover, Richard: letter to, 464

Godfrey, Jacob, 313

Gooding, James H.: letter from, 461–63; protests unequal pay, 461–63

Goodrich, Luther, 257–58

Gordon, George H., 445

Graham, C.: letter from, 408–16

Grand Junction TN: contraband camp at, 186–200; military laborers at, 191–92

Granger, Gordon, 75, 81; letter to, 79–80; policy on fugitive slaves, 76–77

Grant, Ulysses S., 186, 191; letter to, 101–3

Green, Charles: affidavit of, 399

Green, E. H., 399

Green, J. W., 274

Grey, (Mr.) (overseer), 287–89

Grundy, Felix, 500

Hadley, Job, 192

Hadlock, William E., 211

Hail, Wilson, 417–18

Haiti, 521; emigration to, 38–40

Haitian Emigration Bureau, 40n.

Hale, H., 417–18

Hall, James F.: letter to, 305–7

Hall, Joseph: letter from, 376–78

Halleck, Henry W.: letter from, 101–3; letter to, 67–68; order by, 17–18; policy on fugitive slaves, 17–18, 27–29, 32

Halstead, Eminel P.: letter from, 36

Hamelton, Warren D.: appeals court–martial conviction, 485–86; letter from, 485–86

Hammond (Hammend), Edward: letter from, 31–33

Hampton VA: agricultural labor near, 279–82; contraband camp at, 237, 281; impressment of military laborers in, 201–3

Hardenberg, John, 230

Hardin, Jacob: imprisoned for hiring out as a free man, 404–5

Hardin, William: letter from, 438

Harlan, A. W.: letter from, 214–16

Harney, William S.: letter from, 7–8; letter to, 6–7; slavery policy of, 6n., 7–8

Harris, Alexander, 312

Harris, Joseph J.: letter from, 496; requests liberation of family, 496

Harris, William: letter from, 138–39

Harris, William N.: letter from, 148–51

Harrison, Henry: letter from, 153–54

Hatteras Inlet NC: fugitive slaves at, 175

Hawkins, John P.: criticizes federal policy on plantation leasing and agricultural labor, 277–78; endorsement by, 277–78; letter from, 267–68; policy on personal property, 266–68

Hawley, James A., 299

Hayes, Charles, 272

Health: of black soldiers, 459, 477–79, 515–17; in cities, 216–17, 383; *see also* Medical care

Helen, Eli: and education of former slaves, 519

Helena AR, 210–11; fugitive slaves at, 180–82; military laborers at, 181

Henry, Rober: letter from, 208–9

Hergremather, Louis: writ by, 341

Herring, Jack, 282–83

Hicks, Thomas H.: letter from, 15–17

Hill, James, 311

Hill, William B.: letter from, 345–46

Hinks, Edward W., 116; letter to, 115–16

Hitchcock, A. S.: labor proposals by, 305–7; letter from, 305–7

Hodgkin, Thomas: letter from, 345–46

Hodgkins, Theodore: advocates retaliation for Confederate abuse of black prisoners of war, 465–66; letter from, 465–66

Hogarth, William H.: letter to, 379–82

Holloway, Carl, 202

Holly, Calvin: letter from, 523–25; protests treatment of former slaves in Mississippi, 523–25

Holly Springs MS: contraband camp at, 187–200

Holt, Joseph, 382, 412

Hood, Emily, 77–78

Hope, Joseph, 202

Hope, Miles, 202

Hope, Samuel E.: letter from, 144–45

Hope, Willson, 202

House of Representatives, U.S. *See* Congress, U.S.

Housing: in cities, 177, 216–17; in contraband camps, 187; of military laborers, 183–84; in shantytowns, 214

Houston, Robert, 209, 212; testimony by, 210–11

Houston, Samuel, 500

Houston, Ulysses L., 311

Howard, Charles H.: letter from, 11–12

Howard, John, 327

Howard, Joseph W.: letter from, 438

Howard, Oliver O., 528; letters to, 228–29, 376–78, 523–25

Howle, James D.: letter from, 153–54

Hugus, Jacob, 215

Humphrey, (army surgeon), 188

Humphrey, John: threatens to evict black soldiers' families, 525–28

Humphrey, L., 192

Humphreys, Benjamin G., 522

Humphries, Milly, 230

Hunter, David, 179; condemned as outlaw by Confederate authorities, 448; emancipation order by, xxix, 46–47; letters from, 56–59, 448–49; policy on black prisoners of war, 448–49; policy on enlisting black soldiers, xxix, 56–59; threatens retaliation for Confederate abuse of black prisoners of war, 448–49

Hunton, Thomas: letter to, 68–71

Huntsville AL, 265

Hurlbut, Stephen A.: defends policy on agricultural labor, 322–25; free blacks criticize labor policy of, 319–22; letter from, 322–25; letter to, 319–22; policy on agricultural labor, 324; relief policy of, 321n., 324

Hutchinson's Island SC: former slaves on, attacked by Confederate soldiers, 52–56

Indiana: enlistment of black soldiers in, 391

Ingall, Pearl P.: letter from, 180–82

Ingraham, James H.: letter from, 319–22; letter to, 322–25

Ingram, Joseph: and education of former slaves, 519

Iowa: governor of, 67–68

Irby, (Mr.) (Mississippi legislator): letter to, 519–22

Irwin, Anna: statement of, 230

Irwin, Laura, 230

Island 76 (Mississippi River): contraband camp on, 210

Jackson, Alonzo: testimony by, 154–61

Jackson, Andrew, 438, 500

Jackson TN: contraband camp at, 186

Jacob, Richard T., 390, 392

James, Horace: policies of, criticized by former slaves, 222–29; relief policy of, 225–26

James, Thomas: petition from, 406–8

Jefferson, Thomas, 449

Johnson, Andrew, xxxiii, 405; letters to, 408–16, 538–39; petition to, 406–8

Johnson, Cave, 500

Johnson, Hannah: advocates retaliation for Confederate abuse of black prisoners of war, 450–51; letter from, 450–51

Johnson, Hillary, 422, 424

Johnson, John, 313

Johnson, Nancy: testimony by, 124–29

Johnson, Octave: testimony by, 51–52

Johnson, R. M.: petition from, 406–8

Johnson, Reverdy, 466; letter to, 345–46

Johnson, Stewart, 230

Johnson, William R., 202

Johnston, George W.: letter to, 404–5

Jones, (Mr.): helps military laborers liberate families, 117–20

Jones, David L., 187

Jones, William, 281

Jones, William: affidavit of, 510–11

Jones, William A.: letter from, 18–19

Jordan, John, 202

Jordan, Thomas: letter to, 137–39

Kamper, Jane: statement of, 373

Kean, Steele & Co. (proprietors of Louisville Hotel): letter from, 417; letter to, 417

Kellogg, Francis W.: letter from, 105–6

Kelly, A. W.: order by, 216–18; policy on urban labor, 216–20

Kendall, F.: letter from, 151–52

Kenner LA: military laborers at, 182–85

Kentucky: black men from, present petition to President Johnson, 405–8; black soldiers from, 407, 505–6, 518, 538–39; black soldiers from, jailed by civil authorities, 422–24; black soldiers in, 467–68; Confederate invasion of, 73; emancipation politics in, 397–98, 410, 413–14, 422; enlistment of black soldiers from, in neighboring states, 386, 391; enlistment of black soldiers in, xxxii, 387–93, 397–400, 510–11; families of black soldiers in, 393–97, 400–403, 422–24, 493–95, 505–7, 538–39; free labor in, obstructed by law of slavery, 402–5, 416–18; fugitive slaves from, 26, 507; fugitive slaves in, 13–15, 73–83, 413; fugitive–slave law of, 103; governor of, 386–87; martial law in, 405–8; military labor in, 13–14, 386–87; Missouri slaves removed to, 355–57; not subject to Emancipation Proclamation, 106; reenslavement of former slaves in, 103–7; slaveholders in, evict families of black soldiers, 493; slaveholders in, evict slaves, 393; slaveholders in, fear slave insurrection, 82–83; slaveholders in, seek forcible enlistment of slaves, 402; slavery in, 13–15, 103–7; slavery in, after Civil War, 403–22; slavery in, undermined by black enlistment, 393, 400; slavery in, undermined by military policies, 408–16; *see also* Border states; Camp Nelson KY; Louisville KY; Paducah KY; Paris KY

Kirkwood, Samuel J.: advocates enlistment of black soldiers, 67–68; letter from, 67–68

Labor. *See* Agricultural labor; Agricultural laborers; Apprenticeship; Contraband camps, labor in; Marketing by former slaves; Military labor; Military laborers; Nonagricultural labor; Slavery; Urban labor; Urban laborers; Wages

LaGrange TN: contraband camp at, 186–200

Lake Providence LA: contraband camp at, 186–200; military laborers at, 192

Lake St. Joseph LA, 299

Lamb, (Mrs.), 329

Lamberton, E. T.: letter to, 422–23

Lancaster, John: letter from, 386–87

Land: aspirations of former slaves for, 282, 284, 290–93, 314, 331, 535–36; conflict over access to, 242; congressional policy on, xxix–xxx, 331; government sales of, 260, 290–93; independent occupation of, by former slaves, 110–11, 173–74, 212–16, 250, 257–59, 275, 279, 294, 297–300, 302, 308–9, 329–31, 379–82; military policy on, xxxiii, 318; presidential policy on, xxxii; Treasury policy on, 242; *see*

also Confiscation acts; Direct Tax Act; Leasing (government–supervised)

Larke, Alured: letter from, 161–64

Larkin, Samuel, 264–66; testimony by, 265–66

Lathrop, J. H.: letter from, 383–85

Laurence, Samuel: letter from, 438

Lawrence, Samuel B.: letters to, 119–20, 348–49, 374–75

Leach, Patsey: affidavit of, 400–401

Leasing (government–supervised), 294–305; and black lessees, 275, 279, 294, 297–99, 302; disrupted by Confederate raids, 268, 274–77, 295–96, 299–301, 304; military policy on, 254, 268–69, 302–4; military policy on, criticized by Union general, 277–78; *see also* Land; Planters, Northern

Leavenworth KS: fugitive slaves in, 113

Ledbetter & Dent (plantation lessees), 276

Lee, Andrew, 514

Lee, J. F.: letter from, 345–46

Lee, Robert E., xxxiii, 238; supports enlistment of black soldiers, 164

Lee, William H.: letter from, 4

Leib, Herman, 441–43

Lewis, A. W.: letter from, 319–22; letter to, 322–25

Lexington (Union gunboat), 443

Liberia, 39–40

Lilly, H. C.: letter from, 397–98

Lincoln, Abraham, xxvii–xxviii, xxxii–xxxiii, 11, 38, 59, 342–43, 379, 405; colonization policy of, xxix–xxx; emancipation policy of, xxix–xxxi, 4, 47–48, 71, 95, 313–18; issues Emancipation Proclamation, xxx–xxxi, 71, 95; land policy of, xxxii; letters to, 82–83, 222–25, 291–94, 349, 450–51,

461–63, 473–79, 483–84, 486–89, 492, 495; overrules Cameron's report on emancipation and black enlistment, xxviii, 26n.; overrules Frémont's emancipation order, xxviii, 46; overrules Hunter's emancipation order, xxix, 46–48; policy on black prisoners of war, xxxi, 447, 450–52, 465–67; policy on enlisting black soldiers, xxxi, 345; proclamation by, 46–48; reconstruction policy of, xxxii; slavery policy of, 3–4, 6; urges gradual emancipation in border states, xxix–xxx, 47–48; *see also* Emancipation Proclamation; Proclamation of Amnesty and Reconstruction

Lister, F. W., 530; letter from, 531–33

Littlefield, H. H., 271

Locke, J. R., 187–88

Lockwood, Henry H., 379; and apprenticeship in Maryland, 374–75; circular by, 334–35; letter from, 374–75; policy on fugitive slaves, 334–35; policy on military labor, 335

Lockwood, Lewis C.: criticizes policy on military labor and relief, 170–72; letter from, 170–72

Long, Alson B.: circular by, 100

Louisiana: agricultural labor in, 240, 251–59, 319–25; agricultural laborers in, 287–89; black soldiers from, 483–86; black soldiers in, 84, 111–12, 430, 435; emancipation in, by state constitution, xxxii; enlistment of black soldiers in, 111–12, 139–40, 437–38; families of black soldiers in, 112, 496, 525–28; free blacks in, 437–38; free papers issued to slaves in, 71–73; fugitive slaves in, 51–52, 251–52; government–supervised leasing in, 254; land in, occupied by former slaves, 110–11, 257–59, 275, 294,

297; part of, exempted from Emancipation Proclamation, xxxi, 95, 99–100, 453; planters in, 251–54, 287–89; refugeeing from, 111, 139–40; slaveholders in, fear slave insurrection, 84–85; slavery in, undermined by black enlistment, 111–12; slavery in, undermined by Union occupation, 49–50, 99–100; slaves in, abandoned by owners, 110–11; slaves in, expect freedom, 84–85; slaves in, liberated by Union soldiers, 49–50; Union occupation of, 251; *see also* Mississippi Valley; *name of particular place*

Louisville (KY) City Court, judge of: letter to, 404–5

Louisville KY: urban labor in, 417–18

Love, Hiram W., 215

Lynch, James R., 313–14, 318

Lynch, Sancho, 275

McCaleb, Hubert A.: letter from, 417; letter to, 417–18

McCann (Irish laborer): mutilates fugitive slaves, 391–92

McClellan, George B., xxxii, 30; policy on fugitive slaves as military laborers, 70n.

McClenny, Nelson: letter from, 257–58

McConner, Clement: writ to, 341

McCook, Alexander McD.: letter from, 13–14; letter to, 15

McCord, D. O., 188

McDougal, Thomas: attempts to liberate family, 422–24

McElrey, Hervey: letter from, 386–87

McKelvey, H. A.: letter from, 219–20

McMeail, (Sergt.): letter from, 538–39

Major, John H.: letter from, 291–94

Mallard, Robert Q.: letter from, 61–66

Mapson, C. C.: letter from, 345–46

Marketing by former slaves, 176, 237, 250, 271, 298, 306

Marshall, J. M.: letter from, 85

Marshall, Sam: attempts to liberate children, 113–15

Martin, James: letter from, 385; objects to settlement by former slaves, 385

Maryland: abuse of former slaves in, 370–73; apprenticeship in, 370–71, 373–78; black soldiers from, 479–80, 515–17; civil officials in, obstruct black enlistment, 339–41; emancipation in, by state constitution, xxxii, 350; emancipation politics in, 348–50; enlistment of black soldiers in, xxxi, 335–49; families of fugitive slaves in, 120–21; families of military laborers in, 117–20; free blacks in, 336, 338–41; fugitive slaves from, 29–30, 42–43, 120–21; fugitive slaves in, 11–12, 15–17, 31–34, 334–35; governor of, 15–17, 120, 341–44; labor arrangements of former slaves in, disrupted by apprenticeship, 374, 376–78; land in, occupied by freedman, 379–82; legislature of, 30–34; nonslaveholders in, support enlistment of slaves, 338–39; reenslavement of former slaves in, 117–20; slaveholders in, seek forcible enlistment of slaves, 348; slavery in, 8, 12–13, 349; *see also* Antietam MD; Border states

Massachusetts: black soldiers from, 426–27, 431; governor of, 436–37; voting by black men in, 504

Mathews, Thomas: letter from, 257–58

May, (Mr.) (plantation guard), 288

Mayhall, Jefferson A., 363–65

Mayo, William D.: appeals court–martial conviction, 483–84; letter from, 483–84

Medical care: of agricultural laborers, 272; of black soldiers, 476; in contraband camps, 188–89, 271; of former slaves, 181; of military laborers, 183–84; *see also* Health

Memphis TN: contraband camp at, 186–200; fugitive slaves in, 68–71; military laborers in, 192; policemen in, attack black soldier, 514–15; Union occupation of, 210

Meninettee, Jerre: petition from, 406–8

Mercer, Hugh W., 66; letter to, 61–66

Metcalf, J. H.: letter to, 183–85

Michigan: black soldier from, 513–14

Migration: of former slaves to Northern states, 104–6; *see also* Colonization abroad; Mobility; Refugeeing

Military labor, 12, 35, 67, 70, 191–92; congressional policy on, xxx, 60; federal policy on, 101–3, 180; military policy on, 8–10, 13–14, 27–29, 68–71, 167–73, 207–8, 335, 386–87; military policy on, criticized by Northern missionary, 170–72; organization of, 178–80; wages for, 168–69, 171–72, 175–76, 178–79, 244, 467–68; *see also* Military labor (Confederate); Military laborers

Military labor (Confederate), 8–11, 129, 137–39; Confederate policy on, 135; impressment of, 44, 148–54, 193, 210; impressment of slaves for, advocated by slaveholder, 134–35; resistance of slaveholders to requisition of slaves for, 137–38, 148–51; servants, 43–44, 60–61

Military laborers, 167–78, 182–85, 210, 228–29, 232–36, 249, 264–65, 316, 386–87, 394; abused by employers, 171–72, 192; attitudes of, toward work, 176–77, 209; in hospitals, 204–6; housing of, 183–84;

impressment of, 200–203, 208–9, 223, 225–27, 386; jailed by civil authorities, 117–20; as liberators, 97–98, 117–20, 122–23; medical care of, 183–84; on naval vessels, 97–98; nonpayment of, 171–72, 192, 201–4, 209, 226–31; servants, 27–28, 76, 80–81, 97–98, 233; taxation of, 206–8; and Union soldiers, 181; *see also* Families of military laborers; Military labor; Military labor (Confederate)

Militia Act (1862), xxx, 59–60, 67, 180, 334; pay provisions of, 252n., 460–61, 467

Miller, George: threatens to abuse black soldier's family, 493

Miller, James: letter to, 74–75

Miller, Joseph: affidavit of, 493–95; protests eviction of family by Union authorities, 493–95

Milliken's Bend LA: battle at, xxxi, 439, 441–44, 472

Mills, Austin R.: letter to, 508–10

Mills, James, 312

Milton, John: advocates exempting overseers from conscription, 130–32; letter from, 130–32

Minor, Henry, 202

Minor, L. H.: letter from, 43–44

Missionaries. *See* American Missionary Association; Freedmen's aid societies

Mississippi: black soldiers in, 519; discriminatory legislation adopted in, 522, 524n.; former slaves from, reenslaved in Kentucky, 105–7; fugitive slaves in, 90, 96–97; land in, occupied by former slaves, 294, 297–99; refugeeing from, 133; refugeeing within, 140–42; slaveholder in, advocates Confederate enlistment of black soldiers, 132–33; treatment of former slaves in, after Civil War, 523–25; *see also* Mississippi Valley; *name of*

particular place

Mississippi Valley: agricultural labor in, 294–305; agricultural laborers in, 268–77, 294–305; black lessees in, 297–99, 302; black soldiers in, 471–73; contraband camps in, 186–200, 268–72; enlistment of black soldiers in, 210–11; fugitive slaves in, 193, 266–67; government–supervised leasing in, 268–77, 294–305; land in, occupied by former slaves, 294, 297–300, 302; nonagricultural labor in, 271; refugeeing in, 193; relief in 270–72; *see also name of particular state or place*

Missouri, 6–9; agricultural labor in, 368–69, 384; attacks on agricultural laborers in, 368; black soldiers from, 528–29; black soldiers in, 480–82; emancipation in, by military order, 46; emancipation in, by state constitutional convention, xxxiii, 369; enlistment of black soldiers in, xxxi, 345–47, 352–54, 359–60, 362–65, 369, 383; families of black soldiers in, 360–65, 367, 464, 480–82; 493; former slaves in, threatened by guerrillas, 382–85; free labor in, obstructed by law of slavery, 368; fugitive slaves from, 113–15; fugitive slaves in, 17–18, 27–29, 350–52, 354–55, 363–65; governor of, 350; gradual emancipation in, 352, 354–55; military laborers in, 27–29; not subject to Emancipation Proclamation, 352; slaveholders in, evict slaves, 378–79; slaveholders in, remove slaves to Kentucky, 355–57, 464; slaveholders in, seek forcible enlistment of slaves, 366; slavery in, undermined by black enlistment, 352, 369; slaves in, removed to Kentucky, 355–57; smallholders in,

object to settlement by former slaves, 385; *see also* Border states; Columbia MO

Missouri State Militia, 363, 367–68; punishes fugitive slave, 113–15

Mitchel, Ormsby M.: policy on fugitive slaves, 44–45; telegram from, 45; telegram to, 45–46

Mitchell, Aaron: affidavit of, 359–60; punished for attempting to enlist, 359–60

Mobility: of agricultural laborers, 302–3; of military laborers, 229–30; military policy on, 305–7, 409n., 421; restrictions upon, 185, 240, 319–20; *see also* Colonization abroad; Migration; Refugeeing

Montague, Robert V., 275

Montague & Clary (plantation lessees), 275–76

Moody, George A.: helps military laborers liberate families, 117–20

Moody, Laura A.: statement of, 117

Moore, Amy: affidavit of, 103–4

Moore, James E.: letter from, 438

Moore, Orlando H.: policy on fugitive slaves, 106

Moore, William: letter from, 438

Morris, Jack: court–martial conviction of, 486–89

Morris, Merrit, 203

Morton, Oliver P., 469

Moscow TN: battle at, 472

Mosely, (Mr.) (Mississippi legislator): letter to, 519–22

Mundy, Marcellus: denounces interference with slaves of unionists, 82–83; letter from, 82–83; policy on fugitive slaves, 106n.

Nashville TN: battle at, 503–4; black residents of, and reconstruction politics, 497–505; labor in, 264–66

Natchez MS: expulsion of former slaves from, 216–20;

freedmen's aid societies in, 218–20; health in, 216–17; housing in, 216–17; urban laborers in, 218–19

Native Guard (Louisiana), xxx, 437–38; 1st, 111–12, 430, 440–41; 3rd, 438

Neal, Andrew, 312

Needham, Thomas, 202

New Bern NC: fugitive slaves in, 35, 89, 175; housing in, 177; military labor in, 35; Union occupation of, 35

New Orleans LA: emancipation celebration in, 85; enlistment of black soldiers in, xxx; free people of color in, 319–23

New York: black soldiers from, 475, 477–79, 486–89; voting by black men in, 488

New–York Daily Tribune, 444; clipping from, 310–18

Newman, (Mr.) (plantation lessee), 272

Nickerson, Frank S., 183, 185

Nobles, William H., 245–46

Nonagricultural labor, 125, 176, 245–46, 248–49, 271, 308–9; domestic servants, 289; fishing, 305–8; military policy on, 305–7; wages for, 215–16; in wood yards, 210–12, 214–16

Nonslaveholders: advocate Confederate enlistment of black soldiers, 4; employ free blacks, 338–39; employ fugitive slaves, 352; fear slave insurrection, 4; object to settlement by former slaves, 385; and slaves, 124; support black enlistment, 388–89, 391, 397–98; support enlistment of slaves, 338–39

Norcom, (Dr.), 183

Norfolk VA: agricultural labor near, 282–84; impressment of military laborers in, 201–3; schools in, 284–85

North Carolina, 200; black soldiers from, 459–60; black soldiers in, 431, 515–17; free blacks in, 136–37; fugitive slaves from, 107–10, 279; military governor of, 97–98; military laborers in, 174–78;

refugeeing to, 133; relief in, 177–78; slavery in, 142–43; unionists and Confederate deserters in, 136; voting by free blacks in, before Civil War, 500; *see also name of particular place*

Northern states: enlistment of black soldiers in, xxxi, 469; free blacks in, 18–19; free–labor ideology in, 21–25, 178, 278, 303–4; migration of former slaves to, 104–6; *see also name of particular state or place*

Norvall, Henry: letter from, 257–58

Nott, Charles C.: statement of, 259

Oats, Aaron: letter from, 505–6; letters to, 506–7; seeks liberation of family, 505–6

Oats, Lucrethia, 507; letter from, 506

Ocean Wave (Union naval vessel), 98

Officers, black. *See* Black soldiers, as commissioned officers

Ohio: free blacks in, 18–19

Okolona MS: education of former slaves in, 519

Overseers, 279, 282–83; and agricultural laborers, 287–89; proposal to exempt, from Confederate conscription, 130–32

Owen, Robert Dale: letters to, 175–78, 260–64

Paducah KY: battle at, 472–73; enlistment of black soldiers at, 388

Page, Edward, Jr., 184–85; letter from, 49–50

Paige, Nathaniel: describes battle at Fort Wagner SC, 445–47; testimony by, 445–47

Palmer, John M., 418, 422; endorsement by, 423–24; letter to, 403; letters from, 404–5, 418–22; policy on enlisting black soldiers, 400; policy on families of black soldiers, 400, 403; policy on

mobility of slaves and former slaves, 409n.

Paris KY: citizens of, seek to expel former slaves, 418–22; mayor of, 418

Parker, George, 203

Parker, Joseph G.: letter from, 438

Patterson, Martin: protests abuse of family, 362

Pearce, Jon'a: letter from, 140–42

Pearsall, Jere: letter from, 142–43

Peebles, Nathaniel R.: letter from, 153–54

Pennsylvania: black soldiers from, 492, 512–13; families of black soldiers in, 492

Phelps, John W., 51, 71; condemned as outlaw by Confederate authorities, 448; critique of slavery by, 21–25; policy on fugitive slaves, 48–49; proclamation by, 21–25

Philbrick, Edward S.: advocates plantation–leasing system, 244; assesses reorganization of agricultural labor, 259–64; land purchases of, 260, 291–92; letters from, 243–51, 260–64; as plantation superintendent, 242–51; reneges on agreement to sell land to former slaves, 290–93

Phips, Nick: abuses freedwoman, 371

Pickens, J. A., 257; letter from, 255–56

Pierce, Edward L., 244, 246, 250

Pile, William A., 361; letter to, 362

Planters, 242, 251–54, 257, 269–70, 287–89, 294–305; Northern, 254–57, 259–64, 268–69, 294–305; *see also* Slaveholders

Plaquemines Parish LA, planters of: agreement with U.S. government, 251–54

Politics. *See* Emancipation politics; Reconstruction politics

Polk, Burr H.: letter to, 80–81

Port Hudson LA: battle at, xxxi, 439–41, 472; Confederate surrender of, xxxi

Porter, James, 312

Prescott, Asa: letter from, 200–203

President, C.S.A. *See* Davis, Jefferson

President, U.S. *See* Lincoln, Abraham

Price, Sterling: letter to, 139–40

Prisby, Simon: letter from, 512–13

Proclamation of Amnesty and Reconstruction, xxxii

Property (personal): military policy on, 266–68, 307–8, 382; ownership of, by former slaves, 188, 211–12, 240, 264–68, 283, 307–9, 330, 379–82; ownership of, by slaves, 123–29, 155–56; seized by Confederate soldiers, 54; seized by pardoned landowner, 379–82; seized by Union soldiers, 123–29, 188, 211–12, 264–68, 307–9; Treasury policy on, 240

Property (real). *See* Land

Pryor, Hubbard: photograph of, 425

Pyatt, Joseph B., 155

Randall, A. B.: letter from, 221–22

Randall, William H.: letter to, 397–98

Randolph, George W.: letter to, 43–44

Ratliff, R. W., 490

Rawlins, John A.: letters to, 186–200, 267–68, 441–44

Reconstruction politics, xxxii–xxxiii, 496–505

Redpath, James, 40n.

Refugeeing, 110–11, 132–33; Confederate policy on, 142; opposed by slaveholders, 146–48; ordered by Confederate authorities, 139–42, 145–48; resisted by slaves, 140–42, 193; spreads demoralization to Confederate interior, 146–47

Relief, 177–78, 185–89, 215, 224–26, 243–44, 270–72; Confederate, 148–51; federal policy on, 241–42; military policy on, 8–10, 167–69, 171–73, 179, 207–8, 225–26, 306–7, 321n., 324; *see also* Contraband camps; Freedmen's aid societies

Religion, 215–16; of black soldiers, 480–81, 508, 512; churches, 168, 177, 310–13; in contraband camps, 197; of former slaves, assessed by Northerners, 197; ministers, 310–13

Rembert, C. T.: letter from, 138–39

Reynolds, William H., 246

Rice, Cora: letter to, 480–81

Rice, Mary, 481–82; letter to, 480–81

Rice, Spotswood: letters from, 480–82; promises to liberate daughters, 480–82; threatens owner of daughter, 481–82

Richards, (Mr.) (carpenter and teacher), 192

Richards, K., 37–38

Richardson, Samuel: forcibly apprentices freed children, 371

Richmond VA, 87

Risby, Thomas, 203

Roanoke Island NC: contraband camp on, 222–29; families of black soldiers on, 224–29; fugitive slaves on, 175–76; military labor on, 226–27; military laborers from, 223, 225–29; relief on, 224–26

Roanoke Island NC, former slaves on: letters from, 222–27

Roberson, Lewis, 203

Robertson, Wyndham: letter from, 146–48

Robinson, Dick: abandons slaves, 110–11

Robison, E. S.: letter from, 514; protests military treatment of former slave, 514

Rodgers, George: letter from, 475–77

Rogers, Charles S.: letter from, 79–80

Roosa, Samuel: appeals court–martial conviction of ex–slave soldier, 486–89; letter from, 486–89

Rosecrans, William S.: letter to, 113–15; petitions to, 362–66; policy on enlisting black soldiers, 359

Rounds, Jefferson: letter from, 257–58

Rowley, Nimrod: letter from, 475–77

Roxborough, Charles A.: petition from, 406–8

Royster, William: threatens slaves, 394

Rucker, Daniel H.: letter to, 204–6

Ryland, John F.: letter from, 350–52

St. Bernard Parish LA, planters of: agreement with U.S. government, 251–54

St. Helena Island SC: agricultural laborers on, 243–50, 290–94; relief on, 243–44

Salisbury, Alfred, 248

Saltville VA: battle at, 489–92

Sampson, Samuel: letter from, 475–77

Sanders, Jacob, 202

Sanderson, John P., 367; letters to, 367–68

Sargent, William G., 187; letter to, 214–16

Sasscer, R. H.: letter from, 345–46

Saunders, Littleton: letter from, 257–58

Savage, Emanuel, 202

Savannah GA: black leaders meet with Sherman and Stanton in, xxxiii, 310–18

Sawyer, Samuel, 182; letter from, 180–82

Saxton, Rufus, 292

Schenck, Robert C.: policy on enlisting black soldiers, 336

Schofield, John M., 350–52; emancipation policy of, 352; letter to, 354–55; policy on enlisting black soldiers, 354, 359

Scofield, Abisha: affidavit of, 395–97
Scott, Patrick: cultivates confiscated land, 379–82
Scott, Winfield: letter to, 9–10
Scroggins, Jack: murdered by owner, 11–12
Scruggs, Alfred: testimony by, 308–9
Scruggs, James H., 308–9
Sea Islands (region). See Edisto Island SC; Hutchinson's Island SC; St. Helena Island SC; South Carolina
Sears, Alfred F.: letter from, 178–80
Seaton, J. L.: letter from, 388–89
Seddon, James A.: letters to, 130–32, 134–35, 140–42, 146–48
Sedgwick, Thomas D., 394
Sellman, John S.: letter from, 31–33
Sells, D. M.: endorsement by, 423
Senate, U.S. See Congress, U.S.
Sergeant, Phil: letter from, 257–58
Seward, William H., 470; letter to, 469–70
Seymour, Horatio, 469
Seymour, Truman, 445, 447
Shanks, John P. C.: letter to, 11–12
Sharkey, William L., 521
Shaul, John D.: letter to, 36
Shaw, Robert G., 446
Shepard, Charles H., 212–13
Shepley, George F.: letters to, 72–73, 122–23
Sherman, Thomas W., 57; letter from, 173–74
Sherman, William T., 123, 151–52; evaluation of, by black religious leaders, 317–18; land policy of, xxxiii, 318; letter to, 13–14; letters from, 15, 68–71; meets with black religious leaders, xxxiii, 310–18; order by, 318; policy on fugitive slaves, 68–71; policy on military labor, 68–71, 387; policy on

personal property, 268
Ship Island MS: Union occupation of, 21
Shorter, John F.: letter from, 473–74
Sickles, Daniel E.: letter to, 535–36
Singer, John: arrested to prevent enlistment, 340–41; writ for apprehension of, 341
Sipple, Thomas: letter from, 475–77
Slaveholders: abandon slaves, 110–11, 193, 329; abuse families of black soldiers, 360–62, 364–66, 367, 400–401, 463–64, 495; abuse former slaves, 373; advocate Confederate enlistment of black soldiers, 5, 132–34, 151–52; advocate execution of fugitive slaves, 61–66; evict families of black soldiers, 493; evict slaves, 72–73, 366–67, 378–79, 393; fear slave insurrection, 4–5, 82–85, 131, 136; jail slaves to evade emancipation, 336–38; oppose enlistment of slaves, 341–47, 363–65; oppose impressment of slaves, 210; punish fugitive slaves, 11–12, 42–43, 112–13, 357–60, 390–92; punish slaves, 61; pursue fugitive slaves, 15–16, 30, 32–34, 74, 76–81, 142–43, 350–51; relinquish claim to slaves, 308; resist Confederate requisition of slaves, 137–38, 148–51; seek forcible enlistment of slaves, 348, 366, 402; seek to expel former slaves, 418–22; seek to retain former slaves, 125; sue employers of former slaves, 402–3; threaten to murder fugitive slaves, 511; and Union soldiers, 12, 15–17, 30–34, 74, 77–79, 81; unionist, 12, 32–34, 74–76, 79–83, 95, 98–99, 341–47, 350–52, 354–55; warn slaves about intentions of Northerners, 26, 108–9, 349; whipped by former slaves, 115–16; see also

Planters; Refugeeing; Slavery
Slavery, 179; and Confederate mobilization, 4–5, 96, 129–32, 135, 148–51; congressional policy on, xxviii, 38; continues in Kentucky after Civil War, 403–22; critique of, by black soldier, 480–81; critique of, by free–black woman, 451; critique of, by Northern general, 21–25; federal policy on, 3–4, 6–8, 101–3, 168; former slaves' understanding of, 314; military policy on, 6n., 12–13, 16, 100, 254; organization of work under, 260–62; undermined by black enlistment, 111–12, 348–49, 369, 393, 400; undermined by Union occupation, 12–13, 98–100, 241, 308; undermined within Confederacy, 96, 108–9, 129–30, 152–54; see also Nonslaveholders; Slaveholders; Slaves
Slaves: abandoned by owners, 110–11, 193, 329; as Confederate military laborers, 137–39; and Confederate soldiers, 137–39; assist Confederate deserters, 124; assist Union prisoners, 124, 154, 156, 158–63, 503; discipline of, 130–32, 142–44; evicted by owners, 72–73, 378–79, 393; expect freedom, 4–5, 84–85; hired out by owners for military labor, 386–87; impressed for Confederate labor, 14; impressed for Union labor, 386; jailed by owners, 336–38; and nonslaveholders, 124; ownership of personal property by, 123–29, 155–56; personal property of, seized by Confederate soldiers, 54; personal property of, seized by Union soldiers, 123–29; resist refugeeing, 140–42, 193; treatment of, in Confederacy, 61, 123–27, 142–43, 154, 156–61, 193; understanding of the war, 3; and Union soldiers, 12–13,

20–21, 44–45, 49–50; *see also* Fugitive slaves; Slavery

Smallwood, L. W.: letter from, 350–52

Smith, (Sergt.), 171–72

Smith, Charles, 202

Smith, Cornelius, 202

Smith, Daniel W., Jr.: letter from, 438

Smith, E. Kirby: letter from, 139–40; orders removal of slaves, 139–40

Smith, Jerry, 506; letter from, 507

Smith, Pleasant: letter from, 96–97

Smith, William S.: letter from, 99

Smoot, A. J.: affidavit of, 33–34

Smothers, Derinda (Rindy Allen): prosecuted for interfering with apprenticed child, 376–78

Soldiers, black. *See* Black soldiers

Soniat, Pierre: letter from, 84–85

South Carolina: agricultural labor in, 242–51, 259–64, 305–7; black soldiers in, 56–59, 432, 435, 459–60, 514, 535–36; Confederate soldiers in, facilitate escape of impressed slaves, 138–39; Confederate soldiers in, facilitate escape of Union prisoners, 163; emancipation celebration in, 94; enlistment of black soldiers in, xxix–xxx, 316; fugitive slaves in, 55, 247; Hunter declares emancipation in, xxix, 46–47; land in, occupied by former slaves, 173–74, 250; land in, set apart for former slaves, xxxiii, 318; military labor in, 244; military laborers in, 173–74, 249; military laborers (Confederate) in, 137–39; nonagricultural labor in, 245–46, 248–49, 305–8; refugeeing to, 133; relief in, 306–7; relocation of former slaves within, 55; sale of government–controlled land in, 260, 290–93; slaves in,

assist Union prisoners, 154, 156, 158–61; Union occupation of, 173, 242; *see also name of particular place*

Southern Claims Commission, 212; testimony before, 60–61, 124–29, 154–61, 210–11, 265–66, 308–9

Spalding, R. M.: letter from, 386–87

Spalding, Samuel: letter from, 386–87

Sparks, David: abuses family of black soldier, 495

Spotsylvania Court House VA: former slaves at, 239

Sprague, William, 469

Sprewell, Nelson, 202

Stacy, Ezra: letter from, 61–66

Stanly, Edward: letter from, 98

Stanton, Edwin M., xxviii, 208, 222, 342–43; authorizes impressment of military laborers, 200; letters to, 31–35, 56–59, 120–21, 200–203, 207–8, 225–27, 338–39, 465–68, 485–86, 505–6, 512–13, 515–17, 528–29; meets with black religious leaders, xxxiii, 310–18; policy on black prisoners of war, 452; policy on black soldiers, 437; policy on enlisting black soldiers, 388–89; telegram from, 45–46; telegram to, 45

Steele, I. N.: letter from, 402; seeks forcible enlistment of slave, 402

Stevens, Charles L.: letter from, 183–85

Stevenson, Thomas G., 445

Stewart, Richard, 202

Stiles, Hilas: letter from, 110–11

Stone, Charles P.: order by, 12–13; policy on fugitive slaves, 19–21; slavery policy of, 12–13

Stores on plantations, 292

Streeter, Holland, 222, 224–25, 228–29

Strong, George C., 445–46

Strunke, Elias D.: describes battle at Port Hudson LA, 439–41; letter from, 439–41

Stuart, J. E. B., 336–37

Surgeon General's Office, 231

Sweeny, John: letter from, 518; requests school for regiment, 518

Tabb, Henry, 202

Tait, Andrew: petition from, 497–505

Tallmadge, Grier, 171

Taylor, (Sergt.): letter from, 538–39

Taylor, Glasgon, 311

Taylor, Richard: letter to, 139–40

Taylor, Robert N., 313

Taylor, William D.: letter from, 153–54

Tennessee Union Convention: petition to, 497–505

Tennessee: agricultural labor in, 289–90, 325–31; black soldiers from, 429; black soldiers in, 518, 528–29; emancipation in, by amendment to state constitution, xxxiii, 329, 505; emancipation politics in, 497–505; enlistment of black soldiers in, xxxi, 391; exempted from Emancipation Proclamation, xxxi, 95, 98–99; former slaves from, reenslaved in Kentucky, 105–7; fugitive slaves from, 26; fugitive slaves in, 98–99, 112–13; land in, occupied by former slaves, 329–31; military laborers in, 229–30, 264–65, 386–87; reconstruction politics in, 497–505; slavery in, undermined by Union occupation, 98–99; voting by free blacks in, before Civil War, 499–500, 504; *see also name of particular place*

Terry, Alfred F., 445, 447

Texas: black soldiers in, 512–13, 533–35, 538–39; refugeeing to, 111

Thirteenth Amendment, xxxii–xxxiii, 410n., 414n., 422

Thomas, Claiborn: letter from, 257–58

Thomas, George H.: letter to, 530–31

Thomas, Lorenzo, 268; letter from, 471–73; letters to, 173–74, 221–22, 294–305, 489–92; policy on enlisting black soldiers, 393; policy on marriages of former slaves, 221; praises black soldiers, 471–73

Thomas, Samuel, 522–23; assesses prospects of ex–slave laborers, 303–4; letter from, 294–305

Thomass, (Corp.): letter from, 538–39

Thompson, Jacob: letter to, 96–97

Thompson, Martha, 214–15

Thompson, William G.: letter from, 219–20

Thorn, J. G.: letter from, 219–20

Tibbets, Horace B., 276

Tod, David, 469

Tomlinson, Reuben, 292–93

Toombs, Robert, 470

Totten, Joseph G.: letter to, 178–80

Townsend, William: forcibly retains former slaves, 373

Trask, Frank L., 255–56

Treasury Department: land policy of, 242

Truxton, W. T.: letter from, 52–56

Tucker, (Mr.) (slaveholder), 16

Turner, Henry M.: advocates colonization, 42

Tuttle, James M.: letter to, 219–20; meets with Northern missionaries, 218–20; policy on urban labor, 216–20; resigns commission, 220

Tyler, Erastus B.: endorsement by, 117–18; letter from, 119–20

Tyler, John F.: letter from, 378–79

Ullmann, Daniel, 112; letters to, 439–41, 496

Urban labor, 264–66, 417–18; military policy on, 216–20; wages for, 417

Urban laborers, 202–3, 218–19

Valentine, Andrew: letter to, 360–61

Valentine, Ann: letter from, 360–61

Vaughn, Archy: statement of, 113

Vermont, U.S.S., 87

Vicksburg MS: Confederate surrender of, xxxi, 132; families of black soldiers in, 430; former slaves sell vegetables in, 298; military laborers near, 191

Vier, John: military punishment of, 483

Virginia, 18th Infantry (Confederate): resolutions of, 164–65

Virginia: agricultural labor in, 278–86; black soldiers from, 533–35; black soldiers in, 470; Confederate impressment of slaves in, 152–54; Confederate military labor in, 8–11; families of black soldiers in, 533–35; free blacks in, 202–3; fugitive slaves from, 335; fugitive slaves in, 29–30, 43–44, 86, 90, 107–10, 153–54, 279; impressment of military laborers in, 200–203; land in, occupied by former slaves, 212–14, 279; legislature of, 146–48; military laborers in, 122–23; parts of, exempted from Emancipation Proclamation, xxxi, 95; refugeeing in, 146–48; Union invasion of Eastern Shore, 16; *see also name of particular place*

Vogdes, Israel, 445

Volunteers, C.S.A.: 32nd Georgia Infantry, 163; 18th Virginia Infantry, 164–65

Volunteers, U.S.: 9th Army Corps, 512; 25th Army Corps, 513; 10th Illinois Cavalry, 441; 92nd Illinois Infantry, 76–80; 23rd Iowa Infantry, 442; 13th Kentucky Cavalry, 392; 14th Kentucky Infantry, 76–77, 81; 9th Louisiana Infantry (African Descent), 441–43; 11th Louisiana Infantry (African Descent), 443; 25th Massachusetts Infantry, 15–16; 54th Massachusetts Infantry, 426–27, 431, 444–47, 449–50, 461, 473; 55th Massachusetts Infantry, 473–75; 11th Michigan Cavalry, 490; 18th Michigan Infantry, 82; 3rd Missouri Cavalry, 353; 2nd Missouri Infantry, 362; 3rd New Hampshire Infantry, 446; 7th New Hampshire Infantry, 446; 79th New York Infantry, 249–50; 99th New York Infantry, 109–10; 14th New York State Militia, 29–30; 12th Ohio Cavalry, 490; 5th U.S. Colored Cavalry, 400, 489–92; 3rd U.S. Colored Heavy Artillery, 467, 514; 3rd U.S. Colored Infantry, 428; 4th U.S. Colored Infantry, 515–17; 8th U.S. Colored Infantry, 492; 16th U.S. Colored Infantry, 528–29; 18th U.S. Colored Infantry, 528–29; 20th U.S. Colored Infantry, 476–79; 22nd U.S. Colored Infantry, 428; 28th U.S. Colored Infantry, 469; 33rd U.S. Colored Infantry, 535–36; 36th U.S. Colored Infantry, 228–29; 40th U.S. Colored Infantry, 530–33; 44th U.S. Colored Infantry, 425, 528–29; 54th U.S. Colored Infantry, 221–22; 73rd U.S. Colored Infantry, 485–86; 82nd U.S. Colored Infantry, 496; 86th U.S. Colored Infantry, 483; 107th U.S. Colored Infantry, 422–23; 108th U.S. Colored Infantry, 519; 116th U.S. Colored Infantry, 538–39; 120th U.S. Colored Infantry, 399; 124th U.S. Colored Infantry, 394, 493, 510; 2nd U.S. Colored Light Artillery, 429; *see also* Missouri State Militia; Native Guard (Louisiana)

Wade, James F., 490–92

Wages: of agricultural laborers, 253, 263, 273, 276, 280, 290, 302–3,

326–28; of black soldiers, xxxii, 460–63, 467–68, 471, 473–78, 485, 487; of military laborers, 168–69, 171–72, 175–76, 178–79, 244, 467–68; of nonagricultural laborers, 215–16; of urban laborers, 417

Walker, J. E., 274

Walker, Leroy P.: letter to, 5

Wallace, James: letter from, 219–20

Wallace, Lew: apprenticeship policy of, 372; liberates jailed ex–slaves, 120

Wardell, Arthur, 312

Ware, Charles, 293

Waring, George E., Jr.: letter from, 27–29

Waring, John H.: seizes property of freedman, 379–82

Washington DC. See District of Columbia

Washington (DC) City Council: resolutions of, 37–38

Washington, George: letter from, 495; seeks discharge to care for family, 495

Washington NC: fugitive slaves in, 175

Waterproof LA, 299–300

Waters, Emily: letter from, 525–26

Waters, Washington: letter from, 31–33

Watson, George F., 255–56

Wederstrandt, John C. P.: letter from, 72–73

Weeks, J. B.: letter from, 219–20

Welcome, Jane: letter from, 492; seeks discharge of son from military service, 492

Welcome, Mart, 492

Welsh, (Dr.), 189

Whipple, William D.: letter to, 531–33

White, Garland H.: letter from, 469–70; seeks appointment as chaplain, 469–70

White, Henry H.: petition from, 406–8

White, Hugh L., 500

White, William: letter from, 538–39

Whitehouse, Ned, 202

Wickliffe, Charles A., 56–59

Wild, Edward A., 445; authorizes slaves to whip owner, 115–16; court–martial of, 116; letter to, 459–60; letters from, 115–16, 122–23

Wilder, Charles B., 279, 281–82; testimony by, 107–10

Wiley, Nelson, 202

Wiley, Warren: abuses wife of black soldier, 400–401

Wilkinson, Call: letter to, 144–45

Williams, J., 273

Williams, Joseph Enoch: petition from, 38–41

Williams, Parker: letter from, 257–58

Willis, H.: letter from, 26–27

Willis, Rhoda, 230

Willyams, William A.: letter from, 372–73

Wilson, (Dr.), 189

Wilson, Benjamin H.: letter from, 368

Wilson, Henry: letters to, 170–72, 471–73

Winchell, Alexander, 299

Wise, Henry A., 283

Wolford, Frank L., 390, 392

Wool, John E.: order by, 168–69; policy on military labor, 168–72; relief policy of, 168–69, 171–73

Wright (Mr.) (would–be lessee), 258

Wright, Elizabeth: letter to, 470

Wright, Rufus: letter from, 470

Wright, Selig G.: letter from, 219–20

Yancey, William Lowndes, 453

Yewel (Mrs.): forcibly apprentices freed children, 371

Yorktown VA: military laborers at, 234

Young, Ira: forcibly apprentices freed child, 376–77